Rogue Justice

The Rise of Judicial Supremacy in Israel

Yonatan Green

Rogue Justice

The Rise of Judicial Supremacy in Israel

Yonatan Green

Academica Press
Washington

Library of Congress Cataloging-in-Publication Data
Names: Green, Yonatan (author)
Title: Rogue justice : the rise of judicial supremacy in israel | Green, Yonatan
Description: Washington : Academica Press, 2025. | Includes references.
Identifiers: LCCN 2025947951 | ISBN 9781680533132 (hardcover) |
9781680533149 (e-book)

For Shira, Alma, Erel and Ivri

"Beyond all the objections that I have tried to illustrate up to this point is the glaring question regarding the legitimacy of the Court seizing for itself the power of judicial review: By what right?"

— Chief Justice (ret.) Moshe Landau, 1996

Table of Contents

Preface

During my third year of law school at the Hebrew University of Jerusalem, Professor Daniel Friedmann published his monumental critique of the modern Israeli Supreme Court, *The Purse and the Sword.* Friedmann is one of Israel's most renowned and respected jurists – former dean of the Tel Aviv law school, "wrote the book" on contract law and civil law, recipient of the Israel Prize (Israel's highest civilian honor) for legal research, and Minister of Justice under Prime Minister Ehud Olmert. He also stands out as one of the few scholars in the Israeli legal landscape willing to confront the Supreme Court and its supporters dominating the legal establishment. One prominent academic described Friedmann's impact in this regard as follows: "It would hardly be an exaggeration to say that Friedmann's critique of the Court... was *one of the most important developments in the history of Israeli law*."[1]

Between law school, bar exams, and training as a young lawyer, I only got around to reading the book a few years later – but when I finally did, I was shaken to my core. For a recent graduate of Israel's top law school, reading Friedmann's scathing account of a lawless court gone rogue was very much a "red pill" moment, revealing a narrative and perspective to which I had never been exposed in my legal studies. I suddenly felt I had been duped, misled, deceived; that key facts and ideas had been withheld by my teachers. My alma mater, I realized, had presented a simplistic and biased account of historical events and had imparted a distorted version of legal thought which deviated from established Western principles of law and democracy. I recall furiously pacing the room while trying to process what I had just read, or laying awake in bed, unable to fall asleep after finishing another chapter, so disturbed was I by Friedmann's rich, personal and compelling account.

From that moment I began to gradually engage with the thorny and gruesome realities of the Israeli legal system and its debilitating flaws. Parallel to my professional career I wrote legal commentary for various outlets, eventually also interviewing Professor Friedmann himself. One turning point was when I translated Judge Richard Posner's critique of Israeli jurisprudence (an essay aptly titled "Enlightened Despot") from English to Hebrew: the translation was met with immediate and considerable success, demonstrating the appetite of many Israelis for a deeper and more serious discussion of Israel's legal woes. I later published a wide-ranging treatise explaining the Supreme Court's flawed conceptualization of democracy and judicial power.

My passion finally merged with my career when in 2019 I partnered with the Tikvah Fund and Aylana Meisel-Diamant to establish the Israel Law & Liberty Forum, which I ran as executive director for the next four years. The Forum seeks to advance a new Israeli legal discourse based on principles of judicial restraint, separation of powers, individual liberties and limited government. We did so by facilitating informed and respectful debate, by encouraging genuine inquiry and by building a community of like-minded jurists. Daniel Friedmann joined as the first chairman of our advisory board.

My role with the Forum allowed me a unique privilege available to few Israelis – to grapple with the core afflictions of the Israeli legal system through reflection, discussion, and action on a daily basis. I had to familiarize myself with the minute details of individual cases and controversies while always returning to consider the larger overarching scheme within which each individual issue has its place. My perspective on, and insights into, the Israeli legal system are thus informed by scores of educational events spanning the length and breadth of Israel's legal debates; by a substantial mass of scholarly literature assembled for our programming; and by hundreds – perhaps thousands – of individual one-on-one meetings and personal interactions with Israeli jurists from across the political and ideological spectrum. They are born of intense and sustained engagement with our legal system's most pressing problems.

It is not, however, only by my professional experience that I am well-situated to describe the rise of judicial supremacy in Israel to a foreign audience. I am what some may call an archetypical hybrid, my identity a fusion of Israeli, American, and British origins. A bona fide *Sabra*, I was born and raised in Israel and have lived there for almost my entire life – through school and military service, university and career, marriage and the birth of my own children. Yet I inherited a distinct Anglo-American heritage from my parents who immigrated to Israel in their twenties. My Western roots run deep: My British great-grandfather served during World War II with the 8th Army in North Africa; his daughter, my grandmother, became President of the Board of Deputies of British Jews and earned an O.B.E. from Queen Elizabeth II. My American lineage spans eleven generations and predates the Revolutionary War; I am a direct descendant of Gershom Mendes Seixas, known as the "patriot rabbi," who was among the fourteen clergymen to participate in the inauguration of George Washington.[2]

I make no claim to absolute objectivity on any matter. But many will agree that straddling the boundary between different nationalities and cultures provides one with an uncommon near-Archimedean perspective. A perpetual semi-outsider may view their environment with a degree of detachment less accessible to the single-identity native. As an Israeli who is also British and American, my views were always influenced and enriched by the broader parallel worlds which I partially inhabit. Like some similar "hybrids," I believe my culturally varied background and upbringing allow for an approach that is more circumspect and at times more skeptical than that shared by many of my peers. To put things more simply, a person with ingrained American-British sensibilities is less likely to be taken in by meritless distortions of law, justice, liberty and democracy.

The controversies plaguing the Israeli legal system and constitutional order are genuinely complex, and are for the most part entirely inaccessible to all save a small group of Hebrew-speaking lawyers and legal scholars. They transcend and defy typical fault-lines of right and left, religious and secular, hawk or dove. A sizeable global audience is acutely interested in Israel's legal dramas yet lacks the means to pierce their surrounding fog. Similarly, the tale of judicial supremacy in Israel does not crystallize in a "big bang" of any single moment or any particular act; the slow onslaught against Israeli democracy and rule of law rather takes on the form of death by a thousand cuts. Even a cursory explanation must cover an inordinate amount of ground. For these reasons and for many others, a hybrid jurist – licensed as an attorney in both Israel and New York, versed and immersed in Israeli law yet approaching it from an Anglo-American perspective – is well suited to undertake the daunting task of illuminating our legal system in a useful and compelling manner.

There is no shortage of Israeli experts willing to malign Israel on any platform and to proclaim its failings to anyone that will listen. This book does nothing of the sort.

Too many critics of alleged Israeli shortcomings impute such deficiencies to the entirety of Israeli society or to the nature and essence of the State. Too easily do its detractors deride Israel as irredeemably immoral or defective. Some Israelis betray their brethren by denouncing their own homeland under the pretext of "tough love" or of "hard truths" and under the guise of sincere concern. More often than not they do so to impose their own views and policies on an electorate they have failed to persuade, or to reap the accolades and rewards invariably bestowed on anyone willing to smear the Jewish State, or simply out of a baffling and narcissistic compulsion to inflict harm on their native land. Most usually, such disingenuous critiques undermine Israel's security, stability and autonomy far more than any ostensible benefit they claim to provide.

Though the overall tone and tenor of this book is unmistakably critical, it is not remotely a condemnation of Israel or of its people. I love Israel as it is, not as a fantasy I wish it would be. It is my home. I yearn for Israel's success, security, stability, virtue and prosperity, on its own terms. The vast majority of Israel's inhabitants are noble, courageous and kind; its government is generally led and administered by upstanding, well-meaning and capable individuals (even if occasionally mediocre or unrefined). The judiciary and legal establishment at the center of this book's attention are no exception. Let me attest unequivocally and unreservedly – Israel is a fine country, a marvelous place in the most literal sense.

The contrast between genuinely constructive criticism and damaging disparagement is perhaps most evident in their relative approach to outside intervention. Those eager to unduly discredit Israel typically invite – whether implicitly or explicitly – some external imposition of a solution or sanction. They demand that Israel be coerced to align with their own views and prescriptions or that Israelis pay the price for their failure to comply. They encourage the global community – government and individuals, Jews and gentiles – to browbeat Israel until it falls in line with their demands. On the other hand, earnest criticism is addressed to the Israeli people and their government, and the message to outsiders it naturally conveys may be summarized as "hands off." To be sure, sincere input based on nuanced and informed understanding – such as that which this book hopefully provides – is welcome and even crucial. At the same time, Israelis ultimately need to sort out their considerable problems for themselves.

I believe this conclusion emerges unambiguously from a close reading of this book: that the task of confronting the sheer formidable complexity and severity of Israel's legal troubles can only possibly be achieved by the Israeli electorate and domestic societal forces, not by foreign pressure or interference; and that those wishing to guide and counsel Israel in this gargantuan endeavor must first necessarily gain a genuine and thorough understanding of judicial supremacy in Israel and how it came to be.

Introduction

"The amendment before us inherently contradicts the basic tenets upon which the democratic character of our system is based, given the force of its harm to principles of the rule of law and the separation of powers. ... There is no alternative but to declare the amendment null and void."
— Chief Justice Esther Hayut[1]

What the Heck is Going On?

On a sunny September morning in the fall of 2023, fifteen Justices of the Supreme Court of Israel filed into the Court's main chambers. The stakes were as high as they had ever been. The drama and tension in the room were palpable. Against the backdrop of a government-led effort at reforming the Israeli judiciary, and of a parallel and unprecedented mass-protest movement against the proposed reform measures, the Court would now hear oral arguments challenging or defending the constitutionality of an amendment to Israel's "Basic Law: The Judiciary." The enormous public controversy engulfing the entire country for the previous ten months had now crystallized into this single momentous case. In recognition of the event's sheer gravity and significance, the Court would hear the case "en banc" – with all fifteen Justices – for the first time in its history. The arguments were live-streamed to a deeply divided Israeli public, accompanied by frenzied tweeting by scholars and pundits alike.

What was all the ruckus about? The piece of legislation under review sought to limit the Supreme Court's ability to assess whether a particular government action or policy is "reasonable," and was part of a broader head-on collision between the elected government and the Court. It was the only measure the government had successfully enacted thus far as part of its push for judicial reform. Passed by an absolute majority of legislators, the law constituted an explicit, direct, full-throated repudiation of a legal doctrine developed by the Court in recent decades.

Public-interest organizations filed their petitions against the law on the very same day it was enacted in July of 2023. The Legal Counsel to the Government refused to defend the law, but permitted the government to retain independent counsel to represent them before the Court. The hearing itself lasted over thirteen grueling hours.

As an amendment to a Basic Law, the new legislation enjoyed the status of a constitutional provision. The question that now lay before the Court went to the core of Israeli society, jurisprudence and constitutional law – could the Court strike down a constitutional amendment? Would the Court invalidate legislation explicitly designed to curtail its own powers? Will the Court intervene in the most contentious constitutional public debate in the country's history?

On January 1st, 2024, the Supreme Court struck down the amendment in a 736-page decision and with a slim majority of eight over seven Justices.

At this point the reader may well be asking: "*What the heck is going on here?*" – and could hardly be blamed for doing so. Israel doesn't even have a constitution, so how could anyone enact a so-called constitutional amendment, and how could any law be "unconstitutional" in the first place? Can the Court actually veto executive government policy just based on it being "unreasonable"? How can non-profit groups file a Supreme Court petition without any aggrieved party showing a distinct harm? Why would such a challenge start at the Supreme Court and not go through some lower courts first? Why didn't the Court dismiss the petitions as a non-justiciable matter of public controversy and legislative policy? Can the Legal Counsel to the Government just refuse to defend the government's position in court? Would the Court really ignore or invalidate such a clear and determined decision by the legislature?

Indeed, an Israeli legal scholar, time-traveling from the 1980s to our hearing in 2023, would be equally dumbfounded and would likely share many of the reader's bewildered questions. Such a scholar may be familiar with the Court's insistence that "a plaintiff must show a distinct individual harm so as to have standing before the Court" and that "the Court may never entertain a complaint attributable to the general public"; she may recall the Court's refusal to deal with highly-charged political disputes that are better "left with the political branches," while "rejecting the attempt to turn the Court into an arena for such controversies." She may wonder how Basic Laws might be considered "constitutional" in light of the Court's constant reiteration that Basic Laws bear no superior constitutional status, or how the Court could strike down laws after clarifying, time and again, that the Israeli system of government is one in which "the Knesset is sovereign and has the authority to enact any law... The possibility of invalidating a law passed by the Knesset is entirely inconceivable." She would certainly know of the Court's overall approach of deference towards "what the Knesset ordinarily does as a legislative body appointed through democratic elections and reflecting the free will of the People."* She might be asking – what happened?

The answers to these questions lie in the deeply troubling process of which the recent saga of judicial reform is merely the culmination, a process which has dominated the Israeli judiciary and legal system since the 1980s. Anyone trying to make sense of the debate around Israeli legal reform, and indeed of almost any

* The source of these quotes will be provided in due course as we separately address each topic.

issue within contemporary Israeli society, politics, national security, economics and of course Israeli law, must first understand the manner in which the Israeli judiciary attained supremacy over the past forty years. Any opinion, description, or explanation of Israeli democracy and its system of government will remain woefully inadequate without an informed and detailed account of the power accrued and wielded by the Israeli Supreme Court. Further afield, those trying to analyze broader global trends regarding democracy and the rule of law must also consider Israeli judicial supremacy as a crucially instructive case study.

This book seeks to describe that process, and the core of the case of those objecting to it.

The following Introduction will provide necessary context regarding Israel's system of government, its founding moments and its legal culture, and will offer some clarifications and points to take under consideration for the remaining chapters. The book then proceeds in three parts. Part I addresses structural elements of the Israeli legal system which serve as key components enabling judicial supremacy. Part II tracks the Supreme Court's ascent in the 1980s and 1990s as it discarded precedent and developed novel, sophisticated doctrines, revolutionizing Israeli jurisprudence and granting the Court effective control over executive governing power. Part III describes the advent of judicial supremacy, in which the Supreme Court and its proxies became the ultimate and final arbiter on the most consequential and contentious issues in Israeli public life.

All Founders, No Framers

To understand Israel's system of government is first to acknowledge the haphazard, sporadic, fitful and arbitrary manner in which it came into being. Our governing institutions and mechanisms were not the result of some methodical deliberative effort involving the wisest and most learned individuals of the era, nor did they organically evolve through centuries of practical experience. Rather, the modern State of Israel was very much "jump-started" with a hodgepodge of disparate governmental and legal arrangements. Some were inherited from the region's previous rulers such as the British and Ottoman empires; some were adapted from recently-created skeletal institutions of local and international Jewish self-governance; some were born of immediate necessity and were virtually invented on the spot.

Israel was formally founded in 1948, in the midst of a major war for survival which was about to get far worse. Its governing apparatus was roughly adapted from the existing colonial mechanisms set up by the British Mandate, in combination with additional existing semi-autonomous institutions of Jewish self-rule (known broadly as the *Yishuv*) under the British. The new Israeli electoral system mirrored the existing method for representation of Jewish factions in the *Yishuv* institutions. Its legal architecture and culture included significant elements of the Common Law introduced by the British, which were themselves adapted by the British for colonial rule (such as leaving out jury trials); yet also incorporated swaths of Ottoman law, including the existing judicial hierarchy, a complex web of religious courts and an Islam-based Civil Code of private law; and all while most leading Israeli attorneys, judges and jurists had actually been educated and trained in Central and Western Europe.

While Israel's governmental starting point was indeed messy, the founding generation could theoretically have revamped and reshaped the new State's governing order. The Israeli Declaration of Independence stated the intent to draft and ratify a constitution within a short timeframe, but this never came about (this will be discussed in detail in Part III). However, noting that Israel did not adopt a written constitution upon its establishment fails to capture the essential point. More than merely skipping the "technical" act of adopting a legal constitution, the Israeli founding generation simply never engaged in the type of discussion that could have served as its basis – that is, a conscious national conversation about fundamental governmental powers and the institutions wielding them, about checks and balances, about the process and limitations of democratic self-rule, about core shared values and so on. This is especially true with regard to the definition and design of Israel's judicial branch. Those seeking the theoretical origins of Israeli governing mechanisms and the processes by which they were established will return virtually empty-handed; those seeking the writings and deliberations of Israel's political thinkers and learned statesmen to which our institutions and system of government can be traced will be disappointed. Israel had no "Federalist Papers," no Philadelphia Convention, no Hamilton or Madison.

To be sure, Israel was blessed with a formidable array of extraordinary leaders at its founding – towering men and women of deep intellect and enormous capability. But (with some limited exceptions) few had a discernible passion or the requisite experience for "constitutional design," the specialized field of assembling the many moving pieces of an effective and optimal system of government; perhaps more importantly, none had the opportunity to actively pursue such an endeavor. Before the founders of 1948 lay the gargantuan and eminently practical task of state-building under impossible conditions while trying to win an existential war of survival. The critical need to stave off imminent extinction by military foes, while maintaining the societal and economic viability of the precariously fragile new State of Israel, took precedence over what seemed to be lofty goals of a constitutional re-design.

Thus, Israel settled for whatever systems we had in place at the time, and has been plodding along with them, for the most part, to this day. Many if not most of the core governmental arrangements and institutions in Israel were never the product of wise deliberation and acute insight, nor of long-standing practice and hard-earned experience, but rather were born of accident, coincidence and happenstance. Israel had many founders, but no framers.

Fundamental vs. Existential

Fast forward to 2023 – not September, but October. In an event that is by now etched in history, the Palestinian Islamist terror group controlling the Gaza Strip known as Hamas launched a barbaric and highly successful attack against Israel. Such scenes of gleeful civilian slaughter and wanton butchery, such displays of murderous savagery alongside the mass-kidnapping of civilians, had not been experienced by a Western country since the likes of Genghis Khan. More Jews were murdered on October 7th than any single day since the Holocaust, in an event which was to Israelis a combination of Pearl Harbor, 9/11 and the Nanjing Massacre. With far-reaching strategic repercussions, at stake was nothing short of Israeli survival – our enemies and allies were watching closely, and our response would define Israeli national security for generations. Without a decisive victory and the utter annihilation of Hamas, no Israeli could be safe within their borders.

In a single moment of blood-soaked horror, tearful sorrow and resolute determination, the earlier controversy of judicial reform and its opponents were swept aside. Once again, repeating the pattern of 1948, the pressing questions of constitutional arrangements and governing institutions would have to wait. The fundamental must yield to the existential. It is in this context that the current tentative and tenuous hiatus of Israeli judicial reform ought to be viewed. In at least some ways, the suspension of legal reform and its accompanying heated debates in the aftermath of October 7th is reminiscent of the founding generation's deferment of constitutional design to an unknown time in the distant future.

This matters because, precisely as in 1948, such issues are by no means resolved by their neglect, justified and valid as such deferral may be. Whatever negative aspects one might find in the recent controversies surrounding legal reform, they had the virtue of triggering an unprecedented national debate regarding fundamental questions hitherto eluding serious public attention. At least Israelis were grappling with these ideas for the first time, painful as this encounter was. Now this conversation has been overtaken and eclipsed by the unifying horrors of October 7th. But just as the historical reluctance to engage in the fundamental questions of constitutional government ultimately and inevitably led to the reform proposals and ensuing crises of 2023, the current lull in the battles over judicial power can only be considered a temporary cease-fire. The underlying woes and flaws of the Israeli legal system, some of them "baked in" since the State's founding but many of them initiated and exacerbated by judicial action over the past forty years, are simply too consequential to lie dormant for long. As evinced by the Court's striking down of the "reasonableness" amendment, they make the eventual eruption of a renewed national controversy surrounding Israeli judicial supremacy a near-certainty. When that time comes, a genuine understanding of these flaws and the process which led to them will be indispensable.

Heroes or Villains

What has been the role, function and influence of the Supreme Court since the State's founding? Answers typically divide into two competing narratives. The first approach casts the Court as a bastion of civil rights and limited government, upholding values of liberal democracy while acting as a bulwark against rampant government overreach. On this view, the Court has been a central driver for and champion of liberal ideals that has led the way for the rest of Israeli society and institutions, often espousing modern policies and norms before their time. During an era in which no serious challenge could be mustered against a centralized and all-powerful Israeli government and in a system with scarce checks on majoritarian power, the Court was and remains a staunch protector of minorities and individuals from governmental abuses. Accordingly, efforts at curbing or limiting judicial power stem from a desire to undermine the State's liberal-democratic character, to enable limitless authoritarian government and to violate the rights of individuals or minorities. This first narrative is the dominant view of the Israeli legal elite and is typically the one presented by most foreign-facing (i.e., for a non-Israeli audience) descriptions and accounts of the Supreme Court and legal system. It is consistent with a broader global narrative, according to which Western countries today are facing increased "democratic backsliding," including the rise of semi-authoritarian populist governments and the systematic weakening of judicial oversight mechanisms.

There is, however, an alternative view of the history and development of the Israeli Supreme Court, a narrative shared by many common Israelis and jurists alike. The Supreme Court had indeed previously served as an important institution holding government accountable to the law and tempering encroachments upon civil rights. But over a gradual process since the 1980s, the Court has become an essentially rogue and lawless institution, regularly flouting precedent and statutory law, arrogating to itself unparalleled political power, and abusing its status and unique position to impose its own radical values and policies on an unwilling or oblivious electorate. In doing so, the Court has enacted disastrous policies and has consistently exacerbated Israeli societal problems, all while undermining the electorate and circumventing the democratic process.

On this view, the Court has emerged today as a patently illiberal, undemocratic and unaccountable oligarchic political entity causing irreparable harm, disrupting and destabilizing political life and endangering the very viability of the Israeli State. Accordingly, rectifying the many resulting flaws of the legal system and rehabilitating Israeli democracy is an imperative that will require significant and fundamental changes driven by the electorate and legislature. This view tracks with a global narrative critical of the massive expansion of judicial power throughout the Western world, in which unelected judicial elites have themselves eroded established democratic values and institutions, and according to which creating more robust checks on judicial power is a crucial element in reasserting popular democratic governance.[2] Professor Martin Loughlin has described such backlashes as "reasonable responses to how constitutional democracies have been undermined" and an "inevitable political response to the reflexive turn taken by contemporary constitutionalism."[3]

Which of these two narratives is a more accurate portrayal of Israeli legal history and reality? The truth will not be found in the sweeping slogans and blanket assertions which typically dominate discussion surrounding these issues. A serious answer must rely on a rich and detailed account of the mechanisms, events, cases and doctrines which comprise the Israeli legal system and upon which Israeli judicial power rests.

This book lays out the arguments of the latter narrative. It will show how the Supreme Court, through a series of sophisticated but dubious doctrines developed over the past four decades, has methodically and unilaterally accrued political power at the expense of the elected and accountable branches of government to devastating effect. The Court has done so while ignoring or undermining basic tenets of democracy, the separation of powers, and the rule of law. This book will establish and explain this process in detail, exploring its central doctrines and mechanisms through the prism of major cases and events. The book will demonstrate how the primary and overarching characteristic of Israeli jurisprudence throughout this process has been one of lawlessness – the utter contempt for the law itself, subverting existing law or inventing new law out of whole cloth. While the advance of partisan politics and personal ideology have certainly played a part, the main pattern which emerges is one of ultimate judicial supremacy as a goal in its own right. Importantly, the critics who have voiced and who share this view span the political and ideological spectrum, and these critiques are by no means new or limited to specific events or individual circumstances.

An impartial and well-meaning reader will at the very least be deeply discomfited and disquieted, and will acknowledge the profound problems facing the Israeli legal system to which any genuine proponent of liberal democracy ought to object. Taking a cold hard look at modern Israeli jurisprudence, such a reader will likely reach the conclusion of the dire need for comprehensive change, recognizing many of the current arrangements to be indefensible in principle and unsustainable in practice. This book is not about the 2023 proposals for legal reform; but by its end, the reader may understand how such proposals may be the inevitable and eminently predictable consequence of a generation of rogue judicial conduct.

A word to the skeptic. If you lean towards the first narrative described above; if you are suspicious of critical descriptions of the Supreme Court and its role in Israeli society; if you think reports of judicial overreach are partisan and exaggerated; please read on. Such a view may only be enriched by a more nuanced and informed account of the Israeli judiciary. At the very least, this book will familiarize the reader with the arguments of those objecting to the Israeli legal status-quo.

Isolation and Statism

When considering Israeli attitudes towards government and the development of Israeli governing institutions, there are two dominant themes which are neither obvious nor intuitive and which require some elaboration. These serve as an important backdrop to understanding many key issues in Israeli public life and in the collective Israeli mindset.

The first theme is the high degree of relative isolation from the Western-democratic world. When compared with other developed democratic countries, Israel is unusually isolated – geographically, culturally and linguistically. Citizens of most democratic states have some familiar basis for mutual comparison and education, based on effortless and casual interaction with democratic counterparts. Such interaction is typically facilitated by physical proximity, by historical-cultural ties, by a shared language – or often by some combination thereof. A typical Austrian citizen might benefit from sharing borders with eight different countries, some of them speaking the same language, all of which practice different varieties of democratic government. A New Zealander or Canadian enjoys a shared history and culture (along with a shared language) with English Commonwealth-based democracies across the globe. These mutual connections regularly expose ordinary citizens to a diverse range of methods for democratic government and of legal systems (among other elements for comparison), while providing a deeply enriching basis for crucial perspective and for reflective self-evaluation.

Israel has no immediate territorial neighbors with functioning, democratic systems of government. Far from it, all countries sharing a border with Israel sport various versions and degrees of autocracy. With the exception of a sizeable Arab minority, Israelis generally do not share cultural or linguistic ties with their surrounding Arab-Muslim majority states. Cross-border travel or business between Israel and her neighbors is generally limited due to either an actual state of war or an otherwise uneasy and tense relationship.

Israel is the only state with a national Jewish character, an attribute with ethnic, cultural and religious significance not shared (remotely) with any other country. Despite the heavy influence of relatively short British colonial rule, Israel has few cultural ties with the United Kingdom. Ultimately, Israel has no genuine "sister-states" which can be said to share a substantially similar culture or parallel historical development.

Finally, Israel's primary spoken language is Hebrew, one not shared with (and not similar to that of) any other country in the world. Israel is likely the only British-inspired and common-law style developed democracy, in which English is not the dominant official language. All in all, Israel is simply not a natural part of the Western-democratic ecosystem.

For present purposes regarding the Israeli legal system and form of government, these combined factors of isolation have a critical bi-directional effect. Facing outwards, Israelis have a generally limited and highly localized understanding of government structures and legal arrangements. Few Israelis have the kind of enriching, intuitive and automatic access to alternative political regimes which other Western citizens take for granted. The average Israeli simply lacks serious exposure to the theory and practice of other countries in terms of political and legal systems. One tangible effect is that certain ideas and arguments, easily rejected or repudiated under more intellectually diverse circumstances, are able to gain public credibility and prominence.

Facing inwards, Israeli political and legal discourse are generally shielded from meaningful external scrutiny. The hurdles for foreign comprehension and analysis of specific and high-detail Israeli issues are simply too substantial and numerous, such that non-Israeli commentary tends to be superficial and misleading (at best). Nowhere is this truer than in the example of Israeli jurisprudence and legal academia. Israeli scholars and judges may make arguments or statements that would barely pass muster (or, more likely, would be wildly controversial or even ridiculed) if presented clearly to their Western colleagues. But writing in Hebrew in a specialized and insulated intellectual environment provides essential impunity from global criticism, unencumbered by foreign contemporaries capable of providing critical analysis. One example is the scant scholarly writing defending or justifying many of our legal system's most obvious flaws, despite Israeli academics publishing overwhelmingly in English-language journals. Israeli jurists simply have had very little incentive to address these flaws when outsider scrutiny is so inherently limited. When discussing flaws of our legal system with Israeli law students and lawyers, I have playfully argued that the most common way by which people lose faith in the Israeli judiciary is simply by reading their rulings. It is precisely this kind of direct and unfiltered access which is generally unavailable to most outside observers of Israeli law.

A second theme to consider is the dominant Israeli approach to democratic government stemming from its strong statist and socialist formative ethos. Much of Israel's founding generation subscribed to a collectivist political worldview bordering on overt Marxism. This included support for heavily centralized executive state power, while excluding more familiar democratic notions of individual liberty and democratic accountability. For the first three decades of the state's existence Israeli politics were dominated by the distinctly left-wing Workers' Party ("*Mapai*") and like-minded partners. As a matter of historical fact, the story of Israel's establishment simply does not include the same pattern usually central to the founding ethos of the Western political order – emancipation from tyranny (whether imperial or aristocratic) with its emphasis on civilian protection from arbitrary governmental abuse.

This divergence from typical Western democratic thought has significantly influenced the subsequent development of Israeli jurisprudence and political attitudes. The Western classical-liberal point of departure reserves ultimate suspicion for state institutions and organs and is primarily concerned with the abuse of government power. This approach tends to favor popular sovereignty and electoral supervision of accountable government, alongside individual liberty as free as possible from state coercion. The state is to be feared; the people are to be trusted.

In stark contrast, much of Israeli political and legal thought stems from a reverse set of assumptions. The unruly electorate is generally regarded with deep suspicion bordering on contempt, while much faith is placed in the methodical and reliable nature of state institutions and the professional bureaucratic class running them. Electorally accountable officials reflecting public sentiment – politicians and legislators chief among them – are warily regarded as short-sighted opportunists motivated by personal ambition, and as a regrettable-yet-tolerable by-product of the political process. Indeed, it is not unusual to hear Israelis contend that politicians are not to be trusted due precisely to their public accountability and their desire for reelection. The term "political" is more often than not used as a slur. Communal or collective needs as ascertained by civil servants accordingly take priority over both individual interest and democratic political autonomy. Popular supervision of government is not the epitome of democracy but rather a necessary evil. The state is revered; the people are inherently suspect.

These twin themes affecting and informing Israeli public discourse and jurisprudence are crucial to understanding the advent of judicial supremacy and will be evident in many of the book's chapters.

Barak's Shadow

"*Barak left an unprecedented mark on Israeli society. It is difficult to find a parallel in other democracies for a judge who has wielded such influence. Barak is a revolutionary – a soft-spoken revolutionary, but a revolutionary nonetheless... In many respects, under Barak's leadership, the Supreme Court effectively became an alternative government.*"

— Prof. Amnon Rubinstein[4]

A central and recurring character throughout the story of Israeli judicial supremacy is that of Chief Justice Aharon Barak. A Holocaust survivor who came to pre-state Israel at the age of five, Barak served on the Supreme Court for twenty-eight years until 2006, eleven of them as Chief Justice. Before his tenure on the bench he was a star university professor and served as Legal Counsel to the Government. He remains active within the legal and political world to this day – holding a senior university position, publishing academic scholarship, providing media interviews and reportedly advising sitting Justices.

More than any other figure, Barak is identified with the substantial changes to Israeli jurisprudence since the 1980s. His long shadow extends over virtually all areas of Israeli law which saw dramatic transformations under his tenure, with most contemporary Supreme Court decisions still employing the doctrines he created and heavily grounded in his judicial philosophy. For all intents and purposes Barak was the indomitable driving force behind judicial supremacy in Israel and its primary architect. Were it not for Barak, the judiciary and legal system would almost certainly not have developed as they did.

Barak's influence is such that most commentators consider his appointment to the bench as the dividing line between the Supreme Court's two major eras – the pre-Barak "classical" or "restrained" era, and the post-Barak "revolutionary" era. Though the sheer magnitude of the change effected by Barak's rulings and opinions is beyond debate, the impact of his tenure ranges far beyond his case-law and legal decisions. Throughout his judicial career Barak was directly and intensely involved in parliamentary politics, legislation initiatives and contemporary societal issues, making his views known publicly or closely advising key policymakers within and without Israeli government. Further still, Barak broadly re-shaped the Court in his image for a generation, through his involvement in the judicial selection process and the appointment of like-minded Justices; and his enduring sway over Israeli academia meant that almost only Barak-approved candidates were hired or granted tenure at leading law schools.[5]

Nomi Levitzky, Barak's official biographer (and unofficial biographer of the modern Supreme Court), described his tenure in these terms:

> "From the moment he set foot in the Supreme Court, he began leading a profound transformation of Israel's legal landscape. Step by step, he sought to shape the law in his own image, one revolution followed another, and within just one generation there was hardly a legal field in which he had not altered thought patterns and not instilled an entirely new discourse. The revolutions he implemented in various fields granted the Court superior power over the other two branches of government – the executive and the legislative. Israel, which before Barak's time had been a parliamentary democracy in which the legislature had the final say, evolved over the years into a constitutional democracy, in which the foundational discourse created by Barak ensures that the Supreme Court has the last word."[6]

Aharon Barak was and remains a controversial but towering figure of historical proportions. He embodied a rare combination of formidable intellectual capacity, disciplined and strategic planning, and natural charisma. Many attest to his disarmingly affable and friendly character alongside his vast command of legal sources and knowledge. He is certainly Israel's most renowned – and most derided – legal scholar, evoking reverence or contempt but never indifference.

Far from being biographical, this book does not presume to evaluate Barak's underlying motives or to engage in psychological speculation (for Barak or for any other individual). It is, at most, his actions and decisions which concern us and which will feature prominently throughout. Nonetheless, Barak's views, character and persona must inescapably accompany any description of the Supreme Court's transformation over the past forty years.

The Israeli Political System

What follows is a brief overview of the Israeli system of government (the legal system and judicial branch will be described in Part I ahead) so as to provide a baseline familiarity with our political process which serves as the backdrop for many key cases and events. A reader well-acquainted with the Israeli political system (or one that simply finds such descriptions excruciatingly boring) may choose to skip this or to return to it for clarification at a later time.

a. The Legislature: Israel is technically a Westminster-style parliamentary democracy with an electoral system of national proportional representation. The primary elected governing institution is the "Knesset" which serves as the Israeli parliament or legislature. The unicameral Knesset consists of a single chamber with one hundred and twenty elected members, with regular elections for all members held every four years (at most). Elected legislators are usually abbreviated as "MKs" (Member of Knesset). The term "Knesset" refers to the legislative institution itself, but also to a particular session or group of Knesset members elected in a specific elections cycle (e.g., the "Twentieth Knesset" was elected in March, 2015 and served until April, 2019).

The Knesset is tasked with appointing the executive Government, with enacting primary legislation, with approving (by committee) certain regulations ("secondary" legislation), and with routine oversight of government activities and decisions.

b. Elections: Israeli citizens vote with a single ballot for a closed national "list" of candidates submitted by a political party. Lists are "closed" in the sense that they are pre-determined at the time of voting, as opposed to systems with "open" lists in which a vote will influence the list composition. Knesset seats (or "mandates") are then allotted according to the proportion of the vote won by each list, in the order that candidates appear on the list (e.g., the first ten candidates on a list of twenty would become Knesset members if the party is allotted ten seats). A party list winning 10% of the total national vote would receive about twelve Knesset seats (10% of 120 members). A minimal "blocking" threshold of voter-share (adjusted frequently) must usually be met for any members of a list to become MKs – for example, if the threshold is 3.25% and a list receives only 3% of the overall votes, no members of that list will become MKs, and such votes will be evenly distributed among parties which have passed the minimum threshold. Elections are also "national" in the sense that the entire country consists of a single voting district, with no geographic or territorial Knesset constituencies. Israel is relatively unusual in this regard, with only a handful of other developed democracies employing an electoral method of single-district closed-list proportional representation.

The political party and the elections list generally overlap but are distinct – for example, several parties may choose to offer joint candidates on a single combined list, with elected politicians then splintering into their respective parties after the elections. The identity of candidates on a given list is predetermined by each political party through a variety of methods according to a party's structure and by-laws. Some parties have a "primaries" system by which the list itself is the product of a vote by registered party members. Other methods include an "organizing committee" which selects list candidates, or direct selection of candidates by the party leader. Some parties conduct an internal vote by their members solely for party leadership. A candidate's place within the list order typically reflects their level of seniority within the party, and a "higher" list position will often translate to a more senior governmental role once elected.

Unlike regional first-past-the-post electoral systems which usually produce two consistently-dominant parties, proportional representation often leads to a variety of political parties competing for the vote of different swaths and subsections of Israeli society. Some parties appeal to the broad public while others may represent a niche group or interest – examples abound, like the sectorial parties representing Ultra-Orthodox and Arab minorities which are a regular staple of Israeli politics, or the short-lived "Gil" party representing retirees which won 7 Knesset seats in 2006. Some "traditional" parties are long-established while others are of a more temporary or personal nature, focusing on a particular individual (usually leading the party) or on a contemporary issue.

c. <u>Coalitions</u>: Following elections, and in accordance with the parliamentary principle of majority rule, successful parties must then create a "Coalition" to form a new Government, which requires approval by an ordinary Knesset vote (typically of at least 61 MKs, an absolute majority). Failure to form a Coalition and Government triggers a new elections cycle. The ideology and character of coalition partners may be highly uniform (reflecting a coherent political "camp") or radically diverse, depending on the unique circumstances of each Knesset. While some parties have a distinct or rigid political viewpoint, many are less clearly aligned and may cooperate with a range of other parties – such that coalition-building is often a daunting puzzle of competing interests and elaborate game-theory. Coalitions also often have great difficulty in formulating and executing consistent government policy, given the diverse (and at times conflicting) interests and preferences advanced by their members. The remaining parties which do not form part of the governing coalition are jointly referred to as the "Opposition."

While a specific left-wing party ("*Mapai*") had dominated Israeli politics for the State's first three decades, no single party has ever won an outright majority sufficient to unilaterally form a government. Inter-party coalitions alongside a mosaic of disparate political factions are therefore an integral component of Israeli government. As an illustration, 40 (!) lists representing 49 (!) parties participated in the November 2022 elections, with 10 lists (representing at least 15 parties) passing the minimum threshold and attaining Knesset membership, and 6 parties (comprised of 64 MKs) ultimately forming the initial governing Coalition.

Such proportional systems are generally recognized as allowing for a high degree of sector-based representation, especially in a fractured and pluralistic society. On the other hand, such systems and the coalition-based governing they necessitate tend to be ineffective, volatile and unstable. These suffer from a lower degree of overall governing ability and from relatively higher chances of government collapse and of renewed elections. Indeed, while Israeli law requires that elections are held every four years, the actual average since 1948 has been roughly every three years. The average lifespan of a given Government is even shorter, clocking in at under two years, as Governments might collapse and be re-formed without necessitating an elections cycle. Scholars are divided on whether proportional representation encourages higher societal integration by enabling direct democratic participation of distinct factions and minorities; or whether it in fact promotes strife and factionalism by emphasizing political and social divisions, and by disincentivizing broad cooperation and representation within mainstream political parties.

d. The Executive:* The most immediate practical consequence of elections, and at times the most acute function performed by the Knesset, is that of Government formation. Ultimately, the Knesset appoints the executive Government, or Cabinet – consisting of the Prime Minister and the assorted Ministers (equivalent to "Secretaries" in the U.S.) which lead their respective governmental Ministries (equivalent to "Departments" in the U.S.). This is a collegiate body with collective decision-making authority and responsibilities. A Government "resolution" constitutes formal binding policy, akin to an Executive Order in a presidential system. With limited exceptions, the entire executive branch and its agencies, officials and organs all fall under the purview and authority of the Government. Individual Ministers have their own spheres of responsibility alongside their collective role as Government members. Some areas of Government authority are explicitly defined by law, while other areas are more vague or wholly based on custom. Ministers are typically (but not always) senior members of Coalition parties, with the most high-ranking roles usually reserved for party leadership.

The makeup and configuration of each Government generally reflect the election results and power dynamics within the governing Coalition. The bargaining power of prospective Coalition partners is not only a function of faction size (and vote-share), but also of a party's leverage. In this sense large or dominant parties are not necessarily able to dictate Government composition (alongside many other aspects of Government action and policy). A small party may often "punch above its weight" if, to name just one such scenario, it is numerically crucial to the formation and survival of a given coalition (i.e., a "kingmaker"). For many years the religious Ultra-Orthodox parties were thus regarded, and they indeed have previously alternated between left-wing and right-wing Governments. Another example is that of Naftali Bennett, who became Prime Minister in 2021 at the head of a party with only seven MKs as a result of the leverage his party enjoyed against other prospective Coalition partners.

The eventual allocation of government departments and their ministerial supervision is the subject of intense post-election negotiations and is usually formalized in public agreements signed by all coalition parties. A party could conceivably join a parliamentary Coalition without receiving a seat in Government or a ministerial role, or could even "support from without" by

---

* See next section for definition of "The Government" and use of capitalization.

abstaining from certain no-confidence votes and thus enabling a Coalition's existence even without technically joining it, but such cases are rare.

The assumption of Ministerial roles by senior party leadership is an integral part of electoral considerations and strategy. Parties are touted not only for their legislative agendas but also as vehicles for their preferred candidates in Ministerial positions. Indeed, election PR campaigns generally focus on the executive role of candidates rather than a party's legislative vision, and parties usually declare in advance which Ministries they aspire to lead. A party's ambitions may even be limited to its executive accomplishments without any meaningful interest in legislative efforts. The iconic 1999 election slogan of Natan Sharansky's sectorial party aimed at immigrants from the former Soviet Union was *Nash Kontrol* ("our control" in Russian), alluding to the party's stated intent of leading the Ministry of Interior.

Accordingly, a vote for a specific list is essentially a dual selection: Voting for future MKs to (hopefully) form a Coalition and advance legislation, while simultaneously voting for prospective Cabinet Ministers to implement policy in their respective spheres of influence and in line with party-voter ideology or interests. Perhaps more obviously and visibly, a vote for a party list is an implicit vote for the prospective Prime Minister the party has committed (or is expected) to support. In this sense, the executive Government and its Ministers are directly accountable to parliament, while also indirectly accountable to their political party and its voters.

As in any Westminster-style parliamentary democracy, there is a high degree of overlap between the legislative Coalition majority in the Knesset and the executive Government cabinet. The Government serves at the pleasure of parliament and can be dismissed by an absolute majority of MKs. The two branches necessarily and by-definition work in relative synchronization most of the time. The Knesset passes the annual budget enabling, defining and limiting all government expenditures. Most enacted laws are initiated by the executive government, while much government action enjoys the sanction and approval of the parliamentary majority. The Government is dependent on the Knesset's constant and proactive support for a range of decisions and activities, while the Knesset majority (and Coalition) generally follows the Government's lead.

Executive power in Israel is highly centralized in that the national Government and its respective organs control most state action and activity throughout the country at nearly all levels of locality. There are no significant "county" or "district" administrative units between the State and those of cities or townships. Urban municipalities have some limited authority for the administration of local government functions, but the national Government maintains heavy involvement in these as well. As just one anecdotal example, the municipal property tax rate is defined by each municipality, but national legislation defines eligibility criteria for reductions or exemptions; another example is that local public school teachers are often employed directly by the national Ministry of Education.

The President of Israel is a largely ceremonial role which functions as a formal "head of state" but with no executive powers. The President does exercise certain formal duties and does enjoy a degree of statutory authority, which can even be politically decisive in unique circumstances.

e. Oversight: The Knesset conducts some limited supervision of the Executive and of various state organs through dedicated committees. The chairmanships of more influential or prestigious committees are also often sought after by senior politicians and are typically agreed upon as part of overall Coalition-forming negotiations. The composition of these committees is partially defined by statute and usually represents both Coalition and Opposition parties in accordance with their relative size in the Knesset.

Instances of direct democracy are extremely limited and there are almost no occasions for citizens to vote regarding specific governmental decisions or candidates. The Israeli electorate lacks any significant mechanism for direct oversight over specific executive or legislative measures. Aside municipal elections for mayoral and city-council roles and aside national elections for party lists as described above, Israelis generally do not vote on particular legislative propositions, on budgetary measures or on personal candidates for political and administrative roles.

Terminology and Housekeeping

Some terminological clarifications are in order so as to minimize confusion and will hopefully be helpful, without getting bogged down with technical definitions.

"Judicial supremacy" is the state of affairs in which the judiciary or some part thereof wields the power of final determination over the most contentious societal issues involving policies, priorities and values. Prof. Jeremy Waldron recently described this succinctly as "a court, unchecked, having the final say."[7] Judicial decision-making is immune from public sentiment even when communicated in the highest level possible within the legal hierarchy (e.g., through duly enacted legislation or even constitutional amendments). Absent literal governmental overthrow, the electorate is effectively powerless to impose judicial compliance with popular political preference. Correspondingly, "judicial supremacism" is the general desire for virtually unlimited judicial discretion, the belief in judicial infallibility (e.g., judges do not typically share the vices or distortions which afflict elected officials, voters or laypersons), and the preference for judicial resolution of contentious public disagreements on core societal issues, over resolution through the political process.

A related term is that of "judicial activism" which this book will try to avoid for the most part unless quoted from other sources. In the absence of any widely accepted definition, "judicial activism" will usually refer to court decisions inadequately based in law and exhibiting a strong degree of lawlessness (a useful conception borrowed from Prof. Randy Barnett). In this sense, identifying such activism or its opposite of "judicial constraint" is highly contextual and does not parallel the notion of judicial intervention or abstention. In some contexts, a decision to strike down a law might be "constrained" and perfectly lawful, while a decision to defer to patently illegal government action might be "activist." More generally, to follow the Richard Posner definition,[8] an "activist" approach could refer to a belief in, or desire for, constant expansion of judicial power at the expense of other government branches.

The term "constitutional" will often be used in its broader sense to mean the primary institutional arrangements, core governmental mechanisms and fundamental values of a given regime. It is not limited only to the context of a formal written constitution. In this sense, countries with no codified constitution such as the United Kingdom or New Zealand still indeed possess constitutional rules and conventions, and even undemocratic dictatorships typically maintain some form of constitutional structure. For instance, rules defining and governing elections or those regarding the relationship between the executive and legislative branches are also almost always "constitutional" in nature. The history and specifics of the Israeli pseudo-constitution, along with a tighter definition of "constitution," will be discussed in detail in Part III.

"Judicial review" refers to the general phenomenon of judges and courts reviewing (and potentially invalidating) government action and decisions. While in the United States this term is often shorthand exclusively for the striking down of primary legislation, here it will refer to the broader definition and may also include administrative review of executive action, depending on context.

The term "government" can have many meanings in different contexts. In Israel this term is usually reserved for the highest tier of the executive branch comprised of the Prime Minister and all other Ministers heading the different governmental ministries. This sense of "government" is thus a distinct body of roughly a few dozen members, with ultimate executive authority and with specific functions mostly defined by law. The book will follow this specific usage such that "Government" or "the Government" (with a capital "G") will refer to the apex Israeli executive organ described above. Another term employed interchangeably referring to the same body is the "Cabinet."* More generally, the term "government" may also include the governing majority of legislators (typically dubbed "the Coalition") working in tandem with the Cabinet to formulate and enact policy. Other usages will be more context-dependent – "governmental" will usually refer to any part of the State governing apparatus (the various departments, organs, institutions, agencies, officials, etc.), while abstract "government" might often be employed for more theoretical discussions and include all aspects of governing in a political society. The Court (capital C) will refer to the Israeli Supreme Court.

The Legal Counsel to the Government (here mostly abbreviated "LCG") is

* In Israel, the "cabinet" technically refers to a smaller subset of Government Ministers in charge of national defense and foreign policy. In this book "Cabinet" will denote the more conventional notion, identical to the Government.

Israel's top legal official, a civil servant within the Ministry of Justice but generally subordinate only to the authority of the Supreme Court. The role and powers of the LCG will be covered thoroughly in Chapter 8. The LCG (person and office) is often referred to as "Attorney General" in English, though this title is inaccurate and misleading and will generally not be used throughout the book. A separate role serving under the LCG is that of the State Attorney, who heads the various departments representing the government in virtually all litigation, be it civil, administrative, or criminal prosecutions.

Where available, reliable and relevant, this book will usually use official English translations of Hebrew sources. Nonetheless, many instances will require the author's translation from Hebrew or some tweaks to inaccurate official translations. Israeli legislation has no formal English version; most relevant legal scholarship is in Hebrew and only a small fraction of Israeli case law is translated to other languages. English quotes from original Hebrew sources are based on the author's best effort at informed and accurate translation. Of note in this context: a) The Israeli term for the top judge within a given court is "*Nasi*," which technically means "President." This book will refer to the role as "President" in lower-tier courts, and as "Chief Justice" in the Supreme Court. b) One form of Israeli legislation involves Basic Laws, which are titled with a colon and don't state their year of enactment, for example "Basic Law: The Judiciary" or "Basic Law: Human Dignity and Liberty." These will be referred to in first capital letters and occasionally (for clarity) with quotation marks.

Finally – as this book focuses exclusively on the Israeli legal system, the Israeli Supreme Court and Israeli government, the word "Israeli" becomes increasingly redundant. Going forward, references should be assumed to regard the specific Israeli context unless stated otherwise.

How To Read This Book

This book is structured such that each chapter serves as a "standalone" treatment of a distinct legal doctrine or element central to the expansion of judicial power. While no aspect of our judiciary can be fully separated from all others, the chapters will attempt to be relatively independent and to cover each topic comprehensively. Aside from the benefit of coherence and structure, this layout will hopefully allow readers to return to desired chapters in order to refresh their memory on a specific doctrine or issue, or even enable casual readers to gain concentrated (albeit limited) insight by skipping to a desired chapter without reading the entire book.

Parts I to III describe three successive "stages," and the book chapters follow a roughly chronological order, but not strictly so: many key developments occurred side by side, even as at each stage one doctrine often precipitated or enabled the next stage of a different doctrine. In other words, while the advent of certain events may be placed within a linear timeline, the many elements of judicial supremacy developed mostly in parallel. These were not only concurrent but also interwoven and reciprocal with constant mutual reinforcement. For instance, the “standing” revolution, the “reasonableness” doctrine and the Legal Counsel to the Government are all distinct topics but are also deeply interrelated, and the effect of each element cannot be properly evaluated when considered in isolation. The sum is greater than all its parts.

In a similar vein, this book attempts to portray a rather large and highly complex picture with many interrelated elements, such that it is impossible to convey all the information at once. If some parts may be confusing or seem to have missing components, these will usually be resolved or addressed at a later point in the book. Having much ground to cover, including simultaneous and related developments which nonetheless require separate treatment and description, the book must be read in a holistic manner with different elements and themes tying together and the overall picture becoming gradually clearer as the chapters progress.

This book focuses on the “what” and “how” of Israeli judicial supremacy, not the “why” of it. It generally does not address most social and cultural fault-lines or geopolitical circumstances that make up the background and context for the events and cases reviewed. It likewise does not dwell on the many conceivable underlying motives, conscious or less so, that compelled Supreme Court Justices to act as they did. These are all the subject of comprehensive and lively debate – their inclusion here would be not only impractical but would also significantly muddy the waters and cause unnecessary confusion. Justice Robert Jackson famously advocated for “analysis of the statute” instead of “psychoanalysis of Congress” – in similar spirit, this book endeavors to analyze rulings and doctrines, not judges and lawyers.

Furthermore, there is no desire here to demonize the Court or to vilify its members. The Supreme Court has been and remains a critical institution for Israeli democracy and rule of law – resolving disputes, clarifying law, safeguarding rights and holding government accountable. Its members are for the most part highly capable, impartial, professional and knowledgeable jurists, deeply patriotic and upright citizens committed to Israeli justice and prosperity. The Court’s rulings are for the most part rigorous, disciplined, beneficial, coherent and legally sound. This holds true for the vast majority of judges throughout the Israeli judiciary and over the course of Israel’s history.

Nevertheless. The substantial and decisive deviations from the high standards to which the Court has historically adhered have regrettably sprouted and grown such that they tarnish the Court’s legacy. In its relentless pursuit of rogue judicial supremacy, the Supreme Court undermines its own role, harms Israeli democracy, and threatens the stability and viability of our society. Comprehending the extent and severity of Israel’s legal flaws, most of them caused or exacerbated by the Court’s lawless conduct, is the first and most important step towards righting the ship of Israeli jurisprudence and of perhaps even alleviating many related ailments of Israeli society. The devil is in the details – without further ado, let us now confront them.

Part I

Foundation

Two pillars of Supreme Court institutional power jointly serving as structural basis for the expansion of judicial power and the advance towards judicial supremacy

Chapter 1

Judicial Appointments

The Self-Packing Court

> *"The Israeli Supreme Court, by selecting its own successors, is a judicial oligarchy. Kind of like the Guardian Council in Iran, which is not something one would want to emulate."*
> — Prof. Steven Calabresi[1]

(Un)Welcome to the Family

Professor Ruth Gavison was one of Israel's most remarkable legal figures of the past generation. A brilliant scholar, a tireless civil rights activist and a revered educator, Gavison was known for her sharp-tongued style and her political moderation. Of wiry frame and intense disposition, she was defiantly uncompromising in her commitment to her intellectual truth and values while constantly aspiring to find common ground and foster dialogue between Israeli groups and communities.

Gavison had graduated from the Hebrew University law school at the top of her class, a favorite student of then-professor Aharon Barak. When Barak established "Mishpatim," Israel's first American-style student-run law review journal, his student Gavison penned an essay for the inaugural issue. After clerking at the Supreme Court Gavison continued to earn a doctorate in jurisprudence at Oxford under the tutelage of H.L.A. Hart. Parallel to an academic career on the faculty of the Hebrew University law school, Gavison was a founder of the Association for Civil Rights in Israel where she also served as Chairperson and President. A renowned scholar and practitioner in the fields of legal philosophy, human rights and constitutional law, she was eventually awarded the Israel Prize for law and was admitted to the Israeli Academy of Sciences and Humanities.

Ruth Gavison passed away in the summer of 2020. Just one month later, another Ruth died – U.S. Supreme Court Justice Ruth Bader Ginsburg. While these two "Ruth G's" were very different women in many respects, and while they almost certainly maintained divergent conceptions of the judiciary, their shared similarities and the proximity of their passing beg some comparison. Both were fierce Jewish jurists of small stature, outspoken in their views and emphatic in their demeanor, commanding the respect of their peers and opponents by the sheer force of their intellect and personality; both were prominently active in their respective civil rights' legal circles; both were perceived (by others as well as by themselves) at one time as moderates and consensus-builders. Whatever the value of such a comparison might be, it highlights the plainly obvious point, that an attribute the two women never shared was their judicial role – Gavison never became a judge.

It could have turned out differently. Gavison was a leading candidate to join the Israeli Supreme Court in 2005, with the unequivocal backing of the elected branches of government and especially the Minister of Justice, Tzippi Livni. She was universally considered qualified for the job; her appointment would clearly have reflected public sentiment.

Yet her bid was aggressively blocked by none other than Aharon Barak himself. As Chief Justice, Barak wielded an effective veto on all judicial nominations to the Supreme Court. Barak had no reservations about Gavison's professional or judicial capabilities. His unabashed argument objecting to her appointment was that she "has an agenda unfitting for the Court" – a now-famous statement he made at a public conference.

No further elaboration was needed as few could doubt Barak's meaning – Gavison was a consistent and compelling critic of the Court's supremacist jurisprudence spearheaded by Barak. In sprawling law review articles and academic textbooks, she respectfully advocated judicial restraint and warned against the Court's foray into political affairs. So polite was her tone when critiquing Barak's court, that her 1997 mega-essay (eventually published as a short book) taking on the Court's "constitutional revolution" starts out with four apologetic pages cautiously explaining why such criticism is legitimate in the first place.[2]

None of this mattered. In single-handedly blocking Gavison from joining the bench, Barak robbed Israeli society and our legal system of the opportunity to have one of our finest legal luminaries on the country's highest court. Years later when discussing the judicial appointments process at a major legal conference, Barak described the Court as "one family." He explained that "the good of the country requires we have a coherent court… someone not part of the family could not join this system." Barak's phrasing might even be compared to the Don Corleone mafia adage – "never take sides against the family."* While the criteria for belonging to Barak's family was never articulated, it would seem that expressing public views critical of Barak's jurisprudence was sufficient basis for exclusion.

How could Chief Justice Barak have barred Gavison's appointment in the teeth of governmental desire and public consensus? To answer, this chapter will

---

* In the 1972 film *The Godfather*.

explore the unique judicial appointments process in Israel.

Not What, but Who and How

The process for appointing judges is one of the more sensitive and delicate matters usually addressed in a country's constitutional documents. This is especially true for "apex" courts – those at the top of judicial hierarchies with final adjudication powers, often called "Supreme" or "Constitutional" courts. The tension inherent in such appointments derives naturally from the dual modern approach to institutional judicial power.

On the one hand, judicial independence and professional qualifications are a key aspect of how we envision the judicial role in a democracy – an impartial tribunal which settles disputes according to law, insulated and shielded from external influence and public opinion with regard to the outcome of a specific case. By design, judges are not supposed to reflect public sentiment when resolving contentious cases and must work within an institutional framework that enables their autonomy and independence and protects these from undue interference. Their selection therefore ought to be informed not by politics or ideology, but rather by professional considerations relating to legal qualifications, experience, knowledge and judicial suitability.

On the other hand, judges are ultimately government officials wielding state power. As final adjudicators such power tends to be considerable and at times immense. Judicial decisions have binding legal effect, such that unelected judges have the unusual power of altering law or creating new legal rules, outside the accepted democratic process for legislation and policymaking. This sometimes means having final say on specific issues (until perhaps the statutory law itself is changed). Many legal disputes involving the interpretation of ambiguous texts or the application of core societal values will almost certainly be influenced by a judge's personal worldview. It is precisely in the judicial independence from public sentiment and from government control that we find the risk of subtle tyranny – ultimate coercive state power exercised by unaccountable officials. As such, the method of their selection (and conceivably, their removal) must serve as a counterbalance to judicial power and its counter-majoritarian nature.

Another angle from which to approach this question is the recognition that the law itself becomes a dead letter unless faithfully applied by judges. If we accept the democratic premise that lawmaking is primarily the domain of elected and accountable representatives, but that it is judges that will often define the law's actual application, then we must concede that enacting new legislation will be an inadequate method of creating or changing the law. Effecting legal change requires also the (delicate, indirect and gradual) democratic control of judicial personnel over time.

Put simply, identity matters. If the public and government must not interfere directly with *what* the court does in each case, the question of *who* sits on the court and decides these cases becomes paramount. Thus the manner in which judges are selected to their post, the *how*, is universally recognized as a critical component of any governing structure.

The Judicial Selection Committee

Judges in Israel are ceremonially appointed by the President; in practice, they are chosen and promoted by a statutory committee called "the Judicial Selection Committee," which has remained largely unchanged and intact since its formation in the 1953 Judicial Law. Today the selection committee and method are defined in Basic Law: The Judiciary and in the Courts Act (both first enacted in 1984, recodifying many pre-existing arrangements). Prior to 1953, for the first few years of Israel's existence judges were appointed by elected representatives – judicial candidates were nominated by the Minister of Justice and then approved by the cabinet and the Knesset.

The Judicial Selection Committee is currently comprised of nine members as defined by law:

Two members are Cabinet Ministers – one is appointed by the Government while the other, always the Justice Minister, chairs the committee.

Two members are Knesset Members (elected legislators), who are appointed directly by the Knesset in secret ballot. Customarily one of these was often a member of the Opposition, though this is not prescribed by law.

Two members are attorneys appointed by the Israel Bar Association's governing body. The Bar serves simultaneously as both a mandatory lawyers' collective labor union, and as regulator of the legal profession (including the licensing of attorneys and adjudication of ethical misconduct).

Three members are Justices currently serving on the Supreme Court – one is the Chief Justice, and the other two are technically appointed by a majority of the other Justices, while in practice they are selected by the Chief Justice.

Judges in Israel must retire from their judicial post at the age of 70, with some limited exceptions.

The committee is convened by the Justice Minister. The committee appoints judges to all tiers of Israel's primary judicial system – the Magistrate, District, and Supreme Court – as well as to most other courts (see more on the judiciary structure in the next chapter). It promotes judges to various positions between tiers and within their current court. The committee also appoints the Supreme Court Chief Justice. Candidates may be submitted to the committee by the Minister of Justice, by the Chief Justice, or jointly by any three committee members.

A simple majority (typically five out of nine members) is sufficient for most appointments. Since a 2007 amendment, appointments to the Supreme Court require a majority of seven out of nine members. Theoretically each member must exercise individual discretion and must vote independently of the institution they represent; in practice, the Supreme Court members have historically voted as a "bloc," and other member groups on the committee often do the same.

Committee proceedings and deliberations are confidential, including interviews and discussions with candidates. A very recent (2022) change to the internal committee rules mandates that some interviews for Supreme Court candidates will be broadcast live, making them almost like a public hearing – though whether and how this is implemented and to what effect remains to be seen.

Readers following the committee arithmetic will have noticed several striking features. Elected representatives accountable to the public are outnumbered as a minority of four out of nine, with the legal establishment (the Supreme Court and the Bar Association) commanding a majority. If they so choose, this unelected majority can appoint and promote judges throughout the legal system almost at will (provided the Minister of Justice convenes a meeting). When one of the MKs is an Opposition member, the Government and Coalition comprise only a third of the committee. Above all, the Justices voting in unison can block any Supreme Court candidate – without their support, the remaining committee members will not reach the seven votes required.

The effects and consequences of this system are dramatic as will presently be described in detail.

The Judicial Veto

The presiding Justices of the Supreme Court can essentially veto the appointment of their future colleagues and successors. Three Justices voting as one can prevent any new judges joining their bench. One may reasonably wonder at the wisdom or justification of *any* judicial intervention whatsoever within the appointments process. While a body selecting judges should probably consider the advice and professional opinion of other judges, such serving judges having an actual concrete say (i.e., a vote) would likely be considered unusual and problematic in many jurisdictions. But a downright veto – which as we shall see translates into the de facto dictation of who gets the job – seems far more objectionable.

The reasons for this go to the core of democratic governance – the most senior State officials must either be directly accountable to the public or must be appointed by such elected representatives. This principle derives from a number of rationales, chiefly to avoid self-perpetuating replication within professional bureaucratic ranks and to ensure that those wielding power reflect public sentiment (even if only indirectly). It's the same reason that top-ranking military generals are selected, promoted or approved by an elected branch of government and not simply by other serving generals. Granting extensive governmental authority to unelected public servants is one thing, at times even necessary or beneficial; granting them the keys to who joins or replaces them is another thing entirely. The democratic legitimacy of powerful state officials is a central component of modern Western government – the appointment to judicial office being no exception.

This echoes the above point regarding the way laws are applied by courts. If one accepts that legislation will be ultimately applied only to the extent and in the manner that judges choose to, it seems that new laws enacted to direct future judicial conduct would be futile, if it is the judges themselves who appoint their own successors. Under such circumstances new judges may well be chosen in accordance with a desired outcome adverse to any new legislation. What use are new laws if an internal self-sustaining appointments cycle can render them perpetually impotent? Here we find the convergence of these two linked issues – democratic legitimacy of senior government officials, and judicial fidelity to legislation. Both are challenged by a judicial veto over successors.

Many countries and jurisdictions differ in the way that they appoint their judges. There is certainly no single ideal or universal way to go about it. Nonetheless, the vast majority of democratic nations do in fact share some critical insights. One is the acknowledgment that judges in apex courts which can review the validity of legislation are exercising an inherently and inescapably political function; another is that the method of selecting judges must correspond to the court's relative degree of judicial and political power. As will be presently shown, Israel is a marked outlier in both these respects. The Supreme Court can strike down laws (see Chapter 9), yet the inherently political nature of such power is denied while the judicial appointments process remains firmly within judicial – not political – hands.

Professor Yoav Dotan is of one Israel's leading experts in public and administrative law and was Dean of the Hebrew University law school. Politically considered as left-of-center, Dotan is one of the few prominent and consistent academic critics of Israeli judicial supremacy. His work will appear often throughout the following chapters. In a 2007 comparative study regarding the relationship between judicial power and democratic accountability, Dotan concludes that most developed democracies reject the model of a court that can strike down laws without corresponding arrangements ensuring a high degree of democratic accountability.[3] Most European countries follow the Kelsenian model of dedicated "constitutional courts," and recognize that constitutional adjudication requires the application of a political-moral worldview.[4] Accordingly, judges are appointed to these courts by overt political actors in a process which is explicitly political. Judicial appointments in the United States of course follow a similar political model in both Federal and (usually) State contexts, based on similar assumptions. Jurisdictions which prefer a more de-politicized selection process, such as the United Kingdom and some other Common Law countries, opt for a much more limited role assigned to courts – including leaving "final say" authority to the elected legislature.

Similarly, while comparing Israeli judicial selection and constitutional courts elsewhere, leading Israeli sociologist and political theorist Oren Soffer observed that "empirical examination of the main models of judicial review of legislation proves that in most cases the appointment of tribunals has a political base." This serves as "another mechanism that helps to alleviate the idea that non-elected judges are interfering in the legislative process," such that judicial review is "softened by stressing the link of the review of legislation to elected politicians..."[5]

Dotan emphasizes that the democratic accountability problem in Israel is "more severe" than other jurisdictions described above, due to the mismatch between the courts' expansive powers of judicial review and the judicial appointments process essentially sidelining elected representatives. This state of affairs reflects a "significant democratic deficit" at the core of Israeli judicial review.[6]

A recent comprehensive study demonstrated this issue in greater detail.[7] The 2021 study reviewed the judicial appointment process employed by a combination of all OECD member states; the thirty leading countries in The Economist's Democracy Index; and all fifty states of the United States. The conclusion was unequivocal: in almost all developed democracies, the composition of apex or constitutional courts is determined directly by the public or by their elected representatives, especially when such a court enjoys semi-legislative authority in the form of constitutional judicial review. Of all the jurisdictions reviewed, only Israel and five others don't place top judicial selection in the hands of elected officials. Of these five, two (the U.K. and Luxembourg) don't empower courts to strike down laws, and one (Turkey) is not defined as a democracy in the Economist ranking. In other words, as a matter of objective fact, Israel is an extreme outlier when considering the disparity between the Supreme Court's power and the way its members are appointed, sharing this dubious distinction with only two other developed democratic legal systems.

We will return to the question of a political judicial appointments process later in this chapter. The point here is not to advocate for such a process in Israel or elsewhere – it is merely to illustrate the degree to which the Israeli method is unusual, in principle and in practice. And while the lack of political dominance and the effective judicial veto are two sides of the same coin, these are in fact distinct features which must be addressed separately, and we now turn to the more egregious of the two.

Controlling the Bench

The judicial veto under current circumstances means effective control of who gets appointed to the Supreme Court. Of course, one might plausibly argue that mere veto power does not amount to positively choosing colleagues and successors for the bench. While intuitively appealing and technically true, this is not the case in Israel.

The judicial veto power – hardly benign to begin with – translates into the practical ability to dictate who is appointed to the bench. This is due to the imbalance of power and incentives on the selection committee. Indeed, many scholars (including those sympathetic to the Court) casually refer to the Court's de facto control over judicial appointments as a given. The Court has both time and foreseeability on its side enabling a high degree of strategic planning and maneuverability, a luxury the political representatives don't enjoy. Supreme Court judges know precisely how long their tenure is and can plan ahead accordingly – they can therefore sit back and wait for the emergence of more favorable circumstances. In the case of severe disagreement or poor relations between the judicial-legal establishment and the political-elected branches of government, all the former need do is ride out the storm. Politicians on the other hand need to deliver on campaign promises and present some measure of success to voters within a limited timespan, and they must consider the likelihood that they will soon no longer be in power (recall that the average life expectancy of an Israeli government is under two years).

Politicians simply have far more to lose in a standoff, and thus have a strong incentive to yield and avoid rocking the appointments boat. A compromise judge on the bench is better than the ideal judge in the bush. Any such so-called compromise, however, is not a "meeting in the middle" but rather a concession under duress – either appoint someone acceptable to the current Justices or don't appoint anyone at all, otherwise known as "my way or the highway." And like all forms of bargaining leverage, the threat of veto (and ensuing delay and failure) need not be explicitly stated, nor do the various parties need to reach the point of being at actual loggerheads. The shared knowledge of the ultimate endgame – i.e., that if push comes to shove, the Court will double down and thwart any attempted appointment – is sufficient to cow most committee members into submission. In this sense "conservative" judges appointed to the Court are in fact invariably "compromise" judges – approved under the constraints of the existing veto, and not necessarily reflecting public preference or the available pool of conservative judicial candidates.

This dynamic has been demonstrated in reality time and again. In the most well-known confrontation between a Minister of Justice and the Court regarding a specific candidate – that of Ruth Gavison described above – the Court prevailed simply by waiting. In the instance of candidate Nili Cohen, the Court Justices themselves were deeply divided about a particular candidate (see later section) – but the question of selection was considered an internal intra-judicial affair. Indeed, the Minister of Justice at the time, Tommy Lapid (father of current politician Yair Lapid), was hardly considered a relevant factor in the decision to accept or reject Cohen's candidacy, and was barely mentioned in contemporary journalistic reporting of the controversy.[8] His own approach was to meekly accept whatever the Justices might decree.

A more general illustration can be found in the relative ease or difficulty the different political "camps" might encounter when trying to advance their desired candidates. By and large, left-leaning governments will typically find themselves fully aligned with the Court's activist preferences, such that the judicial appointments process will be a relative cakewalk, with displays of goodwill and cooperation abounding as the committee breezes through the candidate list. Right-leaning governments or anyone who desires "restrained" candidates will conversely find themselves fighting an uphill battle, at odds with the Court and in constant tension and conflict throughout the process, at times leading to a full-blown (yet futile and predetermined) public showdown. From a slightly different angle, candidates clearly aligned with the political left – not only ideologically but also actively involved in left-wing party apparatuses – are appointed as a matter of course, while the appointment of similarly bona fide right-wing candidates is virtually unthinkable. Prior to his appointment as Supreme Court Justice in 2007, Hanan Meltzer was a political activist and candidate with a number of left-wing political parties, worked as legal counsel to dominant Labor politician (and eventual Prime Minister) Yitzhak Rabin, and served as Chairman of the highly influential Labor Party Constitutional Committee. In no realistic scenario could a parallel right-wing candidate – with a similar pedigree of political involvement in, say, the mainstream-right Likud party – be feasibly appointed. In an amusing admission, politician Yair Lapid (and leader of the Opposition) described in a 2024 social media post how the left-wing Opposition "secured a majority" in the committee by appointing a single MK – revealing that in his eyes, the judicial and Bar committee members were effectively representing the Opposition in all but name.[9]

While this reality is taken for granted by many, it ought to give one pause to ask what this says about the Court's actual power over the selections process. Quite unrelated to the question of the Court's possible political or ideological bias, the fact that the political Left can appoint Justices far more smoothly than the political Right, and that this is casually accepted in Israel as a "given," likely tells us all we need to know about the way a mere veto translates into decisive control.

Some argue that the Court's veto power is justified by the parallel veto power available to the political representatives on the committee. But it is for precisely the reasons presented above that this argument is erroneous and misleading. While it's true that the four political representatives on the committee may also technically "veto" Supreme Court candidates, the imbalance of incentives and feasible alternatives means that this ostensible veto is anything but mutual. Further still, this argument ignores the more obvious and principled objection – that beyond a certain threshold of legal-political power held by the judiciary, a political veto (at the very least) is democratically justified and even essential, while a judicial veto raises serious concerns regarding democratic accountability and legitimacy, among others. The existence of the former can hardly serve to defend the latter. Lastly, this argument fails to recognize the institutional significance of a veto power regarding one's own institution – unlike the politician's veto, the Justices on the committee veto (and thus control) who joins their own ranks, creating a range of distortions and dynamics typical of such situations.

Others contend that this judicial veto is the politicians' own recent doing. The seven-member majority required to approve Supreme Court nominees, essentially creating the judicial veto, was the result of a late amendment enacted in 2007 under a center-left government – one of only two successful legislative changes to the selection process since introduced in 1953. The amendment was spearheaded by then-opposition member Gideon Saar of the right-wing Likud party and is therefore often referred to as the Saar amendment. So maybe the politicians can only blame themselves for voluntarily handing the veto keys over to the judges?

Not quite. This argument fails to point out that prior to the 2007 amendment, the five-member majority of Supreme Court and Bar Association committee members could unilaterally appoint Supreme Court Justices, as only an ordinary majority was required for such appointments. Instead of a veto, the legal establishment enjoyed pure, direct, de-jure appointment power, in the teeth of any political opposition whatsoever. The elected committee members may as well have been ceremonial observers. This arrangement amounted to a judicial veto in any case, as the likelihood of the Bar Association committee members aligning with the politicians to form a majority against the Justices was extremely low (see next section). In terms of democratic accountability and legitimacy, this prior arrangement was immeasurably worse than the indirect control deriving from a judicial veto. A more accurate description of the 2007 amendment is that it gave the *politicians*, for the first time, some form of veto over Supreme Court appointments – the parallel veto accorded to the Justices was a "downgrade" from their previous clout. The argument faulting politicians as responsible for the veto is thus disingenuous and ignores the preceding circumstances. The 2007 amendment creating a formal judicial veto should correctly be considered a (very) slight improvement, going from a genuinely outrageous judicial selection process to a merely indefensible one.

The elected branches do possess an additional leverage mechanism. By law, the Minister of Justice (serving as committee chairperson) is tasked with convening the committee, and he or she can refrain from convening it at all. Aside from delaying appointments to the Supreme Court, this would also delay appointments to lower-tier trial and appellate courts urgently needing vacancies filled. This can be used as a pressure tactic against the Supreme Court Justices and the judiciary as a whole, as cases accumulate and the administrative burden on judges and courts swells. Indeed, this is precisely the tactic employed by various Justice Ministers (including Daniel Friedmann and Tzippi Livni) over the years when at loggerheads with the bench over judicial appointments.

However, refusing to convene the committee is largely ineffective and will often even backfire.

First, as explained above, politicians simply have more incentive to appoint a candidate, and they risk more by delaying. Second, the courts can shrug off the adverse effects of a judge shortage, as they did in the case of Ruth Gavison and in other instances. Among other reasons, the case backlog causes disruptions in judicial public services (e.g., cancelled hearings, long overdue rulings, etc.) and in overlapping areas such as law enforcement and private commerce. Such a situation directly affecting ordinary people might be tolerable for unaccountable judges but can't be maintained for long by elected politicians.

Third, importantly, the Court might even order the Justice Minister to convene the committee against his or her will (and in direct contradiction of the controlling statute). During the height of the judicial reform controversy in 2023, Justice Minister Yariv Levin's refusal to convene the committee was swiftly challenged in court. Despite clear statutory language establishing the Justice Minister's discretion whether and when to convene the committee, the Supreme Court seemed poised to rule that Levin's delay was illegal (ironically even violating its own procedural rules to issue a preliminary decision)[10] and had set a hearing for oral argument. It is not at all inconceivable that the Court would simply have decreed a time and place for the committee convention – with or without its chairman's approval or participation. This head-on collision was initially avoided after Levin announced he would convene the committee due to the Israel-Hamas war and overall state of emergency in the country.

But the issue resurfaced soon after. In 2024 the Committee was supposed to appoint the Court's new Chief Justice from among the current Justices. Levin refused to convene the committee because he objected to the practice by which the most senior Justice automatically becomes Chief Justice. Some argued this practice was illegal, because the Justices impose their pick and essentially preclude the committee from exercising its own judgment and statutory authority in selecting the Chief Justice. Levin also favored the candidacy of Justice Yosef Elron over that of Justice Yitzhak Amit who would have been selected under the "seniority" rule.

This time the Court assumed a more aggressive stance – after a few back-and-forths, the Court astonishingly ordered that the committee be convened against the Minister's wishes, without his authorization and indeed even in his absence. This was despite the unequivocal statutory language which grants the Justice Minister sole authority to convene the committee. In a manner that can only be called farcical, under the Court's watchful supervision, the committee was convened without Levin or any other Government and Coalition representatives, and it proceeded to formally appoint Justice Amit as Chief Justice by a majority of five votes. Indeed, the Committee didn't even meet in the Justice Ministry (as it would typically do), but instead assembled in the Judiciary Administration offices.* Levin, Knesset Speaker Amir Ohana and many other politicians refused to accept Amit's appointment as valid, and continue to maintain (to this day) that his appointment is legally void.

Whether Levin's or the Court's actions were legal or proper is beside the point. This event simply demonstrates that even the Justice Minister's ultimate power – refusing to convene the Committee if a satisfactory compromise is not reached – may be easily circumvented by the Court. The political stick of refusing to

---

* Amazingly, the Court's insistence on forcibly appointing Amit was entirely unnecessary, as Amit was serving as "acting" Chief Justice in any case per statutory rules, with all the authority and privileges of a permanent Chief Justice. That is, as long as the Committee was not convened by Levin, Amit was de facto Chief Justice anyway.

convene the committee does not pose a genuine threat to the legal establishment and has thus far proven to be little more than a twig.

As a separate matter, the veto also extends to the dismissal – that is, impeachment – of judges. Israeli law stipulates that the manner for impeachment of public officials is usually the same method by which they are appointed. The only way to impeach a Supreme Court justice would be to muster the same seven-member majority required for their appointment. The obvious consequence is that while the prospect of impeaching Justices is extremely unlikely to begin with, the judicial veto makes it nigh impossible.

Without conducting an extensive review of attitudes towards the impeachment of judges, it's worth recalling Alexander Hamilton's argument in The Federalist 81. Hamilton describes the legislature's power to impeach judges as the ultimate safeguard against judicial encroachment on legislative authority. He calls it a "complete security" against the danger of "deliberate" judicial "usurpations" because Congress could remove judges from their post by "punishing their presumption" and "degrading their station."[11] Hamilton considered the power to impeach judges a critical (and indeed the only substantial) democratic check on judicial authority, which served as part of the rationale to empower the judiciary in the first place. In Israel, the formidable Supreme Court is effectively immune from any such threat due to the veto wielded by the Justices themselves.

We have thus far reviewed the direct and immediate effects of the veto power on appointments to the Supreme Court itself. Let us now turn our attention to some broader and more indirect implications of this system.

Lower Tier Judicial Domination

In addition to the veto over appointments to the Supreme Court, the legal establishment committee members – three sitting Justices and two Bar Association lawyers – command a sufficient majority for appointing judges to the lower-tier Magistrate and District courts. The elected branches have no veto power for such appointments and can be easily sidelined.

The Bar aligns itself with the judiciary almost without fail, for a variety of reasons. Senior lawyers and judges often occupy the same socio-cultural milieu – graduates of the same law schools, attending the same conferences and even vacationing at the same resorts (the Bar hosts an annual national lawyer getaway in the resort town of Eilat). They often maintain familial, communal and professional ties well beyond their day-to-day work. As practitioners within the same profession this is to be expected and is hardly objectionable – but must nonetheless be acknowledged. In addition, active lawyers need to keep their relationship with the courts on a friendly footing for practical reasons. Judges are the ones who will try their cases and ultimately define the success or failure of their clients and careers. Considering the transience of politicians versus the permanence of judges on the bench, the legal profession's fealty to the latter is a no-brainer. Crossing the judiciary carries far more personal and professional risk than annoying the Minister of Justice.

This affinity was clearly demonstrated in the most recent elections to the Bar's leadership institutions in the shadow of the judicial reform proposals, held in June of 2023. Every five years licensed attorneys directly elect representatives to the Bar's national and local governing institutions. The anti-reform and outspoken judicial-supremacist candidate for chairmanship was handed a landslide victory by 73% of voters, in what was a clear repudiation (by the professional legal community) of the government's plans to curb judicial power.

There have been some rare exceptions. The Bar chairman during the Barak-era revolutionary court, Dror Hoter-Ishay, took a firm and public stance in the name of the legal profession against the Supreme Court's judicial activism. He was hounded out of office by a series of criminal investigations in the 1990s and his career never recovered, though all charges were ultimately dismissed (see Chapter 7). More recently, Bar chairman Efi Naveh struck a bargain to cooperate with Minister of Justice Ayelet Shaked, much to the Supreme Court's chagrin. He too had to resign, mired in controversy and under suspicion of criminal conduct (most charges were later dropped). The motivation for criminal proceedings against these two figures notwithstanding, the point here is only that instances of the Bar aligning with politicians against the Supreme Court members of the Judicial Selection Committee are few and far between. All in all, the legal establishment members on the Judicial Selection Committee generally act as one.

As a side note, the participation of the Bar Association in the judicial selection process also raises a number of separate problems and objections, though their examination is not required for present purposes.[12] These range from the questionable propriety of lawyers appearing in court before judges whose promotion may be indirectly affected by the same lawyers; all the way to scandals involving sexual misconduct and alleged illicit intimate relationships between judicial candidates and Bar committee members.

One upshot of this legal majority for lower-tier appointments is the ability to insert preferred candidates into the judicial pipeline. The identity of judges throughout the legal system has a considerable aggregate effect quite separate from the Supreme Court's independent influence. Control of who gets appointed to non-apex courts – local and regional, trial and appellate – will impact how legislation and binding precedent will be applied "on the ground," in the vast majority of day-to-day cases and trials throughout the country. But it will also indirectly define the judicial crop from which Supreme Court candidates may be harvested. As most Supreme Court nominees are sitting District Court judges, deciding who gets a judicial career to begin with will broadly define the character of potentially available Supreme Court nominees for years to come.

The potency of the legal establishment majority was aptly demonstrated in December of 2020. Minister of Justice Avi Nissenkorn (formerly leader of Israel's largest organized labor federation) convened a marathon Judicial Selection

Committee meeting to appoint scores of judges – but due to severe disagreement regarding some of the candidates, the three other politicians on the committee boycotted the proceedings. The absent members thought this would prevent further appointments, in light of a statutory provision allowing the committee to function only with a minimum quorum of seven members.[13] Alas, the objectors were blindsided – at the decisive moment Nissenkorn produced a written memorandum issued by the Justice Ministry's legal counsel, stating that as long as seven members had been *appointed* to the committee, no quorum was required for *actual* meetings and decisions. The committee members present – three Supreme Court Justices, two Bar members and Nissenkorn himself – then proceeded to approve the appointment of sixty-one (!) new judges over the course of five hours, against the express wishes of the three (out of four) elected committee members. This was the first time that the committee had ever appointed judges with the support of only six out of nine members. Of course the absent politicians were furious and protested vigorously (among other things, citing Nissenkorn's bad faith in not disclosing the memo in advance), but the damage was done and the new appointments irreversible. Perhaps consistent with his commitment to representing the public (or lack thereof), Nissenkorn resigned as Justice Minister just a few weeks later, and within two months had quit political life altogether.

The legal establishment majority (albeit this time with a complicit Minister of Justice) were thus able to steamroll the political committee members. The reverse of such a scenario – politicians and the Bar members joining forces against the Justices and unilaterally appointing sixty-one judges in a single five-hour sitting – remains virtually unimaginable. First, because in all likelihood the Supreme Court itself would nullify such appointments as an illegitimate and illegal exercise of the committee's authority. Second, as described, because the Bar members would almost certainly not consider opposing the Supreme Court in such a direct confrontation, due to the symbiotic relationship between the judiciary and legal profession.

Finally, the majority for appointing lower-tier judges serves as additional judicial leverage over Supreme Court appointments. Politicians unwilling to cooperate with the judicial members on the Supreme Court front could find themselves bypassed on the lower-tier front.

Who Will Call Foul?

The judicial involvement in the selection and promotion of judges has a devastating effect on the incentives and ability of legal figures and actors to push back against the legal status quo. In any functioning legal system lower-tier courts play an important role as legal laboratories, testing the boundaries of binding appellate rulings and new legal norms in the field and conveying problems upwards through the judicial hierarchy. Trial courts and lower-appellate courts have many more direct and diverse first-hand impressions of real-world scenarios, and of the effects of top-down legal rules devised by apex courts and the legislature. Such courts may convey that a legal precedent is simply not working in a number of ways – by creative application of precedent in a manner inconsistent with the original higher-court ruling; by expressing their discontent explicitly; or even by making defiant decisions that are certain to be overturned on appeal. "Unruly" judges challenging higher-court precedents may be a nuisance, but in fact serve a useful function for judicial fine-tuning and occasionally even to challenge poorly-decided cases.

Despite this, the current Israeli method of judicial appointments serves as a strong disincentive against any such judicial feedback. The pivotal involvement of Supreme Court Justices in promotion decisions means that lower-tier and trial-court judges are reluctant to oppose problematic precedents and to push the boundaries of the judicial status quo, and will therefore avoid challenging rulings made by their senior peers. Any judge deciding a case knows that if she is not sufficiently careful and does not toe the legal line, she could be jeopardizing her future judicial career.

This effect is not limited to judges deciding cases and extends to the entire legal profession. While the majority of Supreme Court candidates are serving District Court judges, a relatively large portion of eventual appointees hail from other areas of the legal world, including law professors, seasoned litigators and senior government lawyers (for instance, both Chief Justices Aharon Barak and Dorit Beinisch had not served a single day as a judge prior to their Supreme Court appointment). The decisive power of serving Justices over judicial selection means that anyone even remotely entertaining the prospect of pursuing a judicial career will tread lightly when dealing with the judiciary and the Supreme Court. Professional litigators in private practice will exercise undue caution when arguing for a change in existing case law or criticizing a specific judicial policy, especially if recently decided or favored by the current bench. Government attorneys will hesitate before representing governmental interests adverse to judicial opinion – or, on the contrary, might prefer judicial favor over faithful adherence to the government's legal position.

Perhaps most troubling is the effect on legal academia, whose chief role is arguably to critique the courts and to expose mistaken and problematic decisions, being the only distinct class within the legal world not directly subject to judicial authority. Yet appointment to the Supreme Court – and at times even to the District Court – is to many law professors the holy grail of legal advancement and the epitome of their legal career. It offers instantaneous elevation from relative obscurity in dreary university hallways to a position of enormous influence and reverence (and indeed of noble public service), all without the grueling legwork of years' practicing litigation and then climbing the judicial hierarchy. What scholar would risk the potential of such an enticing reward by criticizing the court too harshly or thoroughly, let alone by decrying the court's worst excesses? What is an academic to infer from Barak's invocation of "agenda" and "family," justifying his support for the existing judicial veto and his blackballing of Ruth

Gavison? Scholars and academics know full-well where to butter their bread. This is one reason explaining the relative dearth of Israeli legal academics critical of judicial supremacy as such – while at the same time, so-called critics arguing for even greater judicial power are legion.

Qualified Professionals

One claim often raised in this context is that the current judicial selection process with its heavy judicial and professional involvement is required in order to ensure that appointees meet a high level of professional qualification. This applies throughout the judiciary and especially to the Supreme Court in light of its function as a major appellate tier for civil and criminal trials (see next chapter). Elected politicians and other "non-professionals" simply don't possess the requisite expertise to effectively evaluate and select optimal judicial candidates, such that their excessive involvement in the appointments process would degrade the quality of judges. This approach aligns with a preference for a "merit based" appointment process, in which the professional legal establishment plays a significant (and usually decisive) role.

While this approach to judicial appointments has its benefits and is not unheard of in other jurisdictions, let us first put to rest the notion that politicians are incapable of selecting qualified and worthy judges. Throughout the democratic world judges are regularly selected to all judicial tiers by elected politicians (and at times by direct popular vote). Some jurisdictions and judicial mechanisms regularly utilize "lay" judges with no legal background or education whatsoever.

Indeed, politicians are relied upon to appoint or approve highly competent candidates in all areas of government, including those relating to the military, law enforcement, medicine and public health, science and engineering, economics and finance – the list goes on. There seems little reason to believe that the legal-professional qualifications of judges are any different from the vast range of other specialized skills evaluated by politicians for a host of senior governmental positions. Further still, it is worth recalling that a given appointments process may incorporate professional elements without these being decisive – for example, requiring that politicians consult with judges and attorneys in an advisory capacity to obtain their non-binding professional insights.

Taking an ever broader view, empirical studies examining whether so-called "professional" selections processes produce preferable results in terms of appointee quality remain inconclusive – with large-scale research (to date) unable to provide a hard case for merit-based selection, and often indicating that politically-based processes yield superior outcomes.[14] And it's worth recalling that there is no consensus on what even constitutes "good" judging in terms of merit – as Prof. James Allan points out, "there is nothing self-evident at all about what qualities are desirable in a top judge. Knowledgeable people will disagree."[15]

On a side note, many examples of a merit-based non-political appointments process do indeed include an inherently political check to ensure that the process is not abused by the professional class. Chief among these is the well-known Missouri Plan, adopted in a number of U.S. states and in other jurisdictions. Under the Missouri Plan, a non-partisan professional commission selects judges – but these are then subject to a "retention election," in which the public votes on whether the same judges stay in office. In other words, even where merit-based judicial selection is adopted, it is clear that such considerable political power may not be left solely in the hands of the legal establishment evaluating judicial merit, but rather that the public must exercise their will and oversight in one way or another.

Far more importantly, the argument for professional judicial selection fails to withstand the test of Israeli reality. In a number of illustrative cases it was precisely judicial involvement in the selections process which had produced poor results.

It is true that for many years the Supreme Court was comprised solely of Israel's greatest legal minds. Almost without exception, the Justices serving on the Supreme Court were universally regarded as eminently qualified and highly skilled jurists, the elite of Israel's legal world. Most of them had been classically trained in Europe or under the British Mandate. To this day most Supreme Court Justices undoubtedly meet this standard. Yet the gradual increase in its glaring exceptions undermine, and ultimately defeat, any illusion of a consistent commitment to professional excellence. Since the Barak-led revolutionary era the Supreme Court has periodically favored political and personal considerations over professional qualifications. As described by Prof. Menny Mautner: "Many observers came to realize that the appointment of worthy candidates is too often aborted by the Justices, either for fear of being overshadowed by distinguished appointees, or out of concern that appointees not approved by the Court will challenge its prevailing jurisprudence."[16]

Some Justices appointed to the Supreme Court were universally regarded as woefully unfit for the job by the professional legal community. Their relative mediocrity was an open secret as litigators would dread having their case assigned to these Justices. At the same time highly-regarded candidates were passed over. Many of these decisions remain concealed from the public eye due to the manner in which they are made, or are not publicly discussed among the legal profession for obvious reasons of prudence and discretion – yet a handful were brought to the fore of public attention.

Chief Justice Dorit Beinisch was Aharon Barak's successor and judicial protégé. She was appointed to the Supreme Court in 1995 without serving any prior judicial role and remained there until her retirement in 2012. Because of the "seniority" method practiced in the Supreme Court (see next chapter), the timing of her appointment guaranteed her future role as Chief Justice. It would be an understatement to say that the legal community did not regard Beinisch as particularly qualified for the country's top judicial post. At no point in her career climbing the ranks of the State Attorney's office did she stand out as possessing extraordinary skills of legal reasoning and analysis. Her previous position as State Attorney was mired in controversy. Contemporary journalistic accounts reporting her appointment directly reflect the doubts and misgivings within the legal professional community regarding her candidacy.[17]

Indeed, it was the professional legal community itself that led the effort against her appointment – with initial success. Beinisch was already a candidate for appointment to the Supreme Court in 1993, but her candidacy was summarily rejected by the professional committee members – the three Justices and two Bar representatives. Her rejection was semi-publicly spearheaded by the (then-) Chief Justice Meir Shamgar and became an undignified precedent, as this was the first time a Supreme Court candidate had been directly rejected by the committee. Until Beinisch, the committee had traditionally only actually voted on pre-arranged and agreed candidates such that appointments themselves went smoothly, yet Shamgar insisted on holding a vote to actively reject Beinisch's candidacy. Some interpreted Shamgar's doing so as an "ambush" to ensure Beinisch would not be reconsidered for the post in the future. It was Aharon Barak who then placed his full weight behind finally appointing Beinisch in 1995, after himself becoming Chief Justice.

In stark contrast to Beinisch's perceived mediocrity at the time of her appointment, Professor Nili Cohen was and remains among Israel's most esteemed legal scholars. A star throughout her award-peppered career, Cohen served as Rector of Tel Aviv University and "wrote the book" on Israeli contract law together with Prof. Daniel Friedmann. When her candidacy to serve as a Supreme Court Justice was raised in 2003 she was universally considered to be of the requisite character, caliber and experience. Cohen was in many respects the "model" type of academic candidate for a Supreme Court appointment. Even Aharon Barak supported her.

Despite her stellar and unchallenged professional qualifications, Cohen's candidacy was blocked – by none other than Dorit Beinisch herself. Beinisch did not only object to Cohen's appointment, but successfully led a minor mutiny among Supreme Court Justices against Barak's support for Cohen. While Beinisch never made her reasons explicitly known, speculation among the legal community was that Cohen was in fact *too* qualified – and that Beinisch was simply wary of being eclipsed by a new colleague with superior legal standing and expertise. Other versions put it down to petty factionalism and score-settling within Tel Aviv University academic circles. Cohen herself was never afforded the opportunity to appear before the committee to defend her candidacy – once the Justices sided with Beinisch against the appointment, the committee didn't bother with any superfluous hearings or votes. Cohen ultimately continued to succeed in her academic career, was awarded the Israel Prize (Israel's highest civilian honor) and was elected in 2022 to the prestigious American Philosophical Society (the only Israeli jurist to have attained this distinction).

With the torpedoing of Cohen's candidacy still a fresh memory, Beinisch managed to orchestrate the appointment in 2004 of her long-time friend and ally,

Edna Arbel. Much like Beinisch, Arbel climbed the ranks of the State Attorney office until becoming State Attorney herself (though unlike Beinisch, Arbel also served as a District Court judge). To put it as gently as may be appropriate, Arbel was not known for her exceptional qualifications within the legal community. Perhaps partially attesting to the quality of her legal judgment, Arbel's tenure as State Attorney was marked by a series of failed aggressive criminal investigations against senior public figures, including Reuven Rivlin, Avigdor Kahalani, Benjamin Netanyahu, Yaakov Neeman and Rafael Eitan (see Chapter 6). Arbel's candidacy was met with a high degree of public resistance, including a Knesset committee holding a hearing that called for her removal from the candidates list just one day before the scheduled vote. One recurring argument was that had Arbel not been a close friend and political ally of Beinisch, she would never have been considered for the role of Supreme Court Justice. Other troubling issues surfaced during Arbel's candidacy, such as her false claim in her official résumé that she had acquired a Master's (LLM) degree. Arbel was nonetheless appointed by the committee.

What to make of these events? Contemporary commentators pointed out the contrast created by the saga of these four women – Ruth Gavison and Nili Cohen on the one hand, Dorit Beinisch and Edna Arbel on the other.[18] One remarked about Arbel and Cohen that no one has a clue "why the former was appointed or why the latter was rejected."[19] Some speculated more generally that Barak was not interested in capable jurists able to challenge his revolutionary agenda. His official biographer and great admirer, Nomi Levitzky, described Barak's impact on the Court's composition in diplomatic terms: "Perhaps Barak deliberately shaped a Supreme Court devoid of intellectual charisma to ensure the preservation of his jurisprudence and that the path he charted would endure after him. In the post-Barak court, as it now appears, it is doubtful whether the intellectual capacity and originality exist to bring about change and innovation."[20] One way or another, few would deny that since Barak's tenure the presence of true legal "giants" on the Supreme Court is but a distant memory.

One inescapable conclusion is that the judicial involvement, veto and control in appointing colleagues can scarcely guarantee the professional quality of judicial appointees, both in theory and in fact. Israeli experience shows that the contrary may well be true.

It Was Always Political

What of "politicization" of the judicial selection process? The argument against introducing partisan politics into the courtroom is separate from – though in many ways parallel to – the one regarding professional judicial qualifications. Left to their own devices, so the claim goes, politicians will prioritize candidates according to their ideological leaning and partisan affiliation at the expense of judicial independence from popular sentiment and governmental intervention. Elected officials governed by short-sighted and outcome-driven incentives will try and appoint those judges most likely to share their own value preferences, or perhaps those most willing to act according to the interests of a specific political faction. Instead of choosing the best, politicians would choose the biased. Appointed in this manner, judges will issue decisions based on their partisan ideology rather than on law. Granting politicians power over judicial appointments thus allegedly sullies and contaminates both the selection process and judicial impartiality itself, even if the candidates chosen are technically qualified.

Israel's insulation from Western democracies and the lack of familiarity with other jurisdictions contribute greatly to the prevalence of this approach, to the extent that many public figures portray *any* political involvement in judicial selection as fundamentally inconsistent with democratic values, and especially as contrary to judicial independence – a claim that would seem patently ludicrous on its face to anyone even vaguely aware of global practice, as has been discussed above. Yet this approach is regularly used to justify the absolute rejection of attempts to adjust the current system, of which there have been many.

To name just a few recent examples: In 2008, Chief Justice Beinisch publicly warned Justice Minister Daniel Friedmann that his proposed tweaking of the Judicial Selection Committee would "weaken the Supreme Court," would "harm judicial independence" and would bring about the "politicization" of the appointments process.[21] The proposed change to the committee was hardly an overhaul – replacing one sitting Supreme Court justice with a retired judge, and adding two more non-political committee members (an academic and a lay public representative). In 2016, Justice Minister Ayelet Shaked reportedly supported abolishing the judicial veto power over new appointments – by simply returning to the model in force before the 2007 amendment. Speaking out against the plan, the retired Aharon Barak said that if such a change would be enacted he would "call for all Supreme Court Justices to resign" in protest (a puzzling statement by itself, considering this was precisely the system in place throughout his entire tenure).[22] The Chief Justice at the time, Miriam Naor, said that Shaked (merely by not disavowing the reports) had "placed a gun on the table" and informed Shaked she was pausing all collaboration until Shaked publicly denied the plan.[23] And of course, responding to the 2023 legal reform proposals, Chief Justice Esther Hayut dubbed the changes a "fatal blow" to judicial independence and neutrality, saying that their true motivation was the "total politicization" of judicial selection in Israel.[24] Towards a preliminary Knesset vote on changing the committee composition, the headline from a leading commentator read "The First Shot Through the Heart of Democracy: The Government Will Appoint Judges."[25] In a 2024 post-retirement interview, Justice Anat Baron described the "war on democracy" waged by the government, and proclaimed: "Once you politicize the appointment of Justices, you've lost the court, you've lost democracy."[26] The near-hysterical tone and hyperbolic style of these statements and many others are by no means atypical, but rather accurately represent the dominant approach of the legal establishment towards political involvement in judicial appointments.

Without delving further into the theoretical debates surrounding the so-called "politicization" of the appointments process and without repeating the previous discussion on this issue, there are two practical angles worth addressing briefly.

First is the de facto inescapably political nature of judge-dominated judicial appointments in Israel. At least since the 1980s the involvement of Supreme Court Justices in selecting their colleagues has brought more politicization, not less, in the sense that political considerations have factored prominently and indeed often at the expense of professional ones. Barak and others have contended over the years that a judge's personal (or partisan) politics had never been at issue during the selections process. While this claim seems dubious considering the political uniformity of most appointments during the post-Barak era, it deftly evades the more important point – that jurisprudential considerations are no less political than any other. Barak and his successors blatantly (and at times explicitly) preferred Justices who shared the same views regarding the Court's expansive societal role and policy-making powers, and rejected those who criticized judicial supremacism or who sought a more limited judicial function. When considering judicial candidates, no question is more political than their legal philosophy.

A study of "merit-based" judicial selection methods in some U.S. states by Prof. Brian Fitzpatrick reinforces this observation.[27] Fitzpatrick indicates that so-called merit selection – with heavy involvement of the legal establishment, and especially the judiciary and bar association – is no more likely to produce higher-quality judges than political methods. Rather, the actual effect of such merit systems seems to be that the judiciary simply reflects the political and ideological preferences of the legal profession, an outcome hardly justified by merit-based arguments.

The appointments of Justices Beinisch and Arbel (along with several others) in Israel are clear instances in which political attributes – consisting of both jurisprudential commitment to the orthodoxy of judicial supremacy, along with personal fealty to the dominant force on the Court, be it Barak, Beinisch or others – were the deciding factors. Such considerations may of course align with high professional standards and still result in the appointment of skilled jurists. Yet it seems just as likely that prioritizing judicial politics means not only sacrificing professional qualifications per se, but also losing out on the more independent-minded judges willing to go against the grain. In such a system mediocrity becomes a feature, not a bug, of judicial-dominated appointments.

The 1992 *Hamas Expulsion* case serves to illustrate this point.[28] Following a vicious attack by the nascent terror group Hamas, the Labor-led Israeli government under Prime Minister Yitzhak Rabin decided to round up some four hundred known Hamas operatives and to deport them to Lebanon in the dead of night, using explicit statutory authority enabling such expulsion. On-duty Justice Aharon Barak issued an interim order halting the flash deportation after it was challenged, while the buses were en-route to the border. We will return later to the details and repercussions of this case – for present purposes, we will recall only that Dorit Beinisch served as State Attorney at the time. In what was then an unprecedented decision, Beinisch refused to represent the Government in the court proceedings against the deportation decision, arguing that it was patently and egregiously illegal and therefore indefensible – a position that aligned with Barak's.

On that same day the Supreme Court, holding an emergency hearing with an expanded panel, quashed the interim order and ruled that the government acted within its statutory authority and that the case against the deportation was meritless, exposing Beinisch's assertion of blatant illegality to be a wild and unfounded exaggeration. In light of the Court's clear-cut and unequivocal decision, there are two ways to interpret Beinisch's extraordinary refusal to represent the Government: either Beinisch's legal assessment was grossly misguided, exhibiting an utter failure of substantive legal analysis on her part; or her conduct was cynically political, preferring her personal ideology and her alignment with Barak over legal and ethical obligations. The more genuine Beinisch's belief may have been in the validity of her material legal position, the more poorly it reflects on her actual legal judgment; yet the more credit one may afford Beinisch in her professional-legal skills, the more culpable she becomes of knowingly and purposefully putting politics before principle. Many would estimate the reality to be a combination of both.

Beinisch's personal, ideological and jurisprudential loyalty to Aharon Barak in this case and in others was handsomely rewarded and is thought to have contributed to Barak's insistence on her appointment to the bench – but it is only an example of a wider tendency. It exposes "merit-based" judicial selection in Israel to be nothing of the sort, with political ideology and conformation to the preferences of current judicial power-brokers much more decisive than legal acumen. The point here is simple – there is nothing remotely "non-political" about a judicial selection process in which judges choose their own colleagues and successors, with all it entails.

Judicial Independence – From the Law?

The second angle regarding political involvement in the judicial selection process relates to the recurring argument found in Israeli circles, that elected politicians appointing judges would undermine judicial independence. Despite its superficial appeal this argument is also easily revealed as baseless and is worth refuting.

As recently emphasized in the Israeli context by Professor Philip Hamburger, judicial independence is traditionally viewed as the "exercise of independent judgment in cases."[29] The rationale of having courts which are separate from the ordinary governmental hierarchy is that we want judges to resolve individual disputes according to applicable law, uninfluenced by public sentiment or by the desired outcomes of the government itself or other interested parties. Prof. James Allan describes judicial independence as a judge being "wholly free to decide cases independently of the first-order wishes of the government of the day."[30]

Israeli statutory law reflects this well. Section 2 of "Basic Law: The Judiciary" is titled "Independence" and reads simply: "A person vested with judicial power shall not, in judicial matters, be subject to any authority but that of the Law." Thus the Basic Law shares the common understanding of judicial independence, as carrying out the judicial function (resolving disputes under law) without external intervention or interference in specific cases. The test of judicial independence therefore focuses on this question alone – whether such intervention exists during a judge's tenure and performance of their function.

In this light, the selections process and how a judge is appointed – or whatever happens before someone assumes the judicial role – is entirely irrelevant to the issue of judicial independence as typically understood throughout the democratic world. Prof. James Allan explores precisely this issue in an essay regarding the nexus between judicial independence and a "political" or "professional" appointment process, and stresses that judicial independence is a "post-appointment virtue," and rather irrelevant to the question of how judges are appointed in the first place.[31] This is why most countries see no contradiction between judicial independence and politicians appointing judges, and is why Professor Hamburger stresses that "it's a mistake to assume that political control over judicial appointments is by itself an intrusion on judicial independence."

Of course, judges exercising their duties and resolving cases are likely influenced to some degree by extra-legal considerations such as their prospects for promotions and career advancement, and in this sense might be tempted to curry favor with those making such decisions. But this intractable problem is a permanent and inherent feature of any appointments process and is in no way neutralized by the exclusion of elected politicians. Such judges will be beholden to someone, the question simply becomes – to whom. As demonstrated above, owing one's promotion to more senior judges or to the Bar Association is neither a-political nor does it guarantee any level of professional qualifications. Allan describes the "incestuous quality that infuses any system where existing lawyers and judges" are effectively "appointing their successors" – this is no less true regarding promotions. In other words, if an issue of judicial independence exists because judges think about their career path, it is no less problematic if judges are beholden to an unelected legal elite.

Typical arguments in favor of politicians appointing judges range from principled ones, such as those mentioned above regarding the source of democratic authority, to practical ones, such as the crucial public legitimacy derived from important judicial decisions being traceable to appointment by elected officials accountable to the public. Allan argues for "overtly political checks and balances" controlling the appointments process regarding courts with considerable political power, and that an appointments process based on democratic elections results provides a critical type of variability, in that a "changing group of appointers" is desirable in a system-wide sense and reduces the likelihood of "clones of existing judges."

Yet beyond these, another decisive consideration related to judicial independence is grounded in the unpredictability of changing political fortunes.

The high turnover rate – both personal and partisan – of politicians controlling an appointments process means that judges will be hard put to consistently please any one political camp in the hope of better promotion prospects. This serves as an incentive to exhibit one's superior judicial qualities regardless of partisan leaning or affiliation by simply staying true to the law – that is, an incentive for genuine judicial independence. Conversely, a system of promotions subject to judicial veto, controlled by long-serving judges and an entrenched legal establishment with consistent orthodoxies, seems far more likely to incentivize skewed legal judgment and to impair judicial independence.

It would therefore seem that those trumpeting "judicial independence" as an argument against "politicization" of the selection process in Israel are referring to something else entirely. True to judicial supremacist form, what they seek is judicial independence from the constraints of the law itself. In this sense any indirect exposure of judicial decisions to public sentiment is scorned as "political," be it through the enactment of the public will (otherwise known as laws) by elected representatives, or through the appointment of judges whose views and jurisprudence align with those of the electorate. Objections to judicial appointments by politicians should thus be seen within the larger context of what former British Supreme Court Justice Lord Jonathan Sumption has called a "mounting tide of hostility to representative politics," leading to a legal mindset which ultimately "marginalizes the political process" itself.[32] It is not about judicial independence in any traditional or accepted sense, but rather about a distaste for the very notion of the electorate exerting direct influence over contentious and consequential matters of policy and values – a sentiment at the core of judicial supremacism.

Rotten Roots, Infected Branches

The Supreme Court's formidable power over judicial nominations has a corrupting effect, leading the Court to conduct itself in ways that would otherwise be considered deeply objectionable.

Statutory law designates the Judicial Selection Committee as the sole forum for discussing and selecting most judicial candidates. Yet a 2015 journalistic exposé in Haaretz newspaper revealed that the Supreme Court had established a clandestine shadow-committee tasked with vetting lower-court judges up for promotion.[33] Dubbed "the Duo Committee" because it was comprised of two retired judges (at the time one of whom was Edna Arbel), this pair would review candidates for a District Court judgeship and would report directly to the Chief Justice, either recommending or opposing promotion of lower-court judges to the more senior post. The review included interviewing candidates, reading their previous rulings and consulting with their peers and superiors. Those receiving recommendations would then be presented by the Supreme Court to the Judicial Selection Committee as the only candidates being considered for promotion.

The existence of the Duo Committee had not been disclosed to the public or to members of the Judicial Selection Committee and was not authorized or regulated by any statute; the two retired judges, working voluntarily, were periodically chosen by the Chief Justice with no clear requirements or oversight; there were no stated standards or criteria for the Duo Committee's decisions deciding the fate of many a judicial career; and no records of their deliberations were created or maintained. Needless to say, committee members were not pleased to learn they were unknowingly rubber-stamping pre-vetted and post-filtered candidates.

The Duo Committee was reportedly established[34] by Chief Justice Dorit Beinisch in 2007 – coincidentally or not, a time of unprecedented tensions between the Supreme Court and the incoming Minister of Justice Professor Daniel Friedmann, a renowned jurist and former dean of the top-tier Tel Aviv law school. Freedom of Information Act petitions to publicize the committee's deliberations were rejected. In the aftermath of the public uproar which followed the exposé, Chief Justice Esther Hayut was eventually compelled to "formally" establish the committee by way of an internal administrative directive in 2019 (of debatable legal status). Its proceedings remain confidential (though a brief summary of the Duo recommendation is provided to the selection committee members) and the criteria for the Duo's conclusions remain undefined.

Yet it turns out that the Duo Committee mechanism, which further bolstered the Supreme Court's effective control over the career trajectory of most Israeli judges, was not enough. In 2017, Chief Justice Miriam Naor issued a directive forbidding *all judges* from meeting with politicians or with Bar Association members regarding judicial appointments and promotions. This meant that active judges seeking promotion to the District courts or the Supreme Court are prohibited from meeting the political or Bar representatives on the Judicial Selection Committee (or even those indirectly involved), outside the formal interviews held in committee meetings. The directive was "oral" and was not proactively publicized by the Supreme Court – but rather, again, exposed in a Haaretz news report and only later officially acknowledged by the Court. Unlike the Duo Committee above, this rule has yet to be formalized in any way and remains an unwritten instruction retroactively confirmed by the Court and still in force. While ostensibly aimed at judges, the order works *ipso facto* in the other direction, effectively barring politicians from meeting with serving judges.

Putting aside the questionable legal basis the Chief Justice has for making such a directive, the effect is twofold. First, it puts the non-judicial (and especially the political) committee members at a marked disadvantage when evaluating judicial candidates, with whom they are not necessarily familiar. Due to the limited time and resources available to formal committee proceedings, its members require further in-person meetings to evaluate candidates' professional qualities. These may include raising or discussing sensitive matters which need not necessarily be aired in the larger committee forum. They could also include legitimate "strategizing" – that is, preparation for and coordination towards a committee hearing (in the U.S., for example, White House counsel meet with Supreme Court nominees to prep them for Senate confirmation hearings). Israeli Supreme Court Justices naturally enjoy full access to such judicial candidates, have regular professional and personal interactions with them, are usually pre-acquainted with them and may also freely schedule meetings with them as desired. Thus the political committee members (and to a lesser extent the Bar Association members) are far less able to assess the suitability of candidates for judicial promotion.

Second, and more egregiously, the directive conveys a clear message to sitting judges as to who controls their career advancement prospects. Recall that one cannot submit their own candidacy to the committee – rather a candidate must be nominated by the Chief Justice, the Justice Minister or by three committee members jointly. Candidates must therefore personally petition committee members to be considered, which would typically involve some kind of meeting or discussion at the very least; committee members that desire to proactively nominate candidates would also understandably want to meet with them first. Yet the directive, essentially barring contact with all committee members (and more broadly, with all politicians and with Bar Association figures involved with the selection process), means that there is only one realistic avenue for judges to be considered for promotion – through the exclusive approval of the sitting Supreme Court Justices on the committee.

Imagine a judge with known positions adverse to the dominant outlook on the Supreme Court – what realistic chances for promotion does she have through the Duo Committee (to the District Court) and subject to Supreme Court approval? At the same time, how can she otherwise ask to be considered when barred from approaching non-judicial committee members? Further still, the directive puts prospective unorthodox candidates in a classic Catch-22 situation. If they go through the "approved" channels they will likely be filtered out (especially if applying to the District Court and require a recommendation from the nebulous Duo Committee); yet if they avoid the route of judicial pre-approval, they'll be violating official Chief Justice directives (however questionable) and will be inviting opponents to question their judicial suitability, probably even retroactively justifying whatever misgivings such opponents may have raised. Unsurprisingly, one unseemly upshot is that judicial candidates that desire to be considered by the non-judicial committee members must approach them in a variety of secretive ways or through intermediaries.

The Supreme Court thus exerts its power over the promotion of Israeli judges (and indirectly over much else relating to judicial life besides) through the dual mechanism of the Duo Committee and of mandating exclusive access to judges. Combined with the Court's veto over its own appointments on the Judicial Selection Committee and with its near-guaranteed majority for all others, these mechanisms cement the Court's grip on the career advancement of almost all judges throughout the legal system.

What's changed?

The system for appointing judges throughout the legal system, in place since 1953, is inherently flawed and includes problematic elements since its inception. Yet it may have been tolerable, warts and all, if not for two concurrent developments. The first is the increasingly aggressive abuse of the judicial veto and legal-establishment majority from the 1990s onwards. Perhaps there truly was a time when the Supreme Court's involvement in appointing judges was maintained with prudence and moderation, ensuring the genuine professional qualities of candidates, avoiding ideological considerations and striving for consensus-based appointments, all grounded in respect for the electorate represented on the committee. But that era has long passed, giving way to the approach and practices described in this chapter. The second development is the radical expansion of judicial power on which much of this book will focus. As the Court's involvement in Israel's most contested political and social controversies intensified, no matching adjustments were made to the judicial selection process to balance the Court's power with greater public legitimacy and authority.

It is in this context in 1996 that Moshe Landau, a retired Supreme Court Chief Justice and one of Israel's most renowned jurists, warned against "[dragging] the Court into the arena of publicly charged political disputes," as it would likely "encourage the call to alter the judicial appointments process."[35] As judicial supremacy took hold, calls for reforming the judicial selection process indeed became increasingly common and were taken up regularly by political moderates.

The 2025 Amendment

In April of 2025 the Knesset amended "Basic Law: The Judiciary" and altered the structure and procedures of the Judicial Selection Committee, for the first time since 1953. The general scheme of a nine-member statutory committee remains in place and still includes heavy judicial involvement, but with some significant changes: The two Bar Association members are replaced by public representatives, with one selected by each of the Coalition and Opposition; most committee decisions require some kind of consensus between the various factions, including members appointed by judiciary, Coalition, and Opposition; appointments to the Supreme Court require wide political consensus, but not judicial approval (potentially eliminating the judicial veto).

The new law is set to take effect only in the following Knesset (i.e., after the next elections). Much like all elements of legal reform in Israel the amendment was highly controversial. Whether this amendment can accomplish any of its objectives remains to be seen; whether it is justified or desirable is immaterial for the moment. At this point in time, a thorough description and discussion of the amendment and its potential effects would be premature, for two reasons. First, there is the distinct possibility that the law will be reversed or amended again before it ever takes effect, or soon after. The political opposition has vowed to restore the Judicial Selection Committee to its original form at the first opportunity. Some other political compromise might emerge which again amends the law in a way more acceptable to both the Opposition and to the legal establishment. Second, the amendment has already been challenged in the Supreme Court. The Court could conceivably strike down the amendment as unconstitutional (see Chapter 11), and we would be back at square one.

By the time the reader encounters this passage, circumstances may well have dramatically changed one way or another. Whatever changes perish or endure, future developments can only be evaluated based on understanding the history and controversies surrounding the Judicial Selection Committee and the extraordinary appointment power exercised by the Supreme Court.

*

Prof. Stephen Calabresi, one of the world's leading comparative constitutional scholars, sums up the issue in his quote at the start of this chapter. The current judicial selection process in Israel renders the Supreme Court a self-perpetuating oligarchy (a term employed regularly in this context). His comparison with the Iranian Guardian Council likely refers to the fact that half of this judicial body is appointed directly by the Iranian Chief Justice – yet even in authoritarian Iran, such appointments are subject to approval by the Iranian Parliament. By contrast, the Israeli public through their elected representatives enjoy even less influence.

All in all, the Supreme Court Justices' involvement in the judicial appointments process, including the judicial veto over the appointment of members to the Supreme Court bench, was and remains one of the most glaring flaws of the Israeli legal system.

Chapter 2

Structure of the Judiciary

First and Final Say

"Squash This Bug"

Professor Yoram Shachar is one of Israel's leading legal historians, with a strong focus on empirical and behavioral research of Supreme Court decisions. In March of 2001, Shachar attended an academic conference at Bar-Ilan University, where he delivered a keynote lecture about the Supreme Court's institutional structure. In all likelihood he did not conceive of his lecture as especially controversial. Shachar offered a number of mild historical and comparative observations – regarding the original colonial circumstances leading to the establishment of the Supreme Court; the unique and unintended position of the Supreme Court at the top of the judicial hierarchy; the absence of defined procedures for judicial decision-making within the Court; the insular nature of legal government service; and more besides.[1]

Despite the benign nature of Shachar's remarks they raised the ire of a certain audience member – none other than Chief Justice Aharon Barak. Speaking at the podium in response to Shachar and others at the conference Barak was discernibly livid, and proceeded to launch a stream of disparaging vitriol against Professor Shachar. Barak reportedly asked, "Heaven as my witness, where on earth did he get this idea?" and "does he have any clue what he's talking about?"[2] while questioning Shachar's research and conspicuously omitting his academic title. Barak also responded to the idea of establishing a Constitutional Court with explicit authority to strike down legislation, similar to the common European model, by saying – "this is a bug we must squash while still small."

Barak later apologized to Shachar for his conduct, but the lecture had clearly hit a nerve. What was it that elicited such a distraught reaction from the Chief Justice?

The Israeli judiciary, and the Supreme Court in particular, are characterized by a set of unique institutional and organizational features that lead to a slew of problems and complications and which were for the most part unintended or accidental. Despite the detrimental effects caused by these features, the Supreme Court and judicial establishment have vigorously resisted almost all efforts at institutional change. While Barak was certainly a strong representative of this resistant mindset, his reaction reflected broader attitudes of Supreme Court Justices towards any genuine scrutiny (let alone criticism) of the judiciary's institutional infrastructure, and especially towards proposals for improvements or change. In one example, when reformist Daniel Friedmann was appointed as Minister of Justice, the retired Justice Mishael Cheshin famously responded by announcing: "I will sever the hand of anyone raising it against the Supreme Court."[3]

This chapter will describe the overall structure of the judicial system with the Supreme Court at its apex. As we consider these distinctive characteristics, the Court's vested interest in their preservation will become apparent.

The Court System

The principal segment of the Israeli judiciary consists of three tiers. The lowest is the Magistrate Court, which serves as a local trial court for most civil and criminal cases below certain thresholds of value or severity. Unlike similarly named courts in some other countries, there are no lay Magistrate judges, rather all are professional attorneys. The Magistrate courts include various divisions or parallel tiers such as family court, municipal court, traffic court, youth court and small claims court. The Magistrate courts may also review certain decisions of administrative bodies (similar to an appeals process).

The District Courts serve as the intermediate tier with a number of functions. These serve as trial courts of first instance for civil cases with a monetary value exceeding roughly 700,000 USD; for criminal cases involving severe offenses with potential sentences of over seven years' imprisonment; and for a range of other cases (real property title, intellectual property, some administrative cases, most insolvency cases, white collar crime, and more). They are also the courts of "general jurisdiction" and can hear suits for which no other court has been granted clear authority.

There are six District Courts, corresponding to six jurisdictional regions throughout the country. The Tel Aviv District Court has a financial division (or "economic department") with special expertise and authority to hear cases involving corporate disputes; the Jerusalem District Court has special jurisdiction over cases relating to politicians and some key government functions. Most trial-court cases are held before a single judge, though some specifically defined cases are tried by a panel of three judges.

The District Courts also serve as the appellate tier for most Magistrate Court decisions within their geographical district – final Magistrate rulings are generally appealable as of right, while appeals of interim decisions (including most temporary injunctions and other provisional measures) are usually discretionary. Most primary appeals are heard by a panel of three District judges.

The Supreme Court, located in Jerusalem, is the highest tier within the judicial hierarchy and serves two primary functions: as appellate court for District Court decisions; and as the High Court of Justice, hearing direct challenges to government action. We will return to the Supreme Court momentarily.

In addition to the main judicial system there are several parallel specialized court systems. These include the labor courts, which hear both individual and collective labor-related (and some welfare-related) disputes; military courts; administrative tribunals and committees with quasi-judicial (such as disciplinary or regulatory) functions; and religious courts. Each of these typically has a number of local courts on a regional tier, and a single appellate court on a national tier.

The religious courts in Israel have near-exclusive jurisdiction over "personal status" cases including marriage, divorce, inheritance, guardianship, adoption, and religious conversion. This mirrors the administrative jurisdiction held by parallel religious government authorities. Most State-recognized religions have their own distinct court system which resolves disputes in accordance with their respective religious law. These include Rabbinical (Jewish-Orthodox) courts, Sharia (Muslim) courts, Druze courts, and the Ecclesiastical courts of the ten recognized Christian denominations in Israel. The interplay with the overlapping jurisdiction of other courts (such as the family courts in cases of divorce-related child custody and property division) is complex and at times fraught.

The Magistrate-District model as well as the separate religious-courts model were introduced by the Ottoman Empire during their rule over the region, were inherited and incorporated by the British Mandate and subsequently by the State of Israel, and have remained largely intact to this day.

The Highest Court of Justice

The Supreme Court sitting as High Court of Justice (henceforth: the "HCJ" or "High Court") has both original and final jurisdiction for a host of administrative and constitutional issues. Most Israelis refer to the High Court by its Hebrew acronym, "*Bagatz*." The vast majority of petitions against government decisions and policy originate with the Supreme Court as HCJ and there they end. HCJ rulings and decisions are not appealable – there is no additional tribunal or tier with higher authority than the Supreme Court. It is in essence the first and last stop for virtually any consequential challenge to government action, be it executive or legislative, including constitutional cases in which the Court strikes down laws.

The significance and impact of this single feature cannot be exaggerated. Perhaps to state the obvious, such a model is an extreme outlier compared to most other advanced democratic legal systems and is demonstrably inimical to the administration of justice.

First, the notion of (at minimum) two-tier judicial revision is a staple of the modern liberal legal order. Facing "upwards" within the judicial hierarchy, the decision of an initial tribunal ought to be exposed to review by an additional panel of judges. The right to an appeal is thought of as one of the most fundamental within a modern legal system. Among the many justifications for this basic insight, one is that judges are not infallible – they are capable of making mistakes just like anyone else, such that a minimal correction mechanism is required. Further, it is precisely because of their finality – typically having the definitive last say in specific disputes and immune from further challenge – that binding judicial decisions must be scrutinized by at least one extra layer of review. Another justification regards the incentive structure created by the existence, or absence, of appellate review. The first tribunal to deal with a specific case should usually owe an explanation for their decisions, on legal grounds, to a superior authority. Judges, aware that their decisions will be picked apart by appellate lawyers and then reconsidered by a separate group of judges on appeal, will adopt a more cautious and rigorous approach to their judicial conduct and reasoning. At the very least they would take pains to avoid issuing manifestly sloppy rulings. The knowledge that one's judgment may be overturned by a superior court is a critical check against abuse of judicial power.

Facing "downwards," appellate judges are themselves to some extent limited by the arguments employed by lower courts. Appellate review typically does not consider the issues *de novo* but rather assesses the judicial decision being appealed. As such the reviewing court must contend with the detailed reasoning and analysis presented by lower court judges. The lower court ruling frames, directs and confines the legal points of contention, to some degree constraining the appellate court and compelling it to actively and deliberately engage with the lower ruling substance. In other words, a two-tier system of judicial revision means that the final dispute-resolver (the appeals court) is not the first judicial attempt to do so, but rather someone else has already had a crack at it, with all that entails. A two-tier minimum therefore has a mutually enriching effect on both lower and appellate courts.

Second, many apex courts (especially within the common law tradition) enjoy the benefits of "percolation" – the process by which cases are filtered and processed through the legal system until they reach the top of the judicial hierarchy. A given case is initiated in its "raw" form at the lower courts. Perhaps a much-vaunted case founders and falls flat, while an obscure or benign case turns out to hinge on the most consequential of legal determinations. As (and indeed, if) it progresses, the case matures in significant ways – factual and legal arguments become more sophisticated; points of agreement and contention crystallize; affected factors, interested parties and the public can weigh in. Far from being merely numerical and limiting the top-court case load, percolation provides the opportunity for critical reflection and debate, and for the emergence and articulation of varied legal and factual positions, such that the case arrives at the apex court under circumstances much more suitable for final adjudication of controversial issues. Hence the oft-quoted observation that "Justices like the smell of well-percolated cases."[4]

Yet percolation isn't only about improving the quality of final judgments. It also alerts the legal community and the public at large to the fact that something – if we forgive overuse of the metaphor – is brewing. If settled law may be challenged or novel legal doctrines contemplated, percolation puts the public on notice. While such a process pales in comparison with the transparent and gradual nature of primary legislation, it at least offsets a significant failing of high court rulings – that of sudden judicial lawmaking with no public warning or participation. And while some decry percolation as an excuse for apex judges to avoid considering urgent cases, this criticism does not seem to negate percolation per se, but can be addressed with appropriate mechanisms for injunctive relief in extreme circumstances, and by the correct employment of such mechanisms by judges.

As High Court of Justice, the Israeli Supreme Court has none of these balancing benefits. Being both first and last to consider a huge variety of cases, the Court need not be concerned with authoritative scrutiny from above, nor must it contend with the reasoning of other judges below. The temptation for sloppy legal logic, shoddy research and gratuitous musings (or rather, the absence of incentives to refrain from these) is considerable. There is of course no percolation to speak of – cases arrive as newborns, possibly raising issues hardly contemplated and lacking any serious input from the legal community, and are instantaneously catapulted into the adulthood of final, binding decisions with far-reaching consequences. The broader public discovers the changes in law or the adoption of novel doctrine as a *fait accompli.* Poorly and erroneously decided cases are scrutinized by academics only after the fact, and with little tangible impact.

It is true that other jurisdictions utilize first-and-final apex court proceedings in some instances. The Kelsenian model of constitutional courts in Europe usually involves a single tier which hears relevant challenges to legislation. The U.S. Supreme Court has original (and final) jurisdiction in specific types of cases. But the differences are critical. European constitutional courts are a unique judicial phenomenon and are surrounded by an array of mechanisms designed to offset unusual features such as their single-tier design. Their jurisdiction is severely limited in terms of subject matter and of who can bring a complaint or petition to the court. The highly political nature of their appointment process ensures greater public legitimacy for such single-tier decisions. Such courts typically do not fully "adjudicate" cases, but rather rule on particular legal questions and then refer a case back to lower-tier courts for final resolution. The U.S. Supreme Court exercises original jurisdiction in a defined subset of rare cases, such as disputes between States or involving ambassadors, and the Court issues opinions in only a handful of such motions every year. In such cases the U.S. Supreme Court will also often return a case for adjudication by a lower court, after clarifying the applicable constitutional standard or legal criteria. In these instances and others, use of single-tier adjudication is either extremely limited or is acknowledged as problematic and employed with various balancing mechanisms, or both.

The High Court could hardly be more different. Article 15 of "Basic Law: The Judiciary" defines the Court's broad jurisdiction over "matters in which [the Court] deems it necessary to grant relief for the sake of justice and which are not within the jurisdiction of another court." The statute explicitly includes writs of *habeas corpus*, *mandamus*, *certiorari* and prohibition proceedings, but the "sake of justice" clause is widely considered to confer virtually limitless jurisdiction. With the exception of some minor (and inconsequential) categories, the HCJ's original jurisdiction encompasses any and all legal challenges against government in all its forms. It is the "go to" tribunal for administrative and constitutional cases against the executive or legislative branches. From 2012 to 2021, the fifteen Justices of the Supreme Court heard a whopping average of 1,769 new HCJ cases *every year*, which constitute nearly 50% of the overall primary case-load (i.e., cases assigned to panels and not withdrawn or dismissed outright).[5] The High Court does not remotely resemble the type of courts elsewhere in which "first and final say" power can be justified.

Tellingly, the HCJ was not originally designed this way. When founded under the British Mandate for Palestine in 1918 it was roughly based on the English High Court of Justice (from whence it derives its name) which combines appellate and first-instance functions, but was at the time (and still is) subject to additional appellate review. The English High Court of Justice was the third-down from the top of the judicial hierarchy – its decisions were appealable to the Court of Appeal and then again to the House of Lords. Leaving the Magistrate-District system in place, the newly-minted HCJ in pre-state Israel was one of the main British innovations to the existing Ottoman legal system, and was meant to serve a function similar to its namesake, as an appellate tier for lower court decisions and as an administrative court of first instance for suits against the colonial-Mandatory government. Crucially, pre-state HCJ decisions were appealable to the (British) Judicial Committee of the Privy Council, which acted as the final court of appeals for the entire British Empire (excluding the United Kingdom itself).

The HCJ was therefore never intended, even in its original design, to serve as a first-and-final tier for all challenges against government action. As Yoram Shachar observed, the higher appellate tier was abolished upon Israel's founding and "the Court became truly supreme" without anyone making the "necessary adjustments."

In his discussion of the rule of law, renowned economist and political theorist Friedrich Hayek observed that "whether or not the substance of a decision is subject to review… is probably the best test as to whether a decision is bound by rule [of law] or left to the discretion of the judge's authority."[6] The HCJ as court of first-and-last instance fails this test by any measure. Nowhere in the democratic world will one find a similar system where such far-reaching original jurisdiction over society's most publicly contentious matters is granted to a court with no possibility of further review or recourse.

The Appeal of Power

The Supreme Court's other primary function is that of the highest court of appeals for civil, criminal and some administrative cases. District Court rulings and decisions are subject to appellate review by the Supreme Court. Cases that originate in the District Courts are appealable as of right, meaning the Supreme Court is obligated to hear the appeal and decide upon it, whereas cases originating elsewhere (typically in the lower Magistrate tier) and heard in the District Court as an appeal, are subject to Supreme Court discretion whether to grant *certiorari* – that is, whether to hear an additional appeal even though the case had already been through one appellate tier. As is the case in most jurisdictions, the Court has held that such third-round appellate review is to be granted only under rare circumstances. Naturally, then, the appellate role of the Supreme Court is exercised mostly with regard to first as-of-right appeals from District Court rulings.

Between 2012 and 2021, the fifteen Justices of the Israeli Supreme Court heard an average of 1,854 "real" appeals every year (real, as in not dismissed or withdrawn at the outset and which were assigned to adjudication panels). Over the same period an average of 9,329 new cases were opened every year, with a similar number of cases closed (most are relatively minor proceedings which are presided over by a single judge). The Supreme Court finished the year 2022 with 2,791 open, active cases on its docket.[7]

This dominant appellate function is unusual for a supreme court. Most apex appellate courts, whether in common law or civil law jurisdictions, serve as discretionary tiers which can choose what post-appellate cases to hear. At first glance this appellate function would seem to be a benign but tolerable peculiarity, despite the unnecessary burden on an already overstrained court. Yet closer inspection reveals the opposite – that the Court's appellate role further augments its centralized judicial power and has a system-wide detrimental effect.

Simply put, any ordinary case of consequence in the entire country will easily and inevitably find itself in the hands of the Supreme Court, due to the as-of-right and near-automatic nature of the appeals it hears. What does this mean?

First, it doubles the opportunity for politically-minded and agenda-driven Justices to apply their ideology. With a volume similar to HCJ cases, civil and criminal appeals simply create more avenues to instantiate judicial supremacy or just to impose a judge's ideology. Because most appeals are not discretionary the Supreme Court need not show any special cause to justify selecting a specific case for review. The Court thus has access to thousands of cases and can select the most opportune and convenient one out of the dozen (or so) heard each day with the intent to make that particular case an example, to set a new precedent or for any other purpose. Routine and mundane civil and criminal appeals are also subject to far less public scrutiny due to their low profile. An illustrative example is that of the *Bank Hamizrachi* ruling, largely considered the most important case in Israeli constitutional law, which was in fact a civil appeal and not part of an HCJ proceeding. Instead of merely facilitating review of whether lower rulings were properly decided, the appeals function becomes a back door by which the Supreme Court may further advance its desired agenda.

One example of many is the Court's treatment of tort law. Recent research led by Professor Ehud Guttel, among Israel's leading tort law experts, indicates that the Supreme Court actively used tort appeals to achieve general policy goals it was unable or unwilling to advance through administrative HCJ cases. In a comprehensive review of landmark tort cases, the research paper summarized that "when the Court favors arguments it rejects [in its capacity] as HCJ, it may embrace them in its civil capacity... Tort law enables the Supreme Court to 'supplement' its decisions made in administrative proceedings."[8] The paper further finds a "direct line" between novel Supreme Court tort rulings and the limitations inherent in HCJ cases.

Second, aside its potential for intentional ideological mischief, the appellate role makes the development of case law erratic and unpredictable. This is due to the typical disposition of what one might call a "supreme" judge. An ordinary appellate judge may feel more constrained by precedent, more subject to judicial oversight from a higher-tier court, and more inclined to value stability and predictability in the legal system. Conversely, consider the profile of a typical "supreme" or constitutional judge – accustomed to hearing the most publicly contentious and significant cases of their age, to setting new rules and to charting new legal territory. Such judges adjudicating *every single* civil and criminal appeal of consequence in the nation would affect the character of the entire appellate system. Any routine appeal could suddenly become a landmark judicial event if the judge were so inclined. Indeed, many attribute the gradual deterioration of legal consistency and predictability in all fields of Israeli law to Supreme Court meddling through its appellate jurisdiction.[9] Imagine, if you will, the Supreme Court Justices of the U.S. or the U.K. routinely hearing thousands of ordinary civil and criminal appeals, and how their role at the top of the judicial hierarchy might affect the discipline applied to their routine appellate decisions.

As a separate matter, the appellate function is often employed to justify the "professional" emphasis (that is, the dominance of the legal establishment) within the judicial selection process. Explored in a previous section, this argument does not withstand scrutiny – but is nonetheless an additional factor by which the appellate function serves judicial supremacy.

In light of all the above, it should come as no surprise that the Supreme Court has consistently resisted attempts to reduce its appellate jurisdiction and impact, even at the cost of enduring a staggering case load. It's the reason Justice Barak wanted to "squash the bug" of a constitutional court, as the practical implementation would likely have been separating the Supreme Court's HCJ and appellate functions. It's why the judicial establishment has consistently opposed structural institutional reforms to the court system. The Supreme Court benefits enormously from the influence afforded by its dual function as HCJ and as automatic appellate court, while more conventional arrangements closer to those practiced in other countries would ultimately mean less power wielded by the fifteen members of the Supreme Court bench.

Stacking the Deck – Panels, Evidence and Rehearings

The notion that seemingly technical rules and mechanisms reflect a more fundamental allocation and application of power is hardly new or controversial.[10] It's not only about *what* courts decide; *how* they go about deciding matters a lot. Highly irregular procedural elements at the core of the Supreme Court's routine work demonstrate this principle well and serve as critical components bolstering overall judicial power. Here we will describe a handful of these procedural rules, including those involving panel composition, fact finding, and re-hearings. Some were surveyed in a useful recent essay by one of Israel's leading constitutional scholars, Dr. Joshua Segev, to whom this section will occasionally refer.[11]

Panels

The Court hears most of its cases in three-judge panels, though under certain circumstances cases are assigned to expanded panels. The Court had never heard a case en benc with all fifteen Justices, until it did so for the first (and so far, only) time in the recent 2023 "reasonableness" case. At the risk of stating the obvious, the identity of the judges that are to hear a given case can likely determine its outcome, to the extent that an outcome may even at times be predicted according to which judges have been assigned to the case. This common-sense insight has been established in a wealth of academic literature worldwide, and a pioneering empirical analysis in 2011 by Prof. Keren Weinshall-Margel confirmed that Israel is no exception.[12] Hence, the ability to choose which three (or more) judges will hear a case from within a pool of fifteen judges of different ideological and jurisprudential leanings can be tantamount to preemptively deciding a case before a single hearing is held.

Panel composition – that is, which Justices hear which cases – in the Supreme Court is subject to the complete and total discretion of the Chief Justice. Routine cases are generally (and ostensibly) allocated according to calendar availability, expertise, and seniority of Justices. Nonetheless, the Chief Justice wields the indisputably dramatic power to manipulate case outcomes by deciding which Justices will hear it. The Chief Justice can choose any combination of three Justices to hear any case. Critically, the Chief Justice may choose to assign a case to an expanded panel of any odd number higher than three, and she then defines which Justices are on the expanded panel. The Chief Justice may also mandate that a case be heard by the three most senior Justices on the Court.

The decisions surrounding panel composition are shrouded in a fog of vague, bureaucratic mystery. The Court does not publish or record any rationale or reasoning for assignment decisions, and there are no known (statutory or otherwise) principles which guide or limit such panel compilation. In other words, not only does the Chief Justice offer no explanation for the personal makeup of a given panel or for a decision to expand (or even, not to expand) a panel, but there are also no objective tools by which an observer (or party to proceedings) may evaluate whether such decisions were proper. Further still, the very intervention of the Chief Justice in panel composition is often not announced or acknowledged – a litigant usually has no way of knowing whether the three Justices assigned to a case were chosen by the Court registrar (according to some criteria or at random), or whether they were personally assigned by the Chief Justice. Even in an expanded panel, a litigant must guess the organizing principle by which panel size is determined and Justices are assigned, if such exists.

In a combative speech at a 2017 Bar Association conference, Chief Justice Miriam Naor rejected "baseless" claims that panels are composed in a manner intended to bring about specific results.[13] She insisted that the "vast majority" of ordinary (three-judge) cases are "assigned randomly" by the Court's administrative office. In expanded panels, whose composition Naor acknowledged that she indeed decides, the Justices are assigned "almost always" according to their relative seniority (that is, time served) on the Court. Others tend to justify the panel composition method along similar lines.

Naor's contentions are both unconvincing and inconsistent with the available data, to put it mildly. Global research confirms the intuitive assumption that judicial panel composition matters and affects case outcomes, and that the authority to define which judges preside over a case is manipulated easily and often. Within the Israeli context, a major 1999 empirical study by Yoram Shachar and Miron Gross covering three distinct 5-year segments concluded that Supreme Court three-judge panel assignments were consistently not random, and were also not governed by any discernible organizing principle.[14]

Another crucial example is provided in a recent study by Prof. Yehonatan Givati and Israel Rosenberg, regarding the dismissal of HCJ petitions. In order to dismiss an HCJ petition outright, the on-duty Justice that receives the petition appoints two additional judges to then jointly decide on the dismissal.[15] Givati and Rosenberg showed that on-duty Justices choose their panels strategically – they select like-minded judges to join them to achieve desired outcomes (in this case, the dismissal of a petition). The same study showed that Chief Justice decisions regarding panel composition seem to track their previous conduct (as an Associate Justice) for on-duty panel selections. In other words, the Chief Justice assignment of cases to three-judge panels resembled the same strategic type of panel composition exhibited in on-duty dismissals. (As a result of Givati and Rosenberg's study the Court actually changed its method for dismissal-panel selection).

Empirical evidence aside, Naor's defense of the current panel composition regime fails on its own terms. As Dr. Joshua Segev points out, claiming that interventions with panel composition are rare misses the point entirely – it's the big ones that count.[16] Even if we were to take Naor's assertion at face value, what matters is the intervention in those cases that don't belong to the "vast majority," or the exceptions to "almost always," which are likely the most important, controversial and consequential cases the Court deals with. In other words, it's not the volume of cases that matters, it's how you use it. Strategic panel composition by the Chief Justice to achieve a desired outcome is no less of a problem if employed only in a fraction of (key) cases.

And take Naor's word for it we must, as the Court doesn't care to share with the public when such interventions are made (at least regarding routine three-judge panels). We also don't know at what point in the process the Chief Justice decides whether to assign her desired Justices to the case. Does the Chief Justice weigh in only before a panel is randomly set by the registrar, or might she scrap an allocation she deems unfavorable after it has been tentatively made? Perhaps the random allocation of cases is usually satisfactory such that the Chief Justice sees no need to intervene; perhaps if unsatisfactory, the Chief Justice might simply request a new random assignment instead of mandating her own panel. Would that still count as random? Perhaps the Court registrar and administrative staff already have an idea of what panel might be preferred by the Chief Justice, without the need for their direct involvement. The point is that the legal community and public at large don't really know. This renders the claim about "most cases" irrelevant – because we can't know if it's true, and even if it is, we don't know if it matters.

Yet the real misdirection – and potential for manipulation – occurs in expanded panels. Setting aside the black hole of exceptions, the conventional allocation method for expanded panels – based on custom and not mandated by statute – is called "seniority." Justices serving the most time are assigned to a case in descending order. The identity and ordering of judges on the panel are predictable and pre-defined, based on the fact of their respective time on the Supreme Court bench. This is, at first glance, an (albeit discretionary) objective standard limiting the Chief Justice's total power over panel composition. And here, at least, the public is aware that the Chief Justice has intervened.

Despite this, and due precisely to the "seniority" method, the size of an expanded panel may easily indicate the case outcome and can prove decisive. In major cases Justices tend to vote along known ideological lines. All the Chief Justice need do is choose the panel size which secures a majority likely to vote the way she wants. Consider this scenario: The Court announces that a case will be heard in an expanded panel, let's say of seven Justices. Recall that no justification is offered. Why was the panel expanded? (One might reasonably ask, in some instances – why was a panel not expanded?). Why a panel of seven members, and not, say, five or nine? No reasons for such trifles are given. Nonetheless, this new panel creates a majority of four liberal over three conservative judges, whereas perhaps a five-member or nine-member panel would have rendered a conservative majority.

Herein lies the power to tip the scales in favor of a particular result in contentious cases, by determining how many Justices – with their own judicial and ideological inclinations – hear the case. Segev observes that over the past decades senior Justices tended to belong to the progressive camp, such that almost any case assignment to a seniority-based expanded panel ipso facto raised the likelihood of a progressive result.

The following Court composition demonstrates this point. Imagine the following order of seniority, with Justices categorized as either "activist" (A) or "restrained" (R):

Most senior > ARARRAARRAAARAA > Least Senior

In such a scenario, different panel sizes – based on seemingly "objective" seniority – render different ideological majorities with different likely outcomes: 3=A, 5=R, 7=A, 9=R, 11=A.

Of course, for some expanded panels the Chief Justice simply picks whichever panel they desire, without following the seniority method at all and amounting to total arbitrary discretion. The "seniority" method nonetheless offers small comfort. Some might argue it is worse than total panel-assignment discretion because it misleadingly creates the illusion of objective criteria for panel composition.

Regardless of the type of panel being composed and the method employed to do so, panel assignments have consequences that extend beyond substantive case outcomes. First, a petition may have an almost certain outcome – whether accepted or rejected – but the panel membership could affect the reasoning and rationales presented in the final decision. Based on known personal and jurisprudential differences, a panel could be composed with the intent that certain types of arguments emerge (or are avoided), whether as *ratio decidendi* or *obiter dictum*. Including a specific judge could produce an especially fiery minority opinion which may serve a variety of purposes, while choosing a different panel could guarantee unanimous conformity. In other words, the way a decision is presented and justified matters a lot, and therefore so does the identity of those making it.

Second, the power to choose which Justices preside over which cases presents a genuine problem of judicial independence. Supreme Court Justices are beholden to the Chief Justice and can be rewarded or penalized in various ways through panel assignments, creating strong incentives to conform to Chief Justice preferences.

One well-known example is that of Justice Menachem Mazuz, who consistently deviated from established Supreme Court precedent regarding the legality of demolishing the homes of convicted terrorists. After a number of unruly decisions Mazuz was allegedly removed entirely from such cases (while this was almost certainly the case, such decisions are never publicly acknowledged by the Court). To be clear, the panel method creates its own problems, including the very real threat of rogue judges, such that control over panel composition may serve as an important balancing mechanism; and to be sure, Mazuz was egregiously out of line on the merits in the demolition cases. But Mazuz is just an example illustrating a broader phenomenon of panel composition potentially limiting valid judicial discretion, and the effect such composition power has on judicial independence must nonetheless be acknowledged.

Third, regardless of how the composition power is used and whether it's abused, its very existence poses a hazard to the public perception of an impartial and fair judicial process in the Supreme Court. How can judicial decisions be taken seriously when a single individual, the Chief Justice, possesses such considerable influence over outcomes by choosing panel membership, without even the pretense of transparency or accountability? While this degree of power to manipulate outcomes via panel assignments is a distortion of justice in and of itself, public faith in the system is significant collateral damage.

A final aspect of panel composition on the Supreme Court is that of the inconsistent and erratic nature of judicial decisions arising from disparate panel combinations. This is quite unrelated to the problem of strategic panel manipulation and is inherent to the simple reality of different judges hearing Supreme Court cases and appeals. A primary function of an apex court, and especially an appellate court faced with conflicting rulings from lower tiers, is to clarify and unify legal rules and doctrine through the incremental development of the law. The Supreme Court is supposed to set binding precedent which guides all lower courts and the entire legal system. But as Segev notes, a court which routinely hears cases in "hundreds of panel combinations" undermines this function (there are in fact 455 possible three-judge combinations). Hence the oft-repeated warning from different jurists over the years that the Court could become "a court of judges" instead of a court of law, in which there are "as many opinions as there are members."[17] As Shachar and Gross point out, the above warning coupled with urging Justices to respect existing precedent tacitly acknowledges what is obvious to any observer – that each different panel might decide a case differently.[18]

All in all, the reality of varied panels and the power over panel composition wielded exclusively by the Chief Justice enable ever greater manipulation of judicial outcomes and raise serious concerns about judicial impartiality and fairness at the Supreme Court.

Fact-Finding

The Supreme Court does not conduct evidence hearings – virtually all proceedings involve strictly legal argumentation. There is no witness testimony or cross-examination, no expert or physical evidence submitted. The closest the Court comes to fact-finding is through generic affidavits which affirm factual claims alleged in briefings – but even such affiants are not subjected to cross-examination. This might be appropriate for an ordinary apex court and indeed makes sense for the Court's appellate function, based on the assumption that lower courts have already exhausted the adversarial process for presenting evidence and establishing contested questions of fact. But as we have seen, the Supreme Court is not remotely ordinary, especially in its function as first-and-last High Court of Justice. Conflicting questions of fact are often central to HCJ cases and at times even decisive.

Around the world, legal challenges to government action must usually rest on salient and legally established facts. These might regard the procedure undertaken to arrive at a given government decision, the information and data which served as the basis for policy, the harm caused or rights violated by a specific measure, and so on. Almost any administrative or constitutional case will naturally involve factual elements and disputes which require clarification and adjudication. One of the defining differences between common-law Supreme Courts and European Constitutional Courts is, at least theoretically, the preclusion of abstract review in the former group. Common-law courts are supposed to address actual disputes between parties that involve real-world actions and consequences. The adversarial process by which conflicting parties present and scrutinize evidence is central to the notion of an impartial, passive and unbiased judge. Deciding such cases without the benefit of a fact-finding process essentially means that the judges are groping in the dark – relying on sweeping written assertions with no means to ascertain their veracity or filling in gaps with their own assumptions.

Yet this is precisely the case in Israel. Consider the "factual basis" requirement in administrative law – the Supreme Court examines whether government decisions and policy are based on a sufficient factual foundation so as not to be considered arbitrary and therefore illegal. Fair enough. But how can the Court possibly assess whether any factual foundation merited a certain government decision, if the Court lacks the most basic tools to evaluate such alleged facts? Consider also that many rights-related cases before the Supreme Court hinge on the notion of "proportionality." But the core of any serious proportionality evaluation – often balancing harmed rights against valid societal interests – is a factual cost-benefit analysis. How can one assess the degree of harm or potential value of a proposed policy without considering any direct evidence of either? A prime example is the many HCJ cases scrutinizing military policy, including combat rules of engagement during real-time operations – cases which invariably involve complex questions of real-world impact and effectiveness, and which often revolve around technical factual disputes.

One such example serves to demonstrate this problem. In 2018 five female residents of the Gaza Strip asked for entry permits into Israel for the purpose of receiving life-saving medical treatment. While such permits are routinely granted based on medical necessity, the request of these five women was rejected due to their being immediate relatives of senior Hamas (terrorist) leaders. Among other considerations, the government argued that such permits are an important leverage tactic in ongoing negotiations with Hamas regarding the recovery of Israeli hostages in Gaza (and of the remains of two fallen Israeli soldiers held by Hamas). In an HCJ challenge the Supreme Court ruled that the decision to not grant the entry permits was unreasonable and therefore void.[19]

The merits for this ruling are, for the moment, not the point. In a brief concurring opinion, Justice Yitzhak Amit mocked the government's claim regarding bargaining leverage, and used the Hebrew phrase "blessed be the believer" to convey deep skepticism; Amit found a memo filed with the Court unconvincing and thought that such utility of barring medical treatment in Israel was "doubtful." But on what basis could Amit have possibly reached this conclusion? No direct evidence was presented to the Court; neither the authors of the brief nor any other individual from Israel's defense establishment gave testimony; no direct intelligence analysis was presented by qualified experts. In the absence of any evidentiary proceedings and despite having no relevant personal experience and knowledge, Amit styled himself as military tactician and bargaining extraordinaire, simply declaring reality to conform with his desired judicial outcome. Amit's condescending jeer against the military's assertion, oblivious to the Court's own helplessness in ascertaining pivotal facts, is typical of the Court's mentality towards factual disputes at the heart of HCJ cases.

It's worth noting that in this matter too, the Supreme Court was not designed this way. The original Court indeed conducted evidence hearings and held cross-examinations of affidavit authors. The necessity for fact-finding procedures in an administrative court of first instance was clear even to the Court's colonial founders. The practice was later abandoned (around 1960) to streamline hearings and to reduce the Court's workload.[20] Equally instructive is the fact that even the U.S. Supreme Court maintains special evidentiary procedures for the rare original-jurisdiction cases (e.g., appointing a "special master" for some initial fact-finding), precisely due to the importance of fact-finding in the context of first-instance adjudication.

Factual reality being central to certain judicial decisions, the detrimental effects stemming from the absence of evidence hearings in HCJ cases are varied and far-reaching. These include poor judicial decisions insufficiently grounded in objective reality; undermining public perceptions of judicial impartiality and legitimacy; and incentivizing sloppy and inaccurate drafting of affidavits and briefs by the government and public servants, in the knowledge they won't face serious scrutiny by personal cross-examination. But above all, the remarkable lack of any fact-finding process in HCJ cases boils down to being yet another mechanism of judicial discretion – and judicial power. Justices are essentially free to assume any desired set of facts at the outset of proceedings and to stick with them, impervious to any potential contrary evidence and unwilling to acknowledge the limits of their fact-finding abilities.

Rehearings

The closest the Supreme Court comes to an appeal of its own rulings is called a "further hearing" (*Diyun Nosaf* in Hebrew), which we will call simply a "rehearing." A rehearing may be requested for appeals and HCJ rulings issued by the Court. The Chief Justice may grant a rehearing request at their sole discretion, if the original ruling contradicts established precedent or if the ruling is especially "important, difficult or novel."[21] A panel may also conceivably grant a rehearing for its own ruling at the same time the ruling is issued, but this is extremely rare. As a general matter rehearing requests are not usually granted at all – per judicial policy and confirmed by empirical studies, most major Supreme Court cases are decided (and precedents set) by ordinary three-member or expanded panels, and rehearings are not considered a routine or necessary feature of the Court's work.

The Supreme Court rehearing mechanism is similar to that which exists in appellate courts of other jurisdictions but is nonetheless an outlier. Perhaps the most glaring feature is the vast discretion afforded to the Chief Justice in deciding whether a rehearing is granted. In the U.S. Federal Courts of Appeals (also colloquially known as the Circuit Courts), for example, a party may request that an appellate decision be reconsidered. It is then the original panel that decides whether to grant a rehearing and presides over it; any judge on the court can then trigger a vote on whether to hear the case en benc, which requires support of a majority of active judges. In this way the discretion to activate a rehearing is sensibly dispersed – the merits of a rehearing request is weighed by the panel most familiar with the case and intra-judicial meddling is avoided; while any judge on the court has equal power to initiate en benc consideration once a rehearing is granted. In Israel, not only does the Chief Justice effectively decide whether to grant a rehearing but also decides the rehearing panel composition, with all that entails. Whereas elsewhere rehearings can serve as a reasonable and limited correction mechanism, the Israeli version emerges as a means of overturning outcomes disfavored by the Chief Justice.

This concern is supported by yet another recent empirical study by Givati and Rosenberg (the same pair that researched strategic panel composition), which found that "judges who decide to grant a request for a rehearing are much more likely than other judges to reverse the original ruling in the rehearing."[22] The study showed a clear link between the Chief Justice (or another Justice designated by them) granting a rehearing, and the same Justice then voting to reverse the original panel decision. In other words, rehearings in the Israeli Supreme Court can be seen primarily as an opportunity for the granting Justice to reverse a ruling they dislike on policy grounds. The study also found that this tendency was more pronounced in HCJ cases (as opposed to appeals), further supporting the impression that the desire to reverse policy-related rulings bears on a rehearing decision.

The lack of any appeals process for first-instance HCJ cases coupled with the "rehearings" avenue for reconsidering rulings makes for an unusual combination. Rehearings are not designed or intended to serve an appellate function and indeed cannot compensate for the absence of an appeals process; they typically exist and apply only in a post-appellate setting to begin with. In Israel, parties to an HCJ case have no right to, and no option for, reconsideration by a higher tribunal on the one hand, while on the other the Chief Justice can effectively decide to vacate a ruling by way of granting a rehearing request. The non-appellate-yet-final context of HCJ cases is therefore a critical and defining aspect of rehearings by the Supreme Court.

True to form, the Court offers almost no legal reasoning when granting or denying a rehearing request, and litigants are left to guess the legal grounds for such decisions. One factor which seems to make a rehearing more probable is if a minority opinion severely disagrees with the majority, meaning that a rehearing is much less likely to be granted for a unanimous panel decision than for a contentiously split decision. This intersects with the issue of original panel composition, in the sense that the Chief Justice may strategically assign Justices to a panel in a manner designed to make a rehearing more, or less, likely.

One development regarding Supreme Court rehearings deserves our attention. Statutory law limits rehearings to rulings made by standard three-judge panels. Section 30(a) of the Courts Act of 1984 (not to be confused with Basic Law: The Judiciary, also enacted in 1984) which defines the rehearing process explicitly confines rehearings to "a matter in which the Supreme Court has ruled by three [judges]." The practical meaning is that a case decided by an expanded panel – five or more judges – cannot be reconsidered by granting a rehearing. During Knesset deliberation in the 1950s regarding enactment of the original legislation, one legislator explicitly confirmed that "if a case is heard by five judges at the outset… the right to a rehearing is precluded."[23] The 1995 industry-standard treatise on civil procedure also makes this clear – "were there more than three judges, there is no rehearing."[24] Indeed, for much of the Court's history this rule was strictly observed.

The basic rationale was presumably that important cases decided by routine three-judge panels might evade initial detection – that is, their significance or novelty may only become apparent after a decision has been issued. Such rulings would therefore merit an additional review mechanism, allowing the Court to have an extra "go" at it. By their very nature, cases assigned to expanded panels at the outset can't employ the same justification. If a panel has been expanded it means that someone, either the panel members themselves or the Chief Justice, has already identified at the outset that a case possesses some unique quality that merits consideration by a broader panel. The system has "had its chance," so to speak, to accord the case appropriate attention and to assign it to an expanded group of judges. In other words, the overall institutional scheme originally provided the Court one shot to deviate from the ordinary three-judge panel – either by expanding it in advance, or by holding a post-ruling rehearing, but not both.

Such was the rule until 1995. In the groundbreaking case of *Nahmani v. Nahmani* which involved a separated couple going through divorce proceedings, an expanded panel of five Justices ruled in favor of a man who objected to his wife's demand to impregnate herself using a frozen embryo they had jointly fertilized *in vitro* (the embryo was held by a hospital). Following the judgment, Chief Justice Meir Shamgar surprisingly granted an unprecedented rehearing even though the original panel had already been expanded. This procedural decision was itself challenged by the ex-husband, who claimed that Shamgar had no statutory authority to grant the rehearing. In a remarkable 19-page decision dedicated only to this issue, Aharon Barak – who in the interim had himself just become Chief Justice – penned a majority opinion arguing that, against all established precedent and conventional understanding, the words "by three" actually meant "at least three." Per Barak, the statute merely set a *minimum* of three judges, such that also cases decided by larger panels could be reviewed under a rehearing. The original ruling (which had prevented use of the embryo) was ultimately reversed by the eleven-judge panel in the rehearing. The *Nahmani* case remains the controlling precedent.

The merits of the *Nahmani* case, and even of the interpretive flourish by Barak and the Court, are immaterial for the moment. The decision simply illustrates how the Supreme Court utilizes the rehearing mechanism as yet another instrument reinforcing judicial power. If the Chief Justice is displeased with a specific ruling, they have the rehearing tool at their disposal to nudge the Court in the right direction, or even to create groundbreaking precedent.

And indeed, on numerous occasions the Chief Justice has granted rehearings as a form of damage control – if a three-member panel rendered a decision disliked by the judicial establishment (to which the Chief Justice traditionally belongs), the Chief Justice was able to reverse these by initiating a rehearing and then composing a panel which would yield the desired outcome. Such instances have also become much more frequent in recent years (arguably due to the slightly increased presence of conservative or restrained Justices on the Court). In the 2017 *Gini* case (discussed in the next chapter), Chief Justice Naor granted a rehearing which reversed a prior ruling which enforced statutory law governing the way culinary businesses advertise their compliance with dietary Jewish law. In the 2021 *Zeligman* rehearing, Deputy Chief Justice Meltzer reversed a prior ruling that would have afforded increased judicial deference to regulatory bodies in their interpretation of their own legal regulations. In the 2021 *Jane Doe* rehearing, Chief Justice Hayut reversed a prior ruling which had upheld a controversial Rabbinical Court decision in a divorce-related property dispute. In the 2021 *Rafi Rottem* rehearing (discussed later in Chapter 7) Chief Justice Hayut reversed a ruling which would have restricted application of the "reasonableness" standard in criminal cases. In the 2022 *Urich* rehearing (also noted in Chapter 7), the same Chief Justice reversed a prior appellate ruling which provided more stringent guidelines to trial-court judges granting warrants for searches in suspects' smartphones.[25] In each of these cases, a prior Supreme Court panel had rendered a (relatively or arguably) "conservative" outcome, either in its substantive application of the law or in its restricting of judicial discretion and interference; in each one, the Chief Justice directly or indirectly facilitated the ruling's reversal by granting a rehearing with an expanded panel that would predictably provide the desired outcome.

*

The Supreme Court's unique features of panel composition, fact-finding and rehearings all involve seemingly technical procedures which are typically overlooked when examining Israeli judicial power. Yet these elements, individually and especially when combined, afford both the Justices and the institution of the Supreme Court a formidable degree of additional discretion and power, which ultimately translate into greater influence over final rulings in a manner that has nothing to do with application of the law.

Mis-chief Justice

In a bland and matter-of-fact letter to Chief Justice Esther Hayut in late August of 2023, Justice Yosef Elron presented his candidacy to succeed Hayut for the post of Chief Justice – and doing so, triggered a major uproar. Reactions from top commentators belonging to the judicial supremacist camp bordered on hysteria. Anonymous senior judicial sources called the move "a disgrace"; former Deputy Legal Counsel to the Government Dina Zilber labeled Elron a "trojan horse" enabling a "hostile takeover" of the Court; legal correspondents at news outlets opined that Elron had dropped a "bombshell," that he ought to be suspended from judicial duties, that he was "by his own hand" introducing politics into the Court, and that he was "unfit" to be a Supreme Court judge, let alone its Chief Justice; some legal academics weighed in as well – Suzie Navot (of the Israel Democracy Institute) warned of "the harm to the core of judicial independence" and speculated what illicit promises Elron would make to politicians, while Mordechai Kremnitzer (also of the IDI) went further and stated that Elron's move was a step closer to the "destruction of the rule of law in Israel."[26] No less. What was all this really about?

As the astute reader has likely already perceived, the office of the Chief Justice of the Supreme Court occupies a truly commanding role within the Court, the entire judiciary and beyond. One is unlikely to find so much power concentrated within the role of a single individual in any other democratic judicial system. It is therefore worth sketching out in broad strokes the considerable authority reserved uniquely for the Chief Justice, and in its light to describe how Chief Justices are appointed.

We have thus far detailed the Chief Justice's direct and decisive involvement in judicial appointments, in panel composition and in rehearings. Additional authority with which the Chief Justice is endowed includes the following: appointing the Chair (a serving Supreme Court Justice) of the influential Central Elections Committee; appointing the Chair (a serving or retired Justice or senior judge) and all other members of any State Commission of Inquiry, the highest ad hoc mechanism for independent public investigations; appointing the Chair (a retired Justice) to the committee selecting the Legal Counsel to the Government; and much more – this list is far from exhaustive.

The Chief Justice also has direct veto power over a range of appointments nominally made by the Minister of Justice though subject to the former's approval, within both the judiciary and the executive, including: appointing the Director of the Court System; promoting judges to managerial roles (such as Court President) within Magistrate and District courts; appointing Court Registrars; granting "senior judge" status to retired judges; appointing the Judiciary

Ombudsman in charge of receiving complaints against judges; and many more. Additional areas subject to Chief Justice authority or approval involve appointments to various statutory boards and committees, including the Israeli public broadcasting corporation and regulatory bodies within the financial and banking system. Many other appointments and personnel decisions throughout the judiciary and executive are conditioned on consulting the Chief Justice, often with limited maneuverability to act contrary to such "advice" received.

Of course, such veto power remains obscure so long as the Minister of Justice or other actors are aligned with the Chief Justice or choose to comply with the latter's wishes. But its efficacy becomes clear in the event of direct confrontation. In one jarring example from 2024, Minister of Justice Yariv Levin sought to appoint an experienced and respected judge to the role of President of the Southern District Court. The candidate judge, Avi Levi, was vetted and approved by a formal committee of senior public-service jurists headed by a sitting Supreme Court Justice. But the acting Chief Justice, Uzi Vogelman, objected to the appointment on various pretenses. By withholding his approval Vogelman could postpone the appointment indefinitely and effectively veto the Minister's exercise of his statutory authority. The episode turned into a fiasco when Vogelman's stubborn refusal was itself challenged in an HCJ petition, with the Supreme Court on-duty Justice issuing a request for (acting Chief Justice) Vogelman's formal response. Vogelman persisted in his refusal until his retirement from the bench, and an interim District Court President was appointed only in May 2024 (after the role had been vacant for some nine months) after Yitzhak Amit became acting Chief Justice, and reached a compromise with Minister Levin. However, the appointed candidate was not Avi Levi (Levin's original pick), but someone else entirely – meaning that Vogelman succeeded in thwarting an appointment he didn't like.

The Chief Justice also appoints all members of the judicial disciplinary tribunal (responsible for adjudicating ethical and disciplinary complaints against judges) and decides panel compositions for hearings it conducts. The Chief Justice issues ethical rules for judges and appoints a judicial ethics committee authorized to provide pre-rulings to ethical questions submitted by judges.

Finally, as has been referenced above, the Chief Justice publishes Directives (or "procedural instructions") which apply both to the Supreme Court and to the entire judiciary. The authority to issue such Directives is not grounded in any clear statutory source, and the practice of doing so is relatively new, with most Directives issued since 2012. Given the lack of explicit authority there is also no formal obligation to publicize the directives, and it is in fact unclear whether the Court publishes all directives, or whether it considers some official directives to be "internal" and not publicly available.

As these Directives became more common, some were in fact challenged. A 2014 HCJ petition argued that the Chief Justice had no legal authority to proclaim binding (or even non-binding) directives, a position which was even adopted by the Israeli Bar Association. In an opinion by Justice Elyakim Rubinstein the

Supreme Court conceded that no statutory authority existed, but ruled that such authority was "bound up" with the "judicial environment" and was therefore "inherent" to the role of Chief Justice.[27] Per the Court, this is especially the case regarding guidelines or broad principles which don't necessarily limit judicial discretion. Rubenstein also mentioned, without a shred of irony, the maxim that responsibility (for the daily functioning of the courts) must be accompanied by authority (to issue directives) – an argument some found astounding, considering the Court's reputation for usurping the authority of elected officials despite the latter being held responsible for government policy.

Whatever their legal basis, some Directives indeed address technical and practical matters directly related to litigation in court, just as some outline broad guidelines of a discretionary nature – regarding issues such as filing-deadline extension requests, or evidence hearings involving victims of alleged sexual offenses. Yet many other Directives have a distinctly compulsory character and tone, and their Hebrew title is tellingly that of "procedure" (*nohal*) and not "guideline" (*han-haya*). And some Directives, like number 1-19 which formalized the Duo Committee for vetting District Court judicial candidates, create independent rules and mechanisms that have nothing to do with regulation of routine court proceedings.

The very existence of explicit rules also seems to have enabled a practice of "shadow directives" – unofficial and discreet instructions decreed by the Chief Justice as another form of control over judicial conduct. The ban on candidates' meetings with politicians, described in the previous chapter, is one glaring example. Another is that despite the official Ethics Rules allowing lectures by judges in a non-commercial setting, the Chief Justice has demanded that he or she pre-approve any lecture (public or private) by a Supreme Court Justice, and that such lectures may only be delivered in a strictly academic setting. Thus, the power of issuing official directives of dubious legal validity has itself produced a habit of the Chief Justice simply policing judicial conduct outside the court, without even the pretense of public acknowledgement or official sanction.

The singular importance of who is appointed to this role should now be abundantly clear. The Supreme Court Chief Justice personally wields an inordinate degree of official and unofficial authority that extends well and far beyond judicial adjudication. The office of the Chief Justice exerts immense influence within and without the legal world, throughout both the judiciary and the executive, and can easily be considered one of the most uniquely powerful roles in the Israeli system of government. We may now turn to the way that the Chief Justice is appointed – and return to the saga of Justice Yosef Elron.

Section 8 of the 1984 Courts Act mandates simply that the Judicial Selection Committee is to choose the Supreme Court Chief Justice the same way that ordinary judges are appointed – by majority vote of the committee members. Pursuant to a 2007 amendment (following Barak's eleven-year stint), the tenure of Chief Justice is limited to seven years. There are no statutory rules defining how such an appointment is made or limiting eligibility for the role. Yet since the State's founding, there has been an unwritten custom by which the defining criteria is "seniority," according to which the Justice serving on the Supreme Court the longest is appointed as Chief Justice when the position becomes vacant. The seniority method is firmly established, well-known and openly acknowledged. The practical administration of this method depends on uniform cooperation of the Justices themselves – the only person that submits their candidacy is the most senior judge. In this way the Justices of the Supreme Court jointly present the Committee with a sole candidate, which the committee approves for lack of any competing offers.

Throughout the years there have been a number of attempts to change this practice, though none were successful. For present purposes we need not explore the various justifications offered and objections raised regarding such a system. Its benefits or ills aside, one key aspect is the simple transfer of power from the Judicial Selection Committee to the Justices themselves. The former simply performs a ceremonial function by rubber-stamping the candidate jointly offered by the Court, despite the statute clearly granting authority to the committee. This arrangement would almost certainly be rejected by a court in almost any other context of administrative law – a deciding body failing to exercise its discretion mandated by statute, with a parallel conspiracy (in the literal sense of the word) by public officials to guarantee their desired outcome.

Such questions of legality or propriety notwithstanding, the true impact of the seniority method is found in the foreseeability it creates. Recall that judges have limited tenure and must resign at the age of 70, and that the age and seniority of each judge is known at any given time. Barring unexpected resignation and untimely demise, easy arithmetic produces a clear prediction of who will attain the office of Chief Justice, years and sometimes decades in advance. (To illustrate the point – the current Wikipedia page of the Supreme Court lists the expected Chief Justice roster all the way to 2039).[28] One could consider various ways in which such pre-determination of a judge's promotion to Chief Justice is beneficial or detrimental – to the incentives affecting individual judicial conduct, to the relationships and power dynamics between judges, to the way in which the Court operates, and so on. But the simple fact is that the seniority method defines the identity of the Chief Justice far, far in advance of their actual appointment by statutory committee.

Why does this matter? Because the most significant real-world effect of the seniority method links directly back to the judicial appointments process. Under the right conditions, appointing a specific Justice means effectively appointing them also as Chief Justice down the line. And it is precisely this foreseeability that enables yet greater control of the judicial landscape. Under the guise of a seemingly objective and factual criteria for appointing the Chief Justice, the seniority method de facto brings that promotion forward to the time of selection to serve on the Court. In such circumstances, the veto-wielding establishment knows precisely when to compromise over a benign appointment, and when to fight over a specific candidate tooth-and-nail – aiming to block a future Chief

Justice or to ensure their appointment, as the case may be. In this manner the extraordinary power wielded by the Chief Justice is reserved for those candidates favored by the dominant force on the Supreme Court, simply in a subtle way which is less obvious to the casual observer. It is no surprise then, for example, that Aharon Barak insisted so strongly on appointing his protégé Dorit Beinisch to the bench when he did, for it had the de facto effect of ensuring she would also replace him as Chief Justice over ten years down the line.

Back to Justice Yosef Elron, we can better understand why any shift away from the seniority method is met with such vehemence. In January of 2024 retired Justice Yitzhak Zamir wrote an op-ed titled "Without the Seniority Method the Government Will Have Near-Limitless Control."[29] While such hyperbole is plainly false, Zamir provides a glimpse into the way he (and many like him) view the seniority method as vital to manipulating the ultimate identity of the Chief Justice (and the authority that comes with the title), and as yet another instrument by which the Supreme Court solidifies and exercises its own control.

Soft Power

Finally, a number of features and factors defining the environment in which the Supreme Court operates offer it an unusually high degree of leeway, regarding issues in which courts are usually more constrained and providing yet further opportunity for manipulation.

Records. Court proceedings are not kept in a verbatim written record. Despite the law mandating that all courts keep (and publish or make available) an exact record of oral argument conducted before them, and despite this rule being followed meticulously (for the most part) by lower-tier courts, the Supreme Court sees itself as exempt. Pursuant to a 2007 ruling, the Court Office publishes an abridged summary "reflecting the main points" raised, argued or discussed (until 2007, the Court maintained no written record whatsoever). These are typically partial, inconsistent and riddled with errors. They are also not automatically available to the public, but rather only to case litigants and the media. This permissive approach toward accurate minute-keeping makes for flawed review and recollection of oral argumentation (by the judges themselves); prevents public transparency of the legal process; and allows for an undisciplined or careless form of discussion in the courtroom, by both judges and counsel.

For comparison, the U.S. Supreme Court has been recording the audio of all proceedings since the 1950s, and these have been made routinely available to the public since the 1990s. Audio recordings were also transcribed to written format. Since 2010, the audio recordings and written transcripts of all U.S. Supreme Court proceedings are made available on the court website *on the same day*, or very close to it.

In 2020 the Israeli Supreme Court initiated (via a Chief Justice Directive, of course) a live-broadcast pilot in which oral argumentation for a handful of high-profile cases would be broadcast live from the court, online and available to the general public. The decision to broadcast a hearing is made by the judicial panel presiding over the same case, pursuant to a recommendation made by a separate committee. The committee is chaired by a Justice appointed by the Chief Justice, and the Chief Justice must approve any recommendation before being passed to a panel for a final decision.

While the overall step towards greater transparency seems welcome, the initiative "reveals an inch while concealing two" (as a common Israeli saying goes). It provides the illusion of transparency and greater exposure of the Court's workings while in fact the vast majority of cases remain in dark obscurity, still without the most basic functions of accurate record-keeping and public access. The Court itself selects exactly which solitary cases to broadcast out of the many thousands heard each year (and out of scores or even hundreds of cases of indisputable public significance), and can easily discriminate between such cases in a manner serving its own institutional interests. Naturally, the Court rarely provides an explanation or justification regarding which cases are broadcasted and which are not.[30] The pilot itself is limited to a few months and is periodically extended by the Court, such that the entire initiative remains subject to the unilateral discretion of the Chief Justice and can be terminated the moment the Court finds it sufficiently burdensome.

Timing. The Court has no defined timeframes for hearing arguments or issuing decisions. Rulings in some cases may be delayed for years after oral hearings, depending on a range of factors – from the attention each Justice accords them, to delays granted by the Court, to the arbitrary will of the Chief Justice. It is not uncommon for a party to file a motion requesting (really, pleading for) a decision after a case languishes in neglect, though such motions risk raising the Court's ire. In some cases the Court decides to issue a "partial" ruling without any clear legal basis for doing so – publishing a summary of their final decision, with the detailed reasoning published weeks (and even months) later. The problem is exacerbated by the absence of accurate record-keeping, in that a panel may turn to deciding a case long after oral arguments were concluded.

Most significantly, rulings may be strategically timed so as to maximize their effect on real-world events, or conversely so as to avoid public attention and scrutiny for potentially controversial decisions. This is exemplified by the two most dramatic and contentious rulings in Israeli constitutional law – the 1995 *Bank Hamizrachi* ruling was issued five days after the assassination of Prime Minister Yitzhak Rabin which rocked Israeli society to the core; and the 2024 *Reasonableness* ruling was issued at the height of the Israeli-Hamas war, with Israel still reeling from the events of October 7th and the political branches unwilling to engage in squabbles with the judiciary (the unpersuasive explanation offered by the Court in both cases will be addressed in later chapters).

One especially egregious expression of the Court's approach towards timing is the recent "tradition" of farewell rulings by retiring Justices. It has now become common practice for a retiring Justice to coordinate their final ruling so that it involves some case of significant public importance, to "go out with a bang."

Setting aside the mild hubris and narcissism involved (judicial humility is long forsaken), the practice also represents an appalling miscarriage of justice. Timing rulings in such a way means either that they are rushed, resulting in a half-baked and poorly written decision, or more likely, that they had already been completed earlier and must now wait in abeyance until the good Justice is so kind to schedule his or her retirement hearing. Desperate litigants might be counting the days, waiting for their fates to be decided; public cases affecting thousands of lives or millions of dollars hang in the balance; yet a completed ruling will linger on the shelf until the retiring Justice finds it convenient. It has now come to the point that the entire legal community collectively enters a "brace for impact" mode any time a retirement from the Supreme Court bench approaches.

Post-Judicial Career. As noted above, statutory law dictates that Supreme Court Justices retire at the age of seventy. One significant implication (among many others) is that Justices often go on to pursue lucrative careers, in addition to their generous State-funded pensions.* Some go right back into legal practice, serving as commercial arbitrators or even as attorneys representing clients; others might go to academia. The fact that Justices continue with their robust legal-professional careers immediately after leaving the bench raises a variety of questions and concerns, regarding propriety of both pre-retirement and post-retirement conduct. Perhaps the most audacious example in recent memory is provided by Justice Hanan Meltzer. Within a year of his retirement in 2021, Meltzer was appointed as Chairman of Migdal Insurance and Financial Holdings, one of Israel's leading insurance and investment companies, with a whopping compensation package of over half a million dollars a year (the average Israeli salary is around a tenth of that). Only six months prior to his appointment, Meltzer had reportedly ruled in a case in favor of Migdal and other insurance companies.

On-Call Justice. All Supreme Court Justices (aside the Chief and Deputy Chief) serve as "on-call" Justice on a weekly rotating basis. An on-call Justice is the first point of contact for all new petitions, including some categories of single-Justice cases which are decided exclusively by the on-call Justice that happens to receive them. The identity of the on-call Justice might be critical to the chances of a given case – the on-call Justice plays a decisive (and usually, a determinative) role by choosing whether to advance a petition to be adjudicated and heard by a panel, or whether to dismiss the petition outright. Litigants often try to tactically time their petitions so that these are filed while a potentially sympathetic Justice is on-call – instead of "forum shopping," the Supreme Court enables "judge shopping." Historically, the on-call roster at any given time was not published anywhere, but was rather something of an insider secret – those with contacts on the Court or those regularly arguing before the Court (such as select government lawyers) were in the know. Only relatively recently has the Court started publishing its on-call roster in advance. This is, ultimately, just one more way in

* The average judicial pension is the highest in the Israeli public sector by a significant margin.

which the Court may be manipulated to yield inconsistent and partisan outcomes.

Here, too, Justice Hanan Meltzer earns an honorable mention. In a 2024 interview, the retired Meltzer boasted how, as an on-call Justice, he managed to single-handedly foil the implementation of new Knesset legislation by issuing an immediate provisional injunction, and then by assembling a panel (which included himself) that confirmed the temporary injunction.[31] During the delay, circumstances changed such that the law had to be rescinded. Thus, as a single on-call Justice, Meltzer managed to effectively and unilaterally invalidate primary legislation.

*

The Stage is Set

In his ill-fated lecture at Bar-Ilan University, Prof. Yoram Shachar summarized his contention as follows:

> "Israel is unique among civilized nations in its concentration of normative power in one centralized government, in the position of an autonomous and professional judiciary within this government, in the concentration of the entire judicial power in one single unified Supreme Court, in the accumulation of many control mechanisms within the judicial system – and inwards within the court itself, in the hands of one Chief Justice."

It is no coincidence that Shachar also referred in his lecture, as a given, to the "de facto control of the Supreme Court Justices over all stages of the judicial appointments process."

Demonstrating Shachar's argument, this Part has hopefully established the extent and scope of institutional and structural power held by the Supreme Court and its Justices, within the dual contexts of judicial appointments and broader influence within the judicial hierarchy, forms of power quite separate from that which is inherent in the core judicial function of settling disputes according to law. These organizational schemes granting centralized power to a tiny cadre of judges are not the result of wide public consensus or some insightful experiment of government design, but rather were mostly born of accident and happenstance, inherited from multiple colonial rulers or haphazardly assembled and activated.

This anomalous concentration of institutional power went unaddressed for much of Israel's history, primarily due to being balanced by two major factors which had at least partially allayed legitimate concerns. First, Israel was a system of parliamentary supremacy in which the elected Knesset had the undisputed last word. Second, the first generation of classically trained Justices adopted a distinctly restrained and disciplined approach towards their role and the authority they wielded, keenly cognizant of the risks associated with upsetting the delicate balance between the Israeli branches of government. While the "classical" Court boldly challenged unlawful government action and fiercely defended individual liberties from government encroachment, its Justices also maintained clear jurisprudential limits and exercised their institutional power prudently. Thus, despite these organizational arrangements being objectionable in principle and unwise for a host of reasons, they could have conceivably remained tolerable.

All this changed in the Supreme Court's "revolutionary" era commencing in the 1980's. The judicial veto and effective control over appointments along with an institutional structure granting the Court outsized influence throughout the legal system jointly set the stage for the dramatic expansion of judicial power over all areas of Israeli public and private life. All that was needed was a brilliant, charismatic and determined judge on the bench who might be able to harness the Court's considerable power along with its hard-won prestige in the eyes of the Israeli public, in service of the cause of judicial supremacy.

In a 1977 lecture, Legal Counsel to the Government Aharon Barak said the following: "As jurists, we are not limited to the interpretation and application of existing law. We are the vanguard of the aspiration for better, more desirable law. [...] We are the architects of social change. We possess the skills to construct a better, more just legal system. We do not see our roles as limited to that of mere legal technicians. We see our role as incorporating legal statesmanship."[32] He was appointed to the Supreme Court in 1978.

Part II

Ascendancy

The jurisprudential and administrative revolution and the radical expansion of judicial power

Chapter 3

Objective Purposive Interpretation

Statutes as First Drafts

"'When I use a word,' Humpty Dumpty said in rather a scornful tone, 'it means just what I choose it to mean – neither more nor less.' 'The question is,' said Alice, 'whether you can make words mean so many different things.' 'The question is,' said Humpty Dumpty, 'which is to be master – that's all.'"
— Lewis Carroll, *Through the Looking Glass*

At Cross Purposes

The case of *Gini v. The Chief Rabbinate of Israel* revolved around the issue of Kosher certification granted to restaurants and other food-serving businesses in Israel. Jewish religious law as practiced by many Jews – usually referred to as "*Kashrut*" laws – includes a host of rules and prohibitions regarding permissible and forbidden food, relating to sources, methods of preparation, tools used in the kitchen and much else besides. Businesses offering food adhering to these rules will typically display some form of certificate attesting to their Kosher supervision, most often under the auspices of a recognized organization or individual which provides such certification.

In Israel, statutory law grants the Chief Rabbinate – an official state organ – an express monopoly over Kosher certification. Section 2 of the 1983 Kashrut Fraud Act allows for Kosher certificates to be granted only by the national Chief Rabbinate (and its recognized Rabbis) or by an officially appointed local Rabbi. Section 3 reads that a food establishment "shall not represent the food establishment as Kosher, unless granted a Kosher certificate."[1] The dispute in the *Gini* case centered on so-called "private supervision" certificates displayed by certain food-serving establishments – these were granted by unofficial organizations (not recognized by the Chief Rabbinate) and certified that a food establishment was under their "supervision," implying the food complied with

Jewish religious law without expressly using the word "Kosher."* The legal question was thus one of statutory interpretation – whether displaying such a certificate, essentially stating the Kosher status of the food, ran afoul of Section 3 of the Kashrut Fraud Act.

In a rehearing decision issued in 2017 (which overturned an HCJ decision from the previous year), the Supreme Court ruled that displaying the "private supervision" sign was permissible under the law. The majority and dissenting opinions agreed that the statute had a "subjective" purpose (clearly emerging from the legislative history) of granting the Rabbinate a monopoly over all Kosher certification, which likely precluded the use and display of non-Rabbinate "private supervision" certificates. They also agreed that this "subjective" purpose was the more consistent with the statutory text, which does not define Kosher certification as limited only to instances utilizing the actual word "Kosher." At the same time, the majority and dissenting opinions agreed that the law had an "objective" purpose which related more generally to consumer protection and to preventing consumer fraud, and which also included maintaining the liberty and discretion of business-owners and patrons – a purpose which could permit alternative non-Rabbinate certification as long as consumers were not being directly misled.

The Court was divided on which of the above "purposes" ought to prevail, considering their directly conflicting nature and the different outcomes they each produced. Chief Justice Miriam Naor wrote the majority opinion which ultimately preferred the "objective" purpose, and interpreted the law as not granting the Rabbinate a monopoly over all Kosher certification, despite the statutory text and legislative intent mandating the opposite outcome. The Court therefore ruled the alternative "supervision" signs to be lawful. Naor summarized the Court's interpretive theory thus:

> "The final purpose of the law is determined on the basis of two elements: the subjective purpose – "legislative intent" and the objective purpose "the law's intent" [*sic*]. If synthesizing between the subjective purpose and the objective purpose is not possible due to an irreconcilable contradiction between the two, the decisive weight shall be attributed according to the discretion of the interpreter and considering the totality of the circumstances surrounding the law."[2]

Another ruling issued by the Supreme Court in 2017, in the *Abu Arfa* case, regarded four Palestinian residents of eastern Jerusalem who were associated with the Hamas terror organization and who were elected or appointed in 2006 to serve in the Palestinian government.[3] Unlike most Palestinians, those living in eastern Jerusalem enjoy special status and benefits as "permanent residents" of Israel, including free movement throughout Israel and access to many aspects of Israeli

---

* The specific Hebrew word for supervision, "*Hashgacha*," is commonly associated with Kosher dietary supervision.

State-provided health, welfare, and education services. Section 11 of the 1952 Entry Into Israel Law (Israel's primary immigration legislation, henceforth: the "Entry Law") grants the Minister of the Interior express authority to revoke residential permits "at his discretion." Pursuant to the law, the Interior Minister at the time (Roni Bar-On of the centrist Kadima party) revoked the residential permit of these four Hamas-associated Palestinians on the grounds of "breach of faith to the State," such that they would be expelled from eastern Jerusalem and compelled to move to Palestinian-governed areas of the West Bank or Gaza (or out of Israel altogether).

This decision was immediately challenged in the Supreme Court. The membership or active status of the petitioners within the Hamas terror organization was not disputed, and the case focused on legal executive authority. The Court finally ruled (some eleven years later) that the revocation of the petitioners' resident status was unlawful, based on the Court's interpretation of the phrase "at his discretion" in the Entry Law. At the center of the ruling lay the question whether this explicit phrase indicated wide discretion on the part of the Interior Minister to revoke residency status under the law (limited only by traditional principles of administrative law), or whether despite the phrase this authority was nonetheless limited to specific instances and on the basis of particular grounds.

Writing for the majority, Justice Uzi Vogelman first found that the text was ambiguous,* and that the original "subjective" purpose of lawmakers drafting the law in 1952 was directed at recent migrants to Israel and not at long-established residents (indeed, the unique status of eastern Jerusalem residents only arose after the 1967 Six Day War). Vogelman further reasoned that the Entry Law had a number of "objective" purposes that are independent of the purpose contemplated or intended by its original legislators. These purposes included "state sovereignty" and "public safety and security," which supported the Ministers revocation decisions. However, another objective purpose of the law was "advancement of human rights," which included the right to liberty, dignity and to family life, all of which would undoubtedly be impacted were the residency status of the Hamas activists revoked.

When balancing the text, original "subjective" purpose and the competing objective purposes, and in conjunction with additional considerations, Vogelman ultimately decided that the objective purpose of human rights prevailed – such that the phrase "at his discretion" did not include the authority to revoke resident status of the four Hamas activists under present circumstances. A majority of five out of seven Justices accordingly ruled that the revocation was unlawful.

In his dissenting opinion, Justice Neal Hendel stressed the explicit nature of the statutory text; along with the clear desire (the "subjective purpose") of the original legislators to grant expansive authority to the Interior Minister, serving

---

* Presumably, that the words "at his discretion" could include the meaning "*not* at his discretion."

as the primary organ of the executive government and of the State itself regarding matters of citizenship and residency status. Hendel argued that the majority's interpretation essentially amounted to de facto annulment of Section 11 of the Entry Law. In a separate dissent, Justice Rubenstein asked – "is there no line which cannot be crossed?." While both dissents took issue with the majority's reasoning and conclusion, neither challenged the notion of "objective" purposes at a high level of abstraction and as conceived by the judge, which had the power to trump the law's plain meaning and genuine purpose as intended by its creators.

*

Confused? *Gini* and *Abu Arfa* serve as just two examples within a myriad cases in which the Supreme Court employs a technique it calls "objective purposive interpretation." This elaborate form of legal interpretation purports to apply the law in accordance with a so-called "objective" purpose which is determined and defined exclusively by the judge. In the *Gini* case this meant subverting the plain statutory text and the clear legislative intent behind the law in order to arrive at an outcome the Court found more desirable; in *Abu Arfa* this meant limiting statutory executive discretion so as to disallow a ministerial decision of which the Court disapproved. As we shall presently see, this method of interpretation permeates the Court's jurisprudence and serves as the foundation for much of its legal revolutions, and as a key factor enabling the Court to advance its judicial agenda. This chapter will unpack and expose the theory and practice of "objective purposive interpretation."

Law as Words

Before we proceed with the Israeli approach to legal interpretation, we must entertain a brief diversion by laying out some basic concepts within the broader context of interpreting legal texts.

To say that the law is a word-based discipline seems almost trivial. Since the promulgation of the Twelve Tables in Rome the notion of the law as a written text, fixed and consistent, publicly available and observable, stands at the heart of ordered society as we know it. At least in their official capacity, the specialized job of judges, lawyers and those in the legal field can be said to boil down to two fundamental disciplines: interpretation of texts, and something called "legal reasoning." Legal reasoning refers to the unique logical process of applying the law in a consistent manner, especially within the context of adhering to binding legal precedent, and we may set it aside for present purposes.[4]

"The law" has of course historically extended far beyond naked statutes and written texts alone. From Jewish Oral Law to the classical Common Law to the medieval *lex mercatoria*, legal rules embedded in human custom, in tradition and elsewhere have a long and respectable pedigree. Yet these have been largely displaced by statutes in modern societies, in the interest of clarity, justice and democracy. Judicial rulings and opinions bearing legal force are no exception – these too invariably appear in written form, and it is within their words (and operative outcomes) which we may find binding law.

Understanding and enforcing written legal texts – by their interpretation and construction, by parsing the words in context and by utilizing universal rules of interpretation – make up the bulk of legal education and lie at the heart of the legal profession. Applying the written law emerges as distinct from other abstract exercises in understanding the meaning of texts – such as literary interpretation – due to its obligatory governmental function (that is, the outcome of such interpretation has a binding effect, with adverse consequences for disobedience) and due to its grounding in authority (that is, applying law endeavors to implement the will of some legitimate source of authority within a given legal framework, such as legislator or higher court).

The Western legal order has evolved over many generations to produce a set of distinct-but-related approaches to legal interpretation of texts. As with many other aspects of the law these are especially relevant to the work of those using the law to resolve disputes – that is, to the work of courts and judges. It is the judge who must convincingly explain how a binding decision derives from the law itself and not from pure arbitrary whim; in doing so, she must almost invariably present a clear link between the written legal text and the final judicial outcome, based on a valid theory of judicial interpretation.

While legal texts come in many forms (including contracts and wills), our focus here will center on statutory and constitutional texts. In the briefest terms possible,[*] one may identify the major approaches to legal interpretation as follows:[5]

Textualism focuses on the words of the law and their linguistic meaning, primarily as understood at the time a law was enacted. Far from simple or straightforward and rarely consisting of just opening a dictionary, ascertaining the meaning of a legal text may typically involve sophisticated methods of context and comparison, historical investigation, linguistic expertise and other forms of research.

Intentionalism is concerned with the intent of a text's authors or drafters – what did they mean when employing certain words and terms? What content did they believe they were communicating within a given law? Both textualism and intentionalism share a common aim which we may call the *fidelity principle* – they attempt to execute the command of a legal authority as encapsulated within a legal text, and indeed these approaches often overlap. At times the difference between them can be described as a point of departure – the meaning of a text may be strongly clarified by evidence of how it was understood by its drafters; conversely, the intent of a text's drafters is most directly evident in the words they

---

[*] The following description and classification relies strongly on the useful summary presented by Justice Alex Stein in his essay on Legal Probabilism.

chose to enact as law. If the textualist asks the "what does the text mean?," the intentionalist might ask "what did the text's author mean by it?."

Purposivism endeavors to apply the written law in accordance with its purpose – that is, with the goals, aims, or objects that a law is (or was) meant to achieve. Often called "the mischief rule," purposivism asks "what mischief did this law address?," or "what problem is this law trying to fix?," and so on. Much like intentionalism, purposivism often relies on evidence outside the legal text itself, and may even deduce an unstated or implicit purpose. Yet purposivism and intentionalism are clearly distinct and are not to be confused with one another – put simply, intentionalism is about the meaning of a text as understood by its authors, while purposivism is about the end that a legal text's authors aimed to achieve. Text and intent are about the "what?" of a given law; purpose regards the "why?" of it.

Purposivism shares the same core assumption of the preceding two approaches, that of applying or implementing the desire of a valid legal authority, while broadening the scope of resources available to applying a legal text. If textualism seeks to understand the text on its own terms and intentionalism seeks to interpret the text as understood by its authors, purposivism seeks to apply a legal text in a manner consistent with (or more likely to bring about) the stated or unstated goals of the text's authors. These three approaches and their complex application comprise the most common and well-established forms of judicial interpretation throughout the Western and developed world. Perhaps unsurprisingly, they are also mostly complementary – in the vast majority of cases, the plain meaning of a legal text seamlessly aligns with the clear intent of its authors and directly advances the purpose for which it was created. In other words, the vast majority of laws tend to be fairly clear and readily applicable, because they produce the same result irrespective of which interpretive method is employed.

Other interpretive approaches are more difficult to classify, and we may proceed while acknowledging that there is much room for debate and for alternative formulations of the following descriptions.

Pragmatism argues that a legal text has no objective or absolute meaning and is inevitably open to a variety of interpretations; as such a judge may choose an interpretation that best serves current societal interests (as understood or determined by the judge). The pragmatist approach is closely associated with Judge Richard Posner, one of the most renowned legal scholars of the 20th century, but is often justified or employed in many other contexts and by other names. Instead of fidelity to the law and its author, the pragmatist judge serves as a legislator (or a "trustee" for society at large) by infusing a legal text with a meaning meant to achieve some commendable societal end according to a judge's best understanding of what that might be. The judicial philosophy of Ronald Dworkin and of the "Legal Process School" may also be crudely lumped together with pragmatism.

Fiatism similarly assumes the lack of a fixed and ascertainable meaning of a legal text, but sees the interpretive act as an inherently political exercise of naked power and pure discretion, meant to benefit the group or class to which a judge belongs or which the judge has an interest in serving. One might regard fiatism as the most cynical category of approaches, in the sense that it is unwilling to assume a good-faith judicial effort at applying the law or even at serving society as a whole. Critical legal studies, critical race theory, and Marxist and feminist approaches to law may all be broadly grouped under fiatism.

Some have classified pragmatism and fiatism under a joint category of *reformatism*, due to their shared willingness to "reform" existing law so it produces an outcome which the interpreter-judge finds preferable. Their unifying theme, to greater or lesser extent, is their rejection of the fidelity principle, i.e. the notion or the ideal of a judge or interpreter acting as a faithful agent of the legislator or legal authority. They rather consider the judicial role as an independent source of authority or power, which includes interpretation and application of law in a manner separate from any original authority.

Many if not most jurists do not conform to a single exclusive approach or category. Aside the natural overlap between the different methods, some jurists will consciously reserve different methods for different contexts, circumstances, and types of legal texts. Others might choose to apply different methods by a cascade of necessity – referring to plain text, and then to author's intent if the text is too ambiguous, and then to a text's purpose if the intent itself is insufficiently clear, and so on.

Readers across the globe will find echoes of these various interpretive approaches in their own respective jurisdictions. Perhaps most well-known is the debate regarding constitutional interpretation in the United States, between originalism (reflecting various strands of textualism and intentionalism) and living constitutionalism (reflecting some forms of purposivism and reformatism), though similar struggles are commonplace throughout the democratic judicial world.

Needless to say, the question of legal interpretation employed by judges is not solely methodological, but rather reflects the deepest-held beliefs and the most fundamental conception of law, the judicial role, the separation of powers and much beyond. The method of interpretation adopted by a judge or court will dramatically affect their relative degree of judicial discretion in deciding cases and in exercising policy-making power – whether limited to the judicial function of resolving disputes or extending far beyond it.

As a final terminological point of order, one might properly distinguish between "interpretation" and "construction" as two separate activities – the former regards the linguistic meaning of a text, while the latter regards its application in a given set of circumstances.[6] As the Iowa Supreme Court has explained, "interpretation involves ascertaining the meaning of contractual words; construction refers to deciding their legal effect." For the purposes of this discussion, however, the term "interpretation" is used in the broadest sense and encompasses both traditional notions of "interpretation" and "construction." Indeed, this is also more faithful to the practice of Israeli courts and jurists, who typically make no such distinction and use the universal term "interpretation" (*parshanoot*) to refer to all its aspects and stages.

Fidelity

For a significant part of Israeli legal history and throughout its classical era until the 1980s, the Supreme Court adopted a fairly conventional approach towards statutory interpretation which combined overlapping elements of textualism, intentionalism and purposivism, consistent with its broader character as a faithful-yet-restrained agent of the law. This is implicitly manifest in thousands of cases in which the Court simply sought to realize the author's intent as expressed through the legal text, or to apply the law in a manner most consistent with the genuine purpose envisioned by its authors. But more explicitly, the Court's interpretive philosophy was also demonstrated in a series of cases and writings in which judges directly stated their views on the subject.

Justice Moshe Zilberg famously laid out his conception of the judicial role in a 1954 case, stating that "there is no legislator but the legislature" and that the "plotting" of laws is reserved for legislators alone.[7] Justice Zilberg had already exhibited his inclination towards purposivism in a 1949 case, writing that when interpreting statutes one must "delve into the law, and find and fulfill the desired intent of the statute."[8] Similarly, Justice Shimon Agranat wrote in another 1949 case that laws must be interpreted "in a manner which will give force to the legislature's purpose – a purpose which may be gleaned from reading the various statutory provisions" within a law.[9] Note that the notion of "purpose" here clearly contemplates the conscious purpose of the legislators themselves and maintains fidelity to the authority behind the law. For Agranat it is a concrete and discernible purpose which arises from examination of the legal text itself.

The Court at times displayed even stronger textualist and intentionalist tendencies. Prof. Uri Yadin, one of Israel's founding and most prominent jurists during the classical era, described contemporary statutory interpretation as judges asking themselves "what was the legislator's intent? What is the meaning of the words he used?," stating that "the bridge" between legislator and judge is the "word inscribed in the book of laws."[10] Justice Yoel Zussman, possibly the most renowned Justice of the classical era and the most known for his engagement with complex questions of judicial interpretation, was more strident in his commitment to the statutory text and expressed his skepticism of sources external to the text itself. In a 1956 case, while arguing for the general application of English common-law rules of interpretation, Zussman stressed that "where the judge about to interpret a statute finds the intention of the legislator clearly expressed therein, he must give effect to the will of the legislator and no rule of construction, be it English or any other, will stand in his way."[11] In a 1962 case Zussman warned against courts relying on statements made in the Knesset and emphasized that the court's "primary duty is to discover the 'legislative intent' and its purpose from within the statutory text itself."[12] Still, Zussman maintained a nuanced approach and conceded the need to "retrace the steps" of the legislator to understand the meaning of words chosen by them; in the same case, Zussman exhibited his sympathy for purposivism and wrote that "here too we must ask ourselves, based on the statute's known purpose, what the legislator would have decided in the case before us."[13]

Also in 1962, Justice Zussman wrote the following passage perhaps best encapsulating the attitude which prevailed throughout the Court's classical era: "When interpreting the words of the legislator a judge shall not grant the legislative text his own preferred meaning, and shall not seek to achieve the purpose he deems most worthy: such interpretation is akin to sabotage of the law."[14]

While the Supreme Court entertained a variety of voices and held numerous lively debates regarding the correct method of statutory interpretation, the overarching approach as exemplified above was one of judicial restraint, respect for the legal text itself and the authority behind it, and a good-faith effort to understand and implement the will of the democratic legislature which alone possessed the authority to make law. Writing in 1968, one of Israel's leading jurists at the time summarized the Court's contemporary interpretive jurisprudence as follows:

> "The cardinal principle of statutory interpretation is that the intention of the legislature, when clear and unambiguous, must be applied and enforced by the courts. This may be considered a rule of substantive constitutional law illustrative of the supremacy of the Knesset. It emphasizes the principle that once the Knesset has 'clearly spoken,' it must be implicitly obeyed. When interpreting a statute the courts apply the 'golden rule,' that a statute should be construed according to the intent of the legislature. According to the rule that intention must be gathered from the words used and effect must be given to it even though the court considers the result unsatisfactory."[15]

We may keep this description in mind as we proceed.

Barak's Interpretive Revolution

In her comprehensive essay on Aharon Barak's "strategic" court, Prof. Rivak Weill – a leading Israeli constitutional scholar – describes the process by which Barak gradually introduced his own novel theory of interpretation which replaced the approach illustrated above and came to dominate Israeli jurisprudence. There was no single landmark decision which signified the shift from legislative fidelity to ultimate judicial discretion. Rather, the change "occurred in an evolutionary fashion in judicial decisions and through Barak's influential academic work,"[16] which included his magnum opus of five hefty tomes on legal interpretation. Barak built his approach through a series of key cases, one at a time, until it became the primary method practiced by the Court. Yet Weill emphasizes that Barak's interpretive revolution "was a critical building block for later constitutional revolutions,"[17] and Barak later "explained many of his contentious revolutionary decisions as a matter of 'interpretation.'" In this sense, understanding Barak's interpretive approach is important in its own right, but is also key to understanding the broader expansion of judicial power in Israel.

What, then, is this method of legal interpretation pioneered by Barak since the 1980s, adopted by the Court and upon which so much judicial power rests?

Let us first consider Barak's theory in his own words, written in 2002 as Chief Justice at the peak of his judicial career. In a useful summary of his interpretive approach, Barak states that "any legal text is interpreted according to its purpose," and that "the interpreter* extracts the meaning which fulfills the text's core purpose more than any other meaning."[18] Per Barak, the purpose of any legal text is comprised of two elements: the "subjective" purpose and the "objective" purpose. The subjective purpose relates to the actual purpose or goal that the legislator or author of the text sought to achieve – it is a factual assessment of "historical-psychological-biological" reality.† [19]

Barak continues to define the objective purpose of a legal text as "the role of the legal norm within the legal system" at various levels of abstraction, which is "not related in any way to the intent‡ of the text's creator."[20] This might involve the hypothetical purpose that "a reasonable creator of the text" would have wanted to achieve, or the assumed purpose of a particular type of text, or especially the "values and principles" fulfilled by the text. All these purposes may be derived from the "fundamental values of the legal system."

In his lengthy introduction to an issue of the Harvard Law Review, also published in 2002, Barak expands more on his theory of subjective and objective purposive interpretation. Though he distinguishes between statutory and constitutional interpretation, the overall scheme remains the same. The objective purpose of a constitutional text may involve "fundamental contemporary values"[21], that "reflect the deeply held beliefs of modern society"[22] and the "modern views in the movement of the legal system through history."[23] Barak clarifies that these views and beliefs are "not the results of public opinion polls"[24]

* Barak, and the Supreme Court more generally, often use the term "interpreter" as a euphemism for judges.

† However, Barak also explains that implicit but concealed or subconscious "subjective" purpose can conceivably be imputed to the text's author even if this contradicts their stated or express purpose.

‡ Barak at times uses "intent" and "purpose" interchangeably which can lead to some confusion. This is admittedly a broader problem within schools of legal interpretation that do not adequately maintain the distinction between the two terms. The Hebrew word for "intent," *Kavana*, similarly lends itself to being mistaken for "purpose."

and even more so do not reflect "the will of the people" in the ordinary sense but rather the "social consensus that underlies the legal system."[25]

Similarly, the objective purpose of a statute involves the intent a legislature "would have had if it had thought about the matter," or the intent of the "reasonable legislature";[26] it may be derived from the nature of the statute being interpreted; or, finally, the objective purpose of any statute is "to realize the fundamental values of democracy."[27]

Barak cautions against relying exclusively or too heavily on the subjective purpose – that is, on the statutory text and its actual purpose as understood by those that enacted it – because this "freezes" the meaning of a statute at the time of its legislation, in a manner that "may no longer be relevant" to its meaning "in a modern democracy," thus failing to properly treat a statute "as a living organism in a changing environment."[28] Here Barak demonstrates the connection between his interpretive theory and his wider conception of the judicial role, warning the reader of the dangers in remaining too faithful to statutory text and its authentic purpose:

> "The judge becomes merely a historian or archaeologist and cannot fulfill his or her role as a judge, which is to bridge the gap between law and society… The judge becomes sterile and frozen, creating stagnation instead of progress. Instead of acting in partnership with the legislative branch, the judge becomes subordinate… This subservience does not behoove the role of the judge in a democracy."[29]

Importantly, Barak also clarifies that applying the objective purpose of a legal text begins immediately as part of the interpretive process, and does not depend on the ambiguity of the text or of the subjective purpose. Fundamental societal values create "presumptions" regarding statutes that form part of the objective purpose; these presumptions "are not limited to a particular type of legislation or merely to 'unclear' legislation – they apply always and immediately. They accompany the interpretive process from beginning to end."[30] Barak further emphasizes that the objective purpose is never "a guess or conjecture about the original intent of the legislature; in fact, sometimes it is the opposite, because purpose applies even when it is clear that the legislature could not possibly have intended such a purpose."[31] In other words, if the plain meaning of a text is clear and its purpose is known and explicit, the judge must still consider the objective purpose when interpreting and applying the statute – even if it directly contradicts the text and subjective purpose.

What is a judge to do if he concludes that the subjective and objective purposes are at odds, and perhaps even lead to different outcomes? A central part of Barak's theory is the balancing between such competing purposes and determining an "ultimate" unified purpose. Barak explains that "one should take both the subjective and objective elements into account when determining the purpose of the constitution… seeking synthesis and harmony between past intention and present principle,"[32] and further that the judge "must strike a balance between the will of the authors of the constitution and the fundamental values of those living under it."[33] Similarly for statutes, a judge must resolve conflict between purposes "on the basis of constitutional criteria, of which the central one is democracy."[34] (Barak's conception of democracy includes the "supremacy of values and human rights," as we shall soon see.)

Finally, as to the hierarchy of divergent purposes and their prioritization, Barak concedes that a judge ought to "give weight"[35] to the subjective purpose, but that, critically, "greater weight should be accorded to the objective purposes."[36] While this depends on a range of factors, Barak articulates (in theory) and demonstrates (in practice) a clear conviction that the objective purpose generally prevails over the subjective purpose. In the context of constitutional interpretation Barak is more adamant that "minimal weight, even if not none whatsoever" be attributed to the intent of the framers (or to the subjective purpose).[37] Instead, the "central weight" must be reserved for "fundamental modern societal views."

What, indeed, comprises these vaunted "fundamental views" of modern society, or its "values and principles," or the constitutional criteria of "democracy"? We will return to these in short order.

To summarize: Barak's theory of legal interpretation maintains that any legal text includes both "subjective" and "objective" purposes. The former is a matter of fact, the actual purpose envisioned by a law's authors; the latter is a matter of judicial reasoning and deduction, by which judges identify and apply a range of core principles and values which exist independently from the legal text and from its purpose as understood by its authors. The objective purpose generally prevails over the subjective purpose in the event of conflict between them. Going forward we will call this method "Objective Purposive Interpretation," or "OPI."

Before we proceed to assess this methodology, it's worth noting that Barak always had some broad vision of expansive "interpretation," well before it crystallized into the more sophisticated concepts of OPI. Already in 1980, in one of his earliest Supreme Court rulings, Barak presented his view thus:

> "The words of the statute are not fortresses to be conquered using dictionaries, but rather a wrapper for a living idea, one that changes according to the circumstances of time and place, in order to fulfill the fundamental purpose of the law."[38]

Here was Barak's core idea of interpretation long before "objective purpose" had entered his judicial lexicon – demoting the legal text to relative insignificance while elevating a law's "fundamental" (i.e., judicially-determined) purpose as a decisive factor. In other words, it was never so much that Barak inquired into the optimal method of interpretation and arrived at one which radically expands judicial power, but rather that Barak had always sought to release judicial decision-making from the constraints of the law's text and eventually formulated an elaborate theory which allowed him to do so.

Unchallenged

There is much to unpack here. A number of critical features and attributes stand out immediately upon our initial review of (Barak's own description of) OPI. First is its factually undeniable departure from the previously dominant approach on the Supreme Court and in Israeli jurisprudence. If the classical Court valued text, intent, and to some extent actual purpose, OPI considers all three to be markedly inferior. Second is its divergence from more generally accepted approaches to interpretation and from their standard terminology. In both these senses OPI is a genuinely novel theory. Third, and perhaps most glaring, is the extraordinary degree of judicial discretion and ultimate power inherent in such a method.

As we turn to scrutinize OPI and its shortcomings, it is worth noting that OPI is and remains the dominant and virtually the exclusive method of interpretation within the Israeli judiciary and throughout the legal system ever since Barak's initial interpretive revolution. Weill observes that Barak made OPI "into the *only* acceptable judicial interpretation method applicable to all acts of State. Any other method of interpretation… disappeared from judicial decisions."[39] It is utilized and reaffirmed, almost daily and without incident, at all levels of Israeli courts. In legal parlance, OPI is still "good law."

Perhaps most striking is the degree to which OPI has remained unchallenged in intellectual and academic circles. Lively debates regarding the desired method of legal interpretation are often at the heart of the legal and political landscape in many jurisdictions, perhaps most obviously such as the rich and ongoing debate in the United States. Barak pioneered OPI in the 1980s and has since published a small hoard of articles and books on the subject. Despite this, there is a discernible lack of serious engagement with OPI or with the topic of legal interpretation more generally – it is simply not a major component of the Israeli legal conversation. One will be hard put to find *any* academic or scholarly writing which engages with OPI in a direct and analytical manner, let alone comprehensive books and treatises. The past forty years have produced a handful of works – literally, five or so – dealing with OPI and with Israeli legal interpretation.

There have indeed been some recent notable exceptions. In the aforementioned *Gini* case a dissent by Justice Noam Solberg confronted OPI, but only in limited fashion and only by suggesting a reprioritization of how the objective purpose is to apply or to prevail.[40] A more robust challenge has been mustered by Justice Alex Stein in a series of judicial opinions and in an academic article, in which Stein lays out his own preferred interpretive approach called "probabilism."[41] While Stein's approach is much more aligned with traditional notions of legal interpretation and is more firmly grounded in academic theory and literature, his judicial opinions have limited effect, and his academic writing on the matter has appeared primarily in English with a more abstract focus. Finally, a recent formidable book on statutory interpretation by Israeli scholar Shimon Nataf (which has served as a guide for parts of this chapter and for which I am most grateful) has injected an encouraging breath of fresh air into the legal conversation – the first such book to analytically address the topic since Barak published his own books decades earlier. While perhaps evidence of cracks in the edifice of OPI, these are all exceptions that prove the rule of OPI dominance. In light of the novelty of OPI by any measure, this lack of intellectual engagement can only be considered remarkable.

The primacy of OPI in Israel is not to be mistaken for evidence of its genius or perfection. With all the weight Barak and his followers attribute to it (in his Harvard Law Review introduction, Barak modestly suggested that OPI "provides a proper solution" to the "interpretive dilemma" at the heart of American constitutional law),[42] OPI has not been adopted elsewhere in the world and indeed is hardly known or recognized as a valid interpretive method. As we shall see in a moment, it is at times met with deep skepticism (or even hostility), but for the most part is simply ignored.

The Holy Roman Empire

Judge Richard Posner, among the most renowned legal scholars of the 20th century,* published a scathing critique of Aharon Barak's jurisprudence in a 2007 essay titled "Enlightened Despot."[43] We will revisit this insightful essay a number of times throughout the book. As a preeminent expert and intellectual leader in the field of jurisprudence and legal interpretation, Posner seemed especially unsettled by OPI and Barak's "abuse" of the concepts within, and proceeds to denounce OPI in the most strident terms. Among other points, Posner affirms what might be obvious to any reader – that the presumption of OPI to interpret the law according to the fundamental values of democracy "opens up a vast realm for discretionary judgment (the antithesis of 'objective')." Pulling no punches, Posner concludes that "it is thus the court that makes Israel's statutory law, using the statutes themselves as first drafts that the court is free to rewrite." Phew.

Posner is, ironically, known as the pioneer of legal pragmatism – one of the more permissive interpretive methods, considered off-limits by textualists and originalists in the United States. That is to say, Posner's perspective is hardly that of a die-hard legal conservative. His rejection of OPI is all the more potent considering his own flexible approach to legal interpretation.

What, then, is the problem with OPI?

The essential objection to Objective Purposive Interpretation is that it violates core tenets of democratic legitimacy and the separation of powers; that it radically expands judicial authority; and that it does few of the things and serves few of the functions it claims to. More than anything else, OPI simply elevates the status of a judge to that of de facto legislator – just without the nuisance of elections or public accountability. Much like the Holy Roman Empire – which was neither

---

* Judge Posner served on the U.S. Court of Appeals for the Seventh Circuit for some 36 years; he is the most-cited legal scholar of the 20th century and as of 2021 was the most-cited legal scholar of all time.

holy, nor Roman, nor much of an empire – objective purposive interpretation is neither objective, nor does it concern purpose, nor is it even interpretive.

On a terminological level, OPI involves the misleading inversion of a number of core concepts within the field of legal interpretation, as well as within the context of ordinary spoken language. While presented as a "purposive" approach, and often referred to in Israel simply as "purposive interpretation," it is in fact nothing of the sort. While purposive approaches focus on the actual and concrete purpose of a given legal text in an effort to actualize the effect intended by its authors, OPI expressly relegates any tangible purpose to secondary status and subordinates such purpose to the judicial abstractions of "objective" purpose. OPI is, by any measure, much closer to pragmatism and could easily be categorized as reformative by any serious analysis. This terminological misuse, whether incidental or deliberate, is confusing to Israelis and foreigners alike as it accords OPI a semblance of conformity with established "purposive" methods elsewhere and obfuscates OPI's counter-purposive nature and effect.

Further distortion is found in the reversal of the words "subjective" and "objective," used in the opposite sense of their typical and technical meanings.[*] "Objective" usually refers to some fixed fact of reality which may be measured or evaluated by agreed standards, even if disputable or difficult to discern, while "subjective" usually refers to something dependent on the separate perspective and judgment of each individual observer. An "objective" purpose of a legal text in any conventional understanding would refer to the purpose actually intended by its authors; a "subjective" purpose would refer to a different purpose attributed to a legal text by an external observer not involved in its creation. This is why Posner refers to OPI as "the antithesis of objective." More so, as Nataf points out in his book, typical terminology in the discipline of legal interpretation uses "objective" to mean something which may be evaluated by factual criteria – for example, the text itself is likely the most objective element of a law, in the sense that a claim regarding what words are included within the text is easily verifiable according to a clear factual standard; whereas the more an evaluative criterion is subject to personal speculation and differing views (such as "fundamental values of modern society" or "universal human rights"), the more "subjective" it becomes.

But well beyond terminological objections, valid as they may be, lies the fundamental flaw in a system of interpretation that subjects the content and the spirit of the law to utter judicial whim. OPI grants judges license to ignore the law as it is and create it anew by infusing it with a supposed "objective" purpose, which means application of amorphous societal values as perceived or invented by the judge and at the highest level of abstraction. Here we must ask – what precisely are these "fundamental values of modern society" or "general principles

[*] In the previous sections I mostly resisted using quotation marks for these terms despite their counterintuitive use, so as to faithfully convey the manner in which they are employed by Barak and the Supreme Court.

of the law" which a judge may use to interpret any statute in a manner divorced from its text and authentic purpose? Barak has an answer, or rather, a list:

> "Equality, justice, morality… social objectives of the separation of powers, the rule of law, freedom of expression; freedom of procession, of worship, of occupation; human dignity, judicial integrity, public peace and security, the democratic values of the state and its very existence… good faith, natural justice, fairness and reasonableness."[44]

There you have it. Barak even clarifies that such a list is not exhaustive – and indeed, many variations and formulation of such "fundamental" values have been presented by the Supreme Court over the years.

Unfortunately, the only thing one can extract from the above list is proof of its utter vacuity. First – who says these are Israel's fundamental values, or those of any given society? Why these? Perhaps they have others; perhaps "society" might take issue with the inclusion of some values and the exclusion of others. Second – none of these values aid a judge in interpreting a legal text, as the evaluation of their relevance, content, status and application will differ wildly from judge to judge and indeed from person to person, and depends chiefly on their individual moral ideology. Third – not only is their existence in doubt and their abstract content open to dispute (to put it mildly), but there is no accepted formula to balance and prioritize between them, no framework to resolve inherent tensions among them or to ensure their proper interaction.

Accordingly, the primary conclusion emerging from Barak's formulation of OPI and from its practical application by the Supreme Court is this: it is the judge that defines society's fundamental values; it is the judge that decides which of these might be relevant to a specific instance; it is the judge that balances conflicting values and determines how they may be applied. It is the judge, in effect, that rewrites the law as he may see fit. This is exactly why Posner observes regarding OPI that "as a practical matter," the overall values of the legal system (applied be a court) can only mean "the judge's ideal system."

To be clear, few would doubt that judges and jurists must often revert to purpose, principles and even "values" when interpreting a legal text – but Barak goes wildly beyond that, claiming authority to implement entirely open-ended abstractions with no reliance on recognizable legal content. In various jurisdictions a particular principle (e.g., "natural justice") might take on a particular legal meaning, infused with decades (and even centuries) of carefully curated rulings and events; such principles become a legal term of art, supported by a substantial body of case law and scholarship. It makes much sense for a judge to delicately interpret a law so that it conforms – to the extent practicable – with such concrete and distinct principles, and this is by no means unusual. But for Barak, the vaguest abstraction – devoid of, or divorced from, any prior legal substance – is sufficient basis for interpreting and indeed inverting the meaning of statutory text.

Reading Barak's straight-faced list above and his other explanations might have been comical were it not appalling. Without a shred of irony or self-consciousness, Barak writes that the objective purpose of a statute includes "the interests, values, objectives, policy, and functions that the law should realize in a democracy."[45] The pivotal key word here is *should.* By what right, under what theory of democratic government, is it the role of a judge to dictate what values *should* be realized by the law in a democracy? As if it were some kind of exact science, some settled technical rule that needed only a sufficient level of legal expertise to discern, and not the very question at the heart of public dispute and debate. In other words, quite beside the façade of objectivity, there is a clear problem with the idea that a judge ought to determine (and thus impose) any of these values in the first place.

Another critic of OPI – Oregon State Supreme Court Justice Thomas Balmer – put it clearly and simply in a review of Barak's main book on the matter, taking issue with OPI's suggestion of a "wide-ranging judicial role that raises serious concerns about the role of the judiciary in a representative democracy."[46] This is true at every single stage and level of the OPI process – who ought to decide what are society's core values and define their content? Who is to determine which of these apply when and to what extent? Who is to "balance" inconsistent (or irreconcilable) values so as to achieve synthesis and harmony? And why, in the name of all that is holy, would the answer to any of these questions be – "a judge"?

The scope of these questions far exceeds the limited context of interpretation – nonetheless, OPI illustrates precisely why they matter. And if one is unconcerned by judges performing this function by way of so-called interpretation, they must ask themselves – what if we replace "judge" with "military commander." Most would find the notion of an army general imposing their own conception of "fundamental societal values" rather chilling, and a cause for serious unease. If we find an unelected or unaccountable government official in the executive branch performing this role to be objectionable, there seems no reason to make our peace with essentially the same phenomenon within the judiciary.

On a more practical level, one often-overlooked element of OPI is its debilitating effect on the legal system at large.

Put simply, any interpretive method like OPI must inevitably make the law – all law – far less stable, foreseeable and predictable. If no one can predict how the law might be applied by a judge, then no one knows what the law actually is. This effect in Israel is especially pronounced in civil proceedings. Litigants regularly advance frivolous arguments or file baseless lawsuits, because in an environment of OPI virtually any legal claim is valid, no matter how far-fetched. Courts almost never grant a motion to dismiss, because few lawsuits can be found legally meritless on their face under OPI – even the silliest contention without the slightest basis in law must be seriously evaluated. Legal briefs and oral argument become laborious pseudo-philosophical exercises in which lawyers attribute any conceivable abstract purpose to statutory or contractual provisions. Almost any seasoned Israeli litigator or business lawyer will tell their client the same thing – avoid going to court at all costs even if the law is on your side, because litigation under OPI is less William Blackstone and more Russian roulette. Israeli civil courts are notoriously overburdened, with simple trials taking years to conduct and conclude, even though Israel has almost double the judges-per-capita ratio compared to other common-law jurisdictions. These are just some of the practical implications of legal interpretation which has abandoned the law.

While perhaps the most obvious objection to OPI regards the vast judicial discretion and lawmaking power conferred onto judges, another angle addresses the very notion that it is an interpretive method to begin with.

Prof. Stanley Fish is a prolific and well-known literary theorist, and his analytical critique of OPI focuses not on democratic legitimacy, but rather on the function of language itself. In a piercing 2008 review of Barak's book on purposive interpretation, Fish points out that Barak's method doesn't really involve interpretation at all.[47] His core linguistic contention is that the attempt to attribute an abstract purpose to a legal text which is divorced from the intent and authentic purpose of the text's author, as does OPI, simply ceases to be "interpretation" in any sense. Fish explains that being focused on an author's intention is the very essence of interpretation, period: "If you are interpreting you are in search of the purpose or intention informing (and shaping) the text; you are in search of the intention of the author... Interpretation without purpose (intention) at its center is not merely ineffective or incomplete; it is not interpretation."[48]

Fish indirectly points out the fallacy of an "objective" purpose which under OPI is subject entirely to judicial determination, noting there must be "something prior to the interpreter's efforts, something the interpreter is trying to get right, something in relation to which an interpretation can be rejected."[49] In other words, when a judge answers the question "what are the fundamental societal values and how do they apply here?" – is there any wrong answer? How may we prove the judge wrong? The absence of any standard by which to reject the answer as erroneous negates any claim of objectivity.

Fish also challenges Barak's complex theory regarding how the "intent of the legal system" is infused within the text and therefore justifies interpreting statutes in light of this abstract intent. He notes that an author creating a legal text "is already the bearer and representative of the systems norms and intentions," and that the intent of the system is "not an interpretive category and does no interpretive work... you can't offer it as a reason for concluding X rather than Y."[50]

Fish ultimately rejects the notion that moving away from the author's actual, genuine, real intent and purpose can be considered interpretation at all. Such reliance on purposes not attributed to the author "would not be refining or enriching or enhancing the act of interpreting" but rather "would be abandoning it and taking up some form of re-writing or re-fashioning instead."[51] His final repudiation of OPI reads:

> "Substituting for [the author's] meaning a meaning friendly to modern democracy is not interpretation, but re-writing. Modern democracy's needs did not author the text and when you make modern democracy's needs the text's author, you have broken free of any and all constraints on what you then declare the law to be."[52]

At the risk of stating the obvious – neither the fundamental values of modern democracy, nor contemporary societal sentiment, nor any of the ambiguous and vague terms mentioned in Barak's list above, have any concrete or agreed meaning to speak of. Their content is indeterminate; any attempt at their direct application is a farce. A judge may coax almost any desired meaning out of a given statutory text when interpreted or applied in accordance with such abstract concepts. Relying on such moral ideals as the "objective purpose" of a law in a way that trumps the law itself has only one function – the dramatic expansion of judicial discretion, and by extension, judicial power.

Some scholars define judicial supremacy as the court not applying the law, but rather creating the law. OPI meets this definition easily. Barak posits that "a judge who interprets the constitution is a partner to the authors of the constitution"[53] – while no one will contest that judges dramatically influence a constitution's de facto application as a by-product of interpretation, Barak's conception of the judge as *author* seems quite literal. Under OPI, the judge is elevated not only to the status of legislator, not even to the status of constitutional enforcer, but beyond, to the status of Framer and drafter of the constitution itself.

OPI thus reveals itself as a judicial tool explicitly enabling courts to make binding decisions (and hence, to create law) based not on statutory text, nor even on a realistic appraisal of legislative desire, but rather on the entirely personal and prejudiced moral ideology of each and every judge. Under OPI, the noble democratic aspiration of the law being created and controlled by elected officials accountable to the public becomes laughable. The use of OPI renders legislation meaningless, legislators powerless, and the legislative process futile.

Legislative History – Barak vs. Scalia

One noteworthy aspect of Barak's interpretive approach is his view of legislative history – and the surprising intersection between Barak and none other than U.S. Supreme Court Justice Antonin Scalia.

Legislative history refers to information gleaned from the legislative process which ultimately led to the enactment of a law. This might include the background and circumstances surrounding the law, but typically regards more direct aspects of legislation – such as debates within the legislative body and various committees; official memos provided and circulated among legislators; statements made by legislators in various contexts; previous versions of a law being amended or alternate drafts of the law which were considered; and so on. Legislative history can conceivably illuminate key questions regarding a law and provide useful insight into a statute's textual meaning, the author's intent (their own understanding of the text) and the law's (actual) purpose or what it was trying to accomplish. This makes sense – if trying to better understand a law, it would seem only natural to examine the process by which the law came into being.

Justice Scalia was famous for being an ardent textualist and among the keenest proponents of originalism; in many ways his jurisprudence might be considered diametrically opposed to Barak's, and indeed Scalia was often the object of Barak's criticism (Scalia was less preoccupied with what a distant Israeli Justice had to say). Despite this, Barak and Scalia shared similar views regarding legislative history – both were skeptical and dismissive (sometimes even derisive) of legislative history as a relevant tool for statutory interpretation. Yet upon closer inspection their apparent alignment reveals itself as illusory; and the reasons behind each of their respective objections to legislative history could not be more different. In a nutshell, Scalia avoided legislative history in order to safeguard the statutory text from being distorted or ignored; Barak rejects legislative history precisely so that he may more easily abandon the legal text. Their point of departure hinges on reverse attitudes regarding fidelity to the law as-is.

Scalia's suspicion towards legislative history stemmed from its potential manipulation and power to undermine the statutory text. In Scalia's experience, all too often legislative history was utilized by courts to advance a law's interpretation which was contrary to the law's own text. A creative judge might use legislative history to claim ambiguity, even if the text presented none; or legislative history might be used to attribute an alternative meaning to a certain phrase, even if this would seem an implausible reading of the statutory text on its own. For Scalia, the intent or purpose of a statute is to be gleaned from the legal text itself – "it is the law that governs, not the intent of the lawgiver."[54] While theoretically legislative history might be useful in informing statutory interpretation, Scalia laments that in practice lawyers "make no distinction between words in the text of a statute and words in its legislative history."[55] Further still, Scalia warns of a cycle in which the court's very reliance on legislative history makes it less reliable – legislative debate and discussion becomes geared to providing retroactive material for the courts to consider instead of actually deliberating on the matter at hand. Eventually, "legislative history exists because the courts refer to it."[56]

Barak approaches the matter from the completely opposite direction. Barak doubts whether genuine legislative intent can be taken seriously at all, and finds that usually a legislature – a diverse group of individuals with a range of desires and incentives – has no discernible unified intent conducive to interpreting a law. On this point Barak and Scalia are well aligned. And Barak professes agreement with Scalia that the law is the one enacted, not the one contemplated or desired in the minds of its creators. Ironically, Barak warns that if there is no clear or express legislative intent, one should avoid manufacturing an artificial one – which is precisely what he suggests doing for a statute's objective purpose. At the same time, as we've seen, ignoring the legal text is exactly what OPI sometimes requires – "interpreting" it to mean and do something entirely unrelated to its content or its background, but which better serves fundamental values.

How does Barak reconcile his abandonment of the text while maintaining his rejection of legislative history? Simple – legislative intent is substituted with, you guessed it, "the law's intent, which is none other than the general principles of the law."[57]

Barak's aversion to legislative history becomes clearer within the context of OPI. To the interpreter that desires to ignore or distort the explicit meaning of the law, the legislative history will typically be a burden, or even a source of embarrassment. It's one thing to try and apply an ambiguous text with little information about its creation. It's another thing entirely to apply a legal text while flouting the clear, known and unequivocal intent and purpose of its drafters. As noted earlier, most laws are actually rather clear, their plain text aligning with the meaning contemplated by legislators and consistent with their stated purpose. Legislative history thus poses a liability, in most cases, for those that wish to regularly subvert and undermine the law by way of creative (sorry, "objective") interpretation.

Seen this way, the contrast between Scalia and Barak could not be starker – Scalia rejects legislative history in order to maintain fidelity to the law as enacted; Barak evades legislative history so that the legislative text may too be discarded. This contrast also illustrates the broader tendency of OPI – when in doubt, assume greater judicial power and less mechanisms which might constrain it.

OPI in Action

Objective purposive interpretation is used pervasively throughout the legal system and permeates almost every legal field, precedent, rule or doctrine. Here we will examine only a bare handful of examples (in addition to *Gini* and *Abu Arfa*) to demonstrate its effect – not only because an exhaustive review would likely require a book of its own and could furnish an entire academic career, but also because we will encounter OPI on many other occasions and in many contexts in the following chapters.

The reader may recall the *Nahmani* case regarding disputed frozen embryos of a separated couple, in which Justice Barak ruled that a rehearing may be held even for a panel which consisted of five judges, despite the law limiting rehearings to apply to panels of three judges. Now that we are familiar with the rationale of OPI, the case is worth a brief revisit. While not regarding some major issue of public policy, *Nahmani* serves a strong illustration of OPI's remarkable ability to bypass text, legislative history, practice and precedent – and all in the context of a "hard" numerical rule.[58]

First year law students will typically learn about the distinction between legal "rules" and "standards," by which "rules" are more rigid and constraining, typically having some clear-cut "bright line" criterion to guide decision-making.[59] Of these, numerical rules are often considered the prime example. Any American might be familiar with the "two Senators for each state" rule, or the rule defining the minimum age for the United States President to be thirty-five years, both of which are clearly stated in the Constitution. Many would argue that such a numerical rule is hardly open to interpretation – two means two. But under OPI, Barak and his followers could just as well argue that the "age of 35" in the U.S. Constitution must be interpreted according to its "objective" purpose – perhaps adjusting it for life expectancy and applying the constitutional provision as though it reads "55" years; or perhaps adjusting for modern sensibilities empowering youth, applying the provision as though it reads "25." As we shall see in *Nahmani*, this is not far-fetched.

Section 18 of "Basic Law: The Judiciary" permits that a rehearing of five Justices or more may be held regarding "a matter in which the Supreme Court has ruled by three" – that is, three Justices on the original panel. As discussed in the previous chapter, the statutory text, legislative history and legal precedent were all unequivocal – three means three. So how could Barak "interpret" the bright-line rule of three judges to mean "at least" three? By applying OPI, of course.

Barak first asserts that the literal meaning of "by three" can actually mean "by at least three," ostensibly according to the "sense of the language." We may set this bizarre contention aside, while noting that for Barak even the initial stage of parsing the plain meaning of words is inherently malleable. Barak then considers the statute's "subjective purpose" – that is, the purpose contemplated by the actual legislators who enacted the law in question. At various stages legislators raised the point that the law would preclude rehearing if the initial panel numbered more than three members. Though this would typically indicate that legislators were "on notice" and were well aware of the implications of the statutory language they were adopting, Barak ironically (and inexplicably) presents this as evidence of ambiguity. Barak concludes that he "does not know" the subjective purpose of the statute, and that "wc ought not speculate" in this matter.

Barak now turns to the statute's "objective purpose" – that is, the abstract or ideal purpose which is independent of anything the legislature might have thought or intended. Barak reminds us that deducing such objective purpose is informed by the text, the type of matter being addressed, the basic principles of the legal system, the rule's "normative status" and its "normative environment," common sense and logic, the needs of society and the requirements of reality, and much else besides. After a brief historical survey Barak concludes that the objective purpose of the rehearings mechanism is to "allow the Supreme Court… to reconsider" new precedent, regardless of the number of members on the original panel. On this basis Barak concludes that the *Nahmani* rehearing may proceed even though the original decision had been rendered by a five-member panel. Another seven Justices concurred.

In their dissenting opinions, Justices Bach, Orr and Mazza expose the incredible weakness of Barak's argument. Bach dives into the statutory language (and overall framework) which unequivocally limits rehearings to rulings which were issued by three-member panels – no more, no less. Orr's dissent is more pointed, sardonically stating that he "does not share" the same "sense of the language" to which Barak alludes, and that in his eyes "the issue is simple and clear: 'three' are not 'five,' are not 'seven,' and are not any number which is not 'three.'"* Orr also convincingly explains the rationale behind the "by three" rule – that the Chief Justice (and by extension, the Court) has one opportunity to "expand" a panel for cases of great significance. He can do so either at the outset (by assigning the case to an expanded panel) or retroactively (by granting a rehearing after a ruling is issued), but not both.

Orr then raises the obvious objection that the statute has numerous additional "purposes" which a judge could infer, many of which lead to rejecting Barak's position. These might include the speedy resolution of disputes, the stability of precedent and the finality of legal proceedings. On the other hand, Orr correctly notes that Barak's alleged "objective" purpose of allowing for serious judicial consideration of important matters is already fulfilled when the Court hears a case in an expanded panel to begin with – precisely the reason why the statute does not permit rehearings for rulings issued by larger panels. In doing so, Orr demonstrates one of the most basic flaws of OPI – that any purported "objective" purpose is in the eye of the judicial beholder, and that any judge can circumvent the unambiguous statutory text (and its authentic purpose) by conjuring their own perceived "purpose" and excluding others, just as Barak did in *Nahmani*.

Alas, such objections remained a distant and feeble protest, as the majority of the Court (in this case and in general) embraced OPI and the dazzling judicial power it offers. If a clear numerical rule – "rehearings only for decisions by three-member panels" – could be so manipulated, then ordinary statutory language could hardly withstand the "purposive" onslaught.

In the 1999 case of *Elka Holdings*, OPI was used to dilute and disarm economic tax legislation that the judges disfavored.[60] The Israeli tax code provides that a business is not obligated to pay Value Added Tax (known as "VAT") in the event of a "failed or aborted transaction" – i.e., a transaction which was reported but which fell through, was cancelled or was never executed. The *Elka* case regarded a different kind of event, in which a transaction is executed but is *not fulfilled* – one party provides goods or services but the other party can't or won't pay. The statutory phrase of "failed transactions" (literally in Hebrew, "that did not go through" or "that fell through") is a technical term that clearly excludes unfulfilled transactions and instances of "bad debt." Indeed, the legislative history shows unequivocally that the decision to exclude "bad debt" was both deliberate and

* Barak could perhaps have benefitted from the thorough instructions provided by Brother Maynard's brother in Monty Python's *The Holy Grail*: "Then shalt thou count to three, no more, no less. Three shall be the number thou shalt count, and the number of the counting shall be three. Four shalt thou not count, neither count thou two, excepting that thou then proceed to three. Five is right out."

considered – the legislative explanatory notes stress that "the law does not recognize bad debts" and that it does not cover an event in which "a transaction has been made but the customer does not render payment."

Accordingly, in *Elka,* tax authorities argued that an unfulfilled transaction did not qualify as a "failed" transaction, and that therefore a business was still (initially) obligated to pay VAT for that same unfulfilled transaction.* Aside being consistent with statutory language and legislative intent, the position also reflected sound tax policy – the rationale behind this was that the aggrieved party could still enforce their transaction or collect their debt through legal proceedings (like a claim of breach of contract), or might still succeed through other means, such that the income from the transaction is not yet technically "written off." In other words, a breach of contract does not automatically amount to irrecoverable debt or a "failed" transaction for which a taxpayer is exempt from paying VAT. Without getting further into the weeds here, this was a viable tax position which involved factors such as stability of tax collection, a risk of overlapping tax exemptions by multiple parties, and especially the risk of tax fraud.

All this was of minimal interest to the Supreme Court in *Elka.* The argument articulated by Justice Tova Strasbourg-Cohen (writing for the majority) is striking.[61] To begin with, she pretends that "failed transactions" is an ambiguous phrase, though it clearly is not – its meaning within the statutory context irrefutably excludes bad debt. Though Strasbourg-Cohen concedes that the "subjective purpose" undeniably excludes bad debt, she then proceeds to consider the statute's various "objective" purposes. These include, delightfully, "the pursuit of justice," "being reasonable," "legislative harmony," "fundamental rights," and "neutrality." To support the existence of such "objective" purposes, the Justice offers little substantive explanation beyond the bald assertion of "it seems to me." Per the Court, such objective purpose "embodies the goals and policies that any legislation ought to achieve in a modern democratic society." Finally, under such circumstances, the Court explains that "the subjective purpose… must retreat before the objective purpose."

All this leads the Court to apply the statutory phrase of "failed transactions" so that it includes bad debts, such that unfulfilled transactions exempt a business from paying VAT. In doing so the Court rendered the law meaningless and simply replaced the statutory tax policy with something else the judges happened to prefer.

Though in itself relatively inconsequential, the *Elka* case is a masterclass of OPI in action and reflects the casual and routine perversion of law endemic to Israeli jurisprudence. The Court feigns textual ambiguity where there is none. Though conceding an ostensibly subjective purpose (which is in fact the authentic and original purpose usually well-expressed in the statutory text), the Court invents an array of general and abstract "objective" purposes (which are in fact

---

* To be clear, if the debt is truly written off and cannot be feasibly recovered by the business, then the business can of course recover the VAT they had initially paid.

based on nothing but judicial whim). When Strasbourg-Cohen tellingly uses the word "ought" she illustrates what OPI is really about – judges imposing their own arbitrary (and, one might add, subjective) opinions about the ostensibly ideal goals of a given statute, without even the pretense of grounding these in actual legislation or legislative intent. Finally, the Court invariably prioritizes the objective (that is, judicial) purpose over the subjective (that is, authentic legislative) purpose to achieve whatever policy outcome it deems desirable.

The 1996 *Zandberg* case revolved around a 1992 law which retroactively gave force to consecutive increases to television licensing fees. At the time, as is the case in several countries, Israeli residents owning a television set had to pay a fee to a governmental public broadcasting entity. The Israeli Broadcasting Authority had raised the TV license fee on several occasions between 1985 and 1992, though for various reasons the fee increase was of disputed legality. Ultimately these questions were settled by legislation enacted in 1992, which retroactively validated the fee-increases during those years. The *Zandberg* case focused on fines which were tacked on to license fees owed by delinquent TV-owners – according to the new 1992 law, did TV-owners have to also pay statutory fines for failing to pay their disputed TV license fees during the years in question?

The statutory language leaves little room for doubt, stating that any fee increases during those years "are valid for all legal purposes and in all respects from their date of issuance." This would seem to include fines or late-fees for non-payment of the increased TV fees. But the Supreme Court saw things differently. In a unanimous decision penned by Aharon Barak, the Court "interpreted" the statute in light of its objective purpose – gleaned from "society's fundamental values, including the desire and necessity to fulfill values of justice, morality and human rights." After some discussion, Barak summarizes that obligating TV-owners to pay delinquency fines under the 1992 law would be both "unreasonable" and "unjust," and that therefore such fines were to be excluded from the statute's application.[62]

Whether the 1992 law was wise or desirable is a separate matter. What is certain is that Barak's judicial assertions of reasonability or justice are not remotely related to interpretation of the law, but serve, if anything, to simply undermine and replace the law. Of note, Shimon Nataf highlights that not a single Justice – out of thirteen (!) on the panel – saw fit to challenge Barak's interpretive method or conclusion.

The 2004 *Yelena Ganis* case bears some resemblance to *Zandberg*, though in more aggressive form. A 2001 law granted a benefit to purchasers of real-estate in Jerusalem; shortly thereafter, the Knesset amended the law such that its application was postponed to a later date. Purchasers of real-estate in the interim (between the first law and the amendment) were retroactively not eligible for the benefit, a point which the amendment clarifies in painfully unequivocal language: "Despite the provisions of [the original benefit law]... no person shall be entitled to benefits under [the original law]" until after the amended start-date. Unlike

Zandberg which hinged on the phrase "for all legal purposes," here the legal effect of the law was spelled out by the Knesset in the most direct and unmistakable terms.

Nonetheless, the Supreme Court in *Ganis* decided to "interpret" the amended provision such that interim real-estate purchasers would still be eligible to receive the revoked benefit, relying on the law's objective purpose (among other factors). Justice Dorit Beinisch offers the most candid description in her concurring opinion: "Under appropriate circumstances, the legislative purpose, the context, the totality of the text and the fundamental principles of the legal system might compel us to read in [i.e., insert] an exception not specified in the statutory provision."[63] By "inserting" such a judicial exception the Court essentially annulled the statutory provision which dictated the exact opposite outcome. One legal scholar remarked of this ruling: "Is it conceivable that the legislator says 'white' and the Court interprets it as 'black'?"[64] As quoted above, Judge Richard Posner claimed that the Israeli Supreme Court treats statutes "as first drafts that the court is free to rewrite" – it is cases like *Ganis* that demonstrate the point so well.

In the 2017 *Prison Conditions* case, petitioners demanded that all inmates in Israeli prisons receive some defined minimum of average living space within their cell. Primary legislation does not enumerate any mandatory specific size of living area, but rather vaguely requires that inmates are interned "in appropriate conditions which do not harm their health or dignity." Indeed, the legislative history shows that the Knesset deliberately avoided defining specific criteria for inmate living conditions, leaving such decisions up to Executive discretion. Administrative regulations provide more clarity, and stipulate that the average cell area for each inmate must be at least 4.5 square meters (e.g., a cell with four inmates must have a total living area of at least 18 square meters, or 194 square feet). However, the same regulations distinguish between old and new prisons, stating that the regulations (including the minimum living area) will apply only to prison facilities which are approved and built *after* the regulations take effect. In other words, the regulations clarify that their minimum living area requirement does not apply to existing prisons.

In a unanimous decision penned by Justice Elyakim Rubenstein, the Supreme Court held that the 4.5-meter minimum average living area applied in fact to *all* Israeli inmates and prisons, including all existing ones. It did so by purposive interpretation of the legislative "appropriate conditions" requirement. Rubenstein reminds us that the "objective purpose" of a statute "seeks to pursue the intent of the reasonable legislator, one who's guiding lights are the system's fundamental principles, morality, decency and justice."[65] Such interpretation of the primary statute leads the Court to conclude that the law requires a 4.5-meter minimum living area. Conveniently, the Court seems happy to rely on the regulations to arrive at the figure of 4.5 meters, but not so far as to accept their distinction between old and new prisons.

One noteworthy element is Justice Rubenstein's casual dismissal of financial considerations. At one point Rubenstein rejects the idea that the law permits "discrimination" between inmates at old prisons and those at new ones, for "purely budgetary reasons." For the Court, the electorate and legislature are simply not permitted to save money by applying certain standards to future facilities and not to existing facilities. Never mind that the Court was casually mandating an expenditure amounting to billions of dollars at the expense of taxpayers, with no legislative basis or authority. Whether in the context of statutory interpretation, executive discretion or judicial review of legislation, this is a pattern that repeats itself throughout the Court's jurisprudence. Economic frugality or efficiency is routinely rejected as a legitimate or decisive factor shaping governmental decisions. The taxpayers and their elected representatives must yield to budgetary priorities set by judges.

*

Let us concede for a moment the allure of OPI in light of these cases. The Knesset can, and surely on occasion does, enact laws which seem unfair, unjustified or downright wrong. It might neglect to update outdated legal wording, or might deliberately leave archaic rules in place. Perhaps the law places a burden on some while not on others. Perhaps the law prevents a particular policy or outcome clearly favored by public consensus, solely due to out-of-touch legislators or even to petty partisan politics. Faithfully applying the statute "as is" – according to its meaning and as originally intended and understood – might be a hard pill to swallow. OPI grants the judge – and one might argue, society – an instrument with which to "update" the law so that it more closely conforms to current societal preferences, or with which to disarm the law of its more egregiously unfair effects. Is that really so bad? In both *Zandberg* and *Ganis*, the Knesset seemed to penalize law-abiding citizens for its own clumsy lawmaking; in the *Prison Conditions* case the upshot was arbitrary discrimination between inmates in old prisons and those in new ones. In such cases and in many others, the Knesset's indifference (or deliberate decision) may leave the observer acutely uncomfortable.

A full defense of fidelity to statutory law – and the political process by which it is produced – is beyond the scope of our current discussion. For present purposes we will consider only a brief answer. First, the observer must ask themselves whether remedying such transgressions is within the capacity, role and function of a court of law. To recognize the law's failings is one thing; to presume that these may be validly resolved by judicial fiat is another thing entirely. That the law is unfair or obnoxious does not grant any official license to ignore it – even officials wearing robes and tasked with resolving disputes. The law is not a piece of software to be automatically updated at the click of a button. Judges have no superior claim to know the public "mood" or the requirements of "modern" society; and they have no legitimate basis to impose their own (perhaps justified) preference over the (perhaps loathsome) deliberate preference of the elected legislature. Should a military general, police chief, tax clerk, or health inspector ignore the plain words of statutory law and instead apply their own preferred version based on their evaluation of the law's ideal purpose? If not them, then why a judge? This question goes to the core of our understanding of judicial office and the role of courts in any democracy. The validity of binding decisions and mandatory orders issued by judges rests on the assumption that they are channeling the law – no more, no less. Ask not whether you agree with the statute being "interpreted," but whether you can justify a system in which laws are inverted against their plain meaning to match the preferred policy of unaccountable bureaucrats. Best of all, ask whether you would stand by such an interpretive method that has the opposite effect – imposing fines or revoking a benefit despite the Knesset's clear desire to the contrary; or creating a bad (judicial) rule instead of a good (statutory) one.

Second, and perhaps more importantly, this type of interference absolves the Knesset of its responsibilities and essentially lets legislators off the hook. The legislature passes the hot potato to the courts without having to reckon with the consequences of its actions. Such benevolent "interpretation" reduces the incentive of legislators to do their job, and ultimately erodes electoral sensitivity to legislative action and to the democratic process itself. Put simply, if bad laws are regularly "fixed" by unilateral contrived judicial distortion, then what reason does the Knesset have to stop making them? Why would the electorate replace their representatives? And what could trigger real reflection on the failings of a given electoral system which constantly produces bad legislation? A measure of discomfort (and indeed even a public uproar) stemming from an unjust law is sometimes needed to instigate necessary change, topical or systemic. Courts altering statutes to mitigate their harm ultimately serves as a sedative – treating the pain and killing the patient.

The Court v. The Law

Other examples show how "objective" purpose is leveraged by the Court in novel ways and for goals well beyond a law's technical or isolated application.

In the 1991 *National Insurance* case, the Supreme Court applied purposive interpretation in order to assume that the legislature could not possibly have meant the words it had explicitly enacted. A 1970 statute set up State compensation paid to victims of terror attacks. The statute established an approval process for the receipt of such benefits, including a dedicated body which determines whether the event in which an applicant was harmed may be designated as a terror attack. Such determinations are appealable to an Appeals Committee. The statute stipulates that the decision of an Appeals Committee (regarding the designation of an incident as a terror attack for purposes of compensation) is final and binding: "There is nothing beyond the decision of the Appeals Committee." Such phrasing was commonly used to indicate that a decision is not subject to appeal or to judicial review by any further tribunal or body. Despite such an unambiguous provision, Justice Aharon Barak employs its objective purpose to argue that the statute does not rule out judicial review by the Supreme Court (by direct petition to the High Court of Justice).[66]

Shimon Nataf points out the stark contrast between Barak's approach in the *National Insurance* case to a similar case decided by the Court decades earlier. In the 1966 *Ashdod Local Council* case, the Court considered a near-identical provision regarding the "finality" of a certain type of District Court appellate decisions. In that case, the Supreme Court upheld the law to the letter even though the Justices clearly objected to its outcome, and emphasized that the petitioner's valid complaint must be addressed to the legislature, not to the courts. The Court explicitly stressed that litigants could not circumvent the "finality" provision by petitioning the HCJ to review non-appealable decisions.[67] Needless to say, Barak's argument in the 1991 *National Insurance* case – and his deviation from established precedent – served his broader agenda of expanding the Supreme Court's power and removing any statutory limit on its jurisdiction.

The 2020 *Surrogacy* ruling involved a very different – and extraordinary – application of OPI. When contemplating whether a statute was unconstitutional, the Supreme Court relied on a statute's "objective" purpose in order to evaluate whether it met the requirement of "proportionality." In a nutshell, in order for the Court to uphold a law as constitutional such law must meet a series of requirements, including being intended for a "proper purpose" and that the law's harm be "proportional" (this subject, along with the *Surrogacy* case, will be covered thoroughly in Part III). In the 2020 *Surrogacy* decision, Chief Justice Esther Hayut adopted a radically novel approach: While acknowledging the statute's declared "subjective" (i.e., authentic) purpose, Hayut also imputed a contradictory "objective" purpose to the same statute. But unlike other cases, Hayut didn't use this judicially-invented purpose to interpret (and thus mis-apply) the law. Instead, Hayut evaluated the law's "proportionality" against its purported "objective" purpose, and not against the purpose expressly specified by the Knesset. Unsurprisingly, Hayut found the law to be "disproportionately harmful" (and therefore unconstitutional) because it did not sufficiently achieve its *objective* purpose – that is, it did not achieve a purpose for which it was never designed and which lawmakers never had in mind.[68]

This novel approach is truly revolutionary. The Supreme Court may now distort a law's purpose, not in order to achieve a particular outcome in its interpretation, but rather in order to disqualify the law by stating that its harm does not sufficiently achieve its so-called "objective purpose." The logic of such an approach could hardly be more ridiculous – of course a law does not achieve or advance a purpose which is retroactively invented by a judge and which was not intended by the law's authors.

A helpful comparison might be found in the U.S. standard of "strict scrutiny" judicial review. Under strict scrutiny, courts ask whether a particular measure is "narrowly tailored to a compelling government interest." Imagine if a court were to simply ignore the genuine "interest" advanced by the government with a particular law, and instead declare that the law reflects a different, abstract "objective" interest – one which contradicts the original "subjective" governmental interest.* Then, the court rules that the law under review is not "narrowly tailored" to the new "interest" the court had just devised – an obvious result given that the lawmakers never had such an "interest" in mind in the first place. Needless to say, most laws would even fail the permissive "rational basis" test in such a scenario, because a law would rarely be "rationally related" to a post-hoc "interest" dreamed up by a judge (why would it be?).

A very different example may be found in the 2023 *Tiberias* case. In the lead-up to the 2023 nationwide local municipal elections, the Knesset passed an amendment which would permit certain candidates to run for local political office (and for mayor in particular). Prior to the amendment, some municipal bureaucrats were barred from offering their candidacy for local political office – especially such bureaucrats that are appointed by the central national government, as is the case with certain local oversight committees. The law was passed with immediate effect and would influence the upcoming municipal elections, which were about four months away.

The amendment was deeply controversial because it possessed an apparent underlying motive: it was allegedly tailored to benefit a particular member of a particular committee in a particular town. Mr. Boaz Yosef served as chair of the oversight committee for the town of Tiberias, and was widely considered an ally and confidant of veteran politician Aryeh Deri. Though the legislation applied broadly to all municipalities and was generic on its face, it was universally regarded as having been devised solely to allow Boaz Yosef to compete in the upcoming mayoral elections, and was immediately dubbed the "Tiberias Law" by its critics and by the political Opposition. In addition, the elections cycle had for all intents and purposes already begun, and as such the amendment was branded as a corrupt intervention in ongoing elections. The amendment was swiftly challenged in the Supreme Court as unconstitutional, both in its substance and on account of its "personal" nature.

The Court in turn offered an extraordinary solution. Instead of disqualifying the law, the Court "interpreted" it so that the amendment would not apply to the upcoming elections, but would instead only take effect for later subsequent elections. The Court called this novel doctrine "deferred application." As a result, the amended law itself was upheld, but its effects were "deferred" to a later point, so as to remedy its personal nature and its improper intervention in ongoing elections. Justice Uzi Vogelman explains that the amendment does not specify the time it goes into effect, and that though its "subjective" purpose was clear enough, its "objective" purpose included, inter alia: a presumption against retrospective legislation; an aversion to changing rules of ongoing elections; and a principle of

* Note that this does not regard a pretextual or hidden interest. In this example a court concedes the genuine legislative or governmental interest, but then introduces a separate "objective" interest which the legislation ought to advance and against which the measure will be evaluated.

legislative "generality" within "the rule of law." On the basis of these "objective" purposes (which trump the inferior subjective purpose), Vogelman concludes that the law must be interpreted such that it takes effect only after the upcoming elections. The ruling is entirely couched in the language and terminology of statutory interpretation, including Vogelman's summary: "A conclusion that the amendment shall not apply to the upcoming municipal elections is the interpretive alternative that least violates the fundamental principles of our system."[69]

The potential legal basis for such a deferral (and the dubious propriety of the legislation at issue) is beside the point. What is most striking here is the Court's use of "objective purpose" to simply invent a new temporal timeline for a law's application without the most remote anchor in statutory text and directly contradicting the lawmaker's intent in enacting the amendment. The simple rule for all Israeli law is that legislation takes effect from the moment it is published in the *Reshumot* (the official national register or gazette), unless otherwise specified by the statute itself. Nothing in the short and laconic "Tiberias Law" can support a departure from this default formula. In other words, the Court's reasoning cannot remotely be considered an act of "interpretation" even in the most generous and expansive sense – there are simply no words to interpret. The Court's decision does not and cannot rely on any exercise of understanding and applying the content of the law. For all practical purposes, the Court struck down the existing amendment and re-enacted a new one, this time with a different (and delayed) start date, and all under the false label of "interpretation."

The *Tiberias* case demonstrates just how far "objective purposive" interpretation can be stretched to enable virtually any outcome. Though logically absurd and devoid of any interpretive effort or character, the Court's conclusion is consistent with – and is evidence of – the profoundly and inherently flawed nature of OPI. If judges can apply the law in a manner which contradicts the plain statutory text and its clear legislative purpose, then why not go the extra mile and simply invent new statutes, conjuring provisions out of thin air? In this sense courts rewriting the law from scratch is but a natural and inevitable extension of Objective Purposive Interpretation.

A final trend worth our attention is the Supreme Court's interpretation and application of laws which were specifically intended to negate particular judicial decisions and doctrines.

The Deri Doctrine introduced in the 1993 *Deri* and *Pinhasi* cases is discussed at length in Chapter 6. In those cases the Court developed a novel judicial rule which was purportedly based on a legislative lacuna – a statutory ambiguity – of the law which prevailed at the time. However, new legislation in 2001 attempted to clarify the relevant legal rules and to eliminate any alleged ambiguity. The Knesset explicitly sought to abolish the Deri Doctrine, and faithful application of the amended statutory text would have indeed yielded that result. Despite this, the Court ignored the new legislation and continued to apply the Deri Doctrine as though nothing had changed. Though the Court never really contends directly with the 2001 amendment (wisely preferring to simply pretend it doesn't exist), the original Deri Doctrine leans heavily on "objective purpose" such that it owes its continued application to OPI. Criticizing the Court's intransigence, Daniel Friedmann explains that any ruling "which leaves the Deri Doctrine in force following the [2001 legislation] is erroneous and flouts elementary principles of statutory interpretation."[70] In addition to familiar problems with OPI, Friedmann highlights how the Court renders various post-amendment statutory provisions meaningless, because they assume factual situations which can never arise due to the Deri Doctrine. Thus, by insisting on the continued application of the Deri Doctrine after the 2001 amendment, the Court quite literally "erases" entire provisions from the statute.[71]

Peeking briefly into the world of private law, another notable example is the Supreme Court's approach to interpreting contracts. In the famous 1995 *Aprofim* case Aharon Barak applied "objective purposive" interpretation to contract disputes, such that courts are to interpret contractual clauses according to "the parties' intent" and not necessarily adhering to the contract's text.[72] Prior to *Aprofim*, the Court regarded the contractual language as its most important and superior element (consistent with traditional common law approaches), and that additional "external" factors were only to be considered if the contract text was ambiguous. In *Aprofim*, Barak essentially demoted the contractual text such that it was on equal footing with various other factors – allowing judges and courts (and indeed attorneys and parties) to infer all kinds of contractual content without any substantial textual basis. The ruling was highly controversial and drew criticism from many within Israel's commercial and business sectors, and from the majority of legal experts and practitioners specializing in private law. Nonetheless, the Court reiterated its *Aprofim* approach in numerous subsequent cases (most notably in 2006).[73]

In 2011 the Knesset amended Israel's general contract-law statute with the clear objective of cancelling the *Aprofim* ruling. This was the first and only time the contracts legislation had ever been amended since its enactment in 1973. The lawmaker's desire to reverse *Aprofim* was explicit and unmistakable (to understate the matter) – from its inception, through Knesset deliberations and public interviews, and to the bill's official explanatory notes, cancelling *Aprofim* and restoring the primacy of the contractual text was the principal goal of the 2011 amendment.* The final version enacted by the Knesset states that if a contract's text is unambiguous, the contract must be interpreted and applied according to its text and without involving external factors. Soon after its enactment, Justice Danziger (in a dissenting opinion) characterized the legislation as "a substantive amendment to statutory law governing contract interpretation, reflecting a normative position adopted by the legislature, one which grants the contractual

---

* The initial bill's sponsor in 2009 was a relatively new legislator and critic of the Court, named Yariv Levin. The same Levin eventually served as Minister of Justice and introduced the 2023 judicial reforms.

text decisive weight."

Yet quite astonishingly, in a 2012 Supreme Court decision, Justice Eliezer Rivlin concluded that the amendment was nothing but a "confirmation" (just so!) of the *Aprofim* ruling.[74] Rivlin performs a series of logical and legalistic backflips and somersaults: First, he explains that the new law's "subjective" purpose and text are actually consistent with *Aprofim*; Second, Rivlin presents the law's "objective" purpose as consisting of "legal certainty" and fulfilling the intent of the parties to a contract. Rivlin explains that because both subjective and objective purposes support *Aprofim*, so does the final amendment itself. For the cherry on top, Justice Rivlin goes as far as to claim that the amendment's text goes even further than *Aprofim* in decreasing the significance of the contract language, but that he (Rivlin) was benevolently saving the amendment from having such effect by preferring the statute's objective purpose and leaving *Aprofim* intact.

Once again setting aside the merits and flaws of *Aprofim* and its impact, we find here another instance in which the Knesset enacts legislation explicitly aimed at changing a piece of judicial precedent, which the Supreme Court then either entirely ignores or utterly distorts while relying on the law's "objective purpose" to do so.

A final and painful example of the Court thwarting counter-judicial legislation, by way of false interpretation, may be found in the *Unlawful Combatant Detention* cases. Since its inception Israel has contended not only with the scourge of organized terrorism, but also with the singular evil of hostage-taking by its enemies. At a certain point Israel began holding members of terrorist groups in administrative detention as a "bargaining chip" to be used for the negotiation of returning its own hostages held by such groups. In the 1980s Israel had detained numerous members of *Hezbollah* and *Amal* (Lebanese Shiite terrorist organizations in active conflict with Israel) for the purpose of serving as "bargaining chips." Then, in a landmark 2000 ruling, the Supreme Court held such detention to be illegal – in the Court's view, the relevant statutory framework only authorized detention of persons actively posing a threat to national security. Per the Court, merely belonging to *Hezbollah* and similar Islamist terror organizations was insufficient cause for detention; and the desire to obtain leverage in negotiating the return of Israeli hostages could not serve as alternative grounds for detaining terrorists.

Following the ruling, it became increasingly clear that even violent enemy combatants could not be detained by Israel indefinitely under the new legal reality created by the Court. One notorious Lebanese arch-terrorist, Mustafa Dirani, had been abducted from Lebanon in a daring operation by Israeli commandos – he was directly and personally involved in the kidnapping and holding of Israeli aerial navigator Ron Arad. In addition to his potential knowledge of Ron Arad's whereabouts, Dirani was detained in the hope he could be used as a "bargaining chip" in ongoing hostage negotiations. Relying on the Court's recent ruling, Dirani petitioned the Court against his detention. Though the Court dismissed Dirani's initial petitions (holding that the latter still posed a threat to national security), the Court indicated that after a certain period of time the argument of "national security threat" would no longer be viable. Israel now found itself in an untenable situation – its enemies could kidnap Israeli nationals and hold them as hostages indefinitely, while Israel was severely restricted in its ability to detain members of terrorist groups as a means to facilitate the return of its own nationals.

For this precise reason, the Knesset enacted a major piece of legislation – the 2002 Detention of Unlawful Combatants Act. Critically, the new law established a "presumption of threat" by association – if a person is a member of a terrorist group, then they are presumed to pose a sufficient threat to national security justifying their detention. The law clearly and explicitly aimed to create a new legal framework authorizing the detention of terrorist members regardless of how "active" they might be, and potentially as "bargaining chips" for the release of Israeli hostages. The new legislation thus removed the main legal impediment raised by the Supreme Court's ruling in 2000 – statutory law now no longer required that a terrorist member be detained solely on the basis of their "active" threat to national security.

Unfortunately, the Supreme Court saw things differently. The new law was challenged on constitutional grounds, and the Court eventually issued its ruling in 2008. Drawing on international law and domestic human rights legislation, the Court essentially circumvented the new law's main function (i.e. a presumptive "guilt by association" for members of terrorist groups). Instead, by way of creative and convoluted interpretation, the Court insisted that the State must still prove an active threat to national security emanating personally from the individual being detained. The Court further (and arbitrarily) limited the law's application to territories outside Israel's legal control – i.e., only to Lebanon and Gaza but not to Israel and the West Bank. As told by constitutional scholar Joshua Segev, "the Court totally ignored the fact that the [new law] was meant to legitimize the detention of unlawful enemy combatants in order to facilitate the release of hostages and POWs."[75]

Segev describes how these legal battles "prevented or at least hampered any new initiatives to obtain better human assets for a trade deal with *Hezbollah*."[76] Further, Palestinian terror groups became emboldened and "inspired by *Hezbollah* hostage taking tactics," most notably Hamas in Gaza. Segev hints at the irony in the fact that Israel's inability to deal with terrorists taking Israelis hostage inevitably "leads to escalation of the conflict" – negotiated settlements became less likely, and thus military action more necessary. Segev concludes, poignantly and presciently: "We are not exempt in wondering whether the lack of legal tools to counter the terrorist tactics have also contributed to the escalation and to the fact that hostage taking have [*sic*] become a strategic problem and a trigger for war." Segev's observations were made in 2020, three years before Hamas kidnapped hundreds of Israelis on the October 7th attack. Could the use of "bargaining chips" have diminished the incentive of terror organizations to kidnap Israelis? We will likely never know.

Setting aside the security implications of the *Unlawful Combatant Detention* cases, they exhibit the same pattern as other cases reviewed above –

albeit with tragic ramifications. The Court banned "bargaining chip" detention in 2000 on the basis of an alleged statutory requirement; the Knesset reacted by enacting specific legislation in 2002 which granted explicit and clear-cut authorization for such detentions on the basis of association with terror organizations; finally, in 2008, the Court "interpreted" (or as Segev quips, misinterpreted) the new law in a manner which left it utterly neutered, robbing the statute of its plain meaning and thwarting its intended effect.

Dispensing Justice

The simplest way to understand and summarize Objective Purposive Interpretation is to expose the meaning of the Court's terminology for what it really means. The statutory text and its so-called "subjective purpose" is, plain and simple, the law. The "objective purpose" is, plain and simple, arbitrary judicial whim. Under OPI the Israeli judiciary applies the latter as if it were the former, distinguishing itself from (and making a mockery of) any conventional notion of "purposive" interpretation or conformity with overarching legal principles. Even those who are prepared to give interpretive weight to established legal traditions or well-grounded principles must recoil from the utterly ungrounded claims so wantonly deployed by Justice Barak.

Chapter 9 of this book will examine judicial review of legislation and its invalidation on constitutional grounds. But long before the Court began striking down statutes it was wielding OPI to nullify any disfavored law without the need for explicit judicial review. This is the doctrinal baseline of judicial supremacy.

Justice Benjamin Cardozo famously warned against the danger of judges substituting their own well-intended morality for the law, writing in 1921:

> "The judge, even when he is free, is still not wholly free. He is not to innovate at pleasure. He is not a knight-errant, roaming at will in pursuit of his own ideal of beauty or of goodness... He is not to yield to spasmodic sentiment, to vague and unregulated benevolence."[77]

Justice Felix Frankfurter expressed a similar sentiment nearly three decades later, albeit more bluntly. "This is a court of review," cautions Frankfurter, "not a tribunal unbounded by rules. We do not sit like a kadi under a tree dispensing justice according to considerations of individual expediency."[78]

But "dispensing justice" is precisely what Aharon Barak attempts to do with OPI. Barak counsels that the judge interpreting statutes should, when push comes to shove, "aspire to achieve justice." Justice, Barak explains, "guides the entire interpretive process" and "becomes a residual value which can decide hard cases."[79] Though surely a lofty goal, an aspiration to unilaterally impose one's own conception of "justice" has little to do with applying the law. The primary method of interpretation which dominates the Supreme Court's jurisprudence embodies precisely the type of judicial discretion against which Cardozo and

Frankfurter had warned: literally dispensing justice, innovating at pleasure, yielding to vague benevolence – entirely a "tribunal unbounded by rules."

Chapter 4

Standing and Justiciability

Opening the Floodgates

"*There is no 'legal vacuum'... law fills the whole world.*"
— Justice Aharon Barak[1]

From the founding of the State and throughout its classical era, the Supreme Court developed and maintained firm requirements regarding who could petition the High Court of Justice in cases against the government and what issues the Court would be willing to consider. Known as "threshold" requirements or conditions, these were not defined by statute but rather were carved out (somewhat erratically) by successive rulings, drawing heavily on the common-law tradition as well as simply on first principles and common sense. Though at times lacking consistency, the Court's approach aligned with the conventional tradition and practice of threshold requirements in common-law jurisdictions (such as the U.S. and U.K.) and throughout the world.*

Most legal systems require that a petitioner or plaintiff must have "Standing," and that the dispute is "Justiciable." These threshold requirements strive to ensure that only certain kinds of cases are brought for legal adjudication – cases which represent actual disputes for a court to resolve according to actual law. Such requirements are commonly accepted as necessary to prevent courts of law becoming vehicles for abstract supervision of government policy. They help avoid the litigation of publicly contested socio-political matters in a manner which circumvents the deliberative, collaborative, competitive and participatory political process.

The Court established its "Standing" requirement early on, stating in the 1949 *Unterricht* case that it "does not intervene unless convinced that the action under review, of which the petitioner complains, might violate their legal right."[2] In the 1950 *Ariav* case, the Court clarified that a general objection to unlawful government action is insufficient if a petitioner "cannot show that this act will harm his own interest." The Court further emphasized its role as "only to provide

* I am indebted to the many writings of Prof. Yoav Dotan and Dr. Joshua Segev, on which I relied greatly for this chapter.

relief to any citizen in the event his personal right may be harmed by an illegal action,"[3] after reiterating that an electorate dissatisfied with its government ought to approach the elected Knesset for solutions. In the 1965 *Oppenheimer* case the Court ruled that a petitioner may challenge the government for not meeting some broad legal obligation only if he shows that "his own personal direct interest is harmed,"[4] and repeated the importance of a petitioner's "personal interest" in the 1969 *Miron* case.[5]

Especially illustrative of the Court's approach is the 1977 *Bar Shalom* case, which involved clearly illegal and unethical government conduct but which was nonetheless dismissed as the petitioner lacked standing. Justice Shlomo Asher stressed that "the task of the court is one: to do justice between rival parties, and its role is not to resolve problems – even were they serious and of utmost public importance – without the initiating party being entitled to legal remedy." Critically, the Court articulated the rule that to have standing a petitioner must show an interest which is "personal, distinct, tangible and direct."[6]

The Court recognized various exceptions to the Standing condition, such as that one need not show a personal interest in *habeas corpus* cases (demanding timely judicial review of an arrest), or when statutory law grants Standing independent of personal connection to the case, or for clear-cut cases of public corruption. These too were consistent with near-universal legal practice. More notable was the Court's early expansion of standing to include *any* personal harm, not just violations of a clear legal right. Because the Knesset had not legislated a bill of rights enshrining individual liberties, the Court considered protecting "unenumerated" liberties from government infringement to be part of its role. As such, the Court adopted a relatively permissive approach to the type of harmed interest being alleged – though a petitioner had to show a distinct, direct, tangible and personal interest being harmed, he did not have to base the claim on a precise legal right. Exceptions notwithstanding, the Court's overall approach was consistently faithful to the well-established notion that a party must have Standing to sue the government in court.

The Supreme Court's commitment to the Justiciability requirement was equally firm. In the 1951 *Jabotinsky* case following the resignation of David Ben-Gurion as Israel's first Prime Minister, the Court refused to intervene in the President's decision regarding whether to task other MKs with forming a new government. The Court considered the issue "non-justiciable" and "not given to judicial resolution," describing the relations between the State President, the Government and the Knesset as "by their nature outside the judicial sphere" and to be resolved "by parliamentary means."[7] A later case which well-expressed the Court's jurisprudence was that of *Reiner* in 1965, in which petitioners challenged Israel's controversial agreement to establish diplomatic relations with post-war West Germany. Being a matter of pure foreign policy, the Court dismissed the case outright as it was "not a legal matter but rather a distinctly political one" which "cannot be evaluated by legal criteria."[8]

In the landmark 1975 *Ashkenazi* case, the Court was asked to order that the Minister of Defense and the military Chief of Staff conduct a full investigation of failures in the 1973 Yom Kippur War. The Court dismissed the case as non-justiciable due not only to the general impropriety of judicial intervention in senior military discretion, but importantly, due to the Court's institutional unsuitability (and effective inability) to consider complicated and specialized system-wide policy decisions. This included "the organization, structure and preparedness" of the military, its "equipment and operations," its "methods of deliberation and decision-making," and the "training and instruction of its forces."[9] The *Ashkenazi* case represented the prevailing approach regarding non-justiciability of military affairs, but also more broadly regarding the impracticality of judicial intervention in systemic, complex and wide-ranging policy decisions far beyond the Court's capacity to evaluate. The Court also emphasized the responsibility and accountability of military organs and of the "Ministerial authority in charge of them," noting an intuitive link between professional policy-making discretion and public responsibility for the outcomes of such decisions.[*]

As partially demonstrated by the above cases, the Court's conception and application of justiciability meant that certain types of disputes were considered "out of bounds" for adjudication, in a manner broadly tracking established practice throughout the Western democratic world. These included inherently political decisions (both in the technical-institutional sense and in the public-societal sense), pure policy formation at the highest levels of government, discretionary political appointments, allocation of budgets and resources, military and defense affairs, foreign relations, criminal prosecution and enforcement, and internal parliamentary matters.

The handful of examples above regarding both Standing and Justiciability are ones in which the Court directly addressed and reflected upon their application – but these are joined by many hundreds of cases over the years which failed to meet such threshold requirements and were therefore simply dismissed outright.

*

Fast forward to 2020.

In what was the most severe political crisis in Israel's history, five election cycles were held in the three and a half years between April 2019 and November 2022, due to the inability of any parliamentary majority to form a Coalition or sustain a viable Government. At the height of the crisis following the (third) elections held in 2020, and as the first wave of COVID-19 wreaked havoc on the Israeli economy and on society at large, a bi-partisan supermajority of 72 members of Knesset announced they had reached an agreement to form an

[*] As often happens when considering justiciability, in *Ashkenazi* the Court also addressed the Standing test, describing it as a question whether the petitioner is "engaging in a quarrel which is his own."

emergency national unity government, with various power-sharing arrangements and with Benjamin Netanyahu initially at its head as Prime Minister.

The 2020 Coalition was unusual and unprecedented in many ways. One of the most notable was that during the elections cycle, a mere month before voters went to the polls, Benjamin Netanyahu was indicted for alleged bribery along with a number of counts of Breach of Trust spanning three separate criminal cases. Netanyahu in fact ran for office, and was now being appointed Prime Minister, as a criminal defendant. While high-profile investigations against Netanyahu had been ongoing for many years – they had dogged him since 1999 – this was the first time he had been directly charged with criminal conduct, and indeed the first time a criminal indictee would ascend to the premiership.

The Coalition's stated intent to nominate Netanyahu as Prime Minister was immediately challenged in the Supreme Court, with petitioners arguing that an indicted defendant could not serve as Prime Minister. The petitioners themselves were mostly non-profit left wing organizations, an assortment of activist citizens and even Yesh Atid, the main political party headed for the Opposition. No petitioner could claim a personal and distinct interest was directly harmed by Netanyahu's appointment (and indeed none alleged so).

Many agreed that the legal case was far-fetched. "Basic Law: The Government" specifies no requirements or standards for the role of Prime Minister, aside that he or she be a serving (elected) member of Knesset. Further still, amendments made to the law in 2001 explicitly contemplate a scenario in which a criminal defendant becomes Prime Minister (the law addresses procedural arrangements, such as venue for trial), irrefutably indicating that being indicted does not prevent one from serving as Prime Minister. Needless to say, the political stakes were high – a parliament's appointment of Prime Minister is the most immediately tangible consequence of elections, a deeply and inherently "political" decision in which the public is heavily invested.

Yet the petition was not dismissed outright. The Court held two straight days of televised oral argument, and after another two days issued a rushed 21-page unanimous decision. The eleven Justices on the panel dismissed the petition on its merits, noting the statutory law as described above, deliberating on a number of related doctrines, and ultimately finding that there were "no legal grounds to prevent" Netanyahu from forming the government and becoming Prime Minister.[10] The question of standing is not mentioned in the decision, while the issue of justiciability was raised in one single concurring opinion.

We may set aside the legal substance and outcome of the *Netanyahu* case and focus, for present purposes, on its very existence. In any functioning democratic jurisdiction, real or imagined, such a case being fully entertained by a court of law – contemplating whether to effectively reverse the outcome of elections without the faintest legal basis – would not only be unthinkable, but would almost certainly be impossible. This is due to the aforementioned dual threshold requirements of justiciability and standing, found in almost any legal system. How, then, could a case like *Netanyahu* come to be?

The answer is simple. In a small handful of pivotal rulings during the 1980s the Supreme Court effectively abolished both "standing" and "justiciability" and threw open the judicial doors to anyone, on any issue, for any cause. As we shall presently see, despite the many precedents discussed above and uniquely among the nations, Israel has no genuine threshold requirements to speak of, and the Court regularly hears cases not brought by any discernible aggrieved party and not remotely relating to justiciable questions of law.

One cannot overstate the effect of the "threshold" revolution and its centrality to the ascendancy of the Supreme Court's power. Professor Yoav Dotan contrasts this process with other more gradual changes in the Court's jurisprudence, saying that within a short timespan "the Supreme Court initiated dramatic and far reaching changes in all aspects of [administrative] judicial review," in a manner that "may only be described as a genuine revolution."[11] Dotan points out that unlike the well-known "constitutional revolution" a decade later (to be discussed in Part III), this "administrative" revolution didn't rely on any constitutional or legislative changes whatsoever. In fact, "one would be hard put to recall even minor changes" to the statutory framework regarding judicial review – yet this did little to inhibit the Court in its radical departure from its own prevailing jurisprudence. For this reason, and due to the "total breach" of all previous "major patterns of judicial review," Dotan considers these changes to be part of "the more real and important revolution."[12]

Why Standing and Justiciability Matter

While a comprehensive review of the justifications for threshold requirements is beyond the scope of this chapter, we may outline some of the key arguments for Standing and Justiciability which in turn reflect the prevailing approach for most democratic legal systems. These serve as a critical background to understanding the Court's abandonment of both Standing and Justiciability.

A judiciary serves a key and distinct function in any democratic order which respects the rule of law and the separation of powers. Courts don't simply devise rules of conduct for society at large on their own initiative and as they happen to see fit – that is the lawmaking power reserved to the elected legislature. Nor do courts usually announce their opinion on theoretical matters not directly tied to a case brought before them. Rather, a court's function is first and foremost to resolve disputes of a legal nature between distinct parties. In many areas of law this is naturally intuitive – a contract case will typically be between two sides to a contract, where one side perhaps alleges the other side is in breach for not fulfilling their contractual obligations. The issue at question may be factual but determined according to legal rules (did Jack pay Jill? Can Jack prove it?), or it may be expressly legal (do pails of water count as valid payment?), both often requiring the expertise of a skilled lawyer. The parties to litigation have "rivalry" – they are the actual ones between whom a dispute exists.

The same applies in principle to lawsuits involving the government, in what is often called "administrative" law. A dispute may arise between some government organ – an agency, an official, an entity – and another party: perhaps another government organ, but typically an individual or some recognized association of individuals. However, as the government formulates wide-ranging policy which affects multitudes of people, it may be difficult to pinpoint whether a genuine dispute exists between parties, or whether someone is merely demanding that the court give legal force to their personal objection to government policy.

This is where "Standing" (or *locus standi*) comes in – for a suit against the government to be heard in court, for a claim to be adjudicated on its merits, a party must show they have a tangible, discrete quarrel with the government; merely disliking or disagreeing with government policy does not grant standing to sue. Standing is about *who* gets to avail themselves of a court's formidable authority and asks "why are *you* here?" (or as Justice Scalia memorably framed it – "what's it to you?"). If you're the only person that could bring *this* case, then you likely have standing; if, on the other hand, hundreds of thousands of people could have potentially submitted the exact same case in your stead, then it seems less likely the Standing requirement has been met. Standing exists separately from the substantive legal disagreement at issue in a case – we assume that there may conceivably be some unlawful conduct at hand, yet we still insist that a court's authority to consider the question is permitted only in the context of an actual discernible dispute. If Standing is not shown, then a suit is dismissed before proceeding to substantive deliberation of its merits.

Various jurisdictions have developed different approaches and rules regarding Standing. For federal cases in the United States, for example, this has traditionally meant that a party must show an "injury-in-fact" that is "concrete or particularized" and that is actual or imminent, with a causal connection to the governmental action being challenged and which a judicial decision might be able to redress. Other jurisdictions might adopt a more permissive approach. Even in places with a strong commitment to Standing and clear rules, some borderline cases might have no obvious answer to whether a party's grievance is distinct enough to grant them access to the court. Nonetheless, the principle (with specific and limited exceptions) is generally accepted throughout the democratic world: Access to a court's adjudication services (and associated privileges or benefits) is subject to the claimant or petitioner showing they have a direct, personal, individualized harm or grievance which is distinct from mere objection and which is separate from the diffuse desires and misgivings of any large group in society. They must have Standing.

Justiciability reflects the idea that some issues or disputes should not be adjudicated at all, with a variety of rationales yielding different conceptions of the same notion. Underlying this notion is the fact that at times the very litigation of an issue – its very consideration by a court, regardless of relative legal merit and practical outcomes – involves severe societal risks and exacts a hefty price paid both by the public and by the judiciary itself.

One conception regards the legal nature or core of a dispute – is there in fact a legal right to be enforced? Does the law as we know it have anything to say on the matter? Can the dispute be resolved by legal criteria? If a dispute or disagreement has no legal nexus – say, regarding which Häagen-Dazs ice-cream flavor is best – then it may be said to be "non-justiciable." Another conception is grounded in expertise – does a court possess the relevant tools, knowledge, experience, and conditions to decide a certain issue, and would it be the optimal forum for such a decision? Judges are experts in law, but usually in little else. The highly specialized procedures and rules of litigation serve a very specific purpose and are not necessarily conducive to arriving at the wisest policy or best decision. A dispute might thus be "non-justiciable" if it bears no relevance to legal expertise.

Yet another conception, grounded in the separation of powers and in considerations of public faith in the judiciary, may be thought of as political prudence – should a highly contested matter of socio-political importance, hotly debated between competing groups in society, be resolved by a court of law? Or should it be left to the arena of public discourse and for the electorate, civil society and political process to resolve on their own terms? In the United States this is often referred to as the "political question" doctrine. Inherent in this view is the recognition that certain decisions are within the prerogative powers of the executive and legislative branches and ought to properly remain within their domain, or to be determined in the forums of public and parliamentary politics; and that their resolution by judicial fiat would be unjust as well as unwise. This holds even if one could technically find some legal hook enabling judicial involvement.

These three conceptions have much in common and often overlap. An obvious example is the conduct of foreign relations by the executive government, such as whether a country will join a particular international alliance. It is likely that domestic law has "nothing to say" on the matter; that judges have far inferior expertise relating to diplomacy, international relations and the state's foreign interests; and that the question of which alliances a state joins is an inherently political one, properly determined by accountable branches of government. Such decisions might be considered "non-justiciable" in all the senses described, and a court would typically refuse to consider or accommodate any legal objection to them.

Despite the bland label of "threshold requirements," Standing and Justiciability are far from mere technicalities. They jointly speak to the core definition of what a court does, what purpose it serves, and why its decisions deserve compliance. If courts exist to resolve legal disputes, then they must in fact consider only *disputes* and only ones which are *legal*. A lack of adherence to these threshold principles risks the proliferation of judicial decisions based on judges' personal ideology and political preferences, violating the separation of powers and severely diminishing public faith in the judiciary. This is why Justice Antonin Scalia described Standing as "an essential element of the separation of powers." Beyond all these lie practical considerations of efficiency and expediency: Such requirements serve an important role in maintaining a manageable judicial workload. Ignoring them opens the floodgates and invites a deluge of petitions from uninvolved parties on non-legal issues.

Contrary to popular understanding, threshold requirements are not only about limiting which parties have access to the court or what issues are brought before it – they're also about limiting and containing the court's formidable power. Standing and Justiciability are not a bug of legal formalism but a feature of democratic government. Recall that courts and judges wield an extraordinary degree of de facto governmental authority, issuing binding, enforceable and often final decisions. Judicial independence (the necessity of which is not doubted) means that they do so entirely insulated from public sentiment and shielded from any other direct governmental (e.g., executive or legislative) intervention. Legislation and much executive action involve a great deal of transparency, public debate, stringent legal rules, and a laborious process consisting of many stages and hurdles; most of all, they involve ultimate accountability to the electorate or its direct representatives. Judges, on the other hand and as a practical matter, need only write a document on their computer and sign at the bottom (occasionally they must persuade a handful of colleagues). From a functional and institutional perspective courts are among the most independently powerful organs in democratic government. Threshold requirements are consequently about ensuring this power is used for its intended purpose – and not abused to increase judicial power in ever-expanding circles. If judges can accept cases from any*one* and adjudicate any*thing*, any limits on judicial power are drastically reduced.

Quite separate from the question of limiting judicial power, threshold requirements (Standing and Justiciability chief among them) developed in Western jurisdictions as essential features of ordered liberty and a functioning civil society. Aggrieved parties have a right to control their own claims without the intervention of unrelated third parties. Public controversies over policy and values are best served by avoiding the kind of fixed and rigid resolutions established by judicial precedent. Threshold requirements were developed for the most part, especially within the Common Law tradition, by judges and courts themselves, in societies which were not at all suspicious of judicial power. In other words, threshold requirements were not born due to hostility to judicial overreach, but because they just make sense.

As we've seen in the previous section, the Israeli Supreme Court had initially developed and enforced precisely such requirements, well within accepted global standards and loosely based on, and consistent with, the various rationales presented above.[13]

Turning the Tables – Dr. Becker and Mr. Ressler

Israelis serve in the Israel Defense Forces (the "IDF") for a number of years following high-school and often throughout their lives as reservists.* They do so willingly and proudly but are also obligated to by law. The dilemmas and controversies of the compulsory military service have dogged Israeli society since the founding of the State. Among these has been the matter of exemption – who is exempt from the draft, and why? Israeli Arab citizens are exempt as are women who maintain a religious way of life, though both can volunteer.

Most contentious of all is the blanket exemption granted to the Ultra-Orthodox community. Israeli Ultra-Orthodox Jews (also called "*Haredi*") generally adhere to a strict interpretation and application of religious law and dedicate much of their time to study of religious texts. The Ultra-Orthodox represent a significant and active portion of the Israeli electorate and political community, and for many years have been a staple of partisan coalitions in the Knesset for both left-wing and right-wing governments. A key principle in their lifestyle is the rejection of modernity and maintaining their separation from broader secular society (sometimes drawing comparison with the Amish in the United States). They have (for the most part) objected to military service on societal grounds at least as much as on religious grounds, arguing that military service would compel them to mix and integrate with the rest of Israeli society against their will.

Since the State's founding, Ultra-Orthodox men have repeatedly been granted an indefinite draft "deferment" for those enrolled in institutions of religious study – technically not an exemption but clearly amounting to one. This exemption has enjoyed consistent de facto bi-partisan support, even if for narrow reasons of convenience, and has held fast even when the Ultra-Orthodox were not members of the governing Coalition. As the relative size and influence of the Israeli Ultra-Orthodox has grown, so has public discontentment with their military draft exemption (along with other related problems) and so has the issue occupied an increasingly more dominant place in Israeli public life and debate.

As we shall see several times throughout this book, the saga of Ultra-Orthodox exemption and the advent of judicial supremacy are deeply intertwined. Few issues so closely overlap with the Court's expanding power as does that of the draft exemption, to the extent that tracking the topic inevitably means tracking the history of Israeli judicial supremacy. As is the case elsewhere, it was also regarding Standing and Justiciability that the draft exemption provided the Court with the opportunity to radically expand its authority.

The famous 1970 *Becker* case exemplifies the Supreme Court's original approach to threshold requirements within the context of a novel challenge to the draft exemption. A junior reserves officer petitioned the Court and challenged the Ultra-Orthodox exemption as illegal, on the grounds that the Minister of Defense had exceeded his authority by granting the exemption based on partisan-political considerations and not on military needs or other considerations prescribed by law. The petitioner claimed that the exemption prolonged military service for all

* This author included.

other citizens and that he also spoke on their behalf.

Needless to say, the case was promptly dismissed.[14] With a focus on Standing but demonstrating the overlap with Justiciability, the *Becker* ruling reads like a summary of the classical Court's approach to threshold requirements, and is worth reviewing briefly. Regarding individuals litigating matters in which they were not directly involved ("in a quarrel not his own"), the Court warned that on a practical level such interference "in any public or political affair" would inevitably "disrupt" the Court's functioning and "hamper its ability" to carry out its judicial duties. Later the Court states more explicitly that "a person not asking a thing for himself but that rather demands only to deny something from others" has no standing before the court.

On the more principled level, emphasizing the difference between the judiciary and other accountable branches of government, the Court noted that "there is no judicial case except where there exists a 'quarrel' (*lis*) in which one comes and claims his rights," and that entertaining suits by any person claiming to speak for the public at large would "blur the domains" and might "violate the principle of separation of powers." Aware of the overlap with Justiciability, the Court then observes that "the more the public character of a complaint," and the more a case regards matters typically belonging "to the political arena" which serve as a "topic for discussion before the government and the Knesset," the more the Court must "strictly insist" on the Standing requirement. In other words, the more political a case, the more clearly a petitioner would need to show a direct and personal harm for the court to consider their case.

The Court then makes some of its most strident statements on Justiciability to date, refusing to accommodate "public-collective" objections to policy and stating that "the court is wary of being dragged into general public debates" which are "better left in the hands of political actors." Leaving no room for doubt, the Court starkly warns it must "reject the attempt to transform" it into a forum for such public debates. Directly addressing the matter at hand, the Court notes that the objection to the draft exemption is not distinct from "public collective indignation" and that the petitioner is "no different from any other person" that disagrees with the exemption (thus lacking standing); and finally emphasizes the "pure political character" of the issue (rendering it non-justiciable).

All in all, the 1970 *Becker* decision was both an emphatic reiteration of the Court's insistence on firm threshold requirements, and an unequivocal ruling that the Ultra-Orthodox draft exemption was outside the Court's territory.

And then came the *Ressler* cases.

In a series of four consecutive cases between 1981 and 1986, military reservists led by Maj. Yehuda Ressler petitioned the Supreme Court to invalidate the Ultra-Orthodox draft exemption. Though there had been no major factual or legal changes since *Becker* to justify rehashing the same argument, Ressler cited a handful of new cases in which the Court expressed some willingness to modify and relax its threshold requirements.

In the first *Ressler* case in 1981 the Court (Justice Y. Cohen) dismissed the petition, rejecting Ressler's argument while relying on the *Becker* precedent and on substantially the same grounds. The Court unequivocally reiterated *Becker*:

> "The petition clearly attempts to drag this court into a political-public debate regarding a sensitive and volatile issue, about which public opinion is deeply and bitterly divided. The petitioners cannot succeed in doing so, due to their lack of standing, due to the issue being non-justiciable, and because they have not presented legal cause for judicial intervention."[15]

The last part regarding legal cause is notable – aside questions of standing and justiciability, the Court clearly considered the case itself to be meritless (we will return to this). The Court also stressed the lack of any compelling factual evidence showing that an Ultra-Orthodox draft would tangibly affect the petitioner's length of service, much as it found in *Becker*.

Importantly, the Court pointed out that there in fact had been one significant change to the law, but to the petitioner's detriment. Following the *Becker* case, the statute authorizing the Minister of Defense had been amended with the clear effect (and express intent) of greatly expanding his discretion regarding the grounds for granting exemption. After listing various grounds for exemption, the text was changed from "and other similar reasons" to "and other reasons," omitting the word "similar" and indicating the Minister was not limited to grounds of a certain type or category, but was rather widely authorized to grant exemptions as he deemed necessary. The Court did not mention the *Ashkenazi* case which had also been decided after *Becker* and which further limited justiciability of military affairs, though this was another addition to the law which supported the decision in *Ressler*.

Ressler was not dissuaded, and immediately requested a rehearing before an expanded panel, which was decided in early 1982. The Court (Justice M. Landau) denied the request, generally citing the grounds stated in previous rulings, though slightly more sympathetic to the petitioner's claims of standing.[16] The Court especially noted, again, the statutory amendment which it considered sufficient grounds to deny both the request and the original petition. Nonetheless, Justice Landau expressed some surprise that Ressler didn't argue for the exemption to be defined in primary legislation, rather than in the executive decision of the Defense Minister, an argument Landau seemed to hint might have merit.

Not one to back down and encouraged by Landau's comment, Ressler approached the court a third time and filed his petition anew, still in 1982 and only three months since the initial ruling in 1981 – this time dutifully adding an argument about the need for primary legislation explicitly authorizing the draft exemption.* Once again the Court made short shrift of the case and dismissed it on

---

* One may be forgiven for reflecting, again, on the ease with which such petitions are submitted directly to the Supreme Court as High Court of Justice.

the grounds of standing and justiciability, echoing all the reasons given in the previous two decisions.[17] The Court did, however, leave an opening regarding future evidence that might prove a factual connection between the Ultra-Orthodox exemption and the length of service required of enlisted and reserve soldiers.

But Maj. Ressler showed remarkable persistence and did not despair, akin to a gambler certain that perhaps this time the dice will make amends for all prior efforts. In 1986 Ressler filed yet another petition, mustering all the previous arguments and now armed with a new affidavit from a retired officer alleging a factual connection between service length and the Ultra-Orthodox exemption. Against Ressler were arrayed the State's consistent practice over the previous four decades; bi-partisan political support for the exemption; the *Becker* and prior *Ressler* precedents; the underlying jurisprudence regarding threshold requirements; and even the statutory amendment clarifying the wide discretion granted to the Minister of Defense in creating such policy.

Yet Ressler's gamble paid off. In June of 1988 the Supreme Court issued a landmark decision completely sweeping away all previous conceptions of Standing and Justiciability, ruling that the petitioners had standing and that the issue was justiciable.[18] The majority opinion was penned by Aharon Barak. Yoav Dotan describes the decision in *Ressler* as possibly the single most important and dramatic change effected by the Court expanding its powers of judicial review.[19] In one fell swoop the classic threshold requirements were effectively obliterated – *Ressler* became the Mr. Hyde to *Becker*'s Dr. Jekyll.*

Regarding Standing, Barak recognized a wide "exception" for any "public petitioner" – that is, granting standing to parties with no distinct personal harm, but which raise an important issue relating to the rule of law, to civil liberties, to corruption or to any other matter in which the petitioner claims to show a flaw in governmental conduct. Key to Barak's argument was that "the role of the HCJ is to ensure the fulfillment of the rule of law," and that "locking this Court's gates before a disinterested petitioner" impedes the law, as "without a judge, there is no law."[20]

Barak's upending of Justiciability was yet more extreme, and relied on an intricate theory distinguishing between "normative justiciability" – whether a government action falls under the purview of the law; and "institutional justiciability" – whether the court *ought* to refrain from deciding a case for prudential or other reasons. Barak makes clear that any conceivable government action falls under the law because it is either forbidden or permitted, and that "normative non-justiciability" does not exist. In a passage that has since become famous, Barak took pains to articulate his view in no uncertain terms:

> "There is no action to which the law does not apply… Any action may be 'captured' within the framework of the law… There is no 'legal vacuum' in which the law takes no position regarding actions performed

* Going forward, *Ressler* will refer to this last ruling.

> within it. The law extends over all actions… Any action – be it political or a policy matter as it may – is grasped within the world of law, and a legal norm which adopts a position towards it."[21]

Barak's point of departure is thus that *any* dispute is justiciable per se, and all that remains is to determine whether it meets "institutional justiciability" – that is, whether a court ought to decide the case, under the assumption that the law indeed has something to say about it. Yet he proceeds to largely reject the nominal notion of "institutional" justiciability as well, by listing its justifications and rejecting them one by one. Barak explains why unlimited judicial review of any imaginable government action is consistent with the separation of powers and with democracy, will not cause politicization of the judiciary, and is ultimately supported by considerations of public faith in the judiciary.

This was no passing impulse, and Barak subsequently reiterated and clarified the same core stance. In a 1993 law review article, Barak opened with the phrase: "The whole earth is full of law. Any human conduct is the object of a legal norm."[22] The first part is an inelegant allusion to the biblical passage in Isaiah 6:3 "the whole earth is full of His glory." In his 2002 Harvard Law Review introduction Barak again left no room for doubt:

> "In my opinion, every dispute is normatively justiciable. Every legal problem has criteria for its resolution. There is no "legal vacuum." According to my outlook, law fills the whole world. There is no sphere containing no law and no legal criteria. Every human act is encompassed in the world of law… Even actions of a clearly political nature – such as waging war – can be examined with legal criteria… Everything can be resolved by a court, in the sense that law can take a view as to its legality."[23]

This is, in a nutshell, the precedent set by the Supreme Court in the 1988 *Ressler* decision which generally still applies throughout Israeli public law to this day.

Thresholds Abolished

To say that the Court in *Ressler* and ensuing cases departed from its previous approach and diverged from global legal standards seems trivial. Nonetheless, this monumental decision, its implications and its aftermath deserve our close scrutiny.

Regarding Standing, Yoav Dotan explains that despite Barak's framing "public" standing as an exception, the approach in *Ressler* swiftly led to the "almost complete erasure of all Standing limitations" before the Court,[24] noting that within a short time the Court stopped discussing questions of standing altogether, and that the new approach led to a massive increase of HCJ petitions filed by non-profit advocacy organizations and political parties.* Dotan describes the far-reaching consequences of abolishing the standing requirement as "hard to overstate":[25] First, in the Court's new self-conception as supervisor of all government institutions and actions, fashioning itself as an "independent actor in the public arena that takes a position in almost any matter and issue arising in the political branches." Second, the Court transformed itself into a "second round" forum for political, economic or public disputes on the heels of any determination by the Knesset or the government, due to the fact that it may be immediately and routinely subjected by any person to judicial review.

Dr. Joshua Segev has also written extensively on the issue of threshold requirements. Segev makes a critical and illuminating – and far from obvious – point regarding the link between Standing and evidence hearings at the Supreme Court.[26] As discussed in Part I above, proceedings at the Supreme Court are strictly legal (with rare exceptions) – that is, they involve lawyers making legal arguments – and don't allow for fact-finding hearings such as expert testimony or cross-examination of witnesses. Any factual claims, questions or disputes that arise are presented by the attorneys for each side, occasionally backed up by vague affidavits signed by various parties. Further, being the court of first-instance means that this is the only way the Supreme Court ascertains issues of fact – they are not determined in advance by a trial court.

Yet Standing is inherently a factual question. It asks what the real-world harm is to a particular individual in the specific set of circumstances before the court. In other words, at least in principle, establishing Standing is never a theoretical or abstract legal exercise but rather is based on actual evidence. This tension between the Standing requirement and the Court's relative inability to make factual findings makes the latter's discretion – whether to grant standing, whether to recognize a "public petitioner" – all the more arbitrary.

Close examination of the Court's shift regarding Justiciability reveals it to be even more dramatic. The *Ressler* decision not only expanded the scope of justiciable disputes far beyond prior Israeli practice and compared with other jurisdictions around the world;[27] it also redefined and reconceptualized the very notion of justiciability, in the sense that from then-on the Court adopted and applied Barak's framework of (automatic) normative justiciability and (assumed) institutional justiciability. Indeed, no significant case since *Ressler* has in fact been dismissed solely on grounds of non-justiciability.

Though we avoid a full analysis of Barak's (and by extension and adoption, the Court's) theory, we may make a handful of observations. First is Barak's inversion of both the separation of powers and faith in the judiciary, so that they support an expansive judicial role rather than oppose it. This line of argument couldn't be more dubious: Montesquieu's formulation of the separation of powers explicitly argues that judges ought *refrain* from intervening in actions of other

---

* Though "non-profit" is perhaps a misnomer – routinely petitioning the Supreme Court on controversial public issues has become a highly lucrative and well-funded industry.

government branches. Scholars and judges throughout the world consider such intervention to be in tension with the separation of powers (even if justified), not supported by it. Put simply, there is no accepted theory of the separation of powers in which the judiciary enjoys a general veto authority over all questions of public policy and governmental discretion. "In Barak's conception of the separation of powers," explains Judge Posner, "the judicial power is unlimited."[28]

Barak further argues that limitless justiciability is required because the public would lose faith in the judiciary precisely due to non-intervention. That is, non-intervention would harm the court's public perception more than (non-justiciable) intervention. Aside not being supported by any empirical data, Dotan points out that this seems to be a "self-fulfilling prophecy"[29] – the Court constantly intervenes in issues usually considered outside its territory, and thus establishes a public expectation that it do so. Were the Court to refrain from such non-justiciable interference, the public would expect none to begin with and the Court would likely not suffer any damage to its reputation by avoiding adjudication. Far more importantly, Dotan rightly observes that Barak's argument doesn't address (or simply sidesteps) the original problem of public faith – that indeed, judicial intervention in politically loaded issues without solid legal basis will almost certainly diminish (not to say, demolish) the Court's public standing.

Professor Menachem (nicknamed "Menny") Mautner, former dean of the Tel Aviv law school, among Israel's most prominent jurists and a prolific commentator on the Supreme Court's jurisprudence, also rejects Barak's argument regarding faith in the judiciary. Mautner notes that the Court's over-willingness to engage in inherently political and partisan issues meant the erosion of its own legitimacy to act assertively in protecting individual liberties and civil rights.[30] Mautner's political affiliation would be described by most Israelis (including himself) as radical-left, yet he has been a consistent and vocal critic of the Court's political meddling – Mautner has often stated that the Court had deservedly earned the pejorative label of "a *Meretz* branch in Givat Ram" (Meretz is a far-left political party, and Givat Ram is the neighborhood in which the Supreme Court building is located). Mautner argues that the Court has a critical (and properly activist) role in protecting individual and minority rights, but that it could only do so effectively if perceived as non-partisan on the broader societal and political issues of the day. Such perception, and thus the Court's legitimacy to enforce rights against the government and even against popular opinion, is undermined by the Court's refusal to respect traditional boundaries of justiciability.* We will return to the issue of public faith in the judiciary later in greater detail in Chapter 10.

Also central to Barak's theory is his version of the "rule of law," with Barak arguing that without judicial review and intervention in any government action,

---

* Mautner's research also showed the way in which left-wing politicians and political parties directly leveraged the Court to achieve policy goals rejected by the Knesset and the electorate.

large areas of government become essentially lawless. Aside the argument's logical flaw of begging the question (governmental so called "lawlessness" is a feature, not a bug, of policymaking and of democratic discretion), it is also factually false. There are in fact a variety of mechanisms for enforcement of legal norms in government outside courts of law. Chief among these is parliamentary supervision of executive officials and bodies, alongside other state organs (such as the State Comptroller and other ombudsman offices) and informal oversight provided by the media and public. Claiming that judicial intervention is the only way to hold government accountable and to monitor compliance with the law simply does not align with reality, in Israel or anywhere else.

One recurring feature of this same argument regards corruption, which Barak mentions repeatedly as a justification for both limitless standing and justiciability. But as Barak himself concedes, public corruption was (and is) already a recognized exception enabling suits without a show of Standing; and assuming some patently illegal action is involved (or it wouldn't be corruption), allegations of corruption would certainly be considered justiciable under the traditional approach, such that corruption cannot serve to justify the expansion of either threshold requirement.

Regarding the analytical core of Barak's theory, the premise of "normative justiciability" seems shaky to begin with. The argument that any conceivable action is encompassed within the law because it is either permissible or forbidden, Mautner observes, turns justiciability into "a formalistic and hollow concept."[31] It is, technically speaking, nonsense – the fact that an action is "permitted" because no law forbids it can hardly support the claim that the action is therefore "covered" by law. Are "absence of law" and "permission by law" really the same thing?

Interestingly, Barak contends with some previous rulings and specifically calls out the 1965 *Reiner* decision regarding initiation of diplomatic relations with West Germany. He argues that such a question can never be regarded as purely political, and as an example notes that the law might mandate which government organ is authorized to represent the state in foreign relations.* Quite so. But this example is misleading: *Reiner* was non-justiciable precisely because it was the content of the decision itself (entering into diplomatic relations) being challenged, not the legal authority to do so. In presenting this example Barak displays his unwillingness (or inability) to distinguish between arguments against legal authority and government policy. Even more tellingly, Barak claims regarding his example that "it is inconceivable to argue that this is a political matter and not a legal one."[32] It might be inconceivable – but only to Barak. One could indeed easily conceive a scenario in which such legal authority is unclear, the law providing no distinct answer, making it an exclusively political question to be resolved one way or another by the political branches of government and from which a court keeps its

* In similar fashion, Barak says that "no one would argue" a claim of corruption in the *Reiner* case to be non-justiciable.

distance. Barak offers no explanation why leaving a legally ambiguous political matter in the hands of accountable government is so "inconceivable."

Back to his broader theory, we find a more severe flaw in Barak's very distinction between the two forms of justiciability and their ostensibly binary nature. Dotan argues that Barak's theory fails precisely because of the interdependency between the normative and institutional aspects of justiciability.[33] First, Barak presents normative justiciability as binary – either something does or does not fall under the purview of the law. But Dotan shows that justiciability is properly understood as a continuum or spectrum, with a wide set of factors determining the extent to which an action might be considered justiciable. For example, one intuitively understands that a clear-cut legal norm expressly applying to a specific government action strongly supports an argument for justiciability; while a vague and general quasi-legal norm provides weaker support. While Barak essentially argues that one can always find "some" legal norm that can apply, however vague or abstract, Dotan counters that this is precisely the point – the very vagueness of a legal norm might contribute to its non-justiciability, and would at least be a factor in setting the "degree" of justiciability on some sliding scale.

Second, and as a corollary to the above, Dotan stresses that the "institutional" and "normative" aspects are inexorably linked. Whether a court ought to decide a case depends a great deal on the strength of the initial so-called "normative" determination of justiciability, and vice versa, the degree that an issue is "justiciable" should obviously and significantly be influenced by whether judicial intervention is proper or appropriate. In other words, one can't unlink judicial prudence and the nature of the case being decided as though these were mutually exclusive. This seems hardly a controversial idea.*

But beyond all these critiques (and many others) lies the simple and straightforward objection that discarding "justiciability" undermines the very core of what a court is and what judges do. Despite its relative malleability the notion of "justiciability" reflects the assumption – or the imperative – that courts are a forum for adjudication based on law, and that there are vast swaths of private and public life which are beyond the legal frontier and therefore beyond judicial reach. It is expressed by Lord Jonathan Sumption when he writes that "[not] every human problem and every moral dilemma calls for a legal solution."[34] Claiming that a myriad decisions and determinations made by accountable government – such as whether or not to go to war or for what ends the public may spend its money – are automatically justiciable and subject to judicial supervision runs counter to our most basic understanding of democratic power, its sources and its exercise.

---

* As an aside, Dotan also points out that Barak's terminology is imprecise, as his claim for all-encompassing justiciability is analytical (i.e. "anything is either permitted or forbidden, therefore the law applies to all"), not normative (e.g., "the law should apply to all because…").

The *Ressler* decision stands out for other reasons quite separate from the substantive objections above. It serves as an early example of Barak's signature judicial style and modus operandi, largely adopted by his followers in the Court. First is its length and breadth, reading much more like a philosophical treatise than a binding judicial decision. The four previous rulings in *Becker* and *Ressler* consisted of thirty-one pages combined, averaging under eight pages each. The new *Ressler* decision lasts a startling eighty-six pages – all the more surprising considering the same legal territory had been exhaustively ploughed only a few years before. It is replete with theoretical musings and ramblings, such as this one: "A legal norm with no standards for its application is akin to a person with no shadow or a form without content, and no such thing exists in the world of law, which is all bodies and shadows, and forms encompassing content."[35] Second, as in numerous other cases, Barak presents his radical decision in the case as consistent with the Court's current trend and as a natural step forward. As Weill observes, "Barak asserted that the *Ressler* decision was not revolutionary, but an evolutionary development," and indeed Barak "transformed Israeli public law in stages" while he "portrayed [each stage] as a mere constitutional evolution," despite the clearly revolutionary nature of his novel approach.[36]

Far more important is the (initially surprising) fact that the case was actually dismissed. Barak ruled that despite the issue being justiciable and the petitioners having shown standing, the Minister of Defense had acted lawfully and was within his authority to grant the draft exemption. Yet far from reflecting some measure of judicial restraint, the decision simply displays a more subtle (or "strategic") method of effectuating legal change, for which Barak and the Court are widely known.

Dismissing the case meant Barak could elaborate his universal theory and radically expand the threshold requirements without actual intervention (in this case), thus avoiding significant political and public backlash. From a legal standpoint Barak's entire discussion of justiciability and standing was irrelevant – he could simply have written, as the Court had in previous cases, that "even under the assumption the issue is justiciable and that standing is shown, the petition is dismissed on its merits" or something similar. The decision to spell out an entirely novel jurisprudential approach was a calculated one. It established a precedent (of sorts) adopting Barak's approach and laid the groundwork for future cases that would then treat the expansion of threshold requirements as settled law. As we shall later see, this is precisely what happened, not only generally but within the specific context of the Ultra-Orthodox draft exemption.

I add "of sorts" because in principle judicial philosophizing not material to the final case determination (not least when members of the panel don't agree on the legal theory supporting their joint outcome) would typically be considered *obiter dictum* and not part of binding precedent. Yet this didn't stop Barak and the Court from treating *Ressler* as the new golden standard for threshold requirements. Such was the two-pronged method employed by the Court on numerous occasions – using *dicta* (and even dissenting opinions) while dismissing cases, so as to fly well under the public radar despite breaking new legal ground and then later relying on the same *dicta* as if it were precedential.

After *Ressler*

The 1988 *Ressler* ruling fundamentally shifted the scope of judicial power in Israel from one moment to the next. A lack of standing or an issue being non-justiciable ceased to exist as an impediment to litigating public disputes at the heart of societal disagreement. Almost overnight the Court began adjudicating matters that were considered beyond its reach prior to *Ressler* and that are still seen as such in most other legal systems. Yoav Dotan describes the Court's jurisprudence on justiciability as being easily divided between the pre-*Ressler* and post-*Ressler* eras.[37] More broadly, the decision "reflects a deep ideological shift" in the Court's conception of its own role, and marked "a new era not only for judicial review in Israel but also for public and political life more generally."[38] Perhaps needless to say, the aftermath of *Ressler* saw an explosion of petitions and the colossal overburdening of the Supreme Court due to its immediate inundation with thousands of cases each year.

Issues and areas the Court had previously considered outside its purview now became the subject of routine review and intervention. These include internal Knesset parliamentary proceedings and administration, the legislative process itself, military policy and operations, review of clandestine (espionage) services, economic and welfare policy, agreements between political parties and candidates, foreign relations and diplomacy, executive appointments at the most senior levels of government, and public investigations or commissions of inquiry;[39] all of which are still typically considered non-justiciable or immune from judicial intervention in most jurisdictions.[40] To be clear, these are not the subjects of theoretical pronouncements by the Court regarding potential topics for judicial review, but are actual areas in which the Court regularly intervenes in hundreds (perhaps thousands) of cases over the course of decades.

This expansion of authority encompassed not only the area or type of issue open to review, but also which decision-making body or state organ was typically subject to review. Regarding the wholesale expansion of judicial review of the Government itself – that is, of the collective group of Cabinet ministers constituting the top tier of the Israeli executive branch – Dotan observes that the very judicial involvement in all forms of Israeli government decisions is "exceptional by any comparative measure."[41] What many of these decisions share in common is that "in almost no country on the face of the globe do such matters" arrive in court, as "they are considered to be non-justiciable or immune from judicial review." Nonetheless, the same matters are adjudicated regularly in Israeli courts.

In the context of hearing challenges to the appointment of senior officials within the executive government, Dotan remarks that "the Court's willingness to interfere in decisions to appoint or dismiss [high ranking officials] is… without equal in any other legal system" and that it brands the Court as "an outlier by any standard."[42] Over the years the Court has ventured to review the appointment of military Chiefs of Staff and high ranking military officers, the National Police Commissioner, Ministry Director Generals, the State Attorney, municipal mayors, and even government Ministers themselves. We shall explore this issue in detail in the next chapters.

Practical experience in the decades that followed *Ressler* does provide for some instructive insights. One such critical point regards the interplay between Standing and Justiciability. Simply put, a firm commitment to Standing would naturally prevent judicial review of a great many non-justiciable issues. More often than not, purely political decisions yield no distinct injured plaintiff, and thus no one would have Standing to bring a suit. The lack of Standing (i.e. the lack of a petitioner showing personal harm-in-fact) is a fairly reliable indicator that the issue is also non-justiciable. We might add that conversely, in a legal system with a weaker Standing requirement (allowing for "public" petitioners), any Justiciability constraints would have to be all the more stringent to avoid the court serving as an omnipotent adjudicator in all policy disagreements. Ironically, the Supreme Court indeed alluded to this in a number of pre-*Ressler* decisions, stating that a petitioner with clear and distinct standing could justify intervention in issues of a stronger political nature, and vice versa, ambiguous or weaker standing meant less basis for judicial intervention in political issues. *Ressler* inverted this logic entirely and coupled the abolishment of Standing with the expansion of justiciability.

A typical example is that of (inherently political) senior executive appointments. There is rarely a distinct injured party to bring a viable challenge, excluding perhaps an aggrieved runner-up. Think of the *Netanyahu* case – who is the "directly" injured party that could possibly have standing to sue? The same applies to a large range of political or non-legal issues which typically do not generate a discernible aggrieved party (think of diplomatic relations or broad economic policy). In this sense, an effective standing doctrine and a justiciability requirement work in tandem to prevent judicial intervention in inappropriate cases.

While the "public petitioner" was an exception that became the rule, the Court did develop a slew of "counter-exceptions" – instances in which a petitioner would not be granted Standing despite its broad expansion. Joshua Segev observes that due to their highly discretionary nature, such "counter-exceptions" end up yielding the worst of both worlds.[43] On the one hand the Court entertains petitions filed by virtually anyone with no discernible limit; while on the other, it can decide to suddenly enforce a stricter version of its Standing requirement whenever desired. For example, the Court has carved out such an exception – called "another's quarrel" – under which a petitioner will not have Standing if there is a clear and obvious plaintiff that chooses not to sue. The ostensible rationale is that if the genuine aggrieved party decides to not pursue legal action on their own behalf, then it would not be appropriate to allow an unrelated party to try and enforce the former's rights. Yet the Court has repeatedly ignored this exception when convenient (allowing uninvolved parties to file suit even if the clear aggrieved individual is not a named petitioner), with no clear explanation of when such exceptions are applied. The spasmodic use of these counter-exceptions creates an impression of inconsistency bordering on arbitrariness and non-impartiality.

Finally, an important point to threshold requirements regards the Court's coercive power unrelated to the ultimate merits and outcome of a case – merely entering the judicial orbit grants the Court effective methods to impose its will, even if the petition or appeal is ultimately dismissed. Two short examples, involving foreign policy and Cabinet decision-making, suffice to demonstrate the point. In 1999 the Government sought to evict a building known as "Orient House" – which at the time served as the de facto headquarters of the Palestine Liberation Organization in eastern Jerusalem. Because of the PLO's blatant support for terrorism, the Government declared its intention to forbid PLO activity in Orient House and to block further access to the building.

The moment the decision was announced (and eviction notices delivered to Orient House) the Supreme Court was petitioned in an effort to halt its implementation. In "one of the most activist moves in its history" (per Menny Mautner), the Court (Justice Dalia Dorner) issued a temporary injunction which enjoined the Government from implementing its decision.[44] The *Orient House* case demonstrates an important step in the expansion of the Court's authority to questions of pure foreign policy previously considered off-limits – the Government had clearly acted within its legal authority; objections were based on more abstract and vague arguments, and focused on Israel's diplomatic obligations following the Oslo Accords.

Yet perhaps more importantly, the case shows how the Court can leverage newfound "justiciability" for even the most meritless case. A few days after the injunction, the Government lost elections to their political rivals, who then rescinded the eviction order. The Court's temporary order had in fact managed to prevent implementation of the Government decision altogether. If the issue were deemed non-justiciable (as such foreign-policy issues were considered in the past), the Court could never have entertained the suit or granted a preliminary injunction. In other words, the abolition of justiciability empowers the Court to intervene in cases – and indeed, to thwart government action – even when the legal challenge is utterly unfounded and has no chance of success.

In the 2010 *Agenda* case, the Supreme Court issued a temporary injunction which forbade the Government (i.e., the Cabinet) from discussing an item on its agenda and from voting on the same item. The Government was slated to vote on a bill as a preliminary stage before proceeding through the legislative process, like all formal Government bills. A group of environmental organizations petitioned against the Government due to the proposed bill, which the former said they had not received sufficient time to analyze. The Court (Justice Elyakim Rubenstein) issued a temporary injunction against any "discussion" of the bill until further notice – effectively removing the bill from the Cabinet's agenda and prohibiting the Cabinet from debating the bill and from holding a vote.

Yoav Dotan described the injunction at the time as "one of the most far-reaching decisions in the Court's history" and "a precedent in the history of judicial activism in general." Dotan continued: "It is doubtful whether a court in any country ever dared to order its Government what should and what should not be on its agenda." The injunction stayed in place for a jaw-dropping six days until the Court was gracious enough to revoke it. Still reeling and under the realistic threat of another similar injunction, the Government folded and proposed an amended bill which addressed some of the objections raised by the petitioners. Similar to *Orient House*, the 2010 *Agenda* demonstrates the power of limitless justiciability. The agenda of the chief Executive body or Cabinet would typically be considered non-justiciable in any other jurisdiction – yet here, the expansion of justiciability allowed the Court to issue an injunction which ultimately coerced (or at least compelled) the Government to amend a piece of legislation, even though the actual legal case against the proposed bill was unfounded and unlikely to succeed.

The two cases of *Orient House* and *Agenda* illustrate the unprecedented and unparalleled expansion of justiciability both in terms of policy area (foreign affairs) and in terms of the body subjected to review (Cabinet agenda-setting). Further, the very fact of adjudication provided the Court with sufficient leverage to materially influence government policy, entirely regardless of the final case outcome. It's also worth noting that in both temporary injunctions, as is often the case elsewhere, the Court did not bother to explain – even in the most general terms – the prima facie legal basis for its decision.

Judicial review of non-justiciable issues brought by petitioners without standing will be demonstrated naturally through other cases discussed in the following chapters and throughout the book, such that we may forgo a comprehensive survey of examples. Often as not, an important case before the Court is only there in the first place thanks to the abolishment of threshold requirements.

Objections to the effective abolishment of threshold requirements are grounded in a variety of considerations and mirror the justifications for these requirements in the first place. I've alluded above to the separation of powers and to public faith in the judiciary. In addition to the judicial burden and the court's own ability to function under a deluge of petitions, one might consider the effect on other branches of government. Chief Justice Meir Shamgar warned in his semi-concurring opinion in *Ressler*, that "functioning governing systems – including a functioning judiciary – will not be sustainable if all the political problems begin making their way to the Court to be assessed according to legal standards."[45] Shamgar further cautioned against a "a concentration of [judicial] authority" annulling "the ability of other branches to function." We will revisit *Ressler* in the next chapter within the context of "extreme unreasonableness," with contemporary objections to limitless justiciability articulated by towering figures such as Justice Moshe Landau and Justice Menachem Elon.

*

What are the limits to judicial power? What mechanisms, principles and processes might be considered effective restraints on any court? Typical answers might suggest a selections process which ensures that judges appointed to the bench reflect a variety of approaches (including one of restraint), so that a court is not dominated by a single homogenous group and remains indirectly in tune with public sentiment; or a court hierarchy in which cases are filtered through a series of tribunals and are subject to scrutiny and review before ultimate adjudication at the system apex. Further answers might include the text of the law itself which contains words, meanings and intentions to which judges owe a duty of fidelity and faithful adherence. They might prescribe threshold requirements which keep inherently socio-political issues and general complaints against the government out of the courtroom, requirements which ensure that courts are resolving actual, legal, disputes.

For the Israeli legal system some of these never really existed while others lie in tatters after being shredded by judicial decisions. We now turn to examine the manner in which the Supreme Court exercised this unadulterated power in the absence of meaningful limitations, and to the substantive doctrines the Court developed to further its agenda of ultimate supremacy.

Chapter 5

Extreme Unreasonableness

The Court as Chief Executive

"*Using the standard of reasonableness, the High Court of Justice breached the boundaries of law.*"
— Prof. Menachem Mautner[1]

Following Israel's total withdrawal from the Gaza Strip in 2005, Palestinian terrorist groups (Hamas chief among them) rapidly increased their use of rocket attacks aimed at towns and villages in southern Israel. Both by design and due to their indiscriminate nature these rocket attacks mostly targeted civilian sites including schools, hospitals and residences. The primary defensive measure against such attacks at the time (the Iron Dome system had not yet been developed) was to run for the nearest bomb shelter. Civilians typically had fifteen to thirty seconds to find cover between the warning siren and the rocket impact.

In July of 2006 the Israeli Government decided to construct adequate shelter facilities in all schools near the Gaza border, in a joint effort involving the ministries of Defense, Education and Finance. The prevailing method for doing so was called "sheltered spaces" and involved the calculated reinforcement of specific rooms or areas (such as classrooms and hallways) and converting them into effective bomb shelters, while other classrooms and areas were not reinforced. The logic of "sheltered spaces" was that any pupil or staff member was always within a short running distance from such a "sheltered space" and could arrive in one safely before a rocket strikes the school.

In a case which became known as *Wasser*, a number of parents and other parties challenged this government policy in the High Court of Justice. Aside demanding that the existing policy be fully implemented on schedule (the reinforcement project had suffered a series of delays), the petitioners demanded that the government abandon the "sheltered spaces" method and reinforce *all* classrooms. The government in turn defended the policy as being both effective (in that it was sufficient to protect the school community from harm) and that it was cost-efficient, citing the staggering cost of having to reinforce all school classrooms (estimated in the hundreds of millions of Shekels in the near-term and possibly billions in the long-term). The government also warned of far-reaching consequences for broader defense and national security considerations, not least considering the possibility that rocket attack ranges could gradually expand to threaten more and more schools.* From a legal standpoint this was a question of pure executive policy – there were no statutory rules establishing or defining the government's obligation to provide bomb shelters in schools (though the government did have a general legal obligation to provide public education services). From a national security and financial standpoint the decision fell within the much broader strategic dilemmas of addressing such rocket attacks and of weighing various measures (both defensive and offensive, short-term and long-term), their relative costs and risks, and trade-offs inherent in any resource-allocation decision.

In May of 2007 the Supreme Court accepted the petitions and ordered that the government discard its "sheltered spaces" policy and provide full reinforcement to all classrooms (within the designated area bordering Gaza). In a short ruling authored by Justice Dorit Beinisch the Court did not argue that the government had exceeded or lacked legal authority, nor that the government considered irrelevant factors or failed to consider material factors. Rather, the Court held the policy to be "unreasonable,"[2] in that "the balancing between professional-security factors and budgetary factors" performed by the government "deviates significantly from the range of reasonableness."[3] In other words, the government had acted within its statutory authority and had weighed all relevant factors, but had reached the wrong conclusion – which the Court proceeded to correct. In doing so, the Court dictated de facto proactive national security executive policy with no firm legal basis beyond what is "reasonable." Menny Mautner called this "one of the most activist decisions in the Court's history."[4]

*

We now arrive at "extreme unreasonableness" – what may well be the most famous among all the novel doctrines developed and applied by the Supreme Court, and the one most often associated with the Court's activism. The *Wasser* ruling above joins thousands of similar decisions which apply the abstract standard of "reasonableness" to supervise governmental decisions and policy on their merits, at the highest level of the executive branch regardless of subject matter or context. Many consider the Court's "reasonableness" standard to be the original and true judicial revolution in Israel, surpassing even the "constitutional revolution" (to be discussed in Part III) or coming in at a close second. Yoav Dotan argues that "the tectonic shifts of [Israeli] public law occurred in the 1980s with the administrative revolution" of which the reasonableness standard is the cornerstone.[5] It is, to be sure, one of the most formidable legal tools employed by the Supreme Court to review – and to exercise – governmental power.

In this chapter we will dissect, analyze and demystify the "reasonableness"

---

* Needless to say, non-justiciability was not even raised.

doctrine – how it came about, what it does and does not include, its uses and implications, and much more besides. In previous chapters we have thus far examined important features tangential to the law – the Court's structural and institutional environment, its approach to interpreting legal texts, and threshold requirements as barriers to adjudication. Building on all these but also inescapably linked to their advent and development, we now turn to the monumental – and uniquely Israeli – substantive legal doctrine of "extreme unreasonableness."

Governing Within the Law

Review of executive government action by a disinterested and impartial court of law is among the oldest and most elementary attributes of a civilized and liberal society. Since the days of *habeas corpus* we have recognized and adopted judicial review as a mechanism to ensure the lawful use of governmental power.* At its core is the principle that the government must act lawfully and within the legal authority granted to it. The vast and omnipotent government is for the most part not directly accountable to the public; even if it were, such accountability is insufficient to prevent and mitigate immediate irreparable individual harm caused by illegal governmental action. As such there must be a mechanism by which someone harmed by unlawful government action can demand additional review – a hearing – to air their grievance, make their case, and receive remedy or relief as appropriate. The rules controlling executive action are typically (but not always) called "administrative law," while the process by which such action is challenged in court may be called "administrative judicial review" or some variation thereof.

Yet such judicial review is founded on – and limited by – the key dual concepts of legality and restraint. The government is entitled to make decisions and formulate policy that some find objectionable or that even cause harm of some form or another – indeed it inevitably must do so. When reviewing governmental action the court therefore does not ask whether a given decision is wise, or proper, or optimal. Rather the court asks a single overarching question – was the government authorized by law to do so, to make such a decision, to formulate such a policy, to act the way it did? Is this action within the legal authority granted or delegated by statute or by some other lawful source? At the same time, the court exercises restraint so as not to encroach upon valid executive power – it does not presume to reconsider or re-decide the governmental action in question (it does not perform *de novo* review) as though the judges were replacing the executive government themselves; judicial review is not an appeal against governmental action per se. One renowned British scholar of administrative law, H.W.R. Wade, put the point succinctly: "The court's duty is to confine itself strictly to the question of legality. If the administrative authority acts within its power and according to the law, it is no business of the court to interfere."[6] Wade

* In this sense, judicial supervision of criminal law is merely a subset of administrative judicial review, one that is simply triggered automatically whenever the government exercises its specific enforcement powers.

successfully conveyed the overall spirit of the common-law legal administrative tradition which Israel inherited from Great Britain.

Conventional grounds for judicial review clearly reflect this notion. Chief among causes for judicial intervention is illegality (whether inadvertent or deliberate) or "exceeding authority" (*ultra vires*), jointly considered by most to be the "mother" of all administrative judicial review. Other grounds are adjacent to illegality and inquire whether government had exercised its authority in a manner consistent with the power granted to it. These often overlap and may include arbitrariness or irrationality; severe procedural flaws; discrimination; ignoring material factors or weighing immaterial factors; and other similar grounds. Common to all these is the recognition that governing, with all it entails, is left to the (executive) government.

Israeli administrative law generally matched this traditional approach, especially tracking English common-law doctrines. Much like English law at the time, Israeli administrative jurisprudence was (and remains) statutorily undefined – Section 15 of "Basic Law: The Judiciary" grants the Supreme Court broad authority to review government action but does little else to clarify or guide the legal framework for such oversight. It was rather left to the courts to develop an administrative jurisprudence on a case-by-case basis that was therefore very much the creation of the Supreme Court itself.

Yoav Dotan described the Court's original approach thus: "Judicial review by courts in Israel relied on the classical *vires* doctrine" to ensure that the government "doesn't exceed the mandate granted by legislature," and therefore the "central grounds for evaluating legality" was that of *ultra vires*.[7] The adherence to legal authority as the core basis for judicial review made sense especially considering that the grounds for such review were (and still are) themselves not defined by statutory law – meaning that judicial intervention in executive action had to derive its legitimacy from other firm and solid sources.

Michal Shaked, a prominent government litigator and legal biographer, summarizes that the Court "reiterated time and again" that it was not hearing appeals from administrative decisions, that it was not replacing its discretion with that of a duly authorized agency,[*] and that it was not engaging in *de novo* review.[8] The Court limited its review to a handful of traditional, familiar, recognized grounds of review, and refused to intervene without the clear demonstration of such grounds. In a long series of cases the Court recognized the executive's inherent authority to govern (within the law), stating that it does not evaluate the "effectiveness and wisdom" of government action, does not mandate which (legal) measures the government must employ to achieve a stated aim, and does not intervene in the way an agency manages its financial affairs, along with other

[*] The typical term in Hebrew is "*Rashut*," which may refer to a governmental entity, body, authority, agency, branch, office, department, or even official. It generally means any organ performing government functions, and we will use these terms more or less interchangeably.

rules of a similar nature.[9] An instructive expression of the Court's approach can be found in one of its earliest (1948) opinions:

> "The Supreme Court... is not an appeal court for appealing against the actions of government institutions or government officials... As long as the executive branch acts within the boundaries set by the law, it is not within the Court's authority to examine the nature of the action."[10]

And another example in a 1960 opinion by Chief Justice Zussman:

> "This Court's supervision over the administrative authority shall necessarily be exclusively legal, that is, such supervision is limited to the question of whether the authority exceeded its power as defined by statute... While the effectiveness and wisdom of any exercise of discretion – as opposed to its legality – can not be examined by this Court."[11]

This is not to say that the Court was in any way timid in its review of governmental action. Parallel to its permissive standing requirement,* the Court positioned itself as a critical check on governmental power when it came to protection of individual liberties and civil rights – even in the absence of any statutory basis. In other words, the Court was willing to compromise on its commitment to limited "legality" review when it came to government action impacting classic liberal democratic rights, such as freedom of expression and freedom of occupation, despite no existing legislation explicitly enshrining such rights. In this way the Court established itself as an "activist" champion of individual rights exercising spirited judicial review in their service, but also as a "restrained" court generally maintaining the aforementioned focus on legal authority, adhering to established grounds for review, and refraining from intervention in valid executive discretion.

Traditional (Wednesbury) Unreasonableness

What happens when a government action conforms to the letter of the law, and seemingly doesn't fall afoul of any conventional grounds for judicial review, yet is patently "outrageous"? This, in a nutshell, is the standard known as "extreme unreasonableness," or what we will simply call "reasonableness." Behind this standard is the idea that an act may conceivably be outside the bounds of legal authority even when it technically seems to follow the letter of statutory law. A decision may be unreasonable, and therefore illegal, if authority is exercised in a manner clearly never imagined or intended by the original source of that authority (usually, the legislature).

Many jurisdictions have developed some form or other of reasonableness review. The leading and most well-known common-law decision articulating this

* Allowing claims of any harmed interest without showing infringement of a specific legal right (see previous chapter).

standard was in the 1948 *Wednesbury* case in the United Kingdom, regarding restrictions on the operation of a movie theater imposed by a local municipal authority. In that case, the court recognized there were exceptional circumstances in which it could interfere with executive discretion, if a decision was "so unreasonable that no reasonable authority could ever have come to it,"[12] echoing prior rulings that described "something so absurd that no sensible person could ever dream that it lay within the powers of the authority." A later case provided the definitive articulation of the Wednesbury standard as applying to a decision "so outrageous in its defiance of logic or accepted moral standards that no sensible person who had applied his mind to the question to be decided could have arrived at it."[13]

Critically, and despite its potential ambiguity, the underlying logic of "unreasonableness" remains tethered to the grounds of illegality. A decision is not unreasonable merely because it is "outrageous," but rather because it exceeds the authority originally granted by statute, in the sense that the legislature had never conceived it being applied in such a way. Lord Greene in *Wednesbury* begins by emphasizing that a court "can only interfere with an act of executive authority if it be shown that the authority has contravened the law," and that such challenges against executive action can only prevail "in a strictly limited class of case." Lord Greene stresses that when exercised "within the four corners" of the law, executive discretion is "an absolute one and cannot be questioned in any court of law." H.W.R. Wade describes the unifying principle of unreasonableness to be "that powers must be confined within the true scope and policy of the [legislative] act."[14] *Wednesbury* notes the example of a red-haired teacher being dismissed merely for having red hair, while another common example is that of a Prime Minister appointing his horse as a cabinet member. In both examples an authorizing statute may not have explicitly mandated valid cause for teacher dismissal or that ministers be human beings; yet such a decision could be considered outrageous, *never intended by the original statute* and outside the scope of power granted by statute, and therefore legally unreasonable.

In principle and in practice, adherence to both the "outrageous" character of a decision and to its gross violation of original statutory authority sets an extremely high bar for reasonableness review. The court in *Wednesbury* held that proving unreasonableness would "require something overwhelming" (indeed, the challenge to the restrictions in that case was dismissed). In most instances the standard is characterized as "extreme" or "radical" unreasonableness, reflecting an "outrageous" or "absurd" action so beyond the pale that it constitutes a departure from legal authority, employing language like "no sensible person," etc. This of course makes sense – unreasonableness is essentially a problematic and objectionable demand for judicial intervention in executive discretion despite there being no clear violation of the law. And indeed, in most jurisdictions and to this day, unreasonableness is universally considered to be a last resort serving as a far-fetched and unlikely grounds for review, among the least likely arguments to succeed in court.

A point worth clarifying is that unreasonableness is easily confused with other similar grounds for judicial review, especially irrationality or arbitrariness, though these are analytically distinct. "Irrationality" means no logical or factual relationship between a measure taken and its stated or desired outcome (e.g., painting all sidewalks blue in order to reduce inflation). "Arbitrariness" means a random decision amounting to de facto abdication of a decision-making role (e.g., rolling dice to decide the central bank's interest rate). While there might be some overlap, the latter two are relatively defined, and most often irrational or arbitrary actions can be easily categorized as such. They have a relatively clear meaning, such that we know what "arbitrary" means and we have some basis on which to resolve disagreement regarding its application. On the other hand, the scope of unreasonableness – some "outrageous" action that no reasonable person could possibly choose – is far less clear and potentially more broad, and an unreasonable decision may be neither irrational nor arbitrary. To be sure, some jurisdictions do indeed treat these various standards interchangeably, but as we shall see, the Israeli version of "unreasonableness" cannot be mistaken for irrational or arbitrary decisions. Indeed, Justice Aharon Barak himself later emphasizes that reasonableness (especially in its Israeli form) "is not just a matter of logic or rationality."[15]

Finally, the use of a reasonableness standard is naturally not consistent across jurisdictions or even within them. At times it is used as a catch-all term to refer to an assortment of more recognized grounds, such as irrationality or weighing of immaterial factors. Even when employed in its proper sense described above, it is often not considered an exclusive or sufficiently independent grounds for review on its own, but rather is used as a supplement to other well-established grounds. For example, perhaps a showing of extreme unreasonableness might bolster an argument of discrimination justifying judicial review, and might even tip the scales in favor of intervention, but could not do so were it not for the more mature and firm basis for review (discrimination).

Traditional unreasonableness is, then, a strictly limited doctrine for judicial interference with executive discretion in the most extreme circumstances; a "Hail Mary" to be used by litigants when no other grounds are available to them, and enforced by the court only in the rarest of instances involving "outrageous" conduct. More generally, judicial intervention in executive discretion is a disputed and difficult area of law in almost any jurisdiction, often with no clear-cut formula for its application. Still, as we shall now see, the Israeli innovation of unreasonableness is completely different and bears no resemblance to even the most vague and permissive established grounds for judicial review, in any place and under any name.

The Balancing Act – Israeli Unreasonableness

Despite its misleading name and innocuous appearance, the Israeli "unreasonableness" grounds for judicial review of executive action is another creature entirely, not remotely resembling its namesake of Wednesbury or conventional reasonableness. Dotan describes the difference as "categorical."[16] Diverging radically from its English common-law origins and from the Court's own prior practice, the Israeli version of reasonableness review abandons any focus on legal authority and is divorced from the condition of "outrageousness." As we shall presently see, the reasonableness doctrine is nothing more or less than the utter subjection of all executive power, without exception, to judicial whim, whereby judges "weigh" and "balance" any conceivable government decision on its merits, and deem it lawful or unlawful as they see fit. Its story begins, of course, in the early 1980s and with Justice Aharon Barak.

The 1980 *Yellow Pages* case regarded a decision by a public (governmental) broadcaster to renew a contract for advertisement services. At that time the government had general discretion to enter into private commercial contracts as it desired – among other things, there was no legal obligation to hold a public, competitive bidding process.* The Court's own precedent was that it does not interfere in commercial relationships maintained by the State. The decision nonetheless earned a Supreme Court challenge, the petitioners arguing that the government ought to have offered the contract to additional bidders.

The Court dismissed the petition and ruled in favor of the government, yet the three Justices disagreed on their reasoning for doing so. In a landmark concurring opinion Justice Barak articulated a novel reasonableness doctrine applying to all government action, outlined through four core "propositions": 1. That unreasonableness is an independent, standalone grounds for invalidation of executive discretion; 2. That it is evaluated by "objective" standards (meaning, it is determined by the court); 3. That such unreasonableness must be "substantive" or "extreme" to justify invalidation, and; 4. That an unreasonable decision is one in which the executive did not attribute "proper weight" to the various interests and factors under consideration.[17] Barak explains that the purpose of such unreasonableness review is twofold. The first is to properly or correctly "balance interests" in society; the second is to provide a basis for broader judicial intervention in executive discretion. Barak's requirement that all government action be "reasonable" had already been presented briefly in the prior 1979 *Contractors Center* case,[18] but his *Yellow Pages* opinion elaborated and elucidated his theory in a much more detailed, comprehensive and explicit way. Much like the revolution in threshold requirements, the *Yellow Pages* decision was not precipitated by any substantial change in statutory law.

A key feature at the heart of the new unreasonableness doctrine was the "range of reasonableness." There is, Barak explains, in any given scenario, a variety of possible decisions which fall within the "range of reasonableness" and are therefore lawful; while any decision outside said range could be invalidated as "extremely" or "substantively" unreasonable. The range itself is defined in each

---

* Such an obligation was formally enacted by statute in 1992.

individual case by the court. To be clear, this range is typically far more limited and restricted than that which legal (statutory) authority might permit.

Even more central to this conception of reasonableness is the idea of "balancing interests" (or "weighing factors" and similar phrases). In order for an executive decision or action to fall within the range of reasonableness, it must give "proper" or "due" weight to the various factors under consideration. The government must correctly balance the relative and competing interests affected and involved by any decision, while failure to do so will result in judicial intervention. There is no universal test to define what such proper balancing might look like – it is decided from case to case.

While occasionally modified and honed over the years, the unreasonableness standard as roughly defined in *Yellow Pages* has remained the dominant grounds for review of government action by the Supreme Court, both in principle and in practice.[19] (The term of "reasonableness" and its variations will henceforth refer to the unique Israeli version unless stated otherwise.)

The *Yellow Pages* Revolution

In his *Yellow Pages* opinion Barak maintained that the novel unreasonableness standard followed previous Supreme Court rulings and was consistent with broader established notions of reasonableness – though both claims are demonstrably false. As shown above, prior to *Yellow Pages* the Court adhered to judicial review based on *ultra-vires* (lack of legal authority) and refrained from interfering with pure executive discretion or from evaluating the merits of government policy. And of course, "reasonableness" as all-encompassing de-novo review by judicial "balancing" of executive considerations stands completely at odds with the conventional Wednesbury standard. In other words, the dual cornerstone of classic "unreasonable" review was always the link to illegality and the "outrageous" nature of the executive decision – yet it is precisely these two elements which the Israeli unreasonableness standard discards as one does a pair of old socks.

Barak's claim of adherence to preexisting norms is easily refuted by another opinion in the *Yellow Pages* decision – that of Chief Justice Moshe Landau, who recognized the revolutionary nature and inherent perils of Barak's new approach. Objecting both to the new theory itself and to its presentation as reflecting established doctrine, Landau states the obvious – that Barak's formulation "does not represent the law as is," and that it is simply judicial replacement of executive discretion. Landau warns that an ostensibly "objective" test evaluating the reasonableness of government decisions under any circumstances will quickly lead to "material de-novo review, as if the Court were considering the correctness of the decision anew," thus "compelling the Court to perform the role of the public official."[20] He then reiterates that "this is a role the Court never took upon itself," and rejects "a formula which could entangle the Court in checking the wisdom and effectiveness" of administrative decisions. Stressing the dangers of quasi-legal limitations on executive discretion, Landau cautions that even though the government "does not always excel" in all things, a cure will not be found in "the introduction of sweeping and rigid legal concepts."

A similar view (approvingly cited by Landau) had already been voiced exactly seven months earlier by Justice Menachem Elon in the *Contractors Center* ruling, where Barak had first mentioned his approach to reasonableness. That case involved circumstances almost identical to those of *Yellow Pages* – a challenge to a government contractual engagement without a competitive bidding process. In his concurring opinion Elon objected to the "excessive expansion of rules and grounds for our intervention in the actions of the public authority."[21] He opposed the very effort at announcing broad, categorical rules (as Barak was attempting to do) instead of the established common law approach – the gradual emergence of rules and principles born of incrementally resolving individual disputes. To the substance of Barak's new doctrine, Elon warned of "throwing the Court's doors wide open to a multitude of petitions," which would primarily frustrate and impede the executive's ability to govern. Efficient government aside, Elon recalled (in turn quoting Landau in a prior ruling) that supervision of executive action is also found "in the parliamentary responsibility of the Government and its Ministers before the Knesset, and ultimately before the general public" – dismissing the implicit claim that only the Court could serve as a viable check on administrative power, and hinting at the democratic deficit of Barak's approach.

The novel *Yellow Pages* case drew some academic criticism as well. A 1982 law review article written by prominent government attorney Michal Shaked responded directly to the ruling and comprehensively dismantled the emergent unreasonableness standard developed there. Shaked rejects Barak's claims to conformity, demonstrating (among other points) that previous uses of "reasonableness" by the Supreme Court typically referred to a variety of other grounds (such as mistake in fact or bad faith), that it was never used as an independent cause for judicial review, and that it was only employed in the context of protecting distinct legal rights. The new form of judicial review articulated by Barak "expands the use of reasonableness to new circumstances and for new purposes"[22], entirely different from those previously contemplated by the Court. Shaked painstakingly shows how Barak's reasonableness can rely neither on previous Court rulings, nor on theoretical (or comparative) understandings of the doctrine, ultimately stating that it is "severed" from known administrative law and calling it "revolutionary."[23]

Using a similar phrase, Yoav Dotan emphasizes the "severance" of reasonableness from legal authority (or *ultra-vires*), a link (as noted above) considered to be a staple of unreasonableness both in theory and in local jurisprudence. Prior Supreme Court decisions that employed reasonableness in some form or other were invariably "derived from illegality" – that is, their logic was based on the question of whether the legislator had intended to authorize the Executive to act in a certain (perhaps even an unreasonable) way. Following *Yellow Pages*, this link between reasonableness and statutory authority "disappeared almost entirely from the Court's rhetoric,"[24] which "time and again" asserted a hard distinction between authority and reasonableness. Put more bluntly by Mautner, the Court "completely abandoned" its original approach focusing on legal authority.[25]

Importantly, despite Barak's occasional perfunctory reference to "extreme" executive action meriting judicial intervention, his reasonableness standard includes no such requirement. The judicially-defined "range of reasonableness" can exclude a host of decisions and policies with no "outrageous" element whatsoever, and Barak explicitly refuses to condition judicial intervention on a "radical" departure from the aforesaid range, questioning whether a "substantial" departure would be sufficient for review. As Rivka Weill observes, "subsequent law developed in the direction" of the latter,[26] and indeed over the years the Court's terminology subtly shifted from citing "radical" unreasonableness to mere "substantial" unreasonableness, ultimately forgoing such categorization altogether.

In other words, the Court removed the only distinctive feature unreasonableness review ever had – that of an "overwhelming" action discernibly beyond the pale. This is why Dotan distinguishes between conventional "reasonableness as outrageousness," and the uniquely Israeli "reasonableness as balancing."[27] Correspondingly, the permitted range of reasonable decisions might be as broad or constricted as deemed appropriate by the judge, and could even be limited to a single solitary "reasonable" decision to the exclusion of all others ("at times... the solution the Court sees as desirable is also the only solution a reasonable authority would adopt.")[28]

Indeed, Barak's own definition of reasonableness in *Yellow Pages* and the preceding *Contractors Case* was inconsistent and often undisciplined, confusingly alternating between the rigid classic formulation ("so unreasonable that no reasonable authority" etc.) and his flexible novel version ("unreasonable balancing of factors" etc.). Shaked objected to precisely such misleading terminological manipulation as a "dangerous" combination of familiar form with obscure substance, and warned that such blurring might lead, "deliberately or inadvertently," to the "unchecked expansion" of judicial interference in executive discretion.[29] Over a decade later in his essay on "The Reasonableness of Politics," Mautner analyzed the "sophisticated use of an array of legal concepts" which the Court "endowed with new meaning," all with the aim to "confer upon itself new and unconventional powers regarding administrative decisions."[30]

It's worth stressing the subtle, almost imperceptible manipulation employed by Barak regarding the core definition of any reasonableness test. The conventional approach defines an unreasonable decision as one at which no reasonable authority could possibly arrive; Barak's version requires that government acts in the same manner as would a reasonable authority. While similar at a glance and sharing a "reasonable authority," these two formulations are in fact diametrically opposed. The former implies a wide berth given to executive action and assumes the rarity of genuinely unreasonable action; the latter implies that executive action must match a narrowly defined hypothetical (judicial) estimation of reasonable conduct. Put differently, the conventional view is negative, envisions *un*reasonable conduct as the basis for comparison, and suggests a distant scenario which the government must *avoid*; the Barak view is positive, envisions specific reasonable conduct from the outset, and mandates a concrete standard to which the government must *conform*. This is not a trivial semantic difference, but rather a fundamental reversal of perspective.

Michal Shaked points out another important departure from theory and practice, in the shift from legal rights to "public interests." Traditional Israeli reasonableness, in the rare instances it was invoked, regarded an individual legal right unjustifiably harmed by government action. In this sense even an unreasonable action could only be challenged in the service of protecting a legally enforceable right.* In such cases the court may apply established and known methods of legal analysis concerning enforcement of rights against the government. But the novel reasonableness of *Yellow Pages* goes far beyond this by balancing not only rights but also (and even primarily) general "interests" which the executive must consider. Never mind that the defining distinction between a legal right and an abstract "interest" lies in the enforceability of the former and unenforceability of the latter. Shaked highlights the legal tools developed by courts to adjudicate harm to legal rights, and stresses the lack of such tools in the context of balancing "interests."† Considering there is no conventional framework for such balancing of "interests," the result is "a court which determines disputes according to the opinions and intuitions of justice" of individual judges.[31] Unsurprisingly, over the years, the Court added both "principles" and "values" (and not only "interests") as abstract factors being balanced, further demonstrating the departure from traditional balancing of enforceable rights.

Another feature of the new reasonableness standard was its inescapable focus on the outcome (and therefore, the content) of executive discretion and not on the process by which it has arrived. This is because in such cases the Court typically has only the decision itself as a basis for its review – there are rarely external (or objective) indicators which might demonstrate the actual "weighing" performed by the government. The Court assures us that reasonableness entails only re-examination of the government's "weighing" of competing factors and not of the merits of the decision itself, but this is a patent fiction. For one thing, the "balancing" or "weighing" of competing interests is metaphorical to begin with, and even in real time (when presumably performed by the government) evades any serious quantification. All the more so when such "balancing" is performed

---

* In the *Contractors Center* case, Justice Elon makes the point that the petitioners may have an interest that the government choose their suppliers by competitive bidding, but do not have a legal right to demand it.

† Mautner later makes a similar point by dividing the Court's use of reasonableness into separate categories, some utilizing established legal principles, while others lacking any such tools.

retroactively by a court, whereby judges try to artificially deduce the initial "balancing" which led to the ultimate decision or policy. In a later critique of reasonableness, Justice Asher Grunis dubbed it a form of reverse-engineering: "One cannot ignore that a determination of unreasonableness is made primarily by examining the final product... The use of weights as metaphor... often serves, it seems, as a guise for disagreement with the outcome" of such weighing.[32] In other words, a claim to review the validity of pre-decision interest-balancing inevitably amounts to review of the final outcome and its content. This means the Court does exactly what it says it would never do – reviewing the substantive content of a governmental decision or policy.

Regarding the scope (or limits) of such application in terms of the identity of the deciding body or the subject matter and type of such decisions, Barak presents the new rule in *Yellow Pages* as broadly applicable to any administrative authority and to all administrative judgment (or discretion), without elaborating beyond his repeated declarations that "exercise of discretion by an administrative authority must be reasonable."[33] One could in fact conceive of many such distinctions within a theory of reasonableness review. However, subsequent developments and iterations of this doctrine by Barak and the Court clarify that it applies in the broadest sense imaginable – to *any* government decision or action by *any* public official or organ, from the most trivial to the most consequential, from the most inferior clerk to the most senior governmental figures, from ad hoc bureaucratic determinations to broad policy formulation and quasi-legislative regulations. This all-encompassing approach is later spelled out by the Court in the most explicit terms and becomes especially significant in the link between reasonableness and justiciability, to which we will soon return.

One must also keep in mind that reasonableness, on its own terms, only need be used in the event other grounds for review are unavailable. That is, by definition, when the Court employs reasonableness to intervene in executive discretion it does so because the government action in question does not run afoul of any traditional or conventional grounds such as ultra-vires, arbitrariness, procedural flaws, and so on. When one encounters a Court decision invoking unreasonableness, one may assume that there was no other firm or clear-cut basis for judicial intervention (if there was, it would have been applied instead of reasonableness). The significance of this point will become apparent when considering the sheer prevalence of judicial interference in governmental discretion based on reasonableness alone.

Finally, much like the later *Ressler* ruling, *Yellow Pages* is an important case study in Barak's (and the Court's) broader *modus operandi*, showcasing a pattern which will repeat itself many times. Ground-breaking revolutionary doctrine is presented as minor and natural evolution (both in theory and practice); familiar terminology is employed to suggest contiguity with previous decisions while used in utterly different senses; and the radical shift in jurisprudence is performed under the radar – introduced in an inconspicuous case far from public attention, discussed as moot *dicta* immaterial to the final result (Barak held that the government's decision was reasonable and lawful), and dismissing the petition so as to maintain an impression of restraint while avoiding political backlash. Weill notes Barak's "long game," writing that "affirming the [government's] decision while still laying substantive grounds for future intervention" served numerous "tactical advantages."[34] Perhaps most striking is the characteristic denial – deliberate or subconscious, explicit or implicit – of the gravity of the new doctrine or rule being introduced. Reading *Yellow Pages* can almost leave one with the impression that the unreasonableness doctrine is a pedestrian, almost trivial development of administrative law, and not a legal earthquake upending the Israeli legal system and governmental order.

Governing Government

We have credibly established that the reasonableness doctrine presented in *Yellow Pages* and subsequently adopted – hook, line and sinker – by the Supreme Court had no basis in existing Israeli law and jurisprudence, nor does it remotely resemble its namesake of Wednesbury unreasonableness on which it purports to rely. However, such analytical criticism, which is historical, doctrinal and at times technical and even formalistic, fails to capture the true flaws and devastating effects of the novel reasonableness doctrine. After reading the above section one might understandably ask: So what? The Court developed its own standard for review of executive action. Maybe its claims to conformity with preexisting law and with conventional approaches were inaccurate. What of it?

We therefore turn to consider the true objections to unreasonableness, on both political and legal grounds, in principle and in practice, which must be articulated fully and forcefully.

First, most egregious and towering above all other objections: the unreasonableness doctrine constitutes a wholesale, blatant violation of democratic government and of the separation of powers. The executive branch, whether elected directly or appointed by elected officials, is charged with formulating and applying policy and is authorized to do so by law and by public mandate. Its action is supervised by a host of mechanisms, foremost among them the elected parliament and the electorate itself. In carrying out its duty the Executive exercises vast discretion and judgment, both professional and ideological (that is, reflecting specific value-based policy preferences). Any exercise of discretion routinely consists of "balancing" an array of interests, factors, and values. Critically, "values" are not only one subset of considerations material to a decision, but rather they inform the very weighing of competing factors – that is, the determination of which factors to consider and how much weight each receives in a final decision is itself deeply informed by values, by personal preference, by priorities, by morals.

Such balancing performed by the executive *is the very essence of governing.* It is the core function reserved to the executive branch. It's the thing which government does and is authorized to do by law, which the public expects it to do, on which its ability to function depends, and for which it is accountable. Balancing of competing factors, determining their relative weight and finally selecting a decision or policy, one which best reflects an elected government's preferred priorities and values and those of the electorate which put the government in power – this is all precisely what government is for. This is not only the duty and authority of executive government, but also its privilege, prerogative and purview. There is no government without free exercise of judgment, and there is no judgment without balancing factors and determining the outcome. The "balancing of interests" and the very act of governing are synonymous, they are identical, they are one and the same.

By subjecting lawful administrative and executive decisions to limitless judicial review under the shockingly vacuous standard of "reasonableness" and by second-guessing whether "proper" weight was accorded to competing factors, the Supreme Court denies the government its most basic and most fundamental function. Worse still, it appropriates and arrogates that same power to itself. A judicial determination of "reasonable" government policy by "balancing interests" and selecting an outcome reflecting their "proper" relative weight simply replaces executive authority with judicial authority and transfers the core powers of governing to a miniscule group of lawyers on the bench. Barak concedes that "the final resolution is in the hands of the court, because it is the court and none other that determines what decision a reasonable authority might make."[35] Elsewhere Barak declared that "the reasonable person is the Court itself" (though he hurriedly clarifies this to be a metaphor).[36]

Unreasonableness is thus revealed to be little more than a quasi-legal euphemism for decisions and policies which the Court dislikes or to which it objects; reasonable decisions are ones which the Court permits. As combatively phrased by Justice Grunis: "When the Court interferes with a decision due to unreasonableness, it certainly replaces the government's judgment with its own."[37] Menny Mautner's simple summary of reasonableness says it well: "the Court… has resorted to examining administrative decisions on their merits, rather than according to legal criteria. This type of activism is indefensible."[38] No amount of legal acrobatics and judicial sophistry can hide this plain and obvious truth.*

This is why, per Shaked, the Court assumes the role of "super-administration."[39] This is why Yoav Dotan has described reasonableness as "nearly intolerable from the perspective of democratic accountability" with "no parallel in any other legal system in the world."[40] It is why Dotan has called the reasonableness standard a "judicial mechanism for redesigning government policy in Israel,"[41] by which "the Court becomes an additional government that

* The Court indeed routinely denies this, stating it "does not ask itself what it would have decided" (*Yellow Pages*, p. 440), "does not determine what is the optimum" (HCJ 397/84, p. 19) and "does not replace the discretion of government authorities" (*Ressler*, p. 487). Examples are countless.

oversees the elected government."[42] Lord Jonathan Sumption observed that a technique of this nature "puts great power into the hands of judges" with "no clear legal principles to shape" such; any answer "depends on a subjective judgment in which a judge's personal opinion is always influential and often decisive." Yet as this clearly "gives legal effect" to the "opinions and values" of individual judges, Sumption asks – "what is that if not a claim to political power?"[43] What indeed?

A less obvious but no less egregious violation of the Separation of Powers is the undermining of *parliamentary* authority to define the scope and extent of statutory powers granted to the executive and to administrative bodies. Though the reasonableness standard applies to executive or administrative action and not directly to primary legislation, it effectively undermines and negates statutory law conferring executive authority and discretion. It is the legislative branch which enacts laws guiding the conduct of the executive and granting it various powers – this is partially true in presidential systems of government but is undisputably true in parliamentary ones. As part of forming governmental organs and supervising their function, it is the legislature which decides what authority it grants to various executive bodies and officials, whether expansive or restrictive, what to permit and what to forbid.

Yet when the Court examines the "reasonableness" of an executive decision made duly within its legal authority, it in fact challenges the original grant of authority and deviates from it, claiming to restrict, define, and otherwise limit the powers conferred by primary legislation. Doing so effectively amends the statute itself, as though the Court were saying to the Knesset – "look, we know you granted the Executive certain powers by law, but we simply disagree with your choice to do so." Needless to say, this is done without the Court ever explicitly challenging the validity of the original legislation and without offering any reason to consider the initial granting statute unlawful.

The End of Law

The second overarching feature and effect of the reasonableness doctrine is the abandonment of legal rules and of law as a discipline per se. The Supreme Court regularly offers feeble protestations of the purely legal nature of reasonableness: "The standards applied by the Court are legal and not political ones";[44] the Court "examines only the legality" of a political decision "according to legal standards."[45] Though this assertion is repeated countless times across a myriad cases, there is nothing remotely legal in the reasonableness standard in any conventional sense. It is devoid of legal content. Legal training, experience and expertise contribute nothing to one's determination of whether a government decision was unreasonable and whether competing interests were properly balanced. A government action is unreasonable because the Court says so; and the Court says so because the action is unreasonable.

As Mautner notes, by its very definition, unreasonableness "subjects non-legal aspects" of government to the Court's oversight – a function never intended for the Court and for which the Court is ill-equipped.[46] The point is not that legal experts may disagree about what is unreasonable, but that any such disagreement can only be based on the personal perspective, values, convictions and preferences of every individual judge (and person). Different judicial outcomes are born of difference in opinion and in predisposition, not derived of divergent legal analysis.

Michal Shaked addressed this grievous flaw in her 1982 essay. Not only is unreasonableness unanchored from the established tenets of administrative law, but rather it is "detached from any legal rules, norms and nature,"[47] forsaking any objective legal criteria.[48] The questions are not legal and therefore their resolution cannot take on a legal character. "The court ceases to fulfill a judicial role and begins to function as a council of wise people."[49]

Nowhere is this clearer than in the utter lack of predictability relating to any determination of reasonableness. Law is prescriptive – it serves as an advance guide for permitted and forbidden conduct or it serves no purpose at all. Oliver Wendell Holmes Jr. famously described the law as "the prophecies of what the courts will do in fact,"[50] and the role of lawyers as engaging in such prophecy. Yet any prophesizing regarding how a court might apply the unreasonableness doctrine is a futile delusion – or at least, it is entirely about the judge and their specific desired outcome and has no relation to the law. As Yoav Dotan explains, "the concept of reasonableness is not merely vague or 'broad'; it is rather in fact an utterly empty concept in terms of its substantive content. Reasonableness is a concept which suffers from inherent indeterminacy... The content of balancing-reasonableness is redefined every time anew." As a result, "we have no way of knowing or estimating, on a rational basis, how the Court will determine the proper weight of each consideration in any future individual case," and the legality of any action is "evaluated ad hoc and retrospectively, with no prior guidance or direction."[51]

Expressing this sentiment many years earlier, Shaked quotes Justice Benjamin Cardozo and argues that unreasonableness lacks the basic elements which comprise "the essence of the idea of law": certainty, uniformity, order and coherence.[52] Instead, reasonableness yields "a wilderness of single instances."[53] A ruling based on reasonableness provides almost no guide for future judicial decisions and for executive conduct – estimating its precedential significance is nigh impossible,[54] and not even the most learned lawyer can predict which administrative decision might withstand judicial scrutiny. Indeed, Justice Grunis observed in 2007 that the passage of time did not produce a less abstract formulation that might have decreased the absolute uncertainty surrounding any claim of unreasonableness.[55]

The end of law may well be to guide human conduct in an ordered society; a legal standard devoid of any such guiding element signifies the end of law in a very different sense. When entering the realm of reasonableness, any meaningful concept of law is left to wither at its threshold.

*

Yet reasonableness also heralded "the end of law" in a more fundamental sense. Shaked's observation was prescient, though she perhaps did not realize the full extent of its implications. Reasonableness indeed became the dominant form of judicial supervision of the executive; it was indeed used erratically, incoherently and unpredictably to intervene in any and all forms of governing; it indeed remains to this day as devoid of legal substance as it was in *Yellow Pages*.

However, what is often overlooked is that no legal system can sustain such a doctrine for long without being infected by its lawless approach. Since its introduction into the Israeli legal system the reasonableness doctrine has continued to radiate ever outwards, far beyond the formal confines of the doctrine and its explicit use. As a natural consequence of extraordinary judicial power untethered even to the appearance of law, reasonableness became the gravitational center of the Supreme Court's entire judicial culture. After all, if judges can rule on the legality of any conceivable government decision on grounds as vague and abstract as reasonableness, why bother at all with the pretense of legal reasoning to begin with? The introduction of unreasonableness to the Israeli judiciary meant the universal erosion of commitment to legal norms of any kind. Mautner's claim that reasonableness "breached the boundaries of the law" is no understatement.

At times the Court might characterize a decision as unreasonable, but with no attempt to explain how the "balancing" should have otherwise occurred or what alternative "reasonable" decision was available, or without offering any rationale as to how a factor was "improperly" balanced and why it should have been given less or more weight. In some cases the Court never even specifies which exact policy or decision (or which government organ or official) is currently under review. A petition's vaguest charge of unreasonableness might produce a devastating injunction offering no explanations. Sometimes the Court doesn't mention reasonableness at all, and simply fails to articulate any specific legal grounds for invalidating or impeding executive action.* Some such decisions exhibit a deliberate effort to expand judicial power or to impose a policy preference; others just boil down to downright sloppy legal work. These are all reflections of the same phenomena – a Court in which the law is simply not taken seriously.

Mautner has written extensively about the "decline of formalism and the rise of values" in the Court's jurisprudence,[56] but in the context of reasonableness he may as well have called it "the decline of law and the rise of decree." Reasonableness differs from other radical doctrines in its thorough and brazen disinterest in even the remotest formal legal basis for its decisions. As Justice Antonin Scalia observed, while scoffing at the "mindless" allegation that his approach was formalistic: "the rule of law is *about* form… It is what makes a government a government of laws and not of men."[57] If the rule of law is about

---

* This in turn makes it much more difficult to track and scrutinize the use of reasonableness, as such use is not always explicitly stated.

form, unreasonableness is formlessness. The non-formalism of reasonableness simply translates into lawlessness.

Another contemporary critic of reasonableness employed "formalism" in the opposite way. Prof. Ronen Shamir, at one time head of the Sociology and Anthropology department at Tel Aviv University, described the hollow concept of reasonableness as a decidedly "formalistic" effort to bring all socio-political disputes and disagreement under an ostensibly legal framework, their patently political nature notwithstanding.* Shamir argues the conceit of reasonableness to be its framing of government policy as legal questions to begin with, in this sense applying formalistic (or perhaps, formulaic) legal concepts to evaluate decisions with no legal character. This in turn serves as the legitimating basis for judicial intervention in pure government discretion – an objective Shamir had no doubt was the main purpose behind the insistence on developing and maintaining the reasonableness standard.

Mautner's and Shamir's opposing applications of "formalism" don't actually contradict one another. On its own terms, reasonableness is intrinsically non-formalistic because it lacks any substantive legal content; yet viewed from without, reasonableness is extrinsically formalistic in its attempt to apply a rigid legal standard to non-legal issues. One way or another, both scholars seem to agree on Shamir's conclusion, viewing reasonableness as little more than a "rhetorical tactic to empower judges."[58] Ultimately, such an approach to law cannot but have a broader influence on the Court's overall judicial philosophy and practical behavior.

Shamir's most insightful contribution here is perhaps his characterization of the Court's approach as a "mystification" of the law. Reasonableness converts the law from a fundamentally rational, transparent, logical, analytical process into an inscrutable ritual incantation yielding judicial results, indeed more akin to a shaman consulting the depths of unknowable mystical wisdom. This inherent mysticism is manifest both in the substance of unreasonableness, by relegating faux-legal analysis to the hidden judicial psyche, and in its public perception, by creating an aura of mystery and indiscernibility around legal decision-making.

This, then, is the fallout effect of the reasonableness standard – a creeping corruption of legal thought and of the judicial profession, transforming the Court's fundamental DNA and seeping in to almost every corner of the legal system; a mindset which has no interest, ex ante, in offering genuine legal arguments to justifying the use of binding judicial power.

Back to *Ressler* – Reasonableness and Justiciability

A direct line links the 1980 *Yellow Pages* reasonableness standard and the 1988 *Ressler* expansion of justiciability. Weill remarks that the former "enabled" the

---

* Shamir's aptly named essay, "The Politics of Reasonableness," amusingly and probably intentionally appeared alongside Mautner's "The Reasonableness of Politics."

latter's revolution of "eliminating the non-justiciability doctrine."[59] Mautner observes the combined effect of the Court's "limitless justiciability doctrine" and "extensive application of the reasonableness standard" to be "that the Court furnished itself with vast discretion as to whether and in what ways to intervene in political and administrative decisions."[60]

This is of course intuitive. As discussed in the previous chapter, one significant basis of non-justiciability is that actions devoid of any legal nature or character, about which the law "takes no position" or in which "there is no law to apply," are not suitable for adjudication. The reasonableness standard eliminates any such obstacle, by regarding any government conduct as a legal question which may be evaluated by judicial tools. If *all* executive decisions or policy making "must be reasonable" then it is all fair game for legal analysis and for judicial oversight.

Of course there are other grounds for non-justiciability, such as judicial prudence and propriety, democratic accountability, the separation of powers, and more. Had these remained in place, a firm threshold requirement of justiciability could have partially curbed some of the most expansive elements of the new unreasonableness standard, as many issues would typically be considered non-justiciable regardless of their status as legal or non-legal questions. But these were in turn swept away in *Ressler*, thus completing the expansion of judicial power to include oversight of truly (that is, factually) all government action. The twin concepts of unreasonableness review and total justiciability meant that questions hitherto considered neither legal nor appropriate for adjudication very quickly became subject to routine judicial intervention. As described by Dotan, this combined effect meant that "effectively **any government action** may be challenged in court by **any person** on the basis of **any claim** regarding its justification or desirability," while such claims are "cloaked in the generalized and vague guise" of unreasonableness, and are not associated with "any statutory text whatsoever" or "concrete and distinct legal grounds."[61] (Emphasis in source.)

From *Ressler* onwards, no particle of government conduct could escape the all-consuming black hole of reasonableness.

This insight is not only analytical but was expressly stated by Barak himself in *Ressler* and by contemporary critics. When discussing "normative" justiciability, Barak explicitly cites reasonableness as a "super-norm" applicable to all government action and therefore as the legal bridge between any such action and its justiciability. "The existence of the norm of reasonableness means that there are [legal] standards to evaluate the reasonableness of an action."[62] It is the "reasonableness" of instituting diplomatic relations, of going to war and making peace, of military policy, that is legally applicable and that makes such issues justiciable. Recalling that Barak's approach is binary (either something is entirely justiciable or it is not), Dotan describes reasonableness as the "checkmark" that one may place to establish full justiciability.[63] Despite this, Dotan clarifies that Barak's reliance on the so-called "law" of reasonableness is "for appearances only," and does not actually resolve the many flaws of Barak's approach to justiciability.[64]

Barak notably rearticulates his reasonableness doctrine in *Ressler*, reinforcing the manner in which it complements universal justiciability. He starts out by declaring that "all accept that the government must act reasonably" while citing his own controversial *Yellow Pages* opinion dicta (referencing non-binding opinion and pretending it is established precedential law is a signature Barak move and became standard practice for the Court). He then repeats the familiar formula: The range of reasonable decisions is defined by "the proper balancing" of competing "interests and values." These are determined by "the relevant material," and against the background of the (legal?) system's "fundamental values," its "credo" and the view of the "enlightened public" within it.[65] Barak concedes that the "primary difficulty" is found in the judicial attribution of "weight" to the various values and interests and in their "balancing" to reach a final outcome; but he maintains that these are essentially legal questions open to objective judicial evaluation and are in no way arbitrary. To support this claim, Barak presents this extraordinary passage, quoting himself:

> "The judge does not impose his subjective values on society. He must balance the different interests, according to *what he sees to be* the needs of the society in which he lives. He must exercise his discretion, according to *what seems to him* by his best objective evaluation, to reflect the needs of society. The question is not what the judge wants, but what society needs."[66] (Emphasis added.)

Indeed, like the Batman, the judge wielding reasonableness is "not the hero we deserved, but the hero we needed" (The Dark Knight, 2008). Barak presents this without a shred of irony, seemingly quite unaware that his own description depicts the epitome of subjective and arbitrary discretion, centered around what "seems" to the judge to "reflect the needs of society." It's worth emphasizing that the Court never claims to rely on an empirical evaluation of the needs or preferences of society (neither as a whole nor only the select "enlightened public"). Such societal views, preferences and needs are themselves the product of judicial speculation (or imagination). The passage is especially instructive because, if not for its reference to judges, it could easily have been describing the role of the executive branch – the difference being that the latter is populated with accountable public officials who have a better claim to identify and evaluate the needs of society, and greater legitimacy to balance interests accordingly.

The most significant objection following the landmark *Ressler* decision was raised immediately in its aftermath by retired Chief Justice Moshe Landau. Landau's mellow skepticism and disapproval voiced almost a decade earlier in *Yellow Pages* had by now grown into serious alarm and deep opposition, expressed in a speech titled "Justiciability and Reasonableness in Administrative Law." Landau repeats many of the claims and arguments discussed above, including the revolutionary nature of Barak's novel doctrines and their contradiction of previous Court jurisprudence, and proceeds to admonish Barak and the Court in the most strident terms. The use of reasonableness "leads the Court into a dead end of insufferable results" and becomes a "cipher, devoid of defined content," which enables and employs the Court's "subjective judgment, expressed by the task of balancing competing interests as these are perceived by the judge." Landau argues the Court "has no ability" to evaluate executive decisions of forward-looking policy involving social and economic considerations, and that "the primordial concept of reasonableness certainly provides no such tools."[67] Regarding the balancing of interests, he writes: "I struggle to distinguish between what is 'proper' in the eyes of a citizen and what is 'proper' in the eyes of a judge," casting doubt on any difference between such purported judicial balancing and subjective review of the merit of the policy itself (which the Court claims to avoid). Landau also cites other contemporary non-Israeli legal authorities stating that "the incantation of the word 'unreasonable' simply does not provide sufficient justification for judicial intervention." Finally, reflecting his broader view of the judicial role, Landau summarizes that "the flaws of other branches of government cannot be remedied by assigning the judiciary tasks for which it is not suited and which it is incapable of bearing."

We may conclude that the relationship between the two doctrines is symbiotic, each feeding off the other – reasonableness provides the "legal" pretext to review any government action, while justiciability grants permission to do so. From a broader perspective, the combination of justiciability and unreasonableness leads to simultaneous enhancement and degradation of the law. Limitless justiciability (*Ressler)* applies the law to everything and anything, placing any conceivable human conduct under its heel; yet unreasonableness renders the law meaningless, removing any legal foundation from the judicial supervision of executive action. Thus the fabric of "law" is stretched so wide as to cover anything, but so thin as to mean nothing.

An Unreasonable Court

Just as Justice Landau returned to forcefully attack the reasonableness doctrine eight years after his misgivings in *Yellow Pages*, so did Justice Elon take the opportunity to do so in the 1991 *Zarzevsky* case, eleven years after his own criticism of Barak in *Contractors Center*. By this time reasonableness had taken form as the dominant and unqualified method of judicial review in the Supreme Court. Elon's arguments against reasonableness and justiciability, though familiar, stand out both in their severe tone and in the identity of their author – a sitting Supreme Court Justice writing in an official judicial opinion.

The *Zarzevsky* case revolved around a challenge to an agreement between two political parties. Such agreements are standard practice in Israeli coalition government, by which political parties articulate their mutual undertakings and commitments towards their parliamentary and executive collaboration. These were historically considered non-justiciable and legally unenforceable – among other things, political parties are private civilian entities which do not exercise governmental power, and even an agreement to engage in illegal conduct can be scrutinized at the point of its implementation such that the unlawful act itself may be challenged (in other words, the courts can review unlawful government action if such occurs). And the notion of a court "enforcing" a political agreement seems bizarre – will a judge enjoin legislators to enact a certain law pursuant to a political agreement? Still, since *Ressler* the Court had gradually began subjecting such agreements to direct ex ante judicial review, based on some blend of contract law and public administrative law. In *Zarzevsky* the Court essentially ruled that agreements between political parties are both justiciable and enforceable (and that political parties must act "reasonably"), thus inviting sweeping adjudication of political agreements as a regular post-elections feature.

Setting aside its details and outcome, Justice Elon clearly perceived *Zarzevsky* as an opportunity to lay out his objections to the Barak-ean view of reasonableness and justiciability. In doing so, Elon's opinion presents a comprehensive critique which raises angles and arguments previously unaddressed.

Elon warns of both diminishing public faith in the judiciary and of its inability to function, as a result of Barak's universal justiciability and the inevitable resulting "politicization" of judging. Importantly and presciently, Elon warns of the dangers of judicial "approval" for patently odious or improper government action: ultimate dismissal of meritless petitions is interpreted as a stamp of moral validity, making it easier for government to get away with conduct which Israelis might call "Kosher but rotten."* This is a rarely mentioned counter-intuitive argument showing how expansive judicial oversight actually enables elected government to evade public scrutiny for poor conduct. A related point hinted at by Elon is the damage to the standing and status of political and elected branches of government caused by incessant judicial interference. Elon maintains that the "formation and repair of a political culture ought to be, first and foremost, in the hands of political forces,"[68] distinguishing between "public law" of the courts and "public trial" by the electorate. Directly referring to *Ressler*, Elon states that Barak effectively indicted justiciability itself and "sentenced it to exile."[69]

After pointing out the known analytical flaws in Barak's theory of justiciability, Justice Elon turns his attention to reasonableness. He holds Barak's conception of reasonableness to be itself unreasonable. Elon asks bluntly – what in fact *is* evaluated by the reasonableness standard? What distinction is there between "properly balancing interests" and between the logic, wisdom and effectiveness of government action which the Court maintains it is not reviewing? He asks, "is this not a purely semantic distinction with no practical or material

* This may especially resonate with those objecting to Netanyahu's appointment as Prime Minister under indictment in 2020, which was arguably assisted or encouraged by the Court's unanimous 11-member decision not to intervene. Yoav Dotan makes this point more broadly by emphasizing one rationale for non-justiciability, that at times adjudication can incur certain social costs regardless of outcome.

significance?"[70] Alluding to the lack of any coherence or predictability in Barak's own rulings thus far on political issues, Elon remarks that a judge holding an action to be "reasonable" could just as easily have reached the opposite conclusion. In the absence of any useful legal standard to apply, Elon quips that "it is completely unreasonable to reasonably expect that the court will examine the reasonableness of such matters."[71]

Elon's characterization of Barak's overall approach is especially memorable: "The law is omnipotent, and therefore the court is omnipotent, and therefore the judge is omnipotent, and the standard he applies is that of reasonableness, which too is omnipotent." This, Elon says, violates the fundamental democratic tenet of "rule of law and not rule of judge."[72]

Down the Reasonable Rabbit Hole

We will now take the time to examine some illustrative examples showcasing the use of reasonableness in a variety of contexts. Though by no means exhaustive, the following sampling should provide greater clarity regarding the manner in which reasonableness is utilized to devastating effect – a microcosm reflecting countless cases accumulated over four decades of reasonableness review.

Some points are worth keeping in mind as we turn to consider these cases. Due to its vague definition and application, reasonableness itself often escapes detection or categorization. It is routinely employed without explicit reference to the unreasonableness doctrine or to analogous interest-balancing. Its impact is often felt in its absence – when the Court strikes down government action with no discernible legal basis, this is itself an echo of unreasonableness review. At the same time, the Court utilizes reasonableness to intervene in a wide range of decision types and categories – from minute and inconsequential trifles to major policy; from professional-technical determinations to questions of core ideology and values; reflecting public consensus or ruling over heavily-contested public-political controversies. It is tempting to think of judicial intervention as significant or consequential only regarding the latter types – broad policy, ideological issues and public disputes – but this would be a mistake. It is rather the interference with trivial, day-to-day decisions which betrays the endemic pervasiveness of reasonableness review and which belies the myth of a doctrine reserved for significant abuses of governmental power.

The examples below also demonstrate the intersection of reasonableness and the absence of justiciability. Almost any of these cases would be dismissed in other jurisdictions due to their non-justiciability alone, as they regard issues of pure executive discretion and policy preferences. Reasonableness review serves as the pseudo-legal standard which enables judicial supervision of non-justiciable issues, while simultaneously, the abolition of justiciability requirements allows the Court to freely approach any political or policy matter as though it were solely a question of technical legality.

A useful approach to adopt when confronting examples of reasonableness review is to (try and) ignore one's initial reaction to the case outcome or one's approval of the executive policy in question. Rather, the reader ought to ask themselves whether it is the proper function of a Court to make such calls (in the absence of any applicable solid legal standard). The best way to consider this might be the "shoe on the other foot" test – one might imagine the same scenario but with reversed roles, with the executive choosing the (original) judicial result and the Court deciding the way the (original) executive did. After all, this is a core feature of reasonableness – that two people, and indeed two judges, might reach opposite conclusions regarding what government action is reasonable. One might quickly find that they are sympathetic to a judicial decision not because of their legal justification but rather due to their agreeable outcomes.

A final exercise which the reader might find helpful is to apply the case to their own home jurisdiction – would a court intervene so in identical circumstances? Would it be publicly, socially, politically acceptable for a court to apply the same reasoning and reach the same result? While intuitive and speculative, the answer to this question is almost always negative, and effectively demonstrates the degree to which Israeli unreasonableness deviates from global judicial practice.

Lara Alqasem

In the 2018 case of *Lara Alqasem*, the Court struck down a decision by the Minister of Interior to bar a foreign student from entering Israel. This regarded a non-Israeli citizen entering Israel on a student visa and did not involve humanitarian or refugee-related considerations as is sometimes the case with immigration disputes. Lara Alqasem was an activist in the anti-Israel Boycott, Divest and Sanction ("BDS") movement and had previously been a member of Students for Justice in Palestine ("SJP"), a notorious anti-Israel group. The Minister of Interior generally presides over formulation and implementation of Israel's immigration policy, including wide discretion and decision-making power in a multitude of individual cases.

The Minister's decision to bar Alqasem's entry relied on two statutory provisions. Section 2(a) of the 1952 Entry Into Israel Law grants the Minister general, open-ended discretion in granting temporary visitor visas ("The Minister may grant…"). In addition and more pertinently, Section 2(d) of the Entry Law had been recently amended in 2017 to specifically address the BDS movement. The freshly amended statute mandates that "no visa shall be granted" to a non-citizen that had "knowingly published" a public call to boycott Israel or that "is active" with an organization that did so. It's worth noting that Section 2(d) presents a blanket rule forbidding entry to Israel, while the following Section 2(e) grants the Minister authority to deviate from this rule in exceptional circumstances. The recent statutory amendment was enacted with the express purpose of combating the BDS movement by preventing BDS activists (past and present) from entering Israel. Neither provision defines criteria for granting or refusing such entry visas, such that neither sets substantial statutory limits to the Minister's authority.

Alqasem appealed the Minister's decision to an internal Appeals Board, and then to the Tel Aviv District Court. Both tribunals upheld the Minister's decision as a legal exercise of his wide statutory authority consistent with the law's text and purpose. Alqasem then appealed the decision to the Supreme Court.

The *Alqasem* decision illustrates the potent combination of purposive interpretation and reasonableness review. First, the Court reviewed the text, rationales and various purposes of the Enty Law, including the recent anti-BDS amendment. The word "published," which expressly includes actions in the past-tense, is ignored; while the phrase "is active" is elevated to mean that the statute applies only to persons *currently* active in the BDS movement. The statute's purpose is divided into a jumble of concrete, subjective and objective purposes, ultimately leading the Court to conclude that the statute may be applied in order to *prevent* actual BDS activity in Israel by barring entry of foreign BDS activists, but not as a *punitive* measure to punish BDS activists for past behavior. This conclusion is by no means a necessary one – the law could certainly be understood to include a punitive element. More importantly though, the Court never contemplates the question of *deterrence* – that barring past activists from entry is not necessarily punitive, but rather perhaps an effective and important tool combating BDS by conveying that Israel will not welcome visitors that have engaged in such activity. In other words, the Court presented a false dichotomy between preventative and punitive – both in terms of the law's purpose, and in terms of the effect of the Minister's decision – while ignoring the purpose of deterrence which could likely have justified barring Alqasem.

Next, the Court assesses the Minister's decision in light of the law's alleged purposes. The Court sidesteps the recent amendment and its restrictive nature (which essentially establishes a broad rule against entry of BDS activists). The law clearly sets a presumption of non-entry which the Minister may then overcome for reasons he must articulate; that is, that the Minister's discretion is more limited than in general visa-related issues, with a default rule of non-entry for BDS activists. This argument is acknowledged by the Court, yet is relegated to the "concrete" purpose and does not figure in to the Court's calculus. In other words, it seems the Court's final analysis would have been identical if the recent amendment had not existed and the Court were reviewing the Minister's use of his general visa-granting discretion.

After many recitations regarding the "wide discretion" afforded to the Minister by statute, the Court held that the Minister's decision, while acting within his statutory authority, "clearly deviates from the range of reasonableness."[73] This was due to the decision "not advancing the statute's purpose" and "allegedly"*

---

* This argument was made by an Israeli university, which the Court seemed to accept. As is usually the case, no evidence was presented or considered to establish this empirical assertion.

causing harm to Israeli academia (the Court does not offer any further analysis on the correct "balancing" formula). The Court thus struck down the Minister's decision, overturned the rulings of the Appeals Board and the lower District Court, and mandated that Alqasem be permitted to enter Israel.

While avoiding an exhaustive review, we may easily say the following: the Court ignored the past-tense nature of the statutory text which clearly envisioned barring past (and not only current) BDS activists; the Court invented a "preventative" statutory purpose with no basis in the legal text and to the exclusion of other conceivable purposes, including deterrence; and the Court assessed the Minister's decision as detached from the statutory framework clearly oriented towards precisely such outcomes. The reader will also note the lack of any claim to "extreme" unreasonableness or an "outrageous" action, and the absence of any enforceable right alleged by Alqasem.

Ultimately, the Court intervened in an executive decision (by an elected government Minister) taken squarely within his statutory authority and consistent with the law and with government policy. As in so many others, the *Alqasem* case exemplifies how reasonableness review boils down to abstract judicial supervision of minute executive discretion. The Court's ruling ultimately rests on the sentiment that the Justices would have acted differently were they in the Minister's position.

Alternative Remembrance Ceremony

The annual Israeli Memorial Day, officially called "Remembrance Day for the Fallen Soldiers of the Wars of Israel and Victims of Actions of Terrorism," involves a host of commemoration ceremonies and customs at the State, local, communal and individual levels. The national atmosphere is one of deep mourning, mixed with reverence, patriotism, and hope. The vast majority of Israelis memorialized on Remembrance Day were killed in the context of the Israeli-Arab conflict. Since 2006, a group of Israelis and Arab-Palestinians had conducted an "alternative" ceremony on the same day, which spotlighted the loss of Palestinian life alongside Israelis who were killed. While the ceremony conveyed an official message of peace and reconciliation, it was (and is) justifiably perceived as reflecting the fringes of the political and ideological left. Many Israelis found this ceremony to be acutely objectionable and disrespectful, especially when intentionally held on Remembrance Day itself; though no one questioned the right of organizers and participants to proceed with the ceremony.

In 2018, a group of some two hundred Palestinians applied for permits in order to attend the alternative remembrance ceremony. Palestinian residents of the West Bank require special permits to enter Israel beyond the "Green Line" (the 1949 armistice lines separating sovereign Israel and the disputed West Bank), for a variety of purposes including employment, medical care, and much else. These are technically granted by the Israeli military though are ultimately subject to the oversight and discretion of the Minister of Defense.

The Minister of Defense denied the applications, subsequently writing on Twitter that he "would not lend a hand to the desecration of Remembrance Day" and that the ceremony was a "spectacle of poor taste and insensitivity" towards bereaved families. The ceremony would proceed as planned, but without the presence and participation of the two-hundred Palestinians that had requested to attend.* The Minister's decision was later supported by the permanent committee of the Public Soldier Commemoration Council (a statutory advisory council representing the nation's major commemoration associations).

The decision not to grant entry permits was challenged in the Supreme Court (by the Israeli event organizers, not by the denied applicants). After finding that the Minister had acted within his statutory authority, and after reciting the usual bromides about the Minister's "wide discretion" to grant or deny permit applications, the Court held the Minister's decision to be unlawful and annulled it.[74] This was because the Minister had attributed too much weight to "the feelings of bereaved families and the public" which objected to the ceremony, and had attributed insufficient weight to such families and public as supported the ceremony. "Therefore," wrote the Court, "the Minister's decision suffers from a substantial lack of balance and is unreasonable to a degree justifying our intervention." Thus.

The ruling in this case is extraordinary even by contemporary Israeli standards. It intervenes in what is essentially military and defense policy exercised by the Minister of Defense. It's clumsy and simplistic "balancing" of public sensitivities seem almost like an intentional parody: Surely the Court isn't claiming it is better able, or has greater public legitimacy, to balance such public and ideological considerations, as opposed to the elected and accountable Minister of Defense? Yet that is precisely the argument the Court presents. All this in a case where no one had alleged violation of their fundamental rights or some grievous personal harm. And of course, any pretense of an "outrageous" decision being "extremely" unreasonable is abandoned for simple "substantial lack of balance."

But the ruling truly stands out in that the Court doesn't even bother with legal analysis of any kind. Not of statutory text or purpose; not of existing jurisprudence and prior rulings; not of Ministerial authority and responsibility; not of the petitioner's infringed rights. The Court accepts the legal validity of the overall legal framework – that which requires permits to begin with and confers overall authority on the Minister of Defense – yet doesn't seem concerned as to why his specific decision is any different from hundreds of other routine exercises of the same discretion (many of them arguably far more objectionable). At one point the Court waxes poetic about the importance of a "plurality of opinion" in democratic society, as though the case were about preventing the alternative ceremony and

* To be clear, the Minister's decision did not relate in any way to the existence, place and timing of the alternative ceremony itself; and the Palestinian residents were free to organize a similar event within the West Bank.

not simply about a handful of entry permits among thousands – both granted and denied – on a daily basis. Put simply, the Court just doesn't even try to couch its decision in wording or reasoning of a remotely legal nature.

Closer inspection of the ruling reveals itself for what it really is – justification for a political decision on policy and ideological grounds. One could easily replace a few words and the ruling reads like a Ministry spokesperson's press release or the preamble of an official executive order. Had the Minister decided to grant the permits, he likely would have published a substantially similar statement to explain his decision. This realization demonstrates the political nature of the Court's unreasonableness review more strongly than almost any other analysis.

The Court's 2018 decision was not the last word on the matter. The same event repeated itself in almost identical form in 2019, now with a different Minister of Defense from a different political party, who also refused to grant permits for Palestinians to attend the alternative remembrance ceremony. Notably, this time round there was already a "closure" on movement from the West Bank for the duration of Remembrance Day, due to a bout of violence between Israel and Palestinian terrorist factions – meaning that not only were permits required, but also an official "exemption" from the general closure.

In an opinion by Justice Yitzhak Amit, the Court ruled again that the permits (and an exemption from the closure) must be granted.[75] The word "reasonable" is not mentioned in any form throughout the ruling. First, Amit berated the government for its disobedience and expressed his displeasure at the "regrettable" "re-run" of the previous case. He attributes little significance to the difference between general permit-granting discretion and the (new) separate issue of exception-granting within the context of a (legally valid) closure.

After quoting passages from the previous ruling, Amit proceeds to expound on the importance of diverse approaches to mourning and commemoration – "there are ninety-nine paths to commemoration; ninety-nine ways to express bereavement,"[*] again conflating the ceremony's existence and content (which was not at issue) with the specific, technical, legal matter of entry permits for Palestinians. He then goes on to write about "the core of freedom of expression and of individual autonomy" enabling each person "to shape their life-story," stating that "the Minister of Defense must not interfere with the manner in which a family chooses to express its personal bereavement." Alongside the absence of any legal analysis this claim becomes even more befuddling – is Amit saying that the event organizers have an inherent (legally enforceable) right in demanding the presence of Palestinians at their commemoration ceremony? Because, again, the ceremony and "expressions of bereavement" were not at issue. Unfortunately, Amit does not elaborate much beyond this point.

---

[*] Following the ruling, perhaps the petitioners sang "I got ninety-nine problems but the Court ain't one." Who knows.

In a short concurring opinion Justice Anat Baron makes her own vital contribution to the legal debate, by quoting poetry:

> "If we knew how to calm, how to calm
> The enmity, if we only knew.
> If we knew, if we knew how to silence our anger
> Despite our humiliation, to say sorry.
> If we knew to start over."

Disappointingly, these compelling arguments did not succeed in stopping the government's stubborn insistence on governing. And so in 2023 the case repeated itself again, now with a *third* Defense Minister making the same decision refusing to grant entry permits as occurred in the previous two cases, and with the decision again challenged – and voided – in the Supreme Court.[76] I will not trouble the reader with further details, beyond the fact that the Court (again Justice Amit) dutifully followed in the footsteps of the previous two cases, berating the government for its intransience and raising much the same points. The word "reasonable" does not appear in this thin ruling either.

Aside the way these cases demonstrate the bald-faced co-opting of executive discretion in an ideological-political issue of great public sensitivity, and aside the utter abandonment of any semblance of legal argumentation offered by the Court, they also highlight another aspect of Israeli reasonableness review. The original justification for conventional Wednesbury review contemplates an action that "no reasonable authority" could make. It seems plausible that recurring government action would undermine a claim of unreasonableness – if consecutive governments behave the same way over time and across a variety of contexts, could we really maintain that "no reasonable authority" would do the same? In other words, by the very definition of unreasonableness, repeat and consistent government conduct would at least indicate that it is not "unreasonable" on an empirical, factual level. In the *Alternative Ceremony* cases we find three separate Defense Ministers over three years making substantially the same decision within their legal authority, clearly undermining any claim of (conventional) unreasonableness. Needless to say, this factor is not addressed by the Court.

Goldreich – The Israel Prize

The Israel Prize is the State's highest official civilian honor, bestowed upon Israeli citizens recognized for their public excellence and outstanding service in a range of areas and disciplines. It is akin to the Presidential Medal of Freedom or the Congressional Gold Medal in the United States, or to a Knighthood in the United Kingdom (though it is admittedly distributed more liberally and abundantly). The Prize is awarded on the Israeli Independence Day in a special televised ceremony attended by the President.

For historical reasons and despite its prominence and elevated reputation, the Prize technically falls under the auspices and authority of the Education Ministry.

The process and rules for awarding the prize are not defined by statute, but rather are outlined in a set of internal Ministry regulations. The fields and disciplines in which the Prize is awarded are designated each year by the Minister of Education, who also appoints a secret committee that selects the Prize recipient in each field. While Prize recipients are "recommended" by each committee, any award requires the Minister's final "approval," and it is indeed the Minister who formally grants the award.

In 2021, the prize committee for the field of mathematics and computer science recommended one Professor Oded Goldreich for the Prize. On the same day, Education Minister Yoav Gallant asked that the committee reconsider its recommendation – as it turned out, Goldreich had a possible history of support for the BDS movement. He had allegedly joined public petitions advocating for academic boycott of Israel, notably including a letter to the German parliament objecting to the German definition of antisemitism that included boycotting of Israel (the German government had categorized the BDS movement as blatantly antisemitic). He had also allegedly urged the European Union to boycott an Israeli university located in the West Bank. At least some of Goldreich's conduct potentially fell afoul of an Israeli law that made support for the BDS movement an actionable tort and an offense resulting in ineligibility for certain State benefits.

After some back and forth with the committee, which stood by its recommendation, the Education Minister refused to approve Goldreich's selection as prize recipient. Because the Prize regulations require the Minister's approval, this meant effectively preventing Goldreich from receiving the award.

The decision was, of course, swiftly challenged in the Supreme Court. The Court had already established a long and illustrious history of adjudicating objections to Israel Prize recipients. This is in itself striking, considering the explicit language of Section 33 of the Israeli Contracts Law, which states that prizes (including prizes not within a contractual framework) are "not subject to judicial proceedings" – but such explicit statutory non-justiciability clauses had long been rendered dead letters following *Ressler*. The Court deliberated whether Goldreich's actions justified the Minister's rejection of his nomination for the Prize – past rulings in similar cases had stipulated that the Minister could hypothetically consider "external" (non-professional) factors only if they were of an "extreme" nature. Ruling by majority opinion that the Minister had applied the wrong legal test, the Court voided the Minister's refusal to approve the Prize, and returned the decision back to the Minister so that he may reconsider and apply the correct legal standard.[77]

By now the previous government had already been replaced and the Opposition had taken power. The task of reconsidering Goldreich's selection for the Israel Prize fell to the new Education Minister, Yifat Shasha-Bitton. In admirable defiance of many voices within her own political camp, the Minister reached the same conclusion as did her predecessor – that Goldreich's BDS actions rose to the level of "extreme" circumstances that merit withholding her approval and vetoing the committee's recommendation. Naturally, the decision came once again before the Supreme Court.

In a new ruling, the Court deemed the new Minister's decision unlawful and ordered that the Prize indeed be awarded to Goldreich per the committee recommendation.[78] The ruling was unprecedented – while the Court had adjudicated various challenges against Israel Prize recipients, it had never issued a positive decree to actually grant the prize against the Minister's wishes. In doing so, the Court effectively replaced the Minister's explicit legal authority – whether to approve the committee decision – with its own preference, and de facto itself granted the Prize to Professor Goldreich.

Without diving too deep into the Court's reasoning, the dual decisions merit some quick observations. First, the Court insisted (as it so often does) that it was not replacing the Minister's discretion; but this time went further to maintain that it was not in fact relying on the "unreasonableness" doctrine (this itself was a reflection of the growing public consensus against the use of reasonableness). Rather, one opinion explained why the Minister decision was a contradiction of government policy, while another opinion claimed to rely on previous rulings that limited "external" considerations by the Minister only to "extreme" circumstances. These were dubious arguments handily dismantled in a dissenting opinion by Justice Noam Solberg. Yet more importantly, the Court's analytical hairsplitting makes the decision worse, not better. It simply illustrates the manner in which the spirit of reasonableness review permeates the entire judicial culture, even when the standard is not explicitly applied. This is precisely the ripple effect of reasonableness review – subjecting any exercise of government power to arbitrary judicial limitations and ad hoc faux legal standards, whatever guise they might take. In this sense, the Court was correctly indicating that in 2021, it could easily supplant executive discretion for its own without uttering the word "reasonable" a single time.*

Second, the rulings demonstrate important undercurrents in the Court's approach to all Executive action – the suspicion towards "political" considerations and the elevation of technocratic "professional" opinion. The Court often deems ideological, political or publicly-sensitive factors to be foreign or immaterial to government actions and policy; while at the same time, "advice" or "recommendations" made by bureaucratic functionaries are regarded as binding directives which the executive must usually rubber-stamp. Never mind that bureaucrats or "professional" advisors are capable of their own partisan biases (for example – was the recommendation in favor of Goldreich in spite of his politics, or because of them?), or that few considerations are purely technical. Never mind that conferring authority on a politically accountable figure – such as government Minister – reflects the conviction that certain decisions ought to be made by those with a democratic link to the electorate and while taking their

* To be clear – the petitions themselves alleged "unreasonableness" as the main grounds for intervention.

desires and preferences into account. The *Goldreich* case is a small taste of the Court's approach on both planes – the legal text subjecting the award of a Prize to the Education Minister's approval, along with the accountable authority it seeks to confer, is rendered superfluous and may as well not exist.

More to the point, the Israel Prize itself is precisely the kind of government decision one expects to be at least partially "political" in nature – in that it factors various public and ideological considerations beyond mere technical qualifications, and is expected to reflect (to some extent) the governing agenda of the day. Such awards are typically non-justiciable (in Israel and elsewhere) precisely under the understanding that the government ought to enjoy wide leeway in making such decisions and in bestowing such honors. Though many administrative decisions should certainly be free from political considerations, a State's highest civilian honor is obviously not one of them. Just try and imagine a court striking down a Knighthood or a Presidential Medal of Freedom due to it being too "political" – the idea is preposterous, precisely because the "political" is part of the fabric of such awards.

Third, the Court's rejection of "political" considerations as valid is characteristic of its blindness to the deeply political nature of its own decisions. The *Goldreich* rulings were twice political – first, in applying the standard which limits the Minister's discretion to "extreme" circumstances. Creating such a judicial standard is in and of itself a meta-political approach. In his concurring opinion (in the second ruling), Justice Amit finds it "hardly appropriate" that the Israel Prize be subject to "social-moral-ideological-political values" and considerations. Indeed, perish the thought. Who could imagine a State's highest civilian honor factoring in social or ideological considerations? A monstrous proposition to be sure.* Yet this debate obscures the acutely political nature of the Court's piercing intervention to begin with. The law clearly grants the Minister the authority to approve or reject a committee recommendation (and thus to grant or not to grant the Prize). More than any individual ruling in a given case, the Court's very pretension to dictate to the Minister which valid factors are permitted or prohibited is profoundly political.

More importantly still, the Court-developed standard of discerning which action is sufficiently "extreme" to disqualify a Prize candidate is as political as it gets. Clearly, two consecutive Education Ministers from rival parties and opposing political camps thought that active support for the BDS movement met this criterion, but the Court disagreed. The question isn't who was right, but rather why the Court seems to view its subjective determination as any less political than those of both Ministers. Whether such conduct is "extreme" is precisely the kind of determination reserved to the politically-minded Education Minister responsive to public sentiment.

---

* In the same opinion, Justice Amit outdid himself by suggesting that the non-justiciability of prizes defined in the Contracts Law means that the *Minister* was not to interfere with the committee's choice of award.

Proving the standard's arbitrary nature is easy. In the 1997 *Schnitzer* case, which was the first time the Court adjudicated the Israel Prize, the Court *revoked* the prize awarded to renowned journalist Shmuel Schnitzer, and ruled that the decision to grant the award was invalid because it relied solely on his professional achievements and *failed* to consider his unseemly ethical conduct.[79] Certainly, Schnitzer had written a shamefully offensive and implicitly racist opinion column a few years earlier. Is that worse than openly advocating for the academic boycott of your own country? Why does the former entail annulment of the award while the latter is so non-extreme that it compels granting of the award? When are value-based considerations mandatory (*Schnitzer*) and when are they verboten (*Goldreich*)? And how could anyone pretend that the distinction itself is not fundamentally political, ideological, value-based?

As an aside and for the record, the committee's professional recommendation to award Schnitzer the 1997 Prize favorably noted that his essays were "imbued with uncompromising Zionism, with respect for tradition and for secular life, with culture and reflection, with Judaism and love for the Land of Israel." This and many similar statements dispel any myth of a "professional" prize awarded only for technical achievement – the Israel Prize was always about honoring the most upstanding and meritorious members of Israeli society as jointly judged by their professional peers and by the public's elected representatives.

This, then, is the nuclear core of the reasonableness standard and its progeny – political, ideological, value-based judicial decisions and policies under the empty pretense of legal deliberation.

Butter and Tobacco

Some sections of the Israeli economy are characterized by Soviet-era and Soviet-style government intervention in trade and commerce. This includes price controls over a variety of (mostly dairy) essential consumer products, complemented by prohibitive restrictions on competing imports. The final consumer price of "supervised" products is set by order of the Minister of Finance together with other relevant government Ministers, after consulting with an advisory four-member Pricing Committee or after receiving its "recommended" consumer price. Needless to say, setting maximum consumer prices for essential products (such as eggs, milk, sliced bread, cream, butter, etc.) is an inherently political question of high economic policy with ramifications for millions of citizens and for the economy at large.

In mid-2018 Israel's largest dairy manufacturer, Tnuva, petitioned the Supreme Court and demanded that the Minister of Finance (equivalent to Secretary of the Treasury) raise the maximum price of dairy products. An increase in the minimum price paid by dairy producers for raw milk (set by a separate regulatory arrangement) led to a rise in the manufacturing cost of milk-derived dairy products. This meant that selling some dairy products was no longer economically viable – and some items had already started experiencing retail shortages. Tnuva had initially asked the government to raise the supervised prices for dairy products by 4.08%, and the Pricing Committee ultimately recommended raising prices by 3.4%.

However, Minister of Finance Moshe Kahlon rejected the recommendation and did not sign the order. He offered a number of explanations, mainly relating to a planned legislative overhaul of the regulatory framework which would have made the price change superfluous. Such rationales aside, the background for his refusal was clearly political and electoral – Kahlon was elected on a ticket of economic "social justice" and a progressive welfare ideology. His public image, forged out of a major telecommunications reform he oversaw in 2012, was that of a fighter for the working and middle classes and against monopolistic corporate greed. As such, a hike in the cost of supervised products was anathema to his general political posture. The legal proceedings took place parallel to a heavily publicized dispute between Kahlon and dairy manufacturers, as both traded barbs blaming each other for price hikes and for product shortages. Added to all this was an upcoming elections season in which Kahlon was projected to lose a significant portion of his voter support.

The Supreme Court issued its decision in March of 2019, one month before expected elections. In a brief ruling (the majority opinion was five pages long), the Court held Kahlon's refusal to be unlawful, and ordered him to raise the maximum price as recommended, by 3.4%.[80] The word "reasonable" was not mentioned (though neither were any other concrete grounds for intervention); there is no analysis of the statutory text; the Court doesn't even cite prior rulings as relevant precedent.

In a bewildering display of legal denial, the Court simply ignored the statutory framework under which authority to set controlled prices was clearly vested in the Minister of Finance. Section 12(a) of the 1996 Supervision of Products and Services Law states that the Minister of Finance "may" issue and order setting a maximum price – meaning that price controls are the exclusive domain of the Minister and are also fully discretionary. Immediately following the requirement to consult with the Pricing Committee, Section 13(b) states that the Minister is "entitled to partially or entirely reject the Pricing Committee recommendation" while "recording" the reasons for doing so. The law could not be more explicit regarding the non-binding nature of the Committee recommendation. Also noteworthy is that the law decidedly does not require "special reasons" or "exceptional circumstances," which occasionally appear in legislation and are widely considered to impose some limits on the exercise of discretion. Here, the law set an especially low threshold such that any reason is sufficient, so long as it is recorded.

The Court could have argued that Kahlon's reasons for rejecting the recommendation were "improperly balanced" in typical reasonableness fashion, but instead it went further. Justice Uzi Vogelman stated simply that under the circumstances "there do not exist any explanations enabling [the Minister's] deviation" from the Pricing Committee recommendation. That is, not only was the Court ignoring the Minister's legal authority to reject the recommendation for any reason, but the Court held that there was *no conceivably viable* reason that the Minister could have possibly presented. Vogelman then paradoxically declares, in the same paragraph, that the Minister had a "duty" to "exercise discretion" – by this, it seems he meant the duty to forgo any discretion by submitting to the "relevant professional" judgment of the Pricing Committee.

For good measure and almost comically, Vogelman throws in the indispensable disclaimer: "Our ruling does not constitute intervention in the Finance Minister's economic policy."

Despite this comforting reassurance, the facts are undeniable: the Court exercised authority to set maximum prices on behalf of the Finance Minister affecting millions of people, in complete contradiction to the unequivocal statutory text; more broadly, the Court effectively engaged in macro-economic policymaking without the remotest effort at justifying such governmental interference on legal, statutory, or precedential grounds.

This was not Kahlon's first scuffle with the Supreme Court and by no means the latter's only intervention regarding broad economic policy, which took on a routine and almost casual character. In another case regarding pure Ministerial discretion, the Court heard a petition regarding sales taxes imposed on rolling tobacco and cigarettes. Since 2013 (and effectively long before), the sale and purchase of "standard" factory cigarettes included a hefty tax meant to discourage smoking and to improve public health. As it turned out, the same tax was not applied to loose tobacco sold for use in hand-rolled cigarettes, creating a disparity in their relative consumer prices. A number of public health advocacy groups lobbied the Finance Minister – the same Kahlon – to impose the tax on rolling tobacco as well, but he refused to do so, citing his broad policy against raising taxes or imposing new ones. The same groups in turn petitioned the Supreme Court.

In February of 2019, exactly one month prior to the *Tnuva* ruling, the Court ruled that Kahlon must adjust the sales tax as demanded by the petitioners.[81] There was no question that imposing the tax and setting the tax rate was under the Minister's express authority and discretion per the 1952 Sales Tax Law – though the Court seemed uninterested in the statute and mentions it only in passing. Instead, in a fantastic opinion by Justice Daphne Barak-Erez (former dean of the Tel Aviv law school and considered among Israel's top administrative law experts), the Court dictated tax policy to the Minister of Finance without even the pretense of legal grounds.

The Court first clarified that "policy is not a magic word," and then based its ruling (it seems) on a duty of "equality" and on a "right to health." These are of course nonsensical non-legal arguments which the Court nonetheless seems willing to treat precisely as "magic words." It feels strange to spell this out, but the administrative duty of equality (more accurately called non-discrimination) applies to different parties or individuals affected by government action and not to inanimate objects. Is Barak-Erez really saying that factory cigarettes enjoy a valid legal claim to non-discrimination? If not, who precisely was being discriminated against? The Court doesn't bother explaining (and recall, the petitioners were advocacy groups, not cigarette manufacturers). The Court also doesn't see any need to explain the alleged "right to health" (whose?) and how this right trumps the Minister's statutory authority. But why stop at tobacco? It would follow that the Minister is simply obligated to apply *any* tax the Court deems conducive to improving public health. Though the word "reasonable" does not appear in any form throughout the ruling, the Court concludes that the Minister's objection to raising taxes for low-income consumers (the main group affected by such a sales taxes) failed to "weigh" a list of other factors, mainly citing reports on smoking trends and health hazards – as usual, all pure policy considerations relating to the effects of disparate taxes, and none relating to legal authority.

True to form, the Court states that "we are not taking any position regarding tax policy" or the tax rate to be imposed on smoking products. The Court even seems to hint that the Minister could actually lower the taxes on factory cigarettes (instead of raising the tax on rolling tobacco) to achieve "equality" so long as the disparity is eliminated; but then later states its "hope" that future decisions will "ensure maintenance of public health" – in a veiled threat to intervene once again if smoking taxes are lowered. So much for "not taking any position."

Transition Government – Weiss

Section 30(b) of "Basic Law: The Government" is titled "Government Continuity" and states: "Upon the election of a new Knesset or the resignation of the Government, the outgoing Government shall continue to perform its duties until the new Government is formed."

This provision refers to the well-known phenomenon of a "caretaker" (or sometimes called "lame duck") executive government. When new elections are called or the Government resigns, the latter no longer enjoys the confidence of the legislature and by extension, of the electorate. Nonetheless, Section 30(b) clarifies that a "caretaker" Government – literally called a "Transition Government" in Israeli parlance – has the same legal standing and continues to possess all the authority and power of a normal Government. A 1977 commission headed by a retired Supreme Court Justice considered this arrangement and recommended leaving it intact. Until the Barak era, the judicial and political system consistently and unanimously held to this simple and straightforward statutory rule. Indeed, though a fully-empowered "transition government" raises obvious problems and legitimate concerns, the alternative of a restricted caretaker government is in many ways worse. Due to the unique nature of Israel's electoral system and political climate, Governments often collapse (that is, they lose the support of the Knesset, or new elections are called) and a significant amount of all political life is spent under the authority of an interim transition government. Severely limiting the authority of executive Government during its "caretaker" phase would simply mean crippling all of Israeli State administration for extended periods and on a regular basis.

The election cycles of 2018-2020 are a case in point. The Twentieth Knesset was disbanded in December of 2018 and a new Government was not formed until May of 2020, after three harrowing election cycles which produced no decisive political victories. For a full eighteen straight months, the executive Government in power was a "transition" government, technically formed in 2015. Regardless of its justification or objections, the statutory rule regarding Government Continuity is unambiguous and was once fairly uncontroversial.

From 1999 onwards, the Supreme Court methodically chipped away at this principle until it created a broad rule that the authority and discretion of all "transition" Governments are inherently limited. The Court's jurisprudence was based, of course, on reasonableness – all Government must act "reasonably," and reasonableness dictated that caretaker Governments possess an overall decreased legal capacity.

In the 2001 *Weiss* case, the Supreme Court considered a challenge against a Transition Government which was conducting peace negotiations with the Palestinians. The Court dismissed the petition on its merits and permitted the negotiations (and by extension, the possibility of a peace deal being struck) by the caretaker Government. However, in typical fashion, the ruling was qualified in *dicta*, where Aharon Barak held that the discretion of a Transition Government is "narrow" and must be exercised with "restraint and moderation." Virtually overnight, Barak upended the established "continuity" rule of Section 30(b), and subjected a large chunk of Government action to enhanced judicial oversight, once again dramatically expanding the Court's authority over that of elected branches. Needless to say, whether the conduct of a specific Transition Government deviates from its "narrow" range of discretion or is sufficiently "moderate and restrained" is up for the Supreme Court Justices to determine. Though the Court claims to prevent "irreversible" decisions made by a Transition Government, its jurisprudence in implementing this rule has been wildly erratic and inconsistent – permitting decisions which are manifestly "irreversible" in any meaningful sense, and blocking trivial actions which are easily remedied, altered or cancelled by a future Government.[82]

Since *Weiss*, the decisions and policies of "caretaker" executive government have been held to a wholly-invented standard of "narrow" discretion, based solely on "reasonableness" and directly contradicting black-letter statutory law. Critically, these include a wide array of governmental appointments across the length and breadth of civil service roles, including judicial appointments. Scholars have shown how during different Transition Government periods the Court has prevented judicial appointments it disfavored, while approving (and indeed rushing) judicial appointments it found beneficial.[83]

Internal Parliamentary Proceedings

As a doctrine within administrative law, "reasonableness" might naturally be considered as confined to the limits of reviewing executive action. Yet for the Supreme Court, reasonableness served as a basis for expanding its authority to review internal parliamentary decisions and procedures.

Much like almost any legislature the world over, the Knesset doesn't only serve a purely legislative function. The Knesset plenary, committees, and various officers perform a large variety of functions relating to internal parliamentary matters as well to supervision of the executive in numerous ways. Among other issues, these might cover the day-to-day agenda of the Knesset legislative and deliberative process; ethics decisions and disciplinary proceedings against Knesset members; the revocation or grant of parliamentary immunity from criminal proceedings; elections-related decisions; appointing Knesset-related roles and approval of executive appointments; and formulation or approval of quasi-legislative regulations. These are in addition to the routine review, discussion and amendment of proposed legislation. Knesset committees and top officials are reconstituted after every elections cycle, reflecting the current balance of electoral power within parliament.

In most Western jurisdictions internal parliamentary decisions and proceedings are typically not subject to judicial review. One reason for judicial non-involvement is that these are "partisan" in the most literal sense – judicial intervention would typically be to the benefit or detriment of a specific political faction in parliament. Such decisions are "political" not only due to their ideological or value-based character, but also especially because their subject matter is parliamentary politics themselves. Another reason is the lack of legal grounds for review, as these are often policy or discretionary decisions with no conventional legal norms for analysis or scrutiny. In other words, such decisions could rarely violate an actual enforceable legal rule. Still another reason relates to the fundamentally problematic nature of judicial enforcement – will the judiciary issue orders dictating that elected legislators vote a certain way? Will uncompliant legislators be held in contempt of court? Judicial intervention in parliamentary proceedings almost invites unseemly showdowns. Yet another reason is that legislative institutions often have their own internal mechanisms for resolving dispute and disagreement, both on substantive and on procedural levels. These might include some internal appellate process for review of certain decisions. A final reason is that legislators are the most democratically accountable – and at the same time possess the highest degree of democratic legitimacy and authority – among all government officials. Their conduct ought to, and will inevitably, be subject to the scrutiny and approval or censure of the voting public. Many of these rationales come down to basic conceptions of justiciability and of the separation of powers.

For all these reasons, internal Knesset decisions had been considered immune from judicial review – until the 1980s. In the 1981 case of *Flatto-Sharon* the Court overturned a Knesset committee decision to suspend an MK under criminal investigation. The majority opinion reasoned that when a Knesset committee or organ is performing a "quasi-judicial" function its decision must be subject to judicial oversight: "It is inconceivable that when fulfilling this role a Knesset committee will be immune from judicial review, and that the committee will be the one defining the limits of its authority."[84] The fact that this seemed eminently conceivable to many others – including prior generations of the Supreme Court and the jurisprudence of most civilized nations – escaped the Court's attention.

Chief Justice Landau reliably penned the dissenting opinion in *Flatto-Sharon*, questioning the Court's confident assertion it had the power to review internal Knesset decisions. He quotes a Supreme Court decision from only a few months before, which repeated the "known" rule that "this Court does not intervene in procedures of the Knesset and its committees."[85] Nonetheless, Landau's objections left little impression on the Court, which after *Flatto-Sharon* proceeded to adjudicate internal Knesset procedures in routine fashion and with a heavy hand.

The following year the Court issued the 1982 *Sarid* ruling, which extended the Court's jurisdiction to all parliamentary proceedings, and not only "quasi-judicial" decisions as had been established in *Flatto-Sharon*. Aharon Barak proclaimed that the "rule of law" requires judicial review of internal parliamentary decisions, though ostensibly the Court would intervene only in rare cases involving "substantial harm to the fabric of parliamentary life" or violations of "substantive values of the constitutional order."[86] Both rulings, and the Court's subsequent jurisprudence, rely heavily on evaluating the reasonableness of internal parliamentary decisions. Needless to say, such open-ended and ambiguous standards meant little beyond unfettered judicial meddling in parliamentary affairs.

Yoav Dotan describes this novel development as an "unprecedented encroachment of the Court upon the affairs of the legislative branch (both in terms of the history of the State of Israel and in terms of what is acceptable in other Western countries)," which has "no parallel in the democratic regimes known to us."[87] The immediate repercussions were extensive, with all manner of internal parliamentary decision-making routinely challenged and adjudicated by the Supreme Court. Dotan emphasizes that the effect of such litigation reaches far beyond any specific final judicial outcome, incurring "severe societal costs": "HCJ petitions have become a nearly-routine parliamentary instrument through which MKs (and other interested parties) attempt to influence legislative deliberations and obtain various political advantages." Dotan describes how instead of legislators facing off regarding their political differences in the Knesset plenary and committees, they "confront each other armed with attorneys in the courtroom" and while "the final arbiters in such disputes are the HCJ Justices." The adjudication of internal parliamentary proceedings demonstrates, per Dotan, how the Court's "remedy" of limitless justiciability (based on reasonableness review) is "far worse than the ailment" which the Court purports to cure. Incessant judicial intervention in Knesset affairs causes damage to the "fabric of parliamentary life," to the "proper functioning of parliamentary institutions" and to the Knesset's public standing, damage far more severe than that which the Court claims it is trying to prevent.[88]

The issue of internal parliamentary proceedings was at the core of the remarkable 2020 *Edelstein* case. At the height of cross-party negotiations to form a Coalition following the April 2020 elections, a majority of Knesset members attempted to replace the current Knesset Speaker who had been appointed by the previous Coalition. The Knesset Speaker is the nominal and official head or leader of the Israeli legislature, and is one of the most significant and powerful figures in Israeli government. Among other authorities and privileges, the Speaker sets the deliberative and legislative agenda for the Knesset plenary. Typically and historically, a new Knesset Speaker was only ever appointed following the formation of a new Coalition and Government; but in 2020 a tenuous group of parties sought to derail coalition negotiations – and perhaps enact unilateral legislation retroactively skewing the outcome of the recent elections – without themselves willing to jointly form a Government. Critically, if a new Knesset Speaker were appointed and then a new Government formed by a different group of parties, then the new Government and Coalition would have been stuck with a Knesset Speaker they did not appoint and whom they could not remove – because replacing a Knesset Speaker (when not following elections) requires a supermajority of ninety MKs. Indeed, such a scenario – a Speaker not appointed by the governing Coalition and potentially adverse to it – had never happened before.

Due to the highly irregular (not to say, nefarious) nature of this attempt, the serving Speaker (seasoned MK Yuli Edelstein) refused to add the requested vote to the Knesset agenda. Edelstein did not reject the attempt outright, but simply declined to hold the vote in the immediate few days while critical Coalition negotiations were underway. In doing so, he was acting well within the statutory framework which defined Speaker discretion and mandatory timelines for implementing such parliamentary requests.

Edelstein's refusal was of course challenged in the Supreme Court. In one of the most extraordinary and notorious rulings in the Court's history, five Justices led by Chief Justice Esther Hayut unanimously voted to interfere with Edelstein's authority as Speaker, and commanded that he convene the Knesset plenary within two days in order to hold a vote on appointing a new Speaker.[89] In doing so the Court in *Edelstein* assumed the power to proactively dictate to the Knesset its internal legislative agenda, down to minute details of what vote to hold on which day. This was despite the fact that the Court did not hold that Edelstein's decision violated any statute or any of the Knesset's internal procedural rules – in fact, the ruling doesn't even seriously discuss the applicable statutory framework. Instead, the Court simply asserted that Edelstein's decision "deviates from his valid range of discretion" (a familiar shorthand for reasonableness review, with a pinch of "caretaker government" rhetoric for good measure) and "undermines the foundations of the democratic process" (yes, really).

Backed into a corner, Yuli Edelstein chose to resign from his role as Speaker rather than obey the Court's unlawful order. The Court then doubled down and, instead of following statutory procedures designed for such an event, simply issued a new order which appointed another MK as Acting Speaker for the sole purpose of administering the requested vote. Amazingly, the Court even instructed the prospective new Acting Speaker precisely when to assemble the Knesset plenary and to hold the vote.

The Court's interference came within the most fraught and sensitive of all political moments, in the aftermath of viciously contentious elections and while rival political parties were trying to form a Government (and, incidentally, just a few days after the first COVID-19 lockdown order). By facilitating (or supporting) the Speaker's replacement, the Court also waded deep into the partisan-political fray – the factions demanding a new Speaker were largely affiliated with the cause of judicial supremacy, while the opponents of judicial supremacy would have been severely disadvantaged by the appointment of a new (and adverse) Speaker. By extension, the Court itself was a primary beneficiary of such disadvantage to its own political opponents, by effectively facilitating the appointment of a new supremacist-aligned Speaker. Many viewed the Court's decision as thinly veiled self-serving partisan-political meddling.

Edelstein demonstrates many of the points discussed above. The Court subjected parliamentary proceedings of the highest political consequence to its own arbitrary control without the slightest legal foundation aside vague proclamations of "reasonableness" and "democracy." Such interference would be unthinkable in any other Western jurisdiction in the world – in most countries, parliamentary proceedings (and especially Speakership decisions) are explicitly and comprehensively non-justiciable, immune from judicial oversight. The Court did so without the slightest reference to statutory rules or other regulations which might serve as a source for its ruling, while Edelstein indeed had the Knesset procedural rules on his side.[90] Instead, the Court's reliance on an arbitrary "range of discretion" reflects the inherent malleability and vapidity of reasonableness review.

On a side note, the Court's ruling backfired spectacularly. With the threat of an adverse Speaker being appointed and of flash legislation which would retroactively alter the election results, the Knesset's largest parties settled their differences (at least temporarily) and formed the Netanyahu-Gantz unity Government (including a major split between Gantz's center-left party and its farther-left-wing political partners). In other words, the Court arguably facilitated Netanyahu's renewed premiership after three election cycles and eighteen months of political deadlock. It is quite conceivable that Netanyahu's political career might have ended, had it not been for the *Edelstein* ruling and the Court's heavy handed, unfounded and aggressive interference.

Ritual Baths

Religious Jewish law involves an occasional obligation to bathe in a ritual bath called a *Mikveh*, most frequently applying to women at the end of a menstrual cycle. *Mikvehs* in Israel can be privately owned and operated, but are also provided as a public service under the combined auspices of central government (the Ministry of Religious Services), local municipal government and local official rabbinical authorities, among others.

The small town of *Kfar Vradim* (population 6,000) never had its own *Mikveh*. Other nearby *Mikvehs* were a short drive away, though were inaccessible on the Sabbath or on Jewish holidays in which religious law prohibits driving or riding in a vehicle. The overwhelming majority of *Kfar Vradim* residents are secular and do not make use of a *Mikveh* nor strictly observe the Jewish Sabbath. Following requests from numerous families, in 2007 the national government allocated substantial funds for the establishment and operation of a *Mikveh* in *Kfar Vradim*, subject to the approval of the locally-elected municipal government known as the Local Council. After some resistance the Local Council initially approved the construction of a new *Mikveh*, but then revoked its approval for a variety of reasons in 2008. The Council's considerations included available appropriate sites, competing priorities (e.g., other building projects and efforts needed by the town), and unresolved questions surrounding maintenance costs of the *Mikveh*. The Council formed a public committee which held several meetings (including a town hall meeting open to all local residents), and which eventually determined clear criteria for prioritization of public building projects. According to the criteria, a new *Mikveh* scored lowest on almost every metric and was ranked last place out of seventeen potential new building projects.

The Council's decision against a new *Mikveh* was challenged in Administrative (District) Court which ruled in favor of the Council, and the case eventually arrived on appeal at the Supreme Court.

In 2014 the Supreme Court reversed the Administrative Court ruling and found the Council's decision to be invalid. The Supreme Court held that *Kvar Vradim's* refusal to build a *Mikveh* was unreasonable and that it therefore had an obligation to approve and construct one: "The Council's decision does not reasonably balance the needs of the religiously observant female residents to fulfill their obligation of ritual bathing, with the budgetary considerations and the available land resources."[91]

The Court did not find the Council's decision to be irrational or arbitrary, nor did it violate any local or national statutory provision, nor did it involve procedural flaws, nor were any improper or discriminatory factors considered. Rather, Justice Vogelman (writing for the unanimous panel) explained how a local township's decisions regarding the allocation of local resources are subject to the requirements of reasonableness:

> "The allocation of public resources by local authorities must accord with the principles of reasonableness and proportionality...
>
> Reasonableness requires that, in determining the order of priorities

> among various matters... preference be given to those of greater importance."

Sounds sensible enough. But who is to decide which matters are of greater or lesser importance? Not the democratically elected and accountable Council members; not the local residents funding such matters with their local taxes; it is, rather, Justice Uzi Vogelman who must solemnly apply the principle of reasonableness to ensure the Council arrives at the properly-balanced conclusion. And so Justice Vogelman (along with Justices Hayut and Hendel) proceeds to do just that – after a stimulating and edifying discussion of the conflicting factors and considerations to be weighed by the Council in making their decision, the Court turns to consider whether these were accorded their relative appropriate weight. As he does so, Vogelman perfectly encapsulates the Court's false pretense of simple and straightforward application of a technical legal standard: "All that remains is to examine whether the decision reasonably balances between the various considerations."

Not to be accused of excessive self-awareness or of an aversion for irony, Vogelman first waxes poetic about the wide "range of reasonableness" within which administrative decisions can be made, reminding us that the "balancing" of competing factors "does not usually yield one single reasonable result." Alas, *Kfar Vradim* serves as the unlucky exception, and Vogelman finds that "the Council's decision not to pursue the establishment of a town *Mikveh* is not within the range of reasonableness," and as such, the decision is "void." Leaving nothing to chance, Vogelman clarifies that "the required decision is to establish the *Mikveh* without undue delay," ordering that "building commence as soon as possible" and no later than eighteen months after the Court's ruling. Here, indeed, the Court found that reasonableness dictated "one single result."

The *Kfar Vradim* case exemplifies the unrestricted and absurd expansion of "reasonableness" to any conceivable government action and its undermining of elementary democratic norms. Far from solely "negative" review which prevents extreme or "outrageous" abuse of authority, here the Court proactively micromanages the affairs of a small local municipal council, compelling it to expend resources against its will, for a particular purpose in which most local residents have no interest, at the expense of other priorities and preferences, and based solely on the vague and vacuous standard of "reasonableness." The elected Local Council's decision was not corrupt or illegal in any ordinary sense – its cardinal legal error was that it disagreed with the Supreme Court on how best to serve its local constituency and residents, and on how to best use local resources and town funds.

Valiant but Futile

Despite the fierce objections to unreasonableness as presented previously in this chapter, one ought not get the wrong impression. Such critiques within the legal community were few and far between and largely fell on deaf ears. As Dotan notes in a 2015 essay, "the discourse of reasonableness took over the Court's jurisprudence completely."[92] Notable instances of judicial resistance to the empire of reasonableness throughout the four decades since *Yellow Pages* may be easily counted on one hand, appeared sporadically in fits and starts and indeed represent exceptions that prove the rule – what we call in Hebrew, "a voice in the wilderness" (Isaiah 40:3).* For the most part, the judiciary has eagerly embraced and further fortified the reasonableness standard. As Barak and his followers reshaped the Court in their image, the newer judges "have enjoyed the expanded powers bestowed on them by the concept of reasonableness, which enabled them to impose their ideological convictions on the Israeli administration under the thick and vague veil of reasonableness."

Serious academic treatment of reasonableness has been almost as feeble, with the legal academic community ranging in their approach from enthusiasm to acquiescence to indifference, and only a small cadre of critical scholars willing to venture into the fray. In his 1994 essay, Mautner writes that "there has been no wide discussion in Israeli legal literature regarding the severe problems that the [reasonableness] standard raises" – this holds true today as it did then.

This utter lack of engagement has enabled the Court to adopt a "nothing to see here" approach. The Court has never been compelled to grapple with reasonableness in a serious way and has generally refused to address or even acknowledge those severe problems and many fundamental objections associated with the standard. The Court rather maintains its blanket and deadpan insistence that its use of reasonableness is a perfectly viable and ordinary method of judicial review representing an established standard of legal analysis. Per Dotan, "rather than dealing with the hard questions surrounding the very legitimacy of the use of reasonableness," the Court treated reasonableness "as if it were simply a technical tool applied to administrative actions by 'professionals' (i.e., judges) on an ideologically 'neutral' basis."

As Dotan observes, choosing to ignore valid objections to reasonableness was no accident, as engagement would constitute a "genuine impediment" and a "political problem" for acolytes of judicial supremacy. The Court's persistent claim that it is merely enforcing "the law" and its straight-faced denial of plain and obvious truths undoubtedly reach near-Orwellian proportions. Yet it is precisely this façade which allows the Court to impose policy as though it were enforcing clear legal rules and to supersede the highest elected offices as though these were municipal bureaucrats. As we shall see later in Chapter 8, the intellectual vacuum surrounding reasonableness is also an important factor allowing proactive coercion of policy by the Legal Counsel to the Government.

---

* Such objections were also often half-hearted or lacked resolve. For example, despite his criticism of Barak in *Zarzevsky*, Justice Elon ultimately ruled in favor of adjudicating political agreements on other grounds.

*

There is much more to say of the "extreme unreasonableness" standard developed and utilized by the Supreme Court. The reasonableness standard was just one element (albeit the most dominant) within a broader avalanche of jurisprudential shifts initiated by the Barak Court throughout the 1980s and 1990s. The Court developed a robust theory of "proportionality" in reviewing governmental infringement of individual rights; it subjected private entities to strict standards of public law, bringing further institutions and spheres under its control; it annulled many preexisting statutory restrictions and limitations on the Supreme Court's authority. Chapter 8 will address how the Court employed "reasonableness" to subject major prosecutorial decisions to judicial oversight, weaponizing the criminal justice system against political and ideological foes.

In his sprawling concurring opinion in the 2024 *Reasonableness* ruling, Justice Amit emphasizes that instances of direct judicial intervention represent only a fraction of the standard's real effect, the bulk of which is the day-to-day decision-making process throughout all levels of government. Per Amit: "A central aspect of the power and function of the reasonableness standard lies not in the retrospective judicial review of an administrative decision, but in its prospective application within the administrative mechanism itself, during the formulation and design of the decision."[93] Yoav Dotan argues much the same, stating that "there is no correlation between the amount of times the Court issues a binding order in a final ruling, and the amount of times judicial involvement causes a de facto change to the administrative decision or causes the revocation of a government action."[94]

Indeed, the myriad permutations of routine government action influenced by reasonableness form the vast submerged iceberg of which dramatic rulings are merely the visible tip.

The 2023 Reasonableness Amendment (to be examined in Chapter 11), struck down by the Court in 2024, sought to limit the use of reasonableness against Government (i.e., Cabinet-level) decisions. The motivation behind the Knesset's desire to do so is perhaps now clearer.

Chapter 6

The Deri Doctrine of Judicial Impeachment

Subjugation of Government and Criminalization of Politics

> "*The Deri Doctrine... is fundamentally flawed, as it defies most core principles of public law... The procedure created by the Supreme Court through the Deri Doctrine does not exist anywhere else in the world... The Court seized for itself – with no tangible statutory basis – the authority to impeach senior officials in the Executive branch.*"
>
> — Prof. Yoav Dotan[1]

We now turn to what is, without question, the most dramatic and consequential manifestation of the Court's unreasonableness standard at the intersection of administrative, constitutional, and criminal law. It is here that unfettered and immediate access to the Supreme Court, malleability of any statutory language, no standing requirement, limitless justiciability, and substantive review of executive "reasonableness" on its merits all culminate in the most personal and ruthless weaponization of judicial power. This is also where we will inevitably deviate from our examination of doctrine and consider realpolitik – the practical and temporal impact on Israeli politicians and senior officials.

The following chapter will focus on two related legal innovations. Developing and utilizing a mechanism unseen in the free world, the Supreme Court has claimed the power to prevent the appointment – and to order the dismissal – of any conceivable government official, based solely on grounds of reasonableness. More egregiously still, by holding that criminal proceedings against an official are automatic grounds for mandatory removal, the Court has effectively delegated its power of removal to the bureaucratic, highly-autonomous, non-judicial proxy institutions of criminal prosecution and law enforcement. It is impossible to overstate the significance of these developments – individually and jointly – and their profound effect on the Israeli political landscape and on the lopsided interrelationship between the judicial and the elected branches.

Though these mechanisms are nominally and doctrinally based on the reasonableness standard and operate within its contours, their deviation from global democratic theory and practice and the sheer magnitude of their impact demands separate analytical treatment.

Unreasonable Appointments

Through judicial review of executive appointments, the Court "gained for itself direct effective control," explains Yoav Dotan, of "what is perhaps the most important and critical authority held by the government."[2]

The 1993 case known as *Eisenberg* centered on one Yossi Ginosar, an experienced public official and former intelligence officer who had been selected by the Minister of Construction and Housing to serve as the Ministry's Director General. The office of Director General is one of the most senior and influential in Israeli executive government – each Government Ministry has its own Director General, charged with overall management of their respective Ministry and responsible for its performance and professional duties. Enormously demanding but highly prestigious, it is among the most widely coveted and respected managerial positions in Israeli public service. As a key figure in implementing government policy for a given Ministry, the Director General is a discretionary political appointee and is typically replaced by each incoming Government Minister following general elections. On a technical level a Minister selects and nominates their desired Director General for their own Ministry, who is then formally approved by the Government.

Though already a senior public official, Ginosar was known to the public for another reason – he had been implicated in the 1984 "Bus 300 Affair," in which the Shin Bet (Israel's internal security service) had covered up the extra-judicial execution of two arrested terrorists. Ginosar never stood trial, as he had received (along with a slew of other Shin Bet officials) a preemptive pardon from the President. Despite his alleged involvement in the Bus 300 scandal, there was no question that Ginosar was both qualified for the job and that he also met all professional statutory requirements.

Ginosar's selection as Director General was swiftly challenged by a private citizen at the Supreme Court as unreasonable due to his tarnished history. Here then was a perfect storm, a microcosm of the ascendant judicial revolution reviewed so far: an exercise of explicit statutory authority; an inherently political decision within the heart of executive government prerogative; no statutory basis for intervention (or even open to interpretation); no aggrieved party that can show personal injury for redress; a matter typically (and historically) considered non-justiciable; and the absence of any structural filter between petitioner and apex court. For all the obvious reasons, the Court had never before invalidated a high-ranking appointment of this kind and on such grounds.

As the reader might expect at this point, in a first-of-its-kind decision, the Court intervened with little hesitation and ruled that the appointment was unlawful due to the specter of Ginosar's (alleged) criminal past. The unprecedented, 50-page *Eisenberg* decision was penned by Justice Barak and served as the blueprint for the Court's ensuing jurisprudence on executive appointments.

First, Barak attends to any statutory hurdles. The applicable law authorizing a Director General's appointment set no explicit rules or limitations regarding past criminal conduct of appointees. Even so, Barak held that the absence of any textual or statutory limitation relating to an appointee's past criminal actions is not to be understood as the absence of any legal limitation per se. This is because any statute authorizing appointments must be "interpreted" to include an intrinsic obligation to consider a candidate's criminal past. "Any legislation is enacted within a 'normative environment'... which is an aggregate of the views, values, principles and interests which the legal norm is meant to fulfill." Per Barak, this "normative umbrella" includes "the State's democratic character," the "need for public order" and the obligation that all government "must act reasonably and decently."[3]

Here Barak makes the critical and enduring distinction between the statutory requirements regarding executive appointments, which he calls the candidate's "*competence*," and the balancing of various competing factors (based primarily on reasonableness) by the appointing body, which he calls "*discretion*." An appointment might be valid in terms of "competence" but can still run afoul of (reasonable) "discretion." Barak thus effectively redefines statutory requirements as a minimum base for further evaluation, and thereby renders authorizing statutes (which establish core requirements and grant wide discretion for appointments beyond these) virtually meaningless. "Competence on the one hand and discretion on the other" has since become a judicial maxim. All any of this really means is simply the subjection of executive appointments to the familiar judicial balancing act of reasonableness review, by combining purposive meta-interpretation of appointment-related statutes and applying the competence-discretion distinction.[*]

Next, Barak presents two fundamental rationales for the inclusion of a candidate's criminal past in any appointment considerations. One is a principle of "good character" (or literally – "purity of virtue"): Officers and individuals serving in State organs must possess adequate moral standing. Another is the principle of "public faith" in government: State authorities must strive to ensure and maintain "public faith" in the government's institutions and officials. Insufficient weight given to a candidate's criminal past violates both these

---

[*] Notably, Barak cites a different statute relating to ordinary (non-political) government employees, which stipulates that the Civil Service Commissioner may consider a candidate's past criminal conduct when approving an appointment. Barak concedes that this other statute explicitly does *not* apply to political appointments made by the Government, and that the statute relevant to Government appointments (such as Ginosar's) makes no such stipulation. One might take this to mean that the Government has no such obligation for Ginosar, but Barak concludes the opposite – that the Civil Service Commissioner statute somehow bears upon *all* governmental appointments, and that the "may" (for the former) actually becomes a "must" for Government political appointments.

(somewhat overlapping) public interests. In other words, an executive appointment which does not properly factor past criminal conduct in its considerations is unreasonable, due to its violation of the "good character" principle and its damage to "public faith" in government. Needless to say, the relative appropriate weight attributed to past criminal conduct in accordance with these principles is determined by the judge in each individual case. Barak is unconcerned about any feasibility of such balancing, assuring us that "as there is no person without a shadow, thus there is no principle without weight."[4]

Finally, Barak applies his novel theory to Ginosar's appointment as Director General, though this analysis occupies just a single striking paragraph which is well worth quoting. Ginosar's "appointment… is within the Government's [statutory] authority"; "in the absence of any law" to the contrary, "he is competent" to serve as Director General. "The Government weighed all relevant factors," nor did the Court find that irrelevant factors were weighed. "Nonetheless," continues Barak,

> "The Government's decision is invalid. It is inherently unreasonable to the extreme. The Government did not properly balance between the relevant factors."[5]

The Court offers almost no further elaboration on what proper balancing would look like, or what proper weight should have been attributed to Ginosar's past conduct (and why, and how). To the anticipated objection that the Court is simply substituting executive discretion with its own, Barak responds that "the question is not whether the government's decision is wise, but rather whether the government's decision is legal," again conflating discretionary reasonableness with pure legality under the pretense that these are one and the same. Devoid of self-awareness, or perhaps aware and indifferent, Barak then expounds on the importance of the rule of law, declaring that the Government's high rank within the State hierarchy "cannot grant it powers that the law does not grant," without considering that the same ought to apply to the Supreme Court. He concludes – "no authority is above the law, no authority is permitted to act unreasonably."

Barak's new method of reviewing executive appointments throughout all levels of government under the auspices of "reasonableness" balancing quickly became the new norm. Today, it would not be an exaggeration to say that virtually every senior appointment in governmental life is subject to legal challenge and adjudication. Critically, the twin rationales of "good character" and "public faith" are in no way limited to a candidate's criminal conduct, such that any conceivable flaw in the candidate's background may easily trigger judicial review and disqualification. These extend to past ethical and disciplinary proceedings, controversial or offensive public (or even private) comments, allegations of indecent relationships, zoning violations, tax reporting errors and a host of other inconsequential or immaterial transgressions. The doctrine is also not limited to prevention or disqualification of potential prospective candidates but applies also to dismissal of serving officials.

Yoav Dotan notes that since *Eisenberg* and ensuing cases, the Court "has dealt with petitions against appointment of Ministers, deputy-Ministers, top administrative officials, and high-ranking (or even medium-level) positions within the military, the police and other government departments."[6] The Court's intervention with discretionary appointments at all levels of government is a "permanent component" of Israeli public discourse and of any related political controversy. This type of routine intervention in government appointments on such non-existent legal grounds "does not exist in any other legal system."[7]

To Hire and to Fire

To fully appreciate the implications of this development it is worth pausing for a moment to reflect on the nature of government appointments.

While such judicial intervention is in some sense a natural, even inevitable extension of reasonableness review, appointments are not just another category of governmental discretion, but should rather be understood as governing itself. Some might say that as a practical matter, effective executive government boils down to one sole element – the power to hire and to fire. This is because de facto governing (including discretionary decision-making and value judgments) is routinely performed by a host of unelected officials on a variety of levels and in a myriad of instances. Even direct Ministerial authority, such as signing explicit orders or decrees, is channeled and funneled through the bureaucratic network of government officials and employees. In other words, administrators – not Ministers – are the ones primarily tasked with actual day to day governing, and the senior layer of elected government is therefore virtually powerless to ensure its policies are implemented without the active cooperation and alignment of its subordinates. As just one example, what power does the elected government have over its own military forces, if unable to appoint the top-ranking military generals? As the adage goes, "personnel is policy."

It is for this reason that the primary authority of any Minister or Secretary is that of selecting the officials exercising governmental power at various levels of the executive. Ultimately the extent of executive democratic authority is limited to the power to choose who directly implements, oversees and enforces policy. Indeed, it is not only a privilege and prerogative but also the duty of representative government to appoint executive officials who are committed to the faithful implementation of its policies and preferences.

Such control can be achieved through the selection of specific compatible senior officials but is also accomplished in part by the authority (and threat) to remove existing subordinates for unruly, objectionable or ineffective performance. This does not necessarily mean that every government employee be personally and directly appointed by senior politicians, nor that any employee be subject to whimsical or arbitrary dismissal. But it reflects the understanding that the potential for removal from public office is the most effective check on considerable unaccountable executive power, and at times the only genuine guarantee against the flagrant flouting of governmental authority.

Envisioning the reverse is useful here. Without being subject to the risk of dismissal, unelected administrators exercising discretionary authority become a rogue power unto themselves – autonomous nodes that may do as they please (within constraints of the law), a genuine "Deep State" shielded from significant democratic input and with nothing to ensure their adherence to senior governmental command. The example of military leadership aids us again – what assurances are there against the top military general flatly refusing to comply with lawful government orders? None at all, aside from the government's authority to effectuate the general's immediate dismissal. The power of appointment is not only about legitimate authority of elected government but also about accountability of otherwise irremovable and deeply entrenched executive officials. Indeed, in many senses it is the discretionary appointment and the potential for dismissal which confers upon unelected officials the legitimacy to wield governmental power in the first place.

To be clear, there is value in maintaining a degree of professional independence for government employees to protect them from arbitrary or partisan dismissal and to ensure they carry out their duties without fear of reprisal. Nevertheless, many governmental roles are universally considered as subject to total Ministerial (or otherwise accountable) discretion, due to: (A) their inherently political and partisan nature; (B) their close interaction with senior politicians requiring personal compatibility; and (C) the high degree of governmental power afforded to them, requiring direct civilian (political and elected) oversight. For obvious reasons, the more senior the rank of a public official, the more true this becomes.

Appointments are therefore not merely another subset of governmental decision-making, but are rather correctly seen as a precondition to governing or even as its very essence. Governing without appointing is no governing at all.

*

In light of the above, the *Eisenberg* doctrine subjecting any government appointments to the reasonableness standard and thus to arbitrary judicial review is properly understood as the ultimate subordination of executive government to judicial whim. The Supreme Court wields a veto over governmental appointments, may dismiss serving government officials and in certain cases comes close to dictating the identity of a prospective appointee. It's worth repeating that this relates to instances such as the ones described by Barak himself in *Eisenberg*, in which the appointee meets all statutory requirements, the appointment violates no statutory limitations, and the appointing authority considered all relevant and material factors. In a somewhat ironic twist (as if to prove the arbitrary nature of the Court's intervention), immediately following the

Eisenberg ruling, Mr. Ginosar was appointed as the head of the state-run public housing corporation "Amidar," to which the Court had no objection.

A critical element of such judicial intervention lies not necessarily in its employment, but rather in its very existence. Cases of actual direct disqualification by court order are (arguably) rare, yet the routine adjudication of any senior government appointment has a debilitating overall effect. Dotan observes that despite the failure of most such petitions, their impact "cannot be underestimated."[8] The initiation of legal proceedings and the Court's laborious scrutiny in each case gains massive media attention, which in turn often leads to the appointment's failure – either the appointing authority backs off "to save itself the political costs" of following through, or the candidate withdraws so as "to save themselves the embarrassment and negative publicity."[9] In other words, the Court's removal doctrine serves as a tool to intimidate (and ultimately cow) both government and appointee without any need for a final judicial decision.

As a case in point, Dotan notes that in 2011 "all the leading candidates for the three top positions" in the military, the national police and the prison service "were forced to withdraw their candidacy" due to various allegations of misconduct.[10] The failure of these candidacies was not a result of public pressure per se and not derived from the severity of the allegations, but was rather caused by the near-certainty[*] that the Court would disqualify the appointments. Importantly, none of the allegations in this instance actually produced any criminal charges. One allegation against Yoav Gallant, who was then considered the leading candidate to serve as the IDF's top general, regarded a benign zoning violation and was later found to be completely unfounded – though the ship of his candidacy had long since sailed and another general, one Benjamin (Benny) Gantz, had already been appointed.

We will later return to Barak's arguments and the theoretical framework for this doctrine, as well as to its practical application and implications. However, as it turns out, *Eisenberg* was merely the precursor and the prelude to an even greater tectonic shift in the Israeli system of government, to which we now turn.

The Deri-Pinhasi Cases

In September of 1993, hot on the heels of *Eisenberg* and built on the same foundations, the Supreme Court issued a pair of landmark rulings regarding two high-ranking politicians, Aryeh Deri and Rafael Pinhasi. Both were elected legislators and both members of the Labor Government led by Prime Minister Yitzhak Rabin. Aryeh Deri served as Minister of the Interior and was a rising political star, having become the youngest-ever Government Minister in 1988 at the age of twenty-nine. Rafael Pinhasi was Deputy Minister of Religious Affairs. Both belonged to the Shas political party.

---

[*] This certainty is born of the Legal Counsel to the Government's refusal to defend such appointments in court, to be addressed in Chapter 8.

Deri and Pinhasi were each implicated in separate criminal investigations involving varying levels of corruption. At the time, MKs were immune from criminal prosecution unless their immunity was rescinded by a Knesset vote. After the Legal Counsel to the Government filed draft indictments with the Knesset, the latter upheld Pinhasi's immunity and had yet to vote on Deri's. As such neither had yet been formally indicted, though the State Prosecution and Legal Counsel to the Government clearly intended to charge both with criminal conduct.

Immunity notwithstanding, the Legal Counsel to the Government – Mr. Yosef Harish – informed Prime Minister Rabin that he was legally obligated to exercise his authority and to dismiss both Deri and Pinhasi, as leaving them in their current Ministerial position would be "contrary to core principles of law and government." Harish explained that the pair's dismissal was not only required by "public or moral standards," but also by legal ones.

Rabin refused to dismiss Deri and Pinhasi, citing a variety of justifications. Chief among these was the simple fact that there was no discernible legal obligation to do so – applicable statutory law granted the Prime Minister authority to dismiss a Government Minister, but was completely silent on grounds for dismissal, to say nothing of criminal proceedings.* The statutory language – "The Prime Minister *may* remove" – clearly indicated wide discretion. Further, Rabin cited political considerations such as the integrity and survival of his coalition government, not least because of its heavy engagement with the historical Palestinian-Israeli peace process. (Strikingly, the first Oslo Accord was signed a mere four days following the Court's ruling). More specifically, Shas is an Ultra-Orthodox religious party and is generally associated with the political right, such that its support was therefore a critical (and even decisive) element in Rabin's pursuit of public legitimacy surrounding his peace negotiations.

Rabin judged that the momentous occasion and high foreign-policy stakes justified prioritizing the stability of his coalition. Rabin also noted that the allegations and suspicions had been publicly known during the previous elections and the formation of the current Government – such that the criminal proceedings had already been factored in to electoral preferences, and the appointment of both Ministers had received the Knesset's assent. Rabin also felt vindicated by the Knesset's recent decision to retain Pinhasi's immunity: how unreasonable could his refusal be if it tracks with the Knesset's skepticism regarding the allegations against Pinhasi?

Sure enough, Rabin's decision was challenged in the Supreme Court. On September 8th, 1993, the Court issued two simultaneous rulings which were for all intents and purposes one and the same. Both rulings were decided by the same five-member panel; both rulings cross-referenced and quoted each other; both set out essentially the same arguments leading to the same result. The Deri decision was penned by Chief Justice Shamgar, while the Pinhasi decision was penned by

* The law did address criminal convictions (and imprisonment) in the context of criteria for *appointing* Ministers, but did not address grounds for their *removal* after taking office.

Justice Barak. The Court held that Rabin's refusal to dismiss Deri and Pinhasi upon their indictment amounted to "extreme unreasonableness" and was therefore void; and that under such circumstances Rabin had a legal obligation to exercise his discretion and dismiss both Ministers. The Court's rationale relied heavily on the one presented in *Eisenberg*, of "good character," "public faith," the "competence-discretion" distinction, and so on. At this point, there were no biting dissenting opinions from the likes of Justices Landau or Elon – the rulings were unanimous.

After Rabin gingerly complied with the Court's ruling and fired Deri and Pinhasi, the Shas party resigned from his Government, causing it to be a "minority government" in which its constituent political parties did not command a legislative majority within the Knesset, but remained in power as the Opposition could not marshal sufficient votes to replace the Government or to call new elections. The continuation of the Oslo peace process thus also suffered from severely diminished legitimacy as it was conducted by a Government lacking electoral majority support (barely sustained by the backing of anti-Zionist Arab parties). Proceeding with the immensely controversial Oslo process as a minority government and without the legitimacy afforded by the Shas party undoubtedly contributed to massive societal polarization and to the combustible public atmosphere at the time. The government's term ended when Prime Minister Rabin was tragically assassinated in 1995.*

The rule established in the dual cases of Deri and Pinhasi became known as the *Deri-Pinhasi Doctrine*, which we may simply call *Deri.* The doctrine may be thus summarized: If a Government Minister is charged with committing a crime, the Court may order that the Minister be removed by the Prime Minister. It is assumed and understood that any Prime Minister is expected to do so preemptively without the need for an explicit court order. More broadly still, the rule applies to any government official, in the sense that being the subject of a criminal investigation (and certainly being indicted) serves as near-automatic grounds for their removal from office.

Though in some ways an extension of the freshly minted *Eisenberg*, the *Deri* ruling was extraordinary and unprecedented in its own right. First, *Deri* removed a serving official, which is materially different from invalidating a prospective appointee. Second, *Deri* pierced the very heart of the most senior level of Executive appointments – the composition of the Cabinet itself – and intervened with the Prime Minister's discretion regarding who to appoint or dismiss as Government Ministers. That is, based solely on the reasonableness balancing act,

* Some commentators have explicitly drawn a link between the Court's forced dismissal of Deri and Pinhasi, and Rabin's eventual assassination. See Gavison, saying that had the two remained in Rabin's government it "may have spared us from the trauma of a Prime Minister's murder." (Moshe Gorali, Globes, Nov 7th, 2000); and Friedmann, saying that the decision "contributed greatly to the incitement against Rabin." (Daniel Friedmann, Maariv, Jan 5th, 2023).

the Court was willing to dictate to the State's highest office the substance and outcome of the most consequential decision within executive power. Third, *Deri* effectively dismissed elected officials from political office. Fourth, *Deri* created a mechanism in which criminal proceedings automatically trigger an obligation of resignation or dismissal, without the need for any judicial involvement.

In this sense, while under the broad umbrella of the Court's interference with appointments, *Deri* constitutes a distinct rule within the specific context of criminal investigations and indictments employed primarily against elected politicians.

Intimidation as Judicial Power

Deri is a colossal aberration of democracy, of the rule of law, of the separation of powers, and of criminal justice. There is nothing remotely similar to it in the legal system of any civilized nation on earth – as Yoav Dotan observes regarding *Deri*, "there is **no** comparative law."[11] Without any basis in statute or text, the Supreme Court assumed for itself the power to dictate to the Prime Minister when to dismiss (or eventually, to refrain from appointing) a Cabinet Minister, based solely on the subjective judgment of a handful of senior prosecutors. I challenge any reader to imagine the same scenario in their own jurisdiction.[*] It is a severe violation of the presumption of innocence and of criminal due process. It is a brazen infringement upon the most sacred and fundamental electoral rights in representative democracy. More than anything else, *Deri* is a tool to intimidate and neutralize political opposition to judicial supremacy by casually suspending (and often, terminating) the public career of actual or potential dissidents.

The essence and character of the Deri Doctrine as described above will become evident in greater detail as we proceed.

*

Let us start with this last point as it sheds crucial light on the entire edifice of the *Deri* doctrine. Not only is *Deri* impossible to understand without considering its realpolitik implications, but so is the subsequent dynamic between the elected and judicial branches and the evolution of judicial power in Israel. *Deri* signified the dawn of a new era in Israeli political and public life – the era of judicially-encouraged criminal prosecution (or perhaps, persecution) of elected or senior appointed officials. In one of the first responses to the *Deri* decision, Prof. Ruth

---

[*] Impeachment proceedings are of course a separate category involving representative democratic elements and are invariably based on hard black-letter law. The Fourteenth Amendment of the United States Constitution prohibits those that have engaged in "insurrection or rebellion" from holding office, but the U.S. Supreme Court has ruled that it's up to Congress to decide how this rule is implemented (601 U.S. 100 (2024)). More to the point, few would suggest that such a rule might apply in the absence of explicit unequivocal language such as that found in the Fourteenth Amendment.

Gavison wrote the very next day that it "cannot be evaluated only in legal terms. Its main significance is in the relations it creates between the systems"[12] of government. She could not have been more on point.

From *Deri* onwards, every senior public official in Israeli government is exposed to their career being abruptly terminated by the initiation of criminal proceedings. The merit of such proceedings or their outcome is entirely immaterial – their mere existence are sufficient grounds to induce resignation or dismissal. More often than not, direct judicial intervention is not even required, and an investigation or indictment will yield removal from public office instantaneously. We will return to the theoretical and legal flaws of the *Deri* doctrine, but for now we must focus on how the doctrine is wielded in the real world and what it means for the incentives and behavior of actual politicians.

Yaakov Neeman was a leading attorney (a founder and named partner of Israel's preeminent law firm) when he was appointed as Justice Minister in 1996, in the first Netanyahu government. Neeman was known for his critical stance towards the Supreme Court and for his objection to its expansionist jurisprudence that prevailed at the time. He had also expressed his desire to replace the current Legal Counsel to the Government – Michael Ben-Yair – who had been appointed by the previous government. A single day after Neeman was appointed to office, Ben-Yair announced an investigation into alleged crimes supposedly committed by Neeman. Within a few months, Neeman was indicted for perjury – a grossly inflated charge which was based on a minor and inconsequential clerical error in an affidavit he had filed with the Supreme Court. (Mere days before filing the charges, Ben-Yair was overheard saying of Neeman, "I'm going to screw that fascist."[13])

Almost a year later, Neeman was fully acquitted of all charges by a trial court, which severely criticized the Legal Counsel to the Government's decision to indict Neeman in the first place. The so-called "perjury," the court found, was a minor mistake by a different junior lawyer who had initially drafted the affidavit. Amazingly, this lawyer was never even questioned by investigators (indicating perhaps the prosecution's zeal to reach an indictment), though his testimony could have easily voided the entire investigation.

None of this mattered. Adhering to the Deri doctrine, Neeman had no choice but to resign immediately following the bogus indictment. In his stead, the much more amicable, pliable and pro-Court Tzachi Hanegbi became Justice Minister. Neeman's predictable acquittal a year later was meaningless – his tenure as Minister of Justice had been callously blocked, and any challenge he may have posed to the rising tide of judicial supremacy had been nipped in the bud.

Neeman's example is just one of many, but it accurately demonstrates the widespread strategic deployment of *Deri* against public officials. Yoav Dotan summarizes this phenomenon in an arresting article titled "Impeachment by Judicial Review," stating that certain fundamental realities cannot be ignored:

> "A significant number of officeholders in critical positions (such as the Minister of Justice or the Minister of Public Security), some of whom had been considered critics of the activist disposition of the judicial apparatus, have been removed from office by virtue of this doctrine (thus exerting, at the very least, a significant chilling effect against criticism of the judicial establishment)."[14]

Dotan continues that these cases were often "based on light or even petty offences" which could rarely if ever justify a sanction meeting statutory requirements for removal. Writing in 2018, Dotan notes in summary that "all six recent Prime Ministers of Israel were subject to lengthy police investigations (and accordingly to the threat of removal)." Either Israel is a hopelessly corrupt society in which the public insists on repeatedly electing criminally-inclined leaders (and every global corruption index would consistently indicate this is not the case),* or there is something else going on here.

The most comprehensive and candid review of this reality is offered by Prof. Daniel Friedmann in his book *The Purse and the Sword.* Friedmann meticulously catalogues the abuses of *Deri* targeting politicians and senior officials. In addition to Neeman, there is in fact a respectable tally of top-tier politicians, public figures, and legal professionals, all considered adverse to the legal establishment, who have had their careers tanked and worse only to be fully exonerated down the line. All were targeted in what turned out to be spurious criminal witch-hunts.

A partial list may leave an impression: MK (and future President) Reuven Rivlin was investigated as an MK and his appointment as Justice Minister was derailed, though all seven (!) cases against him were eventually closed and no charges were filed (Rivlin memorably reacted by coining the phrase "the rule-of-law thugs").† MK Rafael "Raful" Eitan was indicted and his appointment as Minister of Internal Security was prevented, yet Eitan was acquitted by the trial court with "no case to answer." Minister of National Security Avigdor Kahalani was indicted but fully acquitted with "no case to answer," his acquittal upheld on appeal. A criminal probe against General Gal Hirsch prevented his appointment as National Police Commissioner, though the suspicions turned out to be baseless. The legal vendetta against Bar Chairman Dror Hoter-Ishay will be examined in Chapter 7. And that's just to name a few. All these public figures were considered less-than-sympathetic to the legal establishment status quo and were vocal critics of the Supreme Court and of the Legal Counsel to the Government.

Yet these instances, objectionable as they may be, are dwarfed by *Deri*'s broader impact. Dotan describes the final result as

> "A state of affairs under which the political and bureaucratic systems live

---

* For example, the "Corruption Perceptions Index" consistently ranks Israel as less corrupt than numerous Western democracies. In 1996, the year of the Neeman indictment, Israel was ranked less corrupt than the U.S.A., Austria, Japan and France.

† An alternative translation is "the rule of law street gang."

> under constant threat of intervention by the legal apparatus to end the public career of any officeholder. This threat is exerted by a flexible and somewhat opaque legal doctrine, the exact parameters and counters of which depend largely on the discretion of the organ that applies it."[15]

Yes, the Deri Doctrine is clumsily used to prevent critics, adversaries and undesirables from attaining office or to forcibly remove them. But the real effect of *Deri* is manifest in the myriad decisions left untaken, candidates passed over, words unsaid, objections unvoiced. Its potency is in the politician's and official's fear of losing their job. It exists in the crippling distortion of democratic government by which many of the State's most senior and elected leaders are paralyzed, wary of advancing certain agendas and especially careful not to challenge judicial power, lest they raise the ire of the legal establishment and face the consequences.

The point of this section is not only to emphasize the injustice or to expose the abuse of the Deri Doctrine. It is not only a principled argument, but rather also a factual observation. The point here is to describe the inescapable reality of a political and executive class thoroughly undermined and suppressed by judicial intimidation, with all that entails for its ability to contend with rampant judicial lawlessness. This is the claim that Dotan implies all-too politely in his article – that in the "bottom line," *Deri* serves a "powerful check" over the political branches and "helps the judiciary preserve its autonomy."[16] Dotan delicately frames this as an explanation for how the Court successfully retains its expansive (and often self-granted) powers despite very few statutory protections against political interference. Elsewhere, Dotan is less restrained – in an op-ed for the Haaretz newspaper, he blames the Deri Doctrine for bogus criminal investigations becoming the primary method "for the elimination of opponents in our political and public system."[17]

In the Introduction to this book I emphasized that its focus is on the "what" and the "how." Here we come closest to glimpsing some of the "why." Whenever one wonders at the progression of Israeli judicial supremacy and at the political reaction (or lack thereof) of the elected branches, the shadow of *Deri* looms over any serious explanation or answer. It would be impossible – even dishonest – to discuss the substance of *Deri* without first presenting its overall effect. The irrepressible truth is that the Supreme Court and legal establishment in Israel are all-too-often able to obstruct or prevent valid challenges to their own power because elected and appointed officials are simply afraid. This disturbing reality – hinted at by Dotan, deliberately ignored by the Court, but acknowledged throughout the Israeli political landscape – is therefore much more sinister than detached academic discussion might let on. Phrased in its bluntest form, the Deri Doctrine is one of the primary pillars on which actual Israeli judicial power rests, by abusing the criminal process to terrorize elected and appointed officials in their exercise of legitimate democratic authority.

Dismantling Deri

Having presented the broader implications of the Deri Doctrine for the relationship between judicial and elected branches at large, we may now turn to dissect the substantive doctrine itself.

Policy Justifications. To examine the theoretical justifications for *Deri* offered by its proponents we must return to *Eisenberg* and the more general foundation for review of executive appointments. As discussed in detail above, the Court contends that in certain circumstances a decision to appoint or a refusal to dismiss may amount to "extreme unreasonableness," due to its violation of the "good character" principle and due to the harm caused to "public faith in government."

The first and most obvious objection is that none of this really comes close to a legal argument or to legal grounds for intervention. What might constitute sufficient "good character" or what policies may or may not harm "public faith" in government are open to debate and no legal training or analysis will provide an answer to such questions. More so, the subsequent question of how to correctly balance such factors (even were we to recognize them as bearing legal weight) against other policy considerations is a typical public-political question not remotely governed by law. This point has been sufficiently made above in the broader context of reasonableness review and needs no further elaboration.

A related point is the Court's assumption that its role and duties include the maintenance of these elements. I would venture to say that in no democracy in the world is a judiciary explicitly authorized or empowered to supervise the ethical or moral standards of government officials, nor is any court of law tasked with upholding the public's positive perception of government. That is, the Court's self-conception as responsible for advancing these (perhaps laudable) causes seems divorced from any known theory of the judicial role in representative democracy. Is it the judiciary's job to settle disputes according to law, or to serve as commissar of moral hygiene in government ranks?

Importantly, the Court never quite clarifies whether its idea of "public faith" in governmental institutions is a hypothetical or empirical one, and judges regularly seem unsure of this themselves. If the former, it is unclear why the Court deems itself any better judge of public sentiment and attitudes towards government than any other institution, and especially than politicians accountable to the electorate. One might consider judges to be among the least well-positioned to estimate public faith in government. And a court imposing "judge-made moral requirements," lacking not only any legislative basis but also not grounded in actual popular opinion, raises "serious questions of democratic legitimacy."[18]

Turning to the latter option of empirical (or factual) public faith in government, the Court enters even murkier waters. For one thing, none of the Court's rulings on this issue have ever presented evidence to support its claims. This does not seem an unreasonable expectation for judicial decisions purporting to rely on (and indeed to preserve) a factual reality of public sentiment. More significantly, such reasoning may hold intuitive appeal regarding mid-level bureaucrats, but it collapses entirely when applied to elected politicians and to senior officials appointed (or confirmed, or removable) directly by elected officials and at their discretion. Would it not seem that the best test to evaluate "public faith" in government is the periodic elections in which the public directly and collectively expresses its faith (or lack thereof) in given government institutions and officials? Simply put, the idea of coercing the (elected) Prime Minister Rabin to fire his (elected) Interior Minister in the name of "public faith in government" is plainly ludicrous.

This notion of public faith was put to the test and resoundingly refuted in the extraordinary *Three Mayors Case*. In 2013, three separate mayors (in three different municipalities) were indicted for corruption offences. Mayors in Israel are personally elected by local residents – possibly the only example of direct representative democracy in Israeli politics. All three mayors had been under investigation for some time, and the suspicions against them were publicly well known. The indictments were filed mere weeks before upcoming municipal elections in which the mayors were set to run for reelection, and where the voting public could express their preferences in light of the criminal allegations against the incumbent mayors. Following the indictments, each respective City Council (an elected municipal governing body) declined to suspend its mayor, though it possessed the legal authority to do so.

Following the indictments, a slew of petitions demanded that the Supreme Court apply the Deri Doctrine and remove the mayors from their office and duties. Here was the perfect opportunity for the Court to back off – if public faith mattered at all, then surely this was the occasion to allow the public to directly determine the fate of its allegedly wayward politicians. The elections around the corner meant that the public could express its faith in clear terms.

Amazingly, in a decision issued just a few days before the municipal elections, the Court obliged the petitioners. The legal argument adopted by the Court was that each City Council's refusal to suspend the mayors was unreasonable, and that *Deri* applied fully and mandated the removal of the mayors in light of their indictment. The Court was unswayed by the fact that the City Council members and the mayors were both directly-elected offices; or by the fact that the Councils and mayors were up for immediate reelection. All three mayors were thus "suspended" and effectively dismissed from their post.

But this was not to be the end of the story. In a fantastic turn of events, *all three mayors* were subsequently reelected to their position, despite both the indictments and their suspension by the Court.* One could hardly imagine a clearer public repudiation of the Court's judgment.

---

* Fortunately for the Court it was saved the embarrassment of re-adjudicating the issue again, as after the elections the political careers of all three mayors came to a swift end anyway.

Setting aside the severe objections to *Deri* per se and to its application to elected politicians, the *Three Mayors Case* demonstrates the absurdity of any "public faith" argument on which *Deri* relies. The clear public support for these three mayors meant that proponents of *Deri* must choose between two conclusions: Either the Court is knowingly protecting a judicial fiction of "public faith" in government even if such hypothetical faith plainly contradicts actual, genuine public preferences; or the Court is sincere but abysmally bad at estimating empirical "public faith" and shouldn't be imposing political outcomes in the public's name.

A natural outcome of the *Three Mayors Case* was that any empirical "public faith" argument became implausible. Small wonder then that the Court seems to be swinging back towards a "normative" or hypothetical conception of public faith to support its application of *Deri*. In his concurring *Netanyahu* opinion, Justice Amit approvingly suggests that "public faith" could be understood as a "legal fiction" much like "the reasonable person."[19] Just as a Court may impose a standard of conduct on an individual in torts, the subtext of Amit's view is that the Court may impose an outcome based solely on what the public *ought* to think.

A last point about the "public faith" argument is its selective utilization. The Court presents "public faith" in government as adversely affected only by the appointment or continued tenure of people lacking sufficient virtue, and as only relating to a specific type of elected and appointed officials. But this is by no means the only way to understand or apply "public faith." In his critique on reasonableness, Ronen Shamir argues that the Court's intervention is a self-fulfilling prophecy – that the incessant judicial meddling conveys a message of incompetence and corruption, thus by its own hand steadily undermining public faith in the institutions it purports to protect.[20] Shamir explains that the "inevitable outcome" of the Court's intervention is "a lack of public faith in politics" as such – diminishing faith in both the ability of politicians to make reasonable decisions, and in the public's own ability to influence outcomes (because the only way to right the wrongs of government misconduct is by enlightened judicial intervention, and not "through the mobilization of socio-political supervision mechanisms found in the democratic order").

The Court is also not interested in the way *Deri* might impact public confidence in law enforcement organs, including the National Police, the State Prosecution and the Legal Counsel to the Government, all of whom undoubtedly suffer tremendous loss of public faith due to their perceived (and actual) criminalization of politics. More than anything else, the Court seems least interested in the effect *Deri* might have on "public faith" in the judiciary. While the Court requires that the government attribute immense weight to considerations of "public faith" when deciding whether to dismiss or appoint an official, it entirely ignores the same considerations that ought to influence its own insistence on intervening in executive or political discretion without the slightest formal legal basis. In other words, the Court's elevation of "public faith" in government institutions to a paramount mandatory consideration is never applied to its own rulings. Some might call such an approach inherently unreasonable. Others might be forgiven the suspicion that the Court doesn't take the "public faith" test very seriously.*

Interpretation. Another pillar of the Court's argument is that of "competence versus discretion" within the context of statutory interpretation. A law may establish certain minimum requirements for an individual to serve in a given role or may stipulate certain conditions which preclude it. The Court's view in *Eisenberg*, extended to *Deri* and regularly repeated since, is that an appointment decision (or refusal to dismiss) is always an exercise of government discretion, and as such is always subject to reasonableness review (and to the law's "objective purpose" in general) regardless of technical statutory requirements. An appointee meeting the law's required conditions for hire, or an official's *not* meeting statutory conditions for dismissal, are only the baseline from which the Court proceeds to examine the validity of related decisions.

The problems here are manifold and we may address them briefly, remaining strictly within the context of statutory interpretation. First is the rather obvious point that this does not seem to involve interpretation in any meaningful sense and is closer to anti-interpretation – deducing substance and binding rules from the absence of statutory text. Of course, omission in legal text can at times certainly contain legal significance, but such instances are confined to defined and well-established circumstances which do not apply in the cases contemplated above.[21] In the context of authorizing statutes such as those in *Eisenberg* and *Deri*, the omission of additional requirements would typically be interpreted to mean exactly what it looks like – the absence of additional (legally enforceable) requirements. Such an omission would indicate the grant of wide discretion to the appointing authority, which is empowered by law to select any candidate within objective technical parameters.

This is supported by the fact that such authorizing statutes are ubiquitous throughout administrative (and constitutional) law and vary enormously in their content. Legislators regularly stipulate different requirements and limitations based on the type of role and on the process by which an appointee is selected. Setting a minimum competency standard without any further conditions therefore represents a deliberate choice, a conscious legislative desire to afford wide latitude, in contrast to other laws which might define greater and more specific limitations. Such a conclusion is also supported by broader assumptions regarding executive prerogatives and the separation of powers (as partially discussed above). A more electorally-responsive and democratically-supervised appointing authority justifies greater discretion in their decision on who to appoint, as they will bear ultimate responsibility and accountability for the quality of their pick and for the performance of their appointee. Similarly, a more senior executive role

* We will return briefly to the issue of public faith in the judiciary in Chapter 10.

typically requires a flexible array of skills and experience which is hard to pin down within predetermined rigid statutory qualifications.

Bottom line, from an interpretive perspective, it just makes more sense to understand silence in appointment-authorizing statutes as precisely what it seems to be: the absence of additional limitations or restrictions.

The Supreme Court in *Deri* reaches the opposite conclusion – if the law does not stipulate further conditions for executive appointments, this is merely an opening for the Court to impose any ad hoc conditions it deems appropriate on a case-by-case basis. The Court calls it "competence versus discretion," but a better title might be "silence is license." If the Court's general interpretive method (discussed above in Chapter 3) originally meant ignoring both the meaning of legal text and the intention of its authors, here we have an even more audacious example of judicial legislation – inserting statutory content where none exists. These interpretive acrobatics constitute an obvious violation of the Omitted-Case canon of construction (courts may not fill in legislative gaps with rules of their own),[22] and are why many commentators agree that the Deri Doctrine had no basis in Israeli statutory law at the time it was developed.

I say "at the time it was developed" because the law has since changed. As mentioned briefly earlier in Chapter 3, in 2001 the Knesset passed wide-ranging legislation which largely overhauled many parts of "Basic Law: The Government" and enacted an additional law which addressed related procedural issues. The newly amended Basic Law directly tackled the question of criminal proceedings against Government Ministers: Section 6 prohibits appointing a Minister within seven years since he had completed serving prison time after being convicted of a crime.* Section 23 explicitly regards removal of a Minister for a criminal offense, and mandates that a Minister's position is immediately terminated upon a conviction of a crime involving "moral turpitude." The new legislation clearly contemplates an ongoing criminal trial against presiding government Ministers, by mandating that such trial is held in a District Court; it also includes instructions for a scenario in which an indictment is filed before a Minister takes office. In sum, the new legislation now comprehensively covered the field which *Deri* had previously occupied, and explicitly set criminal *conviction* – not indictment – as the threshold requiring dismissal. Needless to say, the legislators who drafted and debated the new laws were well aware of the judicial Deri Doctrine.

Seeing as the topic of removal due to criminal proceedings was now no longer a matter of statutory "silence," one might be forgiven for thinking that such a direct legislative amendment alters the legal reality and pulls the rug out from beneath *Deri*.

---

* Even then, the Election Committee Chairman may allow such an appointment if neither he nor the convicting trial court defined the appointee's offense as involving "moral turpitude." We will revisit this later.

But one would be wrong.

The amendment to the Basic Law was met with little more than a judicial shrug. Following the legislation the Court proceeded to apply the Deri Doctrine as if nothing, not a single thing, had changed. In a number of ensuing cases the Court either ignored the new law or insisted that the doctrine remained entirely intact. In one of the first cases to do so, in the 2003 *Hanegbi* case, Justice Rivlin explains that the new provisions directly addressing removal from office due to a criminal conviction were related to competence only, and therefore "do not negate the possibility of judicial review of the Prime Minister's *discretion*."[23] Rather, the Deri Doctrine continues to "outline additional instances" on top of those in the Basic Law, in which the Prime Minister's decision regarding a Minister "cannot stand." Per the Court the new provisions set a mandatory threshold (conviction) at which a Minister must be dismissed, but the exercise of discretion at any stage prior to conviction is subject to ordinary reasonableness review and to the Deri Doctrine. In the same case, Justice Cheshin acknowledges that *Deri* was decided before the law had explicitly addressed removal in light of criminal proceedings, but curtly dismisses any objection by declaring simply that "the [Deri] doctrine's logic applies to the matter at hand."[24]

Thus, since 2001, the Court has continuously applied *Deri* despite the fundamental shift in the applicable statutory framework, always using similar bald assertions and offering little substantive justification. In the 2020 *Netanyahu* case, Chief Justice Hayut explicitly reiterated the validity of the Deri Doctrine following the 2001 amendments.[25] Interestingly, for the first time, Hayut tried to support this claim by another source and referred to deliberations about the amendment which took place in the Knesset, claiming that the MKs "saw it the same way." The weakness of this argument is indicated by the fact that it took the Court nearly twenty years to offer even the feeblest statutory support for its dismissal of the 2001 amendments. Daniel Friedmann scoured the legislative history referenced by Hayut, but could not find the remotest evidence that MKs intended to leave the Deri Doctrine intact (if anything, the record indicates that MKs understood the law to mean that an indictment is not sufficient grounds to mandate dismissal).[26] In a concurring opinion, Justice Anat Baron wrote that *Deri* was still "alive and breathing" after the 2001 law with no further explanation.

Friedmann argues that the Court's preservation of *Deri* after the 2001 amendments is unlawful and violates core principles of statutory interpretation.[27] One such principle is the canon of Negative-Implication (*expressio unius*), that "the expression of one thing implies the exclusion of others."[28] The 2001 amendment requiring dismissal after a conviction implies that dismissal is *not* mandatory at any prior stage; yet the Court refuses to view the conviction threshold as exclusive grounds for removal. Another principle is the Rule to Avoid Surplusage, that interpretation should not cause legal provisions to "have no consequence";[29] yet entire sections of the law are rendered moot by the Court's subsequent application of *Deri.* If a Minister is dismissed immediately upon indictment, then no serving Minister need be tried in the District Court nor will she ever be convicted (Section 23 of Basic Law: The Government), because the defendant would no longer be a Minister due to their dismissal. This means that if *Deri* applies, the scenarios contemplated and addressed in these provisions are legal impossibilities and that the statutory amendments themselves were dead on arrival;* or as Friedmann puts it, the Court simply deleted these provisions from the statute.[30]

It's worth stressing that none of these arguments existed in the 1993 Deri-Pinhasi cases. Even if one were to accept the flawed and far-fetched theory of "silence is license" in the original doctrine, surely the 2001 amendments ought to have put the matter to rest. Justice Grunis tried to impress this point upon his colleagues in a 2014 case, where he insisted that following the amendments "there is no statutory vacuum" and that instances not defined by the new law are in no sense "lacunae."[31] Grunis pointedly asks "what's the use" of the new legislation if it is to be ignored, and finally objects to "using the reasonableness standard to turn [judicially] desired law to law-in-fact." Yet Grunis remained in the minority. To the Court and most of its Justices these amendments were worth little more than the pixels they occupy on a screen. As Dotan states, the Court's interpretive argument that the specific and explicit legislative requirements for removal "should be read as enabling the judiciary to supplement (and in fact circumvent)" them with "judge-made" thresholds, is "difficult to accept."[32]

A final point regarding statutory interpretation is well demonstrated in the *Netanyahu* case discussed below. Barak originally argued that the Deri Doctrine is derived from the law's "objective purpose" (see above discussion of *Eisenberg*). But in his concurring *Netanyahu* opinion, Justice David Mintz essentially argues the opposite – that the objective purpose of the relevant provisions (relating to limitations on appointing a Prime Minister) includes ensuring "stability, clarity and certainty," and therefore supports strict adherence to the statutory text without imposing additional judicial limitations.[33] This serves as a useful example showing just how malleable "objective purposive interpretation" has always been, where such purpose exists purely in the eye of the beholder.

<u>Criminal Law.</u> Among the earliest critiques of the Deri Doctrine was its inconsistency with basic norms of criminal law and procedure. The doctrine creates an automatic sanction triggered by an administrative decision to file criminal charges – long before the defendant has had a single day in court, before the evidence evaluated by an impartial tribunal, before having any chance to properly defend herself. This would seem to violate core requirements of due

* The Court adopted much the same approach of "competence versus discretion" in the 2013 *Three Mayors Case* discussed above – similar legislative provisions applied to mayors, requiring removal from office only following a conviction. The same interpretational critiques apply there as well.

process and of the presumption of innocence. *Deri* means that the Court considers officials guilty unless proven innocent.

The Court has defended its position by arguing that the sanction of removal from public office is not a punishment for criminal culpability, but rather an administrative consequence of credible allegations against an officeholder; and that an administrative decision (such as removal of an official) need only be based on adequate evidence and not on evidence beyond a reasonable doubt. Under *Deri*, the indictment itself serves as evidence on which a decision-maker must rely when choosing whether to dismiss a subordinate indicted official. As Justice Edna Arbel once put it, when considering whether to hire a candidate or fire an officeholder, the absence of a criminal conviction "does not allow for ignoring" the criminal proceedings "on a public level," and "does not allow treating the defendant as if clean of all wrongdoing."[34] On this view, dismissing an indicted officeholder is not punishment for a crime, and the very fact of being indicted is, in its own right, sufficient "administrative evidence" to require mandatory dismissal.

This line of argument has been thoroughly debunked and seems, frankly, especially disingenuous. On an intuitive level, while mandatory dismissal from public office is not a classic criminal sanction (such as imprisonment or fines) it involves considerable direct harm to the interests of the dismissed individual. It is, indeed, a severe adverse action taken against a person, directly stemming from the prosecutorial decision to indict.

Prof. Rinat Kitai-Sangero, a leading Israeli criminal law scholar, rejects any argument that *Deri* is not a criminal sanction or is somehow an allowable exception to principles governing criminal jurisprudence. In her systematic analysis of the subject, she explains how the Deri Doctrine (which is "unique to Israel") contradicts core tenets of the presumption of innocence. At its base, the presumption of innocence "prevents the State from taking measures involving guilt against a person whose factual innocence has not been disproved by the court."[35] One crucial element is that it rules out blind acceptance of decisions made by law enforcement agencies, such that until a conviction a defendant (or suspect) is considered no more guilty than the officials investigating and prosecuting him.[36] As such the concept implies that an individual may not be regarded as guilty, even in a partial or temporary manner, "until the end of proceedings."

Kitai-Sangero finds no justification for the exclusion of indicted public officeholders from such a rule, and concludes that "a conviction should be necessary" for (forcing) their removal from office.[37] She also refutes the claim that "good character" and "public faith" can somehow serve as legal basis for suspension of the presumption of innocence,[38] explaining that the former cannot come at the expense of the latter.[39] To be clear, all agree that officials *can* be dismissed for such reasons. The point here is that *compelling* their dismissal by judicial policy (and against the wishes of their superiors) easily violates the presumption of innocence. Kitai-Sangero ultimately concludes that "discharging indicted public officials from their position absent a conviction" – that is, *Deri* – "embodies a presumption of guilt."[40]

Further undermining the Court's argument, Yoav Dotan points out that the statutory framework (defining a final conviction as a condition for removal) reflects a conscious legislative choice to enshrine and safeguard the presumption of innocence within the context of criminal allegations against Ministers – "a choice that the Court ignores."[41] That is, *Deri* not only contravenes broadly accepted norms of presumptive innocence, but also does so in direct contradiction to the law's express goal of upholding the norm in relation to indicted Ministers.

Moving on, the Court's reliance on "administrative evidence" as a basis for removal from office is itself unconvincing, considering the utter lack of significance the Court attributes to actual substantive evidence against an officeholder.

First, *Deri* is based on the "decision to indict" in and of itself – it has no interest in the evidentiary basis for such a decision. In other words, the indictment *is* the "administrative evidence" which serves as the basis for dismissal. Yet an indictment is merely an announcement, a declaration by prosecutors that they believe a defendant to be guilty of alleged offenses, not "evidence" in any substantive sense.* The Court does not require and does not expect an appointing authority to consider the prima facie evidence collected by the prosecution or law enforcement upon which the indictment is ostensibly based – the *Deri* conception of administrative evidence is simply taking the prosecutor's word for it. This is exactly the "blind acceptance" of law enforcement decisions to which Kitai-Sangero alluded.†

Second, recall that the HCJ conducts no evidentiary hearings or proceedings – meaning that even when a case (demanding dismissal) reaches the Supreme Court, there is no actual examination or scrutiny of evidence against an official. The only "evidence" offered is the prosecutorial conclusion that in their own subjective judgment, the evidence they possess justifies a conviction. All in all, the Court's reliance on so-called "administrative evidence" to justify dismissal is unserious at best, as it expects neither the superior authority nor the court itself to actually examine any prima facie evidence against an officeholder.

Dotan points out two additional distortions of due process caused by *Deri* that "cast a shadow on the integrity of the criminal process."[42] First, when the Supreme Court dismisses an officeholder it signals to the lower criminal court (in which a trial is eventually held) that the defendant may be presumed guilty. Meaning, the Court has already put its weight behind the credibility of charges against a

* Israel has virtually no mechanisms which limit or oversee prosecutorial discretion, such as a grand jury. See Chapter 7.

† Somewhat ironically, this entails that a superior authority must *refrain* from exercising discretion (based on substantive evidence against a subordinate) and must rather rely solely on the conclusions and interpretations offered by the prosecution, amounting to arbitrariness and to an abrogation of their duty to exercise independent judgment.

defendant, potentially tipping the scales for a lower court. Acquittal by a lower court also risks keenly embarrassing the Supreme Court. "It would be naïve" to think that the trial court "is capable of ignoring" such a strong message from the Supreme Court. Recall, also, the significant sway the Supreme Court holds over the fate of lower court judges, discussed above in Part I.

Second, once an indicted official is dismissed from their post, the prosecution now has an enormous incentive to achieve a conviction – any conviction – in order to justify the major political and governmental disruption caused by removal. Otherwise, they may be blamed for bringing meritless charges in order to achieve political goals. In other words, the grave political consequences of an indictment motivate the prosecution to zealously pursue a criminal conviction at any cost. This in turn leads to highly questionable (and at times, patently improper or illegal) prosecutorial and investigative practices.

Such practices were on full display in the 2006 case against Minister of Justice Haim Ramon for sexual misconduct. Investigators heavily and unduly pressured an ostensible victim to file a complaint, applied for (and received) wiretaps against senior government officials on bogus grounds, and prosecutors withheld exculpatory evidence from the defense, among other serious breaches of criminal procedure.* Ramon resigned as Minister of Justice and was eventually convicted on minor charges and given a light sentence. The controversial Ramon case drew immense bi-partisan criticism against the prosecution and the trial court, from both the public and legal establishment, including from leading feminists. Friedmann notes that almost no serious jurist was willing to defend the conviction (Friedmann quotes renowned Professor George Fletcher, saying that the criminal law was used to "achieve a political outcome" and that judges should "expunge the conviction in its entirety").[43] For many, the case proved that *Deri* was effective for even the lightest charges or weakest cases, and that a trial court would convict on the scantest evidence; but it especially demonstrated the lengths to which prosecutors would go (with impunity) to secure a conviction.

The Deri Doctrine creates another peculiar paradox by which in some cases, an indictment (unproven guilt) is a more severe stage within the criminal process than a conviction (proven guilt). This is because the law explicitly allows a Minister to be appointed after a conviction of an offense not involving "moral turpitude." The bizarre result is that a Minister may not serve after a mere indictment, but can be appointed after being duly convicted by a court following a full trial. This is precisely what happened with Ramon, who was subsequently re-appointed to the same Cabinet as Deputy Prime Minister. Justice Grunis pointed out a similar effect in the *Three Mayors Case*, in which the law mandated that a convicted mayor be initially suspended (not dismissed) and could also return to their post if their conviction overturned on appeal – yet *Deri* mandates their dismissal already at the point of indictment. This effectively meant that

* The Ramon case is reviewed by Friedmann in painstaking detail in *The Purse and the Sword*, p. 284 onwards.

indictment carried a more severe sanction (dismissal) than conviction (suspension). Further, it once again rendered the law meaningless – the scenario of a mayor returning to office if their conviction is overturned becomes a fiction, because due to *Deri* the mayor is not merely suspended but is actually dismissed and cannot simply bounce back into office.[44]

As an aside, it's worth noting that Haim Ramon – a charismatic leader within the left-wing Labor party in his prime – was a known critic of the Supreme Court's activist jurisprudence. Considering the extremely light sentence and his immediate return to public office, one might say that the case against him achieved the primary effect of removing yet another opponent of judicial supremacy from a position able to challenge it.[*]

The Deri Doctrine thus contaminates and prejudices the criminal process on the whole – discarding due process, establishing a presumption of guilt, influencing future trial outcomes, and incentivizing prosecutorial zeal.

Democratic Rights. One uniquely alarming aspect of the Deri Doctrine is its direct application to democratically elected and accountable officials and the resulting violation of the most fundamental rights in a democracy – the right to vote and to be elected. We've seen this in the Court's routine adjudication of Ministerial appointments and dismissals, in the *Three Mayors Case* and in the review even of the Knesset's appointing Benjamin Netanyahu as Prime Minister. The Court has maintained over the years that because it is not removing an MK from his Knesset seat, but rather only precluding the same person from serving as a Minister in executive government, that *Deri* does not infringe on electoral rights. Yet this distinction is as artificial as it is misleading.

Recall that in the Israeli multi-party system of proportional representation and coalition government, cabinet Ministers are not mere executive appointments made by the Prime Minister at her pleasure and discretion. Rather, their position reflects their relative electoral success, the clout of their political parties within a coalition government, and their own popularity among their party voters. Voters consider this when choosing parties, as they are effectively also choosing candidates for senior leadership positions in executive government. A vote for a given party is also a tacit vote for that party's top-ranking members to be instated in positions of governmental power, usually in the executive branch. For example, a voter may choose the Shas party so that its leader Aryeh Deri may be a cabinet member or Minister of the Interior, just as much as for their desire for Shas to advance a certain legislative agenda.

Think of it this way: a person who is legally barred from becoming a cabinet Minister will be far less likely to run for Knesset; if they did, their chances of success would be significantly diminished. This is true even if they were

---

[*] Though in fairness, another effect was the destruction of Ramon's public image and his ensuing departure from political life.

extremely popular and enjoyed wide public support. There is an inherent link between the electoral desire to see one's candidate gain a seat in the Knesset and the desire for the same candidate to assume an executive governmental role.

This holds true for the Ministerial role itself, which in a system such as Israel's is typically at least as political as it is executive or administrative. A Minister's actions and decisions are supported by the democratic authority of an elected and accountable official. Their political fate and fortunes depend primarily on the degree of popular support they receive in the ballot box. A Minister (usually, but not always, an elected MK and senior politician) is answerable to the public, and if certain conduct (whether potentially criminal or not) is considered beyond the pale then the public can choose to withhold its support or to penalize cooperation with such Minister. The same applies to other Ministers and to the Prime Minister, as they are accountable for their decision to join forces and collaborate with politicians suspected of objectionable conduct.

Another critical factor is that the initial formation of Government after elections, as well as any subsequent appointment of a cabinet Minister, is subject to approval by the Knesset. Aside the personal democratic authority, legitimacy and accountability of most Ministers as politicians, the appointment itself carries the weight of democratic parliamentary assent. The decision to appoint is therefore not merely the pure will of the Prime Minister but reflects approval from Israel's only national representative body and is an extension of the Knesset's accountability to the public. This means that even Ministers who are not elected politicians (such as Yaakov Neeman or Daniel Friedmann) enjoy an outsized degree of public and electoral legitimacy by dint of their parliamentary approval. This also demonstrates why the characterization of Ministerial appointments as a purely "executive" decision is so inaccurate – as parliamentary approval makes it essentially a dual executive-legislature appointment.

The distinction offered by the Court is therefore entirely contrived and unpersuasive. By dismissing (or prohibiting appointment of) government Ministers and other similar roles, the Deri Doctrine essentially robs senior Israeli politicians of their most important value-proposition to their voters: that they can serve in Ministerial positions. At the same time, it subverts voters' intentions and expectations and undermines one of the core factors on which they base their electoral decision-making. Simply put, with no basis in law or in legal theory, *Deri* dictates to voters the identity of who they can elect; dictates to candidates whether they can be elected; and dictates to the Knesset who is eligible for parliamentary approval.

Administrative Review. Another central aspect of *Deri* is the Court's pretense of conducting ordinary, casual, almost mundane administrative review. Returning to basics, the Deri Doctrine relies on the reasonableness standard as applied to government appointments (or dismissals). Review of executive "discretion" exercised by an administrative body is the hook on which the construct of *Deri* precariously hangs – is the Prime Minister's decision not to fire his Interior Minister reasonable? Is the City Council's decision not to suspend the mayor reasonable? Is the Government's decision to appoint a candidate as military Chief of Staff reasonable? The Court has maintained and reiterated, time and again, that it is merely engaging in conventional administrative review. In this way the Court treats its dismissal of elected officials much the same way – or within the same legal framework – as it would the revocation of a small-town business license or the decision of a junior tax clerk.

Yoav Dotan makes the singular insight that the Deri Doctrine is properly understood as an impeachment proceeding. It is, after all, the removal of an elected or highly senior government official, but not through the regular mechanisms for doing so (such as elections or voluntary dismissal). If we accept that a government official is usually either dismissed by superiors or ousted by the electorate, then we must categorize their forced removal from office by other means as a form of impeachment.

This observation matters because impeachment is universally considered to be a fraught mechanism of momentous significance. It pits democratic authority and legitimacy against the rule of law and other considerations. On a practical level it constitutes a glaring (at times crucial, at times dangerous) exception to the democratic rule that government is replaced via the political process and that the electorate alone grants and revokes political power. It naturally carries "grave repercussions for the political system."[45] For this reason and others, impeachment proceedings are almost always "entrenched" in constitutions or at the very least in detailed and explicit statutory arrangements. In order to lend impeachment legitimacy and to avoid its abuse, in almost all cases impeachment proceedings are initiated and conducted by an electorally representative body (such as the legislature) or with its heavy and decisive involvement.[46]

The Israeli Supreme Court routinely and unilaterally "removes politicians" or prevents their appointment "without any defined constitutional procedure or express statutory basis,"[47] in what amounts to "impeachment by judicial review."* In doing so, the Court exercises its impeachment function with none of the typical authorizing, legitimating or balancing mechanisms typically accompanying such extensive counter-democratic power.[48] Dotan's accurate characterization of *Deri* as an impeachment mechanism utterly undermines the Court's feeble insistence it is engaging in mere administrative review, and exposes the Deri Doctrine for what it really is – judicial interference of the most aggressive nature in the most delicate and sensitive matters within a constitutional order, without the slimmest legal or statutory basis.

This distinction is important because the pretense of administrative review shields the Court (at least in its own eyes) from significant scrutiny and spares it

---

* Dotan also remarks on the "astounding" reality that many Israelis simply assume this is a natural and ordinary component of an ordinary legal system. This is a fine example of the "isolation" phenomenon discussed in the Introduction.

the trouble of contending with the full gravity and implications of its jurisprudence. Objections such as those thoroughly discussed above, relating to criminal procedure, democratic rights, impeachment, the separation of powers, interpretation and much else besides are indeed trivialized or casually dismissed while the Court cites the mantra of administrative reasonableness review. This is especially evident in the Court's treatment of democratic (electoral) rights harmed by *Deri*. Dotan notes that in every other context of harm to individual or constitutional rights, the Court invariably applies a "proportionality" test which evaluates the benefit derived from some measure relative to the harm caused to any violated rights. Yet in all the dozens of cases which utilize the Deri Doctrine the Court does "not even bother"[49] to conduct the same evaluation it would otherwise use for harm to individual rights.*

The implausibility of the Court's pretense of administrative review is demonstrated in an often-overlooked point regarding the difference between *removal* of an officeholder and *prevention* of a candidate's appointment. Though at first glance bearing some resemblance, these two actions are inherently distinct. Israeli statutory law in fact recognizes this distinction, and defines very different thresholds for criminal conduct requiring removal as opposed to conduct precluding appointment. Section 23 of the Basic Law mandates removal of a Minister convicted of any offense involving "moral turpitude"; while Section 4 *allows* the appointment of a Minister if sufficient time has elapsed since she had been previously convicted and imprisoned (and if the conviction did not involve "moral turpitude" then she may be appointed immediately after serving her sentence). Because the criteria for removal covers a much wider category of convictions, parallel conditions for appointment can be seen as more lenient.

This makes sense – the appointment is made in full awareness of (and despite) the Minister's criminal past. If the Minister is an elected politician then their criminal past is typically known to the electorate and factored in to the election results. Conversely, removal usually regards new or newly discovered conduct, and therefore can't be said to have informed the original appointment decision.

Critically, the law also provides for different bodies technically responsible for Ministerial removal or appointment. Whether to remove a Minister is a choice given solely to the Prime Minister; while appointing a Minister requires not only collective Government decision but also the Knesset's literal vote of approval. The latter would support greater judicial deference, as the Knesset itself serves as an independent check on any improper appointment decision, reflecting both democratic authority and the same "public faith" the Court purports to uphold. Of course, even serving Ministers are indirectly subject to Knesset supervision in light of the Knesset's permanent ability to dismiss the Government (and form a new one) or call for early elections.

* Dotan also attributes this to the undisciplined nature of the doctrine, based more on "judicial guts and intuitions" than on "solid analytical legal reasoning."

In light of the above distinction – if the Court was genuinely committed to its version of administrative review, it would confine the Deri Doctrine only to the context of removal. Here is a so-called "administrative" decision (if we accept the Court's formulation) taken by the Prime Minister as head of the executive branch. Here the democratic case for retaining a Minister is perhaps weaker, as the charges against the Minister were unknown to the electorate and to the Knesset at the time of her appointment (or at least did not reach the point of indictment). But the Court does no such thing, and casually proceeded to apply the Deri Doctrine to *appointments* in addition to *removals*. This is despite the fact that appointments clearly permit a much broader scope of conduct (allowing for previously convicted and even imprisoned criminals), and despite that such appointments enjoy the support of the legislature and typically the voters.

In the 2003 case of *Hanegbi*, the Court heard a petition against the appointment of Tzachi Hanegbi as Minister of Internal Security, primarily based on conduct for which he had not been indicted (and for which the case had been closed and a future indictment ruled out).[50] In the saga of Haim Ramon discussed above, his 2007 re-appointment to the Cabinet as Deputy Prime Minister was of course challenged in court, though he had been convicted of a crime without "moral turpitude" and without a prison sentence. In both cases the criminal status of each Minister did not approach the statutory threshold for preventing their appointment, and their selection was approved by the Knesset (Hanegbi was appointed directly following the elections as part of the overall formation of the new coalition Government; Ramon was personally approved by the Knesset).

Instead of being dismissed with a few brief lines stating that there are no legal grounds to review the appointments, both petitions were adjudicated with gusto (the rulings reach a combined total of 190 pages). The Court applied the Deri Doctrine to the fullest extent, glossing over the fundamental differences between removal and appointments. The petitions were ultimately dismissed, though not due to their lack of legal merit – rather, the Justices simply deemed the appointments sufficiently reasonable under the circumstances.

Strikingly, in the *Ramon* case a majority of Justices explicitly agreed (in *dicta*) that the Knesset's decision to approve a Ministerial candidate is subject to judicial (reasonableness) review. Justice Ayala Procaccia explains that such a decision is open to "deeper judicial scrutiny" due to its application of "ethical-moral standards" deemed appropriate for a Minister. "A Knesset decision to approve the appointment of a Government Minister, if amounting to an extreme and exceptional deviation from proper ethical standards, could justify judicial intervention."[51] No less. Almost in the same breath, Procaccia launches an impassioned defense of unreasonableness and the Deri Doctrine as "a vital tool of *administrative* judicial review" – as if she had not just argued for intimate intervention in the *legislature's* deeply political (and electorally-supported) decision to approve a candidate. Notably, the word "administrative" appears twenty-seven times over those three defensive pages. Here then is a telling example of how the language of administrative review is used to justify a jurisprudence completely detached from it, as if judicial second-guessing of parliamentary approval could fall under this legal category.

Just as instructive is Justice Miriam Naor's majority opinion in the *Three Mayors Case* discussed above. Naor asks the critical question on everyone's mind: After their dismissal by the Court, what happens if the indicted mayors are reelected to their position, despite the pending indictments and despite their dismissal by the Court preceding the elections? Her answer hopefully comes as no surprise: "The will of the voter cannot serve as a super-consideration which trumps other factors."[52] She continues:

> "In an ideal world there may have been room to decide that the Court would not intervene. From the perspective of the fundamental right to vote and to be voted for – leaving the decision to voters would be fine. However, due to the severe harm to good character, to the core of democratic government, and to the rule of law, we must not set a rule that an elected official is immune from [judicial] dismissal owing to the fact that they were indicted before elections, and that the public voted for them despite this...
>
> I believe a mayor may be [judicially] removed from office also after elections, even if he was indicted before the elections."*

The upshot of these examples is simple – if the Court's claim that it was exercising "mere administrative review" were remotely serious or sincere, then it would not so willingly and casually apply *Deri* to Knesset-approved or public-supported appointments, which are decidedly political or electoral in nature and in which any "administrative" component is either nonexistent or negligible.

The Policing of Politics

Of all the irredeemable and untenable flaws of the Deri Doctrine, the one that stands out as the most egregious is the delegation of dismissal power to the "rule-of-law thugs" (the phrase coined by MK Reuven Rivlin in his pre-Presidential days). Judicial review of executive appointments based on their reasonableness is bad enough; judicial dismissal of government Ministers due to their indictment is certainly worse. Yet neither compare in severity and gravity to the outsourcing of such impeachment power to a bureaucratic layer of lawyers and officials who are neither representative, nor judicial, nor appointed. For the practical consequence of *Deri* is that the power to remove the State's most senior politicians and officeholders is conferred upon a small clique of figures within the law-enforcement apparatus. This is because, by the Court's own conscious

---

* I added the word "judicial" because there was no question that the City Council could voluntarily remove a mayor at any stage; the only actual question addressed was whether the Court could compel the City Council to do so against its wishes. Naor's formulation of the question obscures this point.

jurisprudence and direction, the indictment itself (and at times even an investigation or a mere announcement of suspicion) is sufficient cause to require one's resignation or dismissal, with no judicial involvement whatsoever.

Justice Hanan Meltzer articulated this point clearly (and approvingly) in the *Netanyahu* case: "The practice since the rulings of Deri and Pinhasi is that Ministers against whom an indictment had been filed did not wait for their removal [by the Prime Minister]... but rather chose to resign of their own volition... Such conduct now amounts to an obligatory constitutional custom."[53]

Precisely how many and which senior officials are required to cook up a criminal indictment depends on the details of a specific case, but they may usually be counted on two hands – a dash of police investigators, a sprinkle of prosecutors, a pinch of Legal Counsel to the Government. It is thus that the unfathomable power to bring almost any political career to a screeching halt is granted by *Deri* to a gaggle of top career bureaucrats largely insulated from the electorate as well as from meaningful legislative or executive oversight.

This point is often overlooked even by the Court's critics and is never remotely acknowledged by the Court itself. Yoav Dotan was almost right in dubbing *Deri* as "impeachment by judicial review," but in practice, the impeachment requires no courts or judges at all. It is for all intents and purposes "impeachment by counsel." The above declaration from Justice Meltzer is not followed by a reflection on its implications or significance; neither does Justice Hayut pause to dwell on such implications when she declares unequivocally that *Deri* remains in full force. In the many cases before it the Court has never wondered out loud about the ramifications of vesting a handful of criminal prosecutors with de facto impeachment powers.

To say this is antithetical to liberal-democratic notions of the rule of law and of criminal justice seems inadequate. Since the days of *habeas corpus*, a cornerstone of the liberal constitutional order has been vigilance towards the devastating power of criminal law. At the core of this insight is the permanent suspicion – or even certainty – that criminal law enforcement may easily devolve into abuse serving illegitimate goals, that a thin line separates prosecution from persecution. It is the civilian taming of criminal law enforcement that serves as a precondition for any state of public freedom to exist, just as it is no coincidence that the darkest most repressive totalitarian regimes are dubbed "police states." The viability and vitality of political liberty rises and falls with the ability to curb the excesses of necessary police power.

Perhaps counterintuitively, this approach applies not only to the vulnerability of powerless ordinary citizens, but all the more forcefully to the application of criminal law against serving politicians. We are all too familiar with scenes from authoritarian regimes in which elected officials of all stripes and persuasions are marched off the public stage due to dubious criminal allegations. Politicians in a democracy are especially difficult to remove by anyone but their voters, making criminal prosecution a tempting shortcut to effect change in government personnel. This is one reason that most democracies maintain one form or another of qualified criminal immunity for elected representatives.

Democratic political theory takes a practical and institutional approach, coldly examining the structural distribution of power and the way assorted mechanisms create incentives and potential for abuse. Whether such abuse is deliberate or inadvertent, based on motives sinister or sincere, is of little consequence. For this reason, a core tenet of the classical liberal approach to government is that well-meaning prosecutors in enlightened democracies are no less susceptible to the lure of achieving improper goals through criminal proceedings, and are no less immune from political and ideological bias. Just as importantly, police and prosecutors are as prone to human error as anyone else. The only possible conclusion is to accept the fundamental fallibility of law enforcement, especially when directed toward political actors.

United States Attorney General Bill Barr made this point compellingly in a 2020 speech about the power of federal prosecutors, in which he repeatedly referred to a canonical 1940 speech by (then-)Attorney General Robert Jackson.[54] Barr observes that "the criminal process is a juggernaut… Once it starts rolling, it is very difficult to slow down or knock it off course." This is in itself a critical insight into the self-sustaining momentum of criminal cases, in which genuine and critical judgment is often replaced by automatic self-validation and single-minded tunnel vision. Jackson contended in 1940 that "the prosecutor has more control over life, liberty and reputation than any other person" in the country. This "tremendous power," per Barr, "carries inherent potential for abuse or misuse" and "must be carefully calibrated and closely supervised." Barr warns that such power, if left unchecked, "has the potential to inflict far more harm than it prevents."

Both Barr and Jackson accurately represent the core liberal concerns regarding even the most well-meaning prosecutors. Barr warns that "a prosecutor can become overly invested in a particular goal," and that "there is always a temptation to will a prosecution into existence when the facts, the law, or fair-handed administration of justice do not support bringing charges." Further still, this risk is "inevitable and cannot be avoided" by simply hiring "only moral people with righteous motivations." Robert Jackson put things more bluntly:

> "If the prosecutor is obliged to choose his cases, it follows that he can choose his defendants. Therein is the most dangerous power of the prosecutor: that he will pick people that he thinks he should get, rather than pick cases that need to be prosecuted… It is in this realm… that the greatest danger of abuse of prosecutorial power lies."

Such concerns are amplified – and such flaws are exacerbated – ten times over by granting prosecutors the ability to dismiss political figures at will and with impunity.

In this light it is clear that *Deri* truly places Israel at odds with consecrated principles of liberal democratic government. In the simplest terms, the effect of *Deri* is the unsupervised and uninhibited power of a few senior prosecutors to dismiss most serving politicians from office. Its existence is intolerable enough even were it not for the undeniable evidence of widespread abuse. The many other theoretical and practical objections to the Deri Doctrine pale in comparison with this single consequence.

To be clear, criminal prosecutors are a critical component of public safety and order in civilized society. We need prosecutors who are capable, determined, and sometimes ruthless in order to put criminals behind bars. Prosecutors often have a grueling and thankless task against offenders who are often sophisticated and even dangerous, a task which they carry out for the most part diligently and in good faith. Nothing here should be construed as a general disposition against prosecutors, their role, their motives or their methods.* Nonetheless, prosecutors wield the State's most formidable tools against its citizens, and the bedrock of the Western political order is the assumption of prosecutorial fallibility – that criminal prosecutors are susceptible to the temptations, biases and errors that afflict all other mortals. The notion of prosecutors capable of unilateral political impeachment is no less odious when we afford prosecutors their due respect and appreciation.

The Court's indifference to the most significant and immediate practical effect of *Deri* isn't all that surprising. After all, it didn't start with Aryeh Deri. In 1977, Prime Minister Yitzhak Rabin was forced to resign after it was discovered he had maintained a U.S.-dollar bank account in the United States. It was illegal at the time for Israeli residents to possess foreign currency, though these were leftover funds in an account Rabin and his wife had lawfully opened when Rabin was ambassador to the United States. In most other circumstances such an offense would be resolved with a minor penalty (a fine) imposed by the Minister of Finance – but here the Legal Counsel to the Government clarified he would not defend such a decision were it challenged in court (or perhaps even that he himself would file a legal challenge). As the Legal Counsel to the Government was determined to indict Rabin on criminal charges for this arguably negligible infraction, Rabin resigned from his role as Prime Minister.[55] Soon after, the famous 1977 elections brought about the historic defeat of the Labor-*Mapai* party and the political ascension of the ideological right, the Likud, and Menachem Begin.

Throughout the ordeal the Legal Counsel to the Government was, of course, none other than Aharon Barak.

Burdens and Conflicts

Proponents of the Deri Doctrine both on and off the bench often raise two related

---

* Full disclosure: This author's spouse served as a criminal prosecutor for the better part of a decade.

arguments beyond the scope of public faith and good character. The first is that the burden of a criminal investigation or indictment may at times render an officeholder unable to carry out her duties. Aside the practical claim related to scheduling, depositions, court hearings, distractions and so on, this might even amount to a legal "incapacity" – i.e., that an official may be considered in a state of incapacity akin to a medical condition such as a coma, depriving her of the ability to serve in her current position. For present purposes we need not analyze the full implications and flaws of this line of reasoning. The angle relevant to our current context is that here too, both in legal circles and in public discourse, the point regarding unilateral prosecutorial impeachment is entirely lost. That is, few will raise the question whether it is proper or wise that a handful of investigators or prosecutors can effectively dismiss senior officeholders due merely to the logistical challenges accompanying criminal proceedings.

On the one hand, the argument has some intuitive practical appeal – it's not about a presumption of guilt or "good character" of public office, but is rather an eminently pragmatic observation regarding the impracticability of functioning in a senior government role while a suspect or defendant in a criminal proceeding. But on the other hand, the proposition is in many ways worse than the original *Deri* rationale of good character. It essentially suggests that officeholders may be unilaterally removed by prosecutors without even the claim of some moral or ethical defect to back it up – the frustration of their duties is itself the justification for removal. This idea seems even more arbitrary and unpalatable than dismissing officials "only" due to the severity of the conduct attributed to them. Needless to say, accepting this argument would provide a strong incentive for the active enlargement of any such associated burden, in a cycle of self-reinforcement. That is, increasing the difficulty of serving in office while under investigation would become an aim unto itself.

A second argument intertwined with the practical application of *Deri* but distinct from it relates to "conflicts of interest." When senior officeholders or politicians are involved in criminal proceedings they are deemed to have an intrinsic conflict of interest to the extent that their policy actions might indirectly affect the proceedings or their outcome. The concern is that suspected or indicted politicians might use their influence and government power to hamper law enforcement efforts or otherwise skew their results. Throughout the world, such conflicts of interest are typically remedied by full disclosure, especially for elected officials – it is sufficient that one's cross-interests are announced and publicly known so that official actions taken are subject to enhanced scrutiny, and the public may judge whether these are justified on independent grounds.

In Israel, however, the ostensible (or potential) existence of such conflict is often deemed sufficient to completely bar an official's involvement in related areas of government and policy, especially those with any bearing on the legal system and judiciary. The rules (if they may be called so) regarding "conflicts" for Ministers are set in various regulations and were developed by the Court and by the Legal Counsel to the Government, partially based on reasonableness (it is "unreasonable" for an official to be in a position "with a potential of conflict of interest"[56]), and these remain highly vague and discretionary. In practice, either a legal advisor or a court might simply inform a public official that they are "in conflict" and are prohibited from engaging in certain activities or participating in certain decisions.

The full extent and implications of the "conflicts" policy are beyond the scope of our present discussion, but a few points are worth our brief attention. While *Deri* mandates the dismissal of indicted officials, the "conflicts" policy simply neutralizes their ability to effect change of any kind related to the legal system. This proscription is broadly construed – for example, it would not be limited to direct intervention in an ongoing proceeding or to the appointment of senior investigators and prosecutors involved with a given case, but would include matters such as criminal law legislation and all judicial appointments. In this sense the "conflicts" policy is a more subtle tool by which an opponent or critic of the legal system may be barred from advancing their agenda even without their removal from office. This is especially effective as investigations (or even preliminary "probes") are often held open for extended periods without resolution, allowing for a form of suspended indefinite "conflict" precluding an official from participating in governmental action relating to the legal system. Thus, the "conflicts" policy is separate from *Deri* in that it employs similar means (criminal proceedings) but in service of an adjacent or overlapping purpose – neutralization instead of elimination.

Critically, being in a state of such "conflict" can constitute a chargeable crime in and of itself, under the "Breach of Trust" offense (we will return to this later on). A public official might be under investigation for a given crime, but if they fail to adhere to the "conflicts" instructions given they may well find themselves embroiled in yet a new criminal investigation stemming from the very existence of the alleged conflict. As such a directive to refrain from governmental activities due to such "conflicts" cannot be taken lightly and is not easily dismissed. In the specific context of "conflict" arrangements imposed by the LCG, the Court (Chief Justice Hayut) noted in 2021 that a public official violating the LCG's legal opinion "assumes considerable risks relating to the consequences of such actions, including at the criminal level."[57]

Needless to say, the same approach to conflicts is never, ever applied to officials within the legal establishment, such as prosecutors, LCG attorneys or judges.

The Ramon affair discussed above demonstrated, per Friedmann, a "threefold failure in the justice system – the indictment, the verdict, and the wiretap,"[58] and severely damaged the public prestige of the presiding LCG Menny Mazuz[*] and of the state prosecution organs, while putting a spotlight on the criminal hounding of politicians. Withering criticism from all quarters was mounting against Mazuz and others involved in the affair, with many calling for an official commission of

---

[*] Mazuz was LCG before being appointed to the Supreme Court some years later.

inquiry. The Prime Minister at the time, Ehud Olmert, also supported forming a government inquiry – "but Mazuz forbade him to do so." The reason for this prohibition was that Olmert himself was under investigation in two criminal cases (both of which ultimately ended without indictments).

Mazuz was well aware of the possible fallout for the aggressive prosecution against Haim Ramon and said as much in an interview, admitting that an acquittal would lead to a "tsunami" and would be "devastating for the [legal] system." During the trial, Mazuz ordered a police investigation regarding Olmert's purchase of a house in Jerusalem. Two weeks prior to the verdict in the Ramon case, after the wiretapping malfeasance had come to light, Olmert became the subject of a separate full-scale criminal investigation by order of the State Attorney (Mazuz had recused himself in this matter). As a result, Olmert and his Government were now "conflicted," and therefore unable to initiate any serious investigations or changes following the Ramon trial debacle. According to Friedmann, the dual investigations "crippled the Prime Minister," had "rendered him powerless" to remedy failures of the legal system and "kept the Government from exercising oversight" of the criminal law enforcement apparatus. Though Friedmann does not claim that the decisions were made solely in order to prevent inconvenient inquiries, he assesses that both Mazuz and the State Attorney "had a clear interest in assuring" that the government would not examine the failings of the Ramon case or take action in light of what they learned.

Another striking example is the various arrangements applied to Benjamin Netanyahu throughout his criminal investigations. Following his indictment in 2020, the Legal Counsel to the Government (Avichai Mandelblit) drafted a "conflict of interests" memo requiring sweeping limitations on Netanyahu's governmental activities. These included, inter alia: avoiding "any involvement" regarding senior appointments in the Ministry of Justice and in the National Police and regarding "the performance of their duties," and even in legislative proceedings relating to such appointments; avoiding involvement regarding appointment of judges to the Supreme Court and District Courts; and avoiding involvement in legislation which might have any impact on the criminal proceedings (including laws of general applicability which might have some effect). The memo emphasizes that this "avoidance" duty extends to indirect involvement and to the exercise of proxy authority through other government Ministers, and also applies to political appointees working directly under Netanyahu. In other words – the memo requires that the democratically elected Chief Executive remove himself entirely from some of the most critical and fundamental elements of civilian and political oversight over the legal system and specifically the criminal justice system.

In the *Netanyahu* case discussed in the next section, the Court concluded there were "no legal grounds" for preventing Netanyahu from forming a Government and becoming Prime Minister. Yet in the same breath (literally in the same paragraph), the Court "noted" the LCG's assurance that Netanyahu's tenure will be subject to a "conflicts of interest arrangement." This was a peculiar statement considering that the issue of conflicts had no legal relevance to the case's outcome and was mentioned nowhere else in the ruling. It was perceived by many to be a veiled threat that the Court might see things differently (regarding the legality of Netanyahu becoming Prime Minister) if Netanyahu would not adhere to the extensive limitations imposed by the LCG.

The "conflicts" approach for Netanyahu had far-reaching effects. After the Court ruled that the LCG's memo amounted to binding law (we'll return to this later), Netanyahu effectively withdrew all involvement in matters relating to the judiciary and legal system. This meant that during the 2023 judicial reform crisis Netanyahu was initially completely severed from policy deliberations and from public action or engagement surrounding the controversy. Only in March of 2023, after the crisis had been raging for some months, did Netanyahu choose to flout the "conflicts" memo and enter the fray (noting that at this point the controversy's effects extended to the State's economy and national security).

Finally, we return to Mazuz with a truly instructive and alarming episode during the Olmert Government. One version is relayed by an official who worked in the Prime Minister's Office:[59] Minister of Justice Daniel Friedmann tabled a motion for the Government to split the role of the LCG into separate functions (see Chapter 8). Mazuz, who was the current LCG, attended the Cabinet discussion and requested to speak. He then produced a list and read out the names of about half the Ministers present. Mazuz explained that all those he had named were the subject of criminal investigations and were therefore prohibited from voting on the issue as they had a conflict of interest. For most of the named Ministers this was the first time they had learned of such investigations. The remaining Ministers in the room took the hint and the motion was removed from the agenda.

According to another version,* told by Prime Minister Olmert himself in his memoirs, Mazuz objected to a benign policy decision advanced by Justice Minister Friedmann, which related to how the State Attorney is appointed.† Mazuz had a particular candidate in mind for the position and such a change might have reduced their chances of being appointed. After threatening that he would put up a public fight against the change, Mazuz informed Olmert and several other Ministers that they were not allowed to vote *for* the change due to their being under investigation and "conflicted." At the same time Mazuz saw no problem with Ministers voting *against* the change, which seemed to indicate these "conflicts" limitations applied rather selectively.[60]

If accurate, these stories reflect the overarching use of criminal "conflict of interest" to simply block the ability of elected government to supervise and shape the legal institutions and organizations which wield the State's formidable penal

---

* Or perhaps this was a separate episode. I have little personal sympathy for Olmert, but the account of Mazuz's conduct relayed in Olmert's book is frankly harrowing.

† Friedmann's proposal was that a committee recommends three candidates from which the Government would choose one.

authority. In this way such institutions avoid scrutiny and accountability for their actions and are able to paralyze political agendas they find disagreeable.

Prime Minister, Prime Suspect

In one of the most famous and dramatic cases ever involving the Deri Doctrine, the Court adjudicated challenges to the appointment of Benjamin Netanyahu as Prime Minister in 2020 following his then-recent indictment for criminal offences. The background and leadup to this case are detailed in Chapter 4 above and need not be repeated. Here we will suffice by recalling that Netanyahu was appointed as Prime Minister by a super-majority of 72 MKs representing an emergency bi-partisan coalition, at the height of the dual COVID and political crises (following the third elections in a year), and after the indictments were known to all and featured prominently as part of electoral campaigns.

The legal question before the Court was straightforward – can the Deri Doctrine be applied to the appointment of the Prime Minister himself? After much handwringing and equivocation, in one of the most unnecessary rulings imaginable, after dragging the public and country through some bizarre legal theater, the Court ultimately responded in a unanimous eleven-member decision that *Deri* did not (indeed, could not) apply to the Knesset's selection of its Prime Minister. The Court of course lost face in every quarter – the political Right and opponents of judicial supremacy were appalled at the Court's willingness to even entertain such a flagrant violation of democratic norms; the staunch anti-Netanyahu camp and judicial supremacists were severely disappointed the Court would not magically rid them of their political nemesis and would permit the ascension of a criminal defendant to the role of Prime Minister. The case was in many senses an inevitable culmination of the Court's folly – the abolition of standing and justiciability, the refusal to limit reasonableness review and its routine extension to the Knesset, the expansive and incoherent application of *Deri*, the permissive and arbitrary approach to statutory interpretation – all these ingredients combined to produce a grotesque scenario in which the material and tangible parliamentary outcome of elections are placed under the chopping block of judicial review. One need not have sympathy for Netanyahu the man or his policies to understand the problematic and perilous nature of such adjudication.

The *Netanyahu* case is instructive for a number of reasons, and we will examine some of its aspects briefly and anecdotally. One element is the futile and rather desperate attempt at any degree of legal coherence – reading the opinions in the ruling, one can almost feel the Court fumbling and stumbling around the smoldering ruins of Israel administrative law. Yet any such effort at logic or consistency was in vain. After conceding there was no statutory requirement barring Netanyahu from serving as Prime Minister, the Court turned to consider the application of *Deri*, yet was awkwardly unsure as to precisely whose discretion was under judicial evaluation. In other words, against whom would a Court order be issued? Who is the primary "respondent"?

The Deri Doctrine purports to review discretion exercised by the Prime Minister regarding his subordinate Minister, but here there was no higher administrative authority that might be compelled to "fire" Netanyahu. Is the Prime Minister supposed to commit political *seppuku* and dismiss himself? Is the President supposed to reject the Coalition's official notice that it had successfully been formed? Is the Knesset speaker prohibited from setting the necessary agenda to swear in the new Government? After dismissing these arguments as having not the flimsiest legal basis, the Court was faced with the only one remaining – reviewing the collective discretion exercised by the majority of Knesset members who supported Netanyahu's Government. This was (at the time) a step too far even for the Court, which eventually denied the petitions in a joint sigh of lament. This confusion as to the legal framework's most basic elements further reflects just how unfounded the entire case was to begin with.

Another noteworthy part of the *Netanyahu* ruling is the concurring opinion of Justice Amit.[61] Amit opens with a stirring parable: An aspiring individual named "Reuven" applies for a junior entry-level position with a local public waterworks company. Alas, Reuven's application is rejected due to a criminal indictment filed against him – his would-be boss explains such a hire is "inconceivable." Reuven then proceeds to apply for a variety of positions of a successively more senior nature, but fails each time because of the same indictment. He then becomes a prominent politician and is first elected to the local mayorship, and later appointed government Minister, but is nonetheless dismissed both times due to the Deri Doctrine. Reuven finally becomes Prime Minister. Leaving little to subtlety and plainly rather pleased with himself, Amit spells out the "anomaly" before us – the imaginary Reuven is barred from any position in public service, aside perhaps the most senior position of all. How can this be countenanced?

Unfortunately, this Homeric epic offered by Amit is not quite as compelling as he seems to think, and illuminates Amit's (and the Court's) jurisprudence in a rather unflattering light.

First, in a minor but wonderfully ironic twist, Amit's premise is simply wrong in its description of legal fact. The story's protagonist would *not* be barred from being employed in the waterworks company. The Israeli Civil Service Commission (which oversees all government employment) published general guidelines for evaluating candidates with a criminal past or who are the subject of ongoing criminal proceedings.[62] The directive, in force since 2015 and explicitly applicable to governmental waterworks corporations, concludes simply that employers and recruiters have discretion on how to factor in a candidate's criminal status (excluding statutory limitations of course). As such the directive clearly contemplates (and in no way rules out) the hiring of a criminal defendant. The takeaway is that the waterworks company in Amit's story would in fact have no reason to categorically reject Reuven as a junior employee, or at least had no legal obligation to do so. This is a far cry from "inconceivable." In other words, somewhat embarrassingly, Amit's most basic contention on which the rest of his parable is based turns out to be demonstrably false.

This is no trivial error. Setting aside inferior legal research (in fairness, we may likely blame a clerk), it also demonstrates a lack of judicial sensitivity to the acute flaws in the argument Amit presents. What if Reuven is innocent? What if the charges against him are grossly inflated? What if he is the victim of vindictive or malicious prosecution from a hostile neighbor? What if the indictment was simply a misunderstanding, a clerical error, or gross incompetence? Our fictional Reuven has yet to argue his case before an impartial tribunal even one single time. Amit sketches out an appalling reality in which a unilateral criminal indictment is sufficient to effectively end the career prospects of a junior candidate for an insignificant role, yet Amit doesn't miss a beat. In the best case, Amit seems oblivious to the most basic liberal assumptions of criminal justice. This is from an experienced judge on a Supreme Court which styles itself as a frontline protector of individual liberties and civil rights.

Amit's parable is misguided (and misleading) in yet another troubling way. At no time does it occur to Amit that there is a difference between an employer who refuses to hire a defendant, and an employer who is prevented from hiring someone by judicial order. In Amit's story and presumably in his broader view, a boss *choosing* not to hire a candidate and a Prime Minister being *forced* to fire a Minister are one and the same. To Amit, the fact that the former part reflects the employer's desire while the latter goes against the wishes of the "employer" – be it the electorate, the public, or just the Prime Minister – is of no consequence whatsoever.

Further reflection reveals the more significant logical flaw here: Amit tries to justify the Deri Doctrine by presenting a story which applies… the Deri Doctrine. In an iconic interview from 2012, fresh politician Yair Lapid was asked why he opposes legalization of recreational cannabis – his answer was "because it's illegal."[63] In similarly circular fashion, Amit presents a "common sense" story in which *Deri* causes the recurring dismissal of hapless Reuven, as though this were the only natural reality imaginable. What Amit is not willing or able to concede is that his story itself suffers from all the same objections that make *Deri* so odious in the first place, and in no way reflects the natural order of things. This fine point is obscured by the way Amit treats voluntary dismissal and compelled (judicial) dismissal as if they were the same.*

Finally, we may observe the Court's general state of denial. In all one-hundred pages of its various opinions at no point does the Court raise any concerns about granting a handful of unelected prosecutors the power to unilaterally dismiss a Prime Minister or veto his appointment by the Knesset. This simply does not figure in as a material consideration and is not raised or discussed. It is a non-issue.

---

* One might reasonably object at this point that I make too much of Amit's parable. Is this just petty nitpicking? Maybe. But judges wishing to avoid such scrutiny in the first place might better refrain from writing inane allegorical prose as if a Supreme Court ruling were their social media feed.

The same denial also extends, and is indeed highly relevant, to the Court's complaints that it is called upon to decide such a case to begin with. Throughout the ruling the various Justices are at pains to clarify just how lamentable they find the whole situation to be, and seem to freely scold the public for their choice of Prime Minister. Justice Menny Mazuz captures the atmosphere when he states that appointing Netanyahu as Prime Minister under indictment "reflects a social crises and moral flaw of society and of the Israeli political system."[64] Mazuz naturally sees the Court as enforcer (or at least agent) of moral propriety and as solver of societal flaws, and as such feels free to assign the Israeli public grades for their poor judgment. (One can almost feel his regret when Mazuz continues – "however, the Court cannot replace the public's role…").

Yet Mazuz and most others on the Court are never willing to consider – let alone acknowledge or address – the possibility that its own jurisprudence is at least partially to blame; that *Deri* inevitably created a legal environment which motivates over-eager prosecutors and in which the public is justifiably skeptical of criminal indictments against politicians. Thanks to *Deri* and its ensuing heavy-handed (and at times plainly wrongful) application to public figures, it is small wonder that the public doesn't treat an indictment with the same gravity the Court seems to think appropriate.* The obvious formula is one of natural cause-and-effect – the automatic political outcome of criminal indictments breeds a justified suspicion of politically-motivated cases. Indeed, such a theory doesn't require great creativity or judicial introspection, but was expressly raised by critics of *Deri* from the outset. Nonetheless – as an ultimate mark of its willful ignorance, the Court simply fails to consider the possibility and evidence that perhaps this sorry state of affairs is not only the fruit of a corrupt political order and an incorrigibly indifferent electorate, but has come about also (at least partially) thanks to its homegrown judicial doctrine of unilateral impeachment.

A Ridiculous Mouse

To complete our discussion of the Deri Doctrine we return to none other than its namesake – Mr. Aryeh Deri himself. The continued evolution of Deri's legal entanglement is fascinating as much as it is deeply disturbing and is well worth our attention. Following the famous *Deri* case in 1993, Aryeh Deri was finally convicted of corruption offenses in 1999, for which he served a prison sentence until 2002.† He eventually returned to politics and was elected to the Knesset, once again as leader of the Shas party, in 2013. After the 2015 elections Deri was

---

* The public's skepticism here seems to have been at least partially justified. The District Court judges trying Netanyahu's case recommended that the prosecution withdraw the bribery charge (the most severe levelled against Netanyahu) before the defense even began presenting evidence.

† Deri maintained his innocence throughout and to this day. Many, including Prof. Daniel Friedmann, considered his conviction unjustified, or thought that subsequent developments merited a retrial.

appointed to Ministerial roles – first as Minister of Economy and later as Minister of the Interior.

As had at this point become a natural feature of the Israeli political order, Deri's appointment was duly challenged in the Supreme Court – once for his initial appointment, and then a second time specifically against his serving as Minister of the Interior. Both these cases were meritless – exactly like the *Hanegbi* and *Ramon* cases discussed above, Deri fully met the statutory conditions for his appointment, which required that seven years pass following the end of serving a prison sentence for a crime involving "moral turpitude." Here then was a bright-line, unambiguous, numerical rule which left no room for doubt – an ex-prisoner could become a Minister after seven years and a day. In Deri's case, some thirteen years had passed since his sentence was completed, and most of the transgressions for which he was accused occurred long beforehand. Unlike the original *Deri* case in the 90s, Deri's past convictions were "old news" known to the electorate and the Knesset, and his appointment of course received the necessary parliamentary approval, both times.

Yet much like the *Hanegbi* and *Ramon* cases, this did not stop the Court from adjudicating the matter, fully assuming that the appointment was nonetheless subject to the requirements of "reasonableness" and the Deri Doctrine. In its first ruling, the Court unanimously dismissed the petitions, though clearly uncomfortable with the result. Writing the lead opinion, Justice Hayut seemed to indicate that Deri's appointment had been saved by the skin of its teeth – saying it was "on the boundary of the range of reasonableness."[65] A second petition, only four months later, took specific issue with Deri's role as Minister of the Interior, because his prior criminal conduct occurred when he was at the same Ministry in the 90s. This time, though the matter had been just adjudicated mere months earlier, the Court needed fifty-six pages to dismiss the case, with an even closer shave for Deri, as the decision was not unanimous. Writing for the majority, Justice Salim Joubran felt that the Knesset's personal approval of Deri added weight to the reasonableness of his appointment, though it remained "a borderline case."[66]

Almost immediately on the heels of Deri's appointment as Minister, and even before the second of these two rulings, the Legal Counsel to the Government announced a slew of fresh criminal investigations against Deri. These involved allegations of corruption (fraud and "breach of trust") and later of tax and money-laundering offenses. Eventually Deri reached a plea deal according to which he was convicted, in 2022, of a tax offense, paid a hefty fine (nearly $50,000), and received a suspended prison sentence. As part of the plea deal, Deri resigned from the Knesset.

Despite this, in the subsequent 2023 elections, Deri was reelected to the Knesset and was once again appointed as Cabinet Minister as part of the formation of a new coalition government. As the sun rises in the East, so a petition was filed with the Supreme Court against Deri's appointment. This time, in an expanded panel of eleven Justices, the Court struck down Deri's appointment with a majority of the panel ruling that the appointment was extremely unreasonable in light of Deri's recent conviction.[67] For many observers this confirmed their view of Aryeh Deri as an irredeemably corrupt figure returning to his crooked ways, one who should never have been allowed to return to public service and who the Court finally and rightly prevented from causing further harm.

And yet.

Such things are rarely as they seem at first glance. There is a fundamentally different version of events which deserves our consideration and which the following evidence strongly supports. Let us rewind to 2015 and the Court's characterization of Deri's appointment as "on the boundary" of legality – almost as if to signal to whoever was listening that perhaps all that was required was a little further nudge to push Deri over the edge. As if the Court were saying – give us a little more dirt, something to work with.

The 2016 corruption investigation against Deri was bogus from the start. Friedmann suggests that had Deri not returned to public office, no one would have dreamed of initiating these criminal proceedings.[68] It was clear very early on that the accusations against Deri had no merit because the prosecution kept delaying any decision – it took the police over two more years to finally publish their "recommendation" in 2018, and another three years until the LCG finally closed the corruption case in 2021 without filing any charges. Had there been a strong case to begin with it would have led to a swift indictment instead of fading in a drawn-out whimper.

Yet the questionable corruption investigation enabled a further "fishing expedition" (as Friedmann calls it), and indeed the police found some unrelated personal business dealings (some of them over a decade old) which they hoped might produce an indictable tax offense. Friedmann notes that the prosecutors now had an additional incentive to find some criminal fault in Deri's actions, in light of the corruption case falling completely apart. A leading criminal defense attorney characterized the new tax charges as a "ladder" for the prosecution to "climb down the tall tree" they were now stuck in.[69] One can't help but recall the "prosecutorial juggernaut" described in Bill Barr's speech and of Robert Jackson's warnings against prosecutors "picking their defendants."

The person overseeing this entire prosecutorial initiative – Legal Counsel to the Government Avichai Mandelblit – seemed to agree. In a hair-raising leaked recording Mandelblit was heard fuming about the "bad results" of the corruption investigation and that it "didn't deliver even a tiny mouse, nothing" (referring to the common Israeli phrase "the mountain did not deliver even a mouse," originating in Aesop's fable "The Mountain in Labour").* Mandelblit alludes to the fact that the investigation did not regard tax evasion but that it had now

* The most well-known rendition is likely:
"What could he produce to match his opening promise?
Mountains will labour: what's born? A ridiculous mouse!"
(Horace, Ars Poetica, 138–139)

unearthed some suspicions of tax offenses which "are not concrete," meaning they will not produce a certain conviction.[70]

"Not concrete" seems to have been an understatement. The tax charges against Deri were so spurious that two unlikely figures came to his public defense. The former General Counsel to the Israeli Tax Authority and another former senior department head in the ITA's legal department published a joint op-ed clarifying that Deri was not convicted of tax evasion or fraud.[71] Instead, Deri's conviction regarded "minor" offenses which involved indirect involvement in tax reporting errors – without intent to defraud and without any cost to public coffers. Critically, in the two counts for which Deri was charged neither action resulted in illicit profit nor in reduced tax payments – it seemed hard to understand why Deri was being prosecuted for tax "offenses" in which all required taxes had indisputably been paid. The two attorneys felt certain that if this had not been a high-profile case in which the prosecution had already sunk significant resources, an indictment for such offenses under such circumstances would never have been filed (if anything at all, the ITA could have imposed some minimal civil penalty for inaccurate reporting).

Finally, Deri entered a plea deal in 2022 that deliberately did not include prison time or "moral turpitude." This was to avoid the risk of a trial-court sentence which might have included "moral turpitude," and which would have barred Deri's reelection in 2023. While the plea deal included Deri's resignation (in and of itself a profoundly objectionable punitive measure for benign tax offenses), all parties agreed that it allowed for his immediate return to politics in the upcoming elections. In a later public interview Mandelblit himself emphasized that the plea deal did not include any obligation on Deri's part to refrain from running for office again – and the prosecution officially confirmed this in later court filings.

In this light, the 2023 Supreme Court ruling against Deri's ability to serve as Cabinet Minister takes a more sinister form. The black-letter law unquestionably permitted Deri's appointment, as he had not served a prison sentence in the past seven years; the previous rulings of *Hanegbi* and *Ramon* and even those regarding Deri himself were not willing to intervene in the Knesset's discretion approving a Ministerial appointment. In fact, the only material legal change since Deri's 2015 and 2016 appointments (and the associated rulings) was Deri's deeply dubious conviction (in a plea deal) of indisputably minor tax reporting offenses with no element of corruption or misconduct in public office. But this seems precisely the "nudge" the Court was looking for – a sufficient hook for the Court to rule that Deri's appointment was now invalid due to its "extreme unreasonableness." Of course, one might understandably speculate whether Deri's policies and political agenda during the interim years had also played some part in the Court's determination to be rid of him.

Though portrayed as a natural and almost inevitable evolution of the Deri Doctrine, this was in fact the first time the Court had actually invalidated a Ministerial appointment (and the Knesset's approval) based on its unreasonableness. Of all the instances for such judicial innovation, the flimsy grounds of Deri's latest tax conviction make the invalidation all the more extraordinary (recall that Haim Ramon's 2007 appointment was not invalidated, though he had just been convicted for an indecent sexual act with a subordinate; and Tzachi Hanegbi's appointment in 2014 was not invalidated, though he had recently been convicted of perjury with "moral turpitude"). Adding yet an extra twist is that the Knesset had recently amended the Basic Law specifically to avoid an interpretive question regarding competence conditions,* in order to clear the way for Deri's reelection and appointment. The legal language and associated debates are immaterial – the point here is that not only did Deri's appointment receive parliamentary approval, but that it was also supported by deliberate legislative action. This is the background on which the Court chose to invalidate a Cabinet Minister's appointment for the first time in the country's history.

Somewhat amusingly, the Court heavily relied on the statements made by the Magistrate judge during the trial-court sentencing, which indicated he was under the impression that Deri was quitting political life for good.† Whether this was indeed his impression, whether such impression may have been justified, and whether this would have affected the sentence is another debate (this seems yet another empirical question unsuited to HCJ proceedings which do not allow for evidence hearings). The Supreme Court implicitly felt that had the trial-court judge known Deri intended to return to political life, he would have perhaps handed down a different sentence which may have precluded Deri from reelection. Yet factual objections aside, the Supreme Court's assumption here is in itself deeply troubling. A person convicted of a crime ought to receive the appropriate sentence as prescribed by statute, precedent, sentencing guidelines and other commonly accepted factors related directly to the crime committed. But the Court seems to casually assume that a politician's future plans are a legitimate consideration for a trial judge when determining a sentence for a criminal conviction. In other words, the Court nonchalantly suggests that a judge in a criminal trial considers the future political intentions of the defendant as a sentencing factor. This approach directly contradicts basic rules of criminal justice, such as judicial impartiality and consideration of only material information.

Here then is yet another example, if any were needed, of how the Supreme Court views the criminal justice system as a mechanism to regulate unrelated (non-criminal) political behavior.

Aryeh Deri is a convenient scapegoat representing a sectorial party and community far from the political and cultural mainstream. This author has never

---

* The existing law was unclear whether a "prison sentence" included a suspended sentence. Though many scholars agreed this only regarded actual imprisonment and that an amendment was not required, the Knesset amended the Basic Law so that the seven-year limitation explicitly applied only to actual physical imprisonment.

† Full disclosure, this judge is a distant relative of mine by marriage.

voted for him and finds much to dislike in Deri the person and the politician. Nonetheless, an honest and clear-eyed assessment leads to the inevitable impression that Deri had been unjustly treated and wrongly pursued by the "rule of law thugs." The price isn't paid only by Deri and his voters. Deri is broadly respected by his political foes and allies alike, is one of the most experienced politicians in the Knesset and is considered a cautious, pragmatic and level-headed statesman with a moderating influence – not easily replaced in the Cabinet once forcibly removed. Few were surprised when, following the October 7th massacre and the outbreak of the war in Gaza, Netanyahu returned Deri to the Cabinet as a non-Minister observer (with a voice but no vote).

Zooming out, the gravity of the 2023 Deri decision can't be underestimated and we have yet to see where it leads. The original Deri Doctrine was, with all its flaws and objections, at least theoretically limited to the removal of serving officeholders when indicted for serious and severe crimes; yet now it seems to apply to the ex ante appointment (and Knesset approval) of Ministers for infractions of any kind. And so we come full circle from the first *Deri* of 1993 to the 2023 Deri case nearly thirty years later. The floodgates of judicial impeachment had been opened long ago, but the current deluge vindicates and even surpasses many original dire predictions. The implications for everything discussed above – and especially for the relationship between branches of government, the ability of elected officials to challenge judicial supremacy, and the unilateral power of prosecutors to demolish political fortunes – are immeasurable.

New Frontiers

A final matter worthy of our attention are two dramatic recent escalations – both decided in May of 2025 – in which the Supreme Court has further strengthened its grip over executive appointments.

The *Civil Service Commissioner* case regards the chairman (or "Commissioner") of Israel's Civil Service Commission – the primary body in charge of all government employees, hiring and employment processes. It is one of the most influential roles in Israeli public service, with the ability to significantly affect the character of the government workforce in a variety of ways. After a drawn-out legal saga, the Government appointed its selected candidate to the role of Commissioner. Needless to say, the appointment was challenged in a Supreme Court petition. The petitioners alleged that the Government was obligated to conduct a "competitive process" with a public search for candidates, in which an impartial committee (controlled by the legal establishment) nominates its own selected candidates from which the Government may select their appointee. While numerous roles within the executive government do indeed involve such a process, the Commissioner is appointed directly by Government resolution.

What the petitioners conveniently ignored was that nothing in the law remotely supported their position. Statutory law is unequivocal, stating not only that the "The Government shall appoint the Commissioner," but also that other mandatory "bidding processes" do not apply to this appointment. Better still, *every single* Commissioner in the State's history, throughout six decades since the role was created, had been appointed precisely this way – at the exclusive discretion of the Government. This includes the most recent Commissioner who had been appointed the exact same way in 2018 without a hitch. Further still, the Supreme Court itself had weighed in on precisely this issue in 2011, and had ruled that the Government was under no legal obligation to perform a "competitive" process, as statutory law and precedent were clear on the matter.

None of this was of interest to the current Court. In a remarkable ruling, the Court ruled in 2025 that the current *process* for appointing the Commissioner was no longer acceptable, and that the Government was obligated to formulate a new process which would restrict its own discretion and ability to choose its desired candidate.[72] The Court based its decision on the familiar mashup of "reasonableness," "authority versus discretion," and so on. Justice Yitzhak Amit's concluding sentence is illuminating: "After weighing all the relevant considerations, I am of the opinion that the appropriate and balanced remedy for the aforementioned flaw is that the appointment mechanism for the role of Commissioner should be competitive in nature." It is the judge who "weighs" all considerations; it is the judge who "determines" the "appropriate" mechanism; the fact that the legislature had weighed things differently and had made its own determination on the matter is of negligible consequence. It is the view of the judge that prevails over the law. We will return to the implications of this ruling in a moment.

In an ironic twist, Justice Amit was on the 2011 unanimous panel which had previously held the process to be lawful; yet he also wrote the majority opinion for the Court in the 2025 ruling which held the opposite. Considering that no change had occurred to statutory law in the interim, Amit was in the embarrassing position of having to explain his total (and totally arbitrary) reversal. The excuse offered by Amit does not disappoint. He explains that "the law must adapt itself to the shifting reality," that is, "attempts by the political leadership to undermine" the "a-political and independent" nature of the Civil Service Commissioner, and to "insert political considerations into the ranks of the public civil service." Amit's extraordinary learned legal explanation amounts to an admission that he doesn't like the appointing Government or its policies.

Nine days later, the Court issued another ruling. The *Ronen Bar* case regarded the head of the Israeli domestic security and intelligence service, the Shin Bet (or "*Shabak*"). Ronen Bar headed the Shin Bet in the leadup to the October 7th attack. Perhaps to state the obvious, the failure of the Israeli intelligence community to learn and warn of the attack was a major contributing factor to the attack's catastrophic results – a failure of which the Shin Bet and its leader Bar share a significant portion. In March of 2025 the Government announced its decision to dismiss Bar from his post and to appoint a successor. Here, too, applicable statutory law is unequivocal. The law states that the head of the Shin Bet "shall be appointed by the Government after nomination by the Prime Minister." More to the point, the law clarifies in no uncertain terms that "The Government may terminate the tenure of the Head of the Shin Bet before its completion." It is hard to think of a more explicit expression of discretionary statutory authority.

The decision to dismiss Bar was immediately challenged in the Supreme Court. Despite the unambiguous statutory law, the Court issued a series of preliminary injunctions preventing the dismissal from going into effect. In a bizarre scenario (even in Israeli terms), Bar remained the head of Israel's secret police (which is, incidentally, also in charge of security of the Prime Minister and Government Ministers), despite the Government's decision to fire him, despite the ugly public confrontation, and despite a complete and genuine breakdown of mutual trust and confidence between both sides. This went on for several months, until Bar agreed to "voluntarily resign" on a designated date in June. The Government, in turn, rescinded its dismissal decision in light of Bar's prospective resignation.

The issue was now moot, with no existing Government decision to challenge or to void – but the Court issued a ruling anyway. This was a "principled" ruling in which the Court insists on laying out its view of the law, notwithstanding the fact that there was no longer any legal dispute to adjudicate. In a majority decision the Court held that the Government's authority to dismiss "gatekeepers," head of the Shin Bet chief among them, was generally subject to judicial supervision and to the typical limits of administrative law (that is, to reasonableness, objective purposive interpretation, and the rest).[73] The Court ruled that the original dismissal decision was unlawful (the reader is spared the Court's unpersuasive reasoning) and therefore void. Though the decision regarded a moot issue and had no practical effect (and in principle, no precedential value), it will surely be relied upon for future interventions in the Government's dismissal of similar officials.*

It is tempting to view these two decisions – issued about a week apart by the same Justices – as just more of the same, yet another two examples in a long line of judicial interventions in executive appointments. However, this is not the case. The two decisions represent a radical escalation of the Court's "appointments" jurisprudence and its erosion of valid, democratic appointment powers, an escalation not only in degree, but in kind.

In the *Civil Service Commissioner* case the Court's intervention had nothing to do with the individual candidate selected by the Government. By all counts, including in the Court's estimation (at least as lip service), the selected appointee was fully qualified and was a proper and "reasonable" match for the role. For the first time in its history the Court intervened in the selection *method* – disqualifying not the candidate, but the selection process itself. Critically, the process in this instance was prescribed by clear-cut statute, yet the Court pretends that it is merely

* For a discussion of the role of "gatekeepers" see Chapter 8.

performing administrative judicial review over the exercise of executive discretion. In other words, the Court takes a statutory rule – appointment by Government resolution – and simply pretends that the rule is yet another administrative policy decision subject to the reasonableness standard. For the first time, the Court has seized the power not only to review the "reasonableness" of a particular candidate, but rather to evaluate the justification (for lack of a better term) of a statutory appointment method. This is, without a doubt, a marked departure from the Court's existing jurisprudence and signifies a quantum leap in the Court's lawless interference with the core of executive government. We can expect to see more decisions in which the Court starts dictating to the Government the proper (or reasonable) process for appointing officials without the flimsiest basis in law.

The *Ronen Bar* case is even more extreme. All the Court's prior jurisprudence regarding executive appointments, including the Deri Doctrine, has exclusively involved *prevention* – that is, denying the Government a certain official or candidate. The Court has disqualified (or blocked) the appointment of candidates, or has demanded (or compelled) the dismissal of officials. In all such instances, the Government wanted to hire (or retain) an official, and the Court denied the Government its preference. Here, for the first time, the Court has *imposed* an official against the Government's wishes – that is, the Government was forced to retain an official despite the former's decision to dismiss the latter. This is a dizzying shift from the Court's existing theory and practice. It is one thing to tell the Government it must dismiss an official or that it cannot hire them; it is another thing entirely to compel the Government to retain an official it wants to fire.

This is a good time to recall that the entire current debate takes place within the framework of reasonableness review (or other equally nebulous grounds), and not "illegality" or the violation of some clear-cut rule. It is undisputed that a court can properly compel the Executive to retain an employee if their termination does not meet some required statutory condition, or if it violates other established principles of administrative law (e.g., corruption or arbitrariness). But the Supreme Court's intervention in appointments, both in general and with the Deri Doctrine, as well as in these recent cases, is based entirely on the absence of such conventional grounds. It is based, as has been discussed comprehensively in this chapter, on the so-called "reasonable" exercise of executive discretion, on a judicial evaluation of whether the government has "correctly" or "properly" weighed competing factors, even when the government acts within its statutory authority and does not violate any other recognizable legal principle.

The Court pretends in *Ronen Bar* that everything is "business as usual," and that its decision is yet another natural application of its appointments review – but nothing could be more misleading. For the first time in its history (and likely the first time in the history of modern Western democracy), the Court *imposed* a senior bureaucrat on the Government, in practice for several months and in principle for future cases, in direct contradiction of an unequivocal statute granting the Government an "at-will" termination power.*

This is, for the second time in a single week, a radical and unprecedented escalation of the Court's crusade against democratic authority and accountable executive government. We can be certain that the Court will use this same reasoning for other dismissals in the near future. Further still, the day is not far that the Court will force the Government to appoint a specific candidate – not just forbidding dismissal but imposing a fresh judicially-desired appointment altogether.†

Our consideration of the *Ronen Bar* case thus far has avoided the most obvious and pressing objection – that in any Western democracy the identity of the nation's top military and defense personnel is a non-justiciable issue, under the exclusive and unrestricted discretion of the civilian (and elected) political leadership. The Court's new turn towards "imposed" retention of officials takes a much darker and more sinister character within the current context. It's one thing to block the Government's choice of Police Commissioner or of military Chief of Staff; it is another thing entirely to force the Government to hire or retain senior officials wielding the most dangerous and formidable instruments of State violence. The idea that a secret police chief could continue to function in their role after being dismissed by the State's elected Cabinet – amid a complete collapse of confidence and mutual allegations of severe misconduct – runs contrary to the most basic principles of democratic oversight and of limited government. As discussed earlier in this chapter, one of the most important and effective tools possessed by elected politicians in their supervision of government organs is the ability to dismiss. If a court halts the government's ability to terminate an official's role, it means that for all intents and purposes the official has been granted a license to go rogue. This is not a legal argument and it deserves separate and more detailed treatment, but it simply cannot be entirely ignored.

The Supreme Court of Israel, bearing the standard of individual liberties and governmental accountability, told the State's elected leadership that it simply could not dismiss its head of domestic intelligence. For several months Israel existed in a genuinely appalling limbo, where the country's secret police was run by a person who had completely lost the Government's confidence (and vice-versa), while the Government was unable to replace or remove him. Worse, for a terrifying few months that same person could make decisions and take actions in the knowledge he was, temporarily, completely immune for the Government's primary "stick" of dismissal. Surely no one with the barest understanding of democratic governance (or with just a modicum of plain common sense) can believe this to be an acceptable state of affairs. Yet the Supreme Court

* Recent notable cases in the United States (still undecided) are no exception, in that they turn on clear statutory language, and none involve the most high-ranking national security officials.

† This indeed came close to happening with the Shlomo Lemberger saga, discussed in Chapter 8.

singlehandedly created this scenario without a moment's hesitation – without even addressing, throughout fifty-eight pages, the basic democratic concern of a State secret police being controlled by someone who is un-fireable.*

The *Commissioner* and *Ronen Bar* cases jointly demonstrate how no method of Israeli judicial supremacy is static. Every lawless doctrine, standard and rule contains an infinite potential for radical and reckless expansion.

These two recent cases also serve as a useful demonstration of other issues discussed in earlier chapters. Justice Yitzhak Amit had selected a three-member "seniority" panel (i.e., the three most senior Justices) to hear both cases – with himself, conservative Justice Noam Solberg, and supremacist Justice Daphne Barak-Erez. Both cases were decided by a two-Justice majority against Solberg's dissent. This just incidentally happened to be the *only* conceivable panel composition that would render such radical supremacist decisions – *every single* other seniority-based panel would have almost certainly eliminated the supremacist majority for these cases. Because such high-profile cases are almost never decided by a small three-member panel, Amit's panel-manipulation stood out as plainly transparent.

Both cases were brought by "public" petitioners – that is, petitioners with no standing. But the *Ronen Bar* case is remarkable in the sense that Ronen Bar himself, the Shin Bet head being dismissed, was not a petitioner. Ronen Bar did not personally challenge the act of his own dismissal. In any other scenario this would qualify as "another's quarrel," when the main aggrieved party declines to sue – precisely the type of "counter-exception" that precludes Standing (discussed in Chapter 4) even in the permissive world of Israeli threshold requirements. Yet the Court swiftly disposed of any such objections, because the case qualifies for a counter-counter-exception (yes, really) in which a petition is heard even if the main aggrieved party declines to sue.

In a minor irony, the named "public petitioner" in the *Commissioner* case was one "Louis Brandeis Center." Justice Brandeis was surely spinning in his grave – his own *Ashwander* rules emphasized the importance of Standing in such petitions, stating that the court should not adjudicate cases "upon complaint of one who fails to show that he is injured" by the government measure being challenged.

The Unreasonableness Amendment

These previous two chapters provide some critical substantive context for the "Unreasonableness Amendment" passed by the Knesset in 2023 as part of its effort at judicial reform and struck down by the Supreme Court in the 2024 *Reasonableness* case, described briefly in the Introduction. The semi-constitutional amendment to the Basic Law reads that no court may consider "the

* This ruling also relates to the symbiotic relationship between judicial supremacy and unaccountable law enforcement, discussed in the next chapter.

reasonableness of a decision taken by the Government, by the Prime Minister or by another Minister," including decisions "regarding appointments" or "to refrain from exercising authority." The foregoing discussion of the Court's use of reasonableness review and of the Deri Doctrine throws this amendment and its background into stark relief. Setting aside the broader debate regarding the amendment's justifications and drawbacks, the amendment was clearly geared as a specific, explicit counter against the Court's sweeping and invasive intervention based only on unreasonableness, and against the Deri Doctrine of judicial-prosecutorial impeachment. As we have seen, previous efforts (such as the 2001 amendment setting clear conditions mandating removal of Ministers) were ignored by the Court. Had the 2023 Unreasonableness Amendment remained in force, the Court would have had to finally discard *Deri* or find an alternative method for judicial impeachment (which is more easily said than done). As such, legislative efforts to curb the use of reasonableness review must be viewed first and foremost through the prism of *Deri* and of the Knesset's (thus far, futile) attempts at reasserting the government's most basic lawful powers.

The constitutional context of striking down this legislation will be discussed later in Part III. For present purposes it's worth observing the heights to which *Deri* and reasonableness have been elevated. In his 2023 book, Yoav Dotan presciently estimated that the Court regards reasonableness as a near-constitutional norm.[74] The Court's subsequent decision in the *Reasonableness* case confirmed this estimation and surpassed it.

Consider that administrative law is almost universally regarded as subject to parliamentary design and override, especially judge-made administrative law. In other words, almost any administrative law textbook would confirm that in a parliamentary (non-presidential) system, defining the law that governs and regulates the executive branch is largely the domain and prerogative of the legislature, including the grounds and limits of administrative judicial review.[*] After examining examples from the United Kingdom and United States, Dotan writes (in summary) that "in neither legal system is it doubted that the legislature has the authority to define the standards for judicial review in concrete legislation."[75] Consider also that the Reasonableness Amendment was an explicit legislative repudiation of *Deri*, along with a large chunk of the reasonableness standard as applied to the most senior levels of executive government. One may raise valid concerns or objections regarding the wisdom of such an amendment (though it largely aligned with public proposals made by Justice Noam Solberg, Yoav Dotan, Daniel Friedmann and others), but few would suggest that defining the grounds for executive judicial review is outside the scope of legitimate Knesset authority.

In almost any other country or jurisdiction imaginable, even the most wayward court would likely back down faced with such a blatant, clear-cut, unequivocal expression of parliamentary will. Nonetheless, the Supreme Court decided to

[*] Within, if relevant, the explicit limits of a written constitutional framework.

strike down the amendment and to retain the reasonableness standard and the Deri Doctrine in their fullest form. Considering Israeli law has no formal alternative method of creating or amending legal norms, the immediate implications of the *Reasonableness* ruling are crystal clear: First, the ultimate authority to shape judicial review of the executive branch rests with the Court, not the Knesset. Second, in a contest between the legal standard of administrative reasonableness and the democratic principle of parliamentary legislative authority, the former prevails.

*

The Deri Doctrine props up judicial supremacy by brutally quelling its political opposition in the most chilling and literal sense. It represents a reprehensible stain on the Israeli legal system and governmental order. There is nothing remotely like it in any functioning civilized nation on earth. Despite its towering flaws violating core tenets of the Western liberal political order, despite its weaponization of criminal law against the electorate and their representatives, despite its gross distortion of functioning democratic government, despite its abject lawlessness – it remains, to this day, in full force and effect. Only a tiny minority of judges and legal scholars are willing to speak out against it, and they generally do so in muted and cautious terms. It is the dark, sinister corner of the Supreme Court's jurisprudence and a key part of understanding the reality of Israeli judicial supremacy.

Chapter 7

Criminal Injustice

Undue Process, Lawless Enforcement and the Presumption of Guilt

"They're a gang, these people. A gang like any other street gang – only this gang is called the 'Rule of Law Thugs.'"
— MK (and future President) Reuven Rivlin[1]

The case of Rafi Rotem spanned some seven years and represented a small drama in the world of criminal and administrative law. Rotem, a recognized whistleblower, claimed there was severe corruption within the Israeli Tax Authority at which he had previously worked. He allegedly embarked on a campaign which included extreme disruption and harassment of various government officials, at times also violating judicial restraining orders. He was indicted for offenses relating to these actions in 2013 and was initially convicted in 2016. However, in 2018 some of the convictions were reversed on appeal by the District Court. One argument raised by Rotem and accepted by the appeals court was that the decision to indict Rotem for certain harassment offenses was disproportionate or unreasonable – that is, the decision was invalid not from a perspective of criminal law, but rather that of administrative law. The court thus overturned these convictions due to flaws in prosecutorial discretion, though Rotem's guilt was proven.

The new ruling was further appealed to the Supreme Court. Before the Court lay a significant question of legal principle: under which legal framework can a defendant challenge, on procedural grounds, the very decision to indict them? Israeli criminal law doctrine allows for such preliminary challenges regarding severe procedural flaws which could result in voiding an indictment. On the other hand, the decision to indict is an inherently administrative decision and therefore theoretically subject to the same standards of Israeli administrative judicial review, especially reasonableness and proportionality.

In two consecutive divided decisions (an initial ruling in 2020 and a rehearing with an expanded panel in 2021), the Supreme Court ruled that administrative judicial review is to be left out of the criminal process, and that the proper framework for raising such challenges to prosecutorial discretion is within the constraints of procedural criminal law.[2] As a result, the District Court's reversal was overturned and the original convictions reinstated. Some hailed the ruling as a fresh and welcome challenge to the primacy of reasonableness – here was the Court finally minimizing application of the reasonableness standard (by no coincidence, the more strident opinions on the panel came from Justices Solberg and Stein, both considered relatively conservative and known critics of the reasonableness doctrine). Others condemned the ruling as leaving criminal defendants more vulnerable to illegitimate practices by law enforcement.

The question at the ruling's center is in many ways counterintuitive. Procedural criminal law is almost certainly, and by definition, more assertive and robust in defending individual rights and liberties and in constraining governmental law enforcement authorities. Administrative law typically gives government the benefit of the doubt (this is often enshrined in official doctrine, such as a presumption of administrative propriety or "regularity") and usually grants officials wide latitude as long as their actions remain within formal legal boundaries. Surely a defendant seeking to challenge prosecutorial decisions within a criminal proceeding would be better served by the former and not the latter.

Yet herein lies the broader insight which the *Rotem* case provides regarding the current state of Israeli criminal law. Parallel to the radical expansion of administrative law and the Supreme Court's penetration into all aspects of government action, Israeli criminal law suffers from a host of alarming features which diverge from established norms and accepted practice throughout the democratic world. Much as reasonableness and related doctrines have come to dominate all public affairs, so have the protections and safeguards afforded by criminal law gradually receded. In this sense *Rotem* reflects the troubling sentiment that a defendant might fare better under the invasive canopy of reasonableness than under the permissive and unconfined contours of criminal law.

The previous chapter examining the Deri Doctrine took a turn towards criminal law, such that our focus in this chapter is a natural and necessary extension. The system of Israeli criminal justice contains many elements which are objectionable enough unto themselves. Yet more importantly, it is a crucial piece in the overall puzzle of judicial supremacy and therefore warrants our detailed attention. Some flaws find their origin in the State's historical background and founding arrangements; others may be ascribed to careless or ignorant legislative initiatives and broader public indifference. Yet a chief factor is the Supreme Court's consistent exacerbation of existing problems and the creation of new ones. The deeply centralized nature of Israeli criminal justice and law enforcement, alongside its insulation from meaningful civilian oversight, make it susceptible to direction and manipulation by interested parties, while increasing the likelihood of flagrant abuse. At the same time, the Supreme Court not only neglects to moderate such dangers but instead leverages the formidable institutions of State police power for its own ends and to protect and enhance its own authority, as we shall presently see.

The Institutions – National, Centralized, Autonomous

Before we delve into some specific acute flaws of the criminal justice system, we must review some basic structural and organizational elements which serve as their background. Israel has a single unitary National Police force and a single unified State Prosecution Service with jurisdiction throughout the country, headed respectively by the Police Commissioner and the State Attorney.* (For the sake of convenience we may occasionally refer to these simply as the "Police" and "Prosecution"). Though each agency is to some extent divided into geographical districts, these are still subordinate to the centralized direction and supervision of national headquarters.

This institutional arrangement is in itself unusual in a number of respects. Both National Police and State Prosecution are largely insulated from local public supervision and input. Police District Commanders as well as District Attorneys are unelected and are not directly appointed by the elected branches (national or municipal) – rather, they are directly accountable only to their respective senior bureaucratic leadership. This matters because the most common and severe forms of crime are typically local in nature and require local attention and prioritization. Law enforcement must be acutely responsive to local challenges, preferences and concerns; the local public, in turn, ensures that law enforcement efforts and resources are directed towards addressing their most genuinely pressing issues. This is one reason that most Western countries adopt a "bottom-up" approach and subordinate local policing to the local population in a variety of ways (such as direct elections for regional leadership or their appointment by elected municipal authorities).

Yet addressing localized and individual crime may often conflict with priorities and policies set by senior organizational leadership. To be sure, such tension makes some sense and is a regular feature of large state agencies fragmented into local subdivisions. The problem with Israel's system is that in the absence of effective local input mechanisms, law enforcement efforts will invariably align with the preferences and needs defined by national headquarters. This imbalance results not only in poor local policing and reduced public safety – but also in a highly-autonomous national police force and state prosecution apparatus capable of aggressively pursuing their own institutional goals.

The question is not only one of local crime versus national crime or of valid disagreement about resource distribution. The lines that divide policing from politics and the *polis* are thin and blurry. Senior bureaucrats at the top of the law

---

* The agency representing the state in most litigation is sometimes called the "State Attorney Office" and acts in civil and administrative cases as well as in criminal cases. As our discussion focuses on criminal cases we shall refer to the agency's prosecutorial function and proceed with the label "State Prosecution" or similar.

enforcement hierarchy have their ideological leanings, as well as their own network of interests and personal priorities. They are also (just as any other government official) susceptible to the pressures and influence of their sociological peer-groups, elite opinion, national media and personal interest. That is to say, local law enforcement is sacrificed not necessarily (or not exclusively) to serve indisputable national objectives; and even national law enforcement may be compromised by improper influences.

One easy and obvious example is that of illegal road-blocking protests in Israel, which over the past decade have gone from a minor nuisance to a major disruptive force in the lives of many Israelis.* Blocking main highways and thoroughfares has some broader impact, but mostly affects the immediate road users and the local environment of wherever such blocking may occur. Local communities are tangibly harmed and generally enraged by such illegal protest activities. In any other country local law enforcement would be expected to respond swiftly and decisively to end such practices and to dissuade future offenders; a District Attorney or regional Police commander showing leniency would likely be booted from office. Yet in Israel these are almost always tolerated to an extreme degree and have been effectively normalized by law enforcement acquiescence.

One factor is convenience – clearing determined protesters is an ugly, grueling task which most police forces would happily (and understandably) avoid. This is especially relevant when the furious (but law-abiding) local public aren't nearly as intimidating and pose no serious threat. Another factor is the privileged or protected status of certain protester groups and the Police's concern for media "optics" and its national public image. Policemen and women forcibly removing or arresting wheelchair-bound disabled people, Ethiopian minorities, middle-class students or retired military veterans is a bad PR look. This impression is bolstered by instances in which the National Police clearly feels more comfortable with adopting a more aggressive stance against unpopular protestors, such as right-wing settlers or Ultra-Orthodox youths. The classic example is the harsh (and occasionally brutal) removal of road-blocking protestors against the 2005 Gaza Disengagement plan.

A final important factor is personal or institutional sympathy, by which the law enforcement hierarchy tacitly supports the protest claims or goals. This was clearly on display during the 2023 protest movement against the proposed judicial reforms, in which protestors routinely and flagrantly blocked the main highway running through Tel Aviv – week after week, months on end – but were met with almost no police resistance. The Tel Aviv police District Commander, Ami Eshed, made no effort to hide his sympathy with the protest movement on an ideological and political level, and proudly advocated toleration for illegal road blockings by protestors. Eshed became something of a celebrity among the protestors, and more

---

* This does not, of course, refer to pre-approved marches or protests which on rare occasions include the temporary lawful closure of certain roads.

importantly, among elite media and in influential political circles.* More broadly, many within senior law enforcement ranks felt that the judicial reforms would also strengthen political scrutiny over their own activities and operations, and publicly aligned their institutions against the reforms.

Had Eshed's job been less insulated from local public sentiment he would likely have acted quite differently. More broadly, illegal road-blocking illustrates some of the effects of nationally-centralized law enforcement institutions with limited incentives to directly serve their local population.

The general effects of poor policing and prosecution have been acutely felt across under-enforced areas of Israeli society. In much of the country's less-populated north and south "protection-extortion" rackets against businesses run wild; Tel Aviv's southern neighborhoods of East African migrants have become a no-go zone for police, a hotbed of rampant property and violent crime, drug dealing, and prostitution; Arab communities are plagued by a deluge of unlicensed firearms which every so often breaks out into all-out clan wars; and sophisticated organized crime has been steadily on the rise throughout the country. Even traffic violations and road safety generally receive inadequate attention (as almost anyone with experience driving in Israel will attest). While local communities cry out, these issues owe at least some of their severity to calculated under-policing and under-prosecution as a matter of policy.

One illuminating case-study involves the aftermath of the May 2021 Arab Riots, described briefly as follows:

> "In little more than a week in May 2021, Arab[-Israeli] rioters set ablaze 10 synagogues and 112 Jewish residences, looted 386 Jewish homes and damaged another 673, and set 849 Jewish cars on fire. There were also 5,018 recorded instances of Jews being stoned. Three Jews were murdered and more than 600 were hurt. Over 300 police officers were injured in disturbances in over 90 locations across the country."[3]

Over two years after these events, a damning report shed light on the abysmal approach adopted by the State Prosecution against known perpetrators of these attacks. According to the study published by journalist Neta'el Bandel, 68% of cases were settled by plea bargain, resulting in dropped charges and lenient sentences; only 37% of defendants were charged with a "nationalist" or "racist" motive (which entails a more severe sentence), despite the clear background motivations animating the riots in their entirety and the conduct of most individual rioters. Prosecutors requested relatively lenient sentences even when no plea bargain was reached, which trial judges often reduced even further. The pace of

* In 2024, the judicial-supremacist organization "Movement for Quality Government" awarded Eshed their major annual prize. In March 2025, no longer working for the Police, Eshed was spotted participating in similar protests (successors of the ones he had previously enabled as District Commander).

prosecuting was excruciatingly slow, with a majority of cases still not resolved (i.e., no verdict) two years after the riots.[4]

Consider the case of Yigal Yehoshua, age 56, who was driving home in the city of Lod on May 11, 2021. Seven Arab rioters surrounded his car and bombarded it with stones from a short distance. Yehoshua was mortally injured when a stone crashed through the windshield and struck his head, dying later of his wounds. The seven perpetrators were convicted of their actions nearly *four years* later, in April of 2025. Extraordinarily, they were ultimately not charged by the Prosecution with any form of homicide, but rather only with aggravated battery and lesser offenses.[5]

Setting aside other related issues, the point here is simply that such a scenario would be intolerable (and likely unthinkable) in a system more responsive to local residents who bore the brunt of such riots. That is, an elected or politically-appointed District Attorney under such circumstances would act very differently or would soon be out of a job.

So much for bottom-up public input into law enforcement priorities and practices – but what about top-down political oversight? This is a complex issue to which we will partially return, but for now it will suffice to say that governmental oversight of the National Police and State Prosecution is extremely limited on both an institutional and a personal level. The Police Commissioner answers (in principle) to a Government Minister, while the State Attorney is directly subordinate to the LCG and only loosely and indirectly to Ministerial authority. Elected politicians have very few tools at their disposal to supervise and control law enforcement agencies and activities, even regarding the most senior appointments and the formulation of broad policy. The "internal affairs" outfit charged with investigating police misconduct (called the "Department of Internal Police Investigations" or abbreviated *Mahash*, but which we will simply call "Internal Affairs" for clarity) is subordinate to the State Attorney and therefore more generally to the law enforcement establishment. An independent watchdog reviewing complaints against prosecutors has been established only recently, though its founding was fought tooth-and-nail by the Prosecution hierarchy and it was ultimately defanged of any serious investigative or practical authority (see later in this chapter). Further still, regarding suspicions of more severe wrongdoing, there is currently no external mechanism (such as a "special prosecutor" from outside the system) to investigate allegations against senior prosecutors or police officers. The practical implication is that these agencies enjoy a privileged status of near-autonomy, unencumbered by local-communal public input while also shielded from national-political oversight by accountable elected officials. Not to put too fine of a point on it, but it often seems that the Cabinet Minister nominally in charge of each agency is the figure with the least influence on both policy and practical matters.

One critical element parallel to under-policing of neglected issues is the gargantuan efforts and resources law enforcement agencies expend targeting ostensible corruption at all levels of national and municipal government. While combatting governmental corruption is undoubtedly important, it also ranks far lower than other pressing issues in the eyes of the general public. Even on an objective level, the tangible societal and individual harm resulting from (anything but the most extreme) government corruption is likely far inferior compared to widespread violent and property crime. The agencies involved are never forthcoming regarding the actual (budgetary) cost of sprawling corruption investigations, though these indisputably come at the expense of other policing and prosecution efforts. One politician came under intense fire for saying, in 2018, that "when people are being murdered in the streets it's more important than a Prime Minister receiving a cigar"[6] – yet he was accurately pointing out the unacknowledged price of a systemic obsession for anti-corruption prosecutions.

The benefits of focusing on political and governmental corruption are clear. The physical risk and inconvenience are negligible – politicians and public officials are much more accommodating and demure defendants than mob bosses and clan chieftains. Sitting at a desk and reviewing financial statements is safer than brushing up against gang members or seizing weapons caches. More so, the image of sanitizing politics from corruption is a positive one, and indeed, anyone criticizing such action automatically aligns themselves with the allegedly corrupt. But most significantly, the extensive emphasis on government corruption provides law enforcement with the ideal leverage against meaningful political supervision. As we've already partially seen with *Deri* and "conflicts of interest," investigations and even preliminary "probes" can have a devastating effect against disobedient politicians. More generally, any public official advocating for greater oversight or more accountability for law enforcement agencies (or even simply any measure that such agencies deem undesirable) is immediately branded hostile to the rule of law. Thus, by design, the outsized focus on government corruption diminishes the ability of elected officials to exercise democratic civilian oversight and authority over the single most important state organs requiring such scrutiny.

Few examples better demonstrate the above than the use of consistent and relentless media leaks of prosecution evidence, which have now become a staple feature of high-profile (and especially political) criminal cases. Routine and comprehensive leaks often involve classified and confidential material, including such that would not be admissible at trial, and are universally understood to emanate from the police and prosecution. Examples might include raw evidence such as transcripts (and even recordings) from witness or suspect interrogations, or processed information such as police memos and summaries; and these often occur long before trial or indictment.

Such leaks have an obvious goal of inducing public support for indictment or conviction in given cases or to weaken the public standing of specific opponents or critics. Leaks are also occasionally accompanied by official PR statements alluding to dramatic and severe offenses and iron-clad indictments, though these have many times stuttered and fizzled until little or nothing is left of the original criminal allegations. The illegal leaks had become so endemic to criminal prosecutions that they eventually drew the ire of both the Supreme Court and the

State Comptroller, but to no avail. During a 2015 police probe into his own conduct, Avichai Mandelblit complained to the Supreme Court of the unjust and damaging leaks published to the media; yet after becoming Legal Counsel to the Government, the same Mandelblit refused to investigate leaks of the exact same nature (possibly issued by his subordinates) on the grounds that such a probe had "a very low chance of yielding a result." Despite hundreds (if not thousands) of media leaks from within investigations and prosecutions over the past few decades, and despite such leaks indisputably being a chargeable (and imprisonable) criminal offense, rarely has anyone been demoted, dismissed or charged in relation to them.[7]

The widespread and persistent leaks clearly reflect law enforcement's preoccupation with their own public image, alongside the premium they place on influencing politicians and political decision-making. The leaks also demonstrate something else – the utter powerlessness of elected officials and the public in exercising oversight over law enforcement institutions. If such clear and flagrant abuses can't be investigated (not to mention, penalized or prevented) then one can reasonably infer that serious civilian supervision over the Police and Prosecution doesn't really exist at all.

A final feature of interest involves the ability to place personnel within the law enforcement and especially the State Prosecution. Under the current government job application scheme, senior prosecutorial positions are open only to existing prosecutors within the system, making it nearly impossible to inject "new blood" willing to challenge the status quo. Experienced and respected defense counsel and even seasoned government lawyers from other departments are barred from applying. This means that the Prosecution is able to filter the pool of potential candidates for all managerial positions, ensuring that anyone attaining senior status within the agency has been thoroughly vetted and professionally molded to suit the agency's outlook and needs.

The above illustrates the unique structure of Israel's law enforcement agencies, especially in relation to public sentiment and to democratic-civilian supervision. It goes without saying that the vast majority of police members and criminal prosecutors, of all ranks, are well-meaning, honorable, law-abiding public servants. More so, they fulfill a crucial societal role at great personal sacrifice and must be accorded the fullest recognition and appreciation for doing so. All this is immaterial – the system and its inherent incentives play their part.

"The Israeli Police will not be political!" So warned the National Police Commissioner in 2024 during a public feud with the Minister of National Security, after the Minister announced his intention to relieve the Commissioner of his duties. "The Israeli police must remain autonomous! Independent!" (The exclamation marks are part of the original press release).[8] In most Western countries the notion of an "autonomous" state police would send a chill down the collective national spine – few insights are as basic to modern political liberal thought as the imperative of state violence (the essence of any police force) being placed firmly under civilian, democratic, and ultimately political control. Perhaps even more extraordinary than the Commissioner's statement is the general shrug with which it was met, hardly causing a public or media stir. Both the statement and the (absent) public reaction say a great deal about the way Israeli law enforcement bodies perceive themselves and about general attitudes regarding accountability of state police powers.*

Civil Rights and Wrongs

I took the New York State Bar Exam after qualifying as an attorney in Israel. One of the first things that struck me as I began my course of bar-prep studies was the intrinsic overlap between constitutional rights and criminal procedure. A class in American constitutional law will invariably arrive at the rights to due process and trial by jury and at protections against self-incrimination or unreasonable searches and seizures; by the same token, a class in criminal procedure will likely start off with the 4th, 5th and 6th amendments to the U.S. Constitution. Though I had taken both constitutional law and criminal procedure classes as a law student at the Hebrew University in Jerusalem, this nexus was not obvious to me, and the fundamental connection between the two did not feature strongly in either class.

Israel has no jury trials – at all. To the best of my knowledge it is the only advanced† common-law derived legal system to have no jury trials of any kind. This anomaly is significant as juries perform a critical function in adversarial systems by tempering the worst excesses of prosecutorial abuse. Juries composed of ordinary citizens are a popular check on the criminal justice process and provide one last input before the final result of a criminal conviction. The absence of juries is especially significant considering the minimal public input that goes into appointments and policy formation within law enforcement bodies in the first place. The overall implication is that public preference and sentiment has neither access through the "front end" of selecting senior law enforcement officials, nor through the "middle" of shaping organizational policy through political oversight, nor through the "back end" of juries at the last stage of convicting criminals.

The absence of jury trials in Israel has historically received little to no attention, and this hallowed pillar of the common-law Anglo-American legal tradition (of which Israel is a part) is generally dismissed or even derided.

Criminal suspects have no right to assistance of legal counsel during police interrogation, occasionally resulting in patently illegal tactics employed to secure cooperation or confession. Defendants have only a limited right against self-incrimination, such that refusal to testify is almost always weighed against the defendant.[9] Israel has no "exclusionary rule" doctrine; a judge has absolute discretion over whether to admit evidence obtained illegally. Naturally, any strict

---

* The Supreme Court has actively reinforced these attitudes. See the 2025 *Police Ordinance* ruling in Chapter 10.

† That is, economically developed and not third-world.

"fruit of the poisonous tree" doctrine (forbidding subsequent evidence gained as a derivative of the initial illegal act) is out of the question and not even considered by legislators or courts. Illegally obtained evidence – even if such illegality is severe and undisputed by all parties – is rarely deemed inadmissible in criminal trials and is routinely used for conviction, including in borderline cases and for severe offenses. As a mirror image of using illegally-obtained evidence, the rules regulating search and seizure of one's person and property are lax to begin with and are enforced inconsistently at best.

Finally, there is no second-tier approval process for authorizing severe indictments – no grand jury or impartial public committee – such that the Prosecution has near-total discretion on whether to indict and with what charges.

These attributes reflect the more general approach adopted by the legal establishment towards criminal procedure and individual protections against prosecutorial zeal. And while many of these are statutory features, the overall attitude is very much encouraged and cultivated by the Supreme Court itself. Joshua Segev has observed the dwindling use of *habeas corpus* writs by the Supreme Court, though it is the only Israeli court with explicit *habeas corpus* jurisdiction. Segev ties this to the Court's evolving self-perception, transitioning from protector of individual liberties in concrete cases to benevolent architect of wide societal policy.[10] The shift is noteworthy as *habeas corpus* inherently encapsulates elements of due process, the presumption of innocence, individual liberty, and preventing abuse of police powers, in the most literally physical sense. The Court thus stands as an outlier compared with other apex courts in most democratic jurisdictions. A typical supreme or constitutional court is usually found at the forefront of protecting individual rights and liberties from government encroachment, first and foremost within the context of criminal justice. Yet since the 1980s the Israeli Supreme Court has taken a lead role in diminishing such legal protections and in promoting an aggressive prosecutorial approach.

A few instances relating to shady evidence-gathering – which would likely be considered unlawful (and potentially criminal) in most jurisdictions – serve to demonstrate some of these deficiencies. The admissibility of illegal evidence and unlawful efforts to obtain information are useful indicators of due-process abuses in a given criminal justice system.

In one of the more notorious sagas of recent years, in 2018 the police had arrested and were interrogating a suspect involved in one of the cases against Benjamin Netanyahu. The suspect was Nir Hefetz, a well-known political PR strategist, journalism executive, and confidant of Netanyahu. Hefetz was held in appalling conditions for days without access to medical inspection or treatment, but that was small beans. The real kicker was a novel and controversial "interrogation technique." Many details of what transpired are covered by a gag order, and trial hearings regarding this matter were held behind closed doors, such that the reader might need to infer their own understanding of the dismal episode.

The following description is based only on publicly available information.*

Hefetz, who is married and has children, was warned during his interrogation of a "bombshell" which would "rock his world." The bombshell allegedly involved a woman who was described as "close" to Hefetz and who is not his wife. Detectives followed her and brought her to the police station – it is unclear whether she was actually questioned, and it seems that aside her alleged connection to Hefetz she had no direct personal relevance to the investigation itself. The police then orchestrated a "random" meeting between Hefetz and the woman at the station. Hefetz later became a State witness for the Prosecution in one of their cases against Netanyahu, providing information and statements.

Prior to this "chance encounter," an interrogator said to Hefetz: "Let's just say that we've been with you all along during the days before your arrest. We know where you've been and what you've done. I know where you were the night before I arrested you." Another interrogator said: "There's a very good chance that after this whole story your children will no longer want to be in contact with you, your wife too... Your family unit is right now in peril due to the bombshell I told you is coming soon." And again: "I'm telling you that you are facing an existential threat to your family unit."[11]

Defense attorneys for Netanyahu argue that the "interrogation technique" was an attempt at "extortion" intended to create an implicit threat to Hefetz's "personal life." They believe that the "chance" encounter at the police station was arranged so as to clarify to Hefetz that should he not cooperate with the investigation and provide the police with information they sought, they could cause the disintegration of his family unit by publicizing damning personal information. As a result, they argue that Hefetz was recruited as a State witness (in the Netanyahu cases) under duress and that his original testimony was unreliable and inadmissible. In 2025 Hefetz filed a multi-million-dollar civil lawsuit against the Police and Prosecution for his treatment in custody, including the above "interrogation technique" and attempt to harm his family.[12] Hefetz is the second of two major State witnesses in the Netanyahu cases to file such a civil lawsuit.

The point in the Nir Hefetz case is twofold: First, such intimidation techniques would almost certainly be perceived as completely unacceptable in most Western jurisdictions and would likely have cost the job of those involved. While there is some debate as to whether the Police and Prosecution leadership were informed of the interrogation technique and had approved it in advance, it seems likely that many within the law enforcement hierarchy were (at least) aware of what was going on. The absence of an attorney during criminal questioning further enables illegal mistreatment of suspects in real time. Second, evidence gained from such invasive and likely-unlawful intimidation would be deemed inadmissible in most jurisdictions, and subsequent information derived from such unlawful conduct

---

* MK Amir Ohana violated the gag order by describing the episode in the Knesset plenary, relying on his immunity as legislator. The alleged details are therefore generally known, though still not readily available via public outlets.

would also be unusable. The District Court in the Netanyahu cases has not yet ruled on the admissibility and weight of Hefetz's testimony (it will likely only do so in the context of a final verdict, if one ever materializes). But under Israel's approach to evidence admissibility, it is improbable a court would entirely disqualify the information and statements received from Hefetz. Leaving decisions on evidence admissibility to the end of the trial is a typical habit of Israeli courts, providing a strong incentive for law enforcement to obtain evidence unlawfully and then see what sticks (not to mention contaminating judicial impartiality by routinely exposing fact-finder judges to inadmissible evidence, which they are then supposed to artificially forget or ignore).

Another case involves Efi Naveh, Chairman of the Israel Bar Association and an opponent of the judicial-supremacist camp. In January of 2019 Naveh's personal smartphone was illegally obtained and hacked by journalist Hadas Shtaif, who in turn handed over the phone's content to the police. Naveh's phone was provided to Shtaif by Naveh's wife in the midst of contentious divorce proceedings – though this undoubtedly violated numerous privacy (and marital privilege and confidentiality) laws, Shtaif received immunity from the Prosecution in exchange for handing over the hacked material. Notably, the Police could not have obtained a warrant to search Naveh's phone (and had no basis to try) – such that the Shtaif hacking-immunity deal was widely perceived as a method for the Police to circumvent existing privacy laws and as a form of evidence-laundering. Despite the phone's content being clearly inadmissible, the Police arrested Naveh almost immediately on suspicion of various crimes based on the information found in his phone. Naveh promptly resigned his IBA chairmanship, with his public career indefinitely suspended (if not terminated). In December of 2019 the Prosecution formally indicted Naveh on charges of bribery.

More than two years later, in 2021, after Naveh's public image and career had been thoroughly decimated, the Prosecution dropped all related charges against Naveh.[13] The decision was based solely on the certainty that the evidence against him (obtained from the hacked phone) would not hold up in court. All this was publicly known and patently obvious already in 2019 – yet the Police and Prosecution had no problem arresting and charging Naveh, with no personal repercussions or accountability for any officials involved in the decision-making process. The Naveh phone saga illustrates the propensity for rampant and highly public abuse of criminal justice with few real time due-process protections, even against high-profile and well-connected figures and even when the evidentiary basis for prosecution is illegally obtained and obviously inadmissible. It shows the ease with which law enforcement agencies rely on unlawful evidence-gathering, and a severe lack of commitment to due-process protections and to limits on misconduct by both police and prosecution.

A final instructive evidence-related example is found in the 2022 *Urich* case (mentioned briefly in Chapter 2), involving another advisor of Benjamin Netanyahu, one Jonatan Urich. In 2019 Urich and other companions were questioned by police, and their smartphones were illegally searched without a warrant. As a result of information gleaned from the initial search, police then applied for and received a valid warrant for a more intensive and penetrating smartphone search. The trial-court search warrant was appealed due to being based on the initial unlawful phone search, and after various permutations made its way to the Supreme Court. The illegality of the initial phone search was undisputed by all parties. Quite separate from the individual case of Urich and his compatriots, the appeal raised fundamental and broad questions relating to illegal searches and due process: especially, the legal effect an initial unlawful search should have on a decision to grant a subsequent warrant; the standard and method by which a trial-court must make its determination; whether such warrant may be granted *ex parte* (i.e. without allowing the defendant or suspect opportunity to object); and the proper stage (within the criminal trial) to raise and consider such questions of admissibility. This was the first time the Court seemed to seriously consider something approaching an "exclusionary rule" or even a "fruit of the poisonous tree" evidentiary doctrine. These questions took additional significance in the era and context of computers and smartphones (treated as computers for legal purposes), as their search constituted a relatively new and severe form of privacy-invasion and an acute threat to individual liberties.

An initial Supreme Court majority led by Justice Solberg set a stringent standard for granting search warrants based on prior illegal searches, to be evaluated at the time the warrant is requested. While far from a hard prohibition (and exclusion) of illegal evidence and its derivatives, the Court seemed to establish grounds for rejecting a warrant-request if the request was based on illegally-obtained information. Further, and critically, the refusal of a warrant in such circumstances would likely hinder the police investigation itself – thus establishing a clear incentive against illegal searches in the first place.

But any celebrations by due-process advocates were short-lived – the Court's decision was reviewed and reversed in the 2022 *Urich* rehearing. In an expanded nine-member panel led by Chief Justice Esther Hayut, spanning 132 pages, the Court essentially permitted the issuing of search warrants based on unlawfully-obtained information.[14] The initial unlawful search would be a "factor" in the judge's decision, and could potentially justify refusing a warrant request only "in rare and exceptional circumstances." Further, the Court ruled that any such search-warrant decisions by a trial judge are unappealable, and evidentiary objections (such as the warrant being based on an initial illegal search) may be evaluated at the main trial and verdict; and that a warrant-request hearing may typically be held *ex parte*.

In a notable and scathing dissent, Justice Elron argued that an unlawful search should typically result in a refusal of a subsequent warrant request, unless the police could convincingly prove that the warrant request is based on separate information (not obtained through the illegal search).* The result of the Court's

---

* Elron was the only Justice on the panel, and more largely on the Court, whose primary area of expertise as a trial-court judge and as an appellate judge was criminal law.

approach, per Elron, was that an individual's rights and privacy could be easily violated *ex parte* (without their participation or knowledge), without the opportunity to object, without the ability to appeal – and all even if the individual is only loosely related to suspected criminal activity under investigation, and even if there is no risk of evidence tampering. Further still, the Court's approach entailed that police would face no substantial consequences for unlawful searches leveraged to enable subsequent search warrants.

Elron's dissent turns acerbic when addressing a concurring opinion by Justice Amit. Per Elron, Amit's approach conveys a message that "the end justifies the means" – that allowing greater leeway for law enforcement justifies severe harm to due-process rights. Elron asks, sarcastically, why bother with rules and laws limiting the authority of investigators? Why bother considering suspected violations of suspects' rights? Why bother restraining police and investigators in their pursuit of fighting crime? Highlighting the irony of the *Urich* case, Elron notes that the Court seems to reward police misconduct: though all agreed that the initial phone search was illegal, the case has resulted in the Court expanding the authority of law enforcement officials while restricting the rights of suspects and individuals. In a sharp rebuke, Elron reminds Amit (and the majority) that the Court's job is to "prevent abuse" of law enforcement's considerable power against individuals, and to "offset" such power imbalance by ensuring that police investigators strictly "adhere to the law."

(Incidentally, a questionable indictment against Urich and co. relating to the phone search was filed only five years later, in 2025. The original prosecutor handling the matter reportedly refused to charge them as he believed there was no viable legal case; when this became clear he was replaced, and the new prosecutor filed an indictment almost immediately. The same cooperative prosecutor was soon named District Attorney for Tel Aviv.)

The Court's decision in *Urich* – by a large majority of an expanded panel in a closely-followed high-profile case – effectively gave official sanction to evidence-laundering, allowing police investigators to blatantly break the law and then utilize the results to obtain a lawful, invasive search warrant. The case usefully reflects the Supreme Court's complicity with, and contribution to, the lack of due-process protections in Israeli criminal law.

The Supreme Court's overall approach is somewhat reflected in a parting comment from Justice Amit in a 2021 criminal appeal.[15] Amit decries the "process" by which criminal law has ostensibly shifted its focus from "evidence" to "rights." Per Amit, there was a time that the criminal trial centered around piecing together and reviewing individual chunks of evidence as they gradually translate into a comprehensive picture, all in service of "the ultimate purpose of the law* – the pursuit of truth." Alas, Amit describes (in a regretful tone) how in recent decades this has been neglected in favor of claims regarding "all kinds of

---

* This may also be translated as "the trial" or "the criminal law."

flaws" in the investigation and prosecution, claims of "illegality" during searches and seizures, and so on, all which "divert" the criminal process from its purpose of "pursuing truth." These unfortunate developments put law enforcement agencies on a defensive footing in which they must show the legality of their actions (... the horror!). "The time has come," tells us Amit, for the criminal process to "cast off the burdens" added in recent years and to once again return the quest for factual truth "to center stage." Small wonder, then, that Rafi Rotem would rather place his faith in administrative reasonableness review than in the criminal process.

In all fairness, Amit's frustration is understandable and likely well-merited in the case before him, as well as in others. An inflation of procedural-legal challenges to police and prosecution conduct really can hamper valid law enforcement efforts to the point of severely handicapping criminal justice. Yet this is a critique more commonly voiced by politicians or the police, not by a Supreme Court Justice. I venture to say that very few apex-court judges would be caught making such a statement in most jurisdictions. The prevailing criminal justice climate in most legal systems – geared heavily towards protections against abuse of police powers – would not allow it. The fact that statements in this vein are made by a senior Israeli Justice speaks volumes about our legal culture and attitudes towards criminal law.

The Rule of Severity

The Principle of Legality is regarded among the most "widely held value-judgment[s] in the entire history of human thought."[16] It is known in Latin as *nulla poena sine lege* – "no punishment without law" and is similarly found throughout ancient Talmudic and Jewish texts in the maxim of "no punishment without warning." It expresses a core tenet of modern criminal justice, that one cannot be liable for a criminal act if she has not been sufficiently warned of its criminality in advance. Israeli law enshrines the principle in Section 1 of the 1977 Penal Code: "There is no offense and there is no penalty unless defined by law or under law." In one representative case from 1973, Justice Haim Cohn wrote that criminal offenses not established by law "in clear and express language" cannot be created by "interpretation or analogy or logic."[17]

The interpretive "rule of lenity" or of "strict construction" is directly derived from the principle of legality and requires that ambiguous statutory language be interpreted in the manner most favorable to the defendant. In other words, if a criminal law statute may be reasonably understood in a number of ways, a court must apply the understanding which would yield the best outcome for a criminal defendant. This is because in such a case the defendant has a plausible argument that they understood the statutory text differently from the version offered by prosecutors, and that they could not have known in advance that their conduct was of a criminal nature. As such, the defendant has not been adequately "warned" and can't be convicted for conduct they reasonably maintain they did not know was criminal.

For much of Israel's judicial history the interpretive "rule of lenity" was accepted as the standard for statutory interpretation in criminal law – even if not always faithfully followed, it was never explicitly repudiated or renounced.[18] Yet this approach was undermined and eventually abandoned by the Supreme Court. Let us return to 1980, and to the quote by Justice Aharon Barak presented above at the end of Chapter 3:

> "The words of the statute are not fortresses to be conquered using dictionaries, but rather a wrapper for a living idea, one that changes according to the circumstances of time and place, in order to fulfill the fundamental purpose of the law."[19]

This poetic passage fits in easily with the approach of Objective Purposive Interpretation which has been discussed extensively, and quickly became one of Barak's most quoted. What might come as some surprise is that it was offered in the context of criminal law.

The 1979 *Mizrachi* criminal appeal* regarded a prisoner that had failed to return to prison from approved temporary leave. A few days later he was arrested and returned to prison to complete his sentence. He was subsequently charged for the offense of "escaping" legal custody. The question under appeal was whether his (deliberate) failure to report back to prison (following lawfully approved leave) constituted an "escape." "Some might argue," muses Barak, that the statute ought to be interpreted strictly while ascribing the word "escape" only its literal, "physical" meaning – that is, an active breakout or getaway, a physical egress from custody. Barak continues that he "cannot accept" such a line of argument – a criminal statute, "as any other statute," must be interpreted in order to "fulfill the law's purpose." Accordingly, Barak reasoned the "escape" here included the prisoner's failure to return from approved leave, and the prisoner was therefore liable and guilty of the charge.[20]

Here began the Court's novel and illustrious application of OPI to criminal law. In subsequent rulings Barak and his successors enthusiastically embraced the idea of purposive interpretation of statutory criminal offenses. The Court's core argument was (and remains) that any criminal offense involves a "protected value," and that the crime might include an array of acts which harm said value, even if the act is not explicitly included in the statutory text. Naturally, the definition of a crime's "protected value," of which act constitutes "harm," and what degree of harm amounts to criminality are all questions to be resolved by the judge on an ad hoc basis for each case. This approach radically expands the potential meaning and application of any criminal statute.

The notion of "purposive" interpretation in criminal law is extraordinary even in the unusual environment of Israeli jurisprudence, as one would be hard put to find an idea more diametrically opposed to the rule of lenity. Any criminal statute

---

* Not to be confused with the 1995 *Bank Hamizrachi* case in constitutional law.

can have a plethora of meanings unknown or unimagined by the individual citizen, who might retroactively find themselves in hot water for behavior clearly permitted by plain statutory language. All that's required is for a judge to decide whether the "protected purpose" of some criminal statute had been sufficiently "harmed" and *voilà!* – a new crime (and criminal) is born.

Criminal law scholar Prof. Boaz Sangero reviews this innovative judicial approach extensively and discusses the many ways in which it distorts criminal law, violates core precepts such as the principle of legality, and frustrates the clear intent and explicit instructions of the legislator.[21] Aside examples of expansive interpretation used to criminalize conduct not included by statutory plain meaning, Sangero also notes the way other definitions within criminal law become malleable concepts in the hands of the Israeli judge. In one leading precedent discarding a basic legal distinction, Barak interprets the requirement for criminal "intent" to include actions without "will" or "desire," but which only "foresee" the result while aware that the result will occur "with a high degree of certainty." Barak argues this to be encapsulated within the "literal" (or "plain") meaning of "intent," strongly diverging from the common meaning most people would typically ascribe to "intent." In another example Justice Dalia Dorner seems to endorse, as a matter of policy, an expansive interpretation of a criminal statute precisely so that it covers as many instances and behaviors as possible and rejects a "restrictive" (literal) interpretation precisely because it seems to limit the applicable cases falling under the criminal statute. In other words, Dorner adopts an expansive interpretation *because* it's expansive.

In yet another striking example, Sangero tracks the way in which the Court explicitly and deliberately ignores a major legislative change which distinguished between a criminal "accomplice" and an "accessory" to a crime. Israeli precedent had historically treated both interchangeably, until a new statute was enacted in 1994 making some clear distinctions between the two, especially with regard to the maximal sentence each category carried. Notably, the sentence of an "accessory" was limited to half of the maximal punishment for the primary crime, meaning that being an "accessory" was now statutorily defined as a less-severe offense.

Sangero describes how the Court seemed displeased with the new distinction (and especially with this limitation on judicial discretion), and began to broadly interpret "accomplice" such that it included conduct technically belonging to the "accessory" category (thus avoiding the new statutory limit and maintaining wide discretion regarding sentencing). Justice Mishael Cheshin offers the remarkable suggestion that a judge determine which offense type to apply (accessory vs. accomplice) according to the punishment they deem appropriate – that is, first choose the (intuitively) fitting punishment, and then retroactively categorize the action as falling under "accomplice" or "accessory" so that it corresponds to the (judicially) desired sanction. "Why bother with criminal law," asks Sangero, if we have "judges that know to fit the appropriate sentence for each case." In a later ruling, Justice Cheshin seems to reject the new statutory distinction in clearer terms, stating that "not all that exists in the laboratory can exist in the open air," and that some substances "dissipate" when meeting reality outside the lab – seemingly suggesting that the new law he dislikes must likewise "dissipate" when applied by judges in the real world.

Even more instructive is the legislative attempt to enshrine the rule of lenity in statutory law. A 1992 bill involving some major amendments to the Penal Code passed its first reading and included a "lenity" clause which set out the rule in clear terms: if a criminal statute is given to a number of plausible interpretations, the court is to apply the most "lenient" for the defendant. The legislative history indicates not only a desire to finally enact the "fundamental" rule in clear statutory language, but actually to reject and repudiate the Court's purposive and expansive approach to criminal law. In one committee discussion the Minister of Justice clearly described the amendment as a response to "recent rulings" which interpreted statutes according to "legislative purpose."

Somehow, further down the legislative process, the bill was amended such that it now allowed for a number of interpretations *according to the law's purpose* – with the new purposive language ultimately included in the final enactment in 1994. What happened? Sangero's investigation recounts how Justice Barak was heavily involved with the new law's drafting and its shifting language, including direct and personal contact with the relevant Knesset committee chairman. Barak attested to this himself in a speech some years later, when he relays a "personal memory" in which "at a certain stage" he was "a partner" in shaping the new law.

De jure the law still established a statutory rule of lenity, even with the "purposive" addition. Yet the notion of purposive interpretation and a rule of lenity cannot be reconciled – one of them has got to give. This is because such "purposive" interpretation can (and does) exclude reasonable interpretations which benefit the defendant – the text might bear some meaning that reduces that defendant's culpability under the rule of lenity, but that meaning might not be applied by a court if it does not conform to the law's ostensible "purpose." *De facto* the judicial focus shifted to the "purpose" clause, which Barak and others clearly took to mean the complete subordination of criminal law to Objective Purposive Interpretation.

Just one illustrative example is that of the "functional uncle" which made headlines in 2020. A man had committed an abhorrent crime – the sexual assault of a minor. The perpetrator had previously been the victim's relative, an uncle by marriage; but prior to the sexual assault he had divorced the victim's aunt. Statutory law mandated that sexual assault by a victim's relative was an exacerbating condition which required a harsher sentence; yet the same law was explicitly clear as to the definition of such "relatives," including an exhaustively detailed list. An ex-uncle who had no blood-relation to the victim ceased to be a "relative" upon divorce. Hence the factual circumstances for applying the harsher sentence did not exist.

In nearly any jurisdiction this would have settled the matter. But in the wonderland of purposive criminal interpretation this was just the point of departure. The prosecution did not dispute that the defendant was not an uncle under black-letter law, but nonetheless demanded the harsher sentence by arguing that the defendant was a "functional uncle," and that regarding the defendant as an uncle would better serve the "protected value" underpinning the statutory sentencing condition. The prosecution was not alone – the District Court agreed, and convicted the ex-uncle of sexual assault as a relative. The position adopted by both prosecutor and judge was essentially that despite its unambiguous language, the statutory definition of "relative" should be read as if it included also "functionally similar" quasi-family members; in other words, that they were at liberty to apply the criminal law not as it was, but as they thought it ought to be.

The argument has its intuitive appeal. Of course the perpetrator here was far closer to being a "relative" than just a stranger or a casual family acquaintance; of course the law aims to prevent (or punish) people taking advantage of a victim's familial trust, and this rationale is not limited exclusively to technical family members. But the solution for such a flaw might be a statutory amendment to widen the definition of relatives; and, perhaps, there might be good arguments to refrain from doing so. With all sympathy for the victim, with all revulsion towards the perpetrator, and with much frustration at the (relatively) more lenient sentence, nothing here grants a prosecutor or judge license to rewrite the law anew to attain a desirable outcome. That is the nature of criminal law, of the principle of legality and of strict (or lenient) construction – supported by strong justifications of their own.

A zealous prosecutor is one thing; an experienced District Court judge joining in is quite another. An appeal to the Supreme Court would most likely have failed, considering prevailing attitudes on the bench. Such is the overall spirit and state of Israeli criminal law – just ends by lawless means, a "functional uncle."

As it turned out, the appeal landed in front of Justice Alex Stein, appointed as a conservative (or restrained) candidate. Stein reversed the trial court holding with regard to the uncle's "functional" family relation to the victim (the main conviction of sexual assault against a minor was not at issue).[22] His ruling is a model of textual interpretation and of strict construction in criminal law, and he expresses deep skepticism towards the *Mizrachi* precedent and more generally towards purposive interpretation in criminal law. The two other Justices on the panel agreed with the result and joined Stein's opinion; yet as if determined to prove that Stein's approach was anomalous to the Court, each concurring Justice added a brief opinion reiterating their unreserved endorsement of purposive interpretation in criminal law. Justice Vogelman stands firmly behind *Mizrachi*; Justice Yael Willner offers a useful summary of the Court's position, writing that "the principle of legality, with all its importance, does not stand alone," and that various "subjective and objective purposes" could at times lead to interpretation at odds with the "strict textual meaning" of the law.* At odds indeed.

Pro-secution

The Israeli judiciary is broadly disposed towards criminalization and is widely considered to be overly "prosecutorial," or pro-prosecution. Criminal conviction rates are unusually high by international standards: over 90% of criminal cases end with a final conviction (2020-21 data).[23] The bench is numerically skewed toward ex-prosecutors and other governmental lawyers – nearly half of all Israeli judges were previously government employees, with 20% of judges hailing specifically from the ranks of state prosecution and litigation (a proportion many times higher than their general share in the legal profession).[24] In all fairness, judges coming from prior public service makes sense – yet the high relative proportion in Israel lends credence to claims of a bench unduly sympathetic towards criminal prosecutors.

Such statistics provide a snapshot of the system's prosecutorial bent, reflecting the institutional features discussed above and encouraging such practices as criminal OPI and a restricted conception of defendants' rights. But the truly defining feature of Israel's criminal jurisprudence is the blatant pro-prosecution approach championed by the Supreme Court which trickles down throughout the judicial hierarchy. Perhaps the most glaring example is the routine application of reasonableness to yet a new frontier – review of prosecutorial discretion.

One of Israel's most severe financial crises occurred in 1983 with the total collapse of share values for most major Israeli banks. The collapse was the result of a deliberate and sustained stock manipulation scheme perpetrated by top bank executives in which stock value was artificially inflated in a "loop" of sorts, whereby banks indirectly and discreetly bought their own stock to buoy and increase share prices (and used proceeds to provide loans to third parties to continue buying stock). At the crisis peak and as the bubble of bank shares was bursting, regulators froze the Tel Aviv Stock Exchange for eighteen straight days; radical government intervention was ultimately required, including a massive bailout and partial nationalization of the banks. Thousands of investors had lost their savings or had sold stock at a considerable loss. The Israeli currency had lost

---

* Adjacent to the general issue of statutory interpretation, Dr. Shaul Cohen argues that Israel is rare (and perhaps unique) in its definition of the criminal act itself – the *actus reus*. Per Cohen (himself a seasoned criminal prosecutor), Israeli statutory law formally adopted the "Austinian" approach which separates the *actus reus* into individual components (action, circumstance and outcome), thus enabling much wider application of any criminal offense and a lower threshold for criminalization of conduct. Most other jurisdictions reject this approach (in favor of defining the *actus reus* as jointly consisting of all its elements) or leave it open to judicial discretion. *See* Shaul Cohen, "What is the Criminal Act?," 28 Law and Business Journal 391 (2023) (Hebrew).

some 23% of its value; after the dust settled, the overall damage to the Israeli economy was estimated at some ten billion U.S. dollars.

The most senior bank managers widely considered as primarily responsible* for the crisis were sacked, and were almost certainly guilty of committing severe securities crimes. Yet following a laborious public inquiry and police investigation the Legal Counsel to the Government at the time, Yosef Harish, decided in 1989 not to indict the top bank managers and accountants. Five years had passed since the crisis, including a much broader national economic meltdown and monetary policy realignment, and Harish felt it was "not in the public interest" to revive and relive the stock manipulation saga, from which he felt the public had moved on.

This decision was challenged in the Supreme Court case known as *Ganor*. The general approach in most common-law jurisdictions is that prosecutorial decisions (and those regarding indictments chief among them) enjoy an enhanced level of judicial deference, beyond ordinary deference or restraint towards other forms of administrative action. Such deference is usually justified by concerns of premature judicial over-involvement in the criminal process (into which judges enter later as impartial adjudicators), from perspectives of both due process rights and separation of powers principles; or by the system-wide considerations and expertise bearing on such prosecutorial decisions.[25] Israeli jurisprudence had historically tracked this approach, with the Court willing to intervene with prosecutorial decisions only in cases of clear bad faith or lack of authority (*ultra vires*).

In its precedential 1990 *Ganor* decision penned by Justice Barak, the Court reversed the LCG's decision and essentially instructed him to indict the bank managers.[26] The Court found nothing unique or special about prosecutorial indictment decisions meriting an exception from its approach to reasonableness and government action – whether to indict or not to indict was just one more executive-administrative decision subject to the totalizing reasonableness standard.† As such, any such decision falling outside "the realm of reasonableness" due to "improper" or the "incorrect" balancing of factors became "illegal" and void. To be clear, Barak rejected any claims that the LCG had acted in bad faith, considered irrelevant factors, ignored immaterial factors, and so on; the only basis for intervention in the indictment decision was its "unreasonable" balancing of considerations.

Since *Ganor* the Court has regularly heard challenges against indictment decisions – and in particular, against decisions *not* to indict. In *Ganor* there was

* To be sure, the reality is somewhat more complicated, and others sharing responsibility were government regulatory bodies and the wider dismal economic environment of poor policy and spiraling inflation.

† The *Ganor* case came hot on the heels of a more limited, but highly similar, ruling which compelled the chief military prosecutor to indict a military officer.

little question that the people involved had engaged in criminal activity and that overwhelming evidence existed against them, but the Court's prosecutorial approach is by no means limited to such clear-cut cases.

Among the most recent illustrative examples is that of Naor Yitzhaki. A group of police officers were conducting an arrest in the Arab-Israeli town of Kafr Kana in 2014. Ethno-religious tensions were running high, with the recent conclusion of Operation Protective Edge in Gaza and a spike in terror attacks against Israeli Jews. A man named Hir Hamdan ran towards the police officers waving a 12-inch knife and yelling "Allahu Akbar" and then attempted to attack the group. The police fired two shots in the air after verbal warnings, but to no avail. As Hamdan came closer to the exposed officers, one of them – Naor Yitzhaki – fired a single bullet at Hamdan, injuring him and neutralizing the threat to the policemen. The whole event lasted a number of seconds and much of it was captured on a security camera. Hamdan later died of his injuries.

The shooting and death triggered an automatic investigation according to standard protocol, by both police and the external Police Investigations *Mahash* unit. Yitzhaki was cleared of any wrongdoing on grounds of "lack of guilt," as he had clearly acted in self-defense during the course of performing his law enforcement duties. The decision to clear Yitzhaki was appealed by Hamdan's relatives until it reached the LCG, who also ultimately chose to leave the original decision intact. The case finally reached the Supreme Court (via direct HCJ petition).

In an extraordinary 2019 majority ruling, the Court ordered that charges be brought against Yitzhaki, as the decision not to indict him was an "extreme deviation from the range of reasonableness" due to various evidentiary questions and that indicting the cop was in "the public interest."[27] The minority opinion by Justice Solberg pointed out the embarrassing mistake made by the majority Justices: statutory law allows for "public interest" considerations only after a prosecutor determines that the evidence merits an indictment. The first stage is the evidence-based judgment of culpability; whether charges are justified by "public interest" is then only considered at the second stage. But in Yitzhaki's case, the first condition had not been met – no one seriously thought he had committed a crime. And of course, the Supreme Court holds no evidentiary hearings and is incapable of evaluating evidence first-hand (Solberg points this out and admonishes the other Justices for their attempt at parsing and evaluating the case evidence). The Court's ruling was unprecedented – while it had intervened many times before in prosecutorial decisions, those cases had been initially closed on the basis of insufficient evidence or a lack of public interest. The Court had never before intervened when the prosecution itself (and in this case, the entire hierarchy all the way up to the LCG) determined that there was simply no criminal culpability, a lack of guilt.* And all this hullaballoo surrounding

---

* In Israel the grounds for closing a criminal case is formally recorded and categorized under "lack of guilt," "insufficient evidence" or "lack of public interest."

an active-duty police shooting against an attacker armed with a 12-inch knife yelling "Allahu Akbar."

The whole episode soon turned farcical. The Court had to hold a rare rehearing because though it ordered that charges be brought, Yitzhaki himself had never been questioned as a suspect following an official warning (such that his statements so far were inadmissible). In the rehearing the Court reversed course and ordered that Yitzhaki first be questioned as a suspect, and then an indictment might be reconsidered.[28] Following Yitzhaki's questioning, the prosecution and the new LCG once again determined that no crime had been committed and that an indictment was not warranted.

Once again, the decision was challenged in the Supreme Court. In a 2023 ruling – almost nine years after the original incident – the Court approved the LCG's decision to clear Yitzhaki and the matter was finally put to rest.[29] Justice Stein states the obvious – that under the given circumstances any decision by the LCG would have been "reasonable," and that a decision not to indict could hardly fall under the scope of "extremely unreasonable" or "outrageous" actions. Stein notably tries to pull the Court a step back towards a traditional conception of reasonableness as outrageousness, but that ship has of course long since sailed. And not even Stein (let alone the rest of the bench) suggests that judicial review of indictment decisions be limited to technical or severe grounds such as corruption or bad faith. The *Yitzhaki* debacle demonstrates both how reasonableness is employed in the most casual manner, for the most trivial issues and as executive micro-management at the most minute resolutions; and how the Court pushes law enforcement agencies towards a more aggressively prosecutorial stance.

From *Ganor* to *Yitzhaki*, the Court has become a critical influence pushing prosecutors towards indictment, causing them to resolve doubt in favor of a trial as opposed to dropping the case – a textbook definition of an overly zealous prosecutorial approach. This has a system-wide effect by which prosecutors may often feel that the risks of dropping charges outweigh the risks of indictment (and acquittal), even though they might not believe an indictment is actually merited. Needless to say, the Supreme Court's intervention also likely prejudices trial court judges and pollutes their impartiality by indicating its assumption of a defendant's prima facie culpability. And to be clear, pressure on law enforcement to adopt a prosecutorial posture is fully legitimate – when coming directly from the public or from accountable government responsible for setting policy and responsive to the electorate. But a court breathing down prosecutors' necks and compelling them to file charges more freely is another thing entirely.

This type of judicial pro-prosecution approach is far from benign. Every prosecutor deciding to drop charges or to close a case will need to add to their calculus the prospect of eventual hassle and embarrassment due to reversal by the Supreme Court. Why risk the headache? Better to just keep the ball rolling and pass the buck. And such questions are not limited to pure indictment decisions. If a prosecutor decides to indict a defendant for one offense and not the other, will the Court intervene? What about a decision not to appeal an acquittal – could the Court compel prosecutors to appeal a case they lost in trial court? It seems that at least doctrinally, all such decisions are within the Court's purview. An Israeli commentator drew a link between the first *Yitzhaki* ruling and the allegations (at the time) against Prime Minister Netanyahu – the LCG had not yet filed an indictment, and there was much speculation regarding which charges and offenses would eventually feature there.[30] Perhaps the Court was signaling to the LCG that they would not hesitate to intervene if the Justices thought a certain count or offense was "unreasonably" left out of any indictment.

The astute reader might notice something strange – what about *Rotem*? This chapter opens with the *Rotem* ruling in which the Court held that prosecutorial decisions within the criminal process are not subject to administrative "reasonableness" review. How can this align with the Court's consistent jurisprudence since *Ganor*? The answer is simple and somewhat bizarre: the Court is perfectly comfortable interfering with decisions *not* to indict and is willing to order that charges are filed (per *Ganor* onwards), all on "reasonableness" grounds; at the same time, the Court balks at intervening in positive decisions to file an indictment (on "reasonableness" grounds) such as that in the *Rotem* case – this is verboten and decried as excessive meddling in the criminal process. To the best of my knowledge, the Court has only ever intervened in decisions of non-indictment and has never voided an indictment based on reasonableness; it has always intervened in order to create or sustain, never to terminate or impede, criminal prosecutions. The reader may judge for themselves whether this conscious and deliberate dual approach is consistent or persuasive. At the very least, it is one which undoubtedly encourages prosecutors to lean towards indictment.

To be sure, there is some difference between indictment and non-indictment, in the sense that the former continues the criminal process which is subject to constant judicial oversight (and an innocent defendant may be acquitted) whereas the latter ends the criminal process (and a potentially guilty suspect walks free). This is indeed the excuse typically offered by the Court and its defenders, that an unmerited indictment can still be stopped and remedied further down the line. But this is an easily refuted fallacy. First, and most importantly, anyone within the world of criminal law knows that cases build momentum – the further they progress, the harder it gets to stop them. Each consecutive stage adds further weight to the allegations against a defendant; on an institutional level, the various parties involved become gradually more invested in the case with more incentive to gain a conviction. We can again recall Bill Barr's depiction of the criminal process as a "juggernaut" which is "very difficult to slow down or knock off course" once "it starts rolling." Second, the harm of filing charges – reputational, financial, familial, social, personal, professional, etc. – is immediate and in many ways irreparable. Even if a defendant is acquitted the decision to indict cannot be simply "undone" as if it never occurred. Third, the claim of "finality" is also unconvincing – pre-indictment cases are closed "without prejudice," and can be reopened (within statutory constraints) if some justification arises.

Perhaps the most striking part of the Court's eagerness to compel indictments is the de facto violation of a fundamental tenet in criminal justice within the common-law tradition – that the agreement of all three branches of government is required to convict an individual of committing a crime. Parliament establishes and defines the forbidden act; the executive (a prosecutor) charges an individual with committing the offense; and the judiciary makes a final impartial determination of whether the defendant is guilty. Each of these elements is separately required for the state to wield its formidable power of criminal punishment against its subjects. This basic notion is utterly undermined by the Supreme Court's approach. Through purposive interpretation of criminal statutes, the Court redrafts the law as it sees fit and replaces the legislature; and through compelled prosecution the Court effectively charges a specific defendant (or generally encourages prosecutors to indict), replacing the executive.* Worse than "judge, jury and executioner," we are left with a judicial organ which can effectively "legislate, litigate, and incarcerate."

A final issue here relates to the broader effects of such extensive and invasive judicial intervention. This book rarely addresses the indirect and systemic damage inflicted by judicial supremacy, but the current context presents the opportunity to convey a critical point. The Court arguably had it right in *Ganor*, in the sense that the LCG's decision to let the bank managers off the hook was grossly unreasonable – perhaps even outrageous. But it is precisely the Court's lack of discipline or restraint which perpetuates such flaws. The problem extended well beyond the specific decision in *Ganor*, to questions of the LCG's own accountability and his responsiveness to public input; it also raised broader questions of public and political supervision of law enforcement and criminal prosecution. But to fix such flaws the public requires genuine (and at times convulsive) reflection prompted by the acutely felt outcomes of these defects – "no pain, no gain." Had the LCG's 1989 decision stood perhaps it (or accumulated similar instances) could have triggered a societal discussion or even a political movement towards adjusting and improving the manner in which the LCG and Prosecution make their decisions, their sensitivity to public input, their degree of political supervision, and so on. The Court's swooping in – *deus ex machina* – delays and ultimately prevents meaningful public debate about the underlying flaws plaguing its governing institutions; the problem is salved, though never solved, and the public moves on to more pressing issues. In the longer term the public begins to lose its self-perception as involved and invested agents for societal or governmental change, so long as the Court infuses the system's lesions with the soothing morphine of judicial deliverance. This point applies generally to judicial supremacy and requires much further exploration and elaboration; but it is well demonstrated by the Supreme Court's prosecutorial approach in *Ganor* and elsewhere.

---

* I thank prominent Israeli jurist Gil Bringer for this insightful observation.

*

The Court's expansive application of criminal law is not limited only to purposive interpretation or pro-indictment interference with prosecutorial discretion. It has also included judicial review of wholly political decisions within the context of criminal justice, such as extradition authority exercised by the Minister of Justice or even the pardoning authority of the President.

One last example defies categorization but reflects Israel's singular jurisprudence. Nisso Shaham, former Police Commander of the Jerusalem District, was indicted in 2013 for seven events (or "affairs") which occurred during his various roles in the National Police. The Magistrate trial court rejected most of the charges against Shaham – he was convicted for one event and acquitted of six others. Though his conduct was deeply objectionable and likely constituted breaches of ethical and disciplinary rules (and Shaham was indeed swiftly dismissed from the Police), almost none of his many individual actions amounted to an independent crime. The prosecution knew this well, and had already in their original indictment presented a novel, revolutionary argument that they called the "cumulative thesis." According to this theory, a series of individual unrelated actions can be aggregated into a single crime, even if no single instance can stand alone as a crime (with the required facts and intent proven beyond reasonable doubt) in its own right.

The prosecution's argument was met with greater sympathy when they appealed the ruling to the District court. The District court reversed the trial court ruling, accepted and applied the "cumulative thesis" and convicted Shaham of the Breach of Trust offense. Shaham had allegedly engaged in improper sexual conduct with colleagues and subordinates in several separate unrelated events; he had also allegedly tried to assist with various professional requests (such as unit placement or promotions) by "pulling strings" and using his connections within the Police, while providing no disclosure regarding past or present intimate interactions. While these were clearly reprehensible actions unbecoming of a senior police officer (or anyone, for that matter), the court held that no single instance was in itself a criminal offense (neither a sex-related crime nor an independent Breach of Trust offense). Nonetheless, the overall "aggregate effect" of the various actions meant that Shaham could be convicted of an offense, though his conduct did not rise at any single point to the level of criminality. To be clear, this is not an instance of a single crime requiring a number of behavioral elements (such as an overall plan or design in the service of a specific aim), but rather of multiple distinct behaviors bearing no connection to one another, none of which can be considered an individual crime.

The problems with such a "thesis" ought to be abundantly clear without too much elaboration. Criminal law requires an *actus reus* as the factual component without which no crime exists. If a person's conduct does not meet the objective, empirical, physical reality of the *actus reus* then they have committed no crime (with some very limited and well-known exceptions). This is precisely the distinction between distasteful or repugnant yet lawful behavior (which includes a very wide range indeed), and an action that crosses the legal line and crystallizes into a criminal offense. The effect of the "cumulative thesis" is that any person might find themselves guilty of a crime that they never committed. A person's routine and lawful conduct might suddenly be retroactively "aggregated" into a new crime, though there is no single point in which the conduct amounted to criminality, no discernible moment in which a person's behavior crossed the threshold between legal and illegal. A person would also have little way of knowing in advance what legal (even if dubious) conduct might somehow jointly amount in hindsight to a "cumulative" crime.

Shaham's case was further appealed to the Supreme Court, though he was not as lucky as the "functional uncle" (whose case had been decided exactly one year earlier). In a 2021 ruling, the Court upheld the District court conviction and endorsed the "cumulative" thesis.[31] In his minority opinion, Justice Yosef Elron decried the deviation from existing jurisprudence and tried to convince his fellow colleagues on the panel that – even with all revulsion and contempt for Shaham's conduct – the novel "cumulative thesis" was an aberration of criminal justice and contradicted fundamental principles of legality, lenity, foreseeability and others (much along the lines of the short critique above).

But to no avail. Justice Neal Hendel justified the "cumulative" conviction by arguing that certain other offenses (such as abuse of a helpless person) were recognized as consisting of multiple components which do not separately amount to criminal conduct, yet this was far from convincing. Just because some specific offenses (by their nature) involve sustained conduct over time which is aggregated into a single crime does not mean that the same logic may be applied universally or horizontally to any offense the Court deems appropriate. Further, the crime of abuse (and similar offenses) is ultimately viewed as a single instance, a single crime with a single victim, even if based on incremental conduct spread out over time. Yet Shaham's deplorable behavior was a set of disjointed events of improper consensual relationships or inappropriate sexual advances, on separate occasions with different people – in no way comparable or consistent with the notion of incremental conduct all part of a distinct overarching criminal offense.

Hendel gives away the game when he summarizes that the application of the "cumulative thesis" to the Breach of Trust offense is learned "by analogy" with other offenses, "from its purpose" and from the "interpretation of its elements."[32] So much for Justice Cohn's axiom in 1973 (mentioned above) that no criminal offense can be created by "interpretation or analogy or logic." In this way the newly-minted "cumulative thesis" broadly represents the Court's lack of commitment to fundamental principles of criminal justice, and its eagerness to break new legal ground and indulge in far-reaching judicial creativity while pursuing a goal of ever-expanding criminalization.

To be sure, there is no love lost for Nisso Shaham, whose (mostly undisputed) conduct was despicable and who very much had it coming. But much like the *Ganor* intervention in indictments, the Shaham case has now provided the Court and the State Prosecution with a new doctrine in their quivers with which to ensnare those that have committed no crimes. It remains to be seen how the "cumulative" thesis will be used, to what effect and against whom.

Moral Turpitude as Leverage

When convicting a defendant of committing an offense, a judge may find that the act consisted of "moral turpitude" – that it deviated from accepted moral standards. "Moral turpitude," known in Hebrew as *Kalon*, has been referenced repeatedly in previous chapters and plays an integral role in the nexus between criminal law, political accountability, and judicial supremacy. Here we will address *Kalon* only briefly.

The meaning of "moral turpitude" is not defined by statute, and its application depends on the particular details of each individual case. For example, crimes involving deliberate malice or dishonesty might often justify a finding of moral turpitude; while crimes involving negligence or even strict liability usually would not. However, there is no definitive list of which crimes entail *Kalon*, because it hinges on the individual circumstances of each case. It is a principled and value-based determination whether an act – as committed by the defendant – was not only technically criminal, but also morally reprehensible. "Moral turpitude" is therefore generally subject to the rather arbitrary discretion of the judge, and of the prosecutor who might demand such a finding.

Setting aside other implications, a finding of *Kalon* has dramatic statutory ramifications for the ability to run for public office or to hold senior governmental positions. "Moral turpitude" may categorically restrict one's political or governmental prospects for an extended period of time, entirely regardless of the actual crime committed and the punishment received. Prosecutors and judges thus enjoy a certain joint veto power over the fate of political careers. In a bizarre inversion, judges in criminal trials relating to politicians or to public figures openly consider a finding of "moral turpitude" in light of a defendant's current position and future career intentions. Instead of ruling whether a certain act exhibited "moral turpitude" – as an isolated legal determination, based on the plain facts, objectively and in its own right – judges view their authority as deciding whether the act renders the defendant fit for public office. Put differently, judges don't ask whether the criminal *act* amounts to moral turpitude (with whatever legal consequences such a finding might entail); rather, they ask whether the legal *consequence* is desirable, and then accordingly decide whether to apply the label of "moral turpitude."

The objections to such a scheme are obvious and need little elaboration. A certain offense (e.g., larceny) or sentence (e.g., three years' incarceration) might entail statutory consequences regarding an offender's ability to hold public office. But barring such concrete rules, an arbitrary and abstract finding of "moral turpitude" simply substitutes public accountability with judicial discretion. It is the electorate (or their representatives, or accountable officials appointing their subordinates) who ought to judge whether a certain act, with its individual circumstances and idiosyncrasies, disqualifies the offender from holding public office. Instead of asking "has the defendant deviated from our moral standards by committing this crime," the judge asks "do I approve of this person holding public offense in future" – two profoundly different questions. The deeply problematic nature of attributing criminal liability based on whether one is a public official likely does not even occur to most Israeli judges, who do so routinely and brazenly.

In similar fashion, prosecutors and defendants regularly negotiate over whether a plea deal will include a finding of *Kalon* or not. A prosecutor might graciously agree to drop certain charges, or to strike a deal, as long as the accused will concede to a finding of "moral turpitude" barring their political prospects; or, conversely, a political defendant might forgo a trial and agree to a plea deal admitting culpability, forfeiting their chance to defend their conduct, as long as the prosecutor does not request a finding of *Kalon*.

This twisted approach places an inherently political determination in judicial (and prosecutorial) hands. The institution of *Kalon* has long since become just another mechanism by which the legal establishment can intimidate and coerce political and governmental actors.

Breach of Trust

We have so far encountered the "Breach of Trust" offense sporadically without explanation or elaboration, yet reviewing the nature and use of this crime is key to understanding the broader reality of Israeli criminal justice at the nexus of judicial and political power.

Section 284 of the Israeli Penal Code establishes a punishment of up to three years imprisonment for "a public official" who "in the course of his duties" commits "an act of fraud or breach of trust"* which "harms the public."[33] Commonly known as the "Breach of Trust" offense, it is a verbatim translation of an earlier offense enacted prior to the State's founding under the British Mandate and is loosely based on the English common-law crime of "Misconduct in Public Office." This offense covers improper actions or decisions taken in an official capacity, and is separate from outright bribery or other clear-cut corruption charges. Its language is notably vague to begin with – what precisely is a so-called breach of trust? What constitutes "harm" to "the public," and how does one identify or measure such harm? What actions fall within the scope of "the course of his duties"?

In most jurisdictions there is no parallel offense, but rather a variety of more specific rules regarding official misconduct and abuse of public office.

* The Hebrew term *mirma* is more accurately translated as "deceit" as opposed to "fraud," but the latter is the more widely accepted translation and features in the original statute in English.

Conversely, where a similar law exists it is rarely applied, precisely due to its ambiguity and the risk of over-criminalizing ordinary (or improper but lawful) government conduct. Indeed, in a recent report, the United Kingdom Law Commission recommended entirely repealing the common law offense of "Misconduct in Public Office" due to its vague nature, proposing the crime be split into more definite offenses with clearer language.[34] Further still, similar offenses elsewhere are often treated as a secondary or ancillary crime, and not as an independent crime in its own right – if a public official is charged with a more concrete and tangible offense, a "misconduct" charge might be tacked on, reflecting the additional severity of a crime committed by someone in public office.

Not so for Israeli courts, where the Breach of Trust offense is applied often – spasmodically and inconsistently – to encompass a wide range of actions and behaviors. Many of the allegations, investigations and prosecutions mentioned above, including some of those that turned out to be spurious (see Chapter 6), relied heavily on one claim or another of "Breach of Trust," including most of the counts against Benjamin Netanyahu.* When one hears of a criminal investigation against public officials it more likely than not involves "Breach of Trust." It is hard to overstate the rampant overuse of "Breach of Trust" in Israeli governmental life – one criminal law expert has described its usage as approaching a "moral panic,"[35] and it has been the subject of widespread criticism from legal experts across the political spectrum.[36] Israel's leading criminal law scholar, Prof. Miriam Gur-Aryeh, wrote a damning essay in 1999 calling for legislators to "repeal" the Breach of Trust crime entirely, for prosecutors to "refrain" from using it, and for the courts to "substantially restrict" its scope and application.[37] Gur-Aryeh even argued that the offense ought to be struck down as unconstitutional but for a technicality preventing the Supreme Court from doing so.

To be clear, the Penal Code includes a wide array of other offenses which apply exclusively to public officials and that specifically address governmental corruption and malfeasance, including: bribery (in its many forms); arbitrary "abuse of power" harming someone's rights; theft or embezzlement of public assets; exercising authority affecting one's private commercial or business interests; sharing restricted or privileged documents or information; undue pressure to extract a confession; forgery of official documents; and more. These are in addition to ordinary crimes which of course may also apply to the conduct of any official, such as fraud, extortion, conspiracy, and many others. Conduct of any government official is additionally regulated by a large body of ethical and disciplinary rules and mechanisms which may adjudicate misconduct and impose sanctions outside the context of criminal law (such as fines, reduced pay, suspension, dismissal, demotion or delayed promotion, etc.). In other words, the

---

* The Netanyahu case essentially rests on Breach of Trust charges, as the single bribery charge was always considered far-fetched, and the trial court judges have recommended that the prosecution consider withdrawing the bribery count.

vast majority of potential improper actions by public officials are covered by other statutory offenses and rules, and law enforcement agencies have ample tools at their disposal to combat actual corruption without the need for "Breach of Trust."

Despite its ambiguity, the repeat prosecution and conviction of public officials for "Breach of Trust" has done nothing to clarify the crime's meaning or content. On the contrary, it remains to this day inscrutable and nebulous, and has been (approvingly) referred to as a "catch-all" or "framework" offense.

In a 2004 Rehearing decision known as *Sheves* the Supreme Court attempted to outline and clarify the crime's main elements and components;[38] but the Court deliberately chose to retain the crime's vague character and to leave wide judicial discretion in interpreting and applying the statute, so as not to hamper the state's efforts in combating governmental corruption. In *Sheves* (and its treatment of Breach of Trust) we find a distilled example of the Court's pro-prosecutorial approach and of its expansive "purposive" reading of criminal statutory law. The majority opinion was written by Chief Justice Barak.

What behavior, then, becomes criminal under the Breach of Trust offense according to *Sheves*? Barak explains that here the statutory language is inadequate – "in order to extract the legal meaning from the textual meaning, we must turn to the purpose at its base."[39] Barak presents the Breach of Trust purpose (or "protected values") as threefold: 1) Maintaining public faith in government officials; 2) Ensuring the good character (or transliterally, the "purity of virtues") of government officials; and, 3) Upholding the "public interest."[40] Elsewhere, Barak speaks of the offense as "ensuring the proper conduct of public officials." This preliminary formulation may already give us pause – Barak makes no attempt to anchor these "protected values" in the legal text or even in first principles; they are rather simply judicial extensions of the statute grabbed out of thin air. Linking a judicial rule to the words of black-letter law had long since become passé.

We have already questioned the Court's sincerity in its invocation of "public faith" in the previous chapter, and the same objections apply here equally; we have similarly challenged the notion of "good character" being policed by judicial enforcement. We might briefly wonder how "the public interest" can serve as an objective, impartial basis for ascertaining the criminality of an individual's conduct, considering that what constitutes "the public interest" lies at the heart of governmental discretion and of societal disagreement. Yet for present purposes it's important to stress that unlike the Deri Doctrine, which purports to involve *administrative* considerations governing the reasonableness of government discretion, here we are wholly within the realm of criminal law. This being the case, two glaring objections stand out: The first is that these ostensible "protected values" do nothing to clarify or concretize the nature of Breach of Trust – they are just as vague and open to absolute interpretive discretion as is the original statutory language. It is left to the prosecutor or the judge to determine whether an act undermines public faith, good character or the public interest, based solely on their arbitrary and subjective ad hoc evaluation of a given case. The second objection (as indicated above) is that nothing in the statutory language lends support to the asserted "values": one might easily think that "breach of trust or fraud causing harm to the public" is materially distinct from, and far more limited than, *any conceivable act* which might *potentially* have some adverse effect on public faith and other related "values." That is, Barak's claim regarding these values being the ones "protected" by the offense constitutes, in and of itself, a fundamental and radical expansion of the plain meaning of the statutory text. In light of these objections, the Court's interpretation of "Breach of Trust" is revealed to be an unacceptable deviation from basic norms of Western criminal law.

The term "potentially" here is central to Barak's application. The textual phrase "which harms the public" suggests an outcome-defined element – to be illegal, the Breach of Trust action must cause some distinct, tangible harm to the public. No harm, no foul. Yet the Court interprets this in the opposite way, with Barak explaining that the offense is a "behavioral" one and not outcome-based.[41] In this way Barak annuls the plain requirement of "harm" and replaces it with a "potential" for harm – it is enough that a certain act is by its nature and character harmful to the public. Critically, this is how the very existence of a potential conflict of interest (which elsewhere would usually not be criminal if not yielding material personal benefit or if fully disclosed) can amount to a crime under the Breach of Trust offense. While Barak did not pioneer this approach singlehandedly (it tracks with the Court's prior jurisprudential trend over the previous decades), the *Sheves* ruling solidified the broad and indeterminate application of Breach of Trust for a generation to come.

The Court's reshaping of "breach of trust" into a blanket criminal prohibition of any conflict of interest (or of not properly pursuing the public interest) does actually echo another legal framework – that of fiduciary duties within the context of corporate law. Corporate directors and officers typically owe a fiduciary "duty of loyalty" to the company and to shareholders, which might be violated if they do not exclusively pursue the company's best interests (if they are "disloyal" to the company). Yet, critically, breach of this duty is a civil offense with civil (typically, financial) remedies pursued by private plaintiffs directly affected by a defendant's actions. The conceptual similarities between the vague Israeli Breach of Trust crime and the more universal corporate versions only emphasize the former's odiousness.

The relevance of these objections is on full display within the facts of the *Sheves* case. All the Justices agreed that the defendant (the Director General of the Prime Minister's Office) had acted improperly by making governmental decisions which had directly benefited him and his acquaintances – he had acted in a conflict of interest. Yet they also agreed that no tangible harm had been done to the public, in the sense that the actions were fully justifiable in their own right and would likely have been substantially identical if taken by someone else without a personal stake. And the defendant's conflict was mostly diminished by the fact that he had disclosed his personal interest fully to his superiors, including to the Prime Minister. The only dissenting Justice out of nine, Justice Mazza, thought that this conduct could not meet the "severity" required of a genuine "breach of trust" and also that it didn't "harm the public" in any meaningful sense. Mazza also stressed that existing disciplinary mechanisms were the obvious and appropriate route for addressing such infractions. Barak and the Court thought otherwise – the mere *existence* of a potential conflict could be sufficient cause for conviction (with no real harm required), due to the generic and abstract harm caused to "protected values" by conflicted government conduct.

Mazza pulls no punches in his dissent, admonishing the Court for failing to achieve the one thing it had set out to do – define and clarify the contours and elements of the Breach of Trust offense. The crime "remains as vague as it was." He also wryly points out that the Court's opinion seems to prove his point – though all Justices broadly agreed on the meaning and components of the Breach of Trust crime, they reached opposite conclusions regarding its application in a case that should have been relatively clear-cut and where the facts were virtually undisputed. Mazza's dissent additionally reveals a logical flaw in Barak's treatment of the "harm to the public" requirement: Barak essentially argues that conduct typically having a negative effect on "public faith" (such as a potential conflict of interest) is both the "breach of trust" act itself *and* simultaneously fulfills the requirement for "harming the public." But this makes no sense – not every alleged "harm" is inherently corrupt. The statute clearly establishes the two as separate and distinct elements, such that the ostensible "harm" to public faith cannot also serve as the independent, affirmative, proactive "breach of trust," which must include some form of "corruption" or other "severe" attribute. In other words, Barak's circular argument in *Sheves* is that vague potential public harm caused by a conflict of interest also simultaneously meets the definition for a "breach of trust" on its own, despite the statute's clear distinction between the (severe or corrupt) "breach" and the ensuing "harm." Mazza finally stresses that the legislature is free to enact more specific or restrictive laws regarding undesirable conduct by public officials.

The Court shows its true colors when it tries to justify the crime's admittedly "vague boundaries" while barely acknowledging the widespread criticism against it. Barak explains that were the law to be repealed by legislators or restricted by the Court, "our legal system would lose an important tool for ensuring the proper conduct" of government, and would impede "the public's ability to defend itself" from abuses of power by officials.[42] In other words, Barak essentially admits that the wide application of the Breach of Trust offense by the prosecution and courts, despite its vague language and clear violations of the principle of legality, is not rooted in sound principles of criminal law or statutory interpretation but is rather motivated by a desire to rein in government officials and politicians. Barak further justifies the offense's use by stating "our" desire for "a progressive society" founded on "human interaction based on integrity, decency and virtue" – yet in familiar circular fashion, this is simply one more description of the Court's flawed expansive approach, not a defense of it.

In her concurring opinion Justice Dorit Beinisch outdoes Barak by mounting a defense bordering on the ludicrous. In straight-faced form, Beinisch notes that elected politicians are not subject to the same disciplinary rules as are most government employees (hence their conduct must be subjected to the Breach of Trust offense),[43] seemingly oblivious to the most fundamental arguments regarding direct public accountability of elected officials in a democracy. If we must spell out the objection here – elected politicians are usually not bound by the same disciplinary mechanisms as ordinary government employees precisely *because* they are directly accountable to the public. Their moral and ethical conduct is subject to the much more penetrating and severe scrutiny of routine collective public choice; and, conversely, the public's stamp of approval (or toleration) of potentially borderline conduct is precisely the argument *against* its criminalization.

More amusingly still, Beinisch raises the ante by stating that what's at stake is democracy itself, no less: "We must keep in mind that corrupt government is but a step away from the gradual erosion of the character and resilience of the democratic regime." There we have it – per Beinisch, the Israeli democratic order hinges on judicial supervision of the "good character" of government officials by expansive construction and application of the Breach of Trust offense. Needless to say, the alternative notion that a democratic order relies on protections against arbitrary prosecution and on intrinsic limitations of criminal law enforcement (such as the principle of legality, the rule of lenity and due process) is left to wither in neglect.

Over the years and especially since the *Sheves* ruling, politicians and public officials have regularly found themselves entangled with the Breach of Trust offense, often under ambiguous circumstances for conduct which few had previously (or subsequently) considered of a criminal nature. Often overlooked, the most immediate and tangible effect of the offense and its expansive application is not in the crop of convictions or even indictments it yields – rather, the Breach of Trust offense provides the Police and Prosecution with a formidable tool in the form of criminal investigations. Given the crime's vague nature, endorsed and encouraged by the Supreme Court, any public official can become a criminal suspect at the drop of a hat. There is, quite literally, no rational or technical limit to what conduct might constitute a potential violation and serve as grounds for a full-scale investigation, including arrests, depositions, evidence-gathering, searches and seizures, etc. As has been repeatedly demonstrated above, the end result of dropped charges or of acquittal is of little consequence. The Breach of Trust offense thus arms the legal establishment with an apparatus not so much for the prevention of government corruption as it is for the harassment and intimidation of government officeholders.

In a similar vein, an investigation or indictment for Breach of Trust will almost invariably trigger an alleged conflict of interest and its accompanying restrictions discussed in the previous chapter, including limitations on an official's ability to take any action relating to the legal system itself. Indeed, one could theoretically find themselves in a Kafkaesque loop in which they are charged with Breach of Trust for acting in a conflict of interest (as was the case in *Sheves*); they are consequently deemed in a new "conflict" arising from the indictment; they are then alleged to have violated the restrictions of their new "conflict"; and may now be slapped with a fresh Breach of Trust charge due to the unrelated subsequent violation, *ad infinitum*. While this scenario might seem far-fetched, the real implications are not – a public official will hesitate many times before flouting "conflict of interest" restrictions imposed on them, no matter how unfounded the initial Breach of Trust charge.

Beyond the immediate cowing effects of any criminal proceedings, the Breach of Trust offense is also inseparable from other key mechanisms of judicial supremacy. The Deri Doctrine requires resignation (or dismissal) of indicted public officials, yet such indictment is infinitely more easily secured under alleged Breach of Trust. That is, the aberration of *Deri* enabling prosecutorial-judicial impeachment of public officials is many times compounded by the Breach of Trust offense which provides a near-effortless path to indictment. And the sweeping power of the Legal Counsel to the Government, to be discussed in the next chapter, similarly owes much to the vague and malleable nature of the Breach of Trust offense. The combination of these elements puts much of the political and governmental apparatus at the mercy of near-total prosecutorial and judicial discretion. Every politician and civil servant is under the constant threat of having their governmental authority handicapped or of their public career halted indefinitely or even terminated. The full effect of the Deri Doctrine and of the LCG's political leverage crystallizes in light of the Breach of Trust crime, especially within the context of an aggressively prosecutorial criminal justice system.

Criminal Lawyers

What happens when criminal justice institutions acquire staggering political power, attain near-absolute autonomy and lack meaningful civilian oversight? One effect of such combined features is abuse. Another is impunity for wrongdoers. Both are two sides of the same coin and must be addressed in the Israeli context.

The general impression, observed by many, is that all-too-often the law enforcement apparatus abuses its power to pursue illegitimate goals, and that malfeasors rarely face any serious scrutiny (let alone sanctions) for their transgressions. On the one hand, the vast majority of police officers and criminal prosecutors are undoubtedly faithful civil servants carrying out their duties with diligence and discretion. On the other, there are simply far too many instances of abuse and impunity for these to be easily dismissed as isolated examples or unrepresentative "bad apples." In the best case, even the most well-intentioned and stout-hearted prosecutor or investigator might surrender to the temptations of abuse or bias presented by such accumulated power. In the worst case, police power is deliberately and methodically employed in the service of illegitimate ends. The suspicion of abuse is only augmented by the impression that rarely does anyone answer for questionable deeds and decisions. As Jesse Pinkman teaches Walter White in the TV series *Breaking Bad*, there is at times a very thin line between a criminal lawyer, and a *criminal* lawyer.

Here we will review a handful of such instances and some of the mechanisms further enabling such abuse. All are inherently related to the infrastructure of judicial supremacy and the cowing of civilian and political forces by the legal establishment.

In 2016 journalist Raviv Drucker revealed the existence of an extraordinary document compiled by the police, which came to be known as the *Itzhaki Dossier*. In 2018 journalist Kalman Liebskind revealed further details previously unknown to the public.[44] According to various reports, the *Dossier* was created in 2014 at the initiative of Meni Itzhaki, a senior police officer who at the time headed the Investigations and Intelligence Department within the National Police. Without involving or notifying the Police Commissioner or other senior parties, Itzhaki had asked to compile a comprehensive report on all information regarding potential criminal conduct of Knesset Members. Such a document had never been prepared in the National Police history and previous suggestions in that vein had been vetoed by various senior police figures.

The final *Itzhaki Dossier* included intelligence, information and allegations of severe criminal conduct against some forty (!) elected legislators (a third of the entire Knesset body) and against nearly half of all Government Ministers. Critically, the vast majority of these "leads" were not considered open or active investigations, were not followed up in any way, and their targets were not formal suspects – it seems, rather, that they were collected to serve another sinister purpose. All accounts indicate that the object and function of the *Itzhaki Dossier* was to lie dormant until used, selectively and strategically, by Police or other law enforcement parties in order to pressure, deter or harm elected politicians. This could be achieved by opening an actual investigation based on information in the *Dossier*, by leaking information to the press, and in a variety of other ways. This was, in every respect, the ultimate political "dirt" collection project.[45]

When exposed in 2016 the *Dossier* caused an uproar, with politicians across the political spectrum denouncing the document and drawing comparisons with the FBI blacklists under J. Edgar Hoover. All other considerations aside, there was virtually no question that the document's compilation violated a slew of internal police procedures and likely also various statutory regulations. Some suggested that the order to compile the report was itself a criminal act. In an emergency Knesset Committee meeting, the serving Police Commissioner Roni Alsheikh and representatives for the LCG downplayed the *Dossier*'s significance, defended the report and claimed it was compiled as an anti-extortion effort to prevent blackmail attempts against legislators, or as a general intelligence "review." Few found this explanation persuasive or satisfying.* The 2018 damning exposé by Liebskind further confirmed the worst suspicions – it turned out that the *Dossier* was not alone, with a similar report concurrently compiled against elected mayors and municipal leaders. Apparently, Itzhaki had also requested that the police begin preparing a list of non-politician persons of interest, for their future inclusion in a similar report.

The journalists who exposed the *Dossier* were careful not to name any specific politicians who were on the list. Yet two days after the document was revealed, a single name on the list was leaked to the press – that of Interior Minister Gilad Erdan, who held ministerial responsibility over the National Police. There is little doubt as to who had the strongest incentive to leak Erdan's name (and his alone). Faced with the choice of downplaying and ignoring the *Dossier* or of putting up a fight and risking potential criminal investigation and prosecution, Erdan chose the former. Despite the leak and his alleged inclusion in the report nearly a decade ago, to the best of my knowledge, Erdan has since not been publicly accused of any criminal conduct.

In most countries the very creation and existence of something remotely resembling the *Itzhaki Dossier* would likely have led to severe public and political backlash with material consequences, including rolling heads within the police hierarchy, a reinvigorated effort at civilian oversight of high-level police conduct and perhaps even a major restructuring of law enforcement institutions. In Israel, after the dust settled, nothing happened. The outrage faded and died with barely a whimper. The *Dossier* exists to this day, sitting on a shelf somewhere, and there is little reason to assume that it (or its substantive equivalent) is not being regularly updated, augmented and perhaps even employed. Meni Yitzhaki was never investigated by any formal body, and (after resigning in 2017) currently serves as a fellow with the prestigious Institute for National Security Studies. The Police has provided almost no substantive answers to the many questions surrounding the *Dossier*, including as to its creation, subsequent use and current status.

The *Itzhaki Dossier* is a prime example of the way in which law enforcement is incentivized (by factors such as the Deri Doctrine, the malleable Breach of Trust offense, "conflict of interest" restrictions, and the Court's prosecutorial jurisprudence) to collect "dirt" on public officials; of clear-cut and unabashed abuse of police power by some of the most senior figures within the police hierarchy; and of the total impunity enjoyed by both individuals and institutions within the law enforcement establishment.

The method of dusting off a "dirt" file for use against public figures is in no way hypothetical or far-fetched. In 2015 Interior Minister Gilad Erdan announced his intention to appoint a new Police Commissioner – a decorated retired military general, Gal Hirsch. Some in the senior Police leadership vehemently objected to the appointment, both publicly and in private exchanges which were published

* Both journalists explained in detail why such explanations do not withstand scrutiny.

much later. Reportedly, within hours of the announcement (and notably, precisely during the time the *Itzhaki Dossier* was floating around but had not yet been exposed), a request was issued by Meni Itzhaki's office to receive all intelligence information relating to Hirsch. Almost overnight Hirsch became the subject of various rumored allegations – referred to be the media as a "cloud" of suspicion – regarding past business dealings from years earlier. The LCG announced a "probe" into the suspicions, which they said could take weeks or even months. The Interior Minister eventually folded and withdrew his decision to appoint Hirsch.

Today, the affair is almost universally considered to have been a hit job. A series of investigative news reports in 2018 concluded that Hirsch was the victim of "political elimination."[46] A senior police officer within the Intelligence Department, Guy Nir, became a whistleblower and explicitly described the concerted effort to prevent Hirsch's appointment by raising baseless criminal allegations against him (Nir also provided audio recordings which allegedly showed Meni Itzhaki's proactive fishing for incriminating information). Hirsch was initially attached in 2015 to two criminal investigations: one involving a competitive bidding process, the other involving bribery of a foreign official in Europe. The first case was dropped entirely in 2018; in the second case, the bribery suspicions were dropped and the case proceeded on various charges of tax evasion. At the time of this writing, over nine years since his appointment as Police Commissioner was foiled, Hirsch has yet to be convicted of a single crime. As in many other similar cases, no one has ever answered for the obstruction of democratic government or for the staggering personal harm caused to Hirsch and to others like him.

The Sword of Damocles

The Gal Hirsch affair brings our attention to the issue of protracted, drawn-out investigations which seem to linger for extended periods of time with no progress or resolution. Far from an unfortunate bug, this is in fact a deliberate and calculated feature of Israeli law enforcement. But before addressing prolonged ongoing cases and their effects we must consider one additional mechanism utilized by law enforcement – the "probe."

A criminal "probe" or "review" is usually announced by the Police, State Prosecution or LCG within the context of suspicions against public figures. The "probe" is a pre-investigation stage in which law enforcement bodies might gather some initial evidence, verify the veracity of allegations, conduct informal interviews with witnesses, and engage in other quasi-investigative efforts. The ostensible object of the probe is to assist in deciding whether to open a formal or official full-blown investigation. Over the years, some of its defenders have argued that the "probe" serves the best interests of public officers – they allow for informal inquiry into allegations of impropriety without the tarnishing and damaging label of a criminal investigation. This is, as we shall see, utter nonsense. More generally, the probe serves primarily as another potent – and unlawful –

instrument of prosecutorial intimidation.

To begin with, the "probe" has no legal basis whatsoever. Statutory law allows for the opening of a criminal investigation following a complaint filed with the police, or when the police "discovers that a crime has been committed."[47] When police or other bodies conduct a "probe" in lieu of an investigation they do so absent any legal authority. This is no trivial technicality – both a complaint or any such "discovery" of a crime enabling an investigation must have a firm, credible, plausible basis. This reflects the fundamental notion that law enforcement are not at liberty to investigate any person for any conceivable offense for any reason they deem justified. Properly understood, the initiation of a criminal investigation must overcome some basic hurdles, including being justified by some substantial information or evidence; it should not be undertaken on a whim or based on rumors and hearsay. This of course applies all the more forcefully to public figures of all kinds, against whom many might have a vested interest in triggering harmful criminal investigations.

A preliminary probe simply circumvents any such requirement by conducting what is a de facto criminal investigation based on the scantest or flimsiest evidence. Such probes might be typically initiated following obscure media publications based on unnamed sources, sensationalist claims in anonymous letters or minute scraps of unverified information acquired by questionable means. Critically, they rarely meet the statutory legal requirements of someone filing an official complaint or of "discovering" a "crime"; and effectively anyone can provide the impetus for a new probe if the police or prosecution are inclined to listen. Thus the probe constitutes a criminal investigation for all intents and purposes without the inconvenience of meeting basic conditions stipulated by law and required by fundamental norms of criminal justice. It is simply a way to lower the bar enabling invasive law enforcement scrutiny.

The so-called "probe" has a number of immediate consequences. First, it is often viewed by the public as equivalent to a criminal investigation, such that reputational (and often, more tangible) damage is already inflicted. Second, the probe essentially becomes a fishing expedition – a probe can easily serve as an excuse to search for evidence of unrelated offenses (real or imagined) which might then form the basis for a fresh probe or a formal criminal investigation. This is indeed often the case, with many examples of a probe regarding one claim or allegation, leading to criminal investigations into entirely unrelated offenses which likely would never had existed if not for the initial probe. Third, critically, the "probe" is often treated by the legal establishment as sufficient grounds for imposing many of the sanctions and restrictions discussed extensively above – such as barring appointment to senior governmental office, imposing "conflict of interest" rules, and so on. When Gal Hirsch was prevented from becoming Police Commissioner, it was due precisely to such "probes," without even the courtesy or dignity of a real investigation.

Finally, probes have the habit of being held open indefinitely, keeping the subjects of such probes in a constant state of limbo where they are neither suspects in a formal investigation nor are they entirely outside the ambit of law enforcement attention. Among the many other effects and implications, the persistent probe serves as clear leverage against public figures and as a fixed reminder that a probe could easily become an investigation – or worse – at any time.

The prolonged duration of criminal proceedings against Gal Hirsch is in no way exceptional; and the impression of the criminal process being abused with impunity is in no way limited to the National Police. Daniel Friedmann describes how, time and again, the State Prosecution and the Legal Counsel to the Government seem in no rush to conclude open investigations and criminal proceedings. Cases are instead kept open indefinitely, sometimes for years on end, with little progress and no indication of where the case might be headed. These cases at their various stages hang over the heads of public officials and other figures "like Damocles' sword"[48] – an ever-present reminder and warning that their political fate and fortunes (and much else) lie in the hands of a few senior government lawyers. As we've seen, the very existence of an investigation or ongoing trial can have profound consequences regarding an official's ability to act or to serve in various positions, regardless of any final outcome.

One such official that seemed to feel this way was none other than the Legal Counsel to the Government himself – Avichai Mandelblit. A 2020 bombshell news report exposed phone-call recordings between Mandelblit and his then-friend Efi Naveh (Chairman of the Bar Association) in 2015 and 2016. In a shocking exchange Mandelblit describes being "held by the throat" by the "jerk"* who refused to make a decision in his case – referring to the State Attorney, Shai Nitzan. Mandelblit fumes at the "system" of "holding people by the throat" and complains of being "skewered"† by Shai Nitzan and others.[49] What was this all about?

Mandelblit's appointment to the role of LCG in 2016 was mired in controversy due to an ongoing criminal investigation regarding his suspected involvement in a 2010 episode known as the "Harpaz Affair." In a petition to the Supreme Court against Mandelblit's appointment, a panel of five Justices ruled that the evidence against Mandelblit was scant and the investigation was not an impediment to his appointment. But here things got interesting: the State Attorney (Shai Nitzan) and the State Prosecution did not seem in any hurry to formally close the case against Mandelblit – though the investigation was officially announced as closed, it remained technically open within the Prosecution computerized file system. Mandelblit was adamant that the case be formally closed and also that the official reason be listed as "absence of guilt," as opposed to other reasons (such as "insufficient evidence"). Yet for some reason, Shai Nitzan and others were not willing to do so.

---

* The Hebrew term *manyak* is probably better translated as "asshole" in this context.

† The Hebrew root *tafar* literally means "sew" and can also refer to being framed for a crime.

Mandelblit's outrage expressed in the leaked phone-calls revealed an extraordinary and bizarre reality in which the Legal Counsel to the Government clearly felt he was under the thumb of the State Prosecution – technically his subordinates – due to their control over pending criminal cases against him. It would seem his sentiments were justified – the fact that the case remained open had enormous ramifications for Mandelblit, including affecting his potential future ambitions for serving on the Supreme Court. Shai Nitzan never offered a compelling justification for refusing to close the case, solidifying the impression that Mandelblit had every reason to worry.

It later emerged that in addition to this leverage over Mandelblit, the Prosecution possessed more recordings related to the "Harpaz Affair" which could potentially implicate Mandelblit in a much more dangerous way. The evidence was deemed an illegal wiretap and inadmissible, and the courts issued a gag order against publishing the recording's content, but there is no doubt that Mandelblit was acutely aware of the recordings' existence and of the damage it could inflict on his public standing and future prospects (and Mandelblit was also deeply familiar with the habitual leaking of sensitive case material, about which he had publicly complained prior to becoming LCG).

Over the course of his tenure as LCG, Mandelblit made countless decisions related to criminal cases, including the indictments against Benjamin Netanyahu. Shai Nitzan was one of the strongest driving forces in favor of indicting Netanyahu (and of the shaky bribery charges which the trial court has since recommended withdrawing), among many other decisions for which he required Mandelblit's support and approval. We will likely never know how and to what extent the "leverage" against Mandelblit played a part in such decisions, though it is beyond question that such leverage existed and that Mandelblit clearly felt "held by the throat" at a number of junctures and for an extended period of time – perhaps throughout his entire tenure. It would be hard to argue that Mandelblit's predicament did not affect his judgment at all. Though just one example of many, this instance of prolonging the existence of a criminal case seems especially striking due to the sheer audacity of applying such methods to the LCG himself, a figure ostensibly at the apex of the governmental legal corps, and due to the degree of its artificiality (Mandelblit's case remained open on a technicality even though he was cleared of wrongdoing). Indeed, the method of "Damocles' Sword" in the shape of criminal proceedings hanging over one's neck has been, and still is, regularly employed against both junior and senior public officials.

The System Protects Itself

Shai Nitzan himself is a highly relevant figure in our current discussion and is worth our brief attention. Considered among the most aggressive State Attorneys in recent memory, Shai Nitzan became well-known as a Deputy State Attorney during the infamous 2005 Disengagement from Gaza, when he pursued arrest without bond for minors (including teenage girls) caught engaging in civil disobedience. Interestingly, Nitzan was appointed as Deputy State Attorney and later as State Attorney with no actual prior trial experience as a criminal prosecutor.

In *Menayek*, one of the best Israeli TV shows ever made, an honest Internal Affairs investigator tries to expose a group of corrupt policemen and prosecutors. One of the show's main and oft-repeated themes is that "the system always protects itself" – a chilling insight which has often been proven all-too accurate in reality. The *Itzhaki Dossier* may be viewed in this light – as an insurance policy to be activated in the event that the "system" might need "protection" from an unruly public figure. The following few examples during Shai Nitzan's tenure as State Attorney further demonstrate the manner in which Israeli law enforcement institutions "protect" themselves.

<u>Ruth David and the Vanishing Files.</u> The *Menayek* TV series was loosely inspired by the story of Ruth David – a Tel Aviv District Attorney from 2002 to 2010 who stands at the center of an astonishing corruption affair. In an event that shook the State Prosecution and legal establishment to its core, Ruth David was arrested in 2015 for illegally helping criminal defendants by providing them with confidential internal prosecutorial information and by bribing a police investigator (among other means). She was indicted on several counts and her trial is ongoing.

Yet the Ruth David affair remains shrouded in mystery and suspicion. The current charges against her focus on her time as a private attorney after her tenure as District Attorney. Following her arrest and indictment in 2015, many had raised the concern that cases David handled as a prosecutor (and especially as DA) may also have been marred by corruption.* Some viewed her abrupt resignation and departure in 2010 as a quiet cover-up attempt. Despite these obvious concerns, few seemed eager to look too closely. The investigation into David's previous conduct as DA was removed from under the Internal Affairs department (which had been responsible for the post-DA corruption investigation) and assigned to the Prosecution and Police themselves, despite obvious objections that both the latter have a vested interest in the outcome of any such investigation. In 2014 the official watchdog body responsible for investigating misconduct by prosecutors demanded to receive documents relating to complaints against Ruth David, but the serving Tel Aviv DA and State Prosecutor Shai Nitzan both refused to cooperate and stalled for months; conveniently, the watchdog lost jurisdiction to investigate complaints when David was arrested in 2015.[50]

Some of these complaints regarded a matter of particular interest – a "mega" corruption case which landed on Ruth David's desk in 2004, for her decision on

---

* Interestingly, Ruth David played a role in some of the cases discussed above – she was the trial prosecutor in the bogus case against Yaakov Neeman (for which he resigned as Justice Minister in 1996), and she was the DA involved with the controversial case against Haim Ramon (in which Ramon's phones were wiretapped on dubious grounds, and in which exculpatory evidence was then withheld from the defense). I am not suggesting that Ruth David engaged in corruption in these cases.

whether to proceed to indictments. The case involved allegations of severe corruption within the Israeli Tax Authority and suspicions against senior tax officials for colluding with organized crime and smuggling rings – corruption of the genuine, bona fide, old-school sort.* After only three days, though the case included a 160-page internal memorandum and "crates" of additional documents and evidence, Ruth David decided to close and immediately archive the case.[51] (A few months later, a police informant involved in the same investigation was reportedly found dead in a Tel Aviv hotel room, with signs he had been beaten, two of his fingernails missing, and a nylon bag taped over his head. The death was apparently not investigated, as the police ruled it a suicide.) In retrospect, David's decision to shelve the case seemed to be unusual and alarmingly hasty – described by the formal watchdog body in a 2017 report as "perplexing."[52] Perhaps here was an instance meriting further examination?

Yet efforts at looking into Ruth David's decision proved fruitless. It turned out that the physical case files containing most of the information from the original 2004 investigation had been destroyed – literally incinerated – in 2014, just around the time the complaints and suspicions against David had begun to surface. The incineration decision itself left no tracks – any documentation as to who ordered or approved the incineration or detailing the grounds for incineration, was destroyed along with the main case files.[53] To reiterate: not only the case files were destroyed, but also the official log which recorded actions and decisions pertaining to the case files. Shai Nitzan declared that this was just an unfortunate coincidence, but his assurance seems hard to accept – the files were deliberately *not* destroyed in previous years (and indeed had been regularly tracked) precisely due to the ongoing interest in the 2004 case. The watchdog body was also unconvinced. After stating that the reasons for incinerating the case files were "unclear," the watchdog report expressed bewilderment at the lack of any paper trail regarding the incineration decision itself, calling it "bizarre and mystifying."[54] We will almost certainly never know who ordered that the case files be incinerated or when the order was given – under the circumstances, it seems highly unlikely that such a decision would be taken without the direct involvement of senior leadership within the State Prosecution.

The Legal Counsel to the Government – Avichai Mandelblit of "held by the throat" fame – ultimately decided in 2016 to not pursue further charges against Ruth David for conduct during her tenure as DA, at the recommendation of Shai Nitzan and others, due to insufficient evidence and the statute of limitations.[55] Regardless of whether Ruth David really did or did not engage in corruption during her tenure as Tel Aviv District Attorney, the unfolding of her case – and especially the mysterious destruction of casefiles involving one of her most questionable decisions – provides an instructive glimpse into the way "the system" really does protect itself.[56]

---

* Incidentally, a primary whistleblower in these allegations was the same Rafi Rottem starring in the opening of this chapter.

The Not-So-Subtle Hint. Another example surrounds the death of an Arab Bedouin man (and Israeli citizen), Yacoub Al-Qian, in 2017. During an altercation between police forces and members of an illegal Bedouin village, Al-Qian was shot by police officers while driving his car. The police maintained he had accelerated and had tried to ram policemen; other witnesses claimed that Al-Qian was first shot while posing no threat, and that after being shot he lost control of the car, resulting in the car striking police officers. The police prevented emergency medical teams from reaching Al-Qian and he soon died of his injuries. Al-Qian was almost immediately publicly accused of being a terrorist with ties to ISIS. The accusations were echoed by senior police commanders, by the Police Commissioner Roni Al-Sheik, and eventually by Government Ministers and the Prime Minister himself.

Despite the initial reactions, an Internal Affairs (*Mahash*) unit investigation had found "severe operational failings" in police conduct throughout the Al-Qian affair, and ultimately concluded that Al-Qian acted innocently and that there was "no reasonable basis" for the claim that he was attempting a terrorist attack. Many politicians and public figures, including Prime Minister Netanyahu, publicly apologized to the Al-Qian family – both for the death itself, and for incorrectly echoing the initial police allegations of terrorism (neither Roni Al-Sheik nor Shai Nitzan ever issued an apology). State Attorney Shai Nitzan ultimately decided not to pursue criminal charges against the shooting policemen, though the option of disciplinary action was still available to their supervising commanders within the police.

During the investigation and after Al-Qian's exoneration, Police Commissioner Roni Al-Sheik and the head of Internal Affairs, Uri Carmel, started trading public blows which were rapidly escalating in tone and in severity. Al-Sheik was also reportedly disseminating false rumors (through leaks to the press) that Internal Affairs were concealing evidence from the public; according to some reports, Al-Sheik had threatened to disband the Internal Affairs unit while alluding to his past expertise in "dismantling hostile organizations."[57] In addition, it seems that before any police officers involved in the shooting could be investigated they were shown video footage of the incident, and Al-Sheik himself publicly issued a version of events – actions that would usually be considered obstruction of justice in any other setting.

The head of Internal Affairs, Carmel, apparently complained to his boss, State Attorney Shai Nitzan, and demanded that Nitzan get involved and publicly back Internal Affairs. In an extraordinary email from 2017, exposed in 2020 by journalist Amit Segal, Nitzan refused to back Internal Affairs despite admitting that Al-Sheik's behavior was "scandalous" and "intolerable." The reason? Because such an "escalation" between the Police and Prosecution would "only serve those that bear ill-will towards law enforcement." Critically, Nitzan finished this sentence with a well-known Aramaic adage – "a hint is sufficient for the wise."[58]

What was the hint? Nitzan was almost certainly alluding to the advanced investigations and indictments against Benjamin Netanyahu, and the mounting public criticism against law enforcement for the way the prosecution was being handled. The implication in Nitzan's short sentence was that due to the current precarious public standing of the Police and Prosecution, it would be imprudent timing for airing grievances between the institutions. If this meant complicity in Al-Sheik's attempt to cover up the unwarranted police killing of an Israeli citizen, so be it – the system always protects itself. The deputy head of Internal Affairs at the time (who soon after became acting head), Moshe Saada, understood the message precisely this way. In a 2022 interview after leaving the Internal Affairs unit, Saada accused Al-Sheik of actively covering up the Al-Qian killing, and unequivocally maintained that Shai Nitzan and LCG Mandelblit were in turn supporting Al-Sheik so as not to undermine the cases against Netanyahu.[59] Saada also described Shai Nitzan as "a man for whom truth is not a guiding light."

<u>The Hazards of Expert Testimony</u>. Colloquially known simply as "*Abu Kabir*," the National Institute of Forensic Medicine is administrated by the Ministry of Health and is Israel's only forensic research lab conducting autopsies in cases of non-natural death. The Institute regularly provides Israeli law courts with medical opinions and therefore has a working relationship with the Police and Prosecution. One skilled and experienced forensic analyst, Dr. Maya Furman, was hired in 2014 to join the Institute's team of doctors. At some point before starting her new job, Furman had given testimony as a private expert witness (summoned by the defendant) in the Roman Zadorov trial – possibly the most contested and controversial murder trial in Israeli history. Her position was beneficial to the defendant and contradicted the version advanced by the prosecution.

Furman never imagined that her expert opinion in a criminal trial would land her in hot water, but she soon suspected that something was amiss – her start date at Abu Kabir kept getting delayed. Furman eventually discovered, to her shock, that State Attorney Shai Nitzan was personally lobbying the Ministry of Health to rescind Furman's employment offer.[60] In a well-documented debacle of petty vindictiveness, or perhaps of calculated strategy, Shai Nitzan and much of the Prosecution hierarchy aligned against Furman's joining the Institute, explicitly due to her expert testimony in the Zadorov trial. When the head of the Institute clarified he agreed with Furman's expert testimony and that he had no intention of rescinding the offer, he too became a target of the Prosecution's ire. Prosecutors also misled the trial court by implying that the Institute head disagreed with Furman's expert opinion, though the opposite was true.

Such was the pressure exerted by Shai Nitzan against Furman's hiring that she was eventually forced to take legal action in Labor Court. The court sided with Furman, ordered that she commence work immediately with no further delays or conditions, and awarded Furman compensation of tens of thousands of Shekels.[61] (During the Labor Court proceedings, prosecutors also interfered with the content of an affidavit filed by the Institute head, and demanded he remove statements which clarified he agreed with Furman's expert opinion in the Zadorov trial). The watchdog body for prosecutorial misconduct issued a report following the saga, deeply criticizing Shai Nitzan and the Prosecution's improper meddling with Furman's employment at the Institute.[62]

Perhaps needless to say, the implications of Furman's story extend far beyond her own career. The message conveyed by the Prosecution's conduct (and even more so had they succeeded in barring Furman from her post) was that crossing the Prosecution too strongly could entail deeply damaging personal ramifications. Other expert witnesses watching the events unfold may well have learned to think twice about contradicting the Prosecution's version in court. Ironically, a decade later, the defendant Roman Zadorov was acquitted of all charges in a dramatic retrial, which occurred partially as a consequence of Furman's forensic analysis.

Furman still holds a senior position at Abu Kabir, though she is very much haunted by the experience of being personally targeted by the state's most senior law enforcement officials.[63] The entire episode serves as an example – and a reminder – of the impunity enjoyed by senior law enforcement officials for inexcusable conduct, and of the lengths to which a State Attorney might go to get their way. Needless to say, despite Zadorov's acquittal, the Labor Court ruling, the watchdog report, and even a Supreme Court decision backing Furman's expert testimony, not a single person at the State Prosecution has ever faced consequences of any kind – personal or professional, civil or criminal – for their treatment of Dr. Maya Furman.[64]

Petty and Vindictive Abuse

The notion of a system "protecting itself" through the abuse of law enforcement power at times extends to the broader context of judicial supremacy. The criminal justice system may be enlisted not only against those challenging the autonomy and unaccountability of police and prosecution, but also against prominent opponents of expansive judicial power. As discussed above in Chapter 6, Yoav Dotan described how the Deri Doctrine (and its underlying criminal proceedings) was often directed against "critics of the activist disposition of the judicial apparatus," such as Minister of Justice (and Barak critic) Yakov Neeman or Minister of Justice Haim Ramon. Yet the abuse of criminal proceedings was never limited to public officials or to the *Deri* sanction of dismissal.

One especially disturbing example is that of Dror Hoter-Ishay, a prominent attorney who served as chairman of the influential Bar Association during the heyday of Aharon Barak's judicial expansionism. He was also a member of Israeli legal nobility, as his father had founded the Israeli military's legal branch and had served as the IDF's first chief advocate general. Reflecting reservations within the broad practicing legal community, Hoter-Ishay emerged as a consistent and compelling critic of the Supreme Court's jurisprudential innovations championed by Barak. Hoter-Ishay was reelected in 1995 around the same time Barak was assuming the role of Chief Justice – seen by many as an indication of the legal community's exasperation with the Court's rampant activism and interventionism. In 1996 Hoter-Ishay published a scathing interview with a daily newspaper* in which he complained of a "collapsing" legal system and set out his case against the Barak-era Supreme Court. Everything was there: Hoter-Ishay maintained that "not all is justiciable," that the Court should not become a "super-legislator," that judges preoccupy themselves with "high matters" instead of fulfilling their proper role, that "reasonableness" privileges the policy preferences of judges, and much more. He also criticized the recent shameful charges against Yakov Neeman and his removal as Minister of Justice.

Almost immediately following the interview's publication, Hoter-Ishay was subjected to a series of baseless criminal proceedings, all of which eventually failed but which ultimately led to the end of his role as chairman of the Bar and to the collapse of his own legal and public career. The central case involved an absurd claim that Hoter-Ishay owed taxes for income generated by a property owned by his father. After a year of aimless foot-dragging the Prosecution withdrew the tax charge, but still indicted him with a far-fetched offense of providing an acquaintance with illegal tax advice. He was at first convicted in trial court, but then swiftly acquitted of all charges on appeal.

When he spoke out publicly against the bogus prosecution and the initial conviction in the trial court, Hoter-Ishay was again hounded by spurious charges, this time under the esoteric offense of "offending the court."[65] He apologized, the charges were withdrawn, yet he was charged again after repeating his criticism regarding his initial conviction. This time the charges were dismissed by a trial court, but by now Hoter-Ishay had been in and out of court through repeated criminal proceedings. In another case, State Attorney Edna Arbel (who was later appointed to the Supreme Court) inserted Hoter-Ishay's name in a report alleging his involvement in a separate criminal affair, though there seemed to be no basis for the claim; Hoter-Ishay sued Arbel for libel, and it seems she narrowly avoided civil liability only due to her governmental immunity. These were just some of the groundless criminal proceedings against Hoter-Ishay which materialized following his interview and from which he was eventually exonerated without exception. Even the court-sympathizing mainstream media came to his defense, and American Prof. Alan Dershowitz published a letter in Israeli media defending "the right to criticize."

One incident stands out as both shocking and especially instructive due to the direct and unique involvement of the Supreme Court itself. At some point after dozens of appearances for questioning at police stations, Hoter-Ishay got fed up with the PR stunts and informed the police he would be available for questioning at his home or his office, but would not provide the prosecution with the photo-op they desired by once again visiting the police station. This sent the police into a frenzy – they demanded his immediate arrest, yet he refused to comply. The

* Though himself secular, he interviewed for an Ultra-Orthodox daily paper because he found that mainstream media outlets were not willing to publish criticism of Barak and the Court.

police requested an arrest warrant from the Magistrate Court,* and the judge set a hearing for the next morning, releasing Hoter-Ishay until any future decision. Ever vigilant in their pursuit of justice, the police rushed an appeal to the District Court and again demanded an immediate hearing the same day. The appellate judge rejected the request – there was no rush, nothing in the investigation warranted this kind of urgency, and the police could appeal if they disagreed with the Magistrate Court's substantive decision the following morning. (Technically, the scheduling decision – setting a hearing the next morning – was not even an appealable decision to begin with.)

Not to be outdone, the State Prosecution joined the fray and appealed again – this time to the Supreme Court. What unfolded next is nothing short of astonishing: Hoter-Ishay was summoned to a midnight hearing at the Supreme Court before on-duty Justice Yitzhak Zamir. Though the hearing stretched into the early hours of the morning, no one seemed quite certain what decision was being adjudicated – was it the scheduling decision? The appeal's rejection? The lack of an arrest warrant? The entire episode turned farcical as the original Magistrate Court hearing (for the arrest warrant) was mere hours away and drawing closer by the minute. Justice Zamir, himself a former Legal Counsel to the Government with clear sympathy for the prosecution, unironically pondered over the "difficult" legal questions raised by the case. While Zamir painstakingly considered the arguments offered by the prosecution, he saw no need to address the prosecution's bizarre insistence on an urgent hearing arrest for a person who clearly was no flight risk and posed no danger to the public. Zamir also saw no need to justify his own decision to grant a midnight hearing under these outrageous circumstances.

Eventually Zamir deigned to allow the morning Magistrate Court hearing to proceed as planned (though he did not dismiss the Supreme Court appeal, so that he could keep tabs on events as they unfolded). The case, as in all the other proceedings against Hoter-Ishay, eventually ended with a whimper. Nonetheless, one can hardly imagine a clearer example of rabid, overzealous, vindictive prosecutorial behavior. The message to the entire country throughout the ordeal was resoundingly clear: that the life of any individual could be made a living hell with relentless pursuit by hostile law enforcement bodies, even when based on the shoddiest and flimsiest legal pretense; and that even the State's most recognized attorney serving as the leader of the statutory national lawyer's organization may be dragged before the court in the dead of night and brought to heel. More so, the message was that criticizing the Supreme Court now came with significant risks to one's wellbeing, property and liberty. As one prominent commentator wrote at the time: "Raise your voice against the Israeli Supreme Court, and be prepared for a war of more than just ideas."[66] Despite his expertise and connections, his legal

---

* The police at least had the good sense to not arrest him on the spot, due to the obvious absence of any probable cause justifying a warrant-less arrest.

pedigree, his station as elected head of the Bar Association, and justice so clearly on his side, Hoter-Ishay was simply powerless to stop the harassment against him.

But perhaps the most striking element of all was the Court's complicity in Hoter-Ishay's mistreatment. Here was a textbook case of governmental overreach and vindictive prosecutorial zeal – any judge with an ounce of integrity would have denounced the attempt for what it was and would have refused to take any part in it. Yet Justice Zamir, with all the weight and authority of the Supreme Court and against everything the Court claims to stand for, allied himself and his institution with the transparently groundless persecution of an innocent man. Worse still, the grievance was glaringly personal: Zamir was no doubt acutely aware of Hoter-Ishay's public criticism against the Court, such that the decision to humiliate him was a deliberate and conscious one. The chilling significance for anyone paying attention was that the Court's vaunted safeguarding of individual liberties did not extend to those the system deemed troublemakers. Thus the myth of a Supreme Court chiefly defending human rights from government encroachment loses any credibility after Justice Zamir's nonchalant indulgence of the prosecution's gross abuse of the criminal process. While of little significance in the grand scheme, the Hoter-Ishay midnight hearing is the small, bewildered cry stripping away any illusion of the emperor's regal garments, baring the Court's malice for all to see.

While describing the Hoter-Ishay saga in much greater detail in his book *The Purse and The Sword*, Daniel Friedmann makes a critical observation tying it to another baseless prosecution the same year – the one against Minister of Justice Yaakov Neeman. Neeman and Hoter-Ishay weren't just prominent critics of judicial expansionism – they were also both members of the Judicial Selection Committee. Friedmann described their membership as "a new and discomfiting situation" for the Court and for its newly minted Chief Justice, Aharon Barak.[67] How fortuitous, then, that the Court's two primary critics on the Committee were promptly humiliated and ultimately neutralized. Hoter-Ishay's reputation and standing in the legal community could not withstand the onslaught, baseless though it was, and he lost his chairmanship of the Bar in the 1999 elections. Well beforehand and throughout most of the criminal proceedings against him, Hoter-Ishay either recused himself from the Judicial Selection Committee or was under the shadow of a pending Supreme Court petition demanding that he step down. Much like the new Minister of Justice that replaced Neeman, so Hoter-Ishay's successor at the Bar had a much friendlier and sympathetic view of the Supreme Court under Barak. As Friedmann puts it, the proceedings against Neeman and Hoter-Ishay "changed the balance of power on the Judicial Selection Committee."

The Bar Association chairman is a high-profile participant in a high-stakes environment, but casual meritless criminal proceedings can be employed in much more pedestrian settings – at times, literally, against passing pedestrians. Avichai Mandelblit, the serving LCG, was strolling down the street of his home neighborhood one Saturday morning in 2020 when a neighbor remarked "*the*

Laws portion, shame" as Mandelblit walked past her. The neighbor was Shira Shpitz, a lawyer, fellow local resident and mother of five, and the cryptic expression directed at Mandelblit had a clear meaning. Both Mandelblit and Shpitz are practicing Orthodox Jews, and that week's Torah portion to be read in synagogues was "Laws"; the Hebrew word "shame" (*busha*) in such a context is equivalent to "shame on you" or "disgraceful." Shpitz was probably expressing her disapproval of Mandelblit's recent legal decisions and policies (likely related to the indictments against Benjamin Netanyahu).

Within minutes Shpitz was approached on the street by plainclothes police officers. In front of her family – including her five minor children – the police informed Shpitz that she was suspected of committing the crime of "offending a public figure," and that she was being detained and must be immediately taken to the police station for questioning. As driving a vehicle is a grave violation of the laws of the Jewish Sabbath, Shpitz asked that they question her at her home, or alternatively that she report to the police station that evening once the Sabbath had ended. The police would have none of it, and explicitly threatened that she could either join them voluntarily or would be arrested on the spot and forcibly taken to the station. Not wanting to escalate any further, thoroughly frightened, and with her children visibly distressed, Shpitz acquiesced and rode the police car to the station, where she was booked, fingerprinted, photographed and briefly questioned. At the station she was informed that she was now suspected of committing the crime of "invasion of privacy." She was released home shortly thereafter, but now had a criminal record and pending investigation.

To state the obvious, calmly saying the words "the Laws portion, shame" to the Legal Counsel to the Government on a residential sidewalk violates no Israeli laws. There is likely not a single lawyer, police officer, prosecutor, or judge in the entire country that would argue that such conduct remotely approaches criminal conduct of any sort. The phrase is also easily protected speech under the right to freedom of expression. Suggesting Shpitz committed any crime – let alone questioning her or initiating a criminal investigation or detaining her on the Sabbath – was plainly ludicrous from the first moment.

Despite this, Shpitz's case file was transferred by the police to the State Prosecution where it remained ominously open for another *eight months*.

Shpitz was lucky – her case was picked up by journalist Ayala Hasson who exposed the whole ordeal, which caused a public outcry and was met with immediate wall-to-wall condemnation and alarm. Mandelblit denied any personal involvement. Within a few days of the news report the criminal file was closed by the Prosecution for "lack of guilt." One can only speculate how much longer the case would have remained open but for the national news coverage. Both the police conduct and the prosecution's foot-dragging drew criticism from the official watchdog body, and Shpitz eventually won a respectable sum in a civil suit against the police. The expression "Laws portion, shame" became a common slogan referring to flagrant abuse of police powers by senior law enforcement.

Yet this was not quite a happy ending, and much remains unresolved. The version offered by police is that Mandelblit's bodyguard reported Shpitz's conduct, leading to her being detained; yet it seems a stretch (to put it mildly) to claim that the information was passed along without Mandelblit's knowledge and that the police proceeded so aggressively with no input from him (Shpitz was, after all, his neighbor and acquaintance). Body-cam footage published later showed that the police officer was perceptibly uncomfortable with his treatment of Shpitz, yet that he was receiving clear instructions from his superiors that Shpitz be detained (the body-cam was turned off multiple times while the officer consulted with said superiors). Other allegations of similar treatment towards local residents surfaced after the initial report, supporting the impression that this was no outlier. To this day, no one knows precisely who ordered or insisted that Shpitz be detained or that a criminal record be opened; nor does anyone know why the case remained open so long with the absence of any viable grounds so glaringly obvious. Was the case reviewed and indefensibly left open (and if so, who ordered to do so), or was the case simply ignored, languishing on some shelf; and which is worse? Aside offering only evasive non-answers, no one from the Police or from the Prosecution ever unequivocally condemned the sham criminal proceedings, including Mandelblit himself, who never saw fit to express much unease about the whole affair.

The Shira Shpitz "Laws portion, shame" example is in some ways even more troubling than that of Hoter-Ishay precisely because of its banality. There is something chilling about the mundanity of it all, the ease in which a person might find themselves detained – and potentially much worse – for the lightest imagined infraction. In the end, not a single individual person has been called to task – let alone, faced consequences – for the arbitrary and reprehensible use of police powers against a guiltless woman in the most menacing and illegitimate way. Abuse and impunity were once again proven to be mutually reinforcing.

A Power Unto Itself

The immense power concentrated within the National Police and State Prosecution and centralized in their respective leadership corresponds to the glaring absence of significant oversight mechanisms. As discussed above, local input in the form of elections or appointment by locally-elected officials is non-existent and out of the question. Top-down mechanisms are either ineffectual or severely limited. Knesset committees and subcommittees nominally tasked with supervising law enforcement agencies are generally powerless, to the extent that summons to testify before these are routinely ignored – agency officials just don't show up.* Ministerial oversight or influence over subordinate law enforcement agencies tends to be tangential or is frustrated by a range of factors. The few high-level appointments at the top of the law enforcement hierarchy subject to direct governmental control – such as those of Police Commissioner, State Attorney or

* Knesset committees do not possess subpoena powers.

LCG – are usually filtered through a convoluted process which limits the pool of potential candidates, and are ultimately subject to Supreme Court "reasonability" review. The institution of a "special prosecutor" vested with full investigative and prosecutorial powers to review credible allegations of criminality or severe misconduct within law enforcement agencies does not exist.

Police misconduct is, in principle, subject to review by the Internal Affairs *Mahash* unit. But the unit is directly subordinate to the State Attorney and the LCG, such that its effectiveness is often limited if not undermined entirely. This is especially true regarding issues which bear on the Prosecution's own interests and cases, or which directly involve prosecution personnel, as demonstrated above. Put simply, some of the most egregious instances of sustained police misconduct also involve senior prosecutors, and at times extend to the leadership of both law enforcement bodies. In such cases *Mahash* is obviously ill-suited to investigate related complaints. Indeed, some have alleged that since the departure of Uri Carmel in 2018 following the Al-Qian affair and cover-up, and the appointment of new leadership by Shai Nitzan, *Mahash* has become far more accommodating to the Prosecution's diktats. The new *Mahash* head which followed Carmel in 2018 stated that she viewed her role as "providing a service to the Police" and that the unit ought to "avoid arresting police officers" to the extent possible.[68] After an adolescent was killed in a police chase in 2021 (amid allegations he was intentionally left to die of his injuries without receiving medical care), *Mahash* seemed to do everything in its power to avoid investigating the officers involved[69] – to the point that even the hard-left and judicial-supremacist *Haaretz* newspaper called out the current *Mahash* leadership, stating that "*Mahash* had lost is way" and that the new head was "unfit to lead" the unit.[70]

Following a number of legislative initiatives to establish an independent body tasked with specific authority to review prosecutorial misconduct, the LCG announced his intention in 2012 to proactively establish such a watchdog agency as an independent unit within the Ministry of Justice. The watchdog officially started operating in 2014 headed by Hila Gerstel, a veteran judge with twenty-four years on the bench who had served as President of the Central District Court. The watchdog had a limited mandate – it could investigate complaints against specific prosecutors and could initiate system-wide organizational reviews, resulting in written reports and recommendations, but was ultimately dependent on the collaboration and goodwill of the Prosecution itself with virtually no way to enforce such cooperation.

From its very inception the watchdog was categorically opposed by the State Prosecution, which immediately announced it would not cooperate with Gerstel and eventually went on national strike in protest. Gerstel herself became a target of regular disparaging media briefings by the Prosecution and her work was impeded at every step, often being challenged in court. After a fiery but brief tenure which included the saga surrounding Dr. Furman's employment at the

Forensic Institute and the explosion of the Ruth David affair, Gerstel resigned from her post in exasperation. Following her departure Gerstel gave an extraordinary media interview in which she described the State Prosecution as a "sick" organization, and how her recent experiences shattered her perception of the Prosecution as a straight and just institution, while explicitly speculating that the state had imprisoned innocent people.[71] When asked whether Shai Nitzan was fit to serve as State Attorney, she answered: "No."

The Prosecution eventually got its way – a 2016 statutory overhaul redefined the watchdog body's authority as a generic Ombudsman, such that it could only investigate personal complaints (and was barred from conducting system-wide organizational reviews). Other new rules included that the watchdog could only look into complaints after the conclusion of legal proceedings, that only those directly harmed by misconduct could file a complaint, and that reports could be made public only with permission of the LCG and Minister of Justice. The new watchdog was headed by another retired judge, David Rosen, but he too started clashing regularly with the Prosecution and his work was generally met by determined resistance. Successive petitions to the Supreme Court have further restricted Rosen's oversight ability due to the Court's restrictive reading of his statutory authority. In an exit interview in 2021, Rosen stated that "if the current law is not amended" to enable more robust oversight, "the watchdog may as well be terminated."[72]

One final example combines abuse of police power with a lack of accountability, the absence of meaningful political oversight and the symbiotic complicity of the legal establishment. In 2022 journalist Tomer Gonen published a series of bombshell reports, alleging that the National Police had been using the "Pegasus" cyber software to infiltrate smartphones of Israeli citizens.* Pegasus is an industry-leading military-grade instrument of cyber warfare and espionage, allegedly used by spy services and foreign governments, developed by Israeli cyber company NSO. Using Pegasus, one can "infect" a smartphone and gain access to any and all information contained within: all of its memory, all of its real time data and communications, all phone calls, anything displayed on the screen – anything and everything.

According to Gonen's reports, the Police had begun using Pegasus by a secret and insulated team after 2015 while Roni Al-Sheik was Commissioner. Its use had allegedly become pervasive, employed in thousands of instances against hundreds of devices and individuals (if not more). Pegasus was used against high-ranking government officials, prominent public figures, and also civilians of interest – critically, in many cases the target was not a suspect in any criminal investigation. Target devices were infected by the unilateral and exclusive decision of police officers, without any judicial order or approval (legally required for an audio wiretap). According to Gonen, the method of utilizing Pegasus was

* The facts surrounding the Pegasus saga are disputed and still far from clear. The descriptions here are based on Gonen's reporting and other publicly available sources.

that an infiltrated device would yield valuable information, which would then form the "intelligence" basis for a formal request for a judicial warrant. The system described was one of methodical illicit surveillance-laundering on an industrial scale.

The police and law enforcement establishment were quick to deny and discount the reports, maintaining that all activity was lawful and judicially approved. But the general veracity of Gonen's reports was ultimately confirmed by official sources and statements – Pegasus was indeed used by the Police, against targets who were not suspects of crimes, without judicial pre-approval, in a variety of cases and instances. The question was now (and remains) the extent of its use, its legality and the consequences of its discovery. Another important question concerns who was aware of its use, both within the Police and in broader law-enforcement circles such as the Prosecution and the LCG. The confirmed use of Pegasus on individuals related to the cases against Benjamin Netanyahu – including, allegedly, Netanyahu's sons – indicates that total ignorance of its use within the Prosecution and LCG is highly unlikely.

On the legal side, any assertions of "lawful use" were disingenuous – the whole point was that there is simply no legal authorization for the Police to use something like Pegasus. That is, there is no legal framework or statute or regulation under which the Police may lawfully infiltrate a civilian's smartphone remotely, copy its contents and track its activity. This kind of legal authority is explicitly reserved for spy services such as the Shin Bet and the Mossad. The very most the Police can do (in this kind of context) is apply for audio surveillance of real-time phone conversations (a wire-tap) or for physically copying the contents of a computer (including a smartphone), both of which require an express judicial warrant.

Upon the report's publication, the LCG Avichai Mandelblit immediately announced an internal "inquiry team" which would look into the allegations. But the move was perceived by many as more of a cover-up than anything else. To begin with, the Pegasus exposé potentially implicated the senior hierarchy of the LCG and State Prosecution – such that a team answering to the LCG which was comprised of subordinate legal bureaucrats had an obvious conflict of interests. Further, the team (of dubious legal authority and validity) based its investigation on voluntary cooperation of police personnel – that is, it had no genuine investigative power nor did it seem interested in exercising such. Mandelblit appointed his own Deputy – Amit Merari – to lead the team. Aside herself being neck-deep in the Pegasus controversy (as one of the most senior figures in the criminal justice system), Merari was also married to Eyal Yinon who was a Prosecution witness in the Netanyahu cases. Perhaps needless to say, the "Merari Team" ultimate report downplayed any wrongdoing or illegality and found only "isolated incidents" of unauthorized extraction of phone information, though it did concede the main gist of the Pegasus revelations.

Excluding Merari's superficial investigation, there is currently no official inquiry within the Police or elsewhere which is cataloguing the use of Pegasus to obtain illegal information and evidence. That is, even Merari and the Police do not claim to know the full extent and effect of the use of Pegasus. Subsequent events have utterly undermined Merari's protestations regarding the limited and lawful deployment of Pegasus: in a number of unrelated criminal trials it has emerged that evidence was obtained by Pegasus (or as a result of its use), and the Prosecution was compelled to withdraw the tainted evidence, in some cases leading to acquittal.

In any other Western country such shocking and severe allegations – clearly substantiated at a basic level – would have triggered immediate consequences and a comprehensive, thorough, public investigation. At the very least, officials would be brought before parliamentary committees and compelled to answer direct questions under oath; whistleblower protections would be established for involved officials volunteering information. Such an event would typically lead to the appointment of a dedicated inquiry with full investigative and prosecutorial powers, separate from the law enforcement establishment and answering to elected officials. If no mechanism exists for effective investigation of law enforcement bodies (such as that of Special Counsel in the U.S.) then new legislation can create one.

Yet in Israel, nothing of the sort happened following the Pegasus scandal. Over three years later the entire affair remains shrouded in secrecy and mystery. Neither the Knesset nor the public has received meaningful factual answers to the vast array of questions swirling around the Police's use of Pegasus, both in the past and in the present. Aside partisan politics and general ineptness of political leadership, a number of critical factors have facilitated this evasion so far.

First, public servants – chief among them the LCG Galit Baharav-Miara and other high-ranking officials – have consistently and flatly ignored summons to appear before Knesset committees, or have provided only generic and cagey answers on the rare occasions they've shown up. In Israel the Knesset is virtually unable to compel testimony by public officials, and is entirely unable to sanction uncooperative officials who refuse to provide a straight answer.

Second, the Knesset's slow reaction is at least partially explained by extraneous events. The Pegasus affair broke in 2022 during the Bennett-Lapid Government which leaned heavily towards judicial supremacy and in which any serious investigation of law enforcement malfeasance was unlikely. The Government collapsed in June of 2022 and elections were held the following November, with the new Netanyahu Government sworn in towards the end of the year. Such processes understandably take time to ramp up and gain momentum.

But the third and most important factor has been consistent and direct judicial intervention delaying and hampering efforts at investigating the Pegasus affair. Though the wheels of government turn slowly, the main spoke in those wheels has been thrown, amazingly, by the Supreme Court itself. Following the new Government formation, the Knesset committee charged with legal affairs conducted an initial inquiry and recommended, in June of 2023, that the Government appoint a formal governmental commission of inquiry. In July

Justice Minister Yariv Levin appointed such a committee, chaired by a senior retired District Court judge, and the committee formation was approved by Government resolution in August. The ball was finally rolling.

The committee formation was inevitably, of course, challenged in the Supreme Court. All committee activity was suspended until further notice. The legal wrangling and preliminary proceedings plodded along for weeks – until October 7th and the eruption of the war in Gaza. The Government announced that it was temporarily freezing the committee's work due to the war; the committee lay dormant for months, and was finally reinstated by the Government in January of 2024.

Within a month, the Supreme Court issued a provisional injunction severely limiting the scope of the committee's activity and authority. Among other things, the Court ordered that the committee refrain from investigating any ongoing or existing legal proceedings (these notably include the Benjamin Netanyahu trial and investigations). Since then, for over a year, the committee has been broadly unable to proceed with its work – LCG Baharav-Miara demanded that all aspects of the investigation be coordinated with her and remain subject to her approval. Then, in June of 2025, the Supreme Court issued a decision indicating that the committee must either comply with the LCG's demands – effectively placing it under the thumb of one of the key institutions implicated by the Pegasus scandal – or face its disbandment by the Court itself. As things currently stand, and thanks to the Court's complicity in preventing any meaningful investigation by a lawful Government-appointed committee of inquiry, any chance of uncovering the truth surrounding the Pegasus affair seems to be steadily decreasing.

The Pegasus scandal demonstrates many of the issues discussed above – poor protection of individual liberties from encroachment by law enforcement, the lack of accountability for law enforcement officials and bodies, and the symbiotic relationship between Police, Prosecution, and the Supreme Court. More than anything, the affair has shown the criminal justice system to be a power unto itself, where knowledge of even the most severe, systemic, and patently illegal abuse of law enforcement power may be effectively buried and suppressed.

The Guardians of Good Government

The reality demonstrated in this chapter is directly related to the Court's dramatic jurisprudential shifts described in the previous chapters. The Supreme Court ceased to view itself as enforcer of law and as protector of individual legal rights, very much two sides of the same coin; as a result, it ceased to function as either. Through Objective Purposive Interpretation, abolishing threshold requirements, subjecting all government to "reasonableness," and dictating governmental appointments, the Court gradually came to envision itself as the absolute "guardian of good government": an exclusive oracle of decency and propriety which dictates the policies, outcomes and ends of all governmental activity. Serving the noble cause of judicial perfection, the mundane trifles of individual liberty were quickly and easily discarded as dead weight. Predictably, in arrogating ever-expanding swaths of de facto State power, the Court became more statist; in asserting ultimate executive (and prosecutorial) discretion, the Court increasingly came to resemble the Executive. Small surprise then that in its aggressive pursuit of limitless judicial authority the Court abandoned individual liberties and their protection from governmental abuse. Becoming the judicial accessory and accomplice of State-sponsored persecution and oppression is merely one more inevitable consequence of judicial supremacy.

*

The numerous flaws of Israel's criminal justice and law enforcement agencies are bad enough, in and of themselves, to cause genuine alarm and to justify some radical systemic changes. Israel sharply deviates from the dominant approach ingrained in the Western democratic world, which recognizes the inherent potential for the abuse and manipulation of the State's police powers; which prioritizes judicial protection of individual rights and liberties against misuse of such powers; and which establishes civilian-political supervision, direction and control of such powers.

Yet these flaws take on special significance within the context of the Supreme Court's ascendancy to judicial supremacy. A clear and sinister line connects the Court's omnipotence and the profoundly flawed system of Israeli criminal justice. Judicial domination of politics ultimately depends on elected officials fearing the repercussions of defying judicial lawlessness. In Israel, such fear is well-founded in the far-reaching, unsupervised and unaccountable power of law enforcement agencies – chiefly the National Police, the State Prosecution, and the Legal Counsel to the Government. In turn, the courts incentivize, empower and sustain illegitimate uses of police powers, by developing crippling rules such as the Deri Doctrine, by turning a blind eye to blatant abuses and by shielding law enforcement (and especially its legal components) from meaningful public-political supervision and scrutiny.[*] In the next chapter, we will examine the primary vehicle the Court has fashioned to facilitate this symbiotic relationship.

[*] See, especially, the 2025 *Ronen Bar* case discussed in Chapter 6 and the 2023 *Police Ordinance* case discussed in Chapter 10.

Chapter 8

The Legal Counsel to the Government

Binding Advice, Representation Monopoly, Prosecutor-in-chief

"The Law is the true embodiment
Of everything that's excellent
It has no kind of fault or flaw
And I, my Lords, embody the Law."
— Gilbert and Sullivan, *Iolanthe*

A recurring and somewhat mysterious character throughout our illustration of the Israeli legal system has been that of the Legal Counsel to the Government. We now direct our attention to this singularly formidable institution which stands at the center of the power structure meticulously crafted by the Supreme Court. Though one cannot overstate the role played by the LCG in the ascendancy and preservation of judicial supremacy in Israel, it is often overlooked or downplayed, especially in foreign descriptions of Israel's legal reality.

Proxy Warfare

Our previous account of the dual 1993 rulings regarding Ministers Deri and Pinhasi (Chapter 6) had left out a critical feature to which we may now finally return. Prime Minister Yitzhak Rabin vociferously objected to the demand that he dismiss these two Ministers both on legal grounds and due to political considerations. But his arguments did not merely fall on deaf ears – they were simply never voiced at all. The Legal Counsel to the Government, Yosef Harish, refused to argue Rabin's view before the Supreme Court or to allow Rabin (and his government) any alternate legal representation. Harish in fact argued *for* the petitioners and *against* the government's position, leading to the creation of the Deri Doctrine discussed at length above. Though the demand that Rabin dismiss Deri and Pinhasi lacked any basis in law and was severely flawed on numerous levels, there was simply no one throughout the proceedings that rose to challenge it. There was only the one single position represented in court, the unified opinion of both petitioner and respondents that Rabin must dismiss both Ministers and that his refusal to do so amounted to illegal "unreasonableness."

The Supreme Court led by Meir Shamgar and Aharon Barak agreed with Harish wholeheartedly, and held that the LCG could present whatever position he wished notwithstanding any direct conflict with the actual opinions of the Government in whose name the LCG acts. The Supreme Court reasoned – without the slimmest statutory basis of any kind – that the LCG is the "authorized interpreter of the law" regarding the Executive branch. Consequently, when representing the government in court the LCG must do so "according to his own legal view,"[1] even if this means refusing to defend the government's position and indeed arguing in favor of the petitioners. The Court found nothing problematic about the LCG arguing *in the government's name* against the government's own views, and would not even concede that the government itself was being deprived of any chance to defend its policies or actions in court. The LCG being "authorized interpreter of the law" meant that as a matter of institutional power he speaks for the government on all ostensibly legal matters. According to Justice Barak, Harish was thus indeed representing the "institutional" Prime Minister by arguing against the actual, real-life Prime Minister Yitzhak Rabin. In his own words:

> "It is true, the LCG's view differs from the Prime Minister's view. They tried to convince one another without success... When representing a government entity before the Court the LCG raises the arguments which he believes, according to his legal understanding, justify the entity's actions under the law. Therefore if the LCG considers that the government entity is acting unlawfully he may inform the Court that he refuses to defend the entity's actions... [The LCG] argues before us in the name of a single solitary authorized entity – that of the Prime Minister. It is true, the position of Mr. Yitzhak Rabin, the Prime Minister, was different... But this was not the position represented before us."

The 1993 *Deri-Pinhasi* cases thus constituted an additional novel and groundbreaking precedent entirely separate from the Deri Doctrine discussed above, which dramatically altered the power dynamics surrounding litigation against any government action. The Supreme Court formally recognized the LCG's authority to impose his view on executive government by choosing whether and how to represent any executive action in court, empowering the LCG to unilaterally doom government policy to legal defeat if he so desires.

In the *Deri-Pinhasi* cases we find a snapshot of the singular and unparalleled power wielded by the office and person of the Legal Counsel to the Government. The LCG Yosef Harish was the accuser in criminal proceedings against Deri and Pinhasi; he issued the legal "opinion" that Prime Minister Rabin must dismiss them; and he then argued for his own opinion and against Rabin's, as the government's sole representative in the Supreme Court. We will soon return to each of these components separately in greater detail.

Prof. Shlomo Avineri, one of Israel's most renowned political scientists (also serving twice under Yitzhak Rabin's left-wing Governments), described the LCG in 2009 as "the person wielding the most authority in the democratic world," more so than the presidents of the United States or France, "holding powers unmatched in any democratic state" and plainly at odds with democratic principles.[2] Avineri goes on to label the LCG as "an androgynous, feral creature in the fields of Israeli politics."

*

Though at times complicated or convoluted, and often mired in euphemistic Orwellian terminology, the LCG role is among the most plainly egregious elements of the Israeli legal system. The powers, role and function of the Legal Counsel to the Government deviate so sharply from accepted democratic standards that they emerge as singularly outlandish, defying comparison with any known Western government. These are often glaringly obvious from their description alone, with little need for further elaboration. Simply put, nothing in the world approaches the existing powers of the Israeli LCG, and the acute problems arising from them are plainly and easily discernible, as will soon be apparent. It is also in the role and conduct of the LCG that we find many of the themes discussed so far in the book converging and crystallizing into definitive tangible outcomes.

Before we proceed to examine these powers and their abuse, a brief background and overview are in order.

As mentioned in the Introduction, the Legal Counsel to the Government is an unelected civil servant indirectly appointed by the Government for a fixed six-year term, serving as the nation's chief legal officer and directing most legal aspects of Israel's law enforcement organs. The Office of the LCG constitutes a distinct and highly independent unit within the Ministry of Justice supporting the functions and efforts of the LCG. The unit is formally divided between departments based on subject matter (e.g. criminal law, constitutional-public law, etc.), with each headed by a Deputy LCG. Each department includes both an "advisory" division in charge of providing the government with legal counsel, and a "legislative" division tasked with assisting in the development and drafting of government-sponsored bills. The LCG sphere of authority also encompasses that of the State Attorney (a separate and subordinate role) and the various litigation divisions which represent the government in virtually all actions before a court of law. These include the State Prosecution Service for all criminal and civil proceedings, and the "High Court of Justice" division – the "HCJD" – which represents the government in administrative or constitutional cases before the Supreme Court. The advisory, prosecutorial and representation functions are all technically delegated by the LCG to their respective agencies and departments.

In this chapter and throughout the book, the term "Legal Counsel to the Government" or "LCG" may refer to both the person and the Office of the LCG (including Deputies) interchangeably – the distinction usually being immaterial – though will typically mean the individual official holding the LCG title.

Uniquely, legal opinions are often public and are proactively issued by the LCG. In most jurisdictions the government is entitled to receive confidential legal counsel, and may freely choose whether to publish the advice it received or to keep it under wraps. This is justified by a variety of rationales involving the government's ability to deliberate and consider different options based on comprehensive information, much the same as the government may request confidential economic, empirical or scientific analysis (to name a few) as part of its decision-making process. Legal advice rendered to any client is almost universally treated as privileged information and the government is usually no exception. Yet in Israel the LCG publicizes legal opinions at his discretion, even (and especially) if defying government policy, with such opinions often appearing in the press before their nominal government addressee has the chance to see them.

Similarly, in most jurisdictions legal advice is offered only when sought (or if mandated by statute) – the government may request a legal opinion at its discretion, and a legal advisor may only render such counsel if they're asked to. In the United States, for example, the Office of Legal Counsel does not render a legal opinion if the White House has not asked for one. In Israel, the LCG proactively and unilaterally initiates and issues legal opinions of their own volition – that is, no governmental action or request is required to "trigger" an LCG opinion, and the government cannot prevent one from being issued or refuse to receive such opinion. Virtually any government conduct (or inaction) at any stage of planning or implementation can potentially provoke the issuance (and publication) of the LCG's considered opinion bearing on the matter.

In addition to the separate unit of LCG within the Ministry of Justice, most government organs, agencies and Ministries have their own individual unit providing legal services and advice. Both technically and historically, these legal advice units are meant to be subordinate to their respective Ministry hierarchies in terms of personnel and policy. Nonetheless, an internal LCG directive (backed by Supreme Court rulings) has established that such legal advice units are "professionally" responsible towards the LCG and must follow LCG instructions and guidelines regarding the content and substance of their work. As such, Ministerial or agency legal advice units effectively function as subsidiary departments of the LCG, and must adhere to the latter's general policies and specific legal determinations.

Many often refer to the LCG using the title "Attorney General" though this conflates more than it clarifies. The Hebrew title is *Yoetz* (counselor/advisor) *Mishpati* (legal) *La-Memshala* (to the Government) such that "LCG" is a more faithful-literal translation. More to the point, there is little similarity between the role of LCG and that of "Attorney General" in most jurisdictions. To wit: LCGs are not elected nor are they directly appointed to their role – the position is treated as a-political and bureaucratic, something akin to the head of a Central Bank. Nor is the LCG a Cabinet member. The LCG typically retains their position following elections and a change of government – such that an outgoing administration may well appoint an LCG deeply adverse to the agenda and ideology of an incoming administration, as indeed occasionally happens.* In the United States, the federal Attorney General is a political cabinet-level position at the head of the Justice Department, comparable to the Minister of Justice in Israel and in most other jurisdictions. In separate (U.S.) States the Attorneys General are typically the chief legal officers and occasionally also lead the State Justice Department, though their roles are invariably considered political and they are either directly elected or are appointed by elected political officials. In the United Kingdom, the Attorney General is the government's most senior legal officer, is answerable directly to Parliament, and is appointed by the Prime Minister and serves at their pleasure. For these reasons and others, the title "Attorney General" within the Israeli context is inaccurate and misleading.

The LCG appointment process was established in 2000 by a Government resolution based on the 1998 Shamgar Report, following an alleged corruption scandal that ended with no indictments but drove public demand for a more ordered selection process. An LCG candidate is nominated by a special selection committee and is then approved by the Government – meaning that the Government can only appoint an LCG that is supported by the committee. The five-member committee is dominated by the legal establishment – the Chairman is a former Supreme Court Justice appointed by the current Chief Justice; other members include an attorney appointed by the Bar Association and a scholar appointed by a forum of law-school deans. The other two members, a serving Knesset Member and a former Minister of Justice or ex-LCG, are respectively appointed by a Knesset committee and by the Government. A nominee must technically receive four out of five committee votes to proceed to Government approval, though this is not closely followed.† Importantly, as the legal establishment enjoys a near-veto over nominees, the Government is extremely limited in its ability to appoint desired candidates to begin with, and the entire process is slanted towards candidates that have a realistic chance at passing muster with the supremacy-leaning academia, Bar and Court. The notion of the Government appointing its "own" counsel is therefore largely mythical, with the committee not only filtering or recommending nominees but at least to some extent dictating to the Government its pool of acceptable candidates.

This process was purportedly devised to minimize political shenanigans and to ensure the high caliber of LCG nominees, though whether it succeeds in doing either seems doubtful. In 2016, Avichai Mandelblit was submitted by the

---

* Gali Baharav-Miara was appointed LCG in February of 2022 by a governing coalition which dissolved in June and was replaced following an elections defeat in November.

† In 2009 no candidate obtained four votes, such that all candidates that received three votes were then vetted by the Minister of Justice, who presented his preferred candidate for Government approval.

committee as the single nominee for Government approval, despite the Justice Minister's request to be able to choose from three candidates. A 2024 exposé by journalist Amit Segal revealed how Mandelblit schemed with the Bar Chairman during his approval process to obtain the necessary votes and to undermine alternative candidates, including receiving privileged inside information in the lead-up to his committee interview.[3] In 2022 the leading candidate Gali Baharav-Miara was an unknown lawyer that had previously served as Tel Aviv District Attorney for civil (non-criminal) matters, with no expertise or practical background in criminal or public law. The committee Chairman, retired Justice Asher Grunis, opposed her nomination on the grounds she lacked sufficient professional experience, likening her selection to "appointing a colonel" to lead the military. She was appointed nonetheless. As recent experience reveals, the current committee process prevents neither backstage horse-trading nor unqualified candidates; it would seem that the only discernible outcome is a limitation on the Government's ability to choose its own legal advisor.

As we proceed to describe the role and authority of the LCG, one critical aspect to keep in mind is the utter absence of governing statutory provisions. Here I do not refer to expansive or creative interpretation, but to the general non-existence of applicable legislation. Most of the LCG's powers have been generally defined and expanded by the Supreme Court itself, on highly dubious grounds (if they can even be called grounds at all) and with only the barest pretense of genuine deliberation. As put succinctly by political scientist Shlomo Avineri, the LCG's powers are "not a product of parliamentary legislation that came after public discussion" but are rather derived from "an improbable mélange of Mandate-era colonialist heritage, High Court rulings, committee resolutions that never went through the legislative process, and the legacy of a few powerful individuals who held the post at a time of powerless [political] leadership." This is of paramount importance because even if such arrangements were to exist in other jurisdictions (and they certainly do not), they would only ever be tolerated if firmly established and authorized by explicit primary legislation (or more likely, by constitutional provisions). In Israel, the formidable edifice of the LCG rests primarily on half-baked *dicta* and unfounded judicial ipse-dixits.

Yoav Dotan has called the LCG a "forward base" of the Supreme Court,[4] but if we are to employ military jargon perhaps a more appropriate term is "proxy" – an ostensibly separate entity furthering the interests of its enabling sponsor. The Supreme Court empowers and legitimizes the LCG; the LCG returns the favor by advancing the Court's agenda at every opportunity and using all means at his disposal to assert judicial power over that of elected and accountable government. Universally acknowledged to be a de facto agent of the Supreme Court within the Executive branch and well beyond, the LCG ceased long ago to counsel the Government in any meaningful sense and instead serves exclusively as long arm and enforcer of judicial supremacy.

I – Binding Counsel

"Authorized Interpreter…"

As his title might suggest, the LCG's primary role is that of providing the government with legal advice.* The office and authorities of this role are not defined in any statutory provision, or really anywhere at all, but are rather vaguely alluded to in disparate snippets of legislation, various Government resolutions and a handful of public commission reports. The need of any government for competent and effective legal counsel is obvious – the state requires legal advice, analysis and assistance as it goes about its business. Over the years, in a process which started in the 1980s and has been accelerating ever since, this core function of the "Legal Counsel to the Government" has been entirely undermined and replaced: Today, the LCG provides not counsel but rather *binding directives*, intervenes in matters of *policy* not remotely legal, and blatantly serves not the government but rather the nebulous *public interest.*

The central maxim used in this context is that the LCG is "the authorized interpreter of the law towards the executive government," and that the LCG's legal opinion "binds" the government until a different judicial determination says otherwise. This basic contention is repeated by the LCG and by the Supreme Court to exhaustion, though it has no (to be clear – zero) basis in statutory law and directly contradicts even the slim grounds from which it claims it originates.

A critical point of departure is the 1962 Agranat Report. Following a genuine dispute between the Minister of Justice Dov Yosef and the influential and dominant LCG Gideon Hausner, the Government established a commission to report on the current and desired authority of the LCG and their relationship with the Government. The commission, headed by Justice Shimon Agranat, published its report with an unequivocal recommendation: Though (in the absence of a clear statutory rule) the Government *ought* to view the LCG's legal opinion as "reflecting existing law," the Government may "decide how to act in each given instance according to its own discretion." Notably, the background for the Agranat Report specifically regarded the question whether the Minister of Justice was obligated to comply with the LCG's legal opinion – to which the Report's answer was a resounding "no." The Report also explicitly distinguished between government offices, agencies and organs making up most of the Executive on the one hand, which must follow the LCG's legal opinion; and the Government at the top of the executive hierarchy on the other hand, i.e. the Cabinet and its members, which plainly is not bound by the LCG's opinion.

---

* The LCG's advisory role usually manifests either as "directives" (or guidelines) which resemble forward-looking rules and regulations of a general nature; or as "opinions" which are usually ad hoc memorandums addressing a particular governmental decision or policy. The distinction between these is poorly defined and is of little consequence, and we will refer to them interchangeably.

When the Government moved to adopt the report's recommendations, Prime Minister Ben-Gurion asked the LCG Hausner whether he found these acceptable. Hausner's response is illuminating:

> "I have never claimed to dictate government decisions or to determine its path, and I regret if anyone understood my words in that way… it would be absurd for me to adopt such a stance. If the government seeks my opinion, it will receive my legal opinion as a basis for discussion, as required by law, but from that point on, it is free to decide according to its discretion."

Hausner emphasizes that once his legal advice is given, the Government "can arrive at one decision" but could "just as well arrive at another." Finally, Hausner expressed his "concern" that he was portrayed as placing his opinion above that of the Government or of any Minister as if he were "some oracle" and protested that any such portrayal was "caricaturistic."

The 1962 Agranat Report text and surrounding debate leave no room for doubt – yet somehow the "absurd caricature" of the Government being bound by the LCG's legal opinion came to be. The phrase "authorized interpreter of the law" appears nowhere in the Agranat Report – perhaps "reflecting existing law" comes closest – but suddenly materialized thirty years later in the 1993 Pinhasi-Deri decisions, to support the binding nature of the LCG's opinions. The Justices presenting this rule as a *fait accompli* make no real effort to indicate a legal source of any kind. In his *Pinhasi* decision, Justice Barak cites his own *dicta* from a 1985 case which had nothing to do with the LCG and in which Barak raised this idea, with no citation and as a tangential throwaway comment to make an unrelated point.* In quintessential Barak-style legal reasoning, this served sufficient grounds to be presented eight years later as a consecrated legal precedent.

But Barak ventures audaciously further, and presents the "binding legal counsel" approach as "derived" from the "constitutional tradition" (no less) established in the 1962 Agranat Report. That's correct – the same report which explicitly recommended the exact opposite. Barak and the Court deftly ignore the key distinction made by Agranat, between the senior "Government" and the broader executive. Finally, Barak refers to a speech delivered by former-LCG and future-Justice Yitzhak Zamir, in which Zamir erroneously described the Agranat Report as establishing the "binding legal opinion" – but even Zamir later

* This is no exaggeration. In the 1985 decision, while expounding on *the Court's* role in interpreting any law and in reflecting the law's content, Barak digresses: "It is sometimes customary that the authority to interpret certain matters for a particular organ is assigned to a specific functionary. For example, the authority to interpret the law for the executive branch is vested in the Legal Counsel to the Government, and their interpretation is internally binding." (HCJ 73/85, s. 11). That's it. Barak doesn't bother with any citations and returns to discussing the Court. To say this is textbook *obiter dictum* of no legal significance would be an understatement.

published a correction (notably, before Barak's 1993 ruling) and conceded that he had misconstrued the Report's conclusions.[5]

Thus, Justice Barak's 1993 *Pinhasi* ruling declared a new legal norm: that the LCG is the "authorized interpreter of the law" and that his opinions bind the Government – including Ministers, the Prime Minister, and collective Cabinet resolutions – unless otherwise determined by the Court. Far from a purported "constitutional tradition," this new innovation was loosely based on the Agranat Report (which it contradicted), a speech by Zamir (which was shown and admitted to be erroneous), and on Barak's own previous incidental *dicta* musings. The concurrent 1993 *Deri* decision by Justice Shamgar said much the same and made even less of an effort at justification, referring simply to the *Pinhasi* decision.

The rest, as they say, is history. Despite lacking any legal basis, despite the sheer magnitude of such a rule and despite the severe obvious flaws stemming from it, the notion of "binding legal advice" began taking hold in the Supreme Court. In a contiguous line of rulings the Court has regularly repeated the twin mantras of "authorized interpreter" and "binding opinion," treating the rule as self-evident gospel. Over the years numerous prominent scholars have painstakingly and compellingly shown the rule to be utterly devoid of legal basis, as reflected in just a handful of examples: Ruth Gavison wrote in 1996 that "not only did the Agranat Commission not support" a binding counsel rule, "it expressly rejected it."[6] Retired Justice Miriam Ben-Porat wrote in 2005 no such "legal tradition" (alleged by Barak in *Pinhasi*) existed and that the claim had neither been substantially adjudicated nor is it supported by available evidence.[7] Daniel Friedmann summarized in 2013 that "the rule has no basis in law," "is devoid of reason" and is "not rooted in Israel's legal tradition."[8]

But to no avail. The Court clung to the myth pioneered by Barak in 1993, and still refuses to concede the slightest doubt or uncertainty regarding the rule, its wisdom, its origins and its legal validity. To this day, the Court has never conducted a comprehensive discussion contending with the many flaws and critiques of the "binding opinion" theory – indeed the Court has scarcely acknowledged or addressed them. The notion of "internally binding" legal counsel now permeates Israeli jurisprudence and has gradually metastasized to ever-expanding proportions.

A later commission headed by (retired) Justice Meir Shamgar in 1997 published further recommendations regarding the office and role of LCG. This commission is often perceived as supporting the "binding counsel" rule, and it indeed adopts the phraseology of the LCG as "authorized interpreter of the law," with his legal opinion "reflecting the existing legal reality." Nonetheless, even the Shamgar report emphasized that it "saw no cause" to deviate from the original Agranat report recommendation which excluded the Government from the LCG opinion's binding force. In other words, even as this commission strongly favored an aggressively dominant role for the LCG, it still left the Government and its Ministers outside the vice-grip of binding legal counsel. Notably, this was already after the 1993 Supreme Court rulings which presented the opposite view as settled law. More importantly, unlike the Agranat Report, this report was never adopted by Government resolution (aside one recommendation relating to the appointment process), such that it has no legal force whatsoever. The argument for binding legal counsel remains meritless as it ever was.

One rare moment of candor is uniquely illuminating. In a 2017 interview (published as a law review article), Aharon Barak is asked about the plainly erroneous legal basis for the LCG's legal opinion binding Government.[9] Barak's answer is astonishing – he concedes the weak legal basis and essentially explains that the "source" is solely the Court's own proclamation. First Barak wonders aloud why Agranat in 1962 did not have the good sense to presciently conform to Barak's 1993 ruling (yes, really: "I too see the weakness of the Agranat Report in this matter. I don't know why Agranat had to decide the way he did, and didn't decide the way that I did later on"). Barak then concedes that the innovation is "an Israeli creation"* which is why he "rushed" to establish the ruling in a Supreme Court decision; and that its only source is the Court's say-so. In Barak's words:

> "There are many Israeli creations without a source. If you ask me what is the legal basis for the rule that the LCG's legal opinion properly defines the content of the law for the Government, then my answer is that the legal basis is the Supreme Court's ruling."

One could hardly come up with a clearer articulation of circular *ipse dixit* reasoning.

It's worth noting that even this description from Barak is not quite accurate – there is no *actual* precedent from the Supreme Court which establishes the "binding counsel" rule per se, but rather only the repeated refrain in *dicta*. The Court has certainly ruled against government action and aligned itself with the LCG many times – but in all such instances the Court disagreed with the Government on the merits of the matter. That is, the Court held that the Government was doing something illegal in its own right, separate from the latter's dispute with the LCG. A real precedent establishing the "binding counsel" rule would need to go further – the Court would need to hold that the Government's action was illegal solely due to the LCG's opposition, even if the action was otherwise legally justifiable. This has never occurred. Thus, critically, even the constant assertion that the Supreme Court has "created" such a firm legal rule turns out to be factually false.

The myth is further propagated of course by the LCG himself. Formal guidelines published by the LCG (titled "The Roles of the Legal Counsel to the Government") state that "the LCG instructions bind the entire governmental system, and the LCG's interpretation of the law is the authorized interpretation for all government branches." The LCG regularly maintains the validity and force

* Though this seems either a euphemism for "judicial creation" or a recognition that the "creation" simply deviates from global democratic theory and practice.

of the "binding counsel" rule in internal rules, in public speeches and interviews, in specific opinions rendered and of course in court filings and argumentation.

The LCG has every reason to keep it up. In a display of Orwellian denial and doublethink, the Supreme Court simply insists on sticking to the "binding counsel" mantra as though nothing were amiss. A handful of representative examples serve to demonstrate this. In a 1998 ruling, the Court stated that the Government's position regarding the content of existing law "is determined by the Legal Counsel to the Government," who "is not an advisor in the typical sense." The LCG's opinion "obligates" government organs and his "professional position *is* the position of such organs." The "private opinions" of elected officials regarding the law "are irrelevant." When exercising its authority the government "must obey" the LCG's legal opinions.[10] In another 2004 ruling, the Court described a specific government action taken against the LCG's advice as "tantamount to a decision taken against the law."[11] This is of course but a natural development – if we are to treat the LCG as "reflecting binding law," why not just do away with pretenses and say that his opinions carry the same weight as statutory law? In another 2008 ruling, the Court emphasized that the LCG's opinion obligates the government "as an institutional matter" – its binding force not grounded only in its "reflecting" the law but also now baked into the institutional state hierarchy of authority.[12]

Ironically, an LCG opinion "binds" the Government, but not the LCG himself, who can change his mind or deviate from previous opinions at the drop of a hat. Daniel Friedmann observes that "while the Government lacks the power to 'override' an erroneous legal opinion, the LCG himself can easily do so – just as a future LCG could, by issuing a new and differing opinion."[13] In other words, for the Government an LCG opinion "reflects the law" in perpetuity, while for the LCG such legal opinion reflects the law until he changes his mind.

The reader may themselves judge how best to label the proactive issuance of public decrees which bind – that is, impose mandatory obligations and prohibitions on – their target recipient. Despite employing the associated terms of "counsel," "advice" and "opinion," the LCG's legal determinations under the "authorized interpreter" model may more aptly be called "directives," or indeed – "orders."

"... of The Law"

The LCG's authority to bind the government by "reflecting" the law rests on non-existent grounds. Yet the "binding counsel" model is exacerbated by the other half of the "authorized interpreter of the law" equation – that is, the way in which "the law" is itself conceptualized. Two substantive theoretical and principled flaws inherent in this approach are worth spelling out.

First, as any lawyer (and almost any citizen) knows, cases in which the law and its application are ambiguous are common. One primary reason for the existence of courts and the legal profession is the regular good-faith disagreement regarding the law's content and meaning. Lawyers routinely advance conflicting non-frivolous legal arguments, as do indeed judges and courts in their rulings. The notion that a single version of "the law" always exists is clearly a fallacy – and therefore so is a rule by which the legal opinion of a single actor automatically prevails over any other. Simply put, the government and its organs may well have a valid legal basis for their actions even if the LCG thinks otherwise. Pretending that the LCG's pronouncement is the only conceivable or allowable legal view is based on the façade that the government could not possibly come to a legal conclusion of equal (or even superior) validity to that of the LCG.

This point goes to the core of the phrase "authorized interpreter of the law." It is hardly a novel observation that the putative interpreter of the law is in most senses the law itself – that though the law may be often broad or unclear, its real force lies in the moment it is interpreted, constructed and applied to a given set of real-world circumstances. Democracies already have such an institution which serves as authorized interpreter of the law – it's called the judiciary. The laborious process of legal adjudication involves complicated rules and procedures for compelling reasons, chief among them that the "correct" legal outcome is often not obvious on its face and its determination requires rigorous examination and discussion (usually of an adversarial nature) by experienced and learned jurists and other subject-matter experts. Yet "binding counsel" simply outsources the judicial role – determining the law's application in specific instances – to a single attorney with arbitrary and unilateral power to select the legal argument they find most favorable or expedient. This defies some of the most basic insights and intuitions regarding the nature and practice of law.

Worse still, this façade extends to an "infallibility fallacy" – denying the possibility of bad-faith or clearly erroneous legal positions. According to the "binding counsel" rule, the government is obligated to follow the LCG's instructions even if plainly invalid. An LCG can impose the most unfounded and specious legal position flying in the face of clear-cut black-letter law, and the Government would need to adhere to a manifestly illegal position simply because the LCG says so. Interestingly, even the 1962 Agranat Report rules out such a situation – the key passage regarding LCG opinions binding government organs (but not the Government itself) opens with the words "Where there is no explicit statutory provision regarding the matter at hand…" In other words, if the applicable law is clear, granting the LCG power to impose a contradictory view simply makes no sense. Even for Agranat, the idea of limited "binding counsel" was conceivable only in the event of genuine legal uncertainty. Both the Court and scholars overlook this clause entirely.

There is no shortage of examples in which the LCG displayed poor legal judgment and comprehension. On numerous occasions the LCG has adopted positions adverse to governmental action while insisting that the government was bound to adhere to the LCG opinion, only to be overruled by the Supreme Court itself. LCG Gali Baharav-Miara – universally viewed as deeply and ideologically hostile to the governing right-wing Coalition during much of her tenure –

demonstrated this dynamic in a few recent cases. In the 2024 *Minnes* case, the LCG vehemently opposed a decision by the Minister of Communications to appoint Dr. Odelia Minnes as temporary *acting* Chairwoman of a statutory telecom council. The LCG argued that Minnes had to meet the statutory requirements of a *permanent* chairperson, despite there being no such provision in governing statutes (and against the law's text, clear rationale, past practice and common sense). The Court unanimously approved the appointment of Minnes and rejected the LCG's spurious argument.

Earlier, in 2022, a left-wing interim "caretaker" Government (to which the LCG was sympathetic) tried to appoint a key committee chairman, violating the Supreme Court's many rulings limiting the ability of transitional governments to make significant decisions with irreversible consequences in the lead-up to elections. This time the LCG passionately defended the Government's decision despite its clear contradiction of prior jurisprudence. The Supreme Court invalidated the appointment and criticized the LCG for her oddly inconsistent position which seemed to favor the outgoing Government.[14]

Finally, in the infamous "reasonableness" amendment to the Basic Law (struck down by the Court in 2024), the LCG fervently argued – both during the legislative process and before the Supreme Court – that the amendment was unlawful. The merits of her arguments notwithstanding, they were clearly not inevitable: the Knesset Legal Counsel mustered a comprehensive defense of the amendment's legality, and seven out of fifteen Supreme Court Justices (just under half the bench) voted to uphold it. Clearly, the position supporting the amendment's legality was sufficiently solid to be adopted by senior jurists and judges, undermining the LCG's contention that the amendment was patently and manifestly unlawful beyond redemption.

The point in these examples is simple – the Legal Counsel to the Government is just another lawyer, capable of mistakes and errors of judgment, of politically motivated decisions, and even of petty or vindictive conduct. The LCG may easily make legal arguments which are patently erroneous, or which simply adopt a single view out of a variety of equally valid legal positions – and has indeed done so on many occasions. Subordinating a huge swath of government conduct to such determinations of a single attorney, based on the illusion of a single legitimate legal view, is simply absurd.

A second flaw – and this is the real kicker – is that in the jumble of Israeli jurisprudence the notion of "legal" assumes a life of its own. Simply put, the phrase "authorized interpreter of the law" acquires an entirely different meaning when we recall precisely what the Supreme Court considers "the law." As demonstrated exhaustively in previous chapters, ostensible interpretation includes a law's "objective purpose," and any review of legality includes the reasonableness standard. In such an environment the very concept of a "legal opinion" loses all meaning – any matter of government policy or priorities is framed as a legal question to be determined by lawyers. This means that the "legal opinion" of the LCG may often be nothing more than a policy prescription dressed in quasi-legal language. An LCG opinion can, and often does, prohibit or mandate government action based solely on its alleged reasonableness or on the supposed objective purpose of legislation. As a result the LCG imposes not only their legal view on the government but rather their actual desired substantive ideology.

The glaring flaws in terms of democratic legitimacy and accountability, alongside the immense potential for incompetence or abuse, become all the more apparent when the LCG adopts a posture generally adverse to an elected administration or to specific officials, whether for ideological, personal or other reasons. A Supreme Court intervening in any conceivable government action for any reason it deems sufficient is bad enough, but a single unelected and unremovable bureaucrat that does so without even the barest appearance (let alone substance) of judicial process is another thing entirely. For the LCG to halt any government decision or policy in its tracks, all that's needed is his effortless determination of "unreasonableness."

This is one place where the straight-faced masquerade of reasonableness review as an ordinary legal standard pays off – it allows the LCG to pretend that pure policy prescriptions are no more than the inevitable and irresistible dictates of "the law." As explained by Prof. Moshe Cohen-Eliyah, the "true implications" of the "dramatic warping of the reasonableness standard" are "only fully manifested when paired with the unrivaled powers granted by judicial fiat to the Government Legal Counsel."[15] More broadly still, this conflation of reasonableness with "the law" demonstrates Ronen Shamir's observation (in Chapter 5 above) regarding the mystification of law: a legal opinion from the LCG is impervious to any rational scrutiny because systematic and coherent language-based analysis becomes irrelevant. A declaration of "illegality" assumes mystical qualities, unchallengeable in terms of ordinary human deliberation and comprehension. This seeps into political and public discourse as well, with commentators insisting an LCG opinion reflects "the law" without even the pretense of presenting or understanding underlying justifications.

Much of this is easily recognizable in the 1993 Deri-Pinhasi rulings, discussed at length above. LCG Yosef Harish raised the legally baseless argument that Prime Minister Rabin must dismiss his Ministers, because failure to do so was unreasonable and would contradict "objective purposive interpretation" of governing statutory law. Here is a determination well within the purview of executive government, involving values, priorities, public faith, political and electoral expedience, policy preferences – everything but law. The position taken up by the LCG – which allegedly binds the government and Prime Minister – was both legally meritless and steeped in the ideological quasi-legal realm of reasonableness.

The potent gunpowder of reasonableness thus proves most formidable when used as ammunition fired from the precise weapon of binding legal counsel. The dramatic effect of these two elements combined is impossible to overstate. Wielding both, the LCG crosses the threshold from arbitrary legal power to absolute political domination, limiting or mandating government action by his or her sole judgment.

Today, the LCG routinely issues so-called legal opinions which are easily recognizable as little more than pure policy papers at best, and more often resemble dressed-up editorial columns. Most modern legal opinions issued by the LCG typically contain nothing more than bald moralizing assertions, making no attempt to elaborate a "legal" argument in any familiar sense, not even ones which are creative, unfounded or far-fetched. Indeed, quite often such opinions don't bother even with abstract legal standards such as reasonableness.

A handful of recent examples suffice to illustrate the point. Throughout the legal reforms proposed by the Government in 2023, the LCG issued a comprehensive set of legal opinions regarding the validity of various legislative measures. These opinions spanned hundreds of written pages and dozens of in-person meetings, yet none included what might be remotely considered a legal position or argument. In these opinions the LCG forcefully opposed the draft legislation, but did so entirely on grounds of policy and alleged first principles – not law. In its major formal written opinion regarding the Government's proposed restriction of the reasonableness standard, the LCG claimed that the legislation was "too broad" and does not sufficiently distinguish between different types of decisions; that it "weakens" judicial supervision of administrative decisions and "upsets the balance" between government branches; and that it will reduce legal "foreseeability."[16] Appearing before a Knesset legislative committee, the LCG claimed that the reasonableness amendment would "severely undermine basic democratic values, such as proper administration, good character of the civil service, the rule of law, and public trust."[17] The LCG legal opinion painstakingly explains why they believe the proposed measures to be a Very Bad Idea.

The point is not whether the LCG was right or wrong. One might agree or disagree with such claims, but what is certain is that they are not "legal" in any sense. Even if they were entirely valid and justified, they amount to little more than just one more considered opinion regarding the pros and cons of a hotly debated government proposal. These are patently value-based, principled arguments in the sphere of political theory or good governance; they are relevant as an effort to persuade the reader of the wisdom and advisability of a given proposal. Yet they are entirely irrelevant to answer the question of "what does the law say about this?"; they point to no discernible legal norms, rules or sources; their defense or refutation requires no legal knowledge or expertise; they are, simply, devoid of any legal content. The LCG so-called legal opinion, here as in many other cases, is essentially indistinguishable from a policy white paper. It is utterly divorced from what would be considered "legal counsel" in any other setting.

Immediately following the October 7th surprise attack by Hamas, many Israelis began calling for a formal inquiry to investigate the many failures which enabled the attack and compounded its catastrophic outcomes. While the need for major institutional and systemic investigation is virtually undisputed, a major point of public contention regards what kind of overall inquiry is to be established (in addition to various localized inquiries and reviews already underway). The primary options under the existing statutory framework include a "Parliamentary Commission" appointed by the Knesset, a "Governmental Commission" appointed by the Government, or a "State Commission" appointed by the Supreme Court Chief Justice; another option is to establish, by new legislation, a separate and novel inquiry model to address the unique and unprecedented circumstances. The authority of whether to establish a formal inquiry and what type to choose is essentially up to the ruling Coalition and Government. Naturally, there are valid arguments to support or reject the various modes of inquiry. Just as naturally, nothing in Israeli statutory law or legal precedent compels the Government to prefer one form over the other.

In June of 2024, as the debate on this issue raged on, the LCG informed Prime Minister Netanyahu that in their "professional opinion," a "State Commission of Inquiry is the appropriate lawful mechanism" to investigate the events surrounding October 7th. Further, the LCG stated that any decision regarding an inquiry must be made "without delay."[18] This position was reiterated by the LCG in additional official statements. In a letter to the Government in May of 2025, the LCG "clarified" again that "a State Commission of Inquiry is the designated and unique legal instrument provided by law that is suited to investigate the events of October 7th." The LCG also stated that the Government "must adopt a reasoned decision on the matter" without delay.[19] The LCG's position, then, is that the Government has two legal obligations: It must make a decision (one way or another) regarding the establishment of a Commission of Inquiry; and it ought to choose a "State Commission" as the mode of inquiry.

Describing any of the above as a "legal opinion" seems something of an overstatement – the LCG's position was laid out in a single page and took the form of a letter. Nevertheless, this is the "Legal Counsel to the Government" herself issuing her office's "professional opinion" in her official capacity, presented in terms of legality and legal obligations governing administrative decisions. To the point at hand, the opinion is of course not remotely "legal." The LCG does not even attempt to cite legal sources (such as statutory law or judicial precedent) or to ground her argument in anything beyond the fact of its own existence. The letters state some feeble claims as to why a "State Commission" is the more "appropriate" or "best suited" option, but that is precisely the dispute around which public debate revolved. The LCG further raises the (highly questionable) argument that choosing a "State Commission" would benefit Israel in the context of adjudication by international tribunals (i.e., the International Criminal Court and the International Court of Justice), but this too is an argument of policy, not of law. Frankly, anyone outside Israel reading the LCG's letter would rightly be asking why in the world the Legal Counsel to the Government was even opining on such an issue.

Throughout this chapter and the entire book, the reader will find many other examples of LCG "opinions" covering matters, and raising arguments, which lack even the most distant or vague relation to law.

Finally, in a recent notable development the LCG seems to take the notion of "authorized interpreter" to mean "exclusive interpreter," such that the LCG zealously guards the objects of his counsel – the Government – from receiving alternative legal counsel. During a peak COVID-19 infection wave in 2020, the Government was set to introduce a slew of restrictions which included some limitations on public protests. The LCG Mandelblit presented a particular legal view regarding the government's narrow authority to issue such restrictions. Minister Amir Ohana suspected that the LCG's opinion was superficial, flawed, and one-sided, and he sought to present the Government with an opposing legal view. Ohana summoned Dr. Aviad Bakshi, a respected scholar of public and constitutional law whose name is regularly floated as a candidate for the LCG role (and for judicial office), to present an alternative legal analysis of the Government's authority.

In a brief letter to the Government Secretary the LCG vehemently opposed both Bakshi's physical presence in the meeting and any indirect presentation of Bakshi's legal position to the Government. Mandelblit wrote that it is "unacceptable" for a Minister to present the LCG's legal opinion "as though it were only one opinion of many," wherein the Government is "free to choose amongst them as it pleases."[20] Perish the thought. To drive this overwhelmingly irrefutable argument home, Mandelblit compares Ohana's attempt with an "inconceivable" request to present the Government with advice from an external military expert (alongside the Chief of Staff). So forceful was his opposition that some Ministers threatened to cancel the critical Government meeting altogether if Ohana dared present the alternate legal opinion. Bakshi was left stranded outside the meeting room; and the alternative legal argument was not presented before the Ministers.

For Mandelblit, his role as "authorized interpreter" meant that the Government and its Ministers are not entitled to receive alternative legal viewpoints. Not only must his opinion bind all of executive government to do his bidding, but the fragile minds of government Ministers must be shielded from dangerous competing views lest they harbor rebellious doubts as to the force of his own legal arguments. Thus the LCG demands not only that his pronouncements be followed as though they were the law itself, but also that no competing view may be entertained or considered.

For the Realm

From "counsel" to binding directive; from "legal" to manifestly political. Yet a final component of the power exercised by the Legal Counsel to the Government is that last notion – that the LCG serves "the government" at all. We've seen and considered instances in which the LCG adopts positions diametrically opposing government policy and actively works to undermine and thwart government decisions. Far from an implausible scenario or a dubious conspiracy theory, such conduct is a regular occurrence in which the LCG and legal establishment indeed take considerable pride. Despite the misleading title and without parallel in any functioning democracy, it turns out that assisting the elected and accountable branches of government is viewed by the LCG as a trifling afterthought, even a nuisance; as we shall now see, the LCG rather serves much loftier goals and more forgiving masters.

There was a time in which the Legal Counsel to the Government matched the role suggested by its name – a civil servant within the Ministry of Justice, assisting executive government with its political agenda and providing state organs with necessary legal advice. He was, in short, the government's attorney. Much like any attorney, his first obligation and duty was to serve and further the interests of his client in good faith and to the best of his ability. As the sole legitimate representatives of popular sovereignty and of state power in a democracy, the elected and accountable government not only requires legal service – they deserve and rightly demand it. Surely assisting the government itself was a sufficiently noble undertaking.

Yet precisely along with the advent of our vaunted "authorized interpreter of the law," so emerged the parallel role of "Gatekeeper." In a gradual but comprehensive metamorphosis largely driven by the Supreme Court, the LCG ceased to view the concrete government and its organs as his client – and adopted in its stead a new client in the form of "the public interest." Over the span of a few decades the LCG's self-perception shifted from "government attorney" to "government warden," upholding the rule of law and protecting fundamental societal values – primarily against ostensible threats emanating from the government itself. The LCG and government legal corps over which he presided became self-styled "gatekeepers," supposedly saving the government from committing the most grievous transgressions.

The above description might seem exaggerated to the uninitiated. It most certainly is not. This radical alteration of the LCG's role is well-documented and universally acknowledged. Yoav Dotan describes the self-perception of government attorneys as "not merely the representative" of government agencies in court, "but rather as a supervisory organ that seeks to promote the general values of the rule of law..."[21] It is repeated regularly by the LCG and by the Supreme Court. In one of many internal guidelines issued by the LCG, the role of government attorneys is defined as a "gatekeeper responsible for upholding the rule of law and the public interest."[22] In the same Supreme Court opinion in which Justice Dorit Beinisch described the LCG counsel as "institutionally" binding the Government, she also defines the LCG role as "protecting the public interest and enforcing the law, and advancing the rule of law and fundamental societal values."[23] Justice Anat Baron goes further in a 2016 decision:

> "The LCG and his representatives throughout government Ministries are the gatekeepers of the rule of law... [The LCG] is not merely an

> 'advisor'; he also 'supervises' the government, and serves as 'watchdog' over the rule of law."[24]

Gil Bringer, a prominent Israeli jurist, conducted an extensive forensic study tracking the development of the "gatekeeper ethos." In his 2018 essay Bringer painstakingly shows how the "tangible client" (that is, the actual government organs, officials and Ministries) was discarded in favor of the so-called "genuine client" – the public at large.[25] Justice Yitzhak Zamir made the point explicitly in a 1993 essay aptly titled "The LCG: Servant of the Public and Not of the Government." Bringer shows how the "public interest" swiftly became an abstract and normative ideal, not to be discerned or deduced but rather to be decided (or rather invented) by government attorneys themselves. Thus the "public interest" lost any connection (loose as it may have been) with the actual interest of the public – and the LCG's only "genuine client" is the public interest as conceptualized exclusively by the LCG and Supreme Court. Over time the adjacent and equally vague concepts of "the rule of law" and "fundamental values" were added to the mix.

This significant pivot was of course noticed and criticized by contemporary scholars in real time. Ruth Gavison warned against taking the "public-interest-as-client" metaphor too seriously – to state the obvious, the public is a diffuse, nameless, faceless customer, and its "interest" is as open to interpretation and debate as any question in democratic government can be. Government attorneys indeed ought to serve the public interest, but this is typically understood to mean simply that they need not support actions clearly outside the scope of official state duties – that is, their role is to assist government organs carrying out their designated functions. Turning the limiting factor of "public interest" into the primary so-called client is an immense distortion. Conveniently, this amenable client may never complain, nor protest, nor disagree with the LCG's determination of its best interests; indeed, no LCG has ever been fired, to date, by the public interest. More to the point, identifying or defining the public interest – whether literal or even figurative – is the core challenge of democracy itself. The entire edifice of elections, public discourse, accountable representative government and much else besides is specifically designed for the ambitious endeavor of finding and serving the public interest, which nonetheless remains in a state of constant (likely permanent) flux and dispute. It is stranger still, to say the least, to claim that a group of bureaucrats isolated from the electorate are better judges of the public interest than the people actually elected by and accountable to the public.[26]

Even if we were to accept the wisdom and feasibility of a "rule of law ombudsman" – a separate institution (effectively a fourth branch of government) wholly dedicated to curtailing governmental transgressions – there seems no reason to do so at the expense of the government's own legal services. One can argue (albeit weakly) for a "gatekeeping" apparatus while still conceding the government's need for genuine legal counsel and assistance. Yet by defecting to the other side, the LCG essentially (and quite intentionally) robs the government of its own legal counsel and leaves it stripped of a key governing mechanism. It seems hard to justify depriving the duly authorized and legitimate government of its "assistance of counsel" – a privilege extended to virtually any citizen and even to the common criminal. Gavison wryly notes that there is a tangible "public interest" that the government receive high quality legal advice and support so it can function effectively and can successfully advance the agenda for which it was elected; yet it is precisely this important function which is undermined by the "gatekeepers" denying the government meaningful legal assistance.

Another objection is the simplistic and contradictory allusion to the "rule of law." Purporting to uphold the rule of law, the "gatekeeper" rationale violates that very principle at least three times over: First, by formulating the approach itself without the flimsiest legal basis. Second, as demonstrated throughout this chapter, the substantive positions adopted by the LCG as "gatekeeper" regularly contradict the rule of law by espousing patently erroneous and unfounded legal arguments. Third, at its most basic, the rule of law means that a society is governed by known rules and not by the pure will of individuals, as famously expressed in the phrase "a government of laws and not of men," or as succinctly summarized in Justice Scalia's essay title "The Rule of Law as a Law of Rules." Yet the "gatekeeper" model translates the arbitrary whims of a single unelected and unremovable legal bureaucrat into staggering and centralized de facto policy-making power – reducing the notion of rule of law into something closer to rule of lawyers.

Perhaps the most obvious criticism of all relates to fundamental democratic norms of accountable and lawful government. Liberal-democratic thought rejects any assumption that state officials can competently and faithfully perceive and pursue the "public interest" in a manner detached from the actual public. It's no coincidence that authoritarian regimes claim to speak "for the people" while avoiding tangible popular oversight, or that it is typically countries like China and North Korea that include "people's republic" in their title. By severing the connection between lawyer (LCG) and actual client (executive government), the "gatekeeper" rationale simply seeks to justify a rogue state organ untethered to the law and unaccountable to neither the public nor the elected government hierarchy. A civil servant with the power to impose policies and decisions upon all executive government in the name of "the public interest" is simply incongruous with the democratic order.

The proponents of "gatekeeping" – the Hebrew term translating literally as "threshold guardian" – always appeared blissfully unaware of the resemblance to Platonic "guardians" better known as philosopher-kings. In arguing for the gatekeeping rationale its advocates actively support one of the most famous and ancient anti-democratic models known within the field of political theory. This irony is entirely lost on them. The ignorance of this terminological and substantive point is so pervasive that it yields some amusing (or unsettling) statements: In 2021, during his first speech as newly appointed Minister of Justice, a senior politician favoring judicial supremacy rhetorically asked "who will guard the guardians?" and then answered "I will." Instead of the original and typical meaning of supervising those who wield power, this speaker meant he would *protect* the so-called guardians, thus comically and obliviously inverting one of the most basic precepts of Western political insight.* We can hardly blame him for this faux pas – in a legal environment that champions "gatekeeping" as a valid justification for undemocratic power, the ancient adage of *quis custodiet ipsos custodes* must inevitably lose all meaning.

Despite such objections and others, the "gatekeeping" rationale successfully took hold. Bringer documents this process and notes how the ethos developed and matured swiftly and fairly recently, a late elaboration on the familiar "authorized interpreter of the law." In 2008 the term was virtually unused and almost unheard-of, when a government commission issued a draft report regarding the legal advice unit for individual government Ministries. In the draft, the report authors described the role of a "public" attorney as "gatekeeper against unlawful action and violations of the rule of law," a role which he must fulfill "to the best of his judgment without fear of elected and appointed ranks." Instead of a government employee tasked with assisting government action and policy, the report envisioned legal advisors primarily as a curb on government action. The Minister of Justice at the time, Daniel Friedmann, forcefully objected to such a formulation and the draft report was never adopted. Instead, the Government passed a 2009 resolution stating the exact opposite – that "the public attorney must act to advise and assist" the policies of his respective Ministry and must "do as much as possible to implement" such policies "swiftly and efficiently" within the constraints of the law.

This repudiation made little impression, in a pattern which is by now familiar. Only months after the unequivocal Government resolution, the LCG issued new guidelines for Ministerial legal advice departments. The new guidelines open with the requirement that any government attorney serve as "gatekeeper" and act for the advancement of the rule of law – the first time "gatekeeper" appeared in formal LCG guidelines. The LCG went so far as to claim that these new guidelines were based on the recent Government resolution, even though the "gatekeeper" formulation was expressly *rejected* by that same resolution. Bringer shows how prior to 2009 the term "gatekeeper" was virtually absent from public and legal discourse regarding the LCG and government attorneys, yet from 2009 onwards the phrase rapidly entered into any reference of the LCG's role and duties.

The enthusiastic adoption of the "gatekeeper" myth eventually reached near-farcical proportions. Former-LCG Mandelblit proclaimed in a 2023 speech that Israel's "founding fathers considered the Legal Counsel to the Government and the Supreme Court to be the independent gatekeepers protecting the liberal-democratic system of government in Israel," making it the right and "duty" of these gatekeepers to annul impermissible legislation. Aside this being

---

* The bizarre statement did not go unnoticed, with one commentator in a leading newspaper observing the "political parody" created by the new Minister.

demonstrably false hogwash, it is a useful example of how far the "gatekeeper" myth has come from its obscurity in 2009.

*

Among the many far-reaching implications of such a paradigm shift is the de facto divorce from any commitment to serving or advancing concrete governmental agenda and interests. The LCG and state legal corps came to see the government itself – in all its manifestations – as just one object of their fidelity, and by far not the most important. The gatekeeper ethos supplanting actual government with the putative public interest serves as the theoretical framework for the LCG to directly and diametrically oppose government policy and efforts. No longer was the LCG required to play the ugly caterpillar serving petty politicians and commonplace public officials; he could now emerge from his legal cocoon as glorious gatekeeper, free to flutter amongst his own ideals of the rule of law and fundamental values.

Critically, the practical expression of these vague ideals all comes down to one discernible principle. Dotan explains that the underlying values of the "rule of law" and "public interest" championed by the LCG are simply those "manifested by the institution of the HCJ [the Supreme Court] itself," and that the LCG became an organ "that is primarily accountable to the HCJ and serves as its extension…"[27] In Dotan's words, the "practical expression" of the LCG's espousing of the rule of law is simply "a deep commitment to the positions, the views and the rulings of the Supreme Court Justices"; a commitment to the legal system and judiciary no less important than its duty towards government agencies.[28] Dr. Eitan Levontin (whose work we will encounter later on) observes that this "adoption of the judicial ethos" means the LCG "tends to judge the government instead of representing the government."[29]

Thus, upholding "the rule of law" in the name of "the public interest" is far from vague and in fact carries a distinct meaning – an institutional alignment with the Supreme Court, such that the Legal Counsel to the Government sees itself committed above all else to the Court and its jurisprudence of judicial supremacy. The institution of the LCG endeavors to bolster the Supreme Court at every possible opportunity. The rare occasions in which the two institutions clash stem from differing views on tactics, not strategy, or from the LCG's poor estimation of the Court's expectations and preferences. Here we may observe the full extent of the LCG's extraordinary role-reversal – from faithful organ of the Executive government supporting its interests in the legal sphere, to hostile agent embedded within the Executive in service of the judiciary and primarily its apex tier.

The gatekeeper ethos thus complements our portrait of LCG as Supreme Court proxy within the Executive branch. Not only is their counsel binding; not only do they wield the vacuous legal concepts developed by the Court; they are also unencumbered by any obligation to serve the government and its interests and can indeed exercise these powers to hinder and foil government action. Presumably legal counsel ought assist "tangible" government according to its best effort and by providing the best available legal argument – yet under the gatekeeper ethos, this idea simply does not exist. The LCG and accompanying legal corps have come to view themselves as nothing short of a bulwark *against* government. It is for this reason, and upon this foundation, that the LCG regularly issues legal opinions forcefully opposing government decisions on the flimsiest of legal grounds, even when perfectly valid legal arguments are readily available or where such objections come down to purely ideological extra-legal disagreement.

In the HBO hit series Game of Thrones, Varys the spymaster is asked by Eddard Stark who he truly serves. Varys memorably answers: "The Realm, my Lord. Someone must." Much like our Legal Counsel to the Government, Varys too eschews assisting the Kingdom's actual governing institutions and officials; Varys too professes he serves the abstract, diffuse, inchoate ideals of society at large. In both cases the pretense is equally contrived as it is self-serving. Varys is a ruthless, scheming, sociopathic power-player. The LCG abuses the rule of law in its own name, undermines the public interest by eviscerating the public's elected representatives, makes a gross mockery of legal doctrine and practice, and violates basic norms of democratic self-government common to any free society. Only one of these characters is fictional.

Obstacles Spiritual and Temporal

The Legal Counsel to the Government renders a legal opinion in some matter, adopting a position directly conflicting with the government's intended action or desired policy. What happens next? The practical effects of an allegedly-binding legal opinion are not immediately or intuitively obvious. It is therefore necessary to understand the material consequences of "binding counsel" in the real world.

The single most dramatic implication relates to LCG's representation of government in litigation proceedings. As we shall discuss further on, the LCG monopoly over government representation in court heavily relies on the notion of the LCG's binding legal opinion as "authorized interpreter of the law." This is easily the most significant and most egregious consequence of "binding counsel." One scholar has suggested that the "binding counsel" model only emerged as a post-hoc justification for the litigation monopoly, a contention supported by the chronological order of their respective appearance.[30] However, we will set this issue aside for the moment, as the LCG monopoly over government representation is treated thoroughly and as a separate matter later in this chapter. Nonetheless, the binding counsel model has a number of other practical effects which are isolated from the "monopoly" question and which are worth our attention.

On a side note, the very concept of LCG "opinions and guidelines" is somewhat murky. While constantly maintaining that these effectively possess the force of law, the Court has refused to treat them with the same standards that apply to other legal norms. In one glaring example from 2022, the Court refused to require their publication under the Freedom of Information Act and generally released the LCG from any obligation of officially publishing the legal opinions they regularly issue to government organs and agencies. This would seem odd, as by the Court's own "binding counsel" approach such opinions easily meet the standards of constituting a legal norm requiring promulgation under statutory law.

The Court tried to explain this discrepancy by distinguishing between administrative directives which must be published, and legal opinions which are merely interpretations. In the Court's words, the latter "do not prescribe the manner in which governmental authority should be exercised… but rather clarify the binding interpretation of the law for the government, thereby defining the boundaries of what is permissible and prohibited in its actions."[31] Here as elsewhere, the artificial distinction between "prescribing how authority is exercised" and "defining the boundaries of permissible and prohibited actions" is almost laughable. As one prominent attorney observed, this meant creating a class of de facto "hidden law" which ostensibly binds the government yet which need not be made public and which often remains shrouded in secrecy.[32]

A primary consequence of the "binding counsel" model is that the LCG has become increasingly bold in treating such legal opinions as law for all intents and purposes, at times to devastating effect. In doing so the LCG has recently developed a novel construct called the "legal obstacle." When a government action is deemed unlawful by the LCG he may proclaim a "legal obstacle" and inform the relevant organ or official that they are proscribed from proceeding with such action or policy. The language employed is important, as the term "obstacle" deviates from the notion of a mere legal opinion and poses as an absolute and immovable reality, almost a law of physics as tangible as gravity. A "legal obstacle" conveys that the action under consideration is impossible and cannot be taken, period. Not simply legal advice with which one can disagree, not even just an "interpretation" of the law; an asserted "legal obstacle" treats the action as though a judicial determination has already occurred and the action under review already rendered illegal and void in the most technical and official sense.

The "legal obstacle" was formalized and expanded in recent years under LCG Avichai Mandelblit, who effectively adopted the most extreme version of the "binding counsel" model. In a 2018 speech (among many other instances), Mandelblit stated that "an action contradicting an LCG legal opinion which declares a legal obstacle is an action against the law."[33] As part of this process, Mandelblit also instituted what he called the "traffic light" system in which the LCG informs the government whether it has a green light (no legal objections), a yellow light (some legal "difficulties" that require consideration and review), or a red light (a "legal obstacle" rendering the action illegal). Justice (and former LCG) Menny Mazuz clarified in 2017 that these "traffic light" colors do not at all correspond to the degree that an objection is legally plausible or well-founded – a Yellow or even obstacle-yielding Red light is not necessarily derived from firmer legal grounds (e.g., an explicit statutory provision). Per Mazuz, such a determination by the LCG might be based on a "feeling" that an action is "inconsistent" with "legal principles," and the LCG is at liberty to halt government policy if his "legal intuitions" say it's unlawful, even if he "can't identify a statute or ruling" to support this assertion.[34] Needless to say, such alleged illegality includes the limitless range of policy and value-based objections stemming from unreasonableness, objective purposive interpretation, and other equally vacuous quasi-legal concepts.

The adoption of this new and aggressive posture further demonstrates the manner in which the LCG views itself as a judicial organ – from their perspective, the "legal obstacle" is indistinguishable from a writ of mandamus issued by a court, a direct and mandatory order to refrain from a specific action.* The Hebrew word used for "obstacle" (*meni'a*, from the linguistic root of "prevent") is tellingly the same as the one for a judicial mandamus order. Aharon Garber points out the jarring reality of this new construct – the LCG's power indeed surpasses that of a court of law, as the latter requires a rigid formal process to issue an injunction (typically including public deliberation and reasoning, several filings or hearings, a multi-member panel, and adversarial argumentation) while the former simply requires the unilateral pronouncement of a single individual.

One extraordinary effect of the "legal obstacle" method is its direct application by the LCG to junior executive officials tasked with carrying out their respective duties, completely bypassing the executive hierarchy and governmental chain-of-command. Instead of addressing the *decisionmaker* responsible for a given objectionable action or policy, the LCG simply directs the specific government employee executing policy – employees who are nominally subordinate to the relevant government Minister or decisionmaker. Having asserted a "legal obstacle" regarding a given Ministerial action or policy, the LCG may then proceed to approach inferior executive officials and units with operative instructions superseding those received from their superiors. In one instance in 2020 challenging a series of appointments within the Ministry of Religious Services, the LCG didn't only tell the Minister to rescind the appointments, but also wrote directly to the Ministry's legal office and requested to inform the appointees that their appointment was void. In another instance, a controversial 2015 report by the LCG regarding a major semi-governmental agency included direct and explicit instructions to governmental accountants and financial officers, requiring that they adhere to new funding conditions set out in the report and that they withhold transferring funds when such conditions are not met.[35]

One striking example in 2020 involved an exchange of public and acerbic letters between the LCG office and David Amsalem, a Cabinet Minister in charge of state-owned corporations. Amsalem instructed the Chairman of the Government Companies Authority – his subordinate – to change the way state corporation board-members were selected due to perceived flaws in the existing process. Though this was a decision well within the Minister's statutory authority, the LCG issued a legal opinion that the Minister was not free to restructure the selection process outside

* I thank Aharon Garber for this insight likening the "obstacle" to a mandamus order.

specific guidelines (defined by the LCG). Amsalem rejected this position and ordered his subordinate to proceed. In a remarkable escalation, the LCG then personally directed the Authority Chairman to disregard his superior's instructions.[36] In his enraged reply Amsalem described the LCG's move as an attempt to usurp executive government and to prevent Government Ministers from carrying out their duties as authorized by law. Amsalem clarified that the Chairman's compliance with the LCG's demands would mean the latter is the Chairman's de facto superior and manager. Making good on this statement a few weeks later, Amsalem refused to provide his Ministerial approval (authorizing financial reports and other important proceedings of a specific government corporation), and instead pointed the Chairman to his new "de facto" bosses at the LCG office.[37]

A much more disconcerting event occurred during the 2023 demonstrations against the government judicial-reform proposals. The reader may recall Tel Aviv police District Commander Ami Eshed from Chapter 7 above – Eshed was sympathetic to illegal road-blockings by protestors which were causing constant disruption to local and national daily life. There we had seen how the absence of any local input into the District Commander's appointment or tenure meant that police priorities favored national politics (or at minimum, the internal police hierarchy or other considerations) over the concerns and interests of local residents. We now revisit the affair from a different angle. In March of 2023, the Minister for National Security and the Police Commissioner announced a slew of appointments within the National Police, including the transfer of Eshed to lead the Training and Education Department. Though this was technically a promotion, it was undoubtedly also crafted to remove Eshed from his position as Tel Aviv District Commander in light of his unsatisfactory (and visibly politically-biased) handling of the roadblocks and other illegal protest tactics.

The LCG Gali Baharav-Miara (herself forcefully opposed to the reform proposals and sympathetic to the protest movement) responded immediately by "freezing" – yes, freezing – Eshed's new appointment. In a letter to the Minister and Police Commissioner early the next morning, the LCG expressed her "grave concerns" regarding the "legality" of their decision, including its background and the "material considerations" on which it was based. As such the LCG "instructed" all relevant parties to "freeze any action or decision" regarding Eshed. Her letter concluded by clarifying that "Commander Eshed shall remain in his current position" until a full review is completed. The forceful language used by Baharav-Miara – instruct, freeze, shall remain – is not incidental and accurately reflects the perception of LCG legal pronouncement as indistinguishable from judicial orders. Equally noteworthy is that the legal case for the LCG's position was of course non-existent. Her letter was published before seeking any response or clarification from the Minister himself, such that the "considerations" behind the decision she found so concerning were not known to her or rather only assumed. (Aharon Garber has noted that the weaker the LCG's legal argument, the likelier they are to trot out a claim of "legal obstacles.")

Still, it worked. The Commissioner buckled the same day and announced he would conform to the LCG's "legal opinion" which "obligates" the national police. The decision was rescinded against the Minister of National Security's wishes and Eshed remained District Commander for another five (decisive) months. The Police Commissioner knew precisely where his bread was buttered and where his loyalties lie.

The Eshed saga usefully demonstrates several distinct points. In the context of the previous chapter on criminal justice, we come full circle and see how the elected and accountable Minister is at times utterly powerless to effect change within their respective spheres of legitimate and lawful authority, and how law enforcement agencies and legal institutions can work in tandem to neuter governmental oversight. This extends to (and is most troubling regarding) the fundamental principle of civilian control over police organizations and their personnel. The result was that thanks to LCG intervention and Commissioner complicity, with no legal basis, Ami Eshed was irremovable at the critical moment his superiors required it. Unsurprisingly, the Police Commissioner that folded is the same one who a year later railed against the loss of "autonomy" for the Police and vowed to ensure its immunity from "political" intervention. The implications and consequences of such a system are ominous.

Back to our current subject, the Eshed affair shows just how potent the "binding counsel" model has become in its own right. Any superficial knee-jerk objection to lawful government action may be coated in the terminology of "legal obstacle," which is then addressed directly at career bureaucrats tasked with executing the government policy being challenged. Faced with the excruciating dilemma of disobeying superior orders or risking the wrath of the entire LCG behemoth (or worse), even the most well-meaning and faithful government employees would likely opt for the former. More realistically, it is not uncommon for the subordinate civil servant to welcome such legal intervention and gladly comply against the wishes of their (transient and perhaps distasteful) elected superiors.

A further recent development (partially demonstrated above) is the dilution of legal "opinion" to mean just anything the LCG says or claims – without even the appearance of legal reasoning or form. Legal counsel usually comes in writing, as memoranda or guidelines (however flimsy their legal basis), but at times a "legal obstacle" might be born solely from the bald assertion of illegality. In October 2024, Police Commissioner Daniel Levi announced a reshuffle of senior police roles which included appointing the current Police Legal Advisor, Elazar Kahane, to another position. The move was widely interpreted as Kahane's removal from office, due to his signing a public letter which objected to a controversial police promotion made by the Minister of National Security.

Within hours of the Commissioner's announcement the LCG (Gali Baharav-Miara) issued a letter denouncing Kahane's removal, claiming the decision was "without justification" and that the LCG should have been "involved." Of the document's five short paragraphs, only two had some semblance of legal reasoning: the LCG argued that the Police Legal Counsel was an internal "gatekeeper" and as such any decision regarding their position must be "in consultation with" the LCG. The letter did not refer to any recognizable legal authority to back up this novel claim – statutory provisions, judicial precedent, internal police rules, historical conventions, even LCG guidelines, were all notably absent. In other words, the LCG did not even bother going through the motions to produce something that might qualify as a "legal opinion," even for the sake of appearance. Still, Baharav-Miara concluded the letter by instructing the Commissioner to "freeze" any plans regarding the Police Legal Advisor role. The LCG's language – "do not proceed" – clearly indicated she considered the letter to be a compulsory order.

Commissioner Levi responded that, "respectfully," he was not familiar with any legal obligation to consult with the LCG or let alone receive her approval for the promotion or transfer of senior police leadership, which in this case followed all the standard organizational procedures for such decisions. Levi objected that the LCG's argument would effectively usurp his lawful authority as Police Commissioner. He was of course correct on both counts.

The LCG's astonishing reply was quick to come. Baharav-Miara reiterated that the Police was "obligated" by the LCG's "directives" and accused the Commissioner of ignoring "the law" from which he was "not exempt." She concluded her letter by warning that "any action" proceeding with the planned role change "would be unlawful." This letter exhibited a notable escalation in rhetoric – the first letter described the Commissioner's decision as "unprecedented" and "of questionable legality" but fell short of pronouncing the act illegal. The LCG's shift from "questionable" to "unlawful" only makes sense in the context of binding counsel: while Levi's original decision was problematic, the patently illegal action would be ignoring the LCG's order to freeze Kahane's removal. In other words, the LCG's first letter asserting the need for her involvement and ordering a halt became "the law" upon its inception, a mandamus in the most literal and immediate sense. In the LCG's view the Commissioner was violating positive law simply by non-compliance with the LCG's five-paragraph letter, a document not even approaching the form or substance of a "legal opinion."

The Commissioner caved one week later. Though he offered some excuse for changing tack, and despite initially dismissing the second letter and welcoming a potential showdown, it was clear he had now backed away from the fight. Kahane's thwarted removal is especially instructive as it illustrates the relentless advance (and inevitable conclusion) of the "binding counsel" model, coming ever closer to the most baseless LCG decrees – absurd on their face and without even the pretense of legal justification – becoming "law" for almost all intents and purposes.

These instances (and many others) demonstrate the impact of "binding counsel" and "legal obstacles" without the need of any judicial intervention whatsoever. In all these cases the very assertion of illegality was sufficient to impede or terminate the governmental action in question.

The second significant discernible effect of the "binding counsel" model comes into play with the Supreme Court's use of interim measures – such as Temporary Restraining Orders – to hinder government action. In a growing number of cases involving LCG objections to government policy, the Court has issued temporary orders halting the policy while offering little to no elaboration on their legal reasoning for doing so. While the Court has never conclusively ruled (as explained above) that the LCG's opinion binds the government regardless of its merit, it does indeed seem increasingly willing to treat the opinion as obligatory in ways which are less formal and final.

In February of 2020, acting Minister of Justice Amir Ohana initiated a governmental commission which would report on the state of the *Mahash* Internal Affairs unit, especially in light of dwindling public confidence in the agency. The motion to appoint the commission was expected to be approved by the Government, which served in an interim "caretaker" capacity approaching new national elections. The LCG Avichai Mandelblit objected to this proposal in advance and issued an opinion, not only describing the legal grounds for his objection but also invoking the new "legal obstacle" claim and stating that the Government was simply barred from making the decision. Mandelblit was essentially arguing that his say-so as LCG was binding in its own right, regardless of underlying legal justification, and that the Government was obligated to adhere to his stated position. After having duly considered the LCG's objection, the Government proceeded to vote in favor and appointed the commission.

The resolution was immediately challenged in the Supreme Court, though the material legal argument against appointing the committee was unlikely to succeed. The petition (and LCG) relied on the Court's rule that "transitional" governments could not effect significant long-term irreversible change. Aside from the rule itself being a weak judicial fiction (see Chapter 5 above), it almost certainly would not have applied to the current circumstances. Appointing a committee is hardly a major or irreversible decision – any subsequent government could easily disband it, replace the members, appoint a new competing commission, or just ignore the commission report and conclusions.* If the Court previously ruled that a caretaker government could negotiate a peace-deal with Palestinians, it seems implausible that it can't appoint a commission to examine the organizational structure of a law enforcement agency. In addition, the LCG's objection was especially suspect, as the Internal Affairs unit was formally under his own responsibility and jurisdiction. The commission was tasked with examining a unit which directly reports to the State Attorney and the LCG himself, and had an explicit mandate to consider whether the unit ought to be removed from the LCG's direct authority. As such the LCG had an acute personal and institutional interest in avoiding or delaying such unwelcome scrutiny.

Regardless of all this, both the petitioners and the LCG himself argued that

* The last option would frankly continue a time-honored tradition shared by all established democracies.

the LCG's objections were sufficient grounds to prevent the Government from proceeding with the commission (and its resolution therefore illegal and void), entirely separate from any substantive legal arguments and even under the LCG's current conflict of interest.

Within two weeks from the Government resolution appointing the commission, the Supreme Court issued a temporary injunction freezing any activity of the commission pending further thorough adjudication.[38] The order effectively buried the commission – a new Government was formed following elections, and the incoming Minister of Justice (sympathetic to judicial supremacy) had no interest in advancing the commission's activity. Indeed, the commission remained in limbo until it was finally disbanded by the Court exactly one year after its appointment due to the Minister's clear lack of any desire to initiate its examination.

Just a few months earlier in December of 2019, a separate but weirdly similar drama unfolded with many of the same characters reprising their roles. The beleaguered Shai Nitzan had completed his tenure as State Attorney and was stepping down from his position, while the existing "caretaker" government (same as above) had yet to nominate Nitzan's successor. Acting Minister of Justice Amir Ohana sought to appoint an interim State Attorney – a regular State Attorney could not be appointed, ironically, due to the Supreme Court's jurisprudence limiting the actions of a caretaker government. The applicable statutory law was unequivocal, granting any Minister the authority to appoint an interim official to vacant roles within their Ministry.[39] Ohana announced he was considering five candidates, and eventually named a seasoned and widely respected criminal prosecutor, Orly Ben-Ari, to the post.

LCG Avichai Mandelblit immediately asserted a "legal obstacle," claiming that Ohana's selection was illegal due to its "extreme deviation from the sphere of reasonableness." Whether Ben-Ari was a good pick for the role is immaterial – the authority to appoint her as interim State Attorney was Ohana's alone. Mandelblit nonetheless raised various objections regarding Ben-Ari's suitability and regarding Ohana's duty to heed the LCG's "advice" – and he was just warming up. In a series of legal opinions and public statements, Mandelblit outdid himself and posed the glorious argument that only one such "reasonable" candidate existed: a Mr. Shlomo Lemberger, the serving Deputy State Attorney. Even in the warped world of Israeli lawlessness this was an extraordinary take. Mandelblit was suggesting that his own view regarding the most "reasonable" candidate ought to prevail over the Minister's explicit statutory authority to appoint an interim State Attorney, and that Ohana essentially could make only one, single, solitary lawful choice by appointing Mr. Lemberger. Any choice aside the one imposed by Mandelblit was unreasonable and therefore unlawful. In Mandelblit's own words:

> "It is my position that Attorney Shlomo (Momi) Lamberger – whom I recommended to you for this position – is significantly and substantially

> more qualified for the role in question than Attorney Ben-Ari, whom you chose to appoint."[40]

The LCG's cartoonish argument exposed "reasonableness" for what many critics had claimed it was all along – a blunt instrument used to dictate specific choices and outcomes with no relation to law. Yet his opposition was ultimately successful. Ohana's decision to appoint Ben-Ari was challenged in a Supreme Court petition echoing Mandelblit's assertions of illegality. Only two days after the appointment was announced, during the opening minutes of Ben-Ari's official commencement ceremony, the Supreme Court issued a dramatic temporary injunction freezing Ben-Ari's appointment. The one-line judicial decision from Justice (and former LCG) Menny Mazuz offered no explanation and led to immediate chaos and disarray.

The next day Orly Ben-Ari withdrew her candidacy for the role.

Taken together, these two consecutive confrontations between Mandelblit and Ohana are highly instructive. In both cases a lawful government decision was effectively thwarted by the combination of an asserted "legal obstacle" and a judicial order for ostensibly interim relief. In both cases the legal argument against the government decision was weak bordering on the ludicrous, and it seems doubtful the Supreme Court would have intervened without the additional weight and assistance of the LCG's adverse legal opinion. It is the "binding counsel" and its alleged violation which gives lawful government action the aura of illegality, which in turn is just enough to support an unexplained order crushing the decision in question. The metaphysical-spiritual obstacle conjured by the LCG is translated into an acutely tangible-temporal obstacle in the form of judicial order. The Court avoids any scrutiny or consequences, as the need for presenting legal justification or reasoning evaporates once the temporary order renders the government decision moot or ineffectual, and both decision and litigation are abandoned. Tactical and surgical use of temporary orders – and the Court's willingness to employ them – should thus be seen as yet another important practical effect of the "binding counsel" model.

Both events are useful case-studies in a much broader sense, in that they contain many elements of Israeli judicial supremacy discussed earlier in this book. Both involve first-instance petitions to the Supreme Court by uninvolved NGOs with no standing, on non-justiciable issues of policy and appointments, alleging vague legal grounds of unreasonableness or creatively far-fetched interpretations of unambiguous statutory provisions. These are strong examples of how the doctrines and systems discussed in previous chapters coalesce and crystalize into concrete, tangible results, though in a manner much more subtle than dramatic overt judicial rulings.

Of equal note, both cases demonstrate the reciprocal relationship between judicial supremacy and law-enforcement institutions in which the Supreme Court shields near-autonomous prosecutorial agencies from the oversight of elected government. The previous chapter covered instances of vindictive and at times repressive conduct by law-enforcement towards critics of – or threats to – the expansion of judicial power. Here, as elsewhere, we see the Court returning the favor. The *Mahash* commission could potentially have led to the unit's removal from LCG and State Attorney control, thus exposing the Police to more direct and proactive scrutiny; Ohana's appointment of an interim State Attorney (not from a narrow slate of curated candidates filtered and approved by the LCG) may well have resulted in a State Prosecution less beholden to its own institutional dominance and Court-aligned interests. In the space of just a few months and in just a few lines of judicial orders, the Supreme Court "saved" the country's two primary law-enforcement agencies from increased democratic oversight. The system always protects itself.

While interim measures are a strong (albeit implicit) judicial expression of the "binding counsel" model, some Justices are not content with repeating the mantra and are getting creepingly closer to officially (and explicitly) treating LCG legal opinions as though they were statutory law. A number of dissenting opinions (which have the habit of being treated, when convenient, as binding precedent) have featured the argument that ignoring or defying an LCG "legal opinion" may be construed as a "procedural flaw," thus creating sufficient basis for pronouncing illegality. This new construct utterly conflates the two distinctly separate grounds for administrative judicial review – illegality and procedural flaws. In the *Minnes* case discussed above, a dissenting opinion by Justice Khaled Kabub argued that the government's appointment of Odelia Minnes against the LCG's advice amounted to a flaw in the decision-making process significant enough to render the decision illegal, despite agreeing that the LCG's legal position itself was erroneous. In Kabub's words: "We must not become accustomed to administrative decisions being taken while disregarding legal opinions of the Legal Counsel to the Government, and without substantial justification." Kabub states his view that the fact that the LCG's opinion was patently wrong ought to be given "limited" weight when considering whether there was a procedural flaw.[41] Other Justices have intimated similar sentiments in oral arguments, including administrative-law expert Justice Daphne Barak-Erez.

Treating any arbitrary and often unfounded LCG quasi-legal fever-dream as a black-box shell which obligates the Government no matter its content involves its own deep irony: Four decades of radically expansionist jurisprudence pursued increasingly penetrating review of the substance and content of any government decision or policy against all established precedent and principles of democratic government, yet any unilateral specious pronouncement of the LCG is to be taken at face-value to the extent that elected government must conform or risk their decision be voided due to the resulting "procedural flaw."

Beyond the Executive

We have so far discussed the LCG's considerable power over executive policy and decision-making through the mechanism of binding legal "advice." Yet a large portion of the LCG's activity and influence belongs to a separate category – that of its "legislative" division. The Legal Counsel to the Government is the formal body charged with assisting Executive-initiated legislation in all stages of deliberation and drafting, including statutory regulations and bylaws (also known as "secondary" legislation), through the LCG legislative division and through the separate Ministerial legal advice units (which, as mentioned above, are "professionally" subject to the LCG's authority and oversight). The vast majority of legislation and rulemaking which is ultimately enacted in Israel is "governmental" – that is, initiated by the various Ministries and supported by the governing Coalition in Knesset. As such, input into (and some control over) the final product of government legislation amounts to substantial influence over the entire legislative field. Throughout the process of discussing and drafting new legislation or amending existing provisions the omnipresent "gatekeeper" attorneys actively monitor and participate in every stage to ensure the "public interest" is upheld. All the aforementioned tools, chief among them the "traffic light" system culminating in a decree of "legal obstacles," are employed by the LCG to mold legislation and to direct legislative initiatives so that these conform to the LCG's views.*

There is no question that the government typically requires the assistance of a competent legal department when forming rules and legislation. Indeed, much of the work performed by skilled attorneys at the LCG legislative division is vital and productive, faithfully supporting government initiatives in an ordered, disciplined and professional manner. Yet as is perhaps a recurring theme in the Israeli legal system, the exception undermines the rule – and the LCG's chokehold over government rulemaking becomes yet another power mechanism imposing the views of judicial supremacy.

In 2017 the LCG legislative division circulated an "internal guide" for its work on primary and secondary legislation.[42] The 84-page document is illuminating and chillingly candid regarding how the LCG views itself. The guide predictably defines the division's role as "gatekeeper" responsible for "maintaining the rule of law." The division may object to, delay, or effectively halt government legislation for a host of reasons, many of them blatantly arbitrary or subjective. What might justify the red light of a "legal obstacle" determination which stops a piece of government legislation in its tracks? The guide mentions any objection vaguely based on the State's "existing constitutional framework" or "the legal system's fundamental principles" (these are verbatim quotes). Needless to say, such standards might include various requirements relating to reasonableness, proportionality, justice, equality, alleged human rights and essentially any worthy cause one considers "fundamental." Another option is a "severe flaw" in the "administrative process" which preceded the legislation – as we've learned, this could mean just about anything, perhaps including even an earlier objection by

---

* I am indebted to Gil Bringer for his comprehensive essay and his clarifying comments on this matter.

the LCG himself. A yellow light ("legal difficulty") could stem from an even wider array of causes, including deviations from "standard" legislative templates (themselves defined by the LCG legislative division), contradiction of "accepted principles of legislative theory" (which are defined nowhere), or at times even if a policy or regulation is based on a "problematic" interpretation of the law.

What are the consequences of red "light" from the LCG legislative division? "A legal obstacle regarding a legislative bill means that the legislation cannot be advanced within the legal framework of Israeli law." The guide employs Hebrew passive language (as is often the case in Israeli legal lingo) and treats the LCG pronouncements as an immovable reality, a law of natural physical immediacy, replete with blanket statements such as the one above. The phrase *cannot be* is typical here and throughout the LCG's legal declarations – not an opinion regarding the content of the law, not an estimation of what a court might decide, but simply a decree of that which lies outside the realm of possible action. Per the guide, the legislative or rule-creation process simply cannot proceed without the LCG's permission; like Han-Solo after being captured by Boba Fett, it is frozen in a state of half-life.

A yellow-light determination of a "legal difficulty" is not much better. Though legislation can proceed even if declared "difficult," the courtesy might be short-lived. The legislative division may still delay a "difficult" bill on two grounds: First, if the responsible government attorney senses that the Ministry advancing the bill is not engaging in constructive discussion "with an open heart and a willing spirit." (Again, verbatim). This is not satire – a junior attorney within the LCG legislative division can halt any legislative bill exhibiting signs of "legal difficulty" if they don't care for the Ministry's attitude. Gil Bringer wryly remarks that this amounts to "psychologization of the judicialization" of the legislative process. Second, such a bill may be delayed if the objection stems from a constitutional difficulty or "other substantive difficulty," if the bill contradicts an LCG official guideline or directive, or if the bill does not conform to "professional guidelines" or "legislative templates" provided by LCG legislative division. It would thus seem that a yellow light may halt legislation in its tracks just as easily as would a red light, with one significant difference: while a "legal obstacle" regarding primary legislation can only be declared by the LCG himself, a "legal difficulty" and ensuing block can be determined by just about any government attorney within the legislative division.

In the event of a suspected "legal obstacle" or "legal difficulty" the guide establishes a convoluted and laborious internal dispute-resolution process, the details of which the reader will be spared. Tellingly, the system conceives of an ongoing conversation between the LCG legislative division and the Ministerial legal advice unit – the office of the actual Minister or other professional players involved in the legislative initiative are deemed irrelevant. Under this arrangement the LCG and his Deputies may essentially delay the advance of an undesired bill indefinitely or until rendered moot.

The single most acute practical effect of a "legal obstacle" block or of a "legal difficulty" delay is that the offensive legislation is barred from being approved by a key committee – and thus from progressing through the legislative process. The guide states plainly and matter-of-factly that "the consequence of a legal obstacle to a bill is that it may not be presented to the Ministerial Legislative Committee." This Committee is comprised of various Government Ministers and headed by the Minister of Justice, and it decides the official Government position towards *all* proposed legislation in the Knesset. Any Government-sponsored or Ministry-initiated bill must receive the Committee's approval before advancing to the Knesset floor for debates and votes. In other words, per the LCG guide, the legislative division may prevent any draft bill from being added to the Committee agenda for deliberation and approval. Thus the fictions of "obstacle" or "difficulty" representing the LCG's objections are ultimately translated into the concrete result of being withheld from proceeding through a key stage in the legislative process.

Needless to say, none of this – no part of it – has any basis in existing statutory law or even in Supreme Court precedent. Aside the vague notion of gatekeeping, there is not the flimsiest legal basis for most of the guide's statements and purported rules. Nothing in Israeli law limits the content of a Ministerial bill or the process by which such a bill is composed and eventually proposed; nothing grants the LCG or any associated organ the right to delay (let alone veto) bills they find objectionable. The agenda of the Ministerial Legislative Committee is set by the Government Secretary and Ministers are free to propose any draft bill they please. Yet this hardly seems to matter – the LCG legislative division treats the "guide" as black-letter law, and the executive bureaucratic and political ranks are usually ill-equipped to mount any challenge. Occasionally certain Ministers or top aides are capable of standing their ground and putting up a fight; in most cases the bill sponsors will demurely yield to the dictates of the LCG.

This particular manifestation of the "binding counsel" model further demonstrates the potency of soft legal power in no need of direct judicial intervention. More importantly, the LCG's influence over almost all significant legislation is silent. Unlike most of the controversies discussed above which bore a highly public profile (e.g. closely-watched litigation or resistance against published legal opinions), the relentless interference with the legislative process and its contents by the LCG is mostly hidden from view and far removed from the public eye. Potential controversies are nipped at the bud, challenges against prevailing views within the legal establishment are quelled before they gain any momentum, and fundamental disputes about the content of laws are "resolved" (generally to the LCG's advantage) behind closed doors – all well before a first draft is presented before the Ministerial Legislative Committee or to the public.

Of course, at least in theory, the Knesset and Coalition may advance legislation on its own, without taking the route of a formal government-sponsored bill. After all, the Knesset is the State legislature entirely separate and autonomous from the executive branch. Legislation directly initiated by Members of Knesset are called "private" bills. Private bills are not, in principle, subject to oversight by the LCG and its subordinate sprawling legal bureaucracy, because they are a purely legislative effort which is not drafted or advance by a government department. Such private bills may therefore allow the Coalition (and Government) to advance key legislation outside the reach and without the intervention of the LCG.

Setting aside practical and procedural difficulties and limitations (for example, a Minister may not initiate a private bill), the Court and LCG have recently indicated their intention to clamp down on unruly private bills they perceive to be serving the Government's agenda. In the 2025 *Police Ordinance* ruling (discussed in Chapter 10), Justice Vogelman chastised the Knesset for doing so, explicitly calling out the attempt to avoid the LCG's "supervision," and warned that "private bills are not intended to serve as a 'bypass channel' for the Government to circumvent the mechanisms that apply to government bills."[43] It thus remains to be seen how much longer the Knesset can maintain its independence from direct LCG involvement in purely parliamentary legislative initiatives.

The Big Picture

During the peak of the 2023 protests against the proposals for judicial reform, some had begun to raise sinister questions regarding an ultimate showdown between the Government and the Court. One representative news article described the "nightmare scenario" in which the military, police and espionage organizations would face the dilemma whether to follow orders from their Ministerial superiors even if these contradicted explicit Supreme Court rulings. Implicit in these discussions was also the suggestion that, as has been known to happen from time to time throughout history, the military and law-enforcement would need to step in and depose the country's civil-political leadership. This scenario was indeed a troubling one from a sociological and pragmatic perspective (though I have doubts both as to its likelihood and as to whether the judicial supremacists viewed it as a nightmare) but should have seemed exceedingly simple from a legal perspective. The laws establishing and governing these state organs are explicit and unequivocal – the assorted defense, police and security services answer directly to the Executive. For example, Basic Law: The Military states that the Minister of Defense is in charge of the Military and that "The Military is subject to the authority of the Government." The chain of command is clear.

Yet those raising the "nightmare scenario" question seemed less certain. Some claimed not only that the military ought to prefer a Court order over an Executive order – but also that the military was equally obligated to defer to the Legal Counsel to the Government. The former head of Israel's internal security service said in an interview that "the entire defense establishment" are "bound by the law and act only according to law," which is "usually interpreted for them by the LCG" and the Supreme Court.[44] Even if faced with direct governmental orders these military and law enforcement organs "may not break the law" – as mediated to them by the LCG and the Court.[45] These statements echoed others voiced by legal scholars as well as retired military and law enforcement officials. Setting aside the thorny constitutional question of a clash between Court and Cabinet, here we find a willingness to treat LCG pronouncements as "hard" law regarding the most fundamental and fraught issues imaginable in a democratic regime.

A related controversy surrounds the scenario of an "incapacitated" Prime Minister. Statutory law mandates various arrangements for the event that a Prime Minister is "incapable" of carrying out his duties. The classic example for such an occurrence indeed transpired in 2006, when Prime Minister Ariel Sharon suffered a stroke and entered a coma.

After Benjamin Netanyahu was indicted as Prime Minister in 2020, some commentators began speculating that the LCG could declare Netanyahu to be "substantively incapacitated" due to his alleged conflicts of interest (and especially if he were to involve himself in initiatives affecting the judiciary or legal system). The argument went that the law didn't actually define incapacity and was subject, as a legal term, to the LCG's objective-purposive interpretation which would compel the Prime Minister and government. The LCG could therefore "declare" the Prime Minister's incapacity for a host of factors or causes if he thought the Prime Minister's ability to function (in any sense the LCG chooses) was sufficiently impaired. If ever actually invoked, the result would be that the LCG could end the tenure of any Prime Minister – however healthy and lucid – by simply announcing the latter's "substantive incapacity," once and for all replacing the electorate's role in judging the suitability and desirability (for which "substantive incapacity" really stands) of the State's premier.

The LCG at the time (Avichai Mandelblit) reportedly discussed the issue in internal forums and took care to issue no official denial that this was being actively contemplated. Scholars and jurists added fuel to the fire by arguing the LCG possessed this authority and encouraging the LCG to exercise it.[46] Some on the Supreme Court explicitly endorsed "substantive incapacity" – in a 2021 concurring opinion, Justice Meltzer stated that the authority to issue a "proclamation of incapacity" due to conflicts of interest "is exclusively in the hands of the LCG."[47] Ever since the idea was floated, the prospect of an "incapacity" stand-off has dogged Netanyahu and has cast a shadow over the entire relationship between the Government and LCG. Many understood Netanyahu's reluctance to engage with the 2023 legal reform proposals (or to violate the "conflicts" policy imposed on him by the LCG and Court) to be based on the suspicion that it would lead to a declaration of "substantive incapacity."

The fact that this argument was ludicrous from the outset – from the legal text to legislative history to democratic norms – or that its implementation was certain to set off an unprecedented crisis in a crisis-laden era, provided little reassurance. The Knesset took the initiative in 2023 and amended the Basic Law, specifying that "incapacity" related only to "physical or mental" impairment. Incredibly, the Supreme Court effectively invalidated the law by "interpreting" it to apply only after the next elections (in a move similar to the *Tiberias* case discussed in Chapter

3), leaving the door open for an LCG pronouncement.[48] As Netanyahu prepared to start giving testimony for his trial in 2024, a new petition demanded that the LCG declare Netanyahu temporarily "incapacitated" for the duration of his trial. Though the Court denied the specific petition, two out of three Justices were willing to accept "substantive incapacity" (determined by the LCG) as a legitimate legal construct.[49] Writing for the majority, Justice Ruth Ronen emphasized that: "Even though the statutory provision does not specify who is authorized to declare the Prime Minister temporarily incapacitated, this Court has been willing to recognize the LCG as possessing this authority."*

The conceptualization of LCG as definitive voice of the law has ramifications far beyond any particular instance or legal controversy, as it seeps into the broader psyche of public-political discourse. People that should know better freely broadcast and bandy about the "binding counsel" fiction; people that know no better are gradually taken for a ride, and become accustomed to the notion of an all-powerful shamanic attorney who may simply dictate to the government the outcomes of all political and policy questions based on a mindless and formless notion of all-encompassing non-law. The reckless and shameful conversations surrounding the military subjecting itself to the de facto authority of an unelected and unaccountable bureaucrat, or regarding the top attorney dismissing the Prime Minister with a declaration of "incapacity," perfectly exemplify this danger.

II – Monopoly

> "*The State's view – as presented to us and as is proper – is the one determined by the Legal Counsel to the Government.*"
> - Chief Justice Miriam Naor, HCJ Rehearing 3660/17, s. 45

> "*When I want your opinion, I'll give it to you.*"
> - Navy SEALs Master Chief, "G.I. Jane" (1997)

In the 2018 *Tnuva* case discussed in Chapter 5, the Court intervened with economic policy of Finance Minister Moshe Kahlon and ordered that he raise the regulated price of dairy products against his wishes. The reader might recall the striking declaration made by Justice Vogelman that "there do not exist any explanations" which could justify the Minister's refusal to raise dairy prices. How could he have said so, when the Minister's policy grounds and legal authority were readily available and clearly had some merit? The answer is as simple as it

* This is also a wonderful flourish of disingenuous hypocrisy from Ronen, as the amended law which the Court "delayed" until the next elections in fact defines the exact procedure for a declaration of incapacity, such that any alleged prior statutory ambiguity has already been dispelled.

is bleak: no one in that case actually defended the Minister's position. The Legal Counsel to the Government ostensibly represented the Finance Minister, but did so by *agreeing* with the petitioners and arguing *against* Kahlon's legally-valid policy decision. The only view ever entertained by the Court in the *Tnuva* case was the one alleging illegality of Kahlon's decision.

Justice Vogelman describes how at the initial hearing "the respondent's counsel has stated that the State agrees" to the issuance of a conditional (nisi) order against the respondent (the Minister of Finance); and later, that "the State has noted that under the current circumstances it consents to issuing" a final order (that is, accepting the petition). In other words, the Legal Counsel for the Government – speaking for the Minister of Finance against whom the case has been brought – agreed with the petitioners and encouraged the Court to comply with their demands. The LCG, speaking for "the State," politely noted that the Finance Minister himself objects to this legal forfeit by his own attorneys.

It therefore turns out that Vogelman wasn't entirely wrong. Within the constraints of the courtroom there truly "did not exist" any explanation to support the Minister's actions. This was not because no such explanation was conceivable, and not because of any weakness in the Minister's potential arguments. It was, rather, because the Minister of Finance himself had been shut out entirely from the legal proceedings against him. Though the decision being challenged was one he had made; though he was the named respondent; though he was the target of the final judicial order; Finance Minister Moshe Kahlon was not afforded the luxury of legal representation for his position or views. Instead, Minister Kahlon was silenced by his sole putative "representative" in Court – the LCG – who spoke in Kahlon's own voice against him.

In his decision, Vogelman was entirely unfazed by this state of affairs and dispatched with the matter in one sentence: "The position of the Legal Counsel to the Government as presented to the Court, is the position of the State." This, in a nutshell, is the representation monopoly.

*

In the previous sections we have thoroughly demonstrated the formidable effect and fundamental flaws of the LCG's "binding counsel." Still, as the reader may have discerned, and though it perhaps defies belief, the most significant component of the LCG's power had been left out of our discussion, and it is to this mechanism which we now turn our attention.

The Legal Counsel to the Government holds a near-absolute exclusive monopoly over representing the entire executive government and its organs in all judicial proceedings. This monopoly prerogative has no basis in law yet is strictly enforced by the Supreme Court. Under this monopoly the LCG alone speaks for the government in all litigation proceedings; the LCG alone determines which arguments will be raised in the State's name during trial; he may choose to advance poor or implausible arguments unlikely to succeed or those contradicting government policy; he may refuse to defend the government decision under review; he may argue *against* the decision being challenged, effectively joining the petitioners. The LCG may also elect, at his sole discretion, whether to allow alternative private legal representation for the government – a privilege rarely extended.

Though they have been separated here for analytical purposes, the twin concepts of "representation monopoly" and "binding counsel" are co-reliant and intertwined. The notion of "authorized interpreter" "reflecting the law" towards the government, along with the LCG's role as defender of the "public interest" rather than any particular body or agency,* serve as the normative basis for the LCG's monopoly over what the court will hear in the government's name.[50] At the same time, their monopoly over representation is the enforcement mechanism by which the LCG may ensure – to a near-certainty – that their "counsel" will ultimately prevail, by denying the government any ability to muster a legal defense of its actions. The representation monopoly is the sharp crack at the end of the "binding counsel" whip.

While I have shown that the "binding counsel" model accords the LCG considerable and unjustifiable power outside the context of litigation, there can be no doubt that the monopoly over the government's legal representation is by far its most momentous outcome and expression. The LCG can, if so desired, predetermine the result of litigation against the government and thus control the legal outcome itself. Just as importantly, the mere potential of such veto in court is usually sufficient to avoid actual legal confrontation – few politicians or officials are willing to engage in a legal showdown in which their own attorney dooms their side to failure. This mind-boggling power, used to devastating effect, dwarfs all other expressions of "binding counsel" substantial as they may be. Shimon Nataf convincingly suggests that the "binding counsel" hypothesis is at its core merely a post-hoc rationalization propping up the earlier phenomenon of the LCG monopoly in court. It is at the very least indisputable that the LCG's assertion (and Supreme Court's confirmation) of a representation monopoly predated any discussion of binding counsel; and it is undeniable that without this monopoly the idea of "binding counsel" would lose much of its bite.

Dr. Eitan Levontin has published extensive scholarly research and commentary regarding the history and role of the LCG and is considered among Israel's foremost experts on the subject. Perhaps unsurprisingly, he is rumored to be the only jurist to have had Ruth Gavison as his Ph.D. supervisor. In 2024 Levontin published a comprehensive law review article tackling the question of the government's legal representation in Israeli courts.† His description of the

---

* In fact, while "the State" is the exclusive government party in criminal litigation, all other litigation types involve the specific state official, organ or agency, and never "the State" per se, such that even on a technical level the claim of representing the State at large is incorrect.

† I am indebted to Eitan Levontin and Aharon Garber for their comprehensive recent

representation monopoly is bruising: The LCG chooses "at will" to defend the government or "to join the petitioners and simultaneously deprive the government from presenting its position." The LCG's view is "the State's view," while the actual position taken by the government or agency is "a dissenting view which can be heard only by the good graces and consent" of the LCG. He continues: "Outside the Court 'the State' is the executive government hierarchy, while inside the Court 'the State' is the LCG." Levontin emphasizes that "there is nothing like this" in any other jurisdiction.

The major turning point for the representation monopoly – which we will simply call "the monopoly" – was the *Deri-Pinhasi* cases. As discussed above, the LCG Yosef Harish agreed with the petitioners and proceeded to argue *against* the government he claimed to represent. The Supreme Court granted this farce full license and legitimacy, distinguishing between the "personal" Prime Minister who was effectively silenced and the "institutional" Prime Minister represented by the LCG. As we shall demonstrate and explore in the following sections, the monopoly prerogative has become an embedded feature of judicial supremacy, enabling the Court to dominate the elected and accountable branches of government while maintaining the façade of an adversarial judicial proceeding approximating established notions of justice or fairness.

One last comment before we proceed regards an institutional element. The "High Court of Justice Department" within the State Attorney legal corps serves as the litigation arm of the LCG. The "HCJD" is the elite group of lawyers tasked with actively representing the State in all constitutional and administrative cases before the Supreme Court (parallel departments are tasked with handling appellate civil and criminal cases). Though technically subordinate to the State Attorney and the LCG, this department commands its own fair degree of autonomy, with the department head often considered among the most influential bureaucrats in government.

Soccer with no goalkeeper

In 2018 a professional committee within the Ministry of Science recommended to appoint Prof. Yael Amitai to the governing board of a bi-national statutory scientific R&D fund called the German-Israeli Foundation. Yet their choice for the prestigious posting turned out to be a controversial one – Amitai had previously called for Israeli soldiers to refuse to serve in the West Bank. As this came to light, Minister of Science Ofir Akunis refused to grant his approval, which was required by law and without which the appointment could not proceed. Though the Minister had the clear statutory authority to approve or reject such appointments, the LCG rendered a legal opinion arguing that Akunis attributed "excessive weight" to ethical factors (though these are permissible per se) as opposed to professional-academic factors, and that his interest-balancing was

research on this subject, on which I relied throughout this chapter.

therefore not sufficiently reasonable. The decision was duly challenged in the Supreme Court on the same grounds.

We may set aside the validity or legality of the Minister's refusal and focus on his representation in court. The Legal Counsel to the Government – the only legal representative available to Akunis – refused to defend the Minister's position and indeed maintained that the decision was unlawful and void. The LCG also clarified to Akunis that he was not entitled to receive separate representation by a private attorney. The LCG's written response generously included the Minister's opinion justifying his actions, but simultaneously clarified that the decision was indefensible and could not stand. Consequently, the only legal counsel in court, representing both opposing parties, uniformly favored the petitioners.

Ofir Akunis nonetheless thought that his opinion might carry some weight, and unexpectedly showed up at the Supreme Court hearing (to which he was not invited). We may imagine the Minister of Science, sitting in the back benches while watching his own legal counsel urge the Justices to undo his decision, gingerly raise his hand and ask if he might get a word in edgewise. Against the vocal objections of the LCG, the Court allowed Minister Akunis to (literally) stand and explain, in his own words, why he thought the decision to be legally valid. The Justices were astounded to discover – floored, really – that the "personal" Minister did not see eye to eye with the "institutional" Minister represented by the LCG. Following this revelation the Court asked that Akunis submit his own written affidavit explaining his view, which he proceeded to furnish.

Alas, Minister Akunis lost the case. Not an attorney himself, and without a single attorney pleading his view before the court, he stood nary a chance.

In his concurring opinion Justice Alex Stein agreed with the case outcome but mounted a scathing attack against the LCG's so-called representation, both in general and in the specific *Akunis* case, which is worth our attention. Stein cast doubt on the legal pedigree of the LCG's monopoly, noting that it had never been directly adjudicated and seemed to rely on disparate dicta. Stein mused, not without a hint of sarcasm, that if the Minister's position was indeed "determined" by the LCG and there was in fact full agreement between the litigant parties, then why had they just spent precious judicial time adjudicating a seemingly non-existent dispute? And indeed, Stein wondered, why was there any need for the Court to provide a ruling in light of the supposed consensus between petitioner and respondent?

On the more principled level Stein noted the unique evil of stifling opinion and the importance of competing arguments in the context of judicial proceedings – stating that in a court of law "there is no room for the outright silencing of arguments due to their being weak, objectionable or outrageous" and that truth must be tested in the market competition of thought. While quoting Oliver Wendell Holmes Jr. and John Stuart Mill, Stein remarked rather pointedly that such a proceeding in which a primary party is unable to advocate for their position cannot be called "legal"* even "on the most basic terminological level"; just as a soccer game ceases to be a "match" if one team has no goalkeeper and the rival team gets unlimited penalty shots.

Following a much more nuanced and balanced analysis of the Minister's decision (and thus subtly demonstrating what legal arguments a lawyer for Akunis might have raised), Justice Stein showed that its illegality was far from obvious or straightforward (indeed, Stein disqualified the decision on something of a technicality while leaving much leeway for Akunis to repeat his refusal). This made the LCG's decision to deprive Akunis of representation all the more heinous. First, because even the Court's jurisprudence and LCG policy state that private representation is to be denied only in "rare and extreme circumstances" in which there is "clear and manifest illegality." As this case hardly approached such a threshold – indeed, as the Minister had a strong prima facie claim that his decision was lawful – the LCG was violating his own (and the Court's) established rules. Second, because the Minister's inability to defend his actions (by capable legal counsel) meant that the Court could not be certain that it had heard the best legal arguments on both sides. Further still, how could the Court evaluate the validity of the Minister's "interest-balancing" if he himself was unable to fully elaborate and explain his views?† To drive the point home (and daring to state the obvious), Stein speculates whether Akunis could have in fact won, if only he had an attorney to faithfully represent him and make the case on his behalf.

Audi Unam Partem – Hear One Side

Justice Stein's opinion properly outlined many of the most glaring objections to the representation monopoly, just as the *Akunis* case itself demonstrates some of its flaws. We may use both as a point of departure as we embark on our own examination of the monopoly's fundamental and inherent injustice.

At the analytical level, the Court regularly asserts that the monopoly is anchored in the LCG's role as "authorized interpreter of the law" and in the "binding" nature of his counsel, treating it all as part of a single fused principle. However, setting aside the legal basis for this description and assuming the LCG really does properly fill this function, there is nothing in the notion of "binding counsel" which justifies the representation monopoly. In order to arrive at the conclusion of monopoly, the Court makes a series of enormous logical leaps and assumptions which don't hold up.[51]

(a) First is the leap between advisor and agent – the rules governing the former don't necessarily apply to the latter. A legal advisor communicating their legal opinion to a client is one thing; a legal agent acting on behalf of a client in a court

* Stein used the term "*mishpat*" which can mean "law" or "trial."

† This criticism echoes the point made by Justice Grunis and Yoav Dotan, that reasonableness is really about objecting to outcomes far more than about the reverse-engineered "improper" balancing of interests.

of law is another. These two roles serve categorically different purposes in profoundly different institutional environments (as perhaps demonstrated by the distinction between solicitor and barrister in several common-law jurisdictions). Even if we are to unreservedly accept the "binding counsel" model and that the LCG's legal opinion obliges the government's obedience, there is no reason to assume that this view automatically extends to representing the government in court. The rationales for the ability of any litigant – and especially the government – to control their legal representation before a tribunal imposing prescriptive obligations are wholly separate from rationales relating to the relationship between advisor and advisee. The government is entitled to a good-faith effort at representation of its position in court regardless of any prior stage in which it received opposing legal advice.

(b) Second is the leap between representation and non-representation. As astutely observed by Eitan Levontin, having an exclusive right to represent the government in court does not entitle the LCG to *decline* to provide precisely such representation. Even were we to accept that the government has no choice but to be represented by the LCG (as its "authorized interpreter"), this does not imply that the latter may elect simply to refuse to defend the government's position. (c) Third and (d) Fourth are the consecutive leaps of a government attorney arguing against the government, and of depriving the government of alternate representation altogether. Again, even were we to assume that the LCG enjoys an exclusive representation monopoly and may even refuse to argue in favor of the action being challenged, by no means does it follow that the LCG can then join the petitioners in demanding the Court rule against the government or that they can block the government from having anyone else plead their case instead.

All in all, the Court fails – even on its own terms – to show how it sails from the port of "authorized interpreter" all the way to points (a) through (d). One could indeed imagine a system involving "binding counsel" yet ultimately allowing for full and faithful government representation once a dispute is litigated. The Court simply never bothers to justify or address any of these analytical leaps, pretending that they all flow naturally and inevitably from the LCG's role as "authorized interpreter of the law."

Moving on. Stein doubts whether a one-sided sham can be called a "trial," but the real terminological perversion lies in the use of "representation" as an Orwellian euphemism for its exact opposite. Levontin coins the phrase "hostile representation" to describe this uniquely grotesque Israeli innovation – the claim that the LCG "represents" the government by arguing for the rejection of its position and for its legal defeat. Israeli judicial supremacy is riddled with cynical linguistic manipulations, yet "Attack Is Defense" comes as close as it gets to *1984*. The Court's aforementioned logical gymnastics betray precisely this terminological inversion, as they show the Court is willing to accept (and indeed, encourage) attack posing as defense without so much as batting an eyelid. For at least three decades the Court has employed the word "represent" to describe an action which is the diametric opposite of the word's meaning.

Here we arrive at the core objection to the representation monopoly – that it undermines the most basic definition of any judicial proceeding. A party is not "represented" if their counsel abdicates any duty to defend their position; a judge does not preside over a "trial" if he is willing to prevent one side from making its case (they don't call them "hearings" for nothing). The representation monopoly makes a mockery of both these concepts. These terminological distortions reflect two angles: that of the party and that of the court and judicial process. From the party's perspective we tend to believe in principles of due process which include both "the assistance of counsel" and the opportunity to have one's "day in court" – indeed, the two are distinct but usually inseparable. From a judicial perspective we hold that a court must consider all sides of the case before them and especially the claims of its opposing participants: first, so that those within and without the legal proceeding have cause to comply with the judicial decision and to support it, knowing that the court has considered both sides of a dispute; second, so that the court may reach the best and most accurate conclusion by being exposed to conflicting earnest argumentation. This is especially true for common-law adversarial systems founded on opposing parties making their best case before a passive tribunal. Judicial consideration of all sides through the presentation of adverse views serves both its legitimacy and the quality of its decisions. Since early antiquity legal systems are commanded and shaped by that universally-recognized maxim of natural justice – *audi alteram partem*.

Not so for the Supreme Court of Israel, which seems to champion the ideal of *audi unam partem* – "hear one side." Though the government pleads innocence, its own attorney professes its guilt. The unilateral power of the LCG to act in the government's name in court, at odds with the most basic tenets of fairness and justice, turns many petitions into de facto *ex parte* proceedings resembling the sham trials and kangaroo courts of tyrannical regimes. As Levontin observes, the Court has converted the abomination of "hostile representation" not only into a legal norm but also into an ideal.[52]

This grievance applies to any client or party to a judicial proceeding but is compounded tenfold by the identity of such party being the government and its organs. The considered view and policy of the Government or any of its Ministers carries with it the weight of democratic authority and legitimacy born of public scrutiny and accountability. However clumsily and indirectly, the government channels the wills and preferences of millions of people who have appointed their representatives for this precise purpose; it bears enormous responsibility for its actions and decisions and for their consequences. Should not the government and the multitudes it represents be afforded the opportunity to argue its case when challenged in court?

To use a familiar phrase, any litigant deserves their "day in court." The party whose action is being challenged and reviewed, the party who is the target and object of a potential judicial order, must be able to present, explain and justify their view before the judges deciding the legality of such actions. Under the monopoly prerogative, that "day" is denied to the State and belongs exclusively to the LCG. Gavison and Levontin jointly address this point in a 2003 article:

> "We might say that metaphorically, the government entity is entitled to as many 'days' in court as the number of people that it represents and on whose behalf it acts. But we certainly ought not deprive the government the right to have its case heard at least one single time… If a government decision is challenged and stands under judicial scrutiny, it would add insult to injury to assert that the one opportunity to be heard belongs to an entity [the LCG] that neither made the contested decision nor bears responsibility for its implementation… It is a double and triple mockery to say that the same entity may join the challengers, and by its very participation deny the entity its right to self-defense."[53]

In this sense the representation monopoly is all the more audacious – not just an aberration of law or justice but also of democracy, as the people's representative government is deprived of the ability to defend its duly enacted policies in a critical forum which will decide their fate.*

The many objections discussed at length in the previous section regarding the "binding counsel" model apply equally – or more strongly – to the representation monopoly. These include the fiction of a "definitively correct" legal view in complex cases, the framing of all political and value-based dilemmas as "legal" and their subjection to vague quasi-legal standards, the limitless objective purposive interpretation of the law, and the "infallibility fallacy" – the myth that decision-making by the LCG can only ever be unbiased and objective with no hint of error, improper personal and institutional motives, or conflicts of interest. We need not rehash them now, but their relevance here is critical. The notion of an unelected and unaccountable legal officer unilaterally imposing their arbitrary view of "reasonableness" on the government is bad enough; the idea that they can do so in a legal proceeding backed by the Court and using the hard institutional mechanics of litigation, all while preventing any discussion of genuine difference or disagreement, is immeasurably worse.

Indeed, on a number of occasions government decisions were upheld by the Court despite the LCG's vociferous objections which included "representation" against the government. In the 1992 case involving the deportation of four hundred Hamas operatives to Lebanon, discussed above in Chapter 1, State Attorney Dorit Beinisch refused to represent the government. Her legal opinion was thoroughly and resoundingly rejected by the Supreme Court which allowed

---

* Levontin notes that there is also a personal element involved, in that adverse judicial statements and rulings may well reflect personally on a specific government Minister or other official (such as a determination that the law had been violated), with potential political, professional, financial and reputational consequences. Here, too, the individual person negatively affected by such a ruling has no opportunity to state their case before the court.

for the deportation to proceed, revealing her objections to be utterly misguided and unprofessional.* In the *Minnes* and *Gini* cases (discussed below) the LCG opposed the government decision and effectively joined the petitioners, yet the Court dismissed the petitions, rebuking the LCG's totalizing and binary approach. Even adopting the most sympathetic view towards the LCG's sincerity and good faith, it is clear that government attorneys, like all mortals, can make grievous mistakes and can exhibit poor legal judgment. Conditioning the government's ability to plead its case on the LCG's exclusive approval simply denies this basic precept of law and common sense.

In addition to objections based on justice and (representative) democracy, the LCG's monopolistic role also constitutes a unique outlier on an institutional level, violating core principles of the Separation of Powers. Many critics of judicial supremacy tend to focus on courts assuming legislative and executive authority, yet the LCG presents a reverse phenomenon in which the Supreme Court deliberately delegates judicial authority to an executive official. Judicial institutions around the world have been designed to perform a specific function in accordance with established principles – and practical procedures – of justice and fairness. These include an array of mechanisms and safeguards with the specific purpose of ensuring such principles are maintained. For hundreds of years the prevailing political approach of Western society has warned of the dangers inherent in placing judicial power in the hands of other branches (with some limited and clearly defined exceptions).

Yet the Israeli LCG exercises precisely such judicial authority entirely outside any similar institutional framework and without the faintest glimmer of judicial process. By wielding both "binding counsel" and the representation monopoly as "authorized interpreter of the law," the LCG performs de facto functions of the judicial branch of government. Understood this way, the inherent dangers and flaws of the unparalleled Legal Counsel to the Government become all the more obvious. The Israeli LCG serves as a remarkable and rare case-study of judicial power being outsourced to a member of the executive branch – with the ensuing damage and abuses coming as no surprise.

The Show Must Go On

Just as the "binding counsel" model finds no basis in law or even in the various commission reports over the years, the representation monopoly (resting on identical legal claims) suffers from the same deficit. The Court's and LCG's relentless blank assertions notwithstanding, the monopoly has simply never been

* The fact that Beinisch kept her job following this incident speaks volumes as to the power dynamics within governmental legal institutions and indicates the loose hierarchy subordinating the State Attorney to the LCG. During that time Beinisch was pursuing the investigations against Deri and other Ministers in Rabin's government, likely limiting the perceived ability to dismiss her. To use the term coined by Avichai Mandelblit, Rabin and his LCG were in many respects also "held by the throat."

properly litigated and decided by the Supreme Court itself, nor does it rest on any recognizable legal norm. As Levontin summarizes, the Court's existing doctrine "does not rely on any substantial legal claim – statutory, terminological, analytical, historical, comparative or otherwise." Even in *Pinhasi* itself the question of government representation was incidental and not the main issue adjudicated. What's more, in *Pinhasi* the Prime Minister and government were not permitted to argue their view on the question of representation *itself* – that is, the LCG asserted a novel privilege of representation monopoly in order to block arguments which might challenge the validity of that same assertion. An extensive forensic review by Aharon Garber reaches the same conclusion as Levontin, showing that Barak's original claim in *Pinhasi*, though shown overwhelmingly to be baseless and without merit, created a self-perpetuating cycle in which the Court refers back to *Pinhasi* and relies on a fictitious "legal tradition."[54]

The absence of any statutory source is especially instructive. Setting aside all questions of principle or wisdom, such an arrangement of representation monopoly would simply be unthinkable and untenable in any Western or democratic jurisdiction without statutory authorization of the most explicit nature. This was, for a time, also the approach in Israeli jurisprudence. A typical expression can be found in a 1959 classic essay by a government attorney (and future judge), in which he emphasizes that any authority exercised by the LCG can be based solely on "explicit" statutory language, and that the LCG has no authority in matters of court representation "unless such authority is granted by power of statute."[55]

This brings us to a brief diversion which could be amusing were it not appalling. In the 2019 *Tnuva* case regarding price regulation of dairy products, Justice Stein weighed in and gingerly suggested that the representation monopoly ought not to apply in instances involving vague standards such as reasonableness. Clear-cut and manifest illegality seems especially unlikely in the context of reasonableness, such that there is a greater interest in hearing the government's authentic position. He referred to his more detailed dissent in the *Akunis* case.

Finding such musings intolerable, Justice (and former-LCG) Menny Mazuz penned his own opinion aimed solely at rebuking Stein for his heresy, in which Mazuz inadvertently provides a priceless gem. First, Mazuz proclaims that the LCG's representation of the State in any legal proceeding is "undisputed" – a peculiar statement to say the least, considering not only the consistent scholarly and judicial dissent accumulating over the years, but also that his response was addressing a literal dispute with another Justice just one page earlier. Next, as support for the representation monopoly, Mazuz triumphantly cites a statutory provision – Section 4 of the 1958 Civil Procedure Amendment Act (The State as Litigant). Surely this had some readers scratching their heads or rubbing their eyes: had Mazuz uncovered a long-lost statutory provision establishing the representation monopoly? Was this the legal Holy Grail which could anchor Barak's *Pinhasi* ruling and the LCG's claim to immense power?

To begin with, the fact that in over twenty-five years of monopoly not a single scholar or judicial decision thought to rely on this provision ought to alert any observer to its questionable relevance and to induce considerable skepticism. And indeed, the lawyers and law-clerks running for the bookcase and furiously Googling this mysterious Act were in for a disappointment. Section 4 initially seems promising: "In any proceedings to which the State is a party, the State shall be represented by the Legal Counsel to the Government or his delegate." Unfortunately, Section 1 of the law defines "proceedings" as limited only to *civil* proceedings (such as contracts or torts lawsuits); therefore excluding administrative or constitutional litigation which tends to be the LCG's primary arena for asserting his monopoly. But the real kicker appears just a few lines further down. Section 10 reads: "This law… does not apply to matters before the Supreme Court sitting as High Court of Justice." The provision could not be more plain and unequivocal, and clearly contradicts the claim that Mazuz advanced by referring to a different section of the same law. It so happens that a 1982 Supreme Court ruling even reiterated the clear meaning of Section 10 and stressed that the law in question, in its entirety, does not apply in administrative or HCJ proceedings. In sum – Mazuz cited this law in an HCJ ruling to establish the LCG's representation monopoly over (primarily) HCJ proceedings, despite the law stating in the clearest terms that it could not possibly apply to any HCJ case.*

At first glance this acutely embarrassing legal blunder might seem only comical or farcical, though upon reflection it becomes more startling and raises some genuinely disquieting questions. Was this just a fluke from a careless judicial clerk? This is unlikely for a two-page opinion within the core of Mazuz's expertise. Was Supreme Court Justice Menny Mazuz, formerly the country's most senior legal officer, just extraordinarily sloppy and didn't bother reading a few more sentences to the end of the law he intended to cite? Or, perhaps, was he aware of the plain contradiction obvious to the most casual reader, yet deliberately asserted a manifest legal falsehood in a Supreme Court opinion? Regardless of which is worse, later events indicate the latter to be the likelier. Nearly two years later, Mazuz made the exact same claim in the 2021 *Inmates* case – showing this to be no fluke or accident, and even though the error had almost certainly been called to his attention. Far from an anecdotal incident or a momentary lapse, this event demonstrates both how desperately supporters of the representation monopoly are clutching for statutory straws, and on a broader level, how deeply unserious and undisciplined Israeli judicial reasoning has become in its era of supremacy.

*

* As an aside, Levontin shows convincingly that the law does not establish a monopoly even in civil cases, but was legislated to address a technicality. The 1958 law simply sets a presumption that the government has authorized the LCG to represent it, waiving the need for the LCG to show Power-Of-Attorney authorization in every case.

In an op-ed praising Justice Stein for his *Akunis* opinion, Yoav Dotan sums up the representation monopoly as follows:

> "This extreme (not to say bizarre) doctrine has no basis in Israeli legislation, nor does it have any parallel in any other legal system in the world. It severely undermines not only freedom of expression, the democratic principle, and the fundamental right to representation in court, but also the rule of law and the foundation of our adversarial legal system."[56]

Yet Stein's reservations are the exception and are largely regarded by most Justices and by the legal establishment as heretical. The plain flaws inherent in the representation monopoly are dismissed or more often, ignored. The Court and its supporters charge ever onwards, repeating the mantra of exclusive representation and its contrived origins. Critically, this charade is not merely intellectual or doctrinal but is also enacted in the most immediate physical sense. Comparisons between courtroom dynamics and theatrical drama are something of a cliché, yet few examples come quite as close to performative theater as does the representation monopoly. Proceedings unfold in a pantomime of legal argumentation in which everyone is in on the ruse, while the Court willingly embraces a "suspension of disbelief" and issues binding judgments which are all-but-predetermined. The Supreme Court Justices are not mere spectators in the monopoly travesty but are rather its creators and enablers – fully complicit in the project of monopoly, they wholeheartedly encourage and enforce the LCG's silencing and subjugation of democratic government. The show must go on.

For the illusion to succeed the Justices must maintain the pretense of a plainly ludicrous, legally absurd and democratically repugnant "trial" in which the main party – the State – is not entitled to meaningful participation. The Justices must sit in their leather chairs in the air-conditioned well-appointed courtroom and preside over a faux-adversarial proceeding in which the government's attorney joins the petitioners and demands the Court's intervention against his client. They must pretend that the farce before them is a legitimate and acceptable administration of justice, though they know – or suspect – that the authentic State may likely have valid legal justification for its actions but is nonetheless denied any faithful legal representation. As they read briefs, hear oral arguments and write opinions, over the course of weeks, months, or sometimes years, the Justices must keep up the concerted effort at willful denial of the reality before their eyes. Can this be attributed to woeful and tragic ignorance of the most basic judicial and democratic principles, or is their conduct born of conscious and perverse bad faith? The reader may determine which is worse, and whether it matters.

The Mechanics of Monopoly

When government attorneys consider a government decision challenged in court to be illegal, a number of courses of action are available to them. In most jurisdictions around the world these would be limited to two options: either defending the government action despite one's misgivings (or delegating the defense to a different but equally qualified and competent government attorney); or resigning from one's position just as would any public official that refuses to perform their duty on grounds of principle.

This used to also be the case in Israel. In the leadup to the 1962 Agranat Commission, LCG Gideon Hausner warned that if the Government would not accept his legal view on a specific matter he would resign (and did in fact resign in 1963 due to further tensions with the Government). Another indisputable towering legal figure during Israel's formative years was Haim Cohn – after briefly serving as State Attorney (1948-1949) and Minister of Justice (1950), he went on to serve as LCG for a decade and then as Supreme Court Justice for another twenty years. Cohn explicitly and unreservedly maintained that the LCG's opinion did not bind the government in any sense, writing in 1952 (while himself serving as LCG) that "the LCG's authority is solely advisory… the Government and its various organs may accept or reject his advice."[57] In legal proceedings, Cohn defended government decisions with which he disagreed and which he thought to be of dubious legality, as he believed "it was his duty to grant the State its day in court." Needless to say, Cohn later became a critic of *Pinhasi* and the representation monopoly (and at times of Barak more generally) and objected to the LCG "silencing" the government and "imposing his opinion" by hijacking its legal representation.

Since *Pinhasi* in 1993 neither of the above options (defend or resign) are seriously considered by the LCG. Instead, per the Court's consistent jurisprudence, the LCG enjoys near-absolute discretion to select any one (or a combination) of several possibilities. These include representing the government but defining the content of legal arguments raised, or "hostile" representation in which the LCG argues against the government action and in favor of its judicial nullification. In either case the LCG may choose whether, and how, to present the "personal" (that is – authentic) views of the government organ or official. The LCG might communicate (or paraphrase) the government's views by *incorporating* these in his own briefs and oral arguments through whatever filter he desires (while stressing that this is not the "State's" position but rather the personal view of the officeholder); he might allow the government to submit a *separate document* – such as a short memo or affidavit – of their own; or, rarely, he might permit the government to retain its own outside legal representation by a *private attorney*. Notably, retaining outside private counsel does not replace LCG representation but is rather in addition to it – the LCG continues to represent "the State" (or the "institutional Minister," etc.) while private attorneys represent the "individual" and "personal" perspective of an organ or official.*

---

* In some rare cases the LCG does in fact represent "itself" in court as a separate institutional entity, typically when the LCG is a named party or a respondent in the petition. Even in such cases the LCG usually acts in two capacities – as both the LCG office itself *and* as

Finally, as we know, the LCG may choose to bar the government from expressing its view altogether by not permitting any of the above options. As the Court has emphasized time and again, the question of which path to choose is one of exclusive LCG discretion. The LCG in fact has no obligation to even inform the Court that the authentic Minister or organ being "represented" disagrees with the position the LCG has taken.

We will now briefly examine each of these routes which the LCG might take. One central observation is that even when the LCG does agree to nominally defend the government's decision (that is, to ask the Court to dismiss the petition), such representation may still be a far cry from any recognizable genuine advocacy. As the government has little to no control over the content of its defense, the LCG (and HCJD) might select arguments with lower chances of success, or to which the government objects in principle, or which serve the LCG's institutional interests, or which have adverse repercussions (for the government) in another context. For example, the government might believe its decision fully justified and lawful by any measure, but the LCG thinks it a borderline case where the decision at issue just barely passes the test of legality by the skin of its teeth;* or the government would argue non-justiciability as a political question outside the Court's purview, while the LCG would concede the Court's jurisdiction and argue on substantive grounds.

In all such instances only the LCG's view will be presented in court, however damaging or ineffectual, still at times leading to legal defeat, to a pyrrhic victory, or to new precedents expanding judicial supremacy.† This pattern also helps to explain the development of the Court's jurisprudence and its ability to evade contending with criticism – the LCG proxy simply refrains from raising arguments uncomfortable or inconvenient for its sponsor, allowing the Court to proceed developing its doctrines unencumbered by meaningful jurisprudential challenges.

In the event the LCG joins the petitioners in alleging illegality, the next two options – of "incorporating" the government's view or allowing the government to file a brief memo – do not amount to meaningful representation in any sense of the word. In the *Pinhasi* case Prime Minister Rabin's views were curtly "presented" within the LCG's broad arguments against him. The same was true for the Minister of Science in *Akunis*, the Minister of Finance in *Tnuva* and in a host of other cases – such token representation didn't do any of them much good. The government's ability to draft and file a document of their own is only a fractional improvement, if at all. Levontin calls both options "charity

---

definitive representative for the government.

* This was precisely what happened in HCJ Rehearing 3660/17, where the LCG stated that a Minister's decision "raises significant legal difficulties" but argued to dismiss the petition on technical grounds. The State lost.

† Keeping in mind how easily the Court recognizes "binding precedent" in tangential dicta of concurring or even dissenting opinions.

representation" – the LCG throws the government a bone which may have some limited placatory effect but is otherwise a hollow gesture. In such instances the government's authentic position is presented briefly as a rough outline, filtered by the LCG and positioned as far inferior to any arguments made by the petitioners and the LCG himself. Most importantly, in both cases there is not a single attorney in the courtroom who will make a good-faith oral argument on behalf of the government, who can answer questions from Justices or who can address additional points raised during the hearing. In other words, the government's authentic legal arguments are not represented in any acceptable sense or meaning.

The next option is for the LCG to allow the government to retain its own private counsel for a specific case. This is typically viewed by the Court and its supporters as a sufficient remedy in which the LCG graciously – almost benevolently – permits the government to pay an attorney to plead their case, despite it being so odious that the LCG himself refuses to so sully his hands. By allowing private representation the Court and LCG consider themselves redeemed, as though this is fully equivalent to faithful representation by government attorneys and allays all criticism of the representation monopoly.

It's first worth noting that private representation is by far the exception to the norm. The LCG defines an extremely narrow window allowing for such a scenario. On the one hand, the illegality of government action has to be to a degree that the LCG is unwilling to defend it, and further, deviation from the representation monopoly is permitted only in "extreme and rare circumstances"; on the other hand, the government is *not* entitled to private representation in instances of "clear and manifest illegality." Unsurprisingly, it doesn't happen often that a government decision hits this sweet spot, so illegal that it is rejected outright by the LCG but not so illegal to disqualify private representation. The government mostly has to settle for "charity representation" by the LCG at the very best.

In addition, the fact is that government rarely – if ever at all – makes decisions which are "clearly and manifestly illegal," and the LCG's determination of such tends to be arbitrary and unfounded even in the Court's view (as will soon be demonstrated). Among the many instances in which the LCG denied a request to private representation, I would challenge an impartial observer to find a single example amounting to "clear and manifest illegality." One might also ask, if the alleged illegality is so clear-cut then what's the harm in retaining outside counsel which will undoubtedly fail to persuade the court? Further still, "manifest illegality" is a question of law to be determined by judges – how can the Court evaluate whether private representation is justified if the LCG prevents the adjudication of that very question? As Gavison and Levontin have observed, denying the government separate authentic representation leads to the impression that either the LCG is not as confident in the validity of his arguments as he pretends to be, or that he lacks faith in the Court's ability to rule correctly and lawfully.[58] One can't help the creeping suspicion that "manifest illegality" is reserved for denying the government representation especially when the alleged illegality is actually far from obvious.

More to the point – private representation sets the government-respondent at a clear disadvantage. The government should certainly be free to retain any attorney it desires if it feels its own are inadequate, but the fact is that the HCJD and LCG legal corps form a formidable cadre of elite public lawyers at the top of their game. Few private attorneys engage in constitutional and administrative cases full-time, and no Israeli law firm maintains a public-law department to rival the manpower, resources, experience and expertise of the HCJD and its small army of lawyers. While this key resource is squandered, the taxpayer has to cough up considerable sums to pay outside counsel legal fees and still gets less for more – private attorneys are simply more cost-conscious and don't have the same time and personnel resources available to the HCJD. In addition, the HCJD lawyers appear before the Supreme Court on a daily basis, thus building a rapport and professional relationship with the Justices which simply cannot be replicated by outside private counsel (this unique professional "affinity" is addressed later in this chapter).

Perhaps most importantly, the "dual representation" conveys a clear message to the Court creating an initial impression of illegitimacy by which the government starts on the back foot. The HCJD attorneys (arguing for "the State" but against "the government") represent the noble public interest; the private attorneys are either mere puppets and mercenaries chasing billable hours, or (if acting pro-bono) are politically motivated partisan ideologues. Like parading a criminal defendant in an orange jump-suit before a jury, the very scenario of private counsel representing the government is prejudicial from the get-go. Recall also that the government and its private attorneys must contend not only with the petitioners arguing their case in court, but also with the LCG which still represents "the State" and argues in favor of the petitioners. This not only adds to the government's litigation burden, but also further undermines its outside counsel in the eyes of the Court.

Interestingly, the 1962 Agranat Report also suggests providing a different attorney from within the ranks of the government legal corps, yet the latter route is never entertained by the LCG. This is despite the fact that the legal advice unit of a specific organ – such as that of a Ministry or government agency – often does actually agree with the policy or decision being challenged and is willing to defend its legality both in and out of court. Here is yet another implication of the unilateral judicial policy subordinating all governmental legal advice units to the "professional" authority of the LCG, and centralizing all relevant governmental litigation within HCJD control.

To be clear, private counsel is better than no representation at all (and in rare instances makes all the difference). But cases in which the LCG permits outside private representation are the exception to the rule. Typically, the LCG joins the petitioners on behalf of "the State" and demands the Court's intervention while stating the token "personal view" of the governmental decision-maker being challenged – private representation is either not requested or not granted. *Tnuva* and *Akunis* were hardly unusual in this respect. In another 2017 case against the Interior Minister, Chief Justice Miriam Naor acknowledged the "Court had been presented with the Interior Minister's personal opinion, which differs from the State's opinion," but then rejected any claim that the LCG ought to have approved private counsel for the Minister. "The State's view," insisted Naor, "is the one determined by the Legal Counsel to the Government."[59] In the 2022 *Goldreich* case regarding the Israel Prize, discussed above in Chapter 5, the authentic Education Minister's position received only a perfunctory mention. Speaking for "the State" and representing the "institutional" Minister of Education, the LCG argued against the Minister's decision, stating that "it is not based on adequate evidentiary grounds" and that "therefore, it cannot stand."[60] In his minority opinion Justice Solberg berated the LCG for refusing to provide the Minister with any form of meaningful representation (whether by the LCG himself or by private counsel), considering the decision at issue was nowhere near "clear and manifest" illegality and considering that the entire case hinged on highly subjective standards of reasonableness and interest-balancing. In this sporadic selection of typical cases, as in many, many others, the LCG "represents" the government organ or official by pitting "the State" against them; conveys their "personal" case in a few superficial token sentences; and denies any alternative meaningful representation of their authentic position.

An additional element of interest relates to legal proceedings *between* government organs. Every country in the world is familiar with the issue of intra-governmental litigation. Disagreements of various forms between different government organs and officials can often escalate into direct legal disputes to be resolved by courts (an especially familiar example is between states and their federal government or amongst themselves). In some cases, bringing legal action against other government bodies is not incidental but rather a primary function of a specific organ (such as financial, safety, labor or civil rights regulators). While every jurisdiction adopts different arrangements to address such conflicts, it is universally understood that at times different governmental entities need to resolve contested questions of law in court.

Yet this is not the case in Israel. The LCG monopoly does not involve only defense against legal challenges, but encompasses any and all governmental legal proceedings of any kind, including their initiation. Per the LCG, with no basis in statutory law, disputes between government bodies must be brought before him for his own resolution, and in any case government organs may not initiate legal proceedings (especially against the State) without LCG approval and involvement. We will briefly revisit this later.

One course of action open to the LCG but never taken is notably absent. In most other jurisdictions (and in Israel prior to the era of judicial supremacy), the most obvious route is that of resignation. Much like any other government employee, the LCG role is not one of forced labor and any government attorney can leave their post at any time if they feel they are unable to perform the tasks for which they were hired. Yet since the 1960s this option is simply not contemplated by the LCG and subordinate organs. Even at the highest tensions and antagonism between the Government and its own legal counsel, the prospect of voluntary resignation is not raised, considered or discussed. Like a hereditary title of nobility, the role of LCG seems to contain an intrinsic and inalienable privilege of undermining and impeding government policy, the abandonment of which is tantamount to abdication.

From a broader perspective, one key takeaway from these various forms of faux-representation is this: That in a great many controversial or pivotal cases, including many which have been mentioned and discussed in previous chapters, the authentic government never had the privilege of genuine advocacy. This casts the entire process of Israeli judicial change over the past generation in a very different light and calls into question the validity of scores, perhaps hundreds, of critically decisive rulings which shifted and reshaped Israeli legal reality. Under the absurd shadow of "representation monopoly" in all its permutations, how many Supreme Court rulings can be taken at face value?

Resistance is Futile

Can the Government challenge the representation monopoly and insist, in specific cases, that its position be heard and considered despite staunch LCG opposition? Most officials and organs are unwilling to engage in such a head-on confrontation. A handful of lucky cases yielded limited or temporary success. Yet the obstacles to genuine representation jointly enforced by the LCG and Court have proven to be virtually insurmountable.

In the *Akunis* case above, Minister Akunis got to chime in during his hearing and to file a short affidavit – far below the bare minimum of what anyone might consider representation – and he had the good fortune of Justice Stein taking an interest in his views. He still lost the case.

The 2024 *Minnes* case discussed earlier in this chapter presents a more interesting example. Minister of Communication Shlomo Karhi sought to appoint Dr. Odelia Minnes (a respected law professor) to an interim position at a telecoms agency. LCG Gali Baharav-Miara didn't only claim there was a "legal obstacle" to the appointment – she actively fought the Minister's decision in Court in her capacity as his legal "representative." Ostensibly arguing on behalf of Karhi and the Government (which approved the appointment), the LCG adopted the petitioner's claims in their entirety and urged the Court to void the appointment. The petition (along with the LCG's position) was far-fetched – the applicable statute plainly allowed for an interim appointee without requiring the same qualifications as those of a permanent appointment; more to the point, an identical interim appointment had been made just a few years earlier with the LCG's blessing. Yet when the Government requested private representation the LCG refused, stating that the issue was not of "major public importance" and that the appointment's illegality was "clear and manifest."

Here in *Minnes* we find many elements of issues discussed throughout the book. A discretionary (and relatively benign) executive appointment is lawfully made within a Minister's purview and is approved by the Cabinet; in a transparent effort at frustrating government policy as an end unto itself, the LCG claims illegality on absurd grounds involving reasonableness and purposive statutory interpretation, and proclaims a "legal obstacle"; the non-justiciable Cabinet decision is challenged directly in the Supreme Court by uninvolved non-profit organizations with no distinct harm or personal grievance (i.e., no standing) beyond their general disapproval; the Government's only legal representative, the LCG, joins the petitioners and argues in the Government's name for the undoing of its own actions; finally, the LCG denies the Government its own separate legal defense. With the decision on the chopping block and the Communications Minister powerless to avoid the one-sided sham, the *Minnes* case had all the makings of yet another pre-determined government defeat.

But Dr. Minnes was in luck – she too was a named respondent on the petition and was therefore entitled, as a private citizen, to her own representation. Two highly skilled legal scholars took on her case and proceeded to utterly and successfully demolish the petition, while voicing arguments which the silenced authentic government could not. The three-member panel hearing the case included Justice Solberg, known to have limited tolerance for such antics and a consistent (if mild and grandfatherly) critic of the LCG's megalomania. Writing for the majority, Solberg rejected the implausible petition and scolded the LCG for her patently unjust and unfounded denial of any legal representation. The standard of "public importance" cited by the LCG was invented out of whole cloth – no mention of this standard had ever been made in any Commission Report or in the many previous Supreme Court rulings covering the issue. Regarding any claim of "manifest illegality," Solberg essentially shows that the legal question at issue was, as it were, clearly and manifestly complicated – that is, the Minister's highly reasonable and plausible legal position could not be further from "manifest illegality" even had the Court ruled against it. Solberg managed to enlist another Justice to his view and upheld the Government decision to appoint Dr. Minnes.

The 2016 *Gini* case was more dramatic yet. Discussed in Chapter 3 above in the context of statutory interpretation, the case revolved around whether eateries could implicitly present themselves as Kosher without official certification. The main respondent in the case was the Chief Rabbinate, a distinct administrative agency. The LCG considered the Chief Rabbinate's position legally invalid and refused to defend it in court. Though there was a legitimate dispute as to the law's interpretation and application, and though the petition sought to deviate from decades of established consensus and practice, the LCG refused to permit private counsel for the Chief Rabbinate. The LCG also did not inform the Court in any written briefs that he did not intend to defend the government.

Once again Justice Solberg came to the rescue. At the beginning of the first hearing, Solberg asked the LCG about the Chief Rabbinate's position – the Court had heard "rumors" of their dispute, presumably on the news – and was thoroughly surprised to discover that the Rabbinate's legal view would not be represented or heard at all. The Court first requested that the LCG proceed to present the Rabbinate's position; based on the impression that the LCG's commitment left something to be desired, and seeing that there seemed no justification to deny separate representation (even the LCG did not allege "manifest illegality"), the Court then decided to hold an additional hearing in which the Rabbinate could present its case firsthand. Despite the LCG's objections, at the second hearing the government was represented by the Chief Rabbinate's own legal advisor.

The Court dismissed the petition and ruled in favor of the government (though this was partially overturned in a later Rehearing). It's hard to imagine how this outcome could have been reached, were the Court not willing to proactively probe the LCG and then to order that the authentic respondent be given a chance of genuine legal defense.

The *Minnes* and *Gini* cases demonstrate the decisive potential effect of faithful, authentic, skilled representation – a privilege routinely denied to government respondents. Nonetheless, these are very much exceptions that prove the rule and could easily have gone the other way. Many unlikely factors made a combined difference in both cases: The LCG's aggressive overreach; the glaring weakness in the petition's legal claim; the government's insistence on maintaining its policy despite mounting legal hurdles; Justice Solberg on the bench; and above all, the fact that the respondent had the good fortune of genuine legal representation – Dr. Minnes with separate representation as a private citizen, and the Chief Rabbinate with their Court-approved legal advisor. Even with all these stars aligned, victory was far from guaranteed. In *Minnes*, Justice Kabub dissented in favor of the petitioners and in both cases the other concurring opinion (joining Solberg's) was lukewarm at most. In *Gini*, Justice Uri Shoham emphasized that such separate representation ought only be allowed in "rare and extraordinary" instance due to the "dangers" such representation posed to "the rule of law" and to "public faith in the system of government." Shoham warned of a "slippery slope" in which – heaven forbid – "any public body" disagreeing with the LCG "might request separate representation, with all the severe consequences that entails." Shoham's support for the representation monopoly and hostility towards genuine representation for the authentic government accurately reflects the consensus on the Supreme Court and within the Israeli legal establishment.

This brings us to a truly extraordinary example – the 2020 *Gun Licensing* case. Firearm ownership in Israel is heavily regulated and requires a government-issued license, available only to eligible applicants that meet certain strict criteria. Such eligibility criteria are set and periodically updated by executive order of the Minister of National Security (at the time, called Minister of Internal Security). A 2018 petition to the Supreme Court challenged the existing gun licensing policy on a number of fronts, demanding that such criteria be set by statutory regulations (and not Ministerial discretionary orders) and that a 2018 order expanding the criteria be annulled.*

In mid-2020 Amir Ohana was appointed as new Minister of Internal Security. It became immediately apparent that Ohana and the LCG – Avichai Mandelblit – disagreed regarding the petition. Mandelblit considered the petition generally justified and intended to state so before the Court (in Ohana's name), while Ohana (supported by the Ministry's legal advice unit) tended to retain the current criteria and objected to requiring they be set by legislative regulations. Ohana demanded separate or private representation to make his case before the Court, noting that this was a textbook instance of "good-faith disagreement" regarding "reasonable interpretations of the law," quoting from the 1998 Shamgar Report. Though the LCG's position essentially deviated from established practice of decades with no statutory basis, Mandelblit refused Ohana's request. Unlike *Minnes*, there was no additional party that might stand in for the authentic government; unlike *Gini*, it was clear the Court would not proactively solicit Ohana's genuine views. It seemed Ohana was at a dead end and was about to meet a similar fate to that of Akunis, Kahlon and many past Ministers.

But Ohana stuck to his guns, so to speak. Taking an unprecedented step, Ohana filed an independent brief with the Court in his own name, stating simply that the LCG did not represent the Minister and that he demanded to be represented by his own counsel. Ohana noted that if this request was not granted, the Court would be ruling without having heard the arguments of the primary respondent in the suit. The basic right to assistance of counsel in Court – afforded to the common criminal – was not being extended to senior government officials carrying out their duties as democratically elected representatives of public will. In some sense Ohana was asking to be afforded the privilege that any litigant typically has – the ability to represent oneself directly without intermediaries.

The Court was unsympathetic to Ohana's predicament and his desperate plea for a fair hearing. In a curt decision, the Court noted that Ohana's brief was filed without the consent of the LCG and was therefore impermissible, as the LCG possessed the exclusive discretion to decide whether to approve separate representation. The Court ordered that the brief be stricken from the record and removed from the official case file.[61] (In a somewhat typical display, the only source the Court cited was tangential dicta from a concurring opinion by Justice Mazuz in *Tnuva*, calling it "precedent").

In just a few sentences the Court officially and explicitly held that the government could not dismiss its own rogue counsel, becoming a distinct anomaly in the history of democratic jurisprudence. The primary respondent in the case, whose decision was under review and the putative subject of any prospective judicial order, had less ability to argue his view than an *amicus curiae*. As often happens the Court did not elaborate further, despite the decision being a logical leap: the LCG's exclusive monopoly over representation does not necessarily

---

* Another demand regarded the ability of security guards to carry and store their agency-issued weapons at their homes.

preclude, by definition, an independent and unmediated filing by a respondent (which technically does not involve "representation" per se). It would also seem that the Justices took the drastic measure of striking the brief from the record, instead of simply stating that it was invalid, in order to convey a sharp public message that they would not tolerate blunt challenges to the representation monopoly. The decision was issued by (former LCG) Justice Mazuz, (former HCJD director) Justice Vogelman, and (inexplicably) Justice Solberg.

Ohana was eventually replaced; the next Internal Security Minister sought to comply with the petitioners and LCG; and the Court ultimately resolved the case in favor of the petitioners.[62]

Sometimes, the LCG might argue against the government even when the latter has granted the petitioners their wish. The 2021 *Inmates* case was brought during the height of COVID-19.[63] Interior Minister Amir Ohana had instructed that COVID-19 vaccines be made available first to prison staff, and only then to prison inmates. This decision was opposed by the LCG. Following a petition against this policy, and in the aftermath of the *Gun Licensing* case discussed above, Ohana reversed the policy entirely – presumably he had learned his lesson. The petition therefore became instantly moot – there was no longer any existing policy to challenge. Nonetheless, LCG Mandelblit demanded that the Court issue a ruling anyway – he wanted the Court to smack down Ohana's insolence and to reiterate the government's obligation to adhere to LCG opinions.

The Court was more than happy to oblige, but that is beside the point for present purposes. In the *Inmates* case the LCG didn't simply join the petitioners by arguing for their position – he quite literally took their place, by insisting that the Court render a ruling against the government even though the government had acquiesced to the petitioner's demands. Levontin wryly notes that from that moment the case title may as well have been changed to *LCG vs. Ohana*. Warping the notion of "adverse representation" further than ever thought possible, for all intents and purposes the LCG simply assumed the role of petitioner against the government.

A somewhat similar event occurred in the 2025 *Ronen Bar* case, discussed in Chapter 6. The Government had decided to dismiss Ronen Bar, the head of Israel's domestic intelligence agency (the Shin Bet). After the decision was challenged in the Supreme Court, the incumbent Bar announced he would voluntarily resign at a designated date in the near future. In light of Bar's prospective resignation the Government rescinded their decision and revoked the dismissal. Nonetheless, LCG Baharav-Miara demanded that the Court issue a "principled" ruling which would support her position regarding limits on the Government's authority to dismiss the heads of its security agencies. The Court, once again, obliged. Setting aside all other related matters, the LCG once again assumed the role of the petitioner in all but name, by essentially becoming the primary party on whose behalf the Court was issuing its ruling against the government.

In this sense, then, the government cannot escape the LCG's forced "representation" even when it folds and reverses or cancels the decision being challenged in court.

As the absurdity of the LCG monopoly and its effects reach ever-new heights, so does the struggle over government representation continue to evolve and to break new ground.

LCG Baharav-Miara recently developed a new tactic of stifling governmental representation, by indefinitely delaying her own decision whether and how to defend the government. In a 2024 petition against the Minister of National Security regarding new personal firearm licensing rules which were issued following the October 7th attack, the LCG has consistently declined to state whether she will defend the policy in question and whether she might approve private representation if requested. The petition was filed in January of 2024 – a year and a half later (!), at the time of this writing, the LCG has still not made up her mind. For the entire duration of that time the Minister and his prospective outside legal counsel have been in a bizarre limbo in which they have no notion of whether and how to prepare their legal defense. The Minister, via a personal private attorney, has filed numerous motions with the Court demanding that the LCG make a decision one way or another, to no avail – the Court (primarily Justice Amit) has consistently allowed for delays in the LCG's response.* Throughout this time the legal case has proceeded, mostly on technical issues, with two hearings already taking place and with the LCG having filed a feeble and half-hearted preliminary response.[64] The de facto situation created by the LCG was that without her making any formal decision on the matter, she had effectively denied the Minister any legal representation.

In a separate case also involving the Minister of National Security around the same time, the Minister approved a promotion (to a higher rank) for police officer Meir Suissa, and appointed him as commander of a police station in southern Tel Aviv. A petition was filed in the District Court against the appointment, and the LCG announced she would not defend Suissa's appointment nor would she permit outside counsel. In an unprecedented step, the first of its kind, the Minister himself filed a separate petition in the Supreme Court against the LCG, challenging her decision regarding private representation and demanding that she allow for his authentic position to receive a good-faith defense in court. The Court dismissed the petition and ultimately refused to intervene in the LCG's arbitrary exercise of her monopoly power.[65]

Finally, a peculiar role reversal has led to the LCG herself petitioning the Supreme Court against another government entity. As noted earlier, the LCG monopoly extends to control over all government legal action, including its initiation. Per the LCG, this apparently applies even – and especially – to legal

---

* Almost comically, Justice Amit had initially granted a motion to register the Minister's private attorney as "counsel of record," but then immediately regretted it and backtracked the very next day, "clarifying" this did not mean approval for separate representation.

action *against the LCG* and its subordinate bodies. In a very recent 2024 case, the Overseer of Religious Trusts (a government official) filed a petition against the State and the LCG herself (Gali Baharav-Miara) in Rabbinical Court; the court issued an initial ruling that the official was entitled to do so and that the case would proceed. Baharav-Miara responded by filing an HCJ petition with the Supreme Court, challenging both the original lawsuit and the Rabbinical Court's decision as illegal, and claimed that the official could only file a suit against the LCG with the approval of the LCG herself.[66] Without the need for our deep exploration of this issue, here we find yet another way in which the LCG monopoly blocks any ability to scrutinize or challenge the decisions and authority of the LCG as an institution. Anywhere else in the world, an unelected and unaccountable bureaucrat effectively immune from governmental legal action against them would be considered intolerable.

Representation Monopoly in the United States

In several jurisdictions throughout the world we may find variations of monopoly over government litigation. While these may bear a passing and superficial resemblance to the Israeli LCG monopoly, the most cursory examination reveals no such comparison to be justified. One of the most obvious examples is found in various forms of litigation and representation monopoly in the United States, and so it may be briefly addressed – and disposed of.

Eitan Levontin conducts a comprehensive review of representation exclusivity in the U.S.A., at the state and federal levels, under the Attorney General or Solicitor General, managed by the Department of Justice or other organs, and so on. We need not delve into this exhaustive review as a summary of the salient points will suffice. First, any official vested with strong monopolistic authority over government litigation in the U.S.A. is either directly political (appointed by the executive or elected) or indirectly political in the sense that they answer and are accountable to patently political figures with democratic and electoral legitimacy. In other words, notwithstanding a high degree of professional independence, the chief legal officer wielding such monopoly is either accountable to the electorate or is subject to final decision-making and policy-formation by executive political leadership. Second, any such monopoly authority is granted by express statute in the most unmistakable terms, and the assertion of such authority in the absence of explicit statutory grounding would be universally considered laughable. Third, the purpose and effect of litigation exclusivity is to serve elected government and its policies – not to challenge or undermine it. Representation monopoly centralizes legal arguments under "one voice" in court, but this is the voice of the actual government, not of any abstract diffuse "public interest" or principle of "rule of law." These elements alone are enough to show that the Israeli and American systems of representation monopoly simply defy comparison.

Yet perhaps more importantly, even the strongest forms of representation monopoly in the U.S.A. still adhere to the basic concept of good-faith, best-effort genuine representation of the authentic governmental body and its views (demonstrating well that exclusive representation does not entail a privilege of *mis*representation). This rule is widely observed, but courts are also quick to correct any deviations. In a 1982 ruling the West Virginia Supreme Court of Appeals intervened when the State Attorney General was not faithfully representing his (governmental) client, the Secretary of State.[67] The court stressed the duty of the government attorney "to zealously advocate the public policy positions of his client in pleadings, in negotiations, and in the courtroom," and that statutory authority of exclusive representation "does not authorize the Attorney General to assert his vision of state interest." In a striking rebuke the court states that the government lawyer "stands in a traditional attorney-client relationship" to the governmental organ he is charged with defending, and that he

> "is not authorized in such circumstances to place himself in the position of a litigant so as to represent his concept of the public interest, but he must defer to the decisions of the officer whom he represents concerning the merits and the conduct of the litigation, and advocate zealously those determinations in court."

The West Virginia court states the obvious – that hostile representation (against the State-client) means that the government official "has not received representation to which he is lawfully and ethically entitled," leading to deprivation of his "due process right to counsel" and "right of access to the courts." Critically, the court notes the requirement that "every defendant be given his day in court" as a core element of due process, such that:

> "State officers are entitled to have their lawful public policy decisions vindicated in the courts just as individuals are entitled to vindicate their personal rights at law."

In a different ruling from 1988, the Texas Supreme Court emphasizes that even explicit statutory authorization for exclusive representation does not extend to misrepresentation.[68] Per the court, such statute "does not close either the mouth of the agency or the ears of the court" when the government attorneys "are not in fact fulfilling their duty to *represent*" their client (Minister Ohana and his desperate failed brief struck by the Court comes to mind). The court continues that an attorney's right to represent the government "imposes a corollary duty" of "diligent and faithful representation."

In a much more recent advisory opinion, the Maine Supreme Judicial Court addressed the scenario of a government attorney authorized (by statute) to control and direct government litigation, while simultaneously opposing the government position in question and arguing against it in court. Following both law and common sense, the court states: "Simply put, it is our opinion that the Attorney General cannot formally oppose the Executive Branch's litigation position and, at the same time, direct the Executive Branch's litigation…" The court concludes that "when the Attorney General has declined to represent the Executive Branch and has taken a contrary litigation position, the Attorney General is no longer directing the litigation of the Executive Branch."

Perhaps most pertinent of all is the way Warren E. Burger, retired Chief Justice of the U.S. Supreme Court, praised a former Solicitor General in a 1988 obituary: "He never forgot he was the Government's advocate in the Supreme Court, not the Supreme Court's representative in the Department of Justice."[69] It would be hard to find a more plain antithesis to the Israeli approach.

These illustrative quotes stand in stark contrast to the Israeli doctrine and cases discussed extensively in this chapter. There is likely not a single Israeli judge – even among those deemed restrained or conservative – capable of uttering such basic and common-sense truths: that the client is the authentic government official or organ, or that representation means exactly what it sounds like. Despite the existence of statutory-based and politically-supervised representation exclusivity in the United States, it does not remotely approach the patently unjust and anti-democratic farce of Israeli LCG monopoly.

Bound and Gagged

The representation monopoly employed by the Legal Counsel to the Government amounts to a de facto veto over large parts of government policy and decision-making. The agent that speaks for the government in Court *is* the effective government for most intents and purposes. Once the LCG alleges the illegality of an action or decision, its judicial nullification is a foregone conclusion. Due to the difficulty in challenging any specific LCG decision or the LCG's overall power and authority, and thanks to the Court's unfaltering support for the LCG in the sweeping majority of cases, the fate of almost any government action is sealed in an office within the Ministry of Justice.

The LCG's legal opinion binds the government's hands while the monopoly gags the government's mouth in court. We began our description of the LCG as the Supreme Court's "forward base" or proxy, but the representation monopoly brings us closer to a sleeper cell, a defecting fifth column, an internal saboteur undermining and destabilizing valid government action at every turn. Justice Stein compares the concept of hostile representation to soccer penalty shots in which the defending team has no goalie. Yet a more accurate analogy would be if one goalie joins the opposing side and tries to score against his own team; the match judge defers to the defecting goalie in all disputes, calling him an "authorized interpreter of the rules"; all while the judge insists that the losing team had an effective, genuine defense the whole time. Whatever analogy we choose, the effect and function of the representation monopoly is clear – imposing the LCG's and Court's desired substantive outcomes on the government through a gross distortion of all accepted judicial and democratic norms.

Two practical matters discussed in previous chapters are also relevant. First is the self-fulfilling nature of the LCG's legal opinion in light of the absence of any standing requirement. A legal opinion adverse to government action (and a "legal obstacle" all the more so) is essentially an invitation to litigate – the LCG signals to any potential petitioner what challenges would earn the former's immediate support. Indeed, in almost any of the cases discussed so far in this chapter the petition was preceded by a public legal opinion along the same lines. Legal opinions proactively and unilaterally initiated by the LCG may as well be seen for what they are – precursors and drafts of legal challenges in court, tantamount to the LCG simply filing a petition himself directly against the government. The lack of threshold requirements means that any issue raised by the LCG may be easily and swiftly brought before the Supreme Court – such that the distance between a fictional "legal obstacle" and an actual judicial order is not far. (Of course, immediate and unfettered access to the Court serving as first-and-last tribunal with no percolation is of equal significance.)

Second is the absence of evidence hearings held in the Supreme Court, such that the LCG's monopoly is not only over legal arguments but also over what factual accounts are presented to the Justices. By exercising absolute control over the government's voice in litigation the LCG may determine precisely what version of reality is communicated to the Court. This is important because unlike most typical courts of law, the Supreme Court obtains its understanding of relevant facts almost exclusively through the filter of briefs and arguments drafted and communicated by attorneys. Without firsthand evidence or any kind of witness and expert testimony, it is the LCG who defines the factual picture to which Justices are exposed. In this sense the government is not only barred from making its case in legal terms, but also from asserting the basic facts and circumstances as the government holds them to be.

Though it packs a lethal punch, the muscle of representation monopoly usually needs only to be flexed. The monopoly has been used to devastating effect in litigation, yet its most significant implications lie outside the court. In most instances its mere existence is sufficient to deter any meaningful pushback against legal opinion or intimations – the monopoly is an ever-present specter hovering behind anything the LCG says or does. Holding government policy captive generates enough leverage to induce conformity, such that the LCG rarely has cause to execute its hostage. Inherent in every alleged "legal obstacle" or "difficulty," in every hum or haw, in the slightest gesture of skepticism, is the veiled threat of certain litigation defeat.

The LCG typically need not issue an adverse legal opinion, as many officials and organs will involve the LCG from the outset to secure his approval, such that potential wrinkles are ironed out at the preliminary negotiating table; if an opinion is rendered, the LCG does not need to explicitly state what fate awaits those that defy him – a determination of hypothetical illegality is an implicit prediction of practical illegality in court; and even the more disobedient governmental elements are invariably brought to heel with an explicit threat to withhold defense. Like a boxer entering a match rigged against him, only the most determined (or foolhardy) official or politician would be willing to insist on an action or decision doomed by the LCG to near-certain failure.

More often than not, the government reversing course or backing down from a valid and lawful decision is the result of an LCG threat of legal desertion. It is not public criticism or legal flaws that tip the scales, but rather the resigned recognition that there is little sense pursuing a course of action that the LCG has doomed to legal defeat. The aborted appointments of Yoav Gallant (as military Chief of Staff in 2011) and of Gal Hirsch (as national Police Commissioner in 2015) followed precisely this course – though nothing came of the bogus criminal investigations against them, the Government backed down after the LCG announced their appointment would be "indefensible" if challenged in court. Many other decisions and policies shared a similar fate.

The result is that the litigation monopoly mostly manifests itself long before – and without need for – overt legal confrontation. In this sense its effect is impossible to overstate or indeed quantify as its influence remains overwhelmingly far out of sight. Innumerable day-to-day minor and imperceptible interventions in a myriad ways and issues form the true effect of the litigation monopoly, of which cases like *Pinhasi* or *Tnuva* are only the most visible expression.

III – Unparalleled Power

Chief Prosecutor

The LCG's third major function – in addition to being advisor and representative – is general "Prosecutor in Chief." As we have touched upon this role numerous times throughout previous chapters, and as it follows a more familiar pattern, we will afford it only a cursory description. The LCG is the official head of the government criminal prosecution apparatus and is broadly responsible for the legal administration of criminal justice throughout the nation. This function is the only one firmly, explicitly and extensively grounded in statutory provisions which follow the model of many jurisdictions, in which the chief legal officer is also the most senior prosecutorial decision-making authority within the bureaucracy of executive government.

The LCG's responsibilities and discretion in this role include broad policy-formation, wide-ranging organizational aspects, and also many highly specific and distinctive privileges and prerogatives. For instance, the LCG is of course generally responsible for the overall functioning and conduct of the State Attorney, the State Prosecution, and the subordinate hierarchy of District Attorneys and additional criminal justice units, including the Internal Affairs *Mahash* department. But the LCG also holds exclusive decision-making power regarding initiating or approving key criminal investigations and indictments, including the use of extreme investigative tactics or techniques. A wide range of prosecutorial decisions in routine cases require LCG input or approval. Perhaps most notably, the LCG is the decisive figure regarding all criminal proceedings – "probes," investigations, indictments, plea bargains, etc. – against politicians and high-profile government officials. As we have seen, such decisions can make or break the careers of any but the most senior, popular, and resolute politicians.

In principle, when separated from the LCG's other parallel functions his role as Chief Prosecutor is not in itself unusual or especially objectionable. However, we may concisely note two main practical objections, both of which have been explored in Chapter 7 above. First is the lack of democratic accountability or input of public preferences: the appointment (and dismissal) process, the centralized authority concentrated in a single office, the inability of elected government to influence policy and priorities, and the absence of meaningful alternative methods of popular feedback – all culminate in a problematic degree of power wielded by a single governmental (bureaucratic) figure. Second, related to the first, is the broad and consistent abuse of institutional criminal power which casts a dark shadow over the LCG's function as Chief Prosecutor even when considered in its own right. This ranges from system-wide flaws to petty vindictiveness (with devastating consequences for its victims) to egregiously improper prosecutions against political and ideological foes – such as Yaakov Neeman, Haim Ramon, Dror Hoter-Ishay and others.

The LCG's powers of criminal prosecution cannot be isolated from the other realities of the Israeli criminal justice system discussed above – most notably, the notoriously and irredeemably vague Breach of Trust offense and its weaponization against public and elected officeholders. The LCG's ability to criminalize virtually any government or political conduct is integral to his role as chief prosecutor. In addition, the overall criminal jurisprudence of the Supreme Court leaves little room for comfort, as it has shown time and again that it would not provide safe harbor against severe abuses, and at times would actively cooperate with and enable these. The last and most significant hypothetical constraint on the LCG's prosecutorial authority – an impartial tribunal protecting individual liberties and holding law enforcement accountable in specific instances – is largely ineffectual and unreliable, with all that entails.

Judge, Jury and Executioner

We may now zoom out and turn to address some broader perspectives within our discussion of the Legal Counsel to the Government. The first and most significant of these relates to the cumulative effect of the LCG's several roles and functions.

As advisor-judge, the LCG defines the content of the law "towards the government" in what many have called a quasi-judicial role. As representative-jury, the LCG predetermines the outcome of cases against the government by misrepresenting its case and opposing the government in the name of "the rule of law" and "the public interest." As prosecutor-executioner, the LCG oversees the criminal justice and law enforcement apparatus and directs them toward targets of his choosing. Each of these individual roles raises severe concerns and objections. Taken together, wrapped into one unelected office and title of the Legal Counsel to the Government, they jointly constitute a staggering, eye-watering, jaw-dropping degree of power unparalleled in the democratic world. Dworkin's famed judge has nothing on the Israeli Herculean LCG.

As is natural in such cases, the multiple roles of the LCG enhance and augment each other as they interact and overlap, such that the sum is much larger than its already sizeable parts. We have seen how, for example, the threat of criminal prosecution is explicitly – at times almost casually – used to cow officials and politicians into submitting to the LCG's legal position. In one episode mentioned above in Chapter 6, LCG Menny Mazuz seemed to intimate to Cabinet Ministers that their vote against his view would entangle them in (unrelated) criminal proceedings. Indictment or even investigations initiated by the LCG lead to an official's dismissal under the Deri Doctrine, or at the very least to a "conflict of interest" in which they are conveniently barred from involvement with government actions relating to the legal system. In the *Pinhasi-Deri* cases the LCG indicted the Ministers in question as prosecutor, demanded that they must be dismissed on grounds of "reasonableness" as legal advisor, and as representative silenced the authentic Prime Minister and Government from arguing their case to achieve his desired outcome – leading to both the Deri Doctrine and the official monopoly precedent.

Prof. Rivkah Weill describes the relationship plainly, almost matter-of-factly: "No one ever wanted to disobey the LCG's advice, especially if it pertained to matters that might lead to criminal prosecution."[70] Daniel Friedmann observed the shift in power dynamics following Haim Ramon's 2007 conviction – under LCG Menny Mazuz – after which "fear of the LCG reached a level that is difficult to describe," where Cabinet Ministers were "terrified of voicing any disagreement" with the LCG.[71] This absurd reality in which the entire executive hierarchy is bullied into conforming with bureaucratic policy diktats for fear of arbitrary prosecution is taken by many for granted as though it were a conventional feature of democratic governance.

The parallel LCG roles conflict in many additional ways beyond the intimidation of public officials to induce obedience. On an institutional level the LCG advises and represents the government on issues directly affecting his own function as chief prosecutor. Recall the *Mahash* case in which the LCG Avichai Mandelblit vehemently opposed forming a government commission which would consider whether to transfer the Internal Affairs unit out from under the LCG's authority. Mandelblit did not voice his opposition on material grounds as chief prosecutor, but rather alleged illegality on unrelated and technical grounds ("caretaker Government") as legal advisor. At no point in his written legal opinions does Mandelblit acknowledge that he is also the official responsible for *Mahash* and answerable for its flaws (and stands to lose considerable influence by its removal from his control) – as if he were issuing his legal opinion in a matter of no consequence to him or his office. The same was true in the *Orly Ben-Ari* case involving the appointment of interim State Attorney – Mandelblit alleged illegality as legal advisor (while stating that the only "reasonable" choice was his own preferred candidate), not as chief prosecutor acutely affected by the identity of their (nominally) subordinate State Attorney.* Again, here too the LCG issued a "legal opinion" as advisor on an issue with immense ramifications for their own parallel role as chief prosecutor, without so much as recognizing or addressing the glaring conflict of interest created by the dual functions. (In both cases the Court avoided contending with this inherent institutional conflict of interest, by issuing interim injunctions which effectively scuppered the government decision in question but which required no elaboration.)

Many esteemed Israeli jurists from across the political spectrum have proposed that the LCG office be split into two or three separate entities. It's worth noting that in the United States, the Solicitor General (in charge of government litigation) and the Assistant Attorney General for Legal Counsel (in charge of rendering legal advice) are political appointments serving at the pleasure of the President, and their respective offices are entirely separate. The functions of legal representation and legal counsel are similarly split in almost any other democratic jurisdiction.

When Israel was set to join the OECD in 2011, one condition initially posed by the transnational organization was that Israel had to divide the LCG "prosecution" and "advisory" functions into two separate roles (the condition was eventually abandoned following intense lobbying). The idea was considered mainstream enough that at various times it was included in the agenda of left-wing political coalitions, such as of the 2006 Olmert Government and 2021 Bennett-Lapid Government. Yet these suggestions are met with universal condemnation from supporters of judicial supremacy and especially from LCGs and Supreme Court Justices (both current and former). The opposition to reducing the LCG's authority often reaches tones so hysterical as to become near comical. Mordechai Kremnitzer – a seasoned law professor with the Israel Democracy Institute – described any such attempt as part of a "populist campaign" to "destroy" Israel's "system of checks and balances" which would ultimately lead to "placing government above the law."[72] Former LCG and retired Justice Yitzhak Zamir warned that because the LCG is the crucial "protector" of the rule of law and of democracy, any such split would "harm democracy."[73] Menny Mazuz (also ex-LCG and ex-Justice) cautioned that splitting the LCG's roles would "dramatically weaken the system of Israeli law enforcement."[74] These comments were notably all from 2021 – well before the 2023 legal reforms and opposing protest movement.

There are many subtle and complex ways in which the various LCG roles are mutually enhanced and amplified, but the most intolerable is also the most

* Mandelblit also had his own personal interest in the matter, as he worried that an adverse State Attorney might rekindle the dormant investigations against Mandelblit for his past conduct as Military Advocate General.

obvious one. The LCG may one day investigate and indict government officials and politicians, Cabinet Ministers and the Prime Minister, and the next day be expected to sit by their side and advise them in performing their governing duties. Such (ostensibly binding) advice extends, of course, to exclusive representation in court and covers matters which are directly related to the same ongoing (or potential) criminal proceedings. One could hardly imagine a more straightforward and noxious conflict of interest that goes to the core of any official's judgment and discretion.

Few examples better demonstrate this glaring conflict than does the criminal prosecution against Benjamin Netanyahu – regardless of whatever one thinks of him as a politician or of the validity of allegations against him. When LCG Avichai Mandelblit made the controversial decision to indict a sitting Prime Minister on novel charges in 2019 he indisputably tied his own personal and professional legacy to the outcome of that trial. To say that Mandelblit had a vested personal and institutional interest in a legal victory – whatever form that might take – would be a fantastic understatement. Retired Chief Justice Miriam Naor put it succinctly: "Netanyahu's trial is also the trial of Mandelblit."[75]

Yet under his dual role Mandelblit proceeded to advise Netanyahu's successive Governments as though nothing could be more natural. Let us set aside the wild scenario in which public officials with an extraordinary degree of mutual personal animus are expected to collaborate in productive good faith, on efforts requiring a high level of genuine trust and co-reliance. On a professional level Mandelblit had clear skin in the game in absolutely every aspect of Netanyahu's government agenda and policies, including their success or failure. Netanyahu's trial is undoubtedly influenced by his popularity and public standing, as these guide a host of determinations made by both prosecution and defense (some might say, even by judges); yet such public standing is itself undeniably affected by the success and realization of Netanyahu's governmental decisions and policies. Simply put, if Netanyahu had not performed well in all subsequent elections, had he not become Prime Minister in 2020 and again in 2022, his trial would almost certainly have developed in a very different way.

It was thus in Mandelblit's obvious and palpable interest, from the very moment of indictment, to limit, impede and frustrate the policy goals and efforts of Netanyahu and his Government. This is not a conspiracy theory but just plain logic. Every time the LCG proclaims a government decision is illegal or a law is unconstitutional, are we to pretend that such determinations are made on purely detached and neutral grounds, as though an ongoing prosecution by the same office against the same government is of no material consequence? The answer becomes obvious when the same question is applied to virtually any other role in any other setting.

The conflict between roles applies in much more direct fashion to issues involving the Netanyahu trial itself, with a handful of examples standing out. Following his indictment Netanyahu sought to finance his legal defense costs in June 2020. He requested that the official State Gifts Committee approve a grant of ten million NIS (approximately three million USD) from a long-time friend and financier who had offered to cover the considerable attorney's fees. The funds available to the legal team of any defendant may influence a trial's outcome, but in Netanyahu's case – three separate charges and over three hundred witnesses for conduct spanning a decade – the ability to finance his legal expenses could prove decisive. The LCG as chief prosecutor and as the person most identified with the indictment had a clear interest in limiting Netanyahu's legal defense.

Nonetheless, LCG Mandelblit issued a formal opinion stating that the grant would be unlawful and directing the gift committee to deny the request.* He did so in his capacity as neutral and unbiased legal advisor, without the slightest hesitation or reluctance that perhaps his own direct stake (both personal and institutional) as prosecutor might affect his judgment (or indeed the appearance of propriety). Quite regardless of the legality of Netanyahu's request, the inherent conflict of interest is plainly intolerable. Here was the LCG, the same chief prosecutor overseeing the criminal proceedings against Netanyahu, in his role as legal counsel effectively vetoing the defendant's access to funds for his legal defense. Netanyahu's request was accordingly and predictably denied.

The reader might recall from a previous section how in 2020 the LCG prevented the Cabinet from hearing an alternative legal opinion regarding protest restrictions at the height of COVID-19. Yet this episode was also tied to the Netanyahu trial. The protests in question were primarily – overwhelmingly – in fierce opposition to Netanyahu on a variety of fronts and focused especially on his criminal culpability (they were universally dubbed the "Balfour" protests as they were mostly conducted near the Prime Minister residence on Balfour Street in Jerusalem; one central organizing body behind the protests was the "Crime Minister" movement). The protests were also explicitly supportive of the criminal prosecution against Netanyahu, encouraged an aggressive uncompromising approach in court and advocated for expanding the indictments to further criminal charges.

As prosecutor and leader of the criminal proceedings against Netanyahu the LCG thus had a vested interest in sustaining and indeed maximizing the demonstrations. LCG Mandelblit adopted the unique legal position, grounded on vague freedom of speech principles, that the duly enacted COVID-19 restrictions cannot apply to the anti-Netanyahu (and essentially pro-prosecution) protests – that is, that the Government had a legal obligation to *exclude* protests from the restrictions which otherwise generally applied to all other personal and communal activity (including religious gatherings). It was this peculiar "legal opinion" which Minister Amir Ohana sought to challenge by exposing the Cabinet to an alternative, more nuanced and more balanced view. Setting aside our own personal views on COVID-19 restrictions and on their relation to freedom of speech and of assembly (and other important individual liberties) and ignoring whether the LCG's position had any merit, we again see how the LCG exercises

---

* No one (including the LCG) suggested the sum was excessive.

his role as legal counsel in complete denial of any possible conflict of interest no matter how plain and apparent. By excluding protests from COVID-19 restrictions and by barring the Cabinet's access to an opposing legal view, all under his capacity as legal counsel, the LCG was effectively aiding anti-Netanyahu protests in a manner which unquestionably benefitted his parallel role as chief prosecutor.

Notably, Justice Menny Mazuz addressed the direct connection between the protests and the criminal proceedings against Netanyahu in a 2021 ruling, in which the Supreme Court struck down a statutory COVID-19 regulation establishing location-based restrictions on protests. Mazuz explained that "the protests" which would be affected by the new regulations "did not concern" governmental policy but were rather "personally aimed at the Prime Minister" in light of the criminal allegations against him. Justice Mazuz felt it would have been "proper" for Netanyahu to avoid any involvement in the legislative process towards these regulations, as the Prime Minister had an inherent personal interest in their effect. Simultaneously, the exact same point regarding the LCG's vested interest in bolstering the protests completely eludes Mazuz and many others. In this instance as elsewhere, judicial supremacists are willfully blind to the glaring contradictions and conflicts at the core of the LCG's parallel functions as advisor and prosecutor.

A final example regards the "conflict of interest" arrangement drafted by LCG Mandelblit for Netanyahu in 2020, eventually endorsed by the Court in 2021. This "binding" legal opinion imposed far-reaching limitations on Netanyahu's involvement in a range of executive decisions, mostly relating to the legal and criminal justice systems, justified by his alleged conflict of interests as a criminal defendant. The irony, of course, is that these limitations were devised and applied by none other than the chief prosecutor in the very same criminal case – Mandelblit himself. As legal advisor, Mandelblit could cripple the Prime Minister's governing ability with various "binding" limitations (devoid of legal basis), while at the same time ignoring his own acute interest in undermining the defendant against whom he had just filed an indictment. Needless to say, when Netanyahu claimed the "arrangement" was invalid and not binding, and a petition against him demanded that the Supreme Court enforce the sweeping limitations, it was the LCG who appeared before the Court to argue (in the name of the public interest) that they were both lawful and binding. Thus the LCG indicts the Prime Minister on a Monday, provides legal "advice" restricting his defendant's authority on a Tuesday, and finally appears in Court as "gatekeeper" of "the rule of law" and defends his own advice on a Wednesday – each day exercising a separate function in what we are supposed to believe is a detached and neutral manner.

The Supreme Court ruled that the "conflicts of interest arrangement" imposed by Mandelblit on Netanyahu was indeed binding, just as any other LCG "legal opinion." To be clear, Netanyahu did not deny that he had a conflict of interest or that he was obligated to adhere to some form of "arrangement" – he had proposed that the LCG delegate the task to the State Comptroller or to a retired judge that did not have Mandelblit's personal stake in Netanyahu's case. The Court's decision is remarkable in that it fails to consider or even address the prospect that there might be the remotest problem in the LCG rendering such restrictions against a defendant in an ongoing criminal trial (the most important and fraught in Israel's history) in which the LCG is also the prosecutor. Perhaps conceding the objection in principle was out of the question, but the Court could not even acknowledge the severe conflict created in this specific instance (for example, when determining just how "binding" the LCG's memo ought to be). In the thirty pages of the main opinion by Justice Hayut, the objection is mentioned in passing – as it was previously raised by Netanyahu's attorneys – but is then completely ignored (Hayut does not even grant it the courtesy of a dismissive rejection). In a short concurring opinion Justice Meltzer mentions the objection but responds by simply bleating – sorry, repeating – the mantra of "binding counsel," as though this were somehow a sufficient (or even rational) answer. The ruling in this case demonstrates not only the crude conflict of interest inherent in the LCG's parallel functions, but also and especially reveals the extent of willful blindness that the Supreme Court readily employs, to avoid any reflection on this glaring aberration and to protect the formidable power accrued by its most loyal and effective proxy.

*

Writing in 2021, renowned political scientist Shlomo Avineri summarized once again (as he had in 2009) the most glaring flaws in the combined roles of the Israeli Legal Counsel to the Government at odds with principles of liberal democracy: the staggering "concentration of power in a single individual or institution," and the patent conflict of interest inherent in the LCG's exercise of this parallel functions.[76] As things stand, the LCG is "the most powerful figure in the country's governmental system, with concentrated authority possessed by no official in any other democratic state." Avineri describes the "binding counsel" model as the gradual "creeping annexation of power, granting the LCG a veto over Government decisions and its legislative initiatives." This effectively "places the LCG above the Prime Minister and the Government, leaving the Government with no meaningful way" to mount a challenge. The prosecutorial function meant that "no Minister would dare" defy the LCG too forcefully – "for who knows, perhaps they would find themselves criminally indicted?" The advent of the representation monopoly further solidified the LCG's dominance and set him as "the boss and final decision-maker" on government policy.

Avineri states the obvious objection that "if this is not a conflict of interest, it would be hard to know what is." Such combined concentration of overlapping powers rolled into one official is "intolerable," placing the LCG in situations which are "impossible on a human and moral level" and which stand "contrary to the norms of checks and balances of any democratic regime." At the same time, the parallel functions performed by a single individual "severely violates the separation of powers" and undermines the government and Knesset as "the representatives of the sovereign" electorate. Finally, the LCG's authority contradicts the most fundamental tenet of democratic government – "the limitation of concentrated power not subject to effective oversight."

Symbiosis

Though we will not attempt to review the complex web of personal and professional interactions between the Supreme Court and the Legal Counsel to the Government, some institutional context is illuminating. From 1983 until 2012 those serving at the Court's helm as Chief Justices – with the astronomical influence of that office – brought with them a uniquely sympathetic and expansionist view towards the role and function of the LCG. Meir Shamgar served as LCG before his appointment to the bench, as did his successor Aharon Barak. The latter's protégé Dorit Beinisch served as director of the HCJD and later as State Attorney before joining the Court. Through nearly thirty years – presiding over the era of ascending judicial supremacy – the Chief Justices that radically transformed the LCG role hailed exclusively from the top ranks of the State legal apparatus.

In addition to the Chief Justices, the Supreme Court bench has long been considered a cozy home for those LCGs (and other top government attorneys) finding favor with the Court. Of the eight LCGs that served before Mandelblit got the job in 2016, five were eventually appointed to the Supreme Court – Shamgar, Barak, Zamir, Rubinstein and Mazuz. Other notable Justices in recent memory rising from similar stations were Gabriel Bach (State Attorney), Mishael Cheshin (Deputy LCG), Dorit Beinisch (State Attorney and director of HCJD), Edna Arbel (State Attorney) and Uzi Vogelman (director of HCJD). Crucially, the vast majority of these jurists had never served as judges – not for a single day – before being placed on the Supreme Court bench. While there are understandable reasons why senior government attorneys continue to pursue a judicial career, the Israeli Supreme Court is generally an outlier in the amount (and proportion) of Justices appointed from the ranks of the State legal corps (and with no prior judicial experience). Anyone occupying the role of LCG or State Attorney have a better shot than most at becoming a Supreme Court Justice.

Eitan Levontin describes the effect of this "clear promotion track from the top of government legal service to judicial office in the Supreme Court."[77] The LCG "routinely argues… before judges that likely will directly determine his personal [professional] fate," creating yet another "institutional and personal conflict of interest." Government representation sometimes "demands an important and legitimate argument contradicting an existing judicial view, which might be erroneous or outdated," yet the LCG "would likely keep faith with the judicial view and not with his role as attorney." Aside the obvious impairment of effective representation, this also harms "inter-branch dialogue," the "quality of judicial deliberation" and "the development of substantive law."

The above applies not only to the person of the LCG but to the government legal corps more generally. The symbiotic institutional synergy between the LCG and Court trickles down to rank-and-file attorneys and to line prosecutors in a manner solidifying their self-perception as long arm of the Court. As Yoav Dotan explains, this applies especially to the HCJD – a "relatively small group of career public servants who appear before the Justices on a daily basis" and therefore develop "a relationship of affinity and mutual trust" with the Supreme Court.[78] This affinity has not only "endowed" the LCG and HCJD lawyers "with a high reputation within all governmental and political circles," but has also "translated into personal gains… in terms of promotion to higher posts within the bureaucracy or to the bench."[79]

Much like the LCG, the prospect of career advancement is key to understanding the benefits of alignment with the Court – judicial office is a natural path forward for many government lawyers. Let us recall (from Chapter 1) that the Supreme Court Justices wield decisive influence over all judicial appointments and not only those to the highest court. Dotan observes that "one of the main prospects for promotion for members of the HCJD is to be appointed to the bench," and therefore "it is understandable that for HCJD members, serving the interest of the court is no less important than winning the case for their clients."[80] The fidelity of government lawyers to the Court is thus grounded not only in ideology or sociology but also in practical career considerations. At the same time, the Court has a clear interest in infusing the judiciary with appointees from within the LCG, HCJD and State Prosecution (and these are indeed overrepresented in the judiciary).

The Supreme Court gleans benefits from such "affinity" which go well beyond the LCG and HCJD commitment to further the Court's agenda by legal directive or misrepresentation in trial (or later, on the bench themselves). Over the years, the HCJD developed a pre-trial process (dubbed "pre-HCJ") in which legal controversies are resolved or narrowed before ever reaching adjudication. It has become customary to provide the HCJD a draft petition before filing with the Court, so that the HCJD and LCG may exercise their considerable policy-making influence internally (especially if they are sympathetic to the petition), and potentially bring about the desired result (or a satisfactory settlement) without troubling busy Justices.

Dotan explains in detail how this pre-trial filtering function "informally delegated" to HCJD lawyers also helps the Court manage its overwhelming caseload, including tasking the HCJD with "investigating actions and reporting findings" – findings which ultimately serve as "the principal factual basis" for the Court's decision.[81] This "semi-adjudicatory" function performed by the HCJD on the Court's behalf assists with the "easing of docket pressures" and "enabled" the Court to act as trial court "despite its obvious institutional inaptness and procedural limitations."[82] Though this is clearly "not compatible with the adversarial model of litigation… because lawyers function as affiliates of the court," it is a staple feature of the symbiotic co-reliance between the Court and the legal corps ostensibly representing the government.

As an aside, it's worth noting that the overall alignment between the Court and the various LCG institutions and subsidiaries is so pervasive that the ability of any individual official to effect significant change is extremely limited. Commitment to judicial supremacy and to the reciprocal relationship with the Court is internally enforced while deviations from the norm are disciplined; no government attorney is too senior to be pushed out of the system (or worse) if perceived as a threat to the overall project. Even the LCG himself would have difficulty swimming against the stream – LCG Yosef Harish found himself abandoned by his subordinates in 1986 when defending the government in a specific context, and described how the HCJD not only "did not assist" but exhibited "blatant defiance." Harish paraphrased the HCJD attitude thus: "We will provide no assistance... You will receive no legal advice." Two days after starting his position as LCG Harish was compelled to appear in court on his own,* as no one from the HCJD was willing to accompany him.[83]

How important was the HCJD and LCG contribution to the Court's ascendancy? Dotan estimates that "the rise of judicial activism" during the 80s and 90s (much of which has been the focus of the book so far) was "largely based" on the mutual relationship between these institutions. The government legal corps "provided the court with inputs essential to the expansion of judicial power," "improved the Court's ability to supervise" executive government, and were vital "for enforcement of the Court's decisions." This "collaboration" (including the pre-trial function) allowed the Court to effectively conceal a large degree of its actual intervention in government action and "thus to reduce the political cost of such intervention."[84]

Immovable Objector

We have so far elegantly ignored one critical question lurking in the shadows throughout this chapter: Why not fire the LCG? Why does the Government not simply relieve the LCG of their duties? The answer is tied directly, and somewhat unexpectedly, to the 2023 "Reasonableness Amendment" and its potential frustration of judicial supremacy, to which we return once again.

The amendment, which stated that the Court could not examine the reasonableness of decisions taken by the Government and its Ministers, would surely have indirectly weakened the substantive grounds for the LCG's legal directives – a great many of which relied on the alleged "unreasonableness" of government action. Yet the amendment also posed a much more immediate and tangible threat to LCG dominance.

---

* After stressing that no government attorney has the "luxury" of refusing to defend the State when inconvenient, the same Yosef Harish about-faced nine years later when he himself denied Prime Minister Rabin meaningful representation in the Deri-Pinhasi cases.

The prospect of dismissing an LCG has always been something of a political impossibility for a variety of reasons. Suffice to say that no LCG has ever been fired.* Levontin observes in 2023 that "the Government's authority" to remove the LCG "is so limited as to be close to theoretical," while also noting a nearly identical statement made some four decades earlier.[85] Friedmann adds that any such "complex" decision becomes "impossible" in the common circumstances of the Prime Minister (and other Cabinet Ministers) being subject to criminal investigations or charges, as it would lead to immediate allegations of improper motives (and presumably to further indictments stemming from the resulting ostensible "conflict of interest").[86] The 1998 Shamgar Report which set out the current appointment process also defined a convoluted dismissal process (adopted by Government resolution), in which the Government could fire the LCG based only on a set of specific "causes." Such "causes" are limited to severe (or criminal) misconduct or "substantial and persistent" disagreements and set a high bar – the Shamgar Report explicitly states the desire to avoid the dismissal of an LCG for their insistence on their "good faith" legal opinion, such that the Government would likely need to prove overt bad faith on the LCG's part. Further, the decision to dismiss can come only after "consulting" the judicially-aligned appointment committee, which is almost certain to recommend against dismissal, and only after the LCG himself may state his case in hearings before both the appointment committee and the Government.

Political or formal hurdles aside, any decision to dismiss the LCG would ultimately be subject to the Supreme Court's piercing judicial review – and herein lies the kicker. Few throughout the legal or political establishment would argue that the Court might uphold a Government decision to fire the LCG. The Court invalidating any such dismissal is universally regarded as very likely. The Court would almost certainly intervene and reinstate a judicially-aligned LCG. Critically, such intervention would likely extend even to a Government resolution changing the dismissal process itself.

Thus, the answer to our initial question is exceedingly straightforward – all other factors notwithstanding, the LCG is simply un-fireable, under the assumption that the Supreme Court will reverse any such Government effort of dismissal. Such de facto immunity also better explains the increasing audacity of successive LCG's in their escalating confrontations with elected government.

At the time of this writing, as of July 2025, the Government has initiated numerous efforts to dismiss the current LCG Gali Baharav-Miara. The LCG has announced these attempts to be illegal and void, and has refused to appear before preliminary Government hearings on the matter. Even if the Government follows through with a resolution to dismiss Baharav-Miara (the first such resolution in Israel's history), the Court is sure to become involved, in what promises to be a drawn-out and ugly battle.

---

* Though Yitzhak Zamir stepped down facing the possibility that he might be fired.

This key insight leads us directly to the Reasonableness Amendment. The sole method by which the Court can reverse a Government decision to fire an LCG is undoubtedly the "extreme unreasonableness" standard and its associated jurisprudence regarding executive appointments. Without the basis of "reasonableness" the Court has virtually no grounds to intervene in a Government decision to fire the LCG. Consequently, the amendment would have severely curtailed – and perhaps even blocked – the Court's ability to prevent the LCG's dismissal. Of all the dramatic effects of the controversial amendment, this seems to be the one that most troubled many adherents of judicial supremacy, even more than annulling the Deri Doctrine or limiting the Court's substantive review of administrative action. Indeed, many critics and commentators at the time framed the Reasonableness Amendment as merely a pretextual first stage towards dismissing the LCG, all as part of an overall scheme to save Prime Minister Netanyahu from the criminal charges against him.

Here, again, we find substantive doctrine and institutional power-mechanisms to be intertwined. The familiar reasonableness standard not only grants the LCG power to dictate policy, as comprehensively demonstrated above, but also grants her immunity, by simultaneously preventing the Government from dismissing the LCG.

This intrinsic link between reasonableness review and the LCG's immunity from removal is expressly endorsed by none other than the Supreme Court itself. In its 2024 ruling to strike down the Reasonableness Amendment, numerous Justices plainly stressed the amendment's adverse effects on the protection of "Gatekeepers" (namely, the LCG and State Attorney) from politically-motivated dismissal. Several Justices articulate this point at length and in the most express terms.

Justice Ruth Ronen explains how the independence and objectivity of these Gatekeepers hinge on the Court's ability to review decisions regarding their appointment or dismissal. The existence of such "effective judicial review" is what

> "ensures that Gatekeepers are appointed according to relevant considerations; that Gatekeepers may rest assured that they will not be unreasonably fired; and that their tenure will not be terminated simply because they did not conform to the interests of those who appointed them."[87]

Per Ronen, the reasonableness standard "has a significant part" in this process of judicial oversight – "in practice, the reasonableness standard is the primary ground" employed in review of appointment and dismissal decisions, and indeed is often "the sole ground for intervention to prevent" improper decisions. Ronen summarizes that removing the Court's ability to review the reasonableness of dismissals would "impair the independence of Gatekeepers" and "increase their reliance" on executive government.*

Justice Daphne Barak-Erez also repeatedly emphasized the "critical" impact of the reasonableness standard regarding the dismissal of Gatekeepers, and the "undoubted" threat to the LCG's independence were the Government able to fire him without the constraints of judicial reasonableness review. "It is clear that the annulment of the reasonableness standard with regard to the dismissal of Gatekeepers raises the concern of damage to their independence, in that they may be fired only for presenting a professional view which is unacceptable to the Government."[88]

There we have it from the horse's mouth – even the Court concedes (in fact, it confidently affirms) that the LCG's immunity from ultimate Governmental oversight in the form of dismissal is inexorably linked to the Court's application of reasonableness review against such decisions. This startlingly candid admission yields two useful insights: First, in confirming the primary reason that the Government is unable (and therefore makes no attempt) to fire the LCG; and second, in highlighting yet another potential (and non-obvious) effect of the 2023 Reasonableness Amendment and the Court's corresponding incentive for opposing it.

As a side point, the judicial opinions above (and many others like them) perfectly reflect the fundamental philosophical outlook of the Israeli legal elite as described in the Introduction to this book. The prime suspects deserving of constant restriction throughout the Court's narrative are the elected politicians and the public they represent; the imperiled blameless saints deserving limitless discretion and confidence are the unelected, unaccountable, entrenched legal bureaucrats. While only the former are subject to regular oversight by the sovereign *demos*, it is the latter which are entrusted with authority to impose their views in any conceivable matter and which must be shielded from "unobjective," "improper" and "non-professional" government actions. The people's representatives are assumed to be scheming and nefarious, the insulated clerks credited with propriety of conduct and purity of conscience.

Consequently, the "independence" advocated by the Court is of a very specific nature – the Court envisions so-called Gatekeepers independent from public input, scrutiny, and control, and more broadly from the law and from democracy itself. The notion of sovereign supervision over government authority through elected representatives isn't only absent from the Israeli judicial lexicon – it is anathematic to it. In the Court's eyes, all-powerful Platonic legal guardians of judicial supremacy shielded from any meaningful public oversight are a core feature of democracy, while the ability of elected officials to hire and fire the single most powerful unaccountable executive officer in the Western world actually undermines democracy.

---

* We will set aside the accuracy and validity of this argument for now.

*

I have taken great pains so far to describe – at times in laborious detail – the ascendancy of judicial supremacy in Israel and its component mechanisms and doctrines which preceded the Court's dramatic shift to review the constitutionality of laws. I have hopefully impressed upon the reader that the challenges and shortcomings of Israeli jurisprudence since the 1980s, pioneered by Aharon Barak and cemented by his allies and adherents, extend far beyond the narrow context of constitutional judicial review which tends to be the focus of contemporary debate and to which we soon turn our attention in the next chapter.

Had the Court never embarked on its constitutional project of absolute supremacy the Israeli legal system would still be beset with the most monumental and crippling flaws, the majority of them created or exacerbated by the deliberate, sustained, methodical decision-making of the Supreme Court and its Justices. These include (but are not limited to) the Court-dominated judicial selection process, the centralized position of the Supreme Court within the judicial hierarchy, the prevailing approach of "objective purposive" legal interpretation, the abolishment and absence of threshold barriers to adjudication, the all-pervading standard of "extreme unreasonableness," the Deri Doctrine of impeachment by judicial review, the abuse of criminal justice, and the aberrant proxy institution of the Legal Counsel to the Government. Accordingly, any resolution or improvement addressing constitutional review but ignoring the issues discussed in the previous chapters would be only of negligible value and perhaps even counterproductive.

Political scientist Martin Edelman described judicial activism – in his words, "the judicialization of politics" – as having "proceeded further in Israel than in any other democratic country."[89] Around the same time, two prominent law professors at UC Berkley published a study in which comparative law scholars rated judiciaries according to their degree of activism (or "daring"): Israel was ranked first out of fourteen countries (the United States came second).[90] These estimations, reflecting a broad consensus and recognition, were made in 1995 – *before* the notorious "constitutional revolution" in which the Israeli Supreme Court assumed the power to strike down primary legislation.

Let that sink in.

Part III

Supremacy

The constitutional revolutions
and the consolidation of judicial hegemony

Chapter 9

The Pseudo-Constitution

From Parliamentary Supremacy to the Judicial Revolution

> "*Only in Israel do judges confer the power of abstract review on themselves, without the benefit of a constitutional or legislative provision. One is reminded of Napoleon's taking the crown out of the pope's hands and putting it on his own head.*"
> — Judge Richard Posner[1]

At long last, we arrive at the grand constitutional questions plaguing Israeli society, politics and jurisprudence. Undoubtedly some readers embarked on reading this book for the primary purpose of exploring this specific topic.

The creation of the Israeli pseudo-constitution and the advent of judicial review, around which this chapter revolves, mark the transition from judicial dominance to judicial supremacy. Despite all the foregoing chapters and extraordinary power and influence exercised by the Supreme Court, the public and its elected representatives still had one potent tool at their disposal – that of primary legislation. At least in theory, even with all the Court's formidable institutional advantages and doctrinal innovations, the Knesset could yet assert its will and authority by enacting direct and express rules, using the most explicit and clear language, in the form of parliamentary legislation. Such laws could indeed extend even to addressing the State's institutional structure and curtailing the Court's legal dominance. Thus Israel's sole democratically-authorized elected branch of government could retain its ultimate power of forming the laws of the land, and of final-say authority on contested societal disagreements. Under such a system of parliamentary supremacy the Court's many transgressions might have somehow remained tolerable.

In 1995 and again in 2024, the Supreme Court fundamentally altered this precarious (and already skewed) imbalance of power by claiming the ability to strike down "unconstitutional" legislation. In doing so the Court wrested ultimate decision-making authority from the Knesset, making it the true administrator of State power and the final lawmaker for all intents and purposes. The Israeli parliament and public were robbed of their only remaining instrument of meaningful governance, and the Court became Supreme. It is to this process and phenomenon which we now turn our attention.

The oft-confusing and bewildering tale of Israeli constitutional law – with its convoluted legal intricacies, its comparative peculiarity and its foreign terminology – may pose a challenge to even the most determined reader, as it indeed does even to Israeli legal scholars. This chapter will aim to simplify and clarify, to present the evolution and perversion of constitutional rules in understandable and accessible fashion. In that spirit, lest the many trees block our view of the forest, it is well worthwhile to articulate some overall facts which are to serve as an outline of our ensuing discussion.

Israel was founded in 1948 without a constitution. To this day, Israel has nothing which remotely resembles a constitution in any conventional sense. Consequently, the Israeli governmental order was one of "parliamentary supremacy" in which the majoritarian elected Knesset was sovereign and in which no court could invalidate legislation on legal grounds. In a 1995 ruling which came to be known as the "constitutional revolution" – devoid of legal basis – the Supreme Court unilaterally decided that Israel's unwritten constitution (which included something called Basic Laws) now amounted to a "substantive" constitution which empowered the Court to strike down legislation it deemed unconstitutional. The Court proceeded to enforce its pseudo-constitution and has since nullified dozens of laws based on this newly contrived authority. In 2024, the Court ruled that the Knesset and public are powerless to significantly alter the so-called constitution or to influence its application by the Court. As a result, since 1995 and more markedly since 2024, the Israeli constitutional order is one of judicial supremacy.

We may bear in mind this overarching account as we delve into its respective components.

For analytical purposes the constitutional debate here is treated separately from the issues discussed in previous chapters, though in reality these are all of course deeply and fundamentally intertwined. The Court's control of judicial selection and centralized dominance of the judiciary, the creative misinterpretation of statutes, the unfettered immediate access of any agitator to judicial remedy for any issue, the enfeeblement of elected government by "reasonableness" coupled with the menace of targeted criminal prosecution, and the relentless internal undermining of government by its own legal counsel – these all form the backdrop and context for the decisive and pivotal events described herein, both in the general environment they created and in the specific, concrete, tangible results they produced.

Before we proceed, some concepts require quick elucidation.

The act of "judicial review" in this chapter refers to the typical sense of striking down primary laws or legislative acts.

The noun "constitution" will usually mean what it sounds like – a constitution as conventionally and intuitively understood by most individuals, citizens and scholars alike. While these come in many shapes and forms, all constitutions (as commonly understood) fit a basic description: a formal comprehensive textual document at the peak of a State's legal hierarchy, laying out fundamental principles and rules of government in a given regime, relating to structural allocation of authority between different institutions and to limitations on government (especially with respect to individual liberties and rights), declaring some core shared societal assumptions or values, adopted by a special or unique method, and reflecting wide and deep popular consensus (or at least compromise).

Martin Loughlin describes the modern "documentary" constitution as "a consciously constructed artifact… a document adopted in the name of the people that defines the powers of government, specifies the basic rights of citizens, and regulates the relationships between the established institutions of government and their citizens."[2] Loughlin emphasizes the written form as the "basic template" for the modern constitution, such that "the most rudimentary requirement of constitutionalism is that the exercise of political power is subjected to the discipline of a *text*."[3] A further "basic principle" is that a constitution "is drafted by elected representatives of the people meeting in a constituent assembly" for the specific purpose of establishing the regime's constitutional norms.[4]

There are indeed other conceivable meanings to the word "constitution" beyond the written version, primarily indicating the fundamental agreed framework and mechanisms of a governmental order and perhaps the core limits or curbs on the exercise of government power. Many distinguish these from a conventional constitution by referring to them as "unwritten" or "uncodified"; some contrast the conventional form as a "legal" constitution with the latter as a "political" constitution. For example, there is no doubt that the United Kingdom is a constitutional democracy despite having no written constitution. We will return later to these distinctions and the boundaries between them, and to other variations within the Israeli context, but will otherwise use "constitution" in its typical and conventional meaning as a comprehensive unified written legal document.

*

Throughout the entire democratic world there are three "clubs" with which we might associate jurisdictions by their approach to judicial review. In one club are countries in which no court can strike down primary legislation – these include states with no written constitution, such as the United Kingdom and New Zealand, or states with a constitution that explicitly rules out such judicial review, such as the Netherlands, Luxembourg and Switzerland. In the second club, certain courts may strike down statutes enacted by the legislature based on their violation or contradiction of a written constitution – these include states where such authority is explicitly granted to judges, such as in Canada or many European and Latin

American countries, or states where such authority is inferred from the constitution's "supreme" status superseding other legal norms, such as the United States. Finally, in the third club, a court may strike down laws as "unconstitutional" in the absence of a written constitution. Like Sgt. Pepper's Hearts Club Band, this is a lonely one – Israel is the only member.

We now proceed to examine how this came to be.

I – In the Beginning: 1948-1995

Deciding Not to Decide

The State of Israel was founded without a constitution, and failed to adopt one in the early years following its establishment. The 1948 Declaration of Independence plainly envisaged (though didn't quite mandate) the adoption of a constitution – the Declaration established the Provisional State Council which was to serve as parliament "until the establishment of the elected, regular authorities of the State in accordance with the Constitution which shall be adopted by the Elected Constituent Assembly not later than October 1st, 1948." The Declaration and its authors thus expressed a clear intent that Israel would form, and then proceed to function under, a conventional constitution.

Alas, it was not to be. The initial deadline of October 1948 was missed by default, as national elections for the Constituent Assembly were held in January of 1949 and the Assembly gathered for its first meeting the next month. It quickly emerged that despite the Declaration's assumption regarding the desirability and feasibility of a constitution, the issue was in fact hotly contested amongst Israel's founders and leaders. A further complication was that the Provisional State Council (the initial parliament under the Declaration of Independence) voted to dissolve itself the moment the Assembly was to be established, and that all its parliamentary-legislative authorities be transferred to the Assembly. As a result, the newly elected Constituent Assembly found itself functioning as the State's de facto parliament from day one – not ideal conditions for the detached discussion and drafting usually required for constitution-making. The Assembly indeed embraced its new parliamentary capacity – in its first and only session, on February 16th of 1949, the Constituent Assembly passed the Transition Law, forming the new Knesset as Israel's official legislature and redesignating itself as the First Knesset. In a sign of things to come, the Constituent Assembly mayfly perished on its first and only day of existence.

The First Knesset picked up where the Assembly left off and resumed the constitutional deliberations. Being the former Constituent Assembly elected for that specific purpose, the First Knesset (probably) still possessed the authority to enact a constitution. But as the debate dragged on – in the midst of an existential war, while engaged in marathonic sweeping legislation and attending to other parliamentary duties of a neonatal State – it became increasingly clear that a constitution was not in the cards.

Following a year of almost no progress the Knesset resolved, in the June 1950 "Harari Decision" (to which we will return), that it would abandon the adoption of a written constitution. Ever since, the State of Israel has plodded along without a recognizable constitution.

Though it might seem odd that a modern State established in the mid-twentieth century decided to forgo a constitution, further reflection reveals that the decision was somewhat unremarkable and was indeed based on compelling rationales. The underlying causes preventing Israel from enacting a constitution have been suggested by numerous scholars – these are illuminating whether as justifications or simply as explanations, and reveal the decision to be not all that inexplicable. We may summarize these explanations as follows:[5]

a) After some thirty years under the British Mandate, many Israelis absorbed British sensibilities regarding an uncodified constitutionalism. In light of Great Britain having no written constitution and getting along just fine, the Israeli public were simply not all that concerned about Israel following suit. This held especially true for the Israeli legal elite, many of whom were educated within the context of English common law and British parliamentary democracy, and whose members might otherwise have played a stronger role in advocating for a constitution.

b) More broadly, the trend towards adopting codified constitutions was less globally obvious than it might be considered today. Many validly democratic regimes did not have a constitution such that the refusal to adopt one did not seem especially abnormal. In addition, one of the strongest arguments in favor of a constitution at the time (and to some degree, still today) applied to federative or presidential systems. Both such governmental systems feature overlapping and competing claims of democratic authority and legitimacy – federal versus state, executive versus legislature – due to separate and parallel popular elections. In such countries a constitution becomes virtually indispensable for the clear distribution of structural governing power. In this sense, the argument for constitutional power-allocation is far less applicable for Westminster-style parliamentary democracy, in which parliament is the sole institution vested with direct democratic authority within a single national government.

c) Israel expected to absorb vast immigration following its founding, which indeed transpired – the Israeli population doubled within three years (by 1951) and tripled within fifteen years (by 1963), a demographic surge nearly unparalleled in modern history. Many argued that it was unjust, as well as imprudent, to codify and entrench Israel's core institutions and values without a large part of its potential incoming population having a say.

d) Throughout its formative years (and essentially until at least 1973) Israel was engaged in a military struggle for its physical survival. Some were concerned that a constitution, including a codified bill of rights and robust judicial review, would tie the government's hands in critical issues relating to security and defense, a luxury Israel could not afford against its many existential threats. A related factor was that in the midst of such war and the threat of annihilation, both Knesset and public simply could not prioritize constitutional aspirations and lofty deliberations over their more urgent needs. As observed in this book's Introduction, the fundamental cedes to the existential.

e) Some raised principled, material objections to the idea of a binding, counter-majoritarian constitution enforced by judges. Chief among these was Israel's legendary leader and first Prime Minister David Ben-Gurion himself. Ben-Gurion persuasively argued against a constitution in numerous public forums, including in 1949 before the Knesset committee charged with drafting one.[6] In that memorable speech, Ben-Gurion doubted whether Israel shared the typical circumstances which justify a constitution (such as a federative system, or one evolving from limits on tyrannical or monarchical power), and generally echoed the points noted above. As for a non-binding and unenforceable "ceremonial declaration of principles," Israel already had the Declaration of Independence which adequately served this purpose.

More substantively, Ben-Gurion rejected the idea of a "supreme law" which limits future majorities by requiring additional hurdles for its amendment or repeal, and asked – "are we sure that those who come after us will not have the same wisdom, the same devotion, that they will not understand the needs of the nation as we do? Why should we restrict them?" He continues: "Why would the parliament decide that the majority of today has more power than a majority of the future?" He concludes later that "we have no justification to be so arrogant as to pass laws that people who come after us can't change." Ben-Gurion correctly recognized that the meaning of any supermajority requirement (for passing or amending "superior" laws) simply meant granting veto power to a minority. To this he responded: "We must not allow a minority to prevent the passage of laws on the grounds that a supermajority is required for certain 'special' laws. I think this would be dangerous here... Even the rule of the majority is not so quickly accepted among us. The rule of a minority? This won't be accepted." Not a scholar of political theory, Ben-Gurion still managed to convey some of the basic common-sense objections to an Israeli constitution.

Ben-Gurion was especially dismissive of judicial review. With "all due respect" to judges, he warned that if "seven people designated with the rank of judge" were to "cancel something that the nation wants," this "would lead to revolution." He called this kind of judicial authority "a reactionary thing" (a hard slur within his socialist-progressive *Mapai* movement). Ben Gurion concludes of such a mechanism: "With us this can't exist. The community wouldn't accept it."

f) For the centralized, statist national government dominated by the ruthlessly pragmatic *Mapai* party, the notion of limiting its leeway seemed to provide very few benefits at very great risk. Especially at the Executive level, Israel's early leadership had little incentive to voluntarily limit the scope of their own considerable (indeed, exceptional) state power. Ben-Gurion's principled objections were also likely (at least partially) motivated by more earthly realpolitik concerns that any constitution would come at the expense of his own governing latitude. One Israeli scholar has suggested that Ben-Gurion's approach regarding a constitution in fact shifted, from approval to objection, as a direct response to the Supreme Court's earliest rulings holding executive government accountable.[7]

g) Finally, there were fundamental disagreements regarding some of the core issues and values defining the character of the Jewish State, especially surrounding questions of religion and state. The religious-oriented parties strongly objected to any constitution (though their electoral-political influence was limited). This inability to reach a broad consensus on key issues was considered an insurmountable obstacle to adopting a constitution.

The above explanations are undoubtedly valid and all contributed in varying ways to the final result. Yet ascribing Israel's lack of a constitution to any single factor, and even to all these insular factors combined, misses the mark in a critical way. To understand the ultimate decision to forgo a constitution we need a broader perspective regarding the essence of Israeli society in its earliest days.

Israel was always a genuine outlier in many senses. One of these, often underappreciated by observers and scholars and indeed by Israelis themselves, is the uniquely fragmented and fractured nature of Israeli society at the State's founding and in subsequent years.

Most states established throughout history relied on a critical preexisting foundation: a cohesive population that had consistently inhabited a given territory for generations or for centuries, and that has jointly developed a recognizably distinct national character. The vast majority of modern countries are demographically based on a relatively homogeneous population that share a coherent set of dominant characteristics. These include ethnicity and physical resemblance, a sentiment of familial kinship, territorial affiliation, language, religion, communal history, cultural customs and more. Put simply, the historical stability and very viability of almost all political communities is that most of its members are fundamentally similar in important ways and agree on some very basic issues. This is true for many seemingly "new" states founded in the past century (such as post-Soviet Eastern Europe), as it is true for colonial immigrant countries which were dominated by members of the colonizing culture. The United States of America, often viewed as both heterogeneous and immigrant-based at the time of its founding, is no exception and demonstrates this point well – the American population was predominantly of British ancestry in 1776, by which time Americans had been inhabiting the colonies for over a century (and sometimes considerably longer).

To say Israel is an exception to this rule would be a wild understatement. The modern State of Israel in 1948 was overwhelmingly comprised of recent immigrants, from a paltry Jewish population of some 60,000 in 1918 that expanded tenfold (!) in the interim thirty years. For all practical purposes the nascent State was demographically based on a brand-new social and political community, which had established a significant physical presence only in the few decades preceding statehood (the Israelite and Judaic Kingdoms of antiquity, the Jewish diaspora communities, and the Jewish yearning to return to Israel during the two millennia since 70AD all notwithstanding). Israel was the ancient Jewish homeland, but was still a very new home. This description applies equally to the first four years following 1948 which saw astronomical Jewish immigration into Israel. In this sense alone, Israel posed a notable exception compared with most familiar States, both ancient and modern. The formation of a State without a core populace recently and consistently inhabiting the region is virtually unheard of, and marks Israel as a clear historical outlier.

More significantly, the new Israeli *demos* was fundamentally heterogeneous, with various societal factions diverging in radical and profound ways. Setting aside the formidable challenge presented by a sizeable Arab-Muslim minority during all-out war against multiple Arab-Muslim neighbors, it is hard to overstate the scope and intensity of extreme differences between the many groups within the Jewish majority comprising the new body politic. People hailed from Eastern and Central Europe, but also from North Africa and the Middle East, with clashing cultural norms and assumptions; the many Marxism-inclined pioneers leaned towards a militant atheism that bordered on hostility towards religion in any form, while many traditional Jews (both Zionists and non-Zionists) practiced a strict and uncompromising form of Judaism; the various "labor" factions championed a tightly-controlled centralized economy with widespread nationalization, yet were opposed by the free-market and property-rights orientation of centrist and right-wing movements; and opposing militias reflecting bitter disputes on defense strategy were just barely contained, at one early point (in the 1948 *Altalena* incident) bringing the country to the brink of outright civil war. Critically, no single group sufficiently dominated the electoral scene, and none possessed the kind of majority that approached homogeneity. For these reasons, the focus on the specific disputes relating to "religion and state" echoes this broader perspective but emerges as narrow and simplistic, as it fails to capture the enormity of societal fault-lines throughout Israel's infancy.

All these amounted to severely divergent worldviews regarding values, priorities, resource allocation, the common good, and of course the proper place of government with respect to them all. Simply put, the distance between the many rival groups in the new Jewish State far exceeded anything typically found in emerging polities, and makes some well-known examples of national division elsewhere seem almost trivial.* Jewish heritage and the aspiration for a national home served as the defining common denominator, but it was a thin glue – awkwardly holding together a precarious structure of disparate ill-fitting

* Famously, Ben-Gurion refused to recognize his chief political rival – Menachem Begin – and did not address him by name during Knesset proceedings. This is not conventional conduct within an emerging democracy.

components. Israel's internal societal survival in those first years is as much a marvel (or miracle) as was its military endurance.

Robert A. Dahl, the most renowned political scientist of the twentieth century and the indisputable pioneer of the study of democracies, considered a high degree of "cultural homogeneity" to be among the most critical conditions favorable to the existence and survival of democracy; countries with "sharply differentiated and conflicting subcultures" pose a "special problem for democracy."[8] This is partially because such distinct separate groups view their political demands as "too crucial to allow for compromise" and "nonnegotiable." Though a handful of democracies have successfully navigated such challenges, they did so when other necessary democratic preconditions were strongly in their favor and by implementing unique arrangements which are not likely to emerge or survive in most countries. In Dahl's words: "The disheartening fact is, then, that all the solutions to the potential problems of multiculturalism in a democratic country... depend for their success on special conditions that are likely to be rare." A review of such arrangements listed by Dahl can quickly establish that these are not applicable to Israel – either irrelevant or nonexistent. Israel's "subcultural conflicts" were in many ways more severe than any typical case-studies contemplated by Dahl, for the reasons described above – no (or limited) preexisting permanent population with a coherent cultural character.

Israel's unique circumstances raise the question of their suitability to an Israeli constitution in the first place.

Conventional wisdom of the modern era favors constitutional democracy – justifiably so. But this does not mean that a constitution is always necessarily a good idea. A written constitution seeks to enshrine a polity's core shared values and to entrench a set of fundamental arrangements regarding the machinery of statehood. Its drafting and adoption presuppose, as an essential precondition, the existence of broad public consensus regarding such values and rules. When this condition is met, a constitution is likely an appropriate and beneficial instrument of stability. But in the absence of such consensus a constitution may well prove detrimental and even ruinous to a given society. As constitutions cannot manufacture consensus artificially, the attempt to adopt one without the requisite social cohesion can backfire by emphasizing core differences and exacerbating tensions. Martin Loughlin observes that "the enactment of a constitution is never sufficient to ensure its efficacy because efficacy depends on 'constitutional reality'..." Whether a constitution succeeds "is assumed to depend on social and cultural factors that lie beyond the realm of law."[9] Instead of providing an agreed framework for democratic self-government the forced constitution simply drives a wedge between opposing groups, embitters most of the public and erodes the basis for voluntary collaboration critical to any free society.

In his illuminating discussion of modern constitutional attitudes, former British Supreme Court Justice Lord Jonathan Sumption observes that "any long-term stability" for a "political community" relies on the people having "a reason for obeying laws that they do not like, other than the threat of coercion." A core element of any such reason is the ability to get along in spite of fundamental disputes without resort to violence – people will cooperate if they can tolerate each other despite borderline incompatibility. Sumption concludes that the primary aspiration of any political system is "to provide a method of decision making which has the best chance of accommodating disagreements between citizens as they actually are."[10] Loughlin similarly describes the view that "the main purpose of a constitution is to establish the authority of the system of government, requiring that it maintains social peace among people with different visions of the good society."[11] Yet given certain circumstances a constitution hampers such chances of mutual accommodation more than it aids them. A constitution is a legal document which cements rigid rules and mechanisms and in its judicial enforcement creates clear-cut winners and losers, but it is precisely such rigidity that can be fatal to deeply fragmented societies. Sumption memorably points out the clear shortcomings of legal solutions to societal disagreement:

> "Law is rational. Law is coherent. Law is analytically consistent and rigorous. But in public affairs these are not always virtues. Opacity, inconsistency and fudge may be intellectually impure, which is why lawyers don't like them, but they are often inseparable from the kind of compromises that we have to make as a society if we are going to live together in peace."[12]

Such was the dilemma faced by the First Knesset in 1949 to 1950. The groups making up Israeli society were getting along, just barely, for now – but their cooperation concealed acute tensions simmering beneath the surface. What the fragile Israeli political order needed was stability born of agility and maneuverability, and not the strife and upheaval born of narrow rigidity (or of the attempt to achieve it). Facing extraordinary headwinds, the new State could bend with the former but might just break with the latter. The fiercely conflicting views between Israel's competing factions meant that any so-called resolution of fundamental questions could only be counterproductive – at best alienating some groups, and at worst Balkanizing the entire Zionist project. In the absence of both consensus and homogeneity, faced with the very real prospect of mass disintegration, the Knesset chose to let sleeping dogs lie.

Viewed from this angle the 1950 decision to defer constitutional resolutions becomes far more comprehensible. It was precisely so that it could function that Israel needed to leave many questions unresolved, by opting for constitutional indeterminacy and legal ambiguity, allowing everyone to just "get on with it." Far from negligent dereliction or a regrettable fluke, and not due only to competing priorities or shortsighted realpolitik, the Knesset's decision is properly understood as a deeply prudent move that might have saved Zionism from self-destruction. Even if not explicitly articulated as such, the deferral of constitutional determinations reflected the genuine schisms amongst the new Israelis and recognized the inherent risks in stressing social and ideological fault-lines – and endangering the entire endeavor of Statehood – by an attempt at adopting a fully-fledged constitution.

Joshua Segev, among Israel's most prominent constitutional scholars, calls this "the decision not to decide." In a compelling and comprehensive essay on the matter Segev describes the "central feature" of the Israeli constitutional environment: fundamental disputes between Israeli groups regarding a plethora of substantive policy questions, as well as regarding many basic institutional arrangements of government.[13] Segev shows how this "top to bottom" disagreement pervaded Israeli political culture to the point that "every two Knesset members had three opinions," and precluded the possibility of adopting a constitution. The founding generation "transcended" this "Gordian knot" by "deciding not to decide" – a deliberate and conscious strategy to sacrifice important constitutional aspirations for the sake of societal compatibility and survival. Segev goes on to present the moral and democratic justifications for this tactic, and argues that "the decision not to decide" is superior to alternative descriptions of Israel's overarching constitutional reality.

Justified or not, the absence of an Israeli constitution was never due to a careless oversight. As observed by one prominent jurist in 1969, the Harari Decision against a constitution (and its aftermath) "proves… that there exists in Israel the unexpressed constitutional principle that there should *not* be a written rigid Constitution standing above the ordinary legislator."[14] This fundamental insight provides key context for the founding moments of the Israeli constitutional framework and bears heavily upon its subsequent development.

The Harari Resolution and Basic Laws

Our point of re-entry into orbit is the 1950 Knesset decision to formally defer the task of adopting a constitution to a later time. Known as the "Harari Resolution" (or the "Harari Compromise"), this was a straightforward resolution tabled in the First Knesset by MK Yizhar Harari, and reads in its entirety as follows:

> "The First Knesset instructs the Constitution, Law and Justice Committee to prepare a proposed State Constitution. The constitution will be built chapter by chapter, in such a way that each will constitute a separate basic law. The chapters shall be brought before the Knesset, provided the committee completes its work, and all the chapters together will be incorporated into the Constitution of the State."

The resolution was approved by a plurality of legislators – fifty (out of 120) voting in favor, with two alternative resolutions backed by thirty-nine and thirteen MKs. Only a single vote was held (that is, not the three readings required for enacting legislation) and the decision is not considered a "law" in any strict sense. Nonetheless, this informal and almost casual resolution brought before the Knesset became the bedrock upon which the entirety of Israeli constitutionalism was built.

The rudimentary and almost clumsy wording of *Harari* is confounding and leaves out much more than it contains. It includes the notion of a piecemeal constitution comprised of separate "chapters," each of which being a "basic" (or "fundamental") law. These are to be approved by the Knesset and are to somehow be jointly combined to become a constitution.*

This initial decree immediately begs some pressing questions: Are such basic laws to be submitted to the Knesset separately, or should they only be presented to the Knesset as a complete and unified corpus? If the former, is the Knesset to enact each "chapter" separately as an individual law or to wait until receiving them all and then enact them jointly? What is the timeline for any of this happening – drafting, legislation and eventual "incorporation"? Is there a deadline for execution or is this an open-ended, indefinite mandate? What is the process for the Knesset to enact each "chapter"? What is the relationship between any legislation enacted under this scheme, and all other legislation, if any difference exists? What is the meaning of this contemplated "incorporation" (presumably in the sense of "combination") into a constitution, and critically, what is the process for doing so? The resolution seems to condition ("provided") all of this on the designated committee "completing its work" – what does that mean? What happens if the work is not completed?

No answer to any of these questions was available; almost without question, the resolution drafters themselves had no concrete notion of its precise meaning or application. Indeed, Israeli jurists have shown only the loosest interest in dissecting the resolution's actual content. Parsing and analyzing the words of *Harari* seems incompatible with its innately slapdash and casual character.

In any event, the practical consequence of the Harari Resolution as understood by the political community and legal system was roughly as follows: the Knesset would periodically and gradually legislate an unspecified number of "Basic Laws." These were to form the basis of a future conventional constitution into which they are to be eventually consolidated. And indeed, the Knesset proceeded to enact and amend (and repeal) a slew of Basic Laws over the years, many of which established or regarded Israel's most significant governing institutions, such as the legislature (Knesset), the executive Government, the judiciary, the military, and much else.

Here we arrive at the crux of the matter – what is a Basic Law? Though the term itself was borrowed from the West German constitution, an Israeli Basic Law shares nothing with its original namesake. A Basic Law is best described as an ordinary law to which the Knesset attributed some special importance, or which the Knesset considered a *candidate* for inclusion in a *future* constitution – a draft

* The Hebrew term here is *Hok Yesodi*, meaning "a law of a fundamental/basic nature." The definite noun *Hok Yesod* (dropping the last vowel), known as "Basic Law," was adopted later. The term "*Yit'agdu*" literally means "incorporated" but also bears the meanings "combined" or "aggregated" or "assembled."

chapter, if you will. Basic Laws are legislated by the Knesset in the exact same process and manner as any other legislation, with the same preliminary deliberations and subsequent promulgation, the same three readings, and so on. Critically, Basic Laws are enacted with *any* majority – just like any other law. A Basic Law may technically be enacted with a vote of 2-to-1 or even 1-to-0. The sole, solitary distinguishing feature of a Basic Law is its title – any piece of legislation bearing the title "Basic Law" and omitting the year it was enacted is, by definition, a Basic Law.

In short, "Basic Law" became a label slapped onto ordinary legislation for assorted reasons, but laws labeled as such are otherwise identical to all other legislation in substance, standing, enactment, and any other aspect.

The use of Basic Laws for "fundamental" issues of a constitutional nature has been notoriously inconsistent. Some of Israel's most important statutes regarding the State's foundational ethos or individual rights are *not* labeled as Basic Laws. Thus, the 1950 Law of Return – granting automatic citizenship to any Jewish immigrant to Israel – is considered one of the most fundamental laws to Israel's core Jewish character (just as similar repatriation laws are typically treated elsewhere). The Law of Return was never labeled as a Basic Law, even though it was enacted mere weeks after the Harari Resolution. In 1951 the Knesset passed several laws relating to individual liberty and equal rights, including the progressive (for its time) Women's Equal Rights Act and a batch of labor-protection laws (indisputably "fundamental" to the socialist *Mapai* coalition) – yet none of these were designated as Basic Laws. The foundational 1957 Law Courts Act and 1955 Elections Act were also not enacted as Basic Laws. In fact, in 1955 a law professor teaching constitutional law in Tel Aviv compiled a list of "fundamental" legislation (of a constitutional nature) which included dozens of statutes and ordinances, none of which bore the label of "Basic Law."

On the other hand, Basic Laws have always been treated by the Knesset with pronounced irreverence. Many Basic Laws are replete with mundane and technical instructions which don't match the style or gravity of constitutional rules – most notably in Basic Law: The Government. Some address subjects or institutions which seem inappropriate for constitutional status entirely – such as one establishing the State Comptroller Office. Over the years the Basic Laws were amended regularly and casually as a matter of course, from minor tweaks to sweeping overhauls, more often than not serving immediate political expediency or convenience and without pretenses of principled or broad justification. At times an entire Basic Law was unceremoniously scrapped and replaced with a new one.

This approach to Basic Laws might seem surprising, but only to an observer with a misplaced impression of their "constitutional" status. When properly understood as ordinary legislation bearing a superficial indication of potential future importance, their treatment as such by the legal and political community makes much more sense. Basic Laws were regarded by all as just regular laws – no more, no less.

To this day, there is not a single other statutory source of any kind defining the scheme of "Basic Laws." The 1950 Harari Resolution (itself not quite a law) is the only normative basis for the existence and enactment of Basic Laws in the Israeli system of government, and is indeed the only quasi-statutory source which addresses the topic in any way.

Following the 1950 Harari Resolution, the designated Committee did not "complete its work" (whatever that meant), as the First Knesset ended without passing any Basic Laws at all. Eight years passed before the Third Knesset enacted Basic Law: The Knesset, the first of its kind, in 1958. While this new Basic Law formally (though retroactively) established the Knesset and defined an important State institution, the law is in some ways disappointing. For one thing, the new Basic Law did nothing to clarify the Harari Resolution – it does not address the Knesset's authority for passing so-called "chapters" of a prospective constitution. In fact, it doesn't mention "Basic Laws" at all. Perplexingly, the law didn't even designate the Knesset as Israel's legislature or declare the Knesset's authority to enact legislation, but rather simply defines the Knesset as Israel's "House of Representatives" (literally "House of Electees," which can also fairly be translated as "Parliament"). Although the Knesset's legislative power is duly derived from previous legislation (notably the Constituent Assembly's 1949 Transition Law), this seems like something of a missed opportunity.

Since then, the Knesset has steadily advanced with the vision set out by *Harari* and has legislated a new Basic Law roughly every four years (until 1992). On the one hand the Knesset was implementing *Harari* by enacting separate statutes which could be regarded as draft "chapters" for a future constitution; on the other hand, the Knesset had clearly discarded *Harari's* main proactive push for a conventional constitution. Paradoxically, pursuing the first part of *Harari* meant abandoning the latter for all intents and purposes. As some scholars observed, the "gradual adoption of a constitution" called for by *Harari* "proved to be an abstention" from doing exactly that.[15] By embarking on the Basic Law route the Knesset was consciously shelving any constitutional aspirations. (We will later address whether the Knesset actually retained the authority to pursue a constitution even had it wanted to).

The 1958 Basic Law did include a specific important element which set it apart from other legislation. After listing some core principles of Israeli elections, Section 4 stipulates that "this Section shall not be amended, except by a majority of Knesset Members" – that is, only an absolute majority of legislators (61 of 120) can amend Section 4 of Basic Law: The Knesset. This came to be known as an "entrenchment" clause – a procedural requirement which purports to limit the ability of future Knessets to effect certain changes. At least in theory, this did indeed impose an abnormal limitation, because all other legislative action (including even the creation of Basic Laws) could be performed with any majority and did not require an absolute majority. Such an "entrenchment" clause demanding a special majority certainly resembles "rigidity" rules typically found in the context of constitutional amendments. Further, the idea of "entrenchment" inevitably sets the stage for a superiority contest in which later legislation is evaluated against the procedural entrenchment requirement.

Still, in 1958 and for many decades after, Basic Laws were not viewed as a substitute for a constitution.

Parliamentary Supremacy and Judicial Review

The Declaration of Independence, the Constituent Assembly (folded into the First Knesset), the Harari Resolution, and the eventual enactment of Basic Laws all inevitably raised questions fundamental to the Israeli democratic order. Did Israel have some kind of conventional constitution? Could the Declaration of Independence serve as one? Did the Knesset possess the authority to create constitutional norms? Were there theoretical legal limits to the power and authority of the Knesset? Did there exist an internal hierarchy between different types of legislation enacted by the Knesset? And could a court of law invalidate a statute – exercise judicial review – based on any of the above?

Throughout Israel's formative years and long after, the resounding, emphatic and unequivocal answer to all these questions was – No. The Israeli constitutional order was incontestably one of parliamentary (or legislative) supremacy. As the sole institution of representative democracy, the Knesset possessed exclusive, ultimate and unrestricted rulemaking power. As we shall see, the consensus as to this point was shared by the vast majority of the public, the legal profession, the political establishment, the international community and, importantly, the Supreme Court. Though at times the subject of academic and theoretical discussion, the fact of parliamentary supremacy as the defining feature of Israel's political system was universally undisputed (even if begrudgingly so).

Let us briefly address these questions and dispose of any potential uncertainty, as we will revisit some of them later in our discussion of the 1995 Constitutional Revolution.

Israel clearly had, and to this day has, no conventional constitution. Proving a negative is always something of a fool's errand.* Suffice it to say that the thing most people consider a "constitution" – a unified comprehensive legal document of supreme law at the top of the normative hierarchy consciously and deliberately adopted by a substantial majority and reflecting fundamental consensus of core shared values – does not and has never existed for Israel. No one claims the contrary.

Though the First Knesset likely retained its power as Constituent Assembly (itself a claim deserving of some skepticism), most scholars and jurists at the time did not view consecutive Knessets as possessing the same authority to create a constitution. Alternatively, or at the very least, the Knesset could not do so through the regular legislative process but would need to devise some unique original method to vest a new constitution with legal validity. Suggestions have

* In Israel we say, "prove you don't have a sister."

included adoption by an especially large parliamentary majority and by additional votes or readings, ratification by a number of succeeding Knessets (with national elections in between), endorsement by popular referendum, and various combinations thereof.

The Declaration of Independence was universally acknowledged to have no legal standing or effect (beyond, perhaps, establishing the Provisional People's Council).[16] To be sure, the Declaration enjoyed (and enjoys) paramount symbolic status as a deep and lasting expression of the Israeli and Zionist spirit, especially as captured in those foundational moments of 1948. Yet by any measure the Declaration is simply not a constitution – it bears none of the traditional hallmarks of a constitutional document. The Declaration was not the product of considered public deliberation and debate; nor was it submitted or affirmed through a political mechanism attesting to broad public support or reflecting notions of popular sovereignty, such as a national referendum. Instead, it was drafted in secret by a handful of powerful figures embedded in the Zionist ruling elite, presented to the People's Council as a fait accompli, and then crudely redacted and heavily edited by one man – David Ben-Gurion himself. In other words, nothing in the Declaration's formation or aftermath reflects the conscious, calculated, and deliberate effort of a sovereign people to define and limit their own powers of government – the very essence of any republican constitution. Quite understandably, no one really believed that the last-minute, arbitrary (even if sensible) drafting whims of Ben-Gurion ought to be elevated to an irrevocable, enforceable "supreme law of the land."

The Declaration's own text disavows any constitutional character by mandating the later creation of a different, distinct constitution, as noted above. The fact that this was also clarified in no uncertain terms to the People's Council means that the only democratic involvement in the entire process (the approval of the People's Council) was contingent on the express understanding that they were not approving a constitutional or legal text of any kind. To put it more bluntly, had it been touted as a constitution, the Declaration itself would likely not have been approved.

Further, the Declaration's overly vague and ambiguous substance is barely suitable as a legal text of any kind. Most constitutions require some level of specificity; they prescribe detailed limitations on government, define particular individual rights, and so on. But the content, scope, and application of most rights or principles mentioned in the Declaration are unclear and open to debate, far broader than language found in constitutions elsewhere. And the Declaration famously avoids any allusion to Israel's current or future territorial borders.

All in all, the Declaration's drafting process and content were sufficient for a public statement of intent and for a bold articulation of the national spirit, but woefully inadequate for anything approaching a constitution.

The Knesset was, legally speaking, omnipotent, in the sense that no discernible legal norm existed which set a limit on its power. That is, as a matter of institutional and legal fact, the Israel system of government did not contain any mechanism for blocking the express will of the Knesset. This was of course consistent with Israel's loose modeling on the United Kingdom parliamentary system (with important distinctions), and more broadly on basic concepts of default democratic power in the absence of a written constitution. The two are indeed inexorably linked – parliamentary supremacy is the "central premise" not only of the British unwritten constitution (according to A.V. Dicey),[17] but of any democratic system lacking a written constitution.

An extension of the same question applies to self-imposed limitations – could the Knesset bind or restrict itself? That is, could one Knesset make laws that curtail its own future authority? This conundrum stirs some initial interest because the assumption of parliamentary supremacy perhaps ought to imply that the same "omnipotence" includes the power of self-restriction. Though reminiscent of the old paradox of God creating a rock He cannot lift, luckily there is no need to resort to theological debates – this constitutional question had long-since been resolved. The single most important feature of British parliamentary supremacy is that Parliament cannot bind itself, in the sense that no organ or body may enforce an earlier law against legislation of a newer Parliament, and such was the prevailing view in Israel.

A.V. Dicey is considered among the most authoritative scholars of English constitutionalism. In his seminal 1885 book on the uncodified English constitution, Dicey describes parliamentary supremacy (he uses the term "sovereignty") thus: Parliament has "the right to make or unmake any law whatever;" that "no person or body is recognized" as having the right to "override or set aside" legislation. Practically speaking, this means that "any Act of Parliament… which makes a new law, or repeals or modifies an existing law, will be obeyed by the Courts."[18] Dicey proceeds to quote Blackstone's 1765 *Commentaries*, in turn quoting Sir Edward Coke's 1644 *Institutes*, jointly very much the bedrock of the common-law tradition as we know it:

> "The power and jurisdiction of Parliament is so transcendent and absolute, that it cannot be confined, either for causes or persons, within any bounds… It hath sovereign and uncontrollable authority in the making, confirming, enlarging, restraining, abrogating, repealing, reviving, and expounding of laws, concerning matters of all possible denominations… It can change and create afresh even the constitution of the kingdom and of parliaments themselves… It can, in short, do everything that is not naturally impossible… what the Parliament doth, no authority upon earth can undo."

For from archaic or outdated, Lord Jonathan Sumption echoes and reiterates this foundational principle in 2019, stating that the British political constitution has "only one truly fundamental constitutional rule, which is that Parliament is sovereign. There is no legal limit to what it can do."[19] The basic rationale is simple: no present Parliament has a claim to superior authority over a future Parliament. As such, any Parliament can freely undo what a previous Parliament has done.

Jurisdictions that follow the model of parliamentary supremacy necessarily subscribe to this view, and the Israeli Knesset was no exception. The Knesset could not bind or limit its own future discretion. For this same reason Israeli law recognized no hierarchy of superior and inferior statutes. All Knesset legislation, whether labeled "Basic Law" or not, was of equal legal force and occupied the same legal plane. This is consistent with the other points made above – it was precisely due to the *absence* of a constitution, and within the framework of parliamentary supremacy, that the Knesset was at liberty to legislate the State's governing institutions into existence, to make and remake the rules of the game as it saw fit. The Knesset could freely enact ordinary laws on fundamental issues (and call them "Basic Laws") because it was supreme, and because it was not limited by any existing constitution.

What happens when one law contradicts another? There was nothing novel about the Israeli system of a single legislative "tier" (regardless of a statute's label), and the challenge of applying contradictory laws was hardly unique to Israel. Dealing with such legal conflicts falls to rules of statutory interpretation and construction which are generally straightforward and are widely known. When possible, the contradictory laws may be reconciled by plausible interpretation, assuming the legislature did not intend for one law to violate another. If not possible, or if that presumption is rebutted, then the later and more specific law wins. Lawyers will of course recognize the maxims of *lex posterior* and *lex specialis*.

Finally, as should be obvious by now and for all the reasons above, no court in Israel had the power to invalidate Knesset legislation. Under parliamentary supremacy, with no constitution, and all laws being born equal – what basis could there be for a judge to strike down a statute? What higher legal norm (or institution) could be said to supersede a duly-enacted law of the Knesset? The answer was – none. Indeed, arguably the most distinctive feature inherent to parliamentary supremacy, and the most conspicuous consequence of having no written constitution, is the legal impossibility of judicial review.

The framework described above characterized Israeli government and jurisprudence following *Harari*, throughout the State's first two generations and right up to the 1995 Constitutional Revolution (with one significant exception addressed in the next section). This is generally undisputed and is irrefutably supported by an abundance of evidence. For present purposes we may sufficiently demonstrate the matter by noting some contemporary descriptions intended for non-Israeli audiences, as these helpfully condense and summarize the salient points.

In 1968 Eliahu Likhovski, a prominent Israeli-British attorney and lecturer at the Hebrew University Law School, wrote a number of essays for the (English language) Israel Law Review journal. In one titled "The Courts and the

Legislative Supremacy of the Knesset," Likhovski describes "the doctrine of the legislative supremacy of the Knesset as the underlying unarticulated major premise of Israel's constitution" – a fact he notes is widely recognized "almost without demur."[20] Noting the Knesset's broad omnipotence, Likhovski observes that the Knesset "has provided for its own establishment," has essentially created and defined the primary State organs and institutions in all three branches of government, and that "in fact it has created the entire legal framework of the State." Likhovski stresses that the Knesset's legislative authority includes the power to abridge rights and to announce retroactive legislation. Though the Executive could exercise certain emergency powers which might suspend application of specific laws, Likhovski explains these powers to be "subordinate to and not in derogation of" legislative supremacy, as only the Knesset could declare a state of emergency and the Knesset could legally repeal such emergency powers at any time.

Specifically addressing the judicial consensus on this matter (especially as expressed by the Supreme Court), Likhovski emphasizes that "as far as [courts] are concerned, there is no legal restraint on the legislative power of the Knesset." This is especially evident in the judicial self-imposed approach to statutory interpretation, as the courts "acknowledge clearly the supremacy of the Knesset." Likhovski stresses the similarity to the English system of parliamentary supremacy, noting that "in Israel and as in Britain, the courts must be considered as subordinate to the legislature," and that judges "will not question the supremacy" of the legislator. Likhovski summarizes that the judiciary acts on the basic political assumption that the "will of the majority in the Knesset... if expressed in statutory form... is the supreme law of the land."

Around the same time, Georgetown University professor David M. Sassoon published an article in the American Journal of Comparative Law titled "The Israel Legal System." Sassoon addressed the State's constitutional development and summarized thus: "One fact is indisputable, namely, that together with the United Kingdom Israel shares the practically unique position of having no formal written Constitution... The basic political, economic, social and cultural values of Israel are to be found within, and not above, the legal system."[21]

The year 1968 also saw the publication of a book titled "The Legal System of Israel" by Judge Henry E. Baker. Baker was a British-born and Oxford-educated attorney who emerged as a prominent pillar of the Israeli legal community during the pre-state British Mandate and helped draft the Declaration of Independence. Baker became provisional LCG upon the State's founding, later formally served as Deputy LCG and was eventually appointed to the District Court bench in 1950 (while also concurrently serving as acting Supreme Court Justice). In 1963 he was appointed President of the Jerusalem District Court.

Baker's 1968 book was reviewed in an article (also for the American Journal of Comparative Law), which reflected the overall impression arising from the book. Stressing the differences between the Israeli and American legal systems, the article notes that phrases like "basic law" or "fundamental law" do not share the same meaning as they might in American constitutional jurisprudence, and that "the parts of the Israeli law designated as 'fundamental' do not constitute the supreme law of the land… Whatever the terminology, the Israeli government is essentially a parliamentary type similar to the British."[22] The article further notes that "all Israeli laws, whether designated as fundamental or not, are adopted by a simple majority of the Knesset and are amended in the same way… the Knesset can alter the nature of the regime by a simple majority vote."

A generation later, on the eve of the 1995 Constitutional Revolution (and, notably, after the enactment of the 1992 Basic Laws), this broad approach remained fundamentally unchanged. In a 1993 speech on "Why Israel Has No Constitution," Israeli law professor Amos Shapira explains that "in the legal sphere, Israel has not yet adopted a formal, comprehensive, written constitution endowed with a 'super law' quality, an entrenched bill of rights and a mechanism of constitutional judicial review on legislation."[23] Further describing the Israeli system of parliamentary supremacy, Shapira elaborates that "in a parliamentary system without a written constitution… the legislature is vested with theoretically unlimited legislative powers and may legislate in derogation of basic individual freedoms and right. It can do this because no constitutional super-norm exists to limit its power."

Also in 1993, Israeli political scientist Bernard Susser published an article on recent Israeli constitutional developments in view of the new 1992 Basic Laws. Describing the status and standing of Basic Laws generally, Susser observed that although they "possess a special aura of dignity, in practice they do not have any special legal standing distinguishing them from normal legislation."[24] The original hope was that after enough such laws were enacted, only "relatively simple stitching" would be required to "sew" them into a single authoritative document, though in 1993 this had evidently not yet occurred.

The comments from both Shapira and Susser are of special interest as the two were involved in a famous initiative in the 1980s to draft a comprehensive written constitution for Israel (known as the "Four Professors" project). The detailed proposal later served as a blueprint for sections of the Basic Laws enacted in 1992.

These five anecdotal examples from the late 60s and early 90s accurately represent the Israeli constitutional order as perceived by Israelis and as described to foreigners.

The Supreme Court's jurisprudence espoused precisely the same view. Among the most well-known examples is the 1965 *Bassul* case which challenged a law restricting the raising of pigs.[25] Writing for the majority, Justice Zvi Berenson (Cambridge-educated, drafter of the Declaration of Independence) was unequivocal:

> "I highly doubt that we even possess the authority to invalidate a statute duly enacted by the Knesset, or any part thereof… It is doubtful that the Court may peek behind the curtain of a Knesset law to evaluate its

> propriety… The question before us is not one of interpretation but one of the supremacy of the Knesset and the finality of its determinations… The Knesset is sovereign in the making of laws. It is free to choose the subject matter of any law and to define its content, and any law issued from its workshop is to be given full force and effect…
>
> All agree that the Court may not doubt the judgment of the sovereign legislature as expressed in the laws it enacts. The Court can only interpret a Knesset statute but cannot raise questions as to its validity…
>
> After a law is enacted by the Knesset and promulgated in the official Gazette, we must bow before it and not questions its provisions, determinations or assumptions. The Knesset pours its wine into the vessel of the law, and the court can only, through the interpretation of the law, state the flavor of the wine."

The *Bassul* case was no outlier but rather expressed near-unanimous consensus reiterated by the Court time and again throughout the classical era (though most petitioners rarely bothered raising such a frivolous argument in the first place). A 1970 case conveys the broad sentiment of the Court's deference towards "what the Knesset ordinarily does as a legislative body appointed through democratic elections and reflecting the free will of the People."[26] More explicitly, the Court stated in 1963 that "in the constitutional order of this State, the Knesset is sovereign and has the authority to enact any law and imbue it with content as it sees fit. The possibility of invalidating a law passed by the Knesset is entirely inconceivable."[27] We find the Court expressing the same view in 1981: "It is universally agreed that according to our existing constitutional order… this Court may not assume the authority to review the content of Knesset legislation."[28] The Court clarified on many occasions that the Knesset's ultimate legislative authority extended to the infringement of rights ("the omnipotent legislature may permit harm to the citizen," 1958)[29] or violation of other important principles ("if [a law] causes discrimination, such discrimination is statutory and is therefore permissible," 1973).[30]

These quotes accurately reflect the prevalent approach within the legal system towards Knesset parliamentary supremacy and the absence of any authority for judicial review. To complete the picture, in some of its earliest decisions the Supreme Court rejected any attempt to elevate the Declaration of Independence to constitutional status (or for it to serve as a basis for striking down laws). In the 1948 *Gubernik* case, the Court famously held that the Declaration "served only to establish the fact of the State's founding for its recognition under international law. It reflects the people's vision and their 'credo,' but is in no way a constitutional norm which determines the practical validity of various laws and ordinances."[31] In the 1949 *Al-Kharboutly* case the Court clarified that the Declaration was indeed not solely a "political" instrument, in the sense that it had the legal effect of the State's establishment. Nonetheless, the Court explicitly rejected the argument that "this document" is "the Constitution" under which statutes may be subjected to judicial review.[32]

The quotes above regarding parliamentary supremacy and the absence of a constitution (in whatever form) are almost superfluous. More than anything else, commentators and the Court were simply stating the obvious truth, overwhelmingly and undeniably evident to any observer – Israel did not have a constitution. No creative argument by eager lawyers could change this painfully uncomplicated fact. In the absence of a constitution, no legal or political theory existed that could justify judicial review.

The Israeli system of parliamentary supremacy must be viewed in the context of the previous discussion regarding the fragmented and fragile nature of Israeli society, and of the conscious, deliberate decision of its leaders to prefer adaptable flexibility over hazardous rigidity by delaying (and effectively rejecting) a written constitution. Regardless of any wide-ranging debate over the desirability and wisdom of such a system, parliamentary supremacy was not an accidental bug, but rather a considered feature, of the Israeli governmental order. The decision against a written constitution was just as much a decision in favor of parliamentary supremacy. In addition to setting aside thorny ideological issues and leaving them in ambiguous indeterminacy, this system provided for the kind of technical agility that Israeli governing institutions needed – an ability to adapt to rapidly changing and unforeseeable circumstances; to effect critical compromises and then swap them out for new ones if need be; to evolve gradually (and sometimes, dramatically) in the way best serving the Israeli public and polity.

A relevant element to bear in mind was the staggering complexity of the governmental and legal arrangements which the early State had inherited from its antecedent regimes. The new State required a "transformation from a multiplicity of often conflicting and archaic legal systems to a homogenous modern system."[33] This disentanglement was (and in some senses, remains) no easy task and involves many core government mechanisms and institutions. As no comprehensive solution (such as revamping the system entirely through a fresh constitution) was available, it made sense for the Knesset to have the authority to alter these fundamental features. Parliamentary supremacy meant that these arrangements were not frozen in place, and could be gradually and methodically addressed by the Knesset as it deemed appropriate.

At the same time, Israel's political leaders and founders (as discussed in the Introduction) were far from statecraft prodigies and were operating under challenging circumstances – few had any illusion that the institutions and systems being created met some kind of global gold standard of constitutional government. The new State was not state-of-the-art. Parliamentary supremacy reflected an admirable degree of self-awareness and humility on the part of Israel's leadership (also expressed by Ben-Gurion in his speech above), that their newly-minted governmental mechanisms were not the apex of human political achievement, almost certainly required significant improvement or replacement by future generations, and should therefore be open to change. This predefined and acknowledged transience also removed the concern of inadvertently entrenching poorly-designed and untested mechanisms, and thus allowed the Knesset to "get on with it" unburdened by such concerns.

In sum, parliamentary supremacy was not only a legal institutional fact, but actually made sense for Israel. There was simply no good argument that subsequent political majorities ought to be bound by the hodgepodge unwieldy fusion of multiple colonial legal systems alongside the ad hoc institutions and mechanisms born of pragmatic expedience.

Finally, it's worth noting that just as the primacy of the Knesset and the inconceivability of judicial review were universally acknowledged features of the Jewish State, so it was plainly true that the Knesset had many practical limitations imposed by political forces, and that the Supreme Court also served as a formidable check on governmental power. Throughout its history and despite nominal supremacy, the Israeli parliamentary system was always one of curbed power and of highly limited effectiveness. Proportional representation and factionalism meant constant political instability. No single party has *ever* gained an outright Knesset majority, such that even a so-called "ruling" party had to cooperate with at least one other party (or more) representing separate and divergent interests. In other words, no single political party has ever managed to truly dominate Israeli politics or to entirely control government agenda and policy. As a result, advancing virtually any legislative agenda tends to be excruciatingly difficult. In most cases the Coalition and parliamentary majority is extremely slim and rarely overwhelming, such that dissent by only a handful of backbenchers is sufficient to defeat almost any proposed measure. This is exacerbated by the relatively small total number of legislators – with only 120 MKs, a five percent "advantage" translates to six people (63 versus 57), meaning that only three rogue Coalition MKs can swing a vote to go the other way. Indeed, legislation requiring an absolute majority (61 MKs) – including uncontroversial measures – has historically proven extremely difficult to enact.[34]

Entrenchment – constitutional rigidity, procedural technicality or neither?

The "entrenchment" clause in Basic Law: The Knesset posed something of a challenge to the prevailing approach described above. Unchanged since its legislation by the Third Knesset in 1958, Section 4 reads:

> "The Knesset shall be elected by general, national, direct, equal, secret and proportional elections, in accordance with the Knesset Elections Law; this section shall not be amended, except by a majority of Knesset Members."

The requirement for an absolute majority (61 of 120 Knesset Members) would ostensibly restrict future Knessets – all other legislative acts, including enactment of Basic Laws, normally require only a simple majority of voting members. As such this requirement arguably assumed a "rigid" constitutional character and violated Israel's "core constitutional premise" of parliamentary sovereignty, insofar as subsequent Knessets are bound by it. The entrenchment also raised separate but related questions regarding the status of Basic Laws and the Knesset's authority to enact constitutional norms of any kind and eventually led to important jurisprudential developments. While perhaps somewhat esoteric, the status and significance of entrenchment clauses are central to our understanding of the 1995 Constitutional Revolution such that they merit our close attention.

Can the Knesset legitimately set a future procedural self-limit for amending legislation? If yes, then on what basis? If no, then what might such entrenchment mean? These mirror a parallel and arguably preliminary question – does the Knesset possess the power to enact "constitutional" legislation of any kind? Does that include self-imposed restrictions?

The most radical argument at the time went along the following lines:[35] The First Knesset was elected as a "Constituent Assembly" and had the legal power to enact a constitution. Though the First Knesset refrained from doing so – and passed the Harari Resolution – all successive Knessets "inherited" the same "constituent power" of constitutional rulemaking. As such, any Knesset can enact a written constitution or legislation of a constitutional nature. Though Basic Laws were not (yet) a constitution, they could be vested with such status if the Knesset so chose. Further, the Knesset can freely impose quasi-constitutional restrictions on its own authority, including entrenchment clauses which set "rigid" procedural requirements such as an enlarged or absolute majority vote for amendments. On this view, the Harari Resolution is properly understood as also authorizing bite-sized constitutional legislation – small chunks of binding constitutional rules outside the framework of a comprehensive written constitution – an authority which any future Knesset continues to possess until decided otherwise.

This argument was generally rejected by the legal and political community, and suffers from several fundamental flaws. First, the notion of an ordinary legislature engaging in "constitutional rulemaking" through the same process of routine legislation defies all conventions of constitutional theory and practice. Such rules are supposed to reflect broad consensus, to derive from first principles, to require significant consideration, and to serve the long-term collective public interest; their formulation is to be detached (personally and institutionally) from the ebb and flow of day-to-day ordinary politics. But neither Basic Laws nor entrenchment require any special or distinct legislative procedure – in terms of notice, deliberation, ratification, or any other action. These can notably be enacted by any majority, such that in principle a very small group of legislators (or the slimmest majority) could "entrench" any statutory provision and limit amendments to majorities much larger than the one that enacted the provision in the first place (for instance, a 2 to 1 majority could theoretically pass an entrenched provision requiring an 80 Knesset Member majority for amendments). Basic Laws are created in the thick of pedestrian and partisan politics, that is, by ordinary career politicians typically concerned with issues of the day. This mechanism simply cannot justifiably restrict future parliamentary and electoral majorities, on an intuitive and rational level.

Second, on a more technical and historical level – but far more importantly – the only Israeli body with the "constituent authority" to enact constitutional rules was the First Knesset which was elected for this purpose.* A "constituent assembly" is able to validly enact a constitution because its flesh-and-blood members are personally selected by the electorate for that specific purpose. The 1949 elections were the only ones ever held in which the enactment of a constitution was on the ballot; and the individual people elected to the 1949 Constituent Assembly (which became the First Knesset) were the only delegates in whom the public specifically vested constitution-making authority. Nothing in constitutional theory or practice, and nothing in Israeli legal and political reality, can justify "passing down" this authority from one Knesset to the next.

Frankly, the notion of a "hereditary" constituent authority is patently absurd. The power of constitution-making is not a hand-me-down set of wrinkled pajamas to be "gifted" from one Knesset sibling to another. Among the most known rules throughout the Western legal tradition is *delegata potestas non potest delegari* – a delegated power cannot be further delegated. This seems all the more applicable regarding an authority fundamentally derived from immediate democratic-electoral sanction, resting on the direct link to the people's conscious vote. Even if the First Knesset wanted to "delegate" its constituent power to successive Knessets (and this is far from clearly established), it had no authority to do so. When the Second Knesset was elected and after the First Knesset failed to enact a constitution any original "constituent authority" had evaporated and along with it any power to make a constitution. In other words, Israeli "constituent" powers – which include making a constitution, but also entrenchment or constitution-esque rules that restrict parliamentary supremacy – were limited solely to the First Knesset. From the Second Knesset onwards, the Knesset serves as an ordinary parliament without the power to limit future electoral majorities.

The entire debate is peculiar to Israel and would never arise in most other jurisdictions. A legislature or parliament is not a constituent authority – this much is obvious virtually any time, anywhere. The question in Israel only arose in the first place due to the anomalous evolution in which its first parliament was originally elected as a constituent assembly, and then came up with a cryptic idea (*Harari*) of constitutional "chapter" drafts. If not for this irregular development the argument would likely not exist at all. But the messy history should not obscure the straightforward and uncomplicated legal reality that since the First Knesset, no Israeli institution properly wields the power to make a constitution or constitutional norms.

Did this mean that Israel had forever forfeited its chance to enact a constitution? Of course not. Many have observed and most agree that the Knesset

* One might argue that even the First Knesset lost such authority by shedding its character as Constituent Assembly and becoming a parliament engaged in common politics.

could form a new Constituent Assembly that would be directly elected by the public for the purpose of drafting and submitting a constitution, and a new Assembly could properly assume such a role. We will return to this briefly in the book's concluding chapter.

Third, even were one to accept the outlandish proposition that future Knessets may enact a written constitution, the case for constitutional "chunks" in the form of Basic Laws and isolated entrenched provisions is even less plausible. Proponents of this claim rely heavily on the Harari Resolution, but this provides a highly dubious basis. On its face, the terms and wording of *Harari* are easily understood to refer only to the First Knesset and as conditioned on the Committee "completing" its work to propose a full (albeit segmented) constitution, which never happened. In fact most Basic Laws were not even drafted or submitted by the Committee as mandated by *Harari* (but rather followed a different legislative process) such that its requirements were not followed even on a technical level. More importantly, the Harari Resolution by itself lacks any meaningful constitutional standing – with the support of fifty Knesset Members, *Harari* was not even passed as a "law," let alone as some momentous constitutional norm. The Harari Resolution has no claim of superiority over later laws passed by the Knesset, and nothing in or around it can change the legal reality that only the First Knesset possessed "constituent power" which could not be further delegated.

On a more principled level there are strong arguments against issuing forth separate segments of constitutionally binding rules in lieu of the overall framework of a single unified written constitution. Constitutional arrangements are invariably comprehensive and co-dependent, with their diverse elements balancing each other out in an integrated holistic scheme. As Martin Loughlin notes, the constitutional text is "drafted in the name of the people and designed to be *comprehensive*. It must contain the essential principles on which government is founded, the method by which it will be organized, and the powers it will possess."[36] Indeed, Loughlin lists "comprehensiveness" as the first precept of the modern constitution, quoting Thomas Paine's requirement that a constitution contain "everything that relates to the complete organization of a civil government, and the principles on which it shall act, and by which it shall be bound." It simply makes no sense to "constitutionalize" one part before deciding the rest. The many moving components of any constitution not only complement each other, but their very function and definition are devised in view of the whole apparatus and the complex inter-relationships between its parts. In fact, it seems unlikely that any Constitutional Assembly in any jurisdiction would consciously decide to adopt a half-constitution (or a quarter, or a tenth). Attempting to do so would almost certainly be perceived as a failure to enact any constitution at all.

Finally, even those arguing that any Knesset could enact a constitution believed, for the most part, that it could only do so by way of some special procedure outside the framework of ordinary legislation. Various suggestions included passing a specific Basic Law which would separately define and set in motion the process for enacting a written constitution; submitting a draft constitution for approval by public referendum; having two consecutive Knessets (with national elections in between) ratify a new constitution; requiring a Knesset supermajority for doing so; and most typically, some combination thereof. Almost all seemed to agree that the Knesset could not simply trot out a constitution – partial or whole – the same way it passed all other legislation.[37]

As "rigidity" (procedural hurdles to amendment) is a recognized feature of constitutional norms, some viewed the Knesset's enactment of entrenchment clauses in 1958 and later as proof of its constituent powers.* But this was always an odd and circular argument. The validity of such entrenchment doesn't stem from its own existence, but rather from the Knesset's preexisting authority or lack thereof. Put differently, whether such procedural requirements are in fact validly "rigid" – can they properly obligate a future parliament, etc. – is precisely the question being debated. An attempt at limiting future amendments to a statute does not automatically and retroactively grant the Knesset constitutional powers if they were not there in the first place.

Among the most pointed contemporary critiques of this view was one articulated in 1970 by American Professor Melville Nimmer, who rejects the premise of the Knesset's continuing hereditary constituent power and echoes many of the arguments noted above.[38] "It would be strange," Nimmer muses, "to view this authority as a kind of property right which the owner can freely transfer to others." Arguing that the only body properly authorized to enact constitutional norms was the First Knesset, Nimmer explains that such authority arose

> "from something in the nature of a trust relationship established between the electorate and the particular men whom they elected for the avowed purpose of writing a constitution. Nothing in the creation of the trust implied that the trustees might transfer this power to others who had not been elected for this purpose. Only in the first election was the electorate properly put on notice that their representatives would engage in constitution-making."

More broadly, subsequent Knessets simply lack the type of clear electoral authorization typically required of any constituent body. In this context Nimmer restates the core "theory in any democratic state" that it is "the people" who "adopt a constitution." He continues: "the legitimacy or popular acceptance of a democratic constitution increases commensurately with the role of the electorate in its adoption," a role which is maximized when a constituent body adopting a constitution "is popularly elected for that purpose and the result of its labors is ratified in a general referendum." While there is no definitive formula for constitution-making, "any State that claims to govern itself by democratic principles" would minimally need "some direct line of authority from the

---

* And some Knesset Members criticized the 1958 entrenchment clause, during legislative deliberations before its enactment, for violating parliamentary supremacy.

electorate" to the constituent body enacting a constitution.

Variations of this argument have been raised by numerous scholars regarding both the Knesset's inability to enact constitutional norms and the framework created by the Harari Resolution. In one later example, Mark Tushnet (citing Bruce Ackerman) stresses the requirement for electoral "heightened attention" to "matters of fundamental political significance" which serves as a prerequisite for the creation of constitutionally-binding rules.[39] Per Tushnet, the formula presented by the Harari Resolution "does not satisfy" relevant accounts of constitution-making, because the Knesset – as ordinary legislature conducting routine politics and elected for that purpose – "could not be expected to have the high degree of attentiveness to fundamental matters that constituent assemblies might."

On a more analytical level Nimmer shows why the idea of "continuing" Knesset constitutional authority is simply nonsensical. Even if one Knesset creates a constitutional norm, any successive Knesset can then annul or recreate the same norm by exercising the exact same constitutional authority, such that the norm is not "binding" in any relevant or practical sense. Under such a framework "the concept of constituent power as a source of higher law becomes meaningless." Any Basic Law claiming constitutional status can be subsequently repealed by a regular legislative act (at most requiring the semantic label of "Basic"). Entrenchment poses no exception, because such a rule can only apply to the legislature acting as such and "cannot impede a body with continuing plenary constituent authority" – meaning, entrenchment can be regarded as a constitutional limit only on the Knesset's legislative function, but cannot command the adherence of the Knesset acting in its constitutional capacity, which could properly overcome or ignore any such entrenched majority requirement. Nimmer quotes Alexis de Tocqueville who aptly described the British Parliament as "at once a legislative and a constituent assembly" – perfectly illustrating how the notion of the Knesset's continuing constitutional authority is conceptually indistinguishable from parliamentary supremacy (British or Israeli).

Thus, Nimmer concludes, the claim that Basic Laws (entrenched or not) enacted by subsequent Knesset's held any kind of constitutional status "appears unacceptable as a key to the question of higher law in Israel" and "must be rejected as either meaningless or socially unjustified." Consistent with his conclusion that there is no "external organic law" which binds or restricts Israeli parliamentary supremacy, Nimmer ultimately urges that "a prior entrenched act of the Knesset should not be regarded as a form of higher law which may control later enactments."

As opposed to the radical theory of eternal "inherited" constituent authority, the more common approach, closely resembling Nimmer's arguments, was that "entrenched" clauses were declarative and essentially unenforceable – including Section 4 of Basic Law: The Knesset. While perhaps expressing an admirable preference of legislators that certain provisions are not lightly tampered with, such clauses had no power to bind or restrict a future Knesset which was free to amend (or violate) them by a later statute. This applied regardless of whether one thought the Knesset theoretically possessed "constituent" authority or not: under the prevailing view that the Knesset had no such authority, of course entrenched clauses had no force against a future parliament; while even among those that claimed such authority existed, most agreed that the familiar Basic Laws or entrenched clauses did not meet the criteria to be considered superior norms of a constitutional nature. Either way, a court could not invalidate a newer piece of legislation due to a conflict with an earlier Basic Law or entrenched clause. This is generally the view shared by any system of parliamentary supremacy, including Britain. (Nimmer extensively describes how the notion of procedural "entrenchment" – precisely like the one in Section 4 – had been rejected time and again in British jurisprudence and political thought.[40] The legal futility of any such entrenchment remains true today.[41])

A middle approach was ambivalent, on the one hand, regarding the Knesset's constitutional authority and was willing, on the other hand, to specifically accept entrenched clauses which set procedural requirements (such as an absolute majority) for future Knessets. The rationale for this was that the Knesset was entitled to self-impose prospective procedural rules as a matter which is entirely separate from more complicated constitutional questions. On this view, such entrenchment was not a "superior" law as much as it was a valid technical rule, not substantively different from the Knesset's internal legislative procedures (e.g., three readings to pass a law), and was not "constitutional" in any sense. Entrenchment clauses were hence fully enforceable, including by a court striking down nonconforming legislation, but at the same time had no bearing on – and existed separately from – the debate surrounding the Israeli constitution.

Without debating the merits of this approach, one factor in its favor is that a requirement for an absolute majority – like the one in Section 4 of "Basic Law: The Knesset" – does not necessarily contradict parliamentary supremacy. An absolute majority of Knesset members are still not a supermajority, and a requirement for the former does not grant a parliamentary minority veto over legislation. In Israel's Westminster-style parliamentary system any Government rests on the support of a Coalition numbering at least 61 members – such that at least in theory, any ruling Coalition can muster sufficient votes to amend an entrenched provision. Indeed, controversial legislation might often require 61 votes if the Coalition is committed to passing it despite concerted Opposition efforts at blocking it. One can therefore view an absolute-majority requirement simply as a deliberative mechanism ensuring important amendments receive full attention and commitment of the parliamentary-electoral majority. A determined governing majority is still able to get its way even in the face of unified opposition – as such, the requirement is not a genuine restriction on the Knesset's lawmaking power and is fully consistent with parliamentary supremacy. In this sense viewing entrenchment as a standard procedural requirement can plausibly evade constitutional questions altogether.

Evidence of this approach is further supported by the existence of similar entrenchment clauses in decidedly non-constitutional settings. For example, a major economic crisis in 1985 led to a flurry of legislation which included "entrenched" clauses in statutory arrangements regarding foreign investments and the Israeli central bank. At the same time, numerous Basic Laws enacted between 1958 and 1992 did not include any entrenchment clause, further weakening the argument that entrenchment is inherently linked to quasi-constitutional norms.

Both approaches – rejecting entrenchment entirely or recognizing entrenchment as an enforceable but modest procedural rule – contrast with the "constitutional" approach in that neither accepts the premise of a Knesset exercising constituent authority to create binding semi-constitutional norms.

Bergman and the Seeds of Judicial Review

This brings us to the 1969 *Bergman* case, in which the Supreme Court – kind of, sort of, maybe – struck down a law. The case and its implications are debated to this day.

In 1969 the Knesset passed a campaign-finance statute which provided State funds to cover expenses of existing political parties. The law was passed by an ordinary majority (that is, less than 61 Knesset Members) and was quickly challenged in the Supreme Court on several grounds. Among these was that the law fundamentally violated the "equality" of elections required by Section 4 of Basic Law: The Knesset, because it privileged existing political parties (by providing them with State funds) over prospective political parties which were not entitled to the same funds. This allegedly gave established parties an unfair advantage over potential future parties, rendering elections unequal. Though this case provided the potential for a dramatic constitutional debate because it demanded judicial review of legislation, the sizeable constitutional questions were largely avoided. The LCG (and future-Justice) Meir Shamgar defended the law on substantive grounds (arguing that it did not violate the "equality" requirement) without addressing the Court's authority of judicial review or the status of Basic Laws and entrenched clauses. The Court on its part followed suit and also refused to engage in constitutional debates for its own reasons.

In a curt five-page decision penned by Justice Moshe Landau, the Supreme Court held that the campaign-finance law was invalid because it was not passed by an absolute majority of Knesset Members, which was required (per the Court) by the Section 4 entrenchment clause of "Basic Law: The Knesset" for any significant violation of the "elections equality" principle in the same Section.[42] The ruling took both legal and political circles by surprise for two separate reasons. First, the Court had previously interpreted the "equality" of elections as applying to the individual right of equal electoral weight, e.g. "one man, one vote," but had now interpreted "equality" abstractly as extending to political parties and their relative privileges. Second, the Court had seemingly taken the unprecedented step of striking down a piece of primary legislation.

Yet the *Bergman* ruling is far less dramatic than it might initially seem. Justice Landau explicitly adopted the "middle" approach described above, under which entrenchment clauses are a technical procedural limitation. The Court was not "invalidating" any law in its view; it was rather enforcing the Knesset's own numerical rules. After concluding that the new law violated the electoral "equality" principle enshrined in Section 4, the question of legality became exceedingly simple – was the law enacted by the required absolute majority or was it not. Because the statute in question did not receive support of an absolute Knesset majority, it lacked legal significance and was unenforceable. The heady constitutional questions of Basic Laws, entrenchment, *Harari*, and so on, were simply (ostensibly) irrelevant.

The Court makes its position in this regard abundantly clear and unequivocal. First and most importantly, the material ruling speaks for itself. The Court summarizes that if the Knesset so desires, it may enact the same law again – "despite the inequality within" – if done so with the requisite majority. The operative judicial order provides that the law under review be applied "only if re-legislated by the required majority." Indeed, the Knesset went ahead and enacted the law anew with an absolute majority (albeit also slightly altering the party-funding mechanism), and the Court dismissed a legal challenge because the condition for an absolute majority was met. More generally, the Court clarifies it has been "relieved" of addressing "preliminary grave constitutional questions" by the LCG's decision not to raise the matter at all. Because the LCG argued that the law didn't violate the equality principle to begin with, the constitutional aspects of the case were simply not litigated, not tangibly argued by any party, and not seriously considered by the Court. The Court therefore emphasizes that "obviously, nothing stated herein represents an opinion" on these issues, not to mention binding precedent. The Court stresses that its decision does not involve the "remotest pretense" of "touching in any way the sovereignty of the Knesset" (that is, it does not challenge parliamentary supremacy).

Far from being a monumental decision establishing judicial review or the primacy of Basic Laws, *Bergman* was on its own terms a technical ruling which enforced a mechanical rule of Knesset procedure. It did not address any constitutional matters nor did it presume to (and it explicitly says so). The fact that the five-member panel was unanimous, with no other Justice feeling compelled to comment on the bland five-page decision, further supports the ruling's unremarkableness. Justice Landau, the decision's author, himself expressed this view on many occasions. In a 1972 essay[43] Landau stressed that the Court in *Bergman* "did not rule on fundamental matters" and that one "ought not read into it that which is not there," saying he "did not know from whence came" any "exaggerated estimation" of the decision's implications. He repeated this point in another extensive article (the technical decision "did not require taking a stand on any ideologically or politically controversial issues")[44] and at many other opportunities.

To be sure, the *Bergman* ruling is not without cause for objection. On the merits, the Court adopted an expansive and creative view of electoral "equality" and could easily have interpreted the requirement more narrowly so it would not apply to the campaign-finance law in question. The Court makes no real attempt to justify its interpretation by way of conventional methodology (the kind of judicial debate on such issues that might elsewhere be considered standard – such as parsing the textual meaning and evaluating the legislative process behind the statute, etc. – is absent from the ruling). In addition, the Court conflates the distinct actions of amendment and violation without a moment's hesitation – even if Section 4 requires a certain majority for *amendment*, the same does not automatically apply to its *infringement* by another law. At no point does the Court even recognize the distinction, though the two are separate legal acts and with potentially different outcomes and there may be strong arguments for requiring the former and not the latter.*

And the Court's remedy – pronouncing the law unenforceable unless passed with the required majority – was not necessarily justified. The Court could just as well have issued a form of declaratory relief by stating that the new law should have been passed by the requisite majority, without rendering it legally void. True commitment to parliamentary supremacy perhaps meant that the Court should have dismissed the petition outright, regardless of grounds or merit, under the simple and established rule that the Court does not review the legality of statutes, period. Similarly, the Court's evasion of constitutional debates and its insistence of triviality comes off as somewhat unconvincing, as there's no denying that it had effectively, de facto, ruled a legislative act of parliament to be annulled and unenforceable, and that such a decision was inexorably linked to the questions the Court was ignoring. Nimmer's critique of Israeli "entrenchment" discussed above was a response to *Bergman* and argued precisely this point.

Such criticism notwithstanding, the *Bergman* case was on the one hand significant in that it undeniably created a precedent by which the judiciary "set aside" a statute, while on the other hand it deliberately refused to address (and let alone decide) any of the constitutional questions discussed above. Most crucially, the ruling is indisputably grounded on a simple numerical proposition – that the Knesset may overcome "entrenchment" restrictions by absolute majority vote.

It is tempting to see *Bergman* as expanding judicial power or as tacitly recognizing judicial enforcement of constitutional limits to parliamentary supremacy. Yet properly understood *Bergman* did precisely the opposite. In many senses the decision cut "entrenched" clauses down to size and threw cold water on the quasi-constitutional claims of the more radical theories. On what we may call the minimalist view, either the Court in *Bergman* decided wrongly or the decision is a minor and narrow determination with limited application and no bearing on broader constitutional questions. This seems to be the view espoused by the decision's own author, Justice Landau. But even on the maximalist view,

* Prof. Rivkah Weill observes in this context that a lack of distinction between amendment and infringement is a staple feature of "monistic" constitutional systems (that is, systems of parliamentary supremacy) in which all legislation bears the same legal status and in which there is no hierarchy of superior (or constitutional) norms.

Bergman at most recognized the enforceability of procedural numerical requirements in "entrenched" clauses, and without any reference to constitutional powers that might limit parliamentary supremacy. The Court's refusal to broach the broader issues is in fact a clear rejection of the more creative claims regarding the constitutional nature of entrenched Basic Laws. Indeed, some scholars even responded to the ruling by complaining that the Court did not engage with their law-review theoretical debates, but this seems to be no accident – the Court was evidently aware of such theories and consciously chose to ignore them.[45]

Seen this way the *Bergman* ruling effectively settled the question of Basic Laws and their potential enforcement, by allowing for judicial review while reducing it to a headcount. The much-vaunted rigid "entrenchment" meant nothing more than legislative arithmetic. In the following years *Bergman* became the exception proving the rule: Basic Laws held no special status and were identical to ordinary legislation; "entrenchment" clauses were no more than procedural majority voting requirements; judicial review extended, at the very extreme most, to enforcing these numerical rules; whether the Knesset was exercising alleged "constituent authority" became largely moot. This is strongly evinced by the 1973 *Kaniel* decision (only a few years after *Bergman*): the Court upheld a Knesset statute regarding elections even though it violated the entrenched Section 4 "equality" principle, for the simple and explicit reason that the legislation was enacted by an absolute majority as required.[46] Subsequent Supreme Court decisions reiterated that Basic Laws possessed no superior status over other legislation, and that the limited possibility of judicial enforcement existed only within the procedural context of an entrenchment clause. *Bergman* thus carved out a highly specific and rare outlier to parliamentary supremacy, but in doing so shot down the loftier notions of constitutional status for Basic Laws and bolstered the overall scheme of Knesset omnipotence and immunity from judicial intervention.

Ultimately, *Bergman* and entrenchment were simply not so much of a big deal. None of the Basic Laws enacted between 1958 and 1992 (including regarding the judiciary, the executive Government, the State capital city and more) included entrenched clauses. The single entrenchment clause in Section 4 of "Basic Law: The Knesset" was enforced by the Court three more times (in addition to *Bergman*) and in near-identical circumstances, requiring an absolute majority for campaign-finance legislation which seemed to unfairly privilege some political parties over others.[47] Arguments regarding the Knesset's constitutional powers and ability to impose constitutional restrictions were relegated to legal academia.

*

Cutting through the fog, Israel's constitutional framework on the eve of the 1995 Constitutional Revolution was abundantly clear and exceedingly simple, despite its many confusing components discussed above. It may be summarized as follows: the Israeli system was one of Westminster-style parliamentary democracy; the unicameral Knesset, appointed by national proportional elections and the sole institution with a claim to direct democratic authority and legitimacy, was the sovereign originator of law and enjoyed parliamentary-legislative supremacy; Israel had no written constitution or anything approaching one; the Knesset could not bind or substantively limit its successors. All legislation existed on a single equal tier, including Basic Laws which held no constitutional or superior status. No court could subject laws or statutory provisions to judicial review; the sole limited exception to this rule was the "entrenched" clause in Section 4 of Basic Law: The Knesset which required an absolute majority of Knesset Members, the judicial enforcement of which extended only to counting votes and ensuring the numerical condition was met.

All this was the irresistible, shared and near-unanimous consensus of the legal and political establishment and of the broad public. Alternative theories were advanced by a handful of scholars but generally remained on the fringes of academic inquiry. Thus, despite later arguments to the contrary, the legal and constitutional reality of Israel until 1995 was in fact relatively straightforward and uncomplicated.

Israel certainly had, since its inception and throughout its existence, an unwritten constitution. The content of this constitution need not be fully elaborated here, but it undoubtedly contained various arrangements, principles, conventions and rules relating to its core values and its system of government. These included the State's national Jewish character, its commitment to electoral representative democracy, the Common Law legal tradition including a robust judicial role, and the "status quo" of delicate questions of religion and state. Like any other, the Israeli unwritten constitution was also comprised of some statutory and textual elements, such as the first legal actions taken by the Provisional People's Council and the Constituent Assembly, the Harari Resolution, (some of the) Basic Laws, fundamental legislation like the Law of Return, parts of the Declaration of Independence, select Supreme Court decisions, and more.[48]

II – The Constitutional Revolution: 1992-1995

Against this backdrop, 1992 saw the Knesset enact several new Basic Laws or pass significant amendments to existing Basic Laws. A dramatic amendment to Basic Law: The Government established a new (but short-lived) electoral mechanism by which the Prime Minister (and by extension the Government he appoints) is chosen directly by popular vote, separate from the proportional outcome of parliamentary elections. We may call this the "direct election" amendment, which will be mostly ignored for present purposes.* Basic Law:

* The "direct election" amendment was a well-intentioned but ill-advised effort at alleviating some of the government's systemic woes. Justified or not, the method was abandoned after three election cycles.

Freedom of Occupation enshrined the fundamental right of, as the name suggests, freedom of occupation. Basic Law: Human Dignity and Liberty served as a much broader and more expansive "bill of rights," including protection of one's life, person, and property alongside more abstract values of dignity, liberty and privacy, among other rights. We may call the latter two the "1992 Basic Laws," the "1992 legislation" or the new Basic Laws. These two new laws were further amended in 1994.

In 1995 the Supreme Court handed down the landmark *Hamizrachi* decision which announced a "constitutional revolution." The Court, led by incoming Chief Justice Aharon Barak, held that the enactment of the two new Basic Laws amounted to a dramatic constitutional development which made these Basic Laws (and most other earlier Basic Laws along with them) the supreme law of the land, such that Israel now had (and has) a "substantive" constitution. The Court also held that new Knesset legislation contradicting or violating norms found in these Basic Laws could be struck down by the Court as unconstitutional. These controversial conclusions are deeply and widely contested to this day.

The Court did not invalidate any law in *Hamizrachi*, but in 1997 ruled to strike down a piece of new primary legislation – relating to licensing of investment advisors – due to the law's incompatibility with Basic Law: Freedom of Occupation. For the first time, Israel had experienced substantive judicial review in which judges nullify a law due to the "unconstitutionality" of its contents. Since then, the Supreme Court has consistently and overwhelmingly relied on this newfound "material constitution" to reshape the Israeli legal system and political order in its entirety, including by invalidating duly enacted primary legislation. At least twenty-five laws have been struck down so far, in part or in full, as unconstitutional.*

These are the three components – the 1992 Basic Laws, *Hamizrachi*, and subsequent judicial review – of the infamous "constitutional revolution," with the 1995 Supreme Court ruling as its focal point and center of gravity. The events described herein are very much the watershed moment of judicial supremacy in Israel. In the preceding years the Court, primarily at the initiative and drive of Justice Barak, had consolidated its power by abolishing threshold conditions of justiciability and standing, by developing novel doctrines of purposive interpretation and reasonableness review, by cowing elected officials under the Deri Doctrine, by empowering its proxy the LCG, and by weaponizing criminal justice. With the "constitutional revolution," after having been rapidly and utterly derailed by the Court for over a decade, the Israeli legal order was launched off a cliff and hurled into the abyss, where it still remains in freefall.

We now turn to examine this extraordinary phenomenon, unparalleled in the annals of constitutional democracy. We will first describe the *Hamizrachi* ruling

---

* Most invalidated laws will be discussed in Chapter 10.

in broad (even dry) strokes, and then consider the 1992 legislation and evaluate whether the Court's findings were justified.

United Hamizrachi Bank v. Migdal Cooperative Village

Immediately following the 1992 legislation, in the formulation and enactment of which he was directly and personally involved, Justice Barak announced in various academic and public platforms that a "constitutional revolution" had taken place. A few months after the laws had passed Barak opened a short speech at the University of Haifa thus: "Not everyone knows this, but recently a revolution has occurred in Israel. I am speaking of a constitutional revolution, in which the Knesset, as the constitutive authority, enacted 'Basic Law: Human Dignity and Liberty' and 'Basic Law: Freedom of Occupation.'"[49] The crux of his argument was that the recent Basic Laws ushered in a new constitutional era, in which Israel essentially has a constitution and in which judges can invalidate legislation due to its incompatibility with the new putative constitution. In 1993 Barak published a comprehensive law journal article elaborating his view on the new legislation and its constitutional implications.[50] In a 1994 speech Barak described this revolution has having taken place "silently, almost hidden from view."[51] In the three and a half years between the new Basic Laws and the *Hamizrachi* ruling Barak expended considerable intellectual effort in presenting his case regarding the former's significance, with at least a dozen combined articles and speeches addressing the issue from various angles.

Barak's enthusiastic adoption of (and advocacy for) this supposed authorization for judicial review was hardly surprising and had been brewing for some time. Not only was this something of a predictable progression of his activist jurisprudence, but also just a few years earlier Barak had clearly indicated – and indeed explicitly stated – his yearning for such judicial ability to override legislation. In the 1989 *Laor* case the Supreme Court invalidated another campaign finance law in accordance with the *Bergman* procedural entrenchment rule, as it had not been enacted with the requisite absolute majority (this was the fourth and last such decision). Despite striking down the law the Court reiterated its well-established and long-held view of parliamentary supremacy, while Barak posited a radically divergent approach in a minority opinion.

Writing for the majority, Justice Menachem Elon wrote: "It is our fundamental principle that a law enacted and passed by the Knesset is not subject to judicial review of its validity. A cornerstone of our democratic system, with its three branches of government, is that we do not question the legislative act of the legislature." Barak voted to uphold the law in question but described the question of judicial review in terms entirely foreign to the Court's prevailing jurisprudence (in typical fashion assuming the role of "restraint" while in effect adopting a far more activist position). After a laborious theoretical exposition, Barak concludes that "in principle" a "court in any democratic society" may strike down a law if it contradicts "the system's fundamental values." According to Barak, the Court's current refusal to exercise such judicial review is only the outcome of the "prevailing legal and societal approach" reflecting the "social agreement" in Israel, enjoying the "consensus" of the "enlightened community." Therefore, Barak summarizes, it would be "improper" for the Court to deviate from existing practice by striking down legislation "contradicting the regime's fundamental values."

Though couched in the terminology of restraint, Barak's *Laor* minority opinion entirely undermined and reframed the Israeli paradigm of parliamentary supremacy. Barak essentially argues that the absence of judicial review in Israel is not a legal limit to the Court's power per se, but rather something of a convention which the Court may choose to maintain or discard at its discretion, based on how it perceives the "enlightened" public consensus on the matter. Such social consensus is not only subjective (that is, it is determined solely by the judge) but is also malleable and conditional – Barak qualifies the prevailing approach as applicable only "at this stage of our national life." And indeed, the "next stage" was brought about by Barak in short order.

The 1995 *Hamizrachi* case involved a number of indirect challenges to a legislative amendment regarding debt settlements in the agricultural sector. The amendment, dubbed the "Gal law," made it harder for banks to enforce debt collections against agricultural businesses. In a handful of civil proceedings, some banks alleged that the Gal law had illegally infringed upon their constitutional right to property – enshrined in the 1992 Basic Law – and was therefore invalid. Conflicting District Court decisions were appealed and the issue quickly made its way to the Supreme Court.*

The *Hamizrachi* ruling spans some four-hundred pages of sprawling (and often rambling) legal debate, culminating in the establishment of a de facto Israeli constitution. All nine Justices on the panel wrote separate opinions. The Court was unanimous in the sense that all agreed with the operative outcome – the challenges were dismissed and the "Gal law" was upheld – but in this sense only. The Justices proposed fundamentally distinct theoretical and practical accounts of their reasoning and conclusions. Technically, the vast majority of the ruling's content is universally acknowledged to be obiter dictum – immaterial "background" reasoning not pertinent to the final operative decision.

The case revolved around two core questions. The first is whether Israel has a constitution as a result of the 1992 laws. The second is whether the Court may exercise judicial review of legislation. Folded into each of these (and into their interaction) are numerous additional questions and issues, theoretical and practical. The Justices offered radically different yet expansively elaborate answers to these questions, drawing on constitutional theory, political philosophy and abstract musings. Though the opinions addressed existing Israeli jurisprudence and its historical development,

* *Hamizrachi* was a civil appeals case, not a "High Court of Justice" administrative petition, demonstrating the Court's power as appellate tier discussed in Chapter 2.

only a fraction of the debate featured genuine Israeli legal substance. The larger part of the ruling engages in grueling philosophical debate drawing on the likes of Hans Kelsen and H.L.A. Hart, such that it far more resembles academic or scholarly exploration than a document of ordered legal argumentation.

Eight of the nine Justices agreed that the Court possessed the authority of judicial review and agreed that the 1992 legislation enjoyed some status of superiority, but differed on the basis for such authority and on the nature of the new laws. The three dominant and most oft-cited opinions are those of Justices Barak, Shamgar, and Cheshin. The only real dissenter, Justice Cheshin maintained that the 1992 laws were of no (or limited) significance and could not fundamentally alter the constitutional order; he argued that the Knesset did not possess the authority to enact a constitution; and he likewise held that the Court possessed no power of judicial review exceeding the numerical procedural enforcement rule established in *Bergman.* We will examine his dissent later.

Justice Shamgar was the outgoing Chief Justice and had just retired from the bench, while Justice Barak had just been appointed to the same role. The two Chief Justices presented overlapping theories with similar immediate outcomes, but which were nonetheless fundamentally different in their underlying approach and in their future implications. Despite each judge positing exhaustingly convoluted treatises on constitutional theory, their respective views can be relayed in relatively simple form.

Shamgar's opinion was based on what he called the primacy of the Knesset and can be summarized thus: If the Israeli parliament is supreme, then it is perfectly entitled to create a hierarchy of laws, according to which some laws enjoy an elevated status compared with others. The Knesset may similarly define "tiers" of superior and inferior types of legislation. The practical significance of doing so was that an inferior (or ordinary) statute could not contradict (or violate) a superior statute. According to Shamgar, this is what the Knesset did by elevating the new Basic Laws to superior status, such that from now on any future law could be deemed invalid. A court enforcing the superior law and implementing the Knesset's will is compelled – and fully authorized – to strike down future legislation if it sufficiently violates the superior Basic Laws.

In other words, Shamgar tackled the familiar paradox of parliamentary supremacy, but he resolved it in the direction opposite to the way it has been traditionally resolved in Britain and other jurisdictions. For Shamgar, parliamentary omnipotence included imposing enforceable self-restrictions on future Knessets by creating a hierarchy of distinct legislative tiers. This formulation avoided the framework and terminology of classic constitutionalism.

Justice Barak, on the other hand, took a radically different approach by fully embracing the model of hereditary constituent authority. Per Barak, the First Knesset and every subsequent Knesset possessed and reserved the power of the original Constituent Assembly – that is, the power to enact a constitution or constitutional norms. The Knesset has always performed a dual function, wearing (in Barak's parlance) "two hats" and serving as both ordinary legislature and constituent authority. The Knesset alternates freely between these roles, and at its choosing can enact norms of a constitutional nature by exercising its constitution-making power. The Knesset indicates this functional shift by appending the words "Basic Law" to legislation being enacted, thus vesting legislation with superior constitutional status.

Here Barak makes a critical and novel terminological distinction between a "formal" constitution and a "substantive" (or "material") constitution, the former referring to a familiar written (or codified, or legal) constitution and the latter referring to the Israeli unwritten (or semi-written) constitution. Barak argued that though Israel did not have a formal conventional constitution, the new Basic Laws provided the State with a substantive constitution which is equivalent to the genuine article in everything but name.

In Barak's view, the two new Basic Laws now served as Israel's constitution for all intents and purposes. This conclusion was based on a number of factors. First, the new laws established (or clearly resembled) a "bill of rights" which is a typical feature of constitutional documents, especially regarding human rights of a universal nature. Second, Barak considered judicial limits on legislation a core feature of "substantive" democracy. By enacting the new "bill of rights," Israel had chosen to officially become such a "substantive" democracy with "human rights" at its core. Third, both the new laws featured a "limitation clause" which stipulated the conditions in which the enumerated rights could be harmed or violated. The combination of these elements – limiting government's ability to infringe upon fundamental human rights – bore the mark of constitutional democracy. In passing these Basic Laws the Knesset was finally fulfilling the Harari Resolution and exercising its constituent authority by creating the new Israeli "substantive" constitution. Central to Barak's argument, and in line with his signature method of objective purposive interpretation, was an interpretive method that he called "constitutional interpretation." This was a unique form of interpretation distinct from ordinary statutory interpretation that called for a much higher degree of philosophical and abstract judicial reasoning. Much of Barak's arguments and conclusions in *Hamizrachi* are derived from this mode of "constitutional" legal interpretation.

Finally, per Barak, a court may enforce the "substantive" constitution by striking down primary legislation, precisely as is customary in many other constitutional jurisdictions – a conclusion that flows naturally (for Barak) from the initial premise of the constitution's existence. Aside being based on the nature of legislative inferiority under constitutional norms, Barak's conclusion also relied on the "limitation clause" which could be understood to mean that a law which does not meet the required conditions is rendered invalid. Either way, per Barak, once a court declares such a law to be invalid, it becomes void and all government organs must follow the court's determination.

Simply put, the new Basic Laws enabled judicial review of legislation. Here too Barak makes a key and novel distinction between "formal" entrenchment and "substantive" entrenchment. Entrenchment of the "formal" kind meant the familiar procedural requirement for a specific majority at the heart of the *Bergman* rule. But a "limitation clause" that imposes conditions on violations to the law may serve as "substantive" entrenchment, giving the law another kind of status and force. In this way Barak introduced the notion of judicial review over laws contradicting a Basic Law, even if the latter did not include any "formal" entrenchment which thus far had been (since *Bergman*) the sole exception enabling judicial review.

Though neither opinion was supported by a majority of the bench, Shamgar's "tiered" view technically prevailed in *Hamizrachi*, as his reasoning was likely endorsed by more Justices (a plurality) than those that endorsed Barak's.[52] Indeed, the ruling concludes with the statement "decided according to Chief Justice Shamgar's opinion."* Nonetheless, it was Barak's view – constituent authority, dual-role Knesset, material constitution, substantive entrenchment, and so on – which ultimately carried the day. The Court in subsequent decisions adopted Barak's view more or less in its entirety, as did many in the Israeli legal establishment. Still, it's worth noting that to this day there is no unified theory regarding the nature and source of Israeli constitutional authority, both within the Court and even within Barak's own jurisprudence.

In the thirty years since *Hamizrachi* the Supreme Court has never revisited these central questions. The power of judicial review and the Barak-ean formulation of the Israeli constitution instantaneously became, as far as the Court was concerned, settled law – binding and controlling. The Court and adherents of judicial supremacy, especially in the legal establishment, began referring casually to "the Israeli Constitution" (with a figurative capital "C") as a matter of course, and act (as described by Weill) "as though Israel has a conventional constitution of which the general public is not aware."[53] Since *Hamizrachi* the Court has not officially considered, in any case or decision, the fundamental validity or viability of that ruling, its theories or its conclusions.

The *Hamizrachi* ruling was issued on November 9th, 1995. As the ruling regarded an uncontroversial law focusing on an esoteric issue (banks collecting debts from agricultural businesses), and as the Court ultimately upheld the law and gave no operative order, it is unlikely that the decision would have generated much initial interest or attention. The case proceedings were not closely followed by the public and received virtually no journalistic coverage.

As things turned out, the ruling was overshadowed by truly tectonic and devastating events – four days earlier on November 5th, the Israeli Prime Minister Yitzhak Rabin had been murdered by an assassin. Despite the unprecedented and earth-shattering circumstances, the Court chose to proceed and issued the ruling

* There is some disagreement among scholars as to which of the two opinions received more endorsements. Regardless of the answer, the fact that this was unclear and remains contested demonstrates the obscurity of the various opinions in *Hamizrachi*.

regardless. The national mood of horror and grief and the political disarray stamped out what little chance there was that *Hamizrachi* would provoke public attention. As Prof. Rivkah Weill notes: "No one noticed the decision in real time."[54] The ruling was reported a few days later as a minor item on page nine of the leading daily newspaper "Yediot" – the bottom third of the same page was filled with classified ads for trucks, motorcycles and antiques. The general public obliviousness to the *Hamizrachi* decision is widely acknowledged.

Critics over the years have accused the Court of deliberately issuing the ruling at a time when it would almost certainly pass under the public radar, so as to avoid scrutiny and political repercussions. They argue that the Court should have delayed the ruling's publication by at least a few weeks if not more. The Court in its defense has always offered the same explanation for its questionable timing choices: Meir Shamgar's tenure as Chief Justice had ended, and according to statutory law a judge must conclude his participation in a preexisting case within three months following his retirement. The Court therefore was obligated to publish the ruling (with Shamgar's central opinion) within the allotted timeframe and could not delay further.

Though perhaps not a matter of great consequence, we may render the service of once and for all putting this issue to rest. The explanation offered by the Court and its defenders is so brazenly implausible as to offend the intelligence of any honest observer. First, the law in question mandates only that a retired judge must "complete the hearings" (or the "deliberation") in his cases within three months of his retirement. Nothing in the statutory text suggests that a ruling must be issued or published within that timeframe; a perfectly plausible reading of the text is that the law's requirement is easily fulfilled if a judge completes their opinion in time, even if the ruling itself is published much later. Indeed, it is not uncommon for completed Supreme Court rulings to be signed, sealed, but not delivered – often languishing for months or even longer, waiting for the Court's convenience. Second, Meir Shamgar retired on August 13th, such that even by its own reasoning the Court could have issued the ruling on November 13th, still within the allotted three months. In the colossal fallout of Rabin's assassination every day was an eternity, and four days – between November 9th and November 13th – could have made a significant difference in terms of the attention afforded to the ruling. Why, then, was the Court in such a rush that it could not wait the extra four days?

Yet these objections are mere trifles. The real absurdity in the Court's explanation is less formalistic. The Court was issuing a groundbreaking ruling and was effectively upending the Israeli system of government. The Justices were fully cognizant not only of the ruling's momentous significance but also of its legal audacity – no one could deny that the conclusion reached by the Court required a generous measure of judicial creativity. At the very least, on the most objective and empirical level, the Court was reversing the settled legal jurisprudence of the previous four decades involving the most important constitutional questions, doing so on the basis of highly ambitious legal arguments. At the same time, issuing the ruling later would have made no practical difference, as the law in question was upheld and the matter was moot.

Somehow the same Court that championed purposive interpretation and that flouted rule after rule saw itself bound to strictly follow this trivially technical deadline; the same Court that was about to recognize the world's first "material" constitution was incapable of delaying its decision under the extraordinary circumstances of an assassinated Prime Minister. The claim was and remains preposterous. If the Court was so inclined it could easily have postponed publishing *Hamizrachi* despite the alleged (and unfounded) statutory deadline, and no one would have batted an eyelid. One cannot escape the impression that the timing of *Hamizrachi* mere days after the Rabin assassination was opportune, and that the decision not to delay its publication was a conscious choice to capitalize on the favorable conditions of public and political distraction.*

A Contested Constitution

Having described the 1995 ruling at the heart of the "constitutional revolution," we may now evaluate the strength and validity of its principal arguments. Were the 1992 Basic Laws a genuine constitutional development? Did they actually empower the Court to conduct judicial review? Do the claims of *Hamizrachi* withstand meaningful scrutiny?

Though we will address these questions thoroughly, there is a broader perspective to consider which is perhaps more significant than any analytical or legal answer. From the moment *Hamizrachi* came into this world its central premise and claims were deeply and vehemently contested – including in the ruling itself, with the devastating dissent mounted by Justice Cheshin. Among those rejecting its reasoning and conclusions were some of Israel's most renowned jurists, public figures, and political theorists (as we shall soon see) from across the ideological spectrum, a rejection which is maintained by many eminent legal scholars and practitioners to this day. In this sense Israel is unique in that the very existence of its purported constitution is a central point of intense disagreement. After three long decades, the objections to *Hamizrachi* have only grown in support and in sophistication, while at the same time the notion of an Israeli constitution was never internalized or recognized by the broad public. The average Israeli on the street could not say what a constitution is, whether Israel has one, or what the supposed Israeli constitution consists of. At the time of this writing, the Knesset website states unequivocally that "unlike many States around the world, Israel does not have a constitution."[55]

Yet a "contested constitution" is a profound oxymoron, a contradiction in terms. There are many legal instruments and institutions which can exist in a state of indeterminacy, but a constitution is not one of them. The entire rationale and function of any constitution is premised on the unambiguous fact of its incontrovertible, obvious and irrefutable existence. Whether a State has a constitution is a manifestly observable fact. If the constitution's very existence is

---

* This pattern repeated itself with the 2024 *Reasonableness* ruling.

disputed, one can hardly assert its recognition and support by a wide public consensus – upon which any constitution's claim to validity is based. In no other jurisdiction in the world is the existence of the State's constitution itself the subject of controversy and debate. Both in theory and practice, the question whether a State has a constitution must necessarily yield a binary answer – yes, or no* – such that anything but a decisive "yes" is, by definition, a categorical "no." For a constitution, much like the Force, a partial attempt is not enough – as Master Yoda teaches, "do, or do not; there is no 'try.'"

This inescapable truth dooms the Supreme Court's constitutional innovation in *Hamizrachi* from the outset. The 1995 Israeli constitution was dead on arrival. Even if the ample and intense objections to the "constitutional revolution" were completely unfounded, the readily observable fact of considerable controversy around the constitution's existence utterly undermines – and essentially demolishes – its claim to validity and force. This is perhaps one reason that the Court over all these years has so adamantly avoided engagement with the formidable arguments levelled against *Hamizrachi* and refuses even their basic acknowledgement, as such a concession would necessarily undermine the constitutional endeavor itself. The question being asked provides sufficient evidence of the answer; the very argument proves the proposition to be ludicrous. To paraphrase Margaret Thatcher, being a constitution is like being a lady – if you have to tell people you are, you aren't.[56]

Joshua Segev makes this point succinctly. Segev notes that mere disagreement "does not mean that the existence or absence of a constitution is purely subjective." A constitution "is not person-relative" and its existence "is independent of personal preferences, convictions, and beliefs of scholars, judges, and public representatives." Justice Barak tries to bridge this gap by various elaborate intellectual flourishes which are ultimately "reduced to a list of controversial theories." But as the existence of a constitution "is not a complicated issue that needs to be resolved by theory," "the mere fact the one tries to establish its existence by theory calls its existence into question."[57]

In this sense the material discussion surrounding *Hamizrachi* and the nature of the Israeli pseudo-constitution is something of a red herring, a misleading distraction. Debating the merits of the "constitutional revolution" obscures the fact that the debate renders itself superfluous. As we proceed with precisely such an evaluation, which is nonetheless necessary and appropriate, we may bear in mind that the burden of proof here is low – the point is not just how compelling one finds a particular claim or counterargument, but rather that the severe doubts surrounding the entire project themselves serve to prove the constitution's nonviability.

---

* Israel might just have the dubious distinction of possessing the world's first and only non-binary constitution.

1992 Basic Laws – The Origin Story

To say that the Supreme Court's primary argument in *Hamizrachi* is flawed would be an understatement so gross as to amount to deceit. Prof. Daniel Friedmann famously described Justice Barak's constitutional revolution as "standing on chicken legs."[58] We will now see why this is so.

In assessing the Supreme Court's claims we must necessarily commence with the legislation passed in 1992 – Basic Law: Freedom of Occupation, and Basic Law: Human Dignity and Liberty.* For the sake of convenience we will abbreviate these laws respectively as "BL:FO" and "BL:HDL" (admittedly only slightly less cumbersome than the full name). As we shall see, the straightforward description of these laws makes short shrift of the Court's constitutional revolution.

The new Basic Laws were enacted in March of 1992, during a "caretaker" Government in the runup to elections. The previous Government had collapsed in January, and on February 4th the Knesset called new elections – the country was headed to the ballot. Under such circumstances the Knesset functioned in a state of limbo – still an elected legislature but with no coherent Coalition of parties or constituencies, loose party voting discipline, and no consistent majority on any given issue. Many Knesset Members were busily preoccupied with their upcoming respective party primaries among other distractions.

BL:FO was enacted around 4am on March 12th with a majority of 23 for, and zero against. Out of one hundred and twenty Knesset Members, less than a quarter bothered voting or even showing up for the vote. BL:HDL was enacted on March 17th with a majority of 32 for and 21 against (with one abstaining). Less than half of all Knesset Members bothered voting or even showing up for the vote. The two new laws were simply not considered momentous or important enough for most legislators to register their presence. The BL:HDL vote was held in the middle of the night (in fact, closer to 4am), after most of the legislative agenda for that day had been taken up by a law regarding loan guarantors. The following day, on March 18th, the Knesset officially dispersed in anticipation of the upcoming elections. Thus the two "human rights" Basic Laws were passed by small quorums and smaller majorities, during a period of political and governmental turmoil, within a twilight legislature that had been elected four years earlier suffering from a manifest democratic deficit. Both laws were initiated by individual MKs as private bills and were not originated from the Law, Constitution and Justice Committee as required by the Harari Resolution.

Politicians and the public paid scant attention to the new legislation, even taking into account the diversions of governmental collapse and upcoming elections. For those attuned to legislative affairs and to the political agenda the "direct elections" amendment was much more the talk of the day. The amendment to Basic Law: The Government was passed on March 18th (right before the

* The complete translated text of both laws is available in the Appendix of this book.

Knesset called new elections) by a majority of 57 for, versus 56 against.* The high degree of participation (94% of all Knesset Members) and the tight margin jointly demonstrate that legislators were certainly capable of showing up for legislation of consequence despite much background noise, in stark contrast with the two preceding Basic Laws which were discernibly regarded as not bearing any particular import.

Even legislators directly involved in enacting the laws did not seem to think they were engaging in some abnormal constitutional act. Weill observes that "at the time the Basic Laws were legislated, no one considered the width and depth of legislative support to be of particular importance." While some MKs conceivably perceived themselves to be fulfilling a constitutional function "many others were utterly unaware of their [alleged] role as constituent assembly."[59] For most MKs it was business as usual.

On a broader societal level the public atmosphere was not remotely one of constitutional transcendence. The preceding 1988 elections yielded no clear parliamentary majority, such that the bitterly opposed Likud and Labor parties were compelled to form an awkward "unity" government with the Prime Minister role rotating between candidates (needless to say, the formation of a constitution did not feature in any of the party campaigns). Such was the "unity" between political camps that the Government collapsed two years later in the infamous 1990 "stinking trick" scandal† which ultimately led to a narrow right-wing Coalition. The entire affair further exacerbated widespread distrust of government and revulsion towards shameless political scheming. The "direct elections" amendment was itself in large part considered an attempt to reduce the influence of small sectorial parties, but more broadly also a public rebuke of the current political establishment and its failings. Further in the background was the violence and mayhem of the First Palestinian *Intifada*. This backdrop was in no way a moment of broad public consensus or harmony regarding any issue, let alone supporting fundamental alterations to Israel's systems of government.

The enactment of the two "rights" Basic Laws was generally ignored by the public and, notably, the press. One day after BL:HDL was passed, the leading national daily newspaper *Maariv* simply ignored the new "bill of rights" and reported nothing related to it, despite running a full page on political and legislative affairs. Another national newspaper, *Hadashot*, mentions the new legislation in a miniscule item as part of a "daily headline digest" which involved thirty-five items in a single page (right after a headline about rising divorce rates and before a report that a farmer had been killed in a tractor accident). The public was oblivious to the enactment of these two purportedly constitutional laws. It is to this that Barak was referring when he announced that the constitutional revolution had occurred "hidden from view" and unbeknownst to many.

---

* The decisive vote was cast by a young lawmaker named Benjamin Netanyahu, who four years later became the first Prime Minister chosen under "direct elections."

† Yes, this is the conventional name by which the affair is known.

Weill cites all these factors, and others, to conclude that "the Basic Laws were enacted without widespread and stable popular support."[60] In addition to elements listed above, Weill stresses that the new laws differed significantly from the major constitutional initiative at the time (the "four professors" draft constitution) which might have been familiar to some legislators. She further observes that even if the legislation could somehow be attributed to the parliamentary coalition (and by extension to some coherent electoral majority), the same coalition was rejected by the electorate and lost the ensuing elections – ruling out any claim that the public had somehow endorsed or ratified the new laws. Weill ultimately rejects any claim that this could have served as a transcendent "constitutional moment" as defined by theorist Bruce Ackerman.

In summary, the Government had collapsed, the Knesset was entering new elections, and neither likely possessed a mandate for dramatic constitutional change; the national mood was one of deep division and of dissatisfaction with the current governing class; public and political attention was directed anywhere but at two new obscure Basic Laws; the new Basic Laws were enacted by small majorities in which most legislators were absent; and their enactment elicited almost no response from the press. The new laws did not generate public, political or legal attention and were not closely followed before, during, and after their enactment. They were, by almost any measure, a non-event. Nothing in the above circumstances might indicate that these Basic Laws could somehow serve as Israel's constitution.

What The Laws Say, And What They Don't

We might contend, perhaps, that the social, political and legislative circumstances surrounding the enactment of the new Basic Laws are immaterial, insofar as what really matters is the law itself which the Knesset enacted. This is certainly true for the most part (setting aside the point that constitutional authorization must also rest on broader factual conditions). It is primarily the law itself which concerns us, its text, and the underlying conscious intent of its legislators. Let us examine, then, what the Knesset enacted – or at least, what it thought it was enacting. We will do so while recalling the fundamental claim in *Hamizrachi* that these two Basic Laws represent a constitutional revolution, serve as Israel's new constitution (essentially to this day), and empower the Court to conduct judicial review.

As many have observed, an especially instructive element of the new Basic Laws is not what's there, but rather what isn't. Conspicuous among all the flaws inherent in the new Basic Laws' claim to constitutional status, is the glaring absence of explicit constitutional terminology and authorization typically found in any constitutional text. These omissions may be easily summarized: a) Neither law has any kind of "supremacy clause" declaring its superiority within a legislative or normative hierarchy. b) Neither law confers the power of judicial review on any court, nor does it address the consequences of another law conflicting with the new Basic Laws. c) Even the familiar "entrenchment" mechanism is only partially present – BL:FO contains an "entrenchment" provision requiring an absolute majority for its amendment, but BL:HDL contains no such entrenchment.

Let this sink in for a moment. The mark of any conventional constitution is its assertion of legal preeminence, that it stands above ordinary law. Any constitution in the world establishes its primacy within the legal State hierarchy in one way or another. The U.S. Constitution states that it "shall be the supreme Law of the Land"; the Canadian Constitution states it is "the supreme law of Canada." Other examples abound throughout the democratic world, with constitutions using similar phrasing or conveying the same concept of supremacy. This of course makes sense – if a constitution is a holistic document aspiring to establish and define all governmental power and authority within a State, then surely it must explicitly address its own position relative to other rules and institutions.

Further, the Basic Laws do not declare that conflicting ordinary legislation is void, null, invalid, unenforceable, or anything to that effect, nor do they empower any court to declare a law unconstitutional. Addressing the question of unconstitutional legislation and of judicial review is another staple feature of modern constitutions, directly derived from the constitution's superior legal status.

Yet the 1992 Basic Laws feature no such provisions.

As if this were not enough, perhaps the most glaring omission is the lack of an entrenchment clause in BL:HDL (by far the more expansive and comprehensive of the two new laws). As exhaustively covered earlier in this chapter, procedural entrenchment was the *only* exception to parliamentary supremacy, the *sole* recognized mechanism for judicial review, and the *single* hint of quasi-constitutional rigidity to any Israeli law. Since *Bergman* in 1968 this was settled law, the established rule consistently applied by the judiciary and acknowledged by jurists, politicians and scholars.

Prof. Rivkah Weill summarizes well the core assumptions of the Israeli legal order at the time the 1992 laws were enacted: "The Court treated Basic Laws just like any other regular legislation… a later regular law prevailed over preceding Basic Laws." The sole exception enabling judicial review was to "protect… the election system" from interference "without absolute majority support in the Knesset," per the procedural entrenchment of Section 4 of Basic Law: The Knesset.[61] In other words, in 1992 the Israeli system of government and the Supreme Court's jurisprudence recognized entrenchment as the one exclusive indication of an "elevated" statutory provision; and legislators passing laws in 1992 unquestionably operated under this understanding. The notion that a law – Basic or not – could be afforded constitutional status without the bare minimum of an entrenchment clause was unthinkable.

Though not quite an omission, the pedigree of both laws as private bills is also not inconsequential. Aside violating the basic requirement set out by the Harari Resolution – that Basic Laws be drafted and initiated by the designated

Committee – this too deviates from constitutional form in an important way. One expects significant constitutional legislation to originate in at least some sense from formal State organs, from "the establishment" so to speak. This would easily apply for official Governmental bills, and also holds for bills initiated by the Constitution Committee – a committee explicitly tasked with exercising and representing the Knesset's institutional role in drafting constitutional rules. Bills drafted by the Committee bear the aura of officialdom, of speaking in the name of the Knesset as an institution, and put others on notice as to their nature and significance (one could even posit that the Harari requirement was a prescient and conscious effort at avoiding unsanctioned constitutional schemes by backbenchers or the Opposition). The fact that both new Basic Laws were private bills initiated and sponsored by individual MKs (from the Opposition, no less) further erodes their claim to constitutionality on both technical and substantive grounds. Similarly, of the 32 votes in favor of passing BL:HDL, most came from members of the Opposition – further bolstering the impression of the law as more rogue subversion than institutional approval.

In 1993, American constitutional scholar Gary J. Jacobsohn published a comprehensive study comparing Israeli and American constitutionalism. In the afterword Jacobsohn addresses the recent developments in Israeli law and politics – and especially the passage of the two new Basic Laws in 1992. Noting how Barak had called these a "constitutional revolution," the author states that "it is difficult to see wherein the revolutionary significance of these laws lie." Jacobsohn observes that "aside from being unentrenched" BL:HDL explicitly provides that nothing in it will affect existing legislation, and it includes important qualifications." Of the idea that these new Basic Laws can somehow establish limits on Knesset legislation, the author responds that this is perhaps true "in a moral or political sense"; yet "nothing could be clearer than that the most far reaching of the two Basic Laws [i.e., BL:HDL] does not constitutionally bind the Knesset."[62]

A full-fledged *coup d'état*

More damning even than the absent hallmarks of a constitutional document is the legislative history and process. The drafts and deliberations of the 1992 Basic Laws reveal, irrefutably, that the Knesset had no intention of enacting a "constitutional revolution." Far from some inattentive lapse, the omissions described above were a conscious choice to avoid even the appearance of vesting the new Basic Laws with constitutional status.

Previous draft bills of the new "human rights" legislation included explicit provisions which established supremacy alongside judicial authority to invalidate conflicting legislation – yet these provisions were discarded as part of various compromises which ultimately enabled the legislation's enactment. Similarly, BL:HDL had initially included an entrenchment clause, but this was dropped during a legislative session when enough MKs objected. Weill notes that the legislation sponsors went into "deep mourning" when the entrenchment was voted down, as in their view this extinguished any hope of the Court exercising judicial review to enforce BL:HDL.[63]

In other words, the type of constitutional authorization so conspicuously absent from the new Basic Laws was in fact considered and then rejected. Some version of it appeared in previous drafts and was then intentionally shed in the final law that was enacted. The Knesset didn't merely refrain from including such constitutional provisions – it actively chose to exclude them. This cannot be emphasized enough.

Further still, these determinations by the Knesset were at the core of a political compromise which enabled the enactment of the 1992 Basic Laws. After years of legislative deadlock in which proposed "human rights" bills proved too contentious, the breakthrough emerged through precisely the explicit abandonment of constitutional provisions. Simply put, if the 1992 legislation drafters and advocates had insisted on such provisions – supremacy, judicial review, entrenchment – the laws would simply not have passed. They were all dealbreakers. The 1992 Basic Laws owe their entire existence to the negation of any constitutional aspirations they might have harbored.

The above factual points are broadly acknowledged and remain generally undisputed.

By 1992 Haim Ramon had already been a Knesset Member for nearly a decade, and served as leader of the left-wing Labor party caucus. Because the Labor party leadership was largely absent due to primaries battles, he effectively functioned in the Knesset as leader of the Opposition. Ramon was instrumental in persuading other MKs to support the new Basic Laws – the Constitution Committee Chairman at the time thanked Ramon for his vital contribution in getting the laws passed, writing that "without your leadership we would not have been able to do so."[64] But Ramon is the first to say that these laws were in no way a constitutional revolution. In retrospect, Ramon asks whether the law's sponsors deceived the Knesset (he leaves it to his readers to reach their own conclusions) and ruefully dubs himself a "useful idiot."[65] For Ramon, the explanation for the media and public indifference following the new laws is simple – there was nothing to merit attention. "No one thought that anything of consequence had occurred, since, indeed, it did not occur to the Knesset Members that they had done anything of consequence." Ramon summarizes his view in no uncertain terms:

> "Since 1995 some have debated over whether the Knesset intended to enact Basic Laws that would allow the Supreme Court to strike down legislation. My answer is unequivocal: No. Even [the bill sponsors] admit that had they declared during the proceedings that the court would be empowered to nullify Knesset legislation, they would not have secured a majority."

Reuven Rivlin (who was eventually to become President of the State of Israel) served in 1992 as an MK on the Constitution Committee throughout the legislative process. He strikes a similar tone:

> "Under no circumstances was the idea to transfer legislative authority from the Knesset to another body. No one even discussed changing the balance of power between the Knesset and the court."

Rivlin continues that when he first heard the new laws being referred to as a constitutional revolution, he "was shocked." "There was no constitutional revolution here whatsoever. It never happened." As the Court gradually "assumed more powers" through "creeping annexation," it dawned on Rivlin that "not only had a constitutional revolution occurred, but rather a full-fledged *coup d'état* – contrary to the spirit of democracy and without authorization."

Another example illustrating the way the Basic Laws were perceived is the views of two scholars already mentioned above in our discussion of parliamentary supremacy – Amos Shapira and Ben Susser. Writing immediately after the 1992 laws had been enacted, both scholars clearly did not consider the new legislation to be supreme or constitutional in any way. Indeed, Susser focused primarily on the "direct elections" amendment also passed in 1992 as the only consequential "revolution" of sorts. This is notable because both professors participated in drafting a popular draft constitution on which the 1992 laws were partially based. Nonetheless, it did not occur to them that the new laws somehow amounted to a constitution of any kind.

One of the most intimate and authoritative accounts of the legislative history preceding the 1992 Basic Law: Human Dignity and Liberty was published the following year by Yehudit Karp, in what she called the statute's unofficial "biography." Karp was Deputy LCG throughout the efforts to enact the new "bill of rights" and was directly and personally involved in all its stages, along with other lawyers of the Justice Ministry. Her descriptions and observations are of special interest due to her overall orientation – deeply supportive of the new Basic Laws, Karp is a steadfast champion for the Barak-ean Supreme Court and is easily associated with the judicial supremacist camp. After retiring Karp joined the most radical elements within Israeli left-wing ideological ranks. In this sense the factual and legal portrait she presents is not diminished by any hostility or suspicion towards the Basic Laws and the overall constitutional project. On the contrary, even in the context of this specific "biography," Karp offers a decidedly maximalist view and argues that the new Basic Laws empower the Court to conduct (some degree of) judicial review, including on the basis of unenumerated rights. Though much of Karp's article references events in the public record and reiterates well-known claims, her personal perspective as enthusiast of the constitutional revolution is nonetheless valuable, as she usefully compiles and confirms many of the points elaborated above.*

---

* Though her article focuses on BL:HDL, Karp's observations are highly relevant to both

Karp's description of the underlying assumptions of Knesset Members and the legal community in 1992 is consistent with our discussion above. "Parliamentary sovereignty" (i.e., supremacy) was "adopted in Israeli jurisprudence" and constitutes "the law of the land." While some posited that the Knesset wielded the authority to enact a constitution, this was a "theory" that had "yet to gain a tangible foothold" in Israeli law. The "prevailing approach" shared by politicians and jurists was that "the legislature has no authority to limit its successors in any matter."[66] Such was the paradigm within which legislators operated while enacting the 1992 Basic Laws.

Karp describes the public and political atmosphere as "days of pettiness, days of conflict and compromise," doubting that any "voices emanating" from the Knesset during the legislative "can indicate an awareness" of legislators that they were engaging in a constitutional revolution.[67] Further, Knesset Members were not even acting out of principle – "more than cohesive thought regarding policy and outcomes," their votes were motivated by "considerations of political expedience."[68]

The compromises that ultimately led to the Basic Laws being legislated were "substantial" and not merely "tactical." At the heart of this political compromise was "the non-inclusion" of a provision "that would have granted the court the power of judicial review."[69] Another provision that might have hinted at some form of supremacy, by subjecting preexisting statutes to "interpretation in the spirit" of the new Basic Law, was also deliberately discarded as part of the same compromise. Karp summarizes the "political understandings" (her euphemism for legislative intent) that underpinned the legislative cooperation to enact the new laws: "No constitutional court – with the power of judicial review – is established"; "judicial review of legislation will not be anchored" in the new laws; and BL:HDL "will not be entrenched."[70]

The verbal Knesset exchanges and discussions are the most acutely striking and illuminating. During the law's second reading in the runup to a vote, the Chairman of the Constitution Committee said the following on the Knesset floor:

> "We are not shifting the weight to the Supreme Court… We are not doing that which was suggested [in previous drafts]… No constitutional court is being established, nor is any court being granted special authority to overturn laws."

Some of the present MKs pressed the issue and demanded to verify their understanding that the court was not being empowered to strike down laws. The Chairman replied: "There is no need to invalidate laws. No law is being invalidated... We are maintaining the status quo." He later continued:

> "The power is not being reassigned to the judiciary. The power remains in this House [The Knesset]… I oppose the formation of a constitutional

---

Basic Laws and to their combined effect.

> court… [which] grants expansive powers to a small clique of judges whose judgment determines the viability of laws in Israel. Not this law…"[71]

These explicit and forceful statements, from one of the Knesset Members most associated with advancing the 1992 laws, are etched in collective memory of those opposing the Supreme Court's constitutional revolution. They merit a brief pause. Read them again. Karp mentions additional cryptic remarks made by various legislators which can be understood to indicate an opposite intent, and she states that "deducing any consensus, mindset or common accord regarding" these issues "is challenging." But the quotes above are hardly ambiguous – such unequivocal statements by the law's drafters and sponsors during key debates are simply incompatible with the notion that the Knesset was consciously infusing the new Basic Laws with constitutional status or enabling judicial review. Their impact cannot be diluted by contrasting opaque hints made by sporadic legislators. Even if there were explicit statements to the contrary – and there are none – such extreme duality or disagreement between Knesset Members as to the nature of the new laws would only serve to strengthen the case of insufficient consensus for constitutional change. A "difficulty" to identify consensus is no difficulty at all – it just means the consensus wasn't there.

Returning to Karp's account, she notes that after BL:HDL was passed many of its supporters voiced their disappointment – the advocates of ambitious constitutional projects felt that the final legislation fell far short of its potential. The law's main sponsor (and prominent constitutional scholar), MK Amnon Rubinstein, lamented the final draft as "modest and minimalistic."[72] Karp further attests that following the enactment of the two new laws "there were no displays of jubilation… not in the Knesset and not in the press." She memorably describes "the profound silence which accompanied their legislation."[73]

Despite all the above, Karp raises the possibility of a "discrepancy between the probable political understanding and the legal outcome, when interpreted according to the purposive method."[74] What she means by this, somewhat euphemistically, is that highly creative legal acrobatics could somehow still overcome the clear statutory language and evident legislative intent, to yield all (or most of) the changes that were rejected by the lawmakers themselves. Karp seems to suggest that this route was at least contemplated, and perhaps even fully intended, by the law's proponents all along.

Karp describes the extensive participation of bureaucratic government lawyers in preparing the new laws. The proposed legislation had initially comprised of a single ambitious "human rights" law drafted at the Ministry of Justice by lawyers within the LCG Office. When it failed to receive sufficient legislative support the draft law was split into separate chunks and pawned off to various Knesset Members to propose as private bills, while the Ministry of Justice (essentially, the LCG attorneys) maintained their direct involvement. "As one who was for many years at the potter's wheel" molding the new laws, Karp describes how these were "forged" in the Justice Ministry.[75] Though Karp presents the ambiguities revolving around the legislative process as a mechanism for accommodating differences and enabling compromise, her account indicates that some in the legal establishment also saw the lack of clarity as an opportunity for retroactive judicial manipulation.

Critically, Karp concedes that bureaucrats involved in drafting the legislation shared the same Barak-ean desire for expansive judicial review.[76] Perhaps more candidly than intended, Karp also describes the duplicitous tactics employed by some of the law's sponsors and proponents as including "duality, ambiguity, glossing-over, and legal misrepresentations." Reading between the lines it seems plausible that both the LCG Office and the legislators advancing the draft bills were less concerned with the law's omissions and with the inconsistent legislative process, in the confident knowledge that the Supreme Court would supply the desired outcome one way or another.

The sentiment of suspected subterfuge was indeed expressed by some Knesset Members. Many voiced disapproval at the partitioning of one proposed bill of rights into several bite-sized laws – if the Harari Resolution envisioned drafting constitutional "chapters," these were now individual "verses" being enacted separately and independently. One prominent left-wing lawmaker (who was also a political science professor) dubbed it "guerilla-style legislation," a "half-legitimate half-subversive method of smuggling a constitution onto the agenda" and said it indicated "an overall error in the field of Israeli constitutionalism."[77] Karp's account implies (somewhat smugly) that this suspicion was perhaps justified. It would seem that from the outset Karp, her fellow government attorneys and their collaborating legislators contemplated a manufactured "discrepancy" between the actual law being enacted as understood by legislators and the "legal outcome" as applied by the Court.

Incidentally, this impression of methodical dishonesty is especially supported by a jarring account, retrospectively offered by one of the primary legislators that had orchestrated the new Basic Laws – MK Uriel Lynn. Lynn was chairman of the influential Constitution, Law and Justice Committee which played a pivotal role in advancing the 1992 legislation. In 2017 Lynn published his personal history of the legislative process and efforts surrounding the new laws, in which he seems to proudly brag about the various machinations and ploys which ultimately got the bills through the Knesset.[78] Lynn describes his "dilemma" at the time as follows:

> "How do we create a legal reality which grants courts the power of judicial review, without provoking intense opposition in the Knesset and without it looking like a transfer of legislative authority from the Knesset to the courts?"

His entire account indicates clearly that the law's ambiguity was a deliberate act of deception.* Lynn admits that towards the final reading of the new laws, he "had the support of the entire Opposition, but did not yet succeed in securing the Coalition's support." In order to escape the Coalition's (i.e., the Knesset majority) unwanted attention, Lynn explains that he had to "avoid expressly mentioning within the law that an external entity was being granted the power to annul Knesset laws" because this would be a "red cloth before the eyes of the Knesset Members" and would "foil the law." Lynn was right, and his "avoidance" bore fruit – among the 32 MKs that voted in favor of BL:HDL, twenty were members of the Opposition while only twelve belonged to the Coalition.

This, then, was the process by which the 1992 Basic Laws were enacted. The political background, legislative record, comments by participating legislators and contemporary scholarly reactions all speak for themselves. As opposed to Lynn's apologetics, the factual and pragmatic account provided by Yehudit Karp has many accurate insights – most pertinent among these is Karp's admission of the achingly undeniable: "Basic Law: Human Dignity and Liberty lacks any accepted and recognized feature which might indicate" the Knesset's intention to "enact a supreme law, of a superior constitutional status, which may determine the validity of conflicting statutes."[79]

An important addendum to our analysis is that the 1992 Basic Laws glaringly lack a host of features and attributes one would expect to find in any constitution, many of which are indeed usually considered to be indispensable. These are in addition to the more specific omissions discussed above (such as a supremacy clause or authorization for judicial review). Among the missing elements we may observe just a handful.

Scope. The very contours of the alleged constitution are undefined, and no one (not even the Court) attempts to delineate where the constitution begins and where it ends. Does it include only the two new Basic Laws, all the Basic Laws or some other assortment thereof? Does it include the laws in their entirety or only select provisions? What of other "fundamental" legislation not classified as Basic Laws? None can say. This is a purported "constitution" with no known or agreed textual content. If asked to compile all the textual components of the Israeli "constitution" in a single document, no two jurists would provide the same answer.

Rigidity and Amendments. The 1992 Basic Laws are generally flexible and almost disposable – they may be scrapped by a simple (or absolute) majority, with no requirement for a supermajority or for procedural obstacles to amendments and nullification. Any ruling coalition of 61 MKs can change any provision or simply revoke both Basic Laws. In a similar vein, the Basic Laws contain no "user manual" for changes, amendments or replacement. Presumably this would mean that the prevailing rules apply, allowing for free and unrestricted amendment via ordinary legislation. But the absence of any amendment rules stands out as

---

* From the book's smug tone it's obvious that Lynn thought he was being rather clever.

singularly unusual for any constitutional text. Despite some overlap, these are two distinct features – complete flexibility and no defined process for amendments.

Symbolism. As we've noted above, the Basic Laws were enacted with no ceremony, no symbolic gestures, no public celebrations, and no outward indication of a momentous occasion in a State's national history.

Length and Clarity. The Basic Laws are notoriously short and vague, with only a few sentences listing operative rights at a high level of abstraction. Most modern constitutions span tens of thousands of words – the two new Basic Laws jointly contain, at most, less than a thousand. Adding all previous Basic Laws still falls far short of any conventional length for democratic constitutions. The provisions themselves are extremely nebulous – to the point of meaninglessness – even compared to the typically generic phrasing of constitutional rights. For example, constitutions will typically list a host of specific protections against abuse of criminal law and procedure – relating to search and seizure, due process and trial fairness, detention, representation, self-incrimination, confrontation of witnesses, and so on (think of the 4th, 5th, and 6th amendments of the U.S. Constitution). The Israeli Basic Laws settle for far broader language. As noted above, the provisions and rights contained in the Basic Laws were deliberately diluted (and thus made more obscure) after more explicit statutory language in previous drafts failed to gain legislative traction.

Constitutional Rights. The 1992 Basic Laws lack a series of fundamental and civil rights typically considered to be the hallmarks of any modern constitution. To name a few, these include criminal due process, freedom of speech, freedom of association and assembly, freedom of religion (or of conscience), and equality before the law. The notion of a modern constitutional document omitting such rights is virtually unthinkable, and reflects the incomplete and fractional nature of the Basic Laws and the weakness of their claim to constitutional standing. We will return to some of these missing rights later on.

Though each is not necessarily dispositive as "proof" of a constitution, the aggregate impression from these missing features leaves little room for doubt. Whatever the 1992 laws are, they were clearly, plainly, manifestly not a constitution.

The 1994 Amendments

Our last point of interest as we retrace the footsteps of the 1992 Basic Laws is a series of amendments legislated in 1994.

The Knesset sought to amend both new Basic Laws for a handful of reasons, some related to improving consistency across both laws. Though legislated at the same time, from similar sources, of a similar nature and for a similar purpose, the two laws were marked by various discrepancies – in their preamble, in their retroactivity, in their "limitation clause" and elsewhere. As we have discussed in detail, only BL:FO had an entrenchment clause. In addition, BL:FO included a "grace period" at the end of which offending administrative regulations would be potentially voided – yet the Knesset had not yet managed to amend or adapt the many relevant regulations, such that an extension of the grace period was urgently needed. The amendments were technically enacted by re-legislating BL:FO anew and replacing the 1992 law altogether; while the same legislative act also included "indirect" amendments to BL:HDL.

But the primary motive for amending the laws was, as is often the case, partisan political expedience. A 1993 Supreme Court ruling held that an executive prohibition against importing non-Kosher meat products fell afoul (no pun intended) of Basic Law: Freedom of Occupation. The Court warned that if the Government wanted to maintain the prohibition it would need to amend the Basic Law so as to enable explicit legislative exceptions to the law's enshrined rights. The left-wing Rabin Government was conducting peace talks with the Palestinians at the height of the Oslo process, and desperately needed support from the Shas religious party, who in turn would not tolerate removing the prohibition on non-Kosher meat imports. As a result, the Rabin Government initiated the amendment with the primary aim of allowing the Knesset to shield specific laws from the effects of BL:FO. Thus was born the infamous "override clause," also known as a "notwithstanding clause," at the behest of the Court and with the personal urging of Aharon Barak, a topic which we will later revisit.

Aside this substantial addition to BL:FO for decidedly earthly reasons, the 1994 amendment added a "purpose" clause to BL:FO similar to the one already found in BL:HDL, which referenced Israel's character as a "Jewish and Democratic State." An additional "preamble" was added to both laws, stating core principles and referencing the Declaration of Independence. The "limitation" clause in both laws – stating the permissible circumstances for abridging rights – was amended so that they were now uniform. However, no entrenchment clause was added to BL:HDL.

Because the 1994 amendments were enacted by a sizeable parliamentary majority, some scholars argued that this "remedied" an inherent flaw in the 1992 legislation, which was enacted by awkwardly small quorums and even smaller majorities. They further argued that the amendments were enacted when the Knesset was fully cognizant of the constitutional significance of its actions.

Yet these arguments verge on the disingenuous and are easily dismissed. First, the amendments were enacted before the 1995 *Hamizrachi* ruling, that is, before the Court formally declared the new laws to be Israel's de facto constitution, such that all the previous prevailing assumptions that existed in 1992 still applied. No one in the political establishment considered the Basic Laws in 1994 to be any more "constitutional" than they were in 1992.

Second, on a practical level, the 1994 legislative process was marked by confusion and chaos, in some ways worse than the ambiguity and indifference of the 1992 laws. Prof. Ariel Bendor, former Dean of the Haifa University Law School and among Israel's foremost administrative law experts, describes the "rushed" manner in which the 1994 amendments were legislated.[80] Critically, the original bill that passed its first reading did not include the "indirect amendments" to BL:HDL at all, and did not include the "preamble" (which referenced the Declaration of Independence) for either law. These were added only for the second and third readings. But when the Constitution Committee Chairman presented the bill for a vote on the Knesset floor, he "entirely ignored" the additions and made no mention of them. As a result, "many Knesset members were likely unaware" of the content of the bill for which they were voting. Especially regarding the new "preamble" provisions, the Knesset floor discussion indicates that voting MKs "were not aware of the inclusion of this central provision, the discovery of which, a few days later, created a political storm." (As it turned out, both the Shas party and Prime Minister Rabin claimed they had no knowledge of the preamble provisions at the time they had voted for the law, a point which ultimately prevented Shas from rejoining the Rabin Coalition.)[81]

More bizarrely still, some of the MKs participating in the readings thought they were voting on an entirely different measure – the Frozen Meat Importation Act. This is unsurprising, recalling the political circumstances surrounding the 1994 amendments, which were primarily enacted to maintain Rabin's parliamentary support by excluding meat-import regulations from the restrictions imposed by BL:FO. As such the various laws were enacted consecutively in a hectic, marathonic legislative session, and Bendor describes how the Knesset "hastily concluded" the Basic Law amendments in "order to proceed immediately to the primary vote" regarding meat imports.

Though the amendments did bring some uniformity to the two Basic Laws, they were also rife with terminological inconsistencies and even logical contradictions. Bendor shows that these are not simply "legitimate interpretive questions" that typically arise in broad constitutional language, but are rather avoidable blunders of plain negligence, likely stemming from the "rushed and nontransparent" legislative process. Per Bendor, the 1994 amendments exemplify the broader practice of Basic Laws being enacted "hastily and even covertly, taking advantage of incidental political 'opportunities' alongside Knesset Members misunderstanding the legislation's substance."

Both Bendor and Weill remark that the entrenchment clause in BL:FO requiring an absolute majority for amendments was technically – and ironically – violated. Many key amendments were not included in the first reading at all, such that they could not be said to have been enacted by the requisite majority in all three readings.[82] This misstep calls into question the entire legal validity of the 1994 amendments under the *Bergman* rule.

As a final nail in the coffin of the "remedy" claim, it is especially noteworthy that despite the vaunted effort at bringing the two Basic Laws into alignment, the Knesset still did *not* add an entrenchment clause to BL:HDL. This further supports the impression that the Knesset was yet again refusing to apply any mechanism of procedural "rigidity" to BL:HDL and was not conferring any sort of elevated status upon the law.

All in all, the 1994 amendments do little to alter the basic outlook regarding the 1992 Basic Laws articulated above. If anything, their pedigree seems at some points even more questionable than that of the 1992 legislation (a consequential point in light of the Court's later reliance on the preamble clauses).

*

And so there we have it. To paraphrase the quote often misattributed to Winston Churchill, the 1992 legislation is the empty taxi pulling up at the Supreme Court building, out of which miraculously emerged the constitutional revolution. Our review of the 1992 Basic Laws must inevitably lead to the single irresistible and undeniable conclusion – that these cannot possibly serve as Israel's constitution, or as any functional equivalent thereof; that they do not satisfy the barest minimal conditions to be regarded as such; that their content and the process of their legislation directly contradict such a thesis; and that their enactment was by no remote means a "constitutional moment" (let alone, a revolution).

The two Basic Laws legislated in 1992 were impressive and important statutory initiatives aimed at enshrining a series of fundamental rights and protecting them from arbitrary infringement by executive government. They were enacted within the existing and well-established context of parliamentary supremacy and the absence of judicial review. Various versions including the establishment of a constitutional court or of arming judges with powers of judicial review were considered, debated, and explicitly rejected. The more substantial of the two laws was not even "entrenched," which had thus far been the sole recognized exception to parliamentary supremacy. The 1992 Basic Laws were enacted unceremoniously by a small minority of legislators in small quorums of voting Knesset members, during a "twilight" Knesset after the Government had already collapsed and in the runup to elections. They were not considered of particular constitutional consequence by the Knesset, by those participating in the vote and those absent, by the legal community and by the general public, before, during, and after their legislation. They lack an array of characteristics usually associated with a definitive constitutional document.

The idea that the Knesset could enact a constitution by exercising its "hereditary" constituent power was a far-fetched academic theory not known – and not acceptable – to most legislators and jurists. Even those subscribing to such a theory generally agreed that the enactment of constitutional norms by the Knesset could not be achieved in the ordinary course of legislation and had to involve multiple additional elements.

The overwhelming avalanche of evidence presented above utterly crushes Barak's central claim in *Hamizrachi.* The proposition that the 1992 Basic Laws could somehow upend the entire Israeli constitutional order – that they may serve, in fact, as Israel's new de facto constitution – championed by Barak and wholeheartedly embraced by the Supreme Court, is and always has been plainly ludicrous. The argument flies in the face of Israeli law and jurisprudence, contradicts all known global constitutional theory and practice, and does not withstand the barest scrutiny.

Barak's Conceit – Constitution, Democracy, Entrenchment

Justice Aharon Barak and the Supreme Court jointly demand that we ignore the obvious reality before our eyes. In their claim that Israel has an effective constitution grounded in the 1992 Basic Laws, they require of us to suspend our disbelief, to disregard all that we know, to discard all factual and legal information available to us, and to enter a state of naïve hypnosis in which the preposterous becomes the persuasive. In his claim of a constitutional revolution, Barak would have us believe that if it looks like a duck, swims like a duck, and quacks like a duck, it must be a Tyrannosaurus Rex.

We turn now to briefly examine the Court's central arguments justifying its claim. On what grounds do Barak and the Court impose the constitutional revolution despite the vast and compelling arguments against it?* The following explanation is derived from the *Hamizrachi* ruling itself and from the judicial consensus that emerged and crystallized in its wake.

Critical to understanding the arguments and justifications offered by the Court, it's worth emphasizing that the primary focus of *Hamizrachi* is not whether the Court may strike down legislation but rather whether Israel does or does not have a constitution. Importantly, the two questions are distinct and ought to be addressed separately. This is a key factor which differentiates *Hamizrachi* from other seemingly similar jurisdictions in which courts have debated questions of implicit judicial power afforded under a conventional constitution, the existence of which was never at issue. This difference highlights the unusual nature of *Hamizrachi* and the context for the Court's various claims.

As a preliminary question Barak considers whether the Knesset is a "constituent authority" – that is, whether it has the capacity to enact a constitution. As described above, Barak answers in the affirmative, assigning the Knesset a dual role as both constitution-maker and as legislature. Barak presents three alternate and elaborate theories to support his claim, which we may outline in cursory terms. One relies on the State's "basic norm" as conceptualized by Hans Kelsen; a second relies on the legal "rule of recognition" as defined by H.L.A. Hart; a third relies on the "best interpretation" of Israel's overall "legal and social history," tracking the writings of Ronald Dworkin. The objections to the claim of "hereditary constituent authority" have been covered in previous sections and need not be rehashed here, but it's worth noting that even Barak's theoretical analysis is severely lacking, to put it mildly. Various scholars have pointed out

* Because Barak's view has been adopted and is regularly applied by the Court, and is taught at Israeli law schools as definitive and controlling jurisprudence, I will refer here to Barak and the Court interchangeably. For current purposes, Barak's view is the Court's view and vice-versa.

his clumsy misapplication of legal theory,[83] and Joshua Segev has shown how the consistent inclination against adopting a definitive constitution is a much more faithful "interpretation" of Israel's legal history. Above these towers the inherent and self-defeating flaw of conjuring a constitution (and constitutional authority) out of abstract, convoluted theorizations. Still, we may proceed with the Court's dubious conclusion that the Knesset does indeed possess the power to enact a fully-fledged constitution.

The next hurdle, then, is whether the Knesset in fact did so – whether the 1992 Basic Laws may be regarded as the Knesset's exercise of its constituent power and as the formation of a new constitution. Barak's central arguments expressed both in *Hamizrachi* and in many instances elsewhere all revolve around a common theme of contrasting the "formal" with the "substantive." This dichotomy championed by Barak stands at the core of his constitutional jurisprudence. We may now explore the Court's main contentions employing such distinctions, to justify its claim that the Knesset indeed enacted a de facto constitution.

The Substantive Constitution. Barak distinguishes between a conventional (or documentary) constitution as typically regarded by the ordinary citizen and as we have defined above, which he calls a "formal" constitution, and the fundamental or essential societal arrangements shaping and restricting government power, which he calls a "substantive" (or "material") constitution. At first glance this might seem like just another variation of the familiar distinctions between codified and uncodified, written and unwritten, legal and political. Yet Barak's claim is far more radical and ambitious. As his phrasing implies, the "formal" is conceptually inferior to the "substantive." "Formal" evokes arbitrary formalism, a technicality, a rigid and hollow format, a token gesture, an external vessel; while "substantive" evokes sincere authenticity, the truly essential component, the core feature, the elemental soul, the real deal. The contrasting connotations are unmistakable. Thus Barak's choice of words already betrays, from the outset, a dramatic terminological reversal in which the unwritten constitution is touted as the real thing, while the conventional written constitution is something of a perfunctory formality.

And indeed, Barak implements this logic to its ultimate conclusion. Even in the absence of a "formal" constitution, a judge may treat a "substantive" constitution as its functional equivalent, effectively eliminating all distinctions between the two. A "substantive" constitution may assume the role of supreme law and may be enforced by the judiciary, including the nullification of ordinary legislation – it may, in short, serve as a State's constitution for virtually all intents and purposes. On the basis of his various theories Barak concludes that though the 1992 Basic Laws are obviously not a "formal" constitution in the conventional sense, they meet his criteria to serve as Israel's "substantive" constitution, and – *voila!* – we have the constitutional revolution. Critically, Barak is careful not to claim that the new Basic Laws are the entire constitution – they are rather just one part of the overall substantive constitution, the boundaries of which are undefined and unknown. In the same vein, Barak clarifies that the Israeli constitution is incomplete and is still very much in the making, expecting the Knesset to continue its enactment and amendment of Basic Laws.

Here we have before us the ultimate sleight of hand performed by Barak and his Court, allowing them to elegantly sidestep the obvious objections to constitutionalizing the 1992 Basic Laws. Barak deliberately conflates two vastly different ideas – that of an unwritten constitution, which all concede that Israel possessed, and that of an enforceable "substantive" constitution. Barak pretends these are one and the same; the absence of a constitutional document, of its signature hallmarks, and of an enactment process reflecting broad public assent as its source of authority and supremacy – to Barak these are trivial technicalities, like a missing checkmark on a Social Security form. The fundamental requirement of any constitution, that it be an integrated *text* consciously enacted by a special process for the specific and exalted purpose of serving as a constitution, is for Barak a nuisance and an inconvenience to be reasoned away or ignored. In a truly audacious feat of legal and logical ingenuity, the Court equates Israel's non-constitution with its diametric opposite, a binding and enforceable constitution. It demands that we acknowledge that Israel has no constitution while we accept the Court's power to behave as though there were one.

In so doing, Barak deceptively ignores the fundamental and profound chasm separating the codified "formal" constitution from the unwritten so-called "substantive" constitution. Their many differences are perhaps best demonstrated precisely through the prism of judicial review. It is a universally recognized principle that judicial review is the dividing line between written and unwritten, legal and political, and that without a "formal" constitution to enforce there can be no basis for a court to strike down primary legislation as invalid, unlawful, or unconstitutional – at least within the framework of Western democratic political philosophy and practice. We will return to this soon in our discussion of "substantive entrenchment."

One reason for this is that courts are designed to enforce legal norms, with all their associated characteristics and trappings – a written constitution, even if sometimes vague or obscure, maintains a high degree of specificity and remains such a coherent and comprehensive legal document lending itself to judicial application. A court enforcing an undefined and unbounded "substantive" constitution means nothing more than the Court embodying the constitution itself, while judicial review entirely ceases to resemble a legal exercise. A constitution is, by its very nature and definition, a formalistic legal instrument. The notion of a "substantive" constitution (as conceptualized by Barak) is, in and of itself, fanciful gibberish.

Far more importantly, the core claim of any written constitution to authority and legitimacy is grounded in its adoption by a unique process reflecting overwhelming electoral will. It is the conscious, deliberate, explicit, popular decision – not just in theory, but in fact – to enshrine a specific textual document as the land's supreme legal norm, that vests such a document with constitutional status. A constitution can supersede acts of government and democratic will, and critically, can even limit the actions of a representative democratic majority, only because it can plausibly assert itself as a direct and faithful expression of the people's sovereignty. To the extent that a constitution aspires to assert itself over the objections of an electoral majority, it can only do so on the basis of authority and legitimacy granted by the actual, factual, physical, tangible assent of the people themselves. This is why the requirements for advance notice, for broad public discussion and acute public awareness, for a specific agreed text, and for ultimate enactment or ratification by direct appeal to the people (or equivalent measures evincing genuine wide popular support), are not mere "formalities" to be overlooked. They are the core essence of that which makes a constitution. This is one primary reason that the distinction between the written and unwritten constitution is so stark – the former can assert that it properly channels a public desire to impose and enforce self-limits on democratic governance, while the latter can make no such claim.

In an act of judicial alchemy Barak transmutes the copper of an unwritten constitution into the gold of the "substantive" constitution. Barak glosses over the foundational distinction at the core of judicial review and simply asserts that an unwritten "substantive" constitution is a viable substitute for a conventional one with all that entails – including, especially, empowering a court to strike down laws. The argument boils down to a terminological and conceptual parlor trick – to the artificial, simplistic and contrived distinction between "formal" and "substantive" constitutions.

This view characterizes the Supreme Court's jurisprudence from *Hamizrachi* onwards and is shared by most of its Justices, who conspicuously ignore the core procedural-popular elements which distinguish constitutional norms from ordinary legislation and which lend them their superiority. Some instances are particularly illustrative. As he often does elsewhere, Barak in *Hamizrachi* conveniently avoids any real discussion of what recognizable criteria underly the existence of a constitution (whether formal or substantive). Yet Shamgar is less sophisticated (or perhaps more honest) and attempts at some point to delineate the characteristics of a constitutional text. Delightfully, the unique process undeniably required to enact constitutional norms virtually anywhere in the world is not listed as part of Shamgar's analysis. Though he mentions in passing that a constitution is "usually" enacted "in other jurisdictions" via a "one-time, unique process" (reflecting the "will of the people"), he clearly does not consider this to be a fundamental or required element. This glaring omission is to be repeated by the Court more pronouncedly at a later point.*

Barak couches his "substantive" constitutional jurisprudence in broad universal language. He presents his arguments as though these were established core tenets of global constitutionalism recognized throughout Western legal and political

* See the *Shafir* case discussed in Chapter 11.

communities. He has no choice but to do so, because existing Israeli law and history clearly provide scant support for his claims. Barak must appeal to alleged abstract ideals of constitutional theory and political philosophy to ground his audacious leap from nothing to something, from zero to one, from non-constitution to de facto constitution.

Yet in truth Barak's theory of "substantive" constitutionalism is his alone, known only in the context of Israeli jurisprudence and adopted only by Israeli jurists. The notion of a fully viable and enforceable "substantive" constitution in the sense used by Barak is simply not recognized or even really contemplated anywhere else in the world, in theory or in practice. Outside Israel no school of law or of political science teaches the distinction between "formal" and "substantive" constitutions. Barak's theoretical jurisprudence, in this case as is in many others, is simply divorced from most existing and prevailing scholarly convention and discussion on the matter. "Substantive constitution" – or any functional equivalent – is not a recognized term or concept in any relevant discipline.

While the "substance" of constitutional provisions is certainly debated often (such as the familiar example of "substantive due process" in the 14th Amendment to the U.S. Constitution), this is not remotely related to the idea of an entire constitution being "substantive" in lieu of the formal written document. In the highly rare occasions that legal scholarship employ such terms, these convey the opposite of the Barak-ean meaning: For example, under the entry for "Democracy, Constitutional" in the Encyclopedia of Global Justice, the "substance of a constitution" is simply "the implementation of the formal constitution as intended by the authors…"[84] That is, anywhere but in Israel, the substantive constitution is the degree to which the provisions of a conventional constitution are faithfully applied. The notion of a constitution without "form" nonetheless bearing "substance" is simply inconceivable. Further still, it's not as though Barak's novel jurisprudence is considered elsewhere to be some groundbreaking innovation. Though his legal acumen is undoubtedly respected and appreciated, Barak's constitutional philosophy has inspired no imitation and is not seriously taught, cited, or adopted in any other jurisdiction.

A final point regarding the claim of a "substantive" constitution is its liberating effect on judicial intervention. Constitutions are often correctly seen as a major limiting factor on executive and representative government, but they are also a critical check on the exercise of judicial power. A proper, well-designed and faithfully implemented constitution constrains courts just as much as it does government officials of other branches. This is because judges enforcing a constitution must persuade legal peers, the political community and the public that they are doing so in a manner consistent with the provisions of that constitution. They must frame their deliberations and conclusions as legal reasoning that is ultimately grounded in, and limited by, the constitutional text. Recalling an earlier quote from Martin Loughlin, the idea of power being "subjected to the discipline of a text" applies equally and perhaps especially to judicial power. In a written constitution this feature is built-in – the source authorizing judicial intervention defines the contours and limits of that same judicial authority.

None of this applies to a "substantive" constitution, which does not claim to anchor itself in a definitive legal document. The "substantive" constitution is untethered to "the discipline of a text" to begin with, such that the judge may freely draw upon sources external to any recognizable legal norm. Further, as we will later see, the "substantive" constitution demands only the loosest adherence to whatever minimal textual elements it might possess. The upshot of all this is that Barak's "substantive" constitution serves exclusively to empower the Court in restricting other branches of government while imposing no meaningful constraint on the Court's exercise of such power. This one-way arrangement is reflected in Judge Richard Posner's penetrating admonition of Barak, that "the judicial branch has to be checked by the other branches, and not just do the checking." By adopting the substantive constitution Barak relieves himself and the Court of the many restrictions and limitations a "formal" constitution might have otherwise imposed on judicial decision-making. The Court accepts none of the constitutional constraints yet assumes all of the judicial power.

In sum, Barak and the Supreme Court advance the spectacularly bizarre idea of an enforceable and tangible "substantive" constitution, and the equally brazen claim that Israel has been blessed with one since the enactment of the 1992 Basic Laws. This fallacy is broadly accepted throughout legal academia (though not by the public) and is taught in Israeli law schools to first-year students that hardly know any better. Most importantly, it is employed by the Court routinely, without question or hesitation.

Substantive Democracy. The Court's second sleight of hand, employed to justify the recognition and application of Israel's new pseudo-constitution, is found in its conception of "democracy" at large.

Barak explains that the principles of popular sovereignty, universal suffrage, political equality, periodic elections, accountable representation and majority rule are all part of mere "formal" democracy. Much like his similar distinction regarding constitutions, "formal" democracy is something of a pantomime, a procedural charade. Real, authentic, genuine democracy involves limitations on the will of the majority in order to protect fundamental "values" – human rights and minority rights chief among them. Naturally, Barak dubs this "substantive" democracy. "A democracy of only the majority which is not accompanied by a democracy of values," explains Barak in *Hamizrachi*, "is a formal and statistical democracy;"[85] and further on: "Democracy is not merely majority rule. Democracy also embodies the rule of fundamental values and human rights as enshrined in the constitution. It is a delicate balance between majority rule and the fundamental societal values which rule the majority."[86] In another illustrative quote from a few years later, Barak maintains that "democracy is not only majority rule… democracy is also the rule of values, of principles and of human rights that the majority is not permitted to take away from the minority."[87] This type of view is regularly expressed by the Court and its adherents, in judicial decisions and in less formal settings.

Per Barak, Israel has chosen the path of "substantive" democracy, declaring that "this choice was not made by judges; it was made by the people." (As we have seen, such factual assertions bear little resemblance to reality). Consequently, constitutional limitations on representative government, enforced by judicial review, is an inherent and integral part of Israel's self-definition as a "real" democracy. The 1992 Basic Laws enshrining protection of human rights were the dramatic shift, the pivotal tipping point, which officially and finally constituted Israel as a substantive democracy.[88]

Once again, at first glance Barak's distinction seems to align with familiar concepts, especially those of "liberal democracy" or "constitutional democracy." At the intersection of classical liberalism and democratic government, liberal democracy prioritizes individual liberty and seeks to minimize governmental intervention in the decisions and preferences of citizens. Constitutional democracy is a democratic order that includes some core mechanisms and arrangements ensuring and safeguarding the State's democratic character. Both typically involve hard limits on the will of the majority, often enforced by the judiciary. Both typically enshrine and protect particular human (or natural, or civil) rights. This being the case, Barak's "substantive" democracy can be understood as just another name for the same idea. Right?

Wrong.

"Substantive" democracy skips the most important feature of ostensibly similar concepts – the voluntary popular adoption of self-imposed restrictions. Barak's version does away with this inconvenient nuisance and simply assumes that constitutional limits and abstract human rights are synonymous with democracy itself, with no need for that crucial stage of consent reconciling democracy with its limits. For Barak and the Supreme Court, the judiciary may enforce restrictions entirely regardless of whether they were sanctioned by popular will. Judges imposing "fundamental values" on politics, on the electorate and on society is a built-in and automatic feature of substantive democracy (e.g., "societal values which rule the majority" and rights that the "majority is not permitted" to revoke). In Barak's substantive democracy, the existence of supreme law, its content and its enforcement are not derived from popular will and do not rely on their adoption in a constitution or any other instrument.

This lies in stark contrast to liberal and constitutional democracy, which derive their respective limitations from conscious democratic choice. Constitutionalism is at its core a manifestation of democratic will and of popular sovereignty. It is "we the people" that define their fundamental values and that decide to subject their representative government to various constraints. And liberal democracy is founded upon the recognition that democracy alone does not include inherent limits to majoritarian power or automatic protections of the individual from the arbitrary whims of the State, which is why liberal safeguards are so critical.*

Put differently, liberal or constitutional democracy are ideals of desirable government – their force and legitimacy are based on *persuading* the electorate to accept certain rules and limitations. "Substantive" democracy does nothing of the sort, but rather contains a self-enforcement mechanism of unilateral judicial power to impose and apply "fundamental values" without any grounding in the original public choice to grant such authority. It discards the crucial stage of convincing the public that it needs to impose limits on its own government.

Many have famously compared the democratic constitution to Odysseus being bound to the ship's mast so that he may resist the call of the Sirens; but the heart of this analogy is Odysseus *requesting* that he be tied. In the "substantive democracy" version of that story, Odysseus is strapped to the mast without ever asking for it and despite protesting that he can't even hear the Sirens – his judicial shipmates simply inform him of their decision, gagging and tying their frantically struggling captain to the mast. Critically, they decide on his behalf when the perceived danger of alleged Sirens (real or imagined) is sufficiently imminent to justify tying up poor Odysseus. Far from the prescient wisdom of prospective self-restrictions, this type of naval conduct can only be considered mutinous.

Constitutional and liberal democracies remain "democratic" because they are founded upon the authority and legitimacy of the *demos*; "substantive" democracy seeks to exclude the *demos* from the process entirely. The latter is not an argument of good governance but rather a usurpative assertion of judicial force, an external imposition of constraints on democracy without the assent of popular will. It compels constitutional democracy without a democratic constitution.

"Substantive" democracy is thus analytical misdirection, deliberately conflating two separate concepts – democratic self-government and its commendable counter-majoritarian limits – erroneously and illogically deducing the latter as a self-evident feature of the former. By equating self-government with self-non-government, by skipping the most crucial stage of the public's acquiescence in creating limits on their own power, Barak distorts and inverts the core meaning of democracy as ultimate authority residing in the hands of the people.

Lord Jonathan Sumption alludes precisely to this phenomenon while discussing "two rival conceptions of democracy."[89] The first and familiar version is a "mechanism for arriving at collective decisions and accommodating dissent," the type that Barak dismisses as merely "formal." Sumption describes the

* As an aside, another important difference is that liberal democracy essentially addresses the relationship between individual autonomy and State power, aspiring to limit the latter; while "substantive" democracy rather addresses the allocation of power between the judiciary and representative government, and merely transfers the exercise of such harmful State power to judges.

alternate version as an eerily accurate portrait of Barak's "substantive" democracy:

> "A system of law-based decision-making that would entrench a broad range of liberal principles as the constitutional basis of the state. Democratic choice would be impotent to remove or limit them without the authority of courts of law."

However, Sumption explains, this second notion of democracy is

> "conceptually no different from the rather similar claims of communism, fascism, monarchism, Catholicism, Islamism and all the other great -isms that have historically claimed a monopoly of legitimate political discourse, on the ground that their advocates considered them to be obviously right."

In other words, any such so-called "democracy" is not remotely democratic. Saying that democracy includes, by definition, a set of judicially pre-approved values beyond the reach of the electorate – in Barak's words, "fundamental societal values which rule the majority" – is a claim indistinguishable from communism or fascism, in the sense that it abandons the core democratic condition of determinative popular sovereignty.

Much like his claims of a "substantive constitution," Barak's argument for "substantive democracy" is again phrased in universal abstractions. Barak presents his views as the uncontroversial and irrefutable consensus, as a unanimous philosophical baseline grounded in established theoretical discourse. One of his more well-known books is "The Judge in a Democracy" – democracy at large, and not just Israel or some other particular legal context. Yet once again Barak's terminology and theory are utterly divorced from relevant scholarly discussion and debate, both traditional and contemporary, in theory and in practice. In their extensive treatment of democracy and its definitions Barak and the Court seem completely oblivious of an entire scholarly discipline dedicated to that specific subject. The mass of relevant literature and scholarship unsurprisingly define the essence of democratic (or republican) government precisely by its ostensibly "formal" elements.* More to the point, the concept of "substantive democracy" (as understood and defined by Barak) appears in no classic textbook or lexicon, is adopted by no Western jurisdiction, and is taught in no democratic law school or course on political science. Once again, Barak tries

---

* The extensive writings of Robert A. Dahl are an especially strong example. In "*On Democracy*," Dahl defines democracy as a set of formal criteria for political equality within a system for collective decision-making. Another instructive example is the meaning of "republican government" in Article IV of the U.S. Constitution. *See* Akhil Reed Amar, *The Central Meaning of a Republican Government: Popular Sovereignty, Majority Rule, and the Denominator Problem*, 65 U. Colo. L. Rev. 749 (1994)

to pass off a novel and unorthodox theory as though it were the common and obvious default.

There is admittedly one striking and deeply ironic exception. The nomenclature distinguishing between "formal" democracy of collective representation and "substantive" democracy of specific supreme values was consistently employed by the tyrannical regimes of communist Russia. The U.S.S.R. routinely derided Western democracy as "formal" (that is, as a pantomime or charade) whereas the grand Soviet democracy was "substantive" due to their enlightened elevation of values (such as material equality or distributive justice) over democratic choice. Indeed, while making his point above about the rival conceptions of democracy, Lord Sumption observes that "the democratic label was claimed by the autocratic communist states" established by the Soviet Union. Whether consciously or not, Barak's competing categories of democracy most closely resemble those used by vicious, repressive dictatorships.

A comprehensive analysis of the Court's jurisprudence on "substantive democracy" and its failings is well beyond the scope of our present discussion. Its many deviations from accepted standards and conventions are intuitively obvious to almost any educated Western observer. Here only a few comments will suffice. Among the most penetrating critiques of Barak's jurisprudence is that of Judge Richard Posner who, writing in 2007, states the obvious point that defining democracy by the very thing that "curtails" it is an analytical fallacy. Unimpressed by Barak's "abstract principles that in his hands are plays on words," Posner writes:

> "The leading abstraction is 'democracy.' Political democracy in the modern sense means a system of government in which the key officials stand for election at relatively short intervals and thus are accountable to the citizenry. A judiciary that is free to override the decisions of those officials curtails democracy. For Barak, however, democracy has a 'substantive' component, namely a set of rights... enforced by the judiciary, that clips the wings of the elected officials. That is not a justification for a hyperactive judiciary, it is merely a redefinition of it."[90]

Another illustrative and more technical example comes from Prof. Dan Avnon, one of Israel's leading political scientists and democratic theorists, who in 1998 had sharp criticism for the "the implicit assumption that democratic states have values." Avnon condemns both the statutory formulation in the 1992 Basic Laws ("Jewish and democratic State") and Barak's views on the nature of democracy: "Democratic theory does not support the proposition that established, modern, democratic states have values" which are independent of society itself. Citizens are the ones who "articulate [values] or re-enforce them through... the participatory, deliberative, and representative features of democracy." In other words, there is nothing in the definition of democracy that includes automatic fundamental values which a judge may unilaterally impose on the electorate. Avnon emphasizes that "democratic states are a form of government," "are neutral in respect of the outcomes" of societal decision-making, and he quotes the decidedly formalistic textbook definition of modern political democracy: "A system of government in which rulers are held accountable for their actions in the public realm by citizens, acting indirectly through the competition and cooperation of their elected representatives." Avnon correctly characterizes democracy's so-called formal elements as its very substance – a direct refutation of the Barak-ean approach. Finally, Avnon warns that infusing the democratic form of government with such inherent values "is a dangerous assumption."[91]

At its lowest points, Barak's acute distortion of "democracy" brings to mind the fiendish advice given by agents of evil in C.S. Lewis's *The Screwtape Letters*. Democracy, according to Screwtape, "is the word with which you must lead them by the nose," though those employing it "should never be allowed to give this word a clear and definable meaning." The word should rather be used "purely as an incantation." Once the unsuspecting dupes adopt Screwtape's diabolical inversion of democracy, "it will never occur to them that 'democracy' is properly the name of a political system, even a system of voting."[92] At one point Screwtape remarks: "Is it not pretty to notice how 'democracy' (in the incantatory sense) is now doing for us the work that was once done by the most ancient Dictatorships, and by the same methods?"

Later academic efforts in Israel have tried to rebrand Barak's distinction using more palatable terms, such as one between "procedural" and "liberal" democracy. For example, Prof. Barak Medina, one of Israel's most recognized constitutional scholars, former Rector of the Hebrew University of Jerusalem and a noted judicial supremacist, published a paper in 2020 titled "*Does Israel have a Constitution? On Formal and Liberal Democracy*."[93] Medina argues that Israel's "Basic Norm" (a term of art in legal theory based on the writings of Hans Kelsen) as a liberal democracy entails inherent and insurmountable limitations on representative government deriving from "core principles" of liberalism. Though Medina takes care not to mention "substantive democracy" even once throughout its 26 pages, the article is a transparent rearticulation of the same. Yet any attempt to equate the two concepts must necessarily fail for the reasons elaborated above (and Medina's article does nothing to address them). If anything, Medina's claims to unfounded and unbounded judicial power based on "fundamental principles" further accentuate the distance between Israeli jurisprudence and any familiar notions of democracy. He patiently explains to the (likely bewildered) reader that "the source of validity for these restrictions are not the determinations of the majority" and continues:

> "The constitutional status of these restrictions must be recognized, along with the court's authority to enforce compliance with them, even if they are not enshrined in a written constitution and even if there is no broad public support for their recognition."

By clarifying the primary target of their respective limitations, Medina's formulation successfully demonstrates the profound difference between substantive democracy and actual liberal democracy as conventionally understood. Liberal democracy seeks to limit the *State* in its ability to harm the public and individuals while preserving the people's status as superior to the State. "Substantive" democracy, as coherently articulated in Medina's apologetics, prevents the *public* from arriving at certain decisions affecting "fundamental values" as defined and applied by actors external to the democratic process and insulated from the electorate. (Incidentally, Medina's argument was criticized both for its institutional incompatibility with established democratic norms, and for its conceptual errors regarding the theoretical framework of Kelsen's "Basic Norm.")[94]

The Court's conception of "substantive" democracy has been a significant feature in the development and application of its constitutional jurisprudence. Under this approach, the Court could justify its legal expansionism and rampant judicial review as a natural and inevitable consequence of Israel's definition as a democratic State.

Perhaps of equal importance, this hierarchy – under which traditional democracy (equal political representation, accountable elected officials, majority rule, etc.) is inferior and "formal," while restrictions on popular democratic authority are superior "substantive" democracy – has been vigorously injected into much of Israeli public and political discourse, such that it has become pervasive and commonplace. From high school civics to law school finals, from daily newspaper rags to late night television, Israelis are inundated with the distorted and corrosive idea of democracy's essence amounting to arbitrary "values" invented and applied by the Supreme Court. Throughout Israeli public discourse, the rationales of "counter-majoritarian" checks (mainly consisting of judicial fiat) eclipse and erase the democratic bedrock of self-government by majority rule.

In a 2016 satirical TV show the new Minister of Education is lampooned for suggesting that democracy is majority rule, while a guileless pupil objects and reminds us that democracy is primarily "protection of minority rights."[95] In the 2023 protests against proposals for judicial reform, crowds chanted the rallying cry of "de-mo-cra-cy" to sincerely advocate for greater unsupervised power wielded by unelected bureaucrats at the expense of representative government. In 2024 one of Israel's most prominent lawyers was interviewed on stage as part of a major academic conference. Following a question that characterized democracy as majority rule, the attorney responded without irony: "Majority rule is not the definition of democracy. It is the definition of dictatorship."[96] The audience – comprised of senior Israeli jurists from all walks of the legal profession – applauded. During a discussion with high school students in 2025, Justice Yitzhak Amit has described both "electoral democracy" and "majority rule" jointly as "fourth grade democracy" (a phrase he has also used in court) and as "inferior."[97]

Broadly speaking, the notion of "substantive" democracy is consistent with the foundational skepticism of Israeli elites towards genuine democratic tradition and Israel's cultural isolation from other democratic jurisdictions, as described in the Introduction above. The idea of judicial supremacy being baked-in to the very definition of popular self-government has capitalized on, and exacerbated, Israeli public illiteracy on questions of democratic governance.

Substantive Entrenchment (and Judicial Review). "From whence comes the restrictive power of an un-entrenched Basic Law, the force of which, according to the prevailing view, is identical to that of an ordinary law? This is indeed the problem."[98] (Yehudit Karp.)

The final component of the Supreme Court's "substantive" trifecta regards the entrenchment clause found (or missing) in the 1992 Basic Laws. The issue of entrenchment posed two essential problems for Barak and the Court. The first was that procedural entrenchment of statutory provisions, such as the absolute majority requirement found in Section 4 of Basic Law: The Knesset, had thus far been interpreted as the sole mechanism allowing for limited (numerical-based) judicial review, while also not conferring elevated or constitutional status on legislation. BL:FO included an entrenchment clause but according to current jurisprudence this was unremarkable. The second problem was that the more consequential and extensive of the two laws, BL:HDL, didn't even have a single entrenched provision. How can these laws provide the legal basis for sweeping judicial review?

It's worth reiterating that the question whether Israel has a constitution, and the question whether the Court is authorized to perform judicial review, are two distinct matters to be resolved separately. Comprehensive judicial review is not feasible without a written constitution as discussed above, at least in principle. Yet even armed with the conclusion that the new Basic Laws may serve as Israel's constitution, it by no means follows that judicial review is automatically authorized. We'll return to this point momentarily.

Barak's solution to the Court's quandary was simple and elegant. The procedural absolute-majority clauses provide for "formal" entrenchment; however, both new Basic Laws possess a novel entrenchment mechanism which may be regarded as – you guessed it – "substantive entrenchment." This was the "limiting" (or "restriction") clause which defines the circumstances under which the law's enumerated rights may be infringed upon. Such clauses are found in both 1992 laws. In Barak's view these limitation clauses served a dual purpose – they authorized the Court to strike down inconsistent legislation, and they proved (or even established) the new legislation's superior constitutional standing. And indeed, these clauses and the formula they present became the basis for almost all future cases of judicial review.

Before we proceed to review the many flaws in such an argument, we may examine the relevant statutory text. The following provision is often referred to as a "limitation" clause though its official title is "Violation of Rights," and it might just as properly be called a "permissions" clause. Section 8 of BL:HDL reads roughly* as follows, with BL:FO containing a near-identical provision:

> Rights under this Basic Law shall not be violated except by a statute that befits the values of the State of Israel, is intended for a proper purpose, and to an extent no greater than required, or according to such statute by force of express authorization.

The argument advanced by Barak, by the Court and by their supporters is that this clause clearly limits the circumstances in which rights may be violated, a limitation that extends to primary legislation. A right may be violated only a) by a law, or b) by express authorization (allowing executive or regulatory action, for example) within a law. However, in order to do so such a law must be 1) consistent with Israel's "values"; 2) have a "proper purpose" and; 3) be proportionate in its violation of rights.† This provision therefore implicitly prohibits laws which do not meet the "limiting" requirements, and suggests a hierarchy in which statutes that violate rights but fail the conditions for violation must be considered invalid. Consequently, for the enforcement of this clause courts must be able to examine whether statutes meet the "limiting" criteria, and on certain occasions to declare incompatible laws void.

Importantly, many judicial supremacists in Israel (and the Court with them) consider this clause to be something of a trump card, an irrefutable argument in the debate surrounding the constitutional revolution. If this clause does not authorize judicial review of legislation then it is surely a dead letter – why would the Knesset enact such a provision if they did not mean to subject laws to the conditions it stipulates? How can the rules of this clause be enforced if judges can't strike down offending statutes?

The "limitation clause" serving as "substantive entrenchment" is thus, critically, the central bridge between Barak's "substantive constitution" and the judicial power to strike down laws.

Though the argument certainly has some initial appeal, it nonetheless collapses under only the slightest scrutiny. We may address both the specific interpretive question of implicit judicial review and the broader claim of "substantive entrenchment."

A preliminary and obvious objection is that this entire construction puts the judicial cart before the constitutional horse. As has already been discussed at length, the concept of courts striking down primary legislation is predicated on the clear and unequivocal condition of a written, codified, legal constitution. Writing in 2006, Oren Soffer easily observes that "the most obvious problem… in activating judicial review of legislation in Israel is, quite simply, the lack of a constitution… [In democratic regimes] there is a direct link between the judicial

* There is some room for debate regarding accurate translation.

† This "proportionality test" will be discussed separately later on.

review of legislation and a formal written constitution."[99] Soffer continues to quote a classic textbook on the matter, *Judicial Review in Comparative Law* (Cambridge, 1986), which stated that:

> "[The] judicial review of the constitutionality of legislation... requires at least three conditions for it to function in a given constitutional system: in the first place, it requires the existence of a written constitution, conceived as a superior and fundamental law with clear supremacy over all other laws; secondly, such a Constitution must be of a rigid character, which implies that the amendments or reforms that may be introduced can only be put into practice by means of a particular and special process, preventing the ordinary legislator from doing so; and thirdly, the establishment in that same written and rigid Constitution of the judicial means for guaranteeing the supremacy of the Constitution over legislative acts."

Fantastically, not a single one of these three universal "required conditions" for judicial review exist in the context of Israeli law. There is no written constitution (a point even Barak would concede); and the Basic Laws have neither clear supremacy, nor rigidity, nor judicial means of enforcement.

The attempt to consider whether some statutory provision does or does not authorize judicial review is meaningless in the absence of a wider constitutional framework which serves as the basis for any such conceivable arrangement to begin with. Analyzing the content of a rule is pointless if the authority to enact the rule never existed. Thus the argument that the text of *any* law authorizes judicial review (under whatever convoluted theory one chooses) is something of a decoy: no sprout of judicial review may legitimately grow in the barren soil of a faux pseudo-constitution.

Put differently, even if the 1992 Basic Laws had provided for judicial review in the most direct and explicit terms, it would have remained entirely unclear whether the Knesset possessed the authority to create such an arrangement in the absence of a conventional written constitution. Given this reality, it is bizarre to realize that the Supreme Court never once seriously contemplates the idea that perhaps, maybe, conceivably, the weakness of its claim to a constitution ought to have some effect on the confidence with which it asserts judicial review.

To be sure, the argument that Section 8 authorizes judicial review fails on its own, as we will soon see. But it's worth noting the absurdity of even having this conversation.

Barak's argument of "substantive entrenchment" is in fact worse than merely inferring judicial review. Not only does the "limitation" clause provide for judicial review in its own right, but it also constitutionalizes the entire Basic Law (and others too, as we will see). In other words, the alleged primacy of the 1992 Basic Laws over offending inferior laws may somehow compensate for everything else, and it essentially establishes the constitutional status of the Basic Laws. This matters because, for Barak, the "substantive entrenchment" is an integral part supporting the overall "substantive constitution" – Barak deduces the entire constitutional status of Basic Laws from the purported "entrenchment" of Section 8. This bears repeating and emphasizing: For Barak, the Basic Laws are a constitution *because* they authorize judicial review, while at the same time, the Basic Laws can authorize judicial review because they are a constitution.

But a claim to judicial review can just as much constitutionalize a statute as Baron Munchausen could save himself from drowning by pulling up his own hair. Even if there were a strong case that Section 8 authorizes judicial review, this could have no bearing on the broader presence or lack of a constitution. As one critic put it, in Barak's view, "it appears that it is the existence of a constitution that is proven by supremacy and not supremacy that is proven by the existence of the constitution."[100] That a dubious assertion of judicial review can serve to actually originate a constitution is a dazzlingly novel argument even in Barak-ean terms.

We may now turn to the "entrenched" text itself. What does Section 8 actually say? The literal, logical and legal meaning of the "limitation" clause is in fact far less suggestive of judicial review than the Supreme Court pretends it to be. Section 8 plausibly (and properly) reads as an instruction for the *executive*, not for the legislature – detailing the conditions for violation of rights by administrative government. Government officials or agencies may only violate the specified rights if they are applying a law or acting under explicit statutory authorization, and if they are doing so in a proportionate manner (such that the harm they are inflicting is proportionate to the corresponding benefit). This would be a perfectly rational and credible way to understand the "limitation" clause as restricting the implementation of the law and not the legislative creation of law itself. Such understanding easily lends itself to direct judicial enforcement against the executive, just not to judicial review.

The vague references to Israel's "values" and a "proper purpose" do not pose any serious difficulty. They may be applied as interpretive guides affecting the proportionality test, such that the purpose of government action and its compatibility with Israel's values might in turn inform the court's assessment of its proportionality. Or these might simply be considered aspirational, declarative, not different from the preamble or the statute's "purpose" clause. As it is, the Court currently pays these requirements scant attention and focuses its judicial review of legislation almost exclusively on the proportionality requirement.

A conceivable alternative approach is that the "Violation of Rights" clause is entirely symbolic and unenforceable, establishing broad principles to guide government action but not establishing any legal authority and sanction to enforce such rights. I find this view less plausible. What certainly is plausible, though, is a statutory bill of rights that does not involve the judicial ability to strike down laws.

Amazingly, the Court never really considers these options and never even engages in a textual analysis parsing the actual words of the "limitation" clause. In its hundreds of constitutional decisions since *Hamizrachi* and over thousands of pages, the Court never questions or doubts that Section 8, on a literal-textual level, commands judicial review as a logical certainty.

One might argue, as the Court does in some sense, that the question is not whether the "limitation" clause *necessarily* mandates judicial review, but whether there is a *conceivable* interpretation to support such a conclusion. After all, the Israeli Supreme Court is clearly not the first to recognize the power of judicial review without explicit authorization for exercising such a function, the obvious example being that of case *Marbury v. Madison.* The bedrock of constitutional judicial review in the United States, *Marbury* is indeed cited repeatedly by Barak and his followers as the model for implicit judicial review. After quoting Chief Justice Marshall, Barak insists that "the constitution's purpose is to restrict the legislature" and that such restriction can only have meaning if "an ordinary law cannot overcome" constitutional restrictions.[101] The U.S. Supreme Court reached this conclusion "despite the fact that the U.S. Constitution contains no express provision on the matter," explains Barak. Since *Marbury*, "no one doubts that a law violating the U.S. Constitution is invalid," and that it is the judiciary's role to determine such invalidity based on its interpretation of the law and the Constitution.

But this claim is of course downright silly, and profoundly offensive to the intelligence of any observer. As Chief Justice Marshall memorably observed some years later, "it is a constitution we are expounding" – *Hamizrachi* could not be more different. In *Marbury* there was no question as to the very existence and validity of a written Constitution – the U.S. Constitution had been debated, adopted, and ratified only twenty-four years earlier by clear majorities of the several United States. Its legal supremacy over other statutory law was clearly established in the plain language of the Article VI "supremacy clause." As many scholars have shown, the *Marbury* decision was substantially consistent with prevailing legal approaches (and also had clear textual grounding within the Constitution itself) and therefore caused little controversy. For the purpose of deducing judicial review, as in elsewhere, Barak consistently glosses over the fundamental and irradicable differences between a conventional constitution and the 1992 Basic Laws. In *Hamizrachi* Israel had no constitution, no supremacy clause and functioned under the assumptions of parliamentary sovereignty. The comparison between the two rulings is patently false.

Barak casually continues to cite additional cases and jurisdictions which recognize the importance of judicial review, despite all of them being exclusively in the context of a written (or in Barak's parlance, a "formal") constitution. He even quotes Justice Felix Frankfurter describing judicial review as "an indispensable implied characteristic of a written constitution." For Barak, the fact that Frankfurter clearly refers to a *written* constitution and not the deformed theoretical dumpster-fire of a "substantive constitution" is of no consequence.

Importantly, the Court's interpretive maneuver – that Israel has a de facto "constitution" which must therefore, by definition, be interpreted to include judicial review – is in fact itself defeated by comparative examination of other jurisdictions. A written constitution, even armed with an explicit bill of rights, is no automatic indicator of inherent restrictions on the legislature which are enforced by the judiciary. The constitutions of various countries – including The Netherlands, Switzerland and Luxembourg – explicitly rule out judicial review of primary legislation. Article 120 of the Dutch Constitution states plainly: "The constitutionality of Acts of Parliament and treaties shall not be reviewed by the courts."

In other words, even were we to accept the unfounded proposition that Israel has a constitution (in the form of the 1992 Basic Laws), there is no reason to accept the Court's assertion that this automatically implies judicial review of legislation in the absence of an explicit provision authorizing such power. If anything at all, and certainly for modern constitutions, textual silence on the question of judicial review is properly understood to mean that no such authority exists. As articulated by a critic of Barak's jurisprudence: "The fact that the constitution is mute does not mean... that the courts are competent, but just the opposite, that there is never any unconstitutional law."[102]

This all applies to a detached and impartial textual assessment of Section 8 on its own terms. The text does not indicate legislative judicial review (and is just as well understood to support only review of executive action), nor can it be interpreted to include such implicit authorization (both because the 1992 laws are not remotely a constitution, and because even if they were, silence does not necessarily entail such authorization). Of course, refuting the Court's argument becomes all the more obvious when taking into consideration the many points discussed above – the absence of any supremacy clause throughout the Basic Laws, the legislative history in which judicial review was explicitly considered (and included in prior drafts) and then rejected, and so on. The combined analysis leaves no room for doubt – any ostensible "interpretation" of Section 8 to deduce judicial review of legislation is manifestly groundless.

One finds no greater example of this point than with that of our friend Yehudit Karp – from the horse's mouth, so to speak. In her "biography" of BL:HDL and as one of the law's key architects and facilitators, writing after the 1992 laws were enacted but before the 1995 *Hamizrachi* ruling, Karp espouses the distinctly maximalist and novel view that the Court is authorized to strike down statutes. But she adds a critical qualifier – that this applies only when such legislation does not reflect a clear and deliberate desire to contradict the Basic Law. Karp argues that the Court's alleged newfound authority of judicial review does not extend to outright judicial supremacy over parliament. Per Karp, the Knesset is fully authorized to violate the Basic Laws if it so chooses, by simply stating its intentions clearly. Karp presented what she believed to be an expansive application of the new Basic Laws, stretching their interpretation to the most extreme extent possible; yet even Karp, ardent supporter of Barak's judicial expansionism and of the overall constitutional project, in her specific effort to provide Barak with intellectual legitimacy for his constitutional revolution, couldn't bring herself to propose (and likely did not even contemplate) the type of comprehensive judicial review that *Hamizrachi* introduced.

Karp assumes that even after the 1992 Basic Laws the legal system remains one of parliamentary supremacy, which under "the dominant approach" means that "the legislature may annul or amend any law and has no authority to restrict its successors in any matter." Karp suggests that Section 8 may be interpreted to include a soft form of judicial review compatible with parliamentary supremacy, such that any authority for judicial review "must necessarily be accompanied by the conclusion, that the legislature may deviate from the restriction, if it chooses to state so explicitly."[103]

Karp got this idea from none other than... Aharon Barak. Writing only two months after BL:HDL had been enacted, in May of 1992, Barak examined the significance of the "limitation clause" and (assuming it empowered the Court to strike down laws) raised two alternative approaches regarding the Knesset's ability to avoid or overcome judicial review: The first, that the Knesset may contradict the Basic Laws by enacting another Basic Law; the second, that the Knesset may violate rights in ordinary legislation consisting of an express "notwithstanding" statement. Both alternatives essentially amount to the same thing – that the Knesset may freely overcome any potential restriction of judicial review, both ex ante and ex post, with no special legislative procedure and with any majority. In other words, if the Knesset wants to prospectively preempt or retrospectively override judicial review, all it has to do is say so. This view is of course radically different from the one Barak eventually set out in *Hamizrachi* three years later.

For both Barak and Karp at the time, this was a natural and necessary interpretation of the Section 8 "limitation" clause – insofar as judicial review applied, it was only to *implicit* violations of rights. Accepting that "ordinary legislation may lawfully contradict fundamental rights" found in the BL:HDL, Barak posited that the limitation clause required simply that any such violation be explicit: "It is crucial that a conflicting law (enacted by any majority) will expressly state that it intends to contradict the Basic Law."[104] Barak continues in unequivocal terms: "If the Knesset" as ordinary legislature "desires to infringe upon rights in BL:HDL, it possesses the power to do so" by any majority... "However, the Knesset must state so explicitly." Barak concludes that the limitation clause "functions as a prohibition against deviation from the Basic Law's obligations, unless done so by a statute which expressly states that it is enacted notwithstanding the provisions of the Basic Law."

Karp quotes Barak extensively and advocates for this approach as a mechanism "maintaining parliamentary supremacy," under which the Knesset may choose freely when to "subject itself to the principles of the Basic Law" and when to "deviate from them, as long as its deviation is express and clear." Echoing Barak's argument, in her interpretation of Section 8 Karp essentially conditions the Court's power of judicial review on the Knesset's ability to have the last word. "The Court is empowered to strike down laws which contradict the Basic Laws" due to their "normative superiority" and despite the laws containing no provisions which establish such superiority or which authorize courts to exercise judicial review. "Nonetheless," emphasizes Karp, "neither the Basic Law nor the courts are empowered to overcome the explicit intentions of the legislature," whether expressed as an ordinary law or as a Basic Law. "The Court may not invalidate a statute if it expressly states that it shall be valid despite the provisions of the Basic Law" or any substantial equivalent. "The courts and the Basic Law will retreat in the face of the clear desire of the legislature."[105]

Though these arguments for judicial review are themselves far-fetched, they can be seen as a palatable equivalent of an interpretive rule adopted in other jurisdictions, in which statutes which violate rights are only enforced if they clearly state their deliberate intention to do so. This is based on a rebuttable presumption that the legislature does not desire to infringe upon rights, a presumption which may be negated by a clear statement of parliamentary intent. This formulation (whether as conditional judicial review or as interpretive presumption) also brings Section 8 closer to a "permissions" clause than a "limitation" clause, by simply requiring that rights' violations be explicitly authorized.

By the time of *Hamizrachi* and the constitutional revolution Barak had entirely abandoned any such approach, opting instead for his totalizing vision of ultimate judicial review. No vestige of this more modest version remained in the 1995 ruling or in the Court's later jurisprudence. Yet Karp's (and indeed Barak's own) initial and authentic interpretation of the "limitation" clause demonstrate the sheer implausibility of the Court's subsequent interpretation and application of Section 8.

To summarize some of the points above, the idea that the text or substance of the "limitation" clause supports judicial review – let alone that it elevates the entire law to constitutional status – has always been without foundation. To this day, the Court and its supporters continue under the pretense that the above arguments are self-evidently true. Over the past three decades the Court has not once revisited or reconsidered these fundamental questions, treating it all as uncontroversial settled law.

Returning to Barak's broader theoretical claims in *Hamizrachi*, we may offer two final observations within our current context of "substantive entrenchment."

Barak's formulation of the "limitation" clause as "substantive entrenchment" is analytically flawed and fails on the most rudimentary conceptual and terminological levels. As mentioned above, one of the Court's most central claims is that the Section 8 "limitation" clause ought to be regarded as tantamount to traditional "entrenchment," which had been previously recognized as restricting the Knesset's legislative power and as allowing for limited judicial review. This was necessary for the Court's attempt to frame the constitutional revolution as somehow remotely consistent with existing precedent and jurisprudence. This was also necessary to deviate from the prevailing legal and political consensus that any Basic Law without procedural entrenchment was no different than an ordinary law. Because BL:HDL has no such provision, the Court explains its logical leap by describing both traditional entrenchment and the "limitation" clause as some form of restrictions imposed on the legislature, and thus justified giving them both the same label of "entrenchment." Consequently, per the Court, the "substantive" is not so different from the "formal" and can be ascribed similar legal (or constitutional) significance.

The problem here is twofold and involves the terminological inversion of the literal meaning for both words "substantive" and "entrenchment." Barak's tone and language indicate a recognition of the legal superiority of the "formal" procedural entrenchment which required an absolute majority for certain amendments, versus the inferiority of a "substantive" entrenchment which he concedes to be of lesser legal weight. However, in practice, this is not the case at all. Under the Court's new formulation in *Hamizrachi* and onwards, the "substantive" limitations apply to *any* majority, whereas the "formal" limitations may be overcome (at least in principle) by an absolute majority of 61 Knesset Members. In other words, ironically, according to the Court's jurisprudence the Knesset may utterly amend (and upend) Israel's system of elections and representative democracy by a majority of 61 MKs (or more), but even 90 Knesset Members (a 75% majority) could not "disproportionately" infringe upon the right to privacy (for example). And indeed, relying on the supposedly inferior "substantive entrenchment," the Court has struck down laws enacted by an absolute majority on multiple occasions. Further still, the enforcement of "formal" entrenchment amounts to counting votes, while the enforcement of substantive entrenchment grants judges vast discretion in assessing the constitutionality of statutes based on vague and subjective standards. Barak pretends that his innovation of judicial review is more modest than the *Bergman* rule enforcing numerical voting requirements, but in fact, his "substantive" entrenchment yields judicial review significantly more expansive (and more restrictive of the Knesset) than the ostensibly superior "formal" version.

Barak's second inversion is far more important and lies in his misleading use of the term "entrenchment." The absolute majority requirement in Section 4 of the 1958 Basic Law: The Knesset, very much where Israel's constitutional debate started, is a procedural impediment to statutory amendments. It adds an irregular technical requirement not usually found for the enactment of most ordinary legislation. The law is "entrenched" because changing it is harder than for most other laws. As discussed above, this was recognized as a "rigidity" element which is a typical feature of constitutional legal norms. It is this *rigidity*, the added difficulty of altering the law, which initiated the conversation around Section 4's "constitutional" status in the first place. The entire claim throughout historical Israeli jurisprudence, and the basis for the *Bergman* ruling, is that the law's rigidity is what indicated its potential – and contested – constitutional nature. The sweeping theory of some Basic Laws enjoying quasi-constitutional status and of the Knesset exercising constituent powers has always been inexorably linked to the *rigidity* of a given legal provision. It was for this reason that only entrenched – that is, rigid – provisions were potentially of a constitutional nature, while all other parts of any Basic Law were the same as ordinary legislation.

Similarly, this is the sense in which "entrenchment" is used in constitutional practice and literature throughout the democratic world – it relates to the procedural difficulty of enacting amendments.

Yet Section 8 of BL:HDL contains no such element and can be amended freely by any majority. Barak and the Court might implausibly argue that the "limitation" clause restricts the Knesset's ability to violate certain rights; what is indisputable is that the same clause is not "rigid" in any sense (and indeed, the Court has never claimed so). Section 8 (alongside the rest of BL:HDL) lacks any form of "entrenchment" mounting some obstacle to the law's amendment. A handful of Knesset Members may lawfully amend the law as they wish or even simply scrap the law in its entirety. In the absence of rigidity of any kind, labeling Section 8 as a form of "entrenchment" (substantive, formal, spiritual, temporal, or any other kind) is plain misdirection. By doing so Barak obscures the simple fact that BL:HDL contains no rigidity element, which is not only the defining feature of "entrenchment" but was also the primary theoretical basis for any judicial review in all of Israeli jurisprudence. This is entirely separate from the legal-historical fact, covered above, of the Knesset's deliberate and considered intent to exclude any entrenchment clause from BL:HDL.

Simply put, Barak deliberately conflates "entrenchment" as rigidity (a mechanism which increases the difficulty of amending an entrenched provision) with a "limitation" clause which ostensibly establishes superiority over other laws. Yet it is only rigidity – some irregular procedural legislative hurdle – which purportedly denoted "constitutional" status until *Hamizrachi*. Barak pretends that rigidity and alleged superiority are interchangeable and labels the latter "substantive entrenchment," though the Section 8 limitation clause contains no "rigidity" to speak of, and thus no entrenchment.

Needless to say, Barak and the Court do not give this terminological fallacy a second thought in *Hamizrachi* or since. The description of Section 8 as "substantive entrenchment" is simply assumed; the glaring inversion of the term's literal meaning of rigidity is ignored. In one amusing irony (or hypocrisy) Barak inevitably concedes this point in a different context. Arguing that a constitution must necessarily limit the legislature, while quoting Chief Justice Marshall in *Marbury*, Barak translates* and declares: "There is no middle ground – either the constitution is superior and it cannot be amended or violated by ordinary means, or it is a regular law, which the legislature may alter as it pleases."[106] Quite so. It is precisely for this reason (among others) that BL:HDL could not possibly possess constitutional status – it was always just a "regular law" that could be

* Barak quotes Marshall in English but then repeats his own similar (but not identical) variation in Hebrew.

freely amended, with no rigidity and no actual entrenchment. The utter inconsistency of his own views is of course lost on (or ignored by) Barak.

Our last observation relates to a peculiar logical error at the heart of Barak's reasoning. It will come as no surprise that to justify the many legal acrobatics and mischiefs in *Hamizrachi*, Barak relies heavily on his elaborate philosophy of Objective Purposive Interpretation, which we have covered at length in Chapter 3. Barak goes to great pains to stress, in the ruling and many times elsewhere, that this application of OPI employs a special category of "constitutional interpretation," which is distinct from "statutory" and other forms of legal interpretation. This method is essentially OPI on steroids, privileging the judge's estimation of a constitution's "objective" purpose over its "subjective" (factual) purpose and its (actual) text. It goes farther than even the most activist theories of constitutional interpretation found in other jurisdictions.

A few illustrative quotes serve to convey the gist of Barak's constitutional interpretation: "Preference should be given to the objective purpose that reflects deeply held modern views in the movement of the legal system through history. The constitution thus becomes a living norm and not a fossil..." It is of course "the judge [who] must give expression to the constitution's fundamental values," and though such values ostensibly "reflect the social consensus that underlies the legal system," they are "not the results of public opinion polls or mere populism" but rather of the judge's own personal estimation regarding the selection and application of such values. For Barak, a judge "is a partner to the authors of the constitution" and must "strike a balance between the will of the authors of the constitution and the fundamental values of those living under it."[107] This last sentence especially exemplifies the degree to which, for Barak and the Court, "purposive" constitutional interpretation abandons any aspirational fidelity to the constitutional text, history, and meaning, but rather allows the judge to directly apply his or her own understanding of a society's contemporary fundamental values.

As Weill notes, Barak "framed" many of his "legal revolutions… as matters of interpretation… It was a matter of interpretation how to treat the 1992 Basic Laws."[108] This pseudo-interpretive method is used to explain away all the contradictions, fallacies and flaws detailed in this chapter; it is the glue holding the constitutional revolution together, harmonizing its discordant components. Purposive constitutional interpretation is what allows Barak to classify Section 8 as possessing "substantive entrenchment," which (combined with Israel's fundamental values as a "substantive democracy") inevitably leads Barak to conclude the existence of a "substantive constitution." It is primarily on these interpretive grounds that Barak elevates the 1992 laws to supreme constitutional status.

Critically, according to Barak, this interpretive method – with its high abstractions and boundless judicial discretion – is specifically reserved for constitutional norms. As a "unique legal document" it is the "constitution's unique character" which justifies employing a method that so dramatically and overtly strays from the constitutional text. The judge's role of "seeking synthesis between past intention and present principle" by reference to "the fundamental views and values of modern society" is inherently dependent on the singular attributes of a constitution and its function. At least in principle, the relationship is one of cause and effect – a constitution exists as an observable-empirical fact; it is therefore interpreted in accordance with Barak's "constitutional" method.

The problem here is therefore simple: Though this method is tailored for interpretation of a constitution, Barak employs it in order to determine the constitutional nature of that which he is interpreting. Why do we apply "constitutional interpretation" to the 1992 Basic Laws? Because they are a constitution. How do we know they are a constitution? Because "constitutional interpretation" tells us so. But why did we apply this method of interpretation in the first place? Because the Basic Laws are constitutional. *Ad infinitum*. It is a textbook circular argument, an obvious logical loop. Barak's analysis fails on its own terms, according to its own internal logic, because he applies a unique method of interpretation in order to establish (indeed, to generate) its trigger for being used in the first place. He uses "constitutional interpretation" to deduce that the thing he is interpreting is a constitution.

An easy way to convey this problem is by contemplating the alternative. If we are to take Barak seriously, then mere "statutory" interpretation would not have yielded the same result; that is, if he had applied only "statutory" (or any ordinary) interpretation to BL:HDL, he could not have reached the conclusion that it was a "substantive constitution." Indeed, this is the clear impression which emerges from our analysis above. At the same time, because the law's constitutional status is a product of Barak's interpretation, there was never an original justification to apply "constitutional interpretation" when first approaching the law. The only basis for using "constitutional interpretation" exists post-interpretation, after the determination that it is a constitution being examined. But this stage is logically unreachable; under Barak's interpretive framework the analysis should have permanently remained on a "statutory" level.

This flaw is yet another sleight of hand, just one more ruse used to justify the constitutional revolution. Though marginal and analytical, semantic and perhaps even pedantic, it is a useful example of Barak's lack of commitment to the consistency or coherence of his own doctrines and their application, and of the Court playing fast and loose with its own rickety theoretical constructs to establish judicial supremacy.

To summarize our survey, the Court's core argument in *Hamizrachi* revolving around "substantive entrenchment" and the Section 8 limitation clause fails on all fronts. From the absence of a constitution and of the Knesset's authority to enact constitutional norms or judicial review; to the contradiction of universal democratic theory and practice; to the plain textual meaning (and omissions) of Section 8 unable to support judicial review; to the unserious and disingenuous misuse of terminology such as "entrenchment"; the Court's elevation of the "limitation clause" as a basis for judicial review was erected on pillars of sand.

*

By inverting the plain linguistic and legal meanings of common concepts, the Supreme Court could justify its ludicrous creation of the Israeli constitution out of whole cloth. In adopting Barak's "substantive" terminology the Court's reasoning reaches Orwellian proportions. The "substance" of any familiar term means its direct opposite: a constitution is whatever a judge unilaterally decides it to be; democracy is the coercive imposition of arbitrary limits on the public; an explicit decision to avoid entrenchment is an implicit authorization of judicial review. These are the grounds on which the Court defends its constitutional revolution.

We the Judges

As we conclude our estimation of the constitutional revolution and proceed to examine its aftermath and effects, it is typically at this point in the conversation that some turn to contemplate the propriety and desirability of a constitution, along with its attendant components such as judicial review, for the Israeli State and for Israeli society: weighing the relative pros and cons, considering the potential form and content of such a constitution, and so on.

I believe these questions to be woefully misguided within our current context.

While in itself commendable, a discussion of the merits and shortcomings of a constitution utterly obscures the fundamental objection against a judicial council making these determinations on behalf of the people and in their stead. In all the vast range of constitutional theory and practice throughout the Western world, there is not but one view which crowns judges as the legitimate authors and originators of a constitution. When scholars and statesmen have debated grand constitutional questions throughout history, never did they envision that the definitive answers be provided by unelected and unaccountable courts of law. No one imagines that "We the People" may be legitimately replaced by "We the Judges." Simply put, questions such as "ought we adopt a constitution for our State?" and "what should our constitution say and do?" are not directed at the judiciary and are not meant to be answered by judges.

The *Federalist Papers* were not only a blueprint for constitutional government which includes checks and balances for State power and fundamental limits on popular will – they were also a historical effort at persuading the real-life voters of New York to approve a specific constitutional text. In the same vein, it is not the force of Hamilton's, Madison's and Jay's arguments which made the U.S. Constitution into binding law, but rather only its adoption by delegates in a constitutional convention and its ensuing ratification by the electorate's representatives in each state. Publius would have been appalled at the notion that a judge might impose the proposed system of government on the public just because it was a good idea.

It is undeniably true that most modern democracies have opted for comprehensive constitutions, just as it is widely agreed (with notable exceptions) that a written constitution is the preferred mechanism for safeguarding numerous elements of a democratic regime. Protections for individual liberties, enforcement of democratic rules, guardrails against tyranny of the majority – these are all essential features of any functioning and enduring democracy. But in adopting these complex and delicate mechanisms there can be no shortcuts. It is the people that must be persuaded of their benefits and blessings. They cannot be imposed by gaslighting the public, by undermining the most basic and noble functions of democratic self-rule, or by denying modern democracy's core purpose and justification of popular sovereignty through majority rule of duly elected representatives. As he so often does, Lord Jonathan Sumption summarizes the point effectively:

> "One can believe in rights without wanting to remove them from the democratic arena by placing them under the exclusive jurisdiction of a priestly caste of judges. One can believe that one's fellow citizens ought to choose liberal values without wanting to impose them."

This red herring of constitutional policy is not hypothetical. Such policy arguments are regularly presented before the Supreme Court, with litigants entreating the Justices to adopt their view of preferred constitutional norms. In doing so, the parties and Court are complicit in upholding the charade of constitutional adjudication which is in reality much closer to the deliberations of a constituent assembly, or of a law school second-year seminar.

Debating whether Israel ought to have a constitution is a worthy endeavor, but that is not the conversation in which we are presently engaged. These admirable questions and dilemmas divert our attention from the simple fact that in Israel, the Supreme Court has unilaterally and indefensibly resolved the matter for us. This renders the Court's constitutional revolution profoundly invalid and manifestly unsound, regardless of anyone's respective opinions on the appeal of a constitution and its prospective contents. To paraphrase Monty Python, a handful of unelected and unaccountable ex-lawyers decreeing a fabricated constitution – much like strange women lying in ponds distributing swords – is no basis for a system of government. Asking whether the sword is sufficiently sharp entirely misses the point.

Calling Foul

Though *Hamizrachi* was issued in relative obscurity and was generally ignored by the public, a number of prominent Israeli jurists sounded the alarm in real time. As the constitutional revolution gained momentum and began crashing through the legal and political system other jurists came to recognize and address its flaws and hazards. These critiques are noteworthy not only because of their compelling force and validity, but also because their authors may not be accused of partisan, political or pedestrian motives, and are easily counted among Israel's foremost legal minds. Many of these arguments raised against the constitutional revolution rest on principle, not on passing expedience or incidental experience, and broadly echo the numerous objections covered in our discussion so far. Though we need not fully examine these various critiques in detail, they merit our brief review.

Some of the sharpest criticism was presented within *Hamizrachi* itself by Justice Mishael Cheshin. A brilliant scholar and gifted orator, the son of a Supreme Court Justice and having served as Deputy LCG, Cheshin was very much part of Israeli legal nobility. In his thorough and sprawling dissenting opinion, Cheshin systematically dismantles the many legal, theoretical and practical fallacies found in the Court's other opinions. Cheshin dismisses the distinctions between the Shamgar and Barak opinions, recognizing (correctly) that they have the same functional effect. Though he effectively contends with the Court's convoluted theoretical arguments Cheshin primarily adopts and embodies the voice of plain common sense, calling out the clear and obvious flaws in the Court's many implausible contentions. He rejects any notion that the Knesset possesses the power to enact a constitution, whether derived from hereditary authority passed down from the First Knesset, or from various other novel theories: "I find it difficult to establish an operative authority for the Knesset to enact a constitution for Israel based on these general, vague, and abstract principles." Cheshin also cites an argument from 1972, that even if the Knesset technically possessed constituent authority, this would clearly be an unwise and unsound way to enact a constitution in terms of public legitimacy, considering the time that had elapsed and the many election cycles since the First Knesset – a point of course all the more valid in 1995.

Cheshin objects to the misshapen chimera created by Barak in which the Knesset acts simultaneously as both legislature and constituent assembly. He was also especially concerned about recognizing the Knesset's power to require large supermajorities for certain future amendments (a power implicit in the Knesset's alleged constituent authority), a danger which he regarded as "manifestly anti-democratic." Though majority rule may be validly suspended via constitutional mechanisms, this can be achieved only "knowingly, deliberately, responsibly, through careful consideration, and in a proper legislative process." The Knesset, being the sole democratically-elected institution in the Israeli system of government, is not entitled to limit its own legislative authority "without receiving specific and express permission to do so. But no such permission has ever been granted." If the Knesset were to be authorized to enact a constitution, "we would expect such authorization to be explicit, clear, and unambiguous." Notably, Cheshin considered requirements for an absolute majority of 61 MKs as consistent with parliamentary supremacy and majority rule, further supporting the argument that *Bergman* (i.e., numerical judicial review to enforce such a majority) did not challenge or undermine Israeli parliamentary supremacy. He goes on to describe the legislative process and history leading to the 1992 legislation, expressing "great doubt" as to whether "the MKs themselves were aware of any 'revolution' on their part."

Among the most memorable passages in Cheshin's dissent is his accusation that the Court confuses the *ought* and *is* of the law. In his view the Court is essentially saying that "the Knesset may enact a constitution because it is proper for it to possess such authority." Cheshin continues:

> "These doctrines themselves are driven in no small part by a strong and pressing urge to infuse the desired law into the existing legal framework, to inject a doctrine (worthy in itself) into the veins of the prevailing legal system. The yearning and longing for a formal and rigid constitution are so deep and intense, that a hypothesis born out of wishful thinking is magically transformed into existing law – a wish that is self-fulfilling... Needless to say, the aspiration – however genuine – for a constitution is not sufficient to establish the authority to grant one."

Another striking critique emerged soon after *Hamizrachi* from one of Israel's most renowned jurists. Retired Chief Justice Moshe Landau, widely considered among the greatest Justices to have served on the Supreme Court and a consistent critic of Barak's activism, published a scathing attack on the Court's constitutional revolution. In an essay titled "*Granting Israel a Constitution By Way of Judicial Decree*," Landau lays out his many objections and reservations against the new ruling which in his words "effectively elevates the Court over the Knesset as a senior partner in State legislation" and "grants the Court final say on the validity of Knesset laws."[109] Retired judges typically refrain from commenting on the decisions of their prior courts, and so Justice Landau's statements were especially unusual.

Landau picks *Hamizrachi* apart, starting with the rambling style "resembling the debate minutes of an academic seminar" while warning against judicial rulings turning into "grand academic research." In a similar vein Landau lambasts the Court for its undisciplined and unprofessional practice of citing sources in a selective manner – he notes that Barak freely cites comments made by legislators in "dud" debates which never led to a law being passed, and that Barak cherry-picks quotes from "the vast ocean" of scholarly sources, though the same sources could just as easily yield "other pearls, no less precious" which might prove the opposite point. As author of the famous *Bergman* decision Landau expressly repudiates the claim that *Bergman* could serve as a legal-historical basis for contemporary judicial review; he reiterates the fact that the Court in *Bergman* had expressly avoided resolving any questions of a substantial constitutional nature, and that the decision applies only to the narrow context of counting votes to ensure compliance with the Knesset's numerical procedures.

While stressing the glaring absence of any "supremacy clause" in the new Basic Laws, Landau marvels at Barak's declaration that "the revolution transpired silently, almost hidden from sight." To this Landau responds: "We have yet to hear of a State's constitution established 'hidden from sight.' A constitutional revolution must take place openly and consciously. A constitution that shifts the balance of power between the branches of government cannot be adopted through a legislative ambush." Tackling other core issues throughout *Hamizrachi*, Landau rightly notes that judicial review is by no means a necessary or automatic feature of constitutional democracy per se, wryly recalling that Israel itself had functioned as a perfectly viable democracy for nearly fifty years without such judicial review. He further refutes the claim that only judicial review can counterbalance the risks of "tyranny of the majority," reminding the Court of the inescapable democratic necessity that, in resolving controversial questions, the view of the parliamentary majority must prevail. "I fail to understand what is democratic about handing over the authority to review democratically-enacted laws to an oligarchic body such as the Court."

Regarding the Section 8 "limitation" clause, Landau rejects as "unacceptable" any notion that the provision "indirectly and implicitly" authorizes judicial review, insisting that "even broad purposive constitutional interpretation must have a limit." In light of the clear statements made during the Knesset deliberations, Landau refuses to attribute the Knesset some hidden conscious intent, as that would require "assuming" that the law's sponsors "acted dishonestly and deceived the Knesset." He further addresses the "abstract and vague language" in the Basic Laws, referring both to the enumerated rights themselves and to the "limiting" criteria in Section 8, warning that any judicial objectivity in applying the law's terms would be "entirely illusory," and that the broad phrasing means "nothing but complete judicial discretion to rule according to the judge's personal worldview."

Landau points out that statutory omission can hardly serve as the basis for judicial review, as Barak infers. "I struggle to comprehend how such a revolutionary conclusion – placing the Court above the legislative branch – can be drawn not from an explicit statement by the constituent authority, but rather from its silence." He highlights the error in comparing *Hamizrachi* with *Marbury*, noting the latter's context of an accepted written constitution of supreme legal status. "Yet we have no such constitution, rather all we have is derived from the legal construction of the Court itself."

Reviewing some practical harms that the ruling will incur, Landua summarizes that "the attempt to grant the State a constitution by way of judicial decree will be unsuccessful," casting the judicial system "into a cauldron of confusion and instability." He delivers an especially stark warning, that the Court's willingness to asses the validity of laws will "drag" it into "the arena of publicly charged political disputes," which in turn will irreparably damage public faith in the judiciary; and he further (accurately) predicts that "exalting the Court's power as a senior legislative partner" will "encourage the call to alter the judicial appointments process."

Landau's final rebuke, remarkable in its severity, leaves a lasting impression:

> "Beyond all the objections that I have tried to illustrate up to this point is the glaring question regarding the legitimacy of the Court seizing for itself the power of judicial review: By what right? Who or what

> authorized the Court to do so, in the absence of explicit authorization by the legislature? Absent such authorization, the theories upon which the ruling is founded lack any basis in existing law."

Among the critical responses to *Hamizrachi* few were as comprehensive and forceful as that of Ruth Gavison's. In her 128-page essay describing the constitutional revolution as a "self-fulfilling prophecy," Gavison throws cold water on the Court's many grandiose claims. Gavison observes that "there is no precedent in the world" for a court adopting judicial review "without the existence of a complete constitutional document and with no express authorization," and further that "only in Israel does the debate focus on **whether** Israel has a constitution at all." She objects that such a maneuver is neither proper nor does it reflect a natural development of the Harari-defined constitutional process that had prevailed so far.

Gavison challenges the Court's use of "constitutional revolution" as a term utterly divorced from the facts. Though the Court proceeds under the "implicit assumption that the core decisions regarding a constitution have already been reached," this was manifestly never the case. "The political questions regarding an Israeli constitution were never systematically discussed" and let alone resolved, a "fundamental fact" which is "obscured" by the Court's term of "constitutional revolution." Clearly no such public process, in the sense of "presenting alternatives for wide public discussion and selecting between them," has ever occurred. Gavison illustrates this by presenting the many questions which had never been submitted to public deliberation and determination: "Ought Israel have a constitution? If so, what should it contain? What are the basic principles of the regime? Should it include a Bill of Rights? How should deeply controversial issues, such as religion and state, the status of Arabs in Israel, and the state's socio-economic approach, be addressed? Should the constitution be rigid? If so, what kind of rigidity? What mechanism should ensure the supremacy of the constitution? And lastly, what should be the procedure for adopting such a constitution?" This being the case, Gavison warns, "we must not countenance a process at the end of which we awaken one sunny day and discover we have a rigid constitution, of which we knew nothing, had not heard, had not seen, had not read, and had not been asked our views."

Another point of Gavison's, raised also by Cheshin, Landau, and others, is that the 1992 Basic Laws were simply not as "revolutionary" as Barak seemed to pretend they were, even at face value and on their own terms. The Knesset had consistently enacted statutory protections for individual rights and civil liberties since its earliest days, and the Supreme Court had always pursued the common-law development and judicial recognition of fundamental rights drawing on a wide array of normative sources and foundations. In other words, Barak's claim that the 1992 laws signified a dramatic departure from previous practice and reflected a unique development in Israel's approach to core statutory rights simply doesn't hold up.

The bulk of Gavison's analysis debunks the Court's theoretical innovations while focusing especially on the tangible reality of Israeli society and its constitutional culture. Emphasizing that "the adoption, content and enforcement of a supreme and rigid constitution are political questions which are resolved differently by each society," Gavison rejects the Court's reliance on "substantive" democracy and other similar concepts, explaining that nothing in the essence of democracy or in the ideals of rule of law or limited government yield specific constitutional arrangements as a logical necessity, despite the Court's effort to pretend otherwise. More importantly, within the context of the Israeli public's preferences and divisions, Gavison warns that "a constitution cannot fulfill its unique roles if it does not enjoy broad societal support." As things stand, and especially in light of the consistent "decision not to decide" and the Israeli preference for flexibility and indeterminacy, the faux-constitution becomes a "divisive and agitating document" instead of forming the basis for society's shared mutual commitments. Finally, Gavison accurately predicts that "the Court's inclination to accelerate the constitutional process will cause it's delay... and will also reinforce the impression that the Court is a central political player and not just society's agreed arbitrator."

All three of these legal luminaries – Cheshin, Landau and Gavison – articulated many more arguments, broadly reflecting the ones discussed in our analysis above.

Other prominent jurists opposed *Hamizrachi* to various degrees or expressed extreme reservations immediately following the ruling. These included retired Justice Haim Cohn; academics such as Yoav Dotan, Eli Salzberger, Daniel Friedmann and Menny Mautner; and practicing attorneys such as Yaakov Neeman and Dror Hoter-Ishay. These were joined by many additional leading lawyers and scholars in the years that followed. Yet such objections, vigorous and valid as they were, failed to gain significant momentum or to rally the legal community around them, and they remained the minority. The Court and its attendant legal establishment marched on, welcoming the new dawn of constitutional adjudication. As a popular Israeli saying goes: The dogs bark and the caravan moves on.

Chapter 10

Judicial Review of Knesset Legislation

Enforcing the Pseudo-Constitution

> "*What is the good of telling a community that it has every liberty except the liberty to make laws? The liberty to make laws is what constitutes a free people.*"
> — G.K. Chesterton[1]

In Israel, bad cases make hard law – and so it came to pass that the 1992 Basic Laws became, from the end of 1995, Israel's de facto constitution. Soon after the 1992 legislation Justice Aharon Barak publicly stated that "now we have been given the tools, we will do the work." And he sure did mean it.

A thorough review of the many effects of the Court's constitutional revolution and its aftermath would require a discussion beyond the scope of this book. Nonetheless, we may offer an outline of the Court's direct and indirect impact on Israeli law and society in its subjection of Knesset legislation to judicial review and in the manner in which this power has been exercised. We will first consider the actual legislation struck down by the Supreme Court since 1995, as the Court simultaneously developed its associated constitutional jurisprudence and doctrines. We will then proceed to examine some key implications – and catastrophic consequences – of the Court's constitutional jurisprudence and judicial review.

I – Ground Zero: Invalidated Laws

Some key points are worth bearing in mind as we review the laws invalidated under judicial review. One striking feature is the unbearable ease with which the Court strikes down primary legislation, at times almost as a flippant afterthought and on the flimsiest of pretenses. Justice Barak and others have compared judicial review to an atomic bomb, referring to it as "unconventional" warfare to be employed with utmost caution and only against threats warranting such extreme weaponry. This affected aversion was always mere lip service. The Court gesticulates a great deal in describing its deference for the determinations of elected officials and its herculean efforts to avoid annulling laws – yet in practice, the Court clearly has no qualms about striking down any legislation on a whim, whether insignificant or monumental.

A related point is that most laws that have been struck down divide easily into two categories: Some are utter trivialities – benign, marginal statutes of negligible or speculative impact, which even if problematic would hardly merit judicial intervention elsewhere; conversely, other laws reflect core politics: value-based determinations of the highest order, pure ideological policy and prioritization, issues at the heart of public dispute and controversy, the very stuff for which legislators are elected and accountable. In some cases these categories overlap, where the Court exhibits an almost laughable compulsion for micro-management of minute details within crucial broad policy.

Aside some rare exceptions what the observer will not find are overt violations of enumerated statutory rights. This is a critical point. Among all the instances of judicial nullification of Israeli laws, virtually none represent the kind of textbook "rights violations" one expects to find in the development of constitutional jurisprudence ostensibly centered on the protection of individual rights from arbitrary government encroachment. Most cases come nowhere close to it. Indeed, the Israeli case-study exemplifies the many flaws and objections typically raised against rights-based adjudication. In the hands and minds of Israel's judges, "rights" become abstractions furnishing the Court with an excuse to intervene in any conceivable issue or controversy and to pursue any desired policy outcome. The original alleged right is "identified" (or rather, invented) with no relation to a statute's words or their meaning, while any policy or government decision may be creatively framed in the language of rights; a "violation" is deduced with only the most tenuous connection to reality and the most fluid requirement of severity; and a final determination of validity is based on a law's utterly subjective "proportionality," itself a euphemism for balancing manifestly ideological and non-legal considerations. Enforcing so-called constitutional "rights" becomes shorthand for judicial imposition of personal values and political preferences against the will of the parliamentary majority and the desires of the public.

Many courts exercising constitutional jurisdiction have developed rules of "avoidance" or restraint, reflecting a presumption of legislative validity and establishing a relatively high standard permitting judicial interference. The most familiar of these are the famous *Ashwander* rules articulated by Justice Louis Brandeis in 1936, reflecting an overall inclination towards judicial humility when faced with legal challenges to primary legislation. The rules guide courts to avoid constitutional rulings unless absolutely necessary, by resolving cases on non-constitutional grounds, interpreting statutes narrowly to allow them to stand, limiting decisions to cases of sufficient "ripeness" and to actual controversies between adverse parties, tailoring the decision to resolve the dispute in question and not beyond (while refraining from grandiose or sweeping rulemaking), and broadly deferring to the democratic judgment and authority of the legislature. Brandeis quotes Justice Cooley approvingly: "It must be evident to any one that the power to declare a legislative enactment void is one which the judge, conscious of the fallibility of the human judgment, will shrink from exercising in any case where he can conscientiously and with due regard to duty and official oath decline the responsibility." The *Ashwander* rules were born after a century of experience with judicial review and out of a clear-eyed, pragmatic understanding of the risks inherent in courts striking down laws. Brandeis quotes an older case from 1878: "One branch of the government cannot encroach on the domain of another without danger. The safety of our institutions depends in no small degree on a strict observance of this salutary rule." These guidelines are broadly accepted today in the U.S. and elsewhere as a model of the proper judicial disposition towards duly enacted legislation.

No trace of this approach may be found in the Israeli Supreme Court's jurisprudence. Though Justice Shamgar mentions *Ashwander* in passing in his *Hamizrachi* opinion, and though a handful of scholars have suggested its adoption in constitutional adjudication,[2] nothing resembling *Ashwander* exists in Israeli judicial thought, in theory or in practice.[*] If anything, the Court's consistent decisions over the years present a form of "anti-*Ashwander*," a mirror-image and antithesis of all those rules stand for. No legal argument is too far-fetched; no violation too benign; no intervention too unnecessary. The threshold for striking down any law is abysmally low.

Since 1995 the Court has struck down roughly twenty-five laws or provisions as unconstitutional. An exact count is unfortunately evasive due both to the Court's increasing pace of judicial review and to the ambiguous nature of the Court's decisions in some cases. In the first fifteen years since *Hamizrachi* around eight laws were struck down; in the following fifteen years around seventeen were struck down, the amount nearly doubling over the same time span. There is a marked gradual escalation in the Court's willingness and propensity to invalidate legislation. Needless to say, counting the number of laws formally struck down ignores the Court's more sophisticated methods of annulling statutes or rendering them dead letters, by bogus "objective purposive" interpretation, by "deferring" their application, by subjecting statutory executive authority to reasonableness, and so on.

Israeli judicial supremacists claim the Court's tally – only twenty five invalidated laws – to be comparably low relative to other jurisdictions, showing the Court's prudence and restraint in exercising judicial review. Setting this doubtful empirical assertion aside, any such argument sidesteps the real issue. First, it ignores the fact that the Court has no authority to invalidate even a single law – let alone over a score of laws. The Court's purported relative self-discipline in illegitimate judicial review is akin to the relative restraint of a serial killer that has murdered "only" twenty-five people out of the many thousands he has

[*] Hillel Sommer notes that the Court's mentions of *Ashwander* can be counted on one hand, and that in fact it appears nowhere in Barak's main scholarly treatise on constitutional interpretation.

encountered. In both cases such a defensive plea rather misses the point. Second, and more importantly, the real question is not how many laws, but rather *which ones*? Here the Court's position becomes truly indefensible. Most examples of judicial interference involve either benign and insignificant legislation which could scarcely merit the "unconventional weapon" of judicial review, or regard the most contentious ideological fault-lines in Israeli society which the Court only exacerbates by imposing its legally-unfounded solutions. It is to answer this question which we now turn.

Proportionality

In order to understand the Supreme Court's theory and practice of judicial review, we must first briefly consider the key concept of "proportionality" and the way in which it has been developed and applied by the Court.

As discussed above, both 1992 Basic Laws contain a "limitation clause" which supposedly defines the criteria for evaluating whether a statute (or any government action) may validly infringe upon protected rights and liberties. If a law is found to violate a right, it will be ruled unconstitutional if the State cannot prove that the harm is "to an extent no greater than required." This is known as the proportionality requirement.

In line with proportionality requirements in other jurisdictions, the Supreme Court has split proportionality into three separate tests: First, the governmental measure must be rationally connected to its objective. Second, the measure must be necessary in the sense that it should impair the infringed right as little as possible, i.e., that it be the least-harmful available alternative. Third, the harm must not be excessive in relation to the benefit it seeks to achieve; that is, the degree of harm must be proportional to the actual benefit derived from the measure or to the public interest it seeks to advance. The third test is often called "narrow proportionality."

As might be expected, the third test is where the action is at. It is a classic cost-benefit "balancing" test which aspires to weigh competing interests, and is thus open to a significant amount of discretion and disagreement. Yoav Dotan describes the third test as "the most important and demanding test" and as the "inner heart" of the Israeli proportionality requirement.[3] The Court will often invalidate a law based solely on "narrow" proportionality even if it is held to have passed the first two tests. Indeed, it is not uncommon for the Court to leave its evaluation of the first two tests inconclusive, or to skip them entirely, and to rule in a petition according to the third test alone. As "both a logical and practical matter," the third test is thus synonymous with general proportionality in Israeli jurisprudence and the two may be treated as the same thing. Going forward, "proportionality" will refer to all three tests combined, with a clear emphasis on the third "narrow" balancing test.

The vast majority of Supreme Court rulings which invalidate a statute as unconstitutional are based on a finding that the law is "unproportional," that is, on a finding that the harm to a protected right does not outweigh its anticipated or actual benefits.

Generally speaking, proportionality evaluation makes sense in constitutional evaluation of laws. Almost any right may be infringed to some degree in the service of advancing important societal interests or in the interest of maintaining other competing rights (for example, we routinely violate the right to liberty by incarcerating violent criminals in the interest of public safety). Proportionality functions as an important mechanism which ensures such measures are not utterly arbitrary or unnecessary, and that their benefit is not completely dwarfed by the severe curtailment or violation of protected rights. Sensible application of proportionality in rights' adjudication might consider whether a measure is completely "beyond the pale," if it causes an extreme harm that cannot possibly be outweighed by its benefits.

A critical point to keep in mind within the context of constitutional judicial review is that, in principle, proportionality isn't about whether a certain measure is generally wise or desirable, or even whether one can make an argument that a law serving a public interest infringes upon a protected right. The alleged lack of proportionality must be so intense and excessive that the judicial cost-benefit evaluation takes precedence over the evaluation made by the elected political institutions. The harm must significantly outweigh not only the benefit, but also the authority of the democratic process itself. Proportionality therefore essentially asks whether a certain issue – or a certain judicial conclusion – is in fact beyond the reach of the legislator and even the electorate, with the result that a democratically-enacted law is rendered impermissible, void and unenforceable.

The inherent problem of proportionality is, of course, that it very easily (and perhaps unavoidably) becomes a value-based policy analysis and not a legal standard. Whether to restrict or harm a certain right in order to gain some public benefit or to prioritize some other right, and whether the degree of harm is justified by the degree of benefit, is precisely the essence of policymaking. Such decisions often involve complex, ambiguous and highly contested questions derived of first-order moral beliefs and personal values, or they relate to large-scale policy-tradeoffs which either have no determinative optimum or are inherently speculative. In other words, "narrow" proportionality review is at its core a value-based policy determination far more than it is a legal standard. In its worst manifestations, proportionality review becomes indistinguishable from simple policy disagreement with a given measure, or from the impression that a judge would simply have voted against the measure on ideological grounds had they been a legislator.

Returning our focus to Israel merits some cursory observations. At least in principle, proportionality partially relies on a factual assessment of reality, regarding the *actual* harm to rights versus the *actual* benefit achieved. Here we find yet another effect of Israel's unique structural model. As discussed in Chapter 2, the Supreme Court does not hold evidentiary hearings and does not examine witnesses, relying primarily on competing legal briefs supported by written affidavits; at the same time, it is typically the court of first instance for such constitutional challenges, without the benefit of evidence fact-finding in lower courts. As such, the Court is especially ill-equipped to evaluate the alleged "proportionality" of a measure at issue, because of its institutional inability to conduct empirical analysis.

In turn, this evidentiary blindness also highlights the power of the Legal Counsel to the Government when representing the government's position before the Court. The LCG's portrayal of official facts and data has a pivotal effect on the Court's ultimate conclusion regarding proportionality. As such, the LCG can undermine the government's legal position by selectively presenting facts in a way that supports the petitioners, even while nominally arguing the legal case in the government's favor. This has indeed occurred in several cases which resulted in a law's invalidation.

As a final note, the reader will surely have detected some similarity between "proportionality" and "reasonableness," and the two are indeed often compared and conflated. They both boil down to a judge asking whether the government's "weighing" and "balancing" of competing factors was proper, and whether the outcome reached by the government is justified. Yoav Dotan describes Israeli proportionality review as "a balancing process which is remarkably similar, if not identical, to the process of balancing considerations within the framework of the reasonableness standard." Though the Court's dissection of proportionality into multiple distinct stages creates an "illusion of a more objective standard," both proportionality and reasonableness are "analytically and practically identical," involving "the very same balancing process." In this sense, the many critiques against reasonableness (based on its vagueness, its indeterminacy, and its limitless expansion of judicial power) apply equally to proportionality, and for the purpose of such critiques "the two standards are indistinguishable."[4]

As we shall see, proportionality in the Israeli context all-too-often boils down to pure ideological preferences dressed in legalistic terminology. It represents what Prof. James Allan has called the "mysterious, ineffable process whereby committees of ex-lawyers claim to be uniquely well placed to intuit deep-rooted social values and to know their jurisdiction's – and indeed civilization's – sentiments on where to draw hotly contested lines over disputes about euthanasia, abortion, mandatory detention, gay marriage, and more."[5] It concerns the type of policy dilemmas and ideological issues which Justice Antonin Scalia has described as "[not] known to the nine Justices of this Court any better than they are known to nine people picked at random from the Kansas City telephone directory."[6]

Micro-Management

The first statute struck down by the Supreme Court, in a 1997 ruling, was one regulating the profession of Investment Managers within the financial services industry. The challenged law mandated a written professional exam among new conditions required to become a licensed Investment Manager. The exam requirement applied retroactively to existing Investment Managers, with a temporary ("adjustment period") exception for professionals that had at least seven years of prior experience in the field. In a unanimous eleven-Justice decision penned by Barak, the Court struck down the law as unconstitutional due to the exam's "disproportionate" harm to the BL:FO right to "freedom of occupation" and annulled the exam requirement altogether for prior Investment Managers. This was the first time the principles of *Hamizrachi* were implemented with the result of a statute's invalidation.

The law in question represented a standard regulatory determination that certain relevant technical skills are demonstrated as a condition to engaging in a given profession. In doing so it applied some of the new requirements (which were themselves not at issue) to a defined set of existing practitioners within the profession. This was a conscious legislative choice balancing various considerations, including the ability to freely engage in a desired profession and the risks of unqualified investment managers offering their services to the general public. Such a decision was not of a "legal" nature but rather a question of socio-political economic policy, in which no judge can claim wisdom superior to that of the legislator. Indeed, the legislation was the culmination of a prolonged inquiry process which spanned two decades and involved regulatory bodies and three expert-led governmental committees. The statutory arrangement held unconstitutional – a licensing exam required of existing practitioners – did not remotely amount to the type of grievous infringement which might typically justify judicial intervention. The Court's finding of "disproportionate harm" was an obvious exaggeration.

The 1997 *Investment Managers* ruling is widely viewed as a tactical decision by Barak. As one scholar observed, the statute provided the Court with a "golden opportunity" to strike down an obscure, "unimportant and uncontroversial" law far from the public eye, so as to "solidify its authority to conduct judicial review" without incurring public wrath (or even attention, for that matter).[7] One way or another, the ruling was clearly unjustified on its merits and well-demonstrates the Court's eagerness to interfere with legislation due to harm which is both negligible and which is well within legislative policy-making discretion. Whether the written-exam requirement for existing professionals is excessively burdensome was a matter of personal opinion for the public and its elected representatives, not for the courts.

The next law struck down by the Court was in the 1999 *Tzemach* case. A provision in military law permitted the arrest of a soldier for 96 hours (four days) without a warrant and without being seen by a judge. The Court struck down the law as a disproportionate infringement of the right to liberty. Notably, this was the first law struck down due to a conflict with the non-entrenched BL:HDL (and not BL:FO) – thus truly cementing the Court's *Hamizrachi* doctrines. *Tzemach* may well be the only judicial review case, of all twenty-five, that actually makes sense (within the wobbly construct of the constitutional revolution). The law under review involved an overt limitation of an explicit enumerated right (liberty); the context of criminal arrest is a typical one for judicial intervention and constitutional protections of individual liberty; and 96 hours of arrest with no judicial oversight was objectively high compared to most accepted standards in similar circumstances and jurisdictions. It did not represent a key question of publicly contentious policy, priorities or value-judgments. If ever there may have been a form of judicial review under the constitutional revolution that might have been defensible, and that could have been endured by the public, it was something akin to this case. Alas, *Tzemach* is the exception that proved the rule.

In 1999 the Knesset passed a law granting a radio broadcast license to "any station that had been broadcasting during the previous five years" and whose broadcasts were available throughout most of Israel's territory. The legislation was a clear and explicit attempt to give official government sanction to a right-wing pirate radio station called *Channel 7*. The Israeli telecommunications sector was notoriously dominated by left-wing media outlets, and so the proprietors of Channel 7 sought to offer a new radio station that catered to right-leaning audiences. As the prospects of receiving a state license to operate a new radio channel were slim, Channel 7 commenced in 1988 as an illegal pirate station – broadcasting from a ship outside Israel's territorial waters. The 1999 law enacted by the Knesset effectively legalized the activity of Channel 7 and granted it a formal license as a recognized radio station.

In a 2002 unanimous nine-Justice ruling the Court struck down the law as an impermissible infringement of the right to freedom of occupation. Radio broadcast frequencies being a limited public resource, the statute unfairly distributed a license to a specific recipient without providing other interested parties the opportunity to contend or bid for the same resource. This violated the right of potential bidders to "free competition" – that is, their equal opportunity to participate in a bidding process – which in turn violated their "freedom of occupation." The ruling is remarkable in two ways: First, the alleged right to "free competition" is already a stretch – a highly creative and expansive interpretation of "freedom of occupation." The two are typically considered distinct legal interests and the former is not automatically derived of the latter. Freedom of occupation primarily protects against governmental impediments to an individual's pursuit of their desired professional vocation, not system-wide policy consideration of resource-distribution. In other words, we already find the Court invoking an individual right (essentially, a liberty) in order to impose an entirely separate and unrelated (even if desirable) norm. Second, the ruling simply ignores any considerations of freedom of speech – the issue is not even discussed (despite being raised by the parties). One would expect a constitutional court to recognize and address the free-speech aspects of a ruling which effectively revokes a broadcast license despite the explicit parliamentary decision to grant it.

The *Channel 7* ruling was thus a gross intervention in government legislative policy, based on far-fetched legal interpretation and – for the first time – with a decidedly partisan bent. Many doubted whether such a decision would have been rendered against a law doing the same for a left-wing radio station by a left-wing government.

One of the most extraordinary rulings ever issued by a Supreme Court – anywhere in the world – was in the 2009 *Private Prison* case. Due to a severe shortage of available prison cells throughout the country, alongside complaints of poor living conditions for incarcerated prisoners, the Knesset passed a law in 2004 establishing a single prison that would be administered and operated by a private corporation under State supervision. According to the government this would have significantly improved the living conditions for inmates, would save significant State funds, and would increase the financial feasibility of building much-needed future additional prisons.

In an 8-to-1 majority decision penned by Chief Justice Beinisch, the Court invalidated the law as an unconstitutional violation of a prisoner's right to liberty and to dignity. The Court argued that outsourcing core State functions such as administering a prison – which inevitably includes elements of internment, coercion, punishment and violence – would impermissibly undermine an inmate's liberty, which can only be maintained when such functions are administered by the State. That is, the right to liberty inherently requires that restrictions on liberty be performed by the State itself. In a similar vein, an inmate's dignity is harmed by the mere fact of being placed under the supervision of a for-profit business corporation, for which the inmate becomes but an instrument for generating income. The infringement of a prisoner's dignity – by being subjected to private (and commercial) administration of key State functions – was the primary basis on which the Court struck down the law. The majority and concurring opinions span a cool 118 pages, taken up mostly by philosophical ruminations on the Israeli social contract, on the nature of the State and on its roles in maintaining public order.

The ruling is truly remarkable and stands out for a number of reasons. This was the first time a law had been struck down based on the abstract ideal of dignity (or liberty).* The legal challenge to the law was entirely theoretical – the private prison had not yet been constructed and had not commenced its operations. No one could allege factual harm, and the various violations of rights were either speculative or notional (that is, they applied irrespective of how the prison would be administered in practice). As a result, the main petitioners themselves were not actual inmates who could claim any personal harm or interest – one was a mediocre law school, the other was a retired prison commissioner.

Far more important, of course, was the Court's radically expansive application of "dignity" in striking down the private prison initiative. The notion of dignity may certainly be infused with more specific content – we can all imagine ways in which the State might severely harm a person's dignity, that could even amount to the level of illegality. But for the Court "dignity" quickly became an effective tool, a catch-all phrase, to include any form of objectionable government conduct

* Previous instances involved more concrete violations of property and occupation rights, or on a very tangible sense of physical personal liberty in the *Tzemach* case.

(which one might say is virtually all government conduct). From the moment any personal interest or preference whatsoever may be framed as a desire for "dignity," all that remains is for the Court to step in to determine the constitutionality of almost any conceivable statute.

Yoav Dotan has noted how the right to human dignity has been expanded to include "a litany of rights which are not considered classic political rights, such as the right to family, to marriage, and to adoption." Dotan continues: "A further expansion of 'human dignity' came to incorporate socio-economic rights including the right to a dwelling, the right to minimal dignified living, the right to education, to electricity, and more." Within this context, Dotan observes that courts have come to skipping any evaluation of whether a "protected" right has been violated, and instead move directly to evaluating the degree and justifications for such violation.[8]

To the issue at hand, having one's prison sentence administered by a private corporation is not inherently an extreme indignity. Though one could perhaps make such a case, an opposite proposition is of equal validity – State employees and institutions at times make for very poor caretakers. One could raise many valid theoretical arguments why privately-run prisons might convey and confer more dignity to inmates than State-run prisons – perhaps some convicted criminals harbor deep animus towards the State that now imprisons them, for example. Other more practical observations might involve the relative incentives to comply with welfare norms (a private corporation doesn't want to lose its lucrative government license), or personnel and hiring flexibility (government employees are harder to dismiss for poor conduct). Anyone that has experienced the pleasure of using an Israeli Post Office knows that our government-run institutions do not necessarily exude an aura of upstanding dignity.

The Court's philosophical premise of categorical indignity is absurd on its face – or rather, it is a thinly-veiled personal value-based preference masquerading as a constitutional imperative. An honest legal appraisal would likely conclude that private prisons do not infringe, per se, on an inmate's right to liberty or to dignity any more than any other type of imprisonment.

The Court's next move, concluding that the law's harm is so extreme as to outweigh its potential benefits and is therefore invalid, is even more egregious. To make its case the Court reverts often to the sensibilities of "modern democracy" and to Israeli society's "basic values." Of the latter we may simply repeat the obvious and familiar objection that the Knesset evaluation of societal "values" is at least as accurate and faithful as the Court's. But of "modern democracy" the answer is even easier: Modern democracies throughout the world, including bastions of constitutional or liberal government undoubtedly committed to individual dignity, permit and maintain privately-operated prisons. These include the United States, the United Kingdom, New Zealand, Australia, and many others. Despite being an issue of understandable controversy, in none of these jurisdictions has a Court ever suggested (let alone, ruled) that private prisons are themselves inherently unconstitutional, or that they rise to some extreme level of harm to either liberty or to dignity – a compelling indication of just how far-fetched the Israeli Court's claims are. The Court recognizes this comparative fact but then simply repeats various policy objections to private prisons – as if to prove its own lack of distinction between alleged democratic imperatives and its own subjective ideological opinion.

There may be strong policy arguments against private prisons – I for one would have deep concerns about any such arrangement – but these are not legal arguments in any sense. The question of private prisons is a major and complex issue of public policy involving economics, welfare, crime-fighting, correctional approaches, tangible system-wide needs, and so on. It also raises some conceivable moral dilemmas. These all combine into a valid and legitimate controversy to be resolved by the elected officials and their constituents. Yet by purporting to "balance" whether the law's benefits are properly proportionate to its harms, the Court simply engaged in pure policymaking at the expense of the public's ability to make such determinations. Under the guise of protecting a prisoner's "right to dignity" the Court removed a valid policy decision from the public's hands and rendered it illegitimate. The *Private Prison* case is little more than distilled judicial legislation – and can hardly pretend to be anything but that.

Ironically, as is so often the case trying to resolve genuinely complex challenges by simplistic judicial fiat, the Court's decision backfired. Since the 2009 ruling no new prisons have been erected in Israel – it turns out that financial burdens and other hurdles made new prisons nearly impossible, if not undertaken as a private joint enterprise. Prison living conditions continue to be poor at many facilities. So poor, in fact, that in 2017 the Court issued a separate ruling which ordered the State to increase the minimum "living space" for the average prisoner throughout the country (see Chapter 3). Needless to say, the Court failed to recognize its own contribution to the current crisis by arbitrarily taking one of the primary available solutions off the table. The order to increase "living space" has still not been fully implemented to this day. The Court thus exacerbated any existing harm to the liberty and dignity of real prisoners, for the sake of its megalomanic micro-management of government policy and its lawless pursuit of lofty ideals.

The law that was struck down in the *Private Prison* case contemplated only a single prison, as an initial pilot project. It stipulated mechanisms ensuring robust executive and judicial supervision of the prison administration. It may, or may not, have improved or worsened the lives of prisoners – the Court never asked them their opinion one way or another. In his dissenting opinion, Justice Edmond Levy suggested that the Court allow the prison to begin operating and then evaluate its effectiveness – and its shortcomings – based on empirical knowledge and experience. Would that have been so bad?

The Supreme Court's intervention in legislative economic policy was only getting started. In the 2012 *Hassan* case, a new executive policy conditioned eligibility for certain welfare benefits on non-ownership of an automobile – if you owned a car, you were not eligible for certain welfare benefits. The reasons involved the rationales typically found in decisions to expand or restrict welfare entitlements. The policy was soon incorporated into statutory law via an amendment to the "Income Support Law." Following an inevitable legal challenge the Court invalidated the amendment and annulled the policy, holding that the car ownership requirement unjustifiably violated the beneficiary's right to "a minimum standard of dignified living."[9]

This requires some quick background. Amid a severe economic recession in 2003, the Government decided to reduce various welfare payments. A legal challenge to these welfare cuts argued that the Basic Law right to "dignity" entails a right to "dignified living" which in turn includes a certain basic state-provided minimum income.[10] Though the argument was preposterous – effectively subjecting all welfare policy to judicial supervision under its application of "dignity" – the Court seemed close to accepting the petition, and ordered that the government provide an estimation of what constitutes a minimum income for "dignified living." This potential judicial intervention in pure economic policy during a national economic crisis caused an uproar, and the Government refused to provide such an estimation, arguing that no objective standard for "dignified living" exists. The Knesset initiated retaliatory legislation which would have directly curtailed the Court's authority. Seeing this explicit threat of a showdown between the judiciary and legislature, the Court realized it had overstepped and dismissed the petitions on technical grounds. Nonetheless, the Court recognized in principle a right to "dignified living," essentially a social welfare right, which ostensibly exists under the explicit right to "dignity" in the Basic Law.

This in turn paved the way to the 2012 *Hassan* decision: the Court made good on its recognition of a right to "dignified living" and struck down the Knesset's welfare amendment on those grounds. The Court mandated specific discretionary budgetary expenditures, elevating its own personal agenda and subjective values over those of the legislature and electorate – all under the obscure right to "dignity." Notably, various constitutions around the world do provide some form of social welfare rights under an idea of "dignity" – but these are granted by explicit and detailed provisions. Nowhere else would a court treat vague "dignity" as a blank check to dictate minute eligibility criteria for welfare payments. *Hassan* is a useful example demonstrating the malleability of "rights" enforcement by the Supreme Court – any personal interest becomes a protected right; any wide government policy may be labelled a violation; the balancing of competing societal interests – such as budgetary constraints versus welfare support – is reframed by the Court as a rational judicial exercise.

Yet another case of judicial micro-management appeared in the 2017 *Quatinsky* decision – but this time on radically different grounds and directed at supervising the Knesset itself. Israel has been embroiled in a severe housing crisis for decades, sparking massive protests in 2011 and galvanizing a substantial social movement. The crisis and protests also accentuated broader issues of income inequality. Moshe Kahlon (along with his *Kulanu* party) was one of the politicians most associated with efforts at curbing inequality and resolving the housing crisis (as Minister of Communications he had led a telecoms reform which substantially reduced end-consumer costs for cellphone network services), and he was reelected on precisely such a platform. One of Kahlon's flagship initiatives as Minister of Finance was an increased tax on any "third" real estate property: Real estate owners would pay an additional tax (beyond the ordinary applicable taxes at the time) if they owned three or more properties. The (somewhat questionable) rationale was that flawed tax incentives were exacerbating the housing crises, and increasing the tax burden would encourage property investors (as opposed to ownership for self-residential purposes) to sell their properties, thus increasing market supply and lowering prices.

Kahlon's initiative was incorporated into the general budget legislation for 2017, but the process of its legislation was allegedly rushed. The budget draft was approved by the Government in August of 2016; the draft bill was published by the Ministry of Finance in September; the bill was submitted to the Knesset for a first legislative reading and approved in October. The bill was then discussed in the relevant Knesset Finance Committee, with various amendments and alternations, and after a night-long session was approved by the Committee on December 16th. The final legislation was enacted by the Knesset on December 22nd of 2016. Needless to say, at each stage the law received the necessary voting majority required to proceed.

In August of 2017 the Supreme Court struck down the "third property" tax legislation on the grounds of it being – wait for it – too rushed. The Court held in *Quatinsky* that the "legislative process" suffered from "defects that go to its root," because of the hurried and superficial discussions and because legislators ostensibly did not have sufficient opportunity to review and deliberate the law. This hasty process violated the parliamentary "participation principle" which ensures that legislators are able to participate in the lawmaking process.

The *Quatinsky* ruling was unique in that it struck down a statute without reference to Basic Laws – indeed without any claim that the provision in question violated any specific Basic Law. Though this was the first (and almost only) time that the Court did so, the ruling marked a dramatic departure from the fundamental premise of all judicial review since the constitutional revolution. Until *Quatinsky* any judicial review had only been exercised against laws which allegedly contradicted a Basic Law by violating specific rights within it. The concept underlying judicial review was that Basic Laws enjoyed an elevated constitutional status which trumped ordinary legislation. *Quatinsky* threw this rationale out the window and introduced a new kind of formless judicial review, based solely on the judicial application of abstract principles such as "parliamentary participation" (itself based on some vague notion of "the rule of law"). The Court now saw itself authorized to freely strike down laws without even the pretense of a conflicting superior Basic Law.

The ruling also marked a bewildering role-reversal – the majority opinion was penned by conservative stalwart Justice Solberg, while a devastating dissent was mounted by uber-activist Justice Mazuz. For Mazuz, subjecting the Knesset's legislative procedures to the Court's notion of propriety – with no clear textual statutory basis – conflicted with core principles of democracy and the separation of powers. Mazuz persuasively argues that the majority deviates from the Court's own precedent, which contemplated judicial intervention only in cases where legislators were denied "*any* practical opportunity" to participate in the legislative process and to know what they were voting for. Yet this was clearly not the case with the "third property" tax law, which had been broadly known and discussed for months (even if minor technical changes had been made in the last minute). Mazuz demonstrates the point by presenting multiple cases in which statutes were enacted in a manner even more rushed than the "third property" tax, but in which the Court nonetheless rejected challenges based on their "flawed legislative process." The dissenting opinion reflected the basic insight, shared by virtually any democracy, that it is the prerogative of a parliamentary majority to enact legislation in a hasty and rushed manner if it so chooses, even if undesirable and unfortunate, and the oversight of such poor legislative performance properly belongs in the realms of political and public debate and consequences.

A final example of judicial meddling is the 2021 *Surrogacy* case. A statutory amendment had expanded surrogacy eligibility to single women (but not to men). Surrogacy – an arrangement whereby a woman (the surrogate) carries and gives birth to a baby for another person or couple (the intended parents) – has been legal and regulated in Israel since a 1996 law.* The statute initially permitted surrogacy services only for heterosexual couples – surrogacy outside the statutory parameters and framework is an imprisonable criminal offense. Following a governmental committee report and a series of Supreme Court decisions, the Knesset amended the law in 2018 so that surrogacy services would be essentially available to all women – whether single or in a relationship of any kind. The amendment did not extend permission to single men or to male same-sex couples.

In 2021 the Supreme Court struck down the 2018 amendment due to its alleged discrimination against men (whether single or in a homosexual relationship) and the violation of their "right to equality." In doing so the Court, once again, interfered in the Knesset's valid policy determination (made for legitimate reasons), by employing the totalizing and flattening language of abstract rights.

Setting aside legal nuance for a moment, it's worth noting that democratic countries around the world have varying approaches to surrogacy. For example, in the United States arrangements vary radically from state to state; in France, Germany, Finland, Iceland, Italy and Sweden, surrogacy is entirely illegal. In the United Kingdom surrogacy agreements are technically legal but unenforceable, because the birth-mother (the surrogate) remains the legally-recognized mother of the child unless she chooses otherwise. Many jurisdictions which permit surrogacy limit the option to women only (whether single or in a relationship).

---

* Commercial (for-compensation) and traditional (the surrogate donates the egg) surrogacy was and remains illegal. Only altruistic (no-compensation) and gestational (egg donor is not the surrogate) surrogacy is permitted in Israel.

This variance makes sense because surrogacy raises complicated medical, ethical, moral and economic questions to which there is no universally correct answer. Competing interests that must be balanced include a couple's (or person's) desire for parenthood; the risks for abuse of vulnerable women and of the development of a "gray" market in which women are pressured into serving as surrogates for pay; legal complications and dilemmas arising from disputes between genetic parents and birth surrogates; child welfare and wellbeing; objections to commercialization of pregnancy and birth; medical justifications for seeking surrogacy; and competition between surrogacy-seekers over a limited pool of available surrogates (just to name a few factors). These are complex and difficult policy determinations reflecting public priorities and value-judgments – absolute and universal "rights" simply don't enter into it. Such dilemmas defy typical political categories – for example uniting, as a 2017 article in *The Atlantic* notes, "left-wing feminists and conservative Catholics." Critically, balancing such interests may lead to valid distinctions between eligibility for males and females, or heterosexual and same-sex couples, based on strong policy rationales.

This alone demonstrates the absurdity of the Court's conclusion that limiting surrogacy to women only is inherently "unequal" to the point of unconstitutionality. The 2021 *Surrogacy* case reflects just one more instance of simplistic and superficial judicial reasoning by which legitimate policy determinations are reframed as "rights," and in which the Knesset's (and public's) preference is supplanted by that of the Court's judges.

There is a common theme for the invalidated laws surveyed in this section, and that is the Court's near-megalomanic obsession with legislative minutiae, interfering in valid legislative policy decisions well-within parliamentary lawmaking prerogative. The Court does so on weak (or non-existent) legal grounds, even when utterly and easily avoidable, on matters of negligible importance or limited influence, involving marginal harm to small subsets of the population. To be clear, the pain caused by some of these laws is not trivial, and people may have valid objections and grievances. Yet none of the cases (with one possible exception) amount to a clear-cut infringement of absolute individual rights, and none of them regard broad and substantial national policy with wide-spread impact.

These cases illustrate the Court's inability to just let things lie – even in the face of primary legislation by a parliamentary majority. They signal the Court's view that even issues of reasonable debate and of minor significance are not to be entrusted to the democratic process to the extent the Court dislikes its outcomes; the Court finds the notion of deference to the electorate's will to be intolerable, and the temptation to meddle irresistible. This phenomenon is in some ways more debilitating to democratic culture than the Court's dramatic intervention in major societal controversies and compromises to which we will soon return.

*

The astute reader may have noticed something amiss in the 2021 *Surrogacy* case described above. A statutory amendment was struck down on the basis of its violation of a right to "equality" – but no such right is listed in either of the 1992 Basic Laws. Astoundingly, already a decade earlier, the Supreme Court had begun striking down Knesset laws due to their incompatibility with the *unenumerated* right to equality. More amazingly still (but perhaps at this point unsurprising), the Court did so despite a right to equality being explicitly and deliberately excluded from Basic Law: Human Dignity and Liberty. The *Surrogacy* case thus leads us directly and conveniently to examine the extraordinary right to "equality" in modern Israeli jurisprudence.

Equality, Status Quo, and the Jewish State

The Supreme Court's inclusion and application of an abstract constitutional "right to equality," implicitly contained within the enumerated right to dignity, while blatantly defying the Knesset's explicit decision against doing so, is surely one of the most spectacular innovations in the annals of comparative constitutional history. It is impossible to overstate the colossal, system-wide, multi-level effect of the Court's decision to pursue this path. One cannot understand the constitutional revolution and its effect on the Israeli socio-political order without a firm grasp of the Israeli mega-constitutional right to equality. It is to this mind-boggling saga which we now turn.

The 1948 Declaration of Independence proclaimed that Israel will "uphold the full social and political equality of all its citizens without distinction of race, creed or sex." The Knesset had legislated numerous laws affording statutory protections against arbitrary discrimination. On many occasions the Supreme Court had recognized "the principle of equality" as a central pillar of the Israeli governmental order. Various previous legislative efforts at an Israeli bill of rights prior to 1992 included some explicit formulation of a right to equality.

Nonetheless, any superior right to equality was always a point of enormous debate and controversy for the Israeli public and their elected representatives. It tied directly into fundamental societal fault-lines relating to religion, class, nationality, race, origin, and far beyond. The decision not to decide – to deliberately leave certain contentious issues undefined and unresolved – almost inevitably precluded a sweeping and enforceable right to equality. Indeed, some feared that a legal right to equality would mean eliminating the Knesset's ability to appropriately manage such electoral tensions and would entail uncontrollable judicial imposition of unwanted, inflexible and indelicate norms.

In our above chronicling of the 1992 Basic Laws we discussed the core legislative compromise by which explicit judicial review was rejected and removed from earlier drafts. But I had intentionally left out a critical piece of the puzzle. The same compromise rested on another core condition of even greater importance – the exclusion of a right to equality.

The initial inclusion of "equality" was the primary obstacle to recruiting even minimal support for the new Basic Laws. It was precisely the aversion to "equality" that led the Knesset in 1992 to split its original "human rights" bill into smaller bite-sized chunks of individual statutes addressing different rights separately; and it was precisely the accommodation of this aversion which ultimately yielded the 1992 Basic Laws. Certain factions within the Knesset eventually agreed to support the Basic Laws on the understanding and condition that no "right to equality" would appear in the final statute. This was the basic compromise central to the 1992 legislation – the constitutional revolution could not have existed had the law's sponsors insisted on retaining a right to equality.

This plain fact is universally recognized and admitted by virtually all parties on all sides of the Israeli constitutional debate. It is undisputed. Many authors and scholars have dedicated significant discussion to this key element of BL:HDL. Yehudit Karp, the law's self-styled biographer, describes the issue of an equality provision as "the most concrete front in which the fiercest battles were fought" and as "the principal stumbling block" standing in the way of a prospective bill of rights.[11] The crucial compromise making the law feasible was to "neutralize" the law's "problematic" components by removing the equality provision; the "political understanding" which formed the basis for the new laws was that "the controversial equality principle" would "not be anchored" in BL:HDL. Karp emphasizes, in the most unequivocal terms, that the "absence" of the equality provision from the final draft "was no accidental oversight," and that the entire framework of splitting the original draft bill of rights into separate statutes "existed only to overcome the obstacle" of the equality provision. Indeed, the law's sponsor stated on the Knesset floor that "there is no general equality provision here" because "it was the stumbling block, the obstacle" to enacting the law in its entirety.

Numerous scholars have observed the same, and this description is borne out by the public record of Knesset drafts and deliberations and of contemporaneous legislator testimony.

Almost immediately after the 1992 laws had been enacted, the adherents of judicial supremacy began striking a different tone. In her own essay, Karp argues for an implicit right to "equality" contained within the right to dignity, or alternatively within Israel's "democratic values." Justice Barak also began arguing for the recognition of "unenumerated" rights to be deduced by interpretation of the Basic Laws. The Court did not go quite so far in the *Hamizrachi* ruling itself, with Barak stating that "rights not enshrined in the Basic Law continue to apply according to their current status."* Still, a significant body of scholarly literature and judicial opinions began advocating that the Supreme

* Though when read in context, this does not quite suggest a rejection of unenumerated constitutional rights: Barak's point was that judge-made non-statutory rights were not demoted or downgraded due to their absence from the new Basic Law.

Court should recognize and enforce a right to "equality," as part of the Court's newly evolving jurisprudence regarding the law's existing enumerated rights.

The Court gladly acquiesced. In a series of high-profile rulings, the Court gradually adopted an implicit constitutional right to equality as derived of the right to human dignity. At first the right's enforcement was limited to instances of alleged inequality which were clearly humiliating or debasing – that is, which maintained a rational connection with a right to dignity. Soon enough the Court turned to addressing "inequality" in its own right, with no element of humiliation or indignity, and eventually arrived at applying any obscure and nebulous meaning of equality as the Court saw fit. In 2010 the first law was effectively struck down for violating such a right. The specifics of these cases and their implications will be discussed in the next section.

The Court's "recognition" of an abstract right to equality within the Basic Laws is astonishing for a number of reasons and constitutes something of a judicial revolution in its own right. First, the claim that one might infer a right to equality from a right to dignity as an interpretive exercise is plainly insincere under the circumstances. The legislative history with its conscious and deliberate exclusion of a right to equality is not shrouded in mystery. There was no doubt regarding "original intent" behind the law, its text or its purpose. The letter and spirit of the law are one. The Knesset knowingly decided to *avoid* a right to equality by *not* including it in BL:HDL; this irrefutable fact was always clear as day. Deducing "equality" from the right to dignity is not a genuine interpretive exercise in the remotest sense. The Court's decision to blatantly ignore legal text and democratic intent is simply indefensible on the most naturally intuitive level. Of this exact issue Justice Moshe Landau said it best: "You may not insert these rights into the Basic Law through the window, after they had been shown out the Basic Law through the front door."[12] One does not need a doctorate in constitutional law to understand the problem here.

It's also worth stressing that nothing in human "dignity" necessarily yields an automatic conclusion of equality. As Justice Alex Stein stressed in one case, "dignity" in certain circumstances may well require the protection of human autonomy and agency just as much as the imposition of manufactured equality. The Court interprets dignity so that it contains equality, though any such equation is far from inevitable.

Second, the Court consciously interfered in precisely the issues which the Knesset sought to exclude from judicial jurisdiction in the first place. Those opposing a right to equality were not French aristocrats, plantation slaveholders or primitive reactionaries, nor were they die-hard free-market libertarians. Their objections were not abstract or hypothetical – they had a series of concrete concerns in mind which were explicitly voiced and debated. Many were worried that a right to equality would destabilize various delicate "status quo" arrangements pertaining to matters of religion and State,* or would adversely affect the Jewish Ultra-Orthodox community and its tenuous relationship with other segments of society. Other considerations also involved Israel's substantial "Jewish" character, with implications ranging from religious state institutions to immigration, military service, Sabbath observance, resource distribution, formal state symbols and beyond.

Yet these issues were exactly the issues into which the Court enthusiastically waded once it armed itself with a right to equality. In other words, not only did the Court "infer" a right to equality when it was deliberately avoided – it also proceeded to apply the same right to the specific controversies that the Knesset explicitly named as those it wanted to exclude from judicial intervention.

Third, there is incredible irony and hypocrisy in flouting the text of a purported constitution when the text is the only thing it had going for it. The Court's essential theory of the constitutional revolution is not based on any special legislative process or clear expression of democratic will, but rather primarily on the words of the constitutional legislation itself. Justice Barak frames his *Hamizrachi* opinion as "interpretation" of the 1992 Basic Laws and especially of the "substantively entrenched" limitation clause. As Barak explained in a speech following the law's enactment, the Court must perform its task "in complete subservience to the words of the Basic Laws." Yet the Court's professed reverence for – or "subservience" to – the words of the constitution turned out to be conditional and short-lived. Considering that the legislative text was the main basis for the constitutional revolution, the Court's utter distortion of the very same text is especially egregious and also theoretically unsound. In one breath the Court elevates the Basic Laws to constitutional status based solely on their text, while in the next breath the Court shows utter contempt for the law's provisions by ignoring any meaning or significance they might have. As we shall see, the Knesset is constituent authority and its word is supreme law only to the extent convenient for the Supreme Court and until the latter wants to deviate from the express constitutional text.

The exclusion of a right to equality was just one of three mechanisms by which the Knesset sought to avoid judicial interference with certain crucial political compromises. The other two were the description of Israel's "Jewish" character in the purpose clause of BL:HDL, and the Section 10 "savings" clause.

The allusion to Israel's Jewish character was a later addition to the law – BL:HDL itself displays no particular connection to Judaism or Jewish national values. Indeed, it is a decidedly civil document that enshrines abstract human rights of a universal nature. In this sense the "Jewish" reference in "Israel's values as a Jewish and Democratic State" is conspicuously out of place. Its addition was

* "Status quo" is a phrase used to describe a series of arrangements relating to religion and state, and to the status of Jewish Ultra-Orthodox communities, which were agreed at the founding of the state and which were meant to be altered only by mutual consent.

a compromise to reassure the law's religious opponents and to allay fears of judicial interference in core issues such as those listed above, by serving as a counterweight against generic democratic ideals. The inclusion of "Jewish" alongside "democratic" values ostensibly indicated that the two categories were on equal footing – that the human rights listed in BL:HDL could not supersede the State's Jewish character. Indeed, some initial proposals had placed Israel's Jewish character as an explicit exception to an "equality right" (when the latter was still part of the draft bill). By adding "Jewish" values to the purpose clause, the religious parties also gained, from their perspective, the first express statutory recognition of Israel's inherent Jewishness.

Section 10 of BL:HDL reads: "This Basic Law shall not affect the validity of any law in force prior to the commencement of the Basic Law." The Hebrew word used for law is *din*, meaning "law" in the broader sense that includes regulations, case law, established legal conventions and so on. The meaning of Section 10 was to reject any possibility of retroactive applicability by which the courts would overturn existing statutes, settled law and prior rulings due to incompatibility with the Basic Law. Section 10 was supposed to insulate pre-existing legal arrangements – including religious "status quo" and much more – from judicial intervention. At the same time, the Knesset also rejected the idea that the courts could interpret existing statutes according to the new Basic Laws. Earlier drafts of BL:HDL included a provision that pre-existing laws would be "interpreted in the spirit" of the new Basic Law, but this provision was deliberately scrapped as part of the same compromise.

All in all these three elements of BL:HDL aspired to provide certain existing rules, policies and arrangements with triple protection – no enforceable right to equality; Jewish values on par with universal values; and exclusion of pre-existing laws from the effects of the new legislation (even by renewed interpretation). As Karp notes, the purpose of these was to "remove any trace of doubt" that the 1992 laws might diminish, in any way whatsoever, existing arrangements regarding religion and state in Israel. Though it's easy to dismiss such compromises as self-interested political haggling and partisanship of sectorial parties, another perspective is possible. At least for the opponents to an "equality" right, here was a good faith and legitimate desire to enshrine and protect certain fundamental individual rights without jeopardizing other important interests and while keeping the judiciary away from controversial issues dividing the public. One might ask what more the Knesset could have conceivably done to achieve this result.*

Yet this perhaps-valiant effort was all for naught. Well before it deployed the weapon of "equality" the Court dispatched the "Jewish values" and Section 10 "savings" clauses easily enough, in a manner which may be described here only in passing. The Court construed Jewish values in the most abstract and universal way possible, such that they cozily conformed to any other alleged universal

* In fact, Justice Cheshin asks precisely this question in his dissenting *Ganimat* opinion: "What more could the Knesset have done or said, and didn't?"

values of democracy or human rights. In his 1992 speech a few months after the new Basic Laws were enacted, Justice Barak listed the basic Jewish values to which the law, in his view, was referring: "Love of humanity, sanctity of life, social justice, doing what is good and just, protecting human dignity, the rule of the law-maker, and other such eternal values." Barak concedes these to be "on a universal level of abstraction." The perversion is almost comical. Such values may or may not be "Jewish," but they certainly do not reflect the purpose and rationale for which the Knesset inserted the phrase "Jewish values" into BL:HDL. The notion of "Jewish values" in the Basic Laws under the Court's decisions essentially became synonymous with broad democratic values, and indeed in some cases with a radical progressive agenda.

In similar fashion, the Court simply ignored the Section 10 "savings clause" and engaged in a wholesale overhaul of prior jurisprudence. Early on in 1995 (even before *Hamizrachi*) the Court ruled in the landmark *Ganimat* case that BL:HDL "has an interpretive effect" on all previous law. Barak explained that though Section 10 precludes any effect on the "validity" of pre-existing law, the 1992 Basic Laws should still impact the "meaning" of older law so as to make it more consistent with the rights and values of the constitutional revolution.* This ruling was confirmed in a re-hearing by an expanded bench. The technical rationale per Barak was that, while the "subjective" (i.e., factual) purpose of a law remains constant in keeping with Section 10, the constitutional revolution affects the "objective" (i.e., judicially-invented) purpose of a law, leading to its renewed interpretation and application.

In a 2012 article Hillel Sommer, an Israeli constitutional scholar, identified the Supreme Court's specific and paradoxical disdain for these deliberate constitutional determinations by the Knesset.[13] Sommer argued that when the Knesset as constituent power had explicitly and publicly considered a particular issue and had made a conscious decision in its regard, the Court ought to exercise restraint and respect the constituent authority's unequivocal choice. Excluding a constitutional right to equality and Section 10 shielding pre-existing law from the Basic Law's effects are two prime examples of such decisions. Sommer convincingly shows how the Court in this context "ignores legislative history even when unambiguous" without showing any principled justification for deviating from the Knesset's clear determinations. Its jurisprudence and rulings "utterly contradict" the "conscious decision of the constituent authority" which "formed part of the political compromise that enabled the Basic Law's enactment."

Sommer's point highlights the absurd position taken up by the Court and the alternative approach that it could have adopted. Implicit in Sommer's argument is the Court's untrustworthiness – how can anyone take the constitutional revolution seriously, when the Court itself refuses to maintain fidelity to the constituent authority's basic decisions? One can imagine (albeit with great effort) an alternate reality in which the Supreme Court presided over the constitutional revolution and

* Yes. This is literally the argument Barak presents in *Ganimat*. It is as bizarre and nonsensical in Hebrew as it is in English.

seized the power of judicial review – yet still exercised a modicum of restraint when it came to unequivocal decisions made by the same constituent authority the Court claims to so respect. The Court could have enforced the various enumerated rights, including dignity, without the gross distortion of "reading in" equality; or it could have even derived a right to equality without using it to strike down legislation; or it could have done both but without intervening in the very issues for which the Knesset sought to avoid judicial involvement. The Court could have done the bare minimum to induce faith in the sincerity of its legal arguments. But the allure of judicial supremacy proved too strong – having tasted the forbidden fruit of judicial review the voracious appetite of Barak and his Court would not be satiated by following the Knesset's clear constraints.

Many critics stress the centrality of these arrangements to the compromise which ultimately led to the Basic Law's enactment, though this distinct point is not always clear enough and is well worth properly articulating. Under the most generous and optimistic view of the 1992 Basic Laws and the constitutional revolution, the Knesset as constituent authority chose to exercise its legitimate powers and enact a de facto constitution in the form of the 1992 laws. Like any constitution, the purported Israeli one was born of a *deal* – different factions (including the Court itself) negotiated and reached an understanding as to the terms of the constitution. Even if we unconditionally accept that the Basic Laws were a new constitution empowering judges to invalidate statutes, it is irrefutably obvious that the new Basic Laws also included some unambiguous restrictions on that power. In other words, under the same generous and optimistic view, the new constitution granted the Court *X* and withheld *Y*: It enshrined certain rights and allowed the Court to do certain things, and in exchange, as part of the same deal, it rejected certain rights and forbade the Court from doing other things. This was the essential transaction into which all parties knowingly and willingly entered (allegedly, according to the Court's view).

In this important sense the Court broke its end of the bargain. Even when we take the constitutional revolution's claims at face value and considered on their own terms, the Court and its supporters violated their side of the deal by flouting the elements noted above and especially by recognizing a fabricated right to equality. It embraced *X* and defied *Y*. The judges simply cheated. In its hubris, its disregard of the law and its disdain for norms of democracy or decency, the Supreme Court did more than anyone else to undermine the foundations of its own judicial revolution – and not for the last time.

One final yet dramatic aspect of the Israeli constitutional right to equality is its uniquely sweeping scope. As we will see, the Israeli Court treats "equality" as a blank check to impose and enforce any policy prescription or prohibition the Justices deem broadly related to any notion of equality. But a blanket enforceable right to abstract "equality" per se is virtually unheard-of in democratic constitutions. This is worth repeating: almost no legal system recognizes an actionable right to "equality" at large. The typical expressions of equality in comparative constitutionalism are far more precise – these include equality "before the law," "equal protection" of the laws, and explicit prohibitions against group discrimination. These formulations bear a relatively particular and distinct meaning as opposed to an open-ended exhortation for equality, most often referring to non-discrimination based on group identity.

A handful of familiar examples will suffice to demonstrate this. The Fourteenth Amendment to the U.S. Constitution famously provides for "equal protection of the laws." Section 15 of the Canadian Charter of Rights and Freedoms states that every individual is "equal before and under the law and has the right to the equal protection and equal benefit of the law without discrimination." Article 3 of the German Basic Law is a model, mentioning equality "before the law" and prohibiting that any person be "favored or disfavored" based on group identity, alongside a more tailored requirement that "men and women" have "equal rights." In some cases a constitution might forgo the language of "equality" entirely and opt for direct non-discrimination. The European Convention on Human Rights has no "equality" provision, but rather a "prohibition of discrimination" – Article 15 states that the "enjoyment" of the Convention's "rights and freedoms" will "be secured without discrimination." The French Constitution of 1958, which sets the Republic's maxim as "Liberty, Equality, Fraternity," nonetheless does not include any operative clause regarding equality or non-discrimination. Instead, only the preamble broadly alludes to ensuring "the equality of all citizens before the law, without distinction" and to promoting statutory "equal access by women and men." Most constitutions, old and new, follow a similar pattern.

This habit is not merely semantic. Constitutional (and other legal) mechanisms focus on non-discrimination and on uniform application of the law, simply because broader notions of equality are so vague as to be entirely meaningless. Equality as an abstract philosophical principle or social ideal may encompass a vast expanse of opinions, preferences and policies.* Whether equality is an "essentially contested concept" or not in the technical sense, its meaning and application has certainly always been a matter of enormous debate. Since classical antiquity the idea of equality has been hotly disputed and has been taken to entail or imply a wide range of dilemmas, considerations and outcomes. Different valid conceptions of equality may easily lead to opposite and contradictory prioritizations and policies. To name one example, the familiar distinction between "equality of opportunity" and "equality of outcomes" is well known, especially in the context of economic and welfare policy, and obviously renders utterly different legal arrangements. Another example is the direct (and irreconcilable) tension between political equality (leading to majoritarian democratic mechanisms for governing and rule-making) and almost any other

---

* Similarly, Peter Westen famously argued that equality per se is an "empty idea" because it requires, analytically, a preliminary underlying determination that has nothing to do with equality. Many arguments about equality are nothing but a reflection of an earlier unrelated moral determination.

notion of equality, because virtually any conceivable law (reflecting democratic equality) inevitably contains some inherent elements of inequality (preferring or privileging some over others). In the French Constitution quoted above, the preamble mentioning "equality" also notes the "secular" nature of the Republic – explicitly privileging the interests of secular citizens over those of religious ones, and implicitly reflecting a particular conception of equality which some other jurisdictions would consider to be unacceptable.

Of course, many contend that "equality" contains some distinct conceptual elements, especially within Western political theory and within its democratic tradition. But persuasive universal or philosophical conceptions of equality are extremely limited and particular, and usually regard some notion of *political* equality. Robert A. Dahl defines democracy as a condition of political equality – that is, equal distribution of political power amongst citizens – based on assumptions of broadly equal human ability and competency to participate in collective self-government. Jeremy Waldron's theory of "Basic Equality" takes a similar tack, defining equality as recognizing that humans are fundamentally alike in ways which are relevant for our basic arrangement of society.

One way or another, "equality" per se cannot offer solutions to the dilemmas and tradeoffs of public life. It cannot "do the work." Broad or political conceptions of equality are important and useful, but they are devoid of enforceable legal content which an experienced lawyer could apply. They cannot assist a judge in deciding whether a statute violates "equality" in the vast majority of cases.

This is exactly why constitutional provisions tend to have much more specific definitions of rights or principles related to equality. "Equal protection" of laws or "non-discrimination" of certain classes are infinitely more precise than plain "equality." Much like "Justice," "Truth" or "Virtue," equality is a concept that might or might not have some baseline meaning, but which is itself devoid of concrete content and entirely useless as a binding legal rule for government to follow or for courts to apply. More likely than not, its judicial enforcement can mean only the imposition of a judge's personal opinions and preferences framed as equality-based imperatives. The above applies even more strongly when general "equality" is claimed as an individual, personal right which a court may enforce and supervise. No constitutional democracy subjects government action, let alone primary legislation, to a superior substantive legal norm of abstract "equality."

None, that is, except Israel. The Supreme Court has wholeheartedly embraced a robust and totalizing conception of equality to justify interventions in all forms of government policy, decisions and legislation. It did so, amazingly, in the absence of any enabling statutory language and, as discussed, against the legislature's clear and irrefutable intent to the contrary. In Israeli legal parlance "inequality" has become shorthand for any opposition to government action, expenditure or law. Such legal objections are notably not related to traditional concepts of "equal protection" or of non-discrimination – Israel has a series of non-discrimination statutes which are vigorously enforced, such that in clear-cut discrimination cases there is no need for recourse to abstract "equality." Further still, such challenges are rarely raised in defense of particular individuals or of distinct minorities, but are rather primarily directed towards broad policy plans with no clear "discrimination" against discernible groups or communities. Needless to say, this jurisprudence of vague "equality" has been consistently employed regarding the very same issues that the Knesset sought to exclude from judicial intervention, violating the BL:HDL Section 10 "savings" clause and flouting the deliberate emphasis on the State's Jewish character.

The Ultra-Orthodox Draft Exemption

The invalidated statutes we have surveyed so far were of relative unimportance to the grand scheme of Israeli societal rifts and disputes. We now turn to consider the Supreme Court's judicial review and annulment of laws of a very different kind. These laws either regarded some of the most contentious and controversial issues at the heart of Israeli public debate and disagreement; or involved principal strategic policy with far-reaching long-term consequences impacting millions of people; or usually, both.

In 2012 and again in 2017, the Court struck down separate statutes which had explicitly provided for the exemption of Ultra-Orthodox (also called *Haredi*) men from the military draft, doing so on grounds of equality. There is likely no example more bewildering and egregious than the Court's intervention in the draft exemption, one which even many of the Court's most loyal supporters are often unwilling to defend. It would be no exaggeration to say that the Israeli political order has never recovered from this blow, the effects of which are still acutely felt.

The Ultra-Orthodox exemption from military service in Israel has been discussed earlier in Chapter 4. The exemption, granted en-masse by the Minister of Defense to Ultra-Orthodox Jewish men engaged in religious study (i.e. enrolled in *yeshiva*), is among the most significant points of public contention to exist in Israeli society and politics, surpassed perhaps only by attitudes to the Israel-Palestinian conflict and the territories captured in the 1967 Six-Day War. The majority if Israeli men and women serve in the Israel Defense Forces in their prime of young adulthood – they sacrifice precious years, endure considerable hardship, and at times risk their life and limb. Many continue their service as army reservists. Some feel that the Ultra-Orthodox exemption is profoundly unfair and unjust; many argue that if the Ultra-Orthodox community were to enlist in the military, the added manpower would significantly reduce the burden of those already serving; others see military service as a path for broader integration of the Ultra-Orthodox into Israeli society and workforce.

Despite this and somewhat counterintuitively, the policy has remained relatively stable since the State's inception. Both right-wing and left-wing ruling coalitions have left the exemption broadly intact; at the same time, the Supreme Court had consistently ruled, up until the Barak era, that the matter was one of non-justiciable policy (social, economic and military). As discussed at length in our review of justiciability and the famous *Ressler* cases, a legal challenge to the draft exemption in 1988 was again dismissed, though this time the Court under Justice Barak deemed the issue to be fully justiciable and subject to the Court's judgment.

It is here that we pick up where we had left off. The maneuver initiated by Barak in 1988 bore fruit exactly a decade later in the 1998 *Rubenstein* case. In yet another challenge to the draft exemption, the Court ruled that the Minister of Defense could not rely on his general exemption-making authority in order to grant the blanket Ultra-Orthodox exemption – rather, the Knesset would need to enact new legislation which explicitly authorized such exemption specifically for the Ultra-Orthodox community. In doing so, the Court developed a doctrine under which "primary arrangements" must be enacted by the legislature and cannot be formulated by executive officers under a statutory grant of broad authority – somewhat similar to both the "non-delegation doctrine" and the "major questions doctrine" in the U.S.

Critically, the Court justified its decision – and its sharp deviation from half a century of precedent – by referring, of course, to the 1995 constitutional revolution. The Court argued that the 1992 Basic Laws had altered the Israeli legal system and constitutional order in a manner indirectly requiring that important issues be stipulated via parliamentary legislation and not through executive policymaking.[14] The outcome of *Rubenstein* was that the Ultra-Orthodox draft exemption was illegal and invalid unless officially sanctioned in primary legislation (though the operative order was deferred to allow for the Knesset to enact the required statutes).

Though the requirement that such a policy ought to be set by clear statute might seem reasonable at first, the *Rubenstein* ruling suffers from a variety of problems. Two direct legal objections stand out. Section 10 of BL:HDL shields pre-existing law from the Basic Law's effects in the most explicit terms – this would obviously include the Court's prior rulings regarding the draft exemption's legality, and also the legal framework enabling the exemption (that is, the general statutory authorization for the Minister of Defense to grant exemptions). The Court's excuse that it was "only" requiring clearer legislative authorization for the exemption policy – and therefore not violating the Section 10 "savings" clause – is utter nonsense. *Rubenstein* was thus one of the earliest examples of the Court's willingness to simply ignore the unequivocal limitation imposed by Section 10.

Indeed, it is widely agreed that the ruling was a calculated move on Barak's part, intended precisely to circumvent Section 10 limitations. At least in principle the Court could not strike down a law that was enacted earlier than 1992 – this was (at the time) a step too far even for Barak's court. As such, the Court may have felt it could not invalidate the existing "exemptions" statute entirely. However, enacting new legislation would subject any arrangement therein to fresh judicial review and to the Court's malleable standards of constitutional proportionality. In other words, the Court violated Section 10 and interfered with pre-existing law in a seemingly relatively minor way (i.e., requiring new legislation), in order to expose any new law to the far more penetrating and aggressive mechanism of post-*Hamizrachi* judicial review.

This was not the only sense in which *Rubenstein* violated the 1992 Basic Laws. Hillel Sommer points out that in addition to other examples of deliberate constitutional determinations made by the Knesset and flouted by the Court (discussed above), the Knesset had also specifically rejected a "primary arrangements" doctrine that would restrict executive determinations of important issues.[15] BL:HDL explicitly allows for infringement upon rights both by direct statute and "by force of express [statutory] authorization" – that is, by executive action. A previous version of the law, which would have made infringement permissible only by direct statute and for which Justice Barak had advocated, was debated and rejected by the Knesset. In doing so the Knesset rejected the idea that protected rights could only be infringed by direct statute, and deliberately sought to avoid a situation where the Court nullifies policy due to its executive and non-legislative character. In this sense the Court's attribution of a "primary arrangements" doctrine to the 1992 Basic Laws directly contradicts the conscious decision of the Knesset against adopting any such doctrine.

More broadly, even if such a doctrine were to properly exist in Israeli law, the Court's assertion that it precludes the draft exemption simply doesn't hold water. A typical "non-delegation" doctrine is aimed specifically against the exercise of legislative, rule-making functions by other branches of government, and against a potential conferral of such powers by the legislature to another government organ. But any legal and governmental system concedes that broad policy is determined and formulated by the executive branch, including on issues of major significance. The "non-delegation" test is one of function (e.g., "is this executive action tantamount to lawmaking?") and not one of importance (e.g., "is this a decision so important only the legislature can make it?"). A statutory authorization for the Minister of Defense to grant exemptions from military service would be universally acknowledged as sufficient legislative basis for executive policy making regarding the extent and scope of such exemptions; such a policy is not "legislative" in any sense.

This is all the more applicable in a parliamentary system in which the Minister of Defense and the executive Government serve at the pleasure of the elected legislature and are regularly subject to parliamentary oversight. A "primary arrangements" doctrine makes much more sense for a presidential system in which there is more concern regarding an unrestrained executive or agency creating major (and borderline-legislative) policy. This is one reason the similar "major questions" doctrine has recently played a significant role in U.S. Supreme Court decisions. In Israel, the draft exemptions policy clearly had the consistently broad and bipartisan sanction of the legislature for decades – and the legislature (or the Government it appoints and controls) can simply order the Minister of Defense to change such a policy at any time. As such there was never any plausible concern that the Minister of Defense was determining a "major question" of policy beyond the scope granted by statute and against the legislature's wishes.

It's also worth recalling that despite its broader economic and societal implications, the draft exemption was a question of direct military policy. Treating the issue as a "primary arrangement" requiring legislative authorization therefore makes even less sense. Military policy and decision-making are typically – and deliberately – considered a wholly executive enterprise operating under wide and general legislative authority. The Minister's discretion to grant exemptions as he deems appropriate, subject to supervision of the Government and Knesset, is no exception.

A final element of the Court's "primary arrangements" doctrine is the difficulty in legislative enactment of controversial issues as opposed to the executive's relative agility. Passing almost any legislation of consequence is a major challenge in Israel's polarized and contentious political landscape, which is one reason so much policymaking is entrusted to the executive branch. The doctrine's main outcome is therefore often either deep embarrassment for political actors forced to take a concrete stance on controversial issues, or the indefinite burying of important policy decisions in endless parliamentary debates and committees. These are both almost always the intended effect of the "primary arrangements" doctrine applied by the Court. Through the innocuous guise of requiring explicit statutory authorization, the Court is able to handicap almost any undesired executive measure, to significantly delay its implementation or to exact a major political price from its supporters – or usually all the above.

The 1998 *Rubenstein* ruling set the stage for the eventual judicial invalidation of the draft exemption in its entirety. Following a governmental commission report, the Knesset complied with the Court's demand and in 2002 enacted what became known as the "Tal Law" – clear primary legislation explicitly providing for the Ultra-Orthodox draft exemption. Needless to say, this did little to mollify the Court. In a 2006 ruling Barak's Court decided that the new law violated the fundamental right to equality (we will return soon to examine this rationale); but the law was granted an extension of a few more years to see if it might be implemented in some redeeming way. Yet again and in typical fashion, the decision managed to be groundbreaking without causing too much of stir – the Court "dismissed" the petitions and left the law intact, while establishing a "hard" constitutional right to equality and declaring that the draft exemption was essentially unconstitutional.

Finally, in 2012, the Supreme Court struck down the "Tal Law" and completed the process it had initiated a quarter-century earlier in 1988. The petitioner in that case was, once again, Mr. Ressler. A further legislative amendment was enacted in 2015, following a multi-year and multi-Government effort to draft a law that would withstand judicial scrutiny. Alas, this amendment too was struck down in 2017.

The Court's treatment and nullification of these statutes merits analysis on three levels – legal, partisan and societal.

On the legal plane, the Court based both decisions on the unenumerated right to equality which is derived from the enumerated right to human dignity enshrined in BL:HDL. The bald-faced audacity and profound ludicrousness of this legal argument is staggering. As explained in detail above, an enforceable right to equality – in any form – was manifestly rejected by the Knesset as a key component of the compromise which enabled the 1992 legislation in its entirety. Striking down some clearly discriminatory statute based on a violation of abstract equality would have been problematic enough, yet the draft exemption rulings are more outrageous by an order of magnitude. This is because the exemptions, objectionable and damaging as they may be, were a *benefit* conferred on a distinct demographic *minority* by a parliamentary majority. Let that sink in for a moment. The Ultra-Orthodox community in Israel is precisely the kind of "discrete and insular minority" famously described by the U.S. Supreme Court as deserving heightened judicial attention and protection.[*] Indeed, judicial supremacists throughout the democratic world regularly argue for constitutional respect for (and protection of) the communal "autonomy," "integrity" and "culture" of distinct minorities, including various exemptions or allowances. Yet in these cases the Israeli Supreme Court invoked a broad principle of "equality" to revoke the majority's accommodation of a minority group, bizarrely arguing that the electoral majority was discriminating against itself.

This was precisely the objection made by Justice Grunis in his consistent dissenting opinions in which he argued against invalidating the exemptions laws. Grunis describes the counter-majoritarian function of judicial review as a mechanism "for the protection of the minority and of individuals from the despotism of the majority," and continues to explain that the same rationale is inapplicable to the draft exemption. "We must remember that this privilege was granted to the minority group through a democratic resolution made by the Knesset. This means that the majority group was the one that decided to grant the privilege to the members of the minority group… The law's harm in this instance is collective harm to the members of the majority."[16]

The proponents of judicial supremacy in Israel regularly trot out the Court's essential function in shielding vulnerable minorities and individuals from government overreach and especially from the dreaded "tyranny of the majority." But perhaps more than any other, the Court's draft exemption rulings expose such hollow arguments for the fanciful canards that they are. Bearing no relation to the purported protection of minorities or upholding of individual rights, the Court's decisions in this regard constitute a blatant intervention in broad public policy of the utmost gravity and a judicial veto of a painful socio-political compromise at the heart of Israeli public life. They prove just how little the Court's supremacism is about the rule of law and just how hell-bent its judges are on imposing their preferred policy outcomes on the Israeli populace.

---

[*] In Footnote Four of *United States v. Carolene Products Company, 304 U.S. 144 (1938)*

The unbearably inescapable overall point bears reiterating: The Supreme Court struck down the most important legislative compromise in contemporary Israeli society and invalidated a benefit granted to a demographic minority, based on the non-existent and contentless pseudo-constitutional principle of vague equality – all of which the Basic Laws tried to avoid in the first place by a host of constitutional mechanisms.

To be clear, these rulings can't even be squared with broader Israeli law and practice which easily accept group-based "positive" discrimination. Underrepresented minorities and ethnic groups receive a wide array of distinct statutory benefits and privileges, including race-based or gender-based quotas in public agencies and institutions (a practice disqualified in the United States as unconstitutional, with very limited exceptions). Even more to the point, other specific groups enjoy their own exemption from military service – most notably, Israeli Arab citizens and Jewish religious women upon request. And get this: The blanket exemption for Israeli Arabs isn't set in any statute nor even in any formal order or policy of the Defense Ministry. Rather, it is based on the "discretion" of military "recruiters" who, since the State's inception and as a de facto matter of government policy, have not enforced the military draft against Israel's Arab minority. Though utterly undermining the Court's jurisprudence of minority-exemption as impermissible inequality, the question of Israeli-Arab military exemption is, extraordinarily, completely ignored by the Court itself in its rulings. Needless to say, the Court has never applied its "primary arrangements" doctrine to the Arab Israeli exemption from military service.

On the societal plane the Court's interventions have evidently done little to ameliorate the actual problem they were supposed to address. It is a matter of observable fact that the Ultra-Orthodox community still doesn't serve in the military, making the Court's interventions an epic failure by any practical measure – one reminiscent of the controversy surrounding abortions in the United States. Regardless of anyone's take on *Roe v. Wade*, it seems indisputable that the U.S. Supreme Court did not "resolve" the contentious issue of abortion in any sense, despite that court's ill-fated statement two decades later that "it is settled now." As Justice Antonin Scalia observed in *Planned Parenthood v. Casey*, not only did the court's ruling "not… resolve the deeply divisive issue," it rather "did more than anything else to nourish it," "fanned into life an issue that has inflamed our national politics," "destroyed the compromises of the past" and "rendered compromise impossible for the future."

Scalia in 1992 could not be more relevant to Israel in 2025. The Supreme Court's decisions on the draft exemption have had a polarizing and destabilizing effect which cannot be overstated. As is often the case with judicial resolution of contentious issues, public discourse shifts from a dialogue seeking social compromise to mutual accusations of coercion and of illegality. Both sides of the debate become more dogmatic, radical and entrenched in their respective positions with far less incentive for constructive communication or nuanced perspectives, as their differences are transplanted from deliberative transactional politics into the zero-sum courtroom environment. In a tragically predictable way, the Court has only succeeded in exacerbating the severe political and ideological fault-lines surrounding the issue, with a consensual resolution seeming further away than it has ever been.

The trend has taken tangible political form over the past decade, with Ultra-Orthodox parties far more wary of cooperation with the secular State, and opponents of the exemption adopting uncompromising hardline positions. Indeed, a significant portion of Israel's recent political turmoil is directly tied to the judicially-forced controversies of Ultra-Orthodox military service – a point overlooked by many observers. It was the Court's 2017 ruling which ultimately brought about the Government's collapse in 2019 (after a key partner withdrew from the Coalition over exemption-related disputes), ushering in the worst political crisis in Israeli history with five election cycles over three years. The failure of any consistent Coalition to form a stable Government over that time was directly rooted in the inability to reach compromises regarding the draft exemption under the shadow of the Court's rulings.

The Court's position is also at least to some extent overtly partisan in its repercussions. The sectorial Ultra-Orthodox parties have increasingly become a staple and crucial component of right-wing Coalitions, especially in the era dominated by Benjamin Netanyahu. Yet their political existence and main value proposition to their voters depends a great deal on their ability to deliver on key policies such as the draft exemption. A genuine effort by the government to forcibly enlist unwilling Ultra-Orthodox men, physically dragging them from homes and communities, would necessarily lead to their political representatives withdrawing from the Coalition and causing its collapse. In this sense the Court's rulings put any duly-elected right-wing government in an untenable position – either circumvent the rulings and defy the Court, or comply and commit political suicide. In other words, the Court's jurisprudence on draft exemptions is seen by many a direct assault on the core viability and feasibility of all modern Israeli right-wing Coalitions. In an ironic twist this has started to unexpectedly backfire – Ultra-Orthodox parties have become *more* beholden to right-wing Coalitions and are willing to go to *greater* lengths to avoid their Government's collapse, due to the feared alternative of a left-wing Coalition implementing the Court's hardline approach.

Justice Barak observed in his 2006 opinion that the draft exemption issue "raises complex and difficult problems which are social, military and ideological in nature." These extend well beyond the context of individual exemptions and pose a "general problem" for the Ultra-Orthodox sector and for "all of Israeli society." The issue's solution is "mired in bitter controversy between different segments" of the Israeli public. Without irony, Barak declares that the issue ought to be addressed by "a social and consensual solution, based on toleration and understanding." Yet the Court showed no interest in heeding its own advice, and none of these truths deterred its Justices from their unilateral crusade; and it was precisely such a "consensual solution," arrived at by Israel's elected legislature, that has been time and again unceremoniously sunk by the Court. From 1988 to 2025 judicial meddling has not moved the needle one iota; the Court nonetheless persists to this day with no sign of reflection or remorse.

One's opinion of the Ultra-Orthodox draft exemption is immaterial for present purposes. As do many Israelis, I myself have deep reservations about the current arrangements as they stand. Israeli public life has grappled with the contradictions, dilemmas and tensions presented by the Ultra-Orthodox community since the State's founding, which have increasingly come to dominate electoral and political controversy. Yet these challenges and their dramatic intensification are impossible to understand without grasping their subjection to the Court's incessant, radical, lawless and corrosive interference. In its ambition of socio-political domination, the Supreme Court's hubristic attempt to resolve the exemption controversy by pure judicial fiat is a marvel of impetuous, reckless, indefensible arrogance. It is a stain on the prestige of judicial office anywhere, offensive to the most fundamental precepts of democracy, good government and common sense. More than almost any issue, it is a testament to the trail of chaos and destruction left by Aharon Barak's legacy and by the Court's unbounded quest for ultimate political power.

Core Policy and Judicial Government

The Supreme Court did not limit its appetite to mundane trivialities nor to the centrally contested matter of military exemptions, and found cause to strike down primary legislation reflecting major core policy and affecting millions – all on the shaky and dubious foundation of manufactured "equality," vague "dignity" and deeply subjective "proportionality." As we survey these cases, it's worth again stressing that our review here focuses only on Knesset legislation struck down by the Court, while we skip over the countless instances of relevant judicial intervention in executive State action.

Israel has always been and maintained a sprawling welfare state, with substantial subsidized public services and significant personal entitlements for large swaths of its population. The 1985 "Budget Foundations Law" provides the broad legislative framework for the annual State budget, which is itself enacted as a Knesset statute. Since at least the 1980s, the State annual budget has included a specific appropriation of public funds to provide supplemental income for "Yeshiva" students that met certain welfare eligibility criteria. Typically belonging to the Jewish Ultra-Orthodox community, these are individuals belonging to religious institutions and engaged in religious learning as a full-time occupation. The vast majority of them are resigned to a life of limited income and even of relative poverty (albeit, arguably, by their own choice).

A series of petitions to the Supreme Court challenged this budgetary appropriation due to its "inequality," in the sense that comparable college or university students in secular institutions were not personally entitled to similar benefits. Laws providing for general supplemental income and unemployment benefits explicitly exclude ordinary students engaged in academic study or pursuing professional training.

In a 2010 majority decision,* the Court invalidated the budgetary "supplemental income" provision for Yeshiva students due to its violation of a requirement for "equal distribution" between "public institutions" found in the Budget Foundations Law.[17] The invalidation was prospective, such that it would apply to future budgetary provisions and not the current one in force – once again establishing a dramatic legal precedent while postponing its effects to minimize public scrutiny. In doing so the Court performed a number of creative legal acrobatics – first, because direct welfare distribution to individuals does not involve "public institutions" (the Court extended the "spirit" of this requirement to all distributions); second, because the "Budget Foundations Law" is not a Basic Law and enjoys no constitutional status by the Court's own standards, and therefore occupies the same legal tier as the budget legislation itself (the Court ruled nonetheless that the two pieces of legislation form an internal hierarchy, and in any case found the law in violation of the BL:HDL "right to equality"). These points alone are enough to render the Court's ruling patently groundless. Delightfully, the Court didn't even bother raising the Section 10 "savings clause" that shields pre-existing law from judicial review, even though the practice at issue had existed for many decades.

Such legal convolutions notwithstanding, the more obvious and principled objection is that the elected Knesset is perfectly entitled to appropriate funds for different purposes which reflect its values and priorities, even if such determinations seem arbitrary or objectionable. Virtually any distribution of public funds must inevitably involve some degree of preference for one group or cause over another. This specific appropriation evinced a legislative interest in enabling or encouraging religious learning for its own sake – perhaps ill-advised or even obnoxious to many of us, perhaps a damaging economic incentive against productive education and work, perhaps an unfair neglect of struggling university students (I myself was one such law student), this was nonetheless a valid budgetary decision made by an elected legislature. As stated by Justice Levy in his dissenting opinion: "The budget statute reflects its policy goals, which are determined by the Government and the Knesset and not by the Court." The State is entitled to "provide or not provide" grants of supplemental income or to "privilege or not privilege" specific activities as it deems appropriate, and in doing so may determine "at what sums."

After the budgetary provision was struck down in 2010, and following recommendations of a committee established to report on the matter, the Government once again resolved to provide supplemental income (this time formulated as a "scholarship") and new funds were allocated in the State annual budget. Alas, after the budget was passed into law, the Court once again

* In typical fashion, the petition was filed in 2000; a hearing held in 2007; and the decision handed down in 2010.

invalidated the statutory appropriation as an impermissible form of inequality, in a unanimous 2014 ruling.[18] The main opinion penned by Justice Rubinstein ended with a postscript in which Rubinstein relayed an encounter with a destitute Yeshiva student: the young man was asking for donations towards clothes for his upcoming wedding, and Rubinstein lamented the youth's decision to marry despite being healthy (i.e., able to work), jobless and penniless. Whatever Rubinstein was trying to get at with this yarn, the impression it leaves is perhaps not the one he intended. Justice Rubinstein clearly disapproved of the supplemental income provision as simply bad policy, and so he struck it down. The superfluous previous forty pages of his ruling do little to alter this impression.

The topic of welfare and resource-allocation brings us conveniently to another law struck down by the Supreme Court in the 2012 *tax benefits* decision. A patchwork of Israeli tax legislation granted various benefits (primarily deductions reducing taxable income) to residents of specific towns and villages which were for the most part named on an individual basis. The benefits applied to some 167 towns with no discernible guiding rationales or consistent eligibility criteria – these towns dotted the country's length and breadth (though many were adjacent to high-risk national borders), and were diverse in terms of various socioeconomic and demographic characteristics. Some of these towns had a population which was predominantly Jewish, Arab or Druze.

A slew of legislative tax amendments were eventually challenged as unconstitutional due to their arbitrariness amounting to discrimination – there was simply no clear reason why some towns were eligible and some weren't, why tax deductions were higher for some towns and lower for others, and so on. In a unanimous three-member panel, the Court struck down part of the tax amendments and demanded that the Knesset enact transparent and objective eligibility criteria for towns to receive the tax benefits.[19] The *tax benefits* decision was based, naturally, on the "disproportionate" violation of the unenumerated right to equality.

Some obvious objections are that the Knesset may legitimately choose to grant tax benefits to whomever it pleases; that arbitrary policy privileging specific towns may be deeply disagreeable but hardly rises to grounds for invalidity (especially in light of the wobbly legal basis for constitutional "equality"); and that such criticism ought to be left to public forums and to the electorate's judgment. Setting these aside, the *tax benefits* ruling provides an opportunity to highlight two other aspects of the Court's judicial review.

First is the role of the Legal Counsel to the Government. It seems one reason the Court may have thought the benefits were indefensible was that no defense was offered. In representing the Government and its policy the LCG refused to argue for the tax amendments in any way, explaining to the Court that the legislation was flawed enough to put its legality in doubt and ultimately agreeing that it ought to be invalidated. As the Government received no alternative authentic representation, the ruling provides no real information regarding the Government's actual position – including, and especially, regarding the rationales for selecting the benefit-eligible towns. Some of the towns which were already recipients of tax benefits (and that wanted the law left intact) had indeed filed briefs arguing that the tax selections were not arbitrary at all, but the Court dismissed these in just a paragraph or two (out of forty pages). Perhaps the inclusion of some towns and the exclusion of others was not as arbitrary as the Court claimed them to be; or perhaps the Court felt that the genuine rationales would be acceptable to the public (even if unacceptable to the Court) and that explicitly rejecting these would trigger some popular backlash. One way or another, from the ruling itself it is impossible to discern whether the Government thought it had good reason to choose as it did, what those reasons might have been, or whether the Court considered these at all.

Aside speaking to the merits of the case (if not arbitrary, then perhaps also not unequal and unlawful?), this illustrates a broader point surrounding the Government's legal representation in such judicial review cases. This topic was covered extensively in the previous chapter and does not require further elaboration. Yet it's worth keeping in mind that in many of the cases discussed in the current chapter, on top of any other adverse factor, the Government has often received legal "representation" ranging from the ineffectual, to the abysmal, to the downright hostile. In several cases which resulted in a law being struck down, one can find the "government" (that is, the LCG) offering the weakest arguments, conceding key points, and generally taking great care to assist the petitioners and to provide the Court with ample justifications for overturning legislation under review. The tax benefits case is but one example of many.*

A second point regards the Court's limitless lack of self-awareness. This was a ruling striking down primary legislation in which the Knesset made a series of particular decisions, supposedly with no clear rationales to guide them. The Court demanded that such policy be based on criteria or principles that were clear, public, objective, coherent and consistent. Hopefully at this stage there is no need to explain the irony of such demands, emanating from a court that developed the "unreasonableness" grounds or that fabricated and employs a right to "equality" to invalidate laws. The Supreme Court of Israel censuring the Knesset for a lack of coherent or objective rules surely breaks a record of some kind.

Since 2013 the Supreme Court has struck down no less than five (!) laws which had attempted to curb illegal immigration into Israel.

Towards the end of my mandatory military service, in 2009, my unit was placed on patrol duty along the Israeli-Egyptian border. Though our official mission was to deter and prevent terror-related threats and drug-trafficking across the border, we quickly realized that our de facto job was a sort of welcoming

---

* At some point the Knesset got so fed up it established its own litigation department which was entitled (by statute) to argue on the Knesset's behalf whenever a law was challenged in court. Despite the improvement, the LCG still appears in any such case and often argues against the Government and Knesset.

committee for illegal economic migrants, making the long and perilous journey from sub-Saharan Africa – mostly Eritrea, though also South Sudan and elsewhere – to find work in Israel. The 128-mile Israeli border with Egypt was porous and at the time contained almost no substantial physical barriers. Every few days we would discover a dozen migrants or so, running across the border or sitting by the road (on the Israeli side) waiting to be discovered. They were offered food and drink, shelter, and initial medical treatment if required, before being sent for formal processing with the civilian immigration services. Often some were injured, either from the unforgiving journey through the Sinai desert or from Egyptian fire – the rumor was that Egypt had ordered its military to shoot any migrants they identify crossing the border. I especially recall finding a young man, likely no older than I was at the time, lying sprawled by the border after being hit by an Egyptian bullet. He had already died when we arrived.

Until 2006 illegal immigration across the Egyptian border – technically termed "infiltration" – was extremely rare, with approximately 2,000 migrants *ever* recorded over the course of nearly six decades. The numbers then suddenly skyrocketed, almost overnight. In 2007 alone there were over 5,000 such migrants crossing the border. Then nearly 9,000 entered in 2008. In 2010 the number jumped to 14,000 and in the following year to over 17,000. By that time it was clear that Israel had an acute border infiltration crisis.

Illegal immigration from third-world countries to developed economies has become one of the most contentious issues in the Western world. In the United States this has become a central – perhaps *the* central – point of policy disagreement between broad political camps. Despite this, the U.S. is something of an outlier due to the issue remaining broadly within the spheres of public debate and government policy. In many (even most) other Western jurisdictions, the question of how to address illegal immigration has been acutely judicialized – that is, it has been subjected to intense judicial scrutiny and involvement, typically under various frameworks of human rights and international law. To say Israel is no exception would be an understatement – few areas of Israeli government policy have received quite so much judicial attention as has that of immigration.

In some senses Israel's illegal immigration dilemmas reflect those faced by many other contemporary Western countries. Similarly, the inherent tension between individual human rights (especially such rights as afforded to non-citizens entering a jurisdiction illegally) and valid governmental immigration policy presents genuine legal difficulties which each jurisdictions might confront differently. In other senses, however, the Israeli case stands out with some unique characteristics.

Perhaps most significantly: Israel is the only economically developed country to share a land border with continental Africa.* While many Africans migrants cross the Mediterranean Sea to reach European shores, there is in fact only one comparable country which migrants might reach without the need to cross a large body of water – the State of Israel. In this sense the Israeli-Egyptian border bears

* The only partial exception being the Spanish territories of Melilla and Ceuta.

the potential for mass immigration from Africans seeking better living conditions or escaping hardship, in a way which is distinct from that affecting European countries. Further, Israel has never colonized territories in Africa or historically dispossessed African people, such that it does not share in any "colonialist guilt" which might drive, at least in some part, European acquiescence to (or justification of) African immigration. Israel is also a relatively small country in both size and population. Unlike typical targets of mass immigration (such as France, Germany, Italy, the U.S., Canada, etc.), Israel's demographics are at the risk of profound alteration or destabilization with only a fraction of the immigration numbers faced by larger countries. In addition, Israel is isolated geographically and politically from its neighbors – such that migrants are generally unable to smoothly continue onwards to another country, and the likelihood of reaching some regional framework for distribution and dispersion of migrants is extremely low. Finally, Israel faces unique security and defense challenges in its conflicts with immediate neighboring countries and with terrorist entities, such that an inability to control who enters the country poses a direct and untenable security threat (and the fact that many migrants came from Sudan, a country intensely hostile to Israel, is also relevant to this point).

These considerations are added to the ordinary factors with which many countries contend in formulating official immigration policy and in dealing with challenges of illegal immigration. We may proceed with this background in mind.

Since gaining public attention in 2005 consecutive Governments attempted to address the issue of migrant infiltration in a variety of ways. Some were successful, some ineffectual. Physical barriers erected throughout the border were only partially effective. Many executive measures (such as immediate "hot return" of migrants back to Egyptian custody) were disqualified or limited by the Supreme Court. These developments unfortunately cannot be covered here in detail. Finally, in 2012, the Knesset enacted a major legislative initiative meant to directly tackle – and significantly restrict – the phenomenon of illegal infiltration into Israel. The new statute essentially provided that illegal migrants could be detained in a special facility (somewhat akin to imprisonment) for up to three years. Primarily due to this component of detention, the law was challenged by numerous legal petitions.

In the unanimous 2013 *Adam* ruling, the Supreme Court struck down the law as an unconstitutional violation of the migrants' right to liberty (including physical freedom of movement), among other constitutional rights (such as dignity and privacy).[20] The majority decision from Justice Edna Arbel is a typical example of rights-based "proportional" reasoning – ultimately concluding that three years of detention was disproportionate, in the sense that the harm to migrant rights far outweighed the alleged policy benefits. We will return to this conclusion momentarily.

A separate declaration by the Court, noteworthy in itself, was the relatively rare disqualification of the statute's "purpose." The BL:HDL limitation clause requires that a right may be violated only for a "proper purpose," though the Court has historically avoided exploring what that might mean, and has instead usually focused on its familiar proportionality tests. Yet in the *Adam* case the Court identified two separate purposes for the law in question: One was to prevent the specific detained migrant from "settling" in Israel (and presumably to better enable their departure or expulsion if legally warranted); the other purpose was to "curb" broader illegal immigration by creating migration (and income-earning) less feasible and therefore less attractive to potential future migrants. This was essentially a purpose of deterrence, though the Government didn't use that specific word. Relying on Kantian philosophy, Justice Arbel reasoned (in *dicta*) that the "deterrent" purpose was in and of itself unconstitutional, because using a human-being as a "means" to achieve a separate "end" was a severe violation of their own personal human dignity, which required that any human be treated as an "end-in-itself."

Setting aside analytical errors (a harm to dignity seems more appropriately analyzed in the proportionality stage, and does not render the "deterrence" purpose as per se improper) Arbel's argument here is illustrative of a broader point. The Court's rejection of "deterrence" as a viable purpose of immigration policy on the one hand, and its conclusion that the harm in detention was disproportionate to the benefits of reducing illegal immigration, on the other hand, are both essentially pure value-based determinations of a public and moral nature. "Balancing" or "weighing" *in principle* the harm caused to liberty by a three-year detention period, against the benefit of substantially curbing illegal immigration – that is, prioritizing individual interest versus broad public welfare – is a classic question of public policy to be considered and decided by the electorate and its appointed government. It is not in any sense a legal question, and no amount of legal training or experience will yield a "correct" answer prescribing the appropriate balance. By the same token, whether "deterrence" is necessarily an "improper" consideration (or purpose) for policymakers is a question of values, not law. Put differently, whether Emmanuel Kant's abstract principle of humans as "ends-in-themselves" ought to apply to parliamentary legislation is a manifestly political and ideological matter to be determined by the political process, not by judges. Yet the Court sees no problem with stating, categorically, that a purpose of "deterrence" is unconstitutional per se, with the outcome of invalidating primary legislation – a declaration not derived of any form of legal reasoning or principled legal analysis.

Just a few months following the Court's decision, the Knesset re-legislated the law with substantial changes. Now the maximal detention period was for one year (instead of three), and only new illegal migrants could be detained. Existing migrants that had entered previously would be partially restricted at a separate "open" facility – they would have to sleep there and to "check in" multiple times daily, but were permitted to leave during the day and move freely throughout the country.

In 2014 the Supreme Court struck down this new statute for similar reasons it had invalidated the previous one, though this time it needed a cool 216 pages.[21]

The Chief Justice, Asher Grunis, dissented forcefully (though he had concurred with the majority in the previous ruling). Grunis points out the arbitrary nature of the Court's reasoning – it was now saying that a maximum detention of one year was too much and disproportionate, without disqualifying the act of detention itself. The violation was therefore one of quantity, not quality. What, then, per the Court, is an "appropriate" amount of time for maximum detention? And why is the Court's judgment of this issue to be preferred over that of the Knesset? Grunis maintains that the Court has no real answer to either question. Indeed, the majority opinion itself concedes that numerous other countries (including Australia, Italy, Greece and Malta) employ mechanisms far more restrictive than the one proposed by the new law – such that there is no clear or obvious degree of "proportionate" detention. And three of the nine judges on the panel thought that the one-year detention limit was acceptable and constitutional, further demonstrating the arbitrary and subjective nature of any such evaluation.

Grunis also emphasized that this was no ordinary law or legal challenge – the Knesset was responding immediately, directly and explicitly to the Court's previous ruling and had taken the Court's position into account. As such the new law now had the added weight of the Knesset's deliberate desire to insist on a particular policy (though materially tempered from its first iteration) in full view of the Court's earlier *Adam* decision. This was not comparable to judicial review of a "fresh" law in which the Knesset may not have been sufficiently cognizant of alleged violation of rights. Here, the Knesset chose to proceed with a particular policy while fully aware of the Court's objections. Per Grunis, this justified an especially heightened degree of judicial deference and restraint.

Following that ruling, the Knesset attempted – now a *third* time – to pass legislation addressing illegal immigration. The maximum time for detention of new infiltrators was reduced to three months; the maximum time for requiring that existing migrants report to an "open" facility was capped at twenty months, and the amount of daily "check-ins" reduced to one.

In a 2015 ruling the Court invalidated the law yet again. The three-month detention time was technically "approved," though only on the condition that it be interpreted to mean that the maximal detention time would only be reached in extreme circumstances. The maximal time for attending the open facility was reduced from twenty months, to twelve months. The only real dissent was mounted by Justice Neal Hendel (Grunis had retired by then), who noted that the Knesset had incorporated significant changes and had clearly made an effort to comply with the Court's restrictions while trying to maintain their own policy goals.

Thus, over the course of three short years, the Supreme Court had struck down the Knesset's three primary legislative attempts to address the crisis of illegal immigration. It is indisputable that absent the measures the Knesset had tried to adopt, African migrants were far less deterred to make their way to Israel, and existing migrants had far less incentive to return to their home countries. Perhaps the Court's decisions were beneficial or more humane; perhaps they caused much greater suffering for all those involved (current migrants, future migrants and local communities that were heavily affected). What is certain is that the Justices that decided these cases were never appointed by the public to determine such questions of policy; and that they will never be held accountable for the consequences of their fateful decisions.

The *Adam* ruling and its successors demonstrate some of the typical and universally recognized problems with rights-based judicial review of broad government policy, especially within the context of immigration. Framing such judicial review solely through the prism of individual (migrant) rights distorts some of the key factors in any such policy. For one thing, also the rights of others are acutely affected – allowing unfettered illegal immigration will materially affect the rights and interests of current citizens (especially those belonging to particular groups or localities). More importantly, any immigration policy in the world is by definition aimed at affecting the incentives of potential future migrants – though this view might lead to decisions which are sometimes tragic and unpleasant, focusing only on those who have already arrived necessarily obscures the bigger picture. This is one reason the Court's disapproval of "deterrence" is so bizarre – all immigration policy is, in some sense, deterrence. The Israeli immigration cases show precisely how a personal human right to "liberty" or "dignity" (alongside the purported balancing of competing interests) is easily translated into virtually any judicially-desired immigration policy – or, more typically, into a non-policy which grants an effective license of unrestricted immigration.

Regardless of whether one is persuaded by the Court's arguments or supports the outcomes of these cases, one has to acknowledge the abject helplessness of the Knesset and the electorate that appoints its members. Here were public representatives trying to address a genuine and severe problem of enormous consequence, with immediate effects felt by millions and with long-term repercussions even more dramatic. Three times the Knesset tried enacting effective laws to address the problem as legislators saw fit; three times a panel of nine Justices voided these laws and sent the Knesset back to square one. What viable course of action was available to the Knesset so it could implement the policy it considered best, for which it was elected and for which it was accountable? In 2015 the answers clearly seemed to be – none.

Incidentally, or not, 2015 was the first year in which legal reform became a major part of a political elections campaign. The 2015 election results brought about the appointment of Ayelet Shaked as Minister of Justice, who in many respects introduced (or at least re-introduced) legal conservatism into the mainstream political agenda.

To complete our description, two more laws related to illegal immigration were struck down by the Supreme Court. As the Knesset became increasingly desperate it enacted a statute to create an economic incentive for illegal migrants to return to their home country or to resettle elsewhere. Part of the 2014 legislation included a "deposit" scheme by which roughly twenty percent of a migrant's income would be withheld as long as they remained in Israel; the funds were to be released upon leaving Israel. Twenty percent was not substantially more than what most Israeli citizens are required (by law) to set aside for their pension funds, social security, universal healthcare, and so on.

The Court invalidated the "deposit" scheme in 2020, as an impermissible violation of the migrants' property rights.

Another form of illegal immigration unrelated to border infiltration had developed as part of Israel's foreign worker program. Workers from foreign (usually third-world or underdeveloped) countries were granted temporary visas to live in Israel and work in specific industries and occupations for a limited period of time. A growing proportion of these workers would stay in Israel and continue work after their visa had expired, becoming illegal economic migrants by default. One mechanism for dealing with such "overstays" was financial. Statutory law (since at least 2000) required that employers deposit additional supplemental wages for their foreign worker employees (again, similar to social security and pension fund supplements), to be saved and managed in a separate bank account and not accessible to the workers. Workers may receive these funds upon leaving Israel on time or early – but if they stay beyond their visa expiration, the State may confiscate the funds by increasing proportion. According to the statute, the longer a worker overstays the less funds will be available for them to recover, from 15% confiscated after one month and the entire deposit (100%) after six months (with various grace periods, delays and discretionary exceptions).

In a 2023 seven-Justice ruling the Supreme Court struck down the statutory confiscation mechanism, holding it to disproportionately violate the workers' property rights.[22] The single dissent came from Justice Solberg, who points out a number glaring flaws in the Court's reasoning. Chief among these is that the foreign worker enters Israel as part of a voluntary contractual arrangement under which they are informed and fully aware of the statutory deposit and its potential for confiscation in the event of the worker staying past their visa expiration. This is a consensual deal struck between the foreign worker and the temporary host state, the terms of which are known and into which the worker enters as a competent adult. Further still, the worker may reasonably be expected to bear the consequences for their own decision to remain in Israel past their visa expirations, consequences to which they had already agreed in advance. Per Solberg, the legal significance of this arrangement is that the worker's constitutional "right to property" is, to begin with, not nearly as expansive as it might typically otherwise be, especially with regard to such "deposit" funds. In this sense the protected right to property was not violated at all by the deposit-confiscation mechanism.

Solberg also compellingly argues in his dissent that even were one to conclude that the statute infringed upon the worker's property rights, the infringement clearly and easily passes any proportionality test. This includes various mitigating procedures, exceptions, grace periods and appeal challenges. Chiefly, the limited (and conditional) harm to property rights were easily outweighed by the significant and legitimate governmental interest in ensuring that foreign workers adhered to the law and to the terms of their entry into Israel, and that a permit for foreign employment did not become an alternative avenue for illegal immigration.

As always, whether one agrees or disagrees with the statute in question or with the ruling outcome – in both these cases – is immaterial. In both cases the elected legislature made a policy determination which involves a host of factors and considerations, many of them ideological and moral as much as they are economic or empirical. Though perhaps debatable and even objectionable, neither arrangement remotely approaches some standard of severe violation of human rights and individual liberties, and both easily fall within the valid and legitimate policy-making power exclusively reserved to the only elected and accountable branch of government. In both cases the Court casually overstated the severity and impact of the alleged violation, while it downplayed the significant policy interests and implications and while it ignored the critical factor of contributory personal culpability on the part of those being harmed. The Court's reframing of such issues as purely objective legal questions regarding rights, which may be resolved (and annulled) by way of neutral judicial "balancing," is deceptive as it is illusory. Once again the Court foisted its preferred policy preferences on an unwilling parliament and electorate, on issues of tremendous national gravity and of negligible (or easily tolerable) individual harm.

The last case within our current review of interventions in core governmental policy regards civilian and Ministerial control of the National Police. The issue of Police autonomy and a lack of effective civilian control has been broadly discussed in Chapter 7. To partially address some of the significant flaws in the way the Police is subject to civilian political oversight, the Knesset enacted a number of legislative amendments in 2022. These amendments were based on similar existing statutes regarding the military and Defense Minister, and were aimed at clarifying and specifying the hierarchy between the superior Minister and subordinate National Police. The new statutory language is straightforward and set out in clear terms that the general policies and priorities of the Police are subject to the broad authority, supervision and direction of the relevant Government Minister.

Naturally, the amendments were challenged almost immediately; and needless to say, the legal challenges were entertained despite there being no aggrieved party with standing, no discernible person that was affected or harmed, no clear legal right alleged, and despite the question being one of foundational political and governmental policy regarding the State's primary law enforcement agency. In the 2025 *Police Ordinance* ruling, the Supreme Court struck down one of the statute's key provisions, in a divided majority decision of five versus four Justices. The disqualified provision of 8D is worth quoting in its entirety:

> "The Minister may stipulate general policy in the field of investigations, including the determination of priority principles, after hearing the position of the Legal Counsel to the Government and consulting with the

> Police Commissioner and with Police officials responsible for investigations."

The same provision states that such authority does not affect the Police's discretion and autonomy to conduct any investigation, including its initiation and conclusion. In other words, the law clarifies the Minister's authority to define the Police's investigative policy in broad principled strokes, and does not enable the Minister to issue orders regarding any particular investigation at any stage. Such a law would seem almost obvious, and is certainly standard in almost any democratic regime, under the fundamental precept that law enforcement must be subject to broad civilian-political direction and directly accountable to elected officials. Any police organization is ultimately limited by finite resources and must make determinations regarding areas on which to focus police activity. Some examples of different areas vying for police attention might include traffic and driving violations; local property crime; bureaucratic and political corruption; violent gang crime; financial fraud and white collar crime; organized crime and racketeering; manufacture, smuggling and sale of contraband or narcotics; domestic abuse; general public safety; and many, many more. The list is as endless as the human capacity for mischief. It is the role of accountable and elected government – not of career bureaucrats – to define some general prioritization of police efforts addressing each of these areas of criminal conduct. As discussed in Chapter 7, an institutional lack of law enforcement responsiveness to local public needs and desires makes such national oversight especially crucial.

Nonetheless, the Court invalidated this provision as unconstitutional. The reasoning presented by the Court's majority is remarkable (though frankly, at this point we may be grateful that the Justices bother with offering any reasoning at all). The Court's decision rests on two arguments. First, the statute has the *potential* to conceivably lead to actual abuse of police power and to introduce improper considerations in police decision-making (e.g., trying to please the Minister), which might in turn bring about the violation of various liberty and dignity rights. Second, more broadly, the statute allegedly "alters the balance" between Ministerial authority on the one hand, and Police autonomy and professional discretion on the other hand (though the Court never really explains why or how this is). Combined with the aforementioned *potential* for abuse or improper considerations, this "imbalance" diminishes the public standing of the Police in a manner which constitutes its own "distinct and independent violation" of human dignity. In other words, the risk of creating a subjective image or *perception* of a Police force beholden to improper or undue Ministerial influence is, in and of itself, a violation of human *dignity* for anyone affected by police conduct.

If the reader is scratching their head, they are not alone. At least four other Justices on the Court felt the same way. The first argument is easy enough to dismiss – throughout the world and indeed in the Court's own prior jurisprudence, speculative harm is never sufficient cause for judicial intervention, let alone for striking down a law (!). The assertion that a statute *may* enable abuse (itself an unsubstantiated estimation) is patently unremarkable, and likely applies to large swaths of all laws concerning human government conduct (including, as one Justice observed, to all police powers to arrest or search individuals). The majority opinion admits that nothing in the new statute itself permits *a priori* abuse or misconduct. As the dissenting Justices stress, any police (or Ministerial) conduct and decisions would be directly subject to all the typical administrative and constitutional supervision mechanisms, including of course direct judicial review. Potential future harm on speculative grounds is a preposterous and profoundly baseless justification for invalidating otherwise-valid legislation.

The second argument is more difficult to address because of its sheer silliness (if the reader will pardon the legal jargon). The alleged subjective perception of a "compromised" police force is a severe violation of human dignity? What does that even mean? In English or in Hebrew, the words are clear yet they are incapable of forming a coherent rational claim. There is simply no logical link between propositions A and B insofar as any of the involved words possess discernible meaning. Gibberish is always hard to refute.

Though the Court's unintelligible argument here is beyond comprehension, its motivation is no great mystery. With the limited exceptions of *Quatinsky* (a fundamental procedural flaw) and of the *Reasonableness* ruling (to be examined later), the Court still maintains the façade of judicial review based on protection of individual human rights set out in (or derived of) the quasi-constitutional Basic Laws. As such it is reluctant to strike down a law based on abstract principles or just, well, "because." For this reason the Court feels compelled to justify its decisions within the framework of right-infringements, proportionality analysis, et cetera, and must impose the rights paradigm on cases to which it bears no relation. This best illuminates the Court's peculiar and nonsensical argument – in the absence of any familiar grounds for judicial review, and with a clear lack of anyone's rights being actually violated, the Court had to concoct a contrived connection between broad police accountability to the public and a "right to human dignity."

Of course, this tactic is counterproductive to the Court's larger ambitions. The *Police Ordinance* decision demonstrates precisely what many critics of rights-based adjudication have argued all along – that a purported "right" may be asserted to support virtually any pure policy prescription. The Court seems determined to prove them right. The illegal immigration cases discussed above were at least anchored in tangible individual rights that were indisputably harmed by – and indeed were the immediate target of – the government policy in question; they involved a clear question of rights versus public interest. But the *Police Ordinance* case shows the extent to which both "rights" and "harm" can be conceptualized at a high level of abstraction justifying judicial intervention in any issue imaginable.

The point crystallizes when the Court's reasoning is phrased in reverse: The individual constitutional "right to human dignity" contains an inherently fundamental and inviolable *collective public right* to the *subjective perception* of *proper and impartial police conduct* which is *uninhibited* by direct oversight of elected officials. This is the Court's actual claim, and it's as looney as it sounds. There might be strong arguments in favor of maintaining positive public perceptions of law enforcement, but these have nothing to do with judicial enforcement of human rights (to the extent of striking down legislation, no less). Can anyone still take the Court seriously in its claim of protecting fundamental rights from unlawful government encroachment? From this broader perspective, the *Police Ordinance* decision is just one more step in the Court's undermining of its own constitutional project.

The Court no doubt had its own institutional reasons for sacrificing credibility for the sake of the particular outcome in that case. We had observed the reciprocal relationship and mutual backscratching between the Israeli judiciary and law enforcement agencies in Chapters 7 and 8. From this angle, the Court had a clear enough motivation to shield police investigative policy from elected governmental oversight. After all, from personal harassment and "probes" to judicial impeachment under the Deri Doctrine, the police investigation is a key element of Israeli judicial supremacy.

As a last point in this matter, the Court's opposition to elected civilian control of law enforcement agencies (in the *Police Ordinance* case and elsewhere)* highlights its contempt for genuinely fundamental principles of universal democracy. Robert A. Dahl, likely the most highly regarded political scientist of the twentieth century and the authoritative scholar of modern democracy, defines five "essential conditions" without which democracy is either "unlikely to exist" or is in a "precarious" state of existence. This is not the "substance" of democracy in the sense that it is not a component of democracy itself – these are rather background prerequisites which serve as the vital foundation of any viable democracy.

First among these conditions, Dahl lists "control of military and police by elected officials." Dahl explains that "the most dangerous internal threat to democracy comes from leaders who have access to the major means of physical coercion: the military and the police." According to Dahl, if the military and police are not "under the full control of democratically elected officials," democratic institutions are unlikely to endure and their "prospects are dim."[23] Though Dahl's seminal book is available in Hebrew translation, it would seem the Justices of the Supreme Court have not read it.

We conclude this section with an honorable mention of the 2019 *Kan* ruling, in which a law was almost struck down. In 2017 the Knesset enacted legislation regarding the Public Broadcasting Corporation, Israel's primary public broadcasting entity also known as "*Kan*" (which in Hebrew means "Here"). *Kan* operates both general media and news broadcasting. The new legislation would have split Israeli public broadcasting into two distinct and separate units – *Kan*

* Consider the recent *Ronen Bar* case, discussed at the end of Chapter 6.

for general media, and a new entity for news and current affairs. As the reader might have guessed, the new law had clear partisan and ideological undertones: many on the political right perceived *Kan* to be irredeemably biased to the left, while the political left claimed the law was politicizing Israel's public broadcasting.

Due to reasons irrelevant for present purposes, the legislation was ultimately rescinded by the Knesset before it could go into effect, and *Kan* remained a unified public broadcaster with both media and news units.

The law was challenged in the Supreme Court before it was rescinded. Though the issue quickly became moot the Court saw fit to issue a ruling anyway, six months after the law had been scrapped. In a unanimous nine-judge ruling penned by Justice Hanan Meltzer, the Court held that the law was unconstitutional in principle, would have been struck down were it still in force, and will be struck down if attempted again. Meltzer's reasoning is truly marvelous: after waxing poetic about the importance of a diverse and free media landscape, and about its centrality to open inquiry and debate in a democracy, Meltzer concludes that Israeli citizens at large possess an enforceable collective right to independent public news broadcasting. Yes, really. In his own words:

> "Public broadcasting, including news and current affairs, must remain independent and free from political interference and interests. This principle reflects, among other things, **a public right**... The outcome we have reached flows necessarily from **the democratic worldview**...
>
> State interference in [public] media entities... effectively amounts to a prohibited subjugation of the press."[24] (Emphasis in source.)[*]

Meltzer quotes a smattering of comparative scholarly writing and rulings concerning the importance of an independent press to free speech (and the principle of governmental non-intervention), without acknowledging that all such discussions refer to private media entities, and not to public (State-funded and State-run) broadcasters. More to the point, in announcing an enforceable "public right to public news broadcasting" which can trump primary Knesset legislation, Meltzer doesn't bother referencing a single Israeli statutory source to support his claim – not even a Basic Law.

The Israel-Palestinian Conflict

A final category of laws struck down by the Supreme Court relates directly to the prolonged violent conflict between Israel and the Palestinians. Statutes connected in one way or another to the conflict were invalidated by the Court in 2005, 2006, 2010, 2015, 2020 and 2021.

The minute details of these cases and their legal arguments tend to be

[*] Justice Meltzer is fond of bold type.

excruciatingly complex, involving multiple legal disciplines and areas of expertise (from international humanitarian law to property and tort law), disparate and conflicting bodies of applicable law (from Israeli domestic regulations to archaic Jordanian civil codes), and factual and legal history that is obscure or disputed. We will therefore examine these cases from a relative distance and at a high level of generality. As we do so there are three points we might take into account.

First, these cases are broadly related to what is easily the most important and consequential issue to exist in Israel, tied directly both to Israel's physical survival and to its core ethos, narrative and self-perception. This fact alone does not render related cases non-justiciable, but clearly bears on their fundamentally political nature, on the public passions they invoke and on the gravity of their consequences. Second, as the Israeli-Palestinian conflict ultimately boils down to a century-old war, the implications of almost any decision or policy – whether direct or indirect – may be measured by a body count. The raw physical environment of these cases is one of terrorism, violence, territory and risk to life and limb. Third is the centrality of democratic responsibility and accountability of government officials charged with decision-making and policy determinations in this area. This stands on its own but is also derived from the previous two points. Whether directly involving military action or not, the potentially grave consequences of any decision pose an especially strong justification for judicial restraint – that is, they justify leaving policy to elected representatives who are responsive to public sentiment, and who will ultimately bear responsibility for any harms suffered by the public as a result of their actions.

Similarly, the point to consider in all cases is not whether one agrees with the law under review or with the judicial result. Reasonable people will rightly disagree on issues of such dramatic consequence, on their relative merits or objections, on their benefits and harms. The question we might ask ourselves is rather, in every case, whether it is the Court that ought to be making these decisions on the public's behalf and on dubious or vague legal grounds. We may proceed with this in mind.

In 2005 the Israeli Government adopted the "Gaza Disengagement" plan – withdrawing all troops and military presence from the Gaza Strip, dismantling existing Israeli communities there, and evacuating their residents, by force if need be. The plan was passed as primary legislation and was predictably challenged in the Supreme Court. The Court showed no hesitation in adjudicating one of the most fraught controversies that Israel had ever known or in considering the constitutionality of strategic foreign policy of the highest order. In the *Gaza Beach* decision the Court ruled that the proposed "disengagement" was constitutional, but struck down a number of statutory mechanisms relating to compensation claims by evicted residents (which had infringed on their right to property).[25] The unsigned majority opinion (jointly attributed to ten Justices) extends over two hundred and fifty pages, while the dissenting opinion by Justice Levy was no less essentially activist, arguing that the law be struck down as unconstitutional. This case stands out not because of its unremarkable result, but rather due to the Court's very contemplation of striking down a law of such central long-term military and geo-political strategic significance.

The violent waves of Palestinian terrorism and Israeli military responses from 2000 to 2005, known as the Second *Intifada*, led to another major legislative initiative. Palestinian residents were regularly filing civil tort lawsuits against the State of Israel, demanding compensation for personal injuries and property damages caused by Israeli military operations throughout the Gaza Strip and West Bank territories. In 2005 the Knesset enacted legislation granting the State sovereign immunity from tort claims arising from military activity in these areas. Such a policy involves financial, moral and military considerations, and is not unusual from a comparative perspective. An obvious example is that of Section 2680(k) of the U.S. Federal Tort Claims Act, under which the United States enjoys total immunity for "any claim arising in a foreign country." The U.S. Supreme Court has held that this sovereign immunity "bars all claims based on any injury suffered in a foreign country."[26] Similar rules are easily found in additional common-law jurisdictions, especially in the context of military action.

The Israeli Supreme Court struck down the statute on the grounds that it violated the property rights of Palestinians.[27] In the impressively short 2006 ruling, Justice Barak concludes that the overall benefits of tort immunity in this case do not outweigh the harm caused to constitutional rights. That these benefits include de-incentivizing Palestinian clashes with the Israeli military – and so contributing to the safety of soldiers, as well as Palestinian and Israeli civilians – is at no point considered by Barak. The right is simply asserted as a trump card superseding all other conceivable factors, though the question of which factors ought to prevail was never a legal one.

The *Torts Immunity* case most acutely demonstrates the way in which ineffectual government legal counsel sabotages State interests. Justice Grunis reluctantly concurred with Barak (making the nine-member decision unanimous) but clearly thought the Court's position suffered some fundamental flaws. His problem, however, was that the government lawyers didn't bother raising them (or indeed, explicitly refused to present any position in their regard). Grunis laments the fact that some of the most basic and obvious questions were not addressed by government lawyers – more than venting his frustration, Grunis was plainly hinting that a sincere effort may well have yielded a result more favorable to the government, but that as these were not discussed he "had no choice but to concur" with Barak's suggested outcome. Specifically, the LCG lawyers did not address whether Israeli law even applied to tort events occurring in the West Bank – Grunis seemed open to the argument that "conflict of laws" rules lead to the applicated of Jordanian law, not Israeli law, with various potential implications; more importantly, the State representatives did not even challenge the assertion that BL:HDL applies to the West Bank. This was an extraordinary (or deliberate) blunder, as it seemed (at least at the time) that there was scarce legal basis to apply BL:HDL outside Israel's formally recognized borders. Here was a clear example of government counsel simply refusing to raise the most obvious legal objections in defense of legislative policy, to the point one Justice felt compelled to call them out on it.

The next statute in our present context regarded *ex parte* arrest hearings for suspected terrorists, and was invalidated by the Court in 2010. The ever-constant struggle against Palestinian terrorism has necessitated various unique legal arrangements of criminal procedure. Many have argued that ordinary paradigms and norms of criminal law and procedure are simply not applicable to a scenario which resembles low-intensity warfare much more than criminal law enforcement. The principled rationales and the incentive structures usually invoked for typical criminal law are profoundly different in the context of an all-encompassing ethno-religious-territorial armed conflict. The State does not have the luxury to afford all standard protections and privileges to suspected terrorism operatives – both for reasons relating to the nature and complexity of criminal investigations under such circumstances, and more importantly, for reasons of immediate security and intelligence, as investigations often yield time-sensitive information regarding other operatives and impending terror activities. Simply put, the U.S. or U.K. do not grant standard "due process" criminal rights to detained suspected Taliban insurgents in Afghanistan or ISIS terrorists in Syria or Iraq. This reflects clear necessity, global practice and plain common sense.

A temporary statutory amendment enacted by the Knesset in 2006 (and extended in 2007 for an additional three years) concerned certain detainment-related hearings for individuals arrested on suspicion of terrorism. One key provision authorized courts to extend a suspect's detention for a limited time (up to an overall total maximum of 20 days) without the detainee's presence. Such hearings were to be permitted only if the suspect was present for the original detention hearing, were limited to specific circumstances – involving immediate prevention of terror attacks, imminent risk to human life or significant impediment to the investigation – and were held with the suspect's legal counsel in attendance. Following the initial experience and towards extending the temporary statute, the Knesset and military stressed that the law's provisions were "crucial to law enforcement engaged in the investigation and prevention of terrorist offenses" and that these have "often contributed to thwarting terrorist attacks, identifying criminals and bringing them to justice."

The Supreme Court struck down the statutory amendment as a disproportionate violation of the detainee's right to appear before a judge during criminal proceeding, as part of the constitutional right to liberty and criminal due process.[28] The conventional norms of liberal democracy certainly require that criminal defendants be able to appear personally (and usually, physically) in court in matters materially affecting their rights; and as such, *ex parte* criminal proceedings are generally prohibited. But all jurisdictions reserve some exceptions to such rules. The Court's view was that a highly specific exception, in the context of terrorism and warfare, within limited circumstances, and for a maximum of twenty days, was constitutionally unjustifiable. To say that such a view was not legally inevitable is an understatement – it is rather, yet again, just one conceivable opinion among many, that comes down to policy preferences and value judgments much more than to law.

In reference to our earlier mention of accountability, we may reasonably ask – how many terror investigations have been thwarted due to the invalidation of this statute? How many Israelis have been killed or harmed as a result? The Court assumes total authority to make such determinations on behalf of the Israeli public, but is willing to bear none of the responsibility for their potential or actual consequences.

Another front in Israel's conflict with the Palestinians is that of international legitimacy and global economics. The infamous "Boycott, Divestment and Sanction" (or "BDS") movement devised by Palestinian leadership in 2001 seeks to both delegitimize Israel in the international public arena, as well as to cause direct harm to Israel's economy, by demanding that countries and corporations refuse to do business with Israel and with Israeli entities. As part of the Israeli effort to counter the BDS movement, in 2011 the Knesset enacted a law under which certain calls to boycott Israeli individuals or entities, based solely on their affiliation with Israel, would become an actionable tort. In other words, the individual or entity could sue the boycott-caller for damages in Israeli court.

One provision granted a plaintiff "statutory" damages – i.e., automatic compensation without needing to show actual damage – under certain circumstances and if the boycott call was "malicious" (though the law does not name specific sums, and largely leaves the award amount to judicial discretion). In a 2015 ruling the Supreme Court struck down this provision as unconstitutional due to its disproportionate harm to freedom of speech.[29] The ruling is perplexing in many respects: Israeli law mandates statutory damages for libel and other speech-related activities, and various jurisdictions include restrictions similar to the one in question (indeed, one can argue that a boycott-call is essentially a form of libel).

Further, much like the right to "equality," "freedom of speech" is deliberately not included in BL:HDL or in any Basic Law. By 2015 the judicial enforcement of implicit (i.e., invented) "unenumerated" rights to strike down primary legislation had become casual and commonplace. Finally, the Court's concern for freedom of speech is slightly less persuasive given its dubious record on the matter across a long string of cases, in which the Court displayed indifference or even hostility towards the same right – most notably, the Court's invalidation of the *Channel 7* law (licensing a radio station) on vague grounds of "freedom of occupation," and without even mentioning freedom of speech as a relevant consideration.

In 2017 the Knesset enacted the *Settlements Regulation* law to address an acute legal problem plaguing Israeli towns and settlements in the West Bank. Real estate property rights in the West Bank are subject to a complex web of archaic Jordanian (essentially Ottoman) civil laws, while historical legal records and documentation are often patchy or disputed. This leads to regular competing claims regarding property rights over specific plots of privately-owned land. A recurring pattern emerged, by which Israeli homes and infrastructure (at times extending to an entire neighborhood) were built on land plots of unclear legal status; at some point, Palestinians would appear and claim prior ownership rights to the same real property, demanding to demolish the buildings. The problem was arguably exacerbated to some extent by the Supreme Court's rulings in various cases, in which it adopted a zero-sum approach and at times ordered that many homes be vacated and demolished (though they had long since been occupied by residents), despite extremely weak and disputed ownership claims, and while rejecting alternative mechanisms such as monetary compensation.

The 2017 law sought to offer "an unconventional solution for an unconventional problem" (as described by the Knesset). It did so by combining elements of eminent domain (with compensation) and a "bona fide purchaser" doctrine common in many jurisdictions. If someone built structures on a plot of private land in good faith and without notice of any competing claims (similar to a bona fide purchaser), or if they did so with express permission and authority granted by State institutions, they would be entitled to continue using the property. If a Palestinian subsequently proved valid ownership and if the newly-built structures exceeded the value of the real estate property itself, the owner would be entitled to generous compensation from the government (125% of the property market value), or to receive an alternative comparable plot of land if available. The law was a landmark piece of the Government's ideological agenda, and was naturally also deeply controversial due to its underlying political implications. Its supporters saw it as a fair and necessary solution, removing a painful stumbling block to the valid and lawful effort of founding and expanding communities in the West Bank; its opponents argued it was a cynical discriminatory ploy to dispossess Palestinians of their land ownership rights to make way for Jewish settlements.

In 2020, three years after the law was enacted and two years after the last court hearing was held, the Supreme Court struck down the law as a violation of the property and equality rights of Palestinians.[30] The LCG Avichai Mandelblit, as had become customary, joined the petitioners and argued against the law, though he was gracious enough to permit the Government private representation. The Court split unsurprisingly down ideological lines, with eight Justices on one side (broadly conceived of as activist or progressive) and Justice Solberg forcefully dissenting on the other. As a matter of legal argument the Court's conclusion is peculiar: Israeli law broadly allows for "eminent domain" – government taking of private property for just compensation, including real estate, to serve what it deems to be important public interests. It's unclear why the harm in question was so different from the same harm ordinarily tolerated in the context of eminent domain. The Court's assertion of illegality is simply inconsistent with a significant body of existing Israeli law, a point that the majority opinion just ignores.

It seems likely that the Court's reasoning relied primarily on more political and ideological grounds. But deciding such matters is precisely the role of the Knesset, not the Court. As Solberg points out, the Knesset's policy sought to resolve a complex problem with an innovative and (in its view) just solution. The elected legislature had deliberated at length and in depth over a matter of significant public controversy, had weighed and balance the competing factors and considerations, and had arrived at its decision which it cemented as primary legislation. The fact that eight Supreme Court Justices preferred a different policy has nothing to do with law. Solberg also observed and predicted, correctly, that annulling the statute would leave thousands of people – plaintiffs and defendants, Palestinians and Israelis – with the same severe problem, tied up in prolonged litigation and with no end in sight.

Our last example of conflict-related laws invalidated by the Court is a statute enacted by the Knesset in 2015, which regarded welfare payments to parents of minors convicted of terrorism crimes. The background was the growing penchant of Palestinian youths and teens for throwing large rocks at Israeli civilian cars as they drove by, causing accidents, injury and death. Aside tightening the criminal law framework for tackling these crimes, the Knesset wanted to incentivize families – and especially parents – to discourage or prevent their wayward youths from engaging in this thrilling activity. To that end, the Knesset's amendment to Israel's National Insurance (e.g., Social Security) legislation revoked various welfare benefits received by parents or guardians for their dependent minors, if the minor was convicted of assorted terrorism crimes and received a prison sentence (think seventeen year-old brutes, not toddlers; the minimum age for imprisonment is fourteen). This was especially relevant for eastern Jerusalem neighborhoods, inhabited mostly by Palestinians who are also lawful Israeli residents and who receive the comprehensive blessings of the Israeli welfare state – including free healthcare, free education, and various forms of direct financial support.

The law meant that if a minor was convicted of terrorism crimes and was imprisoned, their parents would stop receiving specific welfare benefits tied to the culprit minor for the duration of the minor's imprisonment. The law's rationale was not only incentivization – it makes sense that if someone is in prison with all their physical and sustenance needs cared for, there is no justification that someone else receive state funds on their behalf. Indeed, a similar law already existed for imprisoned adults, which revoked some of their own welfare benefits as long as they were incarcerated. It's also worth noting that the law applied to Israelis and Jews just as much as it did to Palestinians or Arabs, both in theory and in practice.

Alas, in the 2021 *Benefit Revocation* case the Supreme Court struck down the amendment as an unconstitutional violation of – wait for it – the right to equality.[31] This was because the law applied only to specific terrorism-related crimes, while parents of other minors imprisoned for various crimes could retain their dependent welfare benefits. Justice Daphne Barak-Erez based this conclusion (in her majority opinion) on two mind-boggling arguments: one was that the law had the disparate effect of targeting Arab minors and families. Fortunately, Barak-Erez clarified this was not her main argument;* unfortunately, her primary argument was even stranger – that the revocation of welfare benefits had the effect of "branding" (or "stigmatizing") the convicted terrorists and their families (or perhaps all Arabs in Israel – her argument is not so clear). The negative stigma is itself a violation of equality rendering the law unconstitutional.

The sheer implausibility of this argument by Barak-Erez compels us to look elsewhere for an explanation – and we find it in the opinion of Justice Yitzhak Amit. The *Benefit Revocation* case was one of those rare instances where Amit's broken clock was spot on, and he joined three conservative Justices in dissenting. Amit argued that no right was violated to begin with, because the law itself was simply so inconsequential. He stresses that throughout the five years since the law was enacted, it had been applied (that is, welfare benefits for minors were revoked) in *seven* cases. You read that right – seven, more than six, less than eight. Amit does some math and shows that the monthly benefit of which parents are deprived amounts to – hold on tight – a maximum of sixty-two dollars and change. Because imprisonment spared parents many expenses, amounting to savings far above sixty-two dollars a month, there was simply no factual basis for the claim that anyone was being "harmed" one way or another.

Amit's point demonstrates the Court's megalomanic micro-management – hundreds of judicial pages by nine Justices, four years of prolonged proceedings, striking down primary legislation, and all for what? Because the parents of seven minors (imprisoned for terrorism) were "deprived" of sixty bucks a month in welfare payments that they saved anyway by not having to sustain the same minors. This is what the Israeli Supreme Court spends its time on. But Amit's point also sheds light on the "branding" argument presented by Daphne Barak-Erez. The individual "harm" to any aggrieved party was so miniscule, in fact so non-existent, that Barak-Erez had to concoct an elaborate theory of "stigmatization" to justify her interference with a policy she simply did not like. On this understanding her ludicrous argument makes much more sense.

And so yet another law directly tied to the Israel-Palestinian conflict was struck down by the Court, for vague and amorphous reasons that amount to policy preferences and ideological values. The ruling was split five to four. How much terrorism activity by minors would have been prevented by the statute had it remained in force? We will never know. To this day the parents of a minor convicted of terrorism charges and serving a prison sentence will still receive benefit payments on his behalf.

---

* If we must spell out the absurdity briefly: It's like arguing that a law targeting Mafia organized crime has a disparate effect on Italians, but worse. Any Israeli law targeting terrorism in one way or another will have a disparate affect on Arabs (primarily Palestinian ones), because the Israeli-Arab conflict involves, as the name suggests, a clear ethnic divide and Palestinian Arabs are the primary perpetrators of terrorism against Israelis. Duh.

As is now customary, we conclude our overview with another honorable mention – the *Family Unification* cases, in which the Court almost struck down a law which just managed to withstand scrutiny by the skin of its teeth.

As is common practice in many countries, a foreign national may attain Israeli "resident" status or citizenship if married to an Israeli citizen, in a process called "family unification." A similar process exists for other immediate family members. During the early 2000s, as Palestinian terrorism reached new heights, it dawned on Israeli authorities that the spousal privilege of granting resident status was being abused to facilitate a form of creeping Palestinian immigration from disputed territories into Israel. In only six years between 1994 and 2002, some one hundred and forty thousand Palestinians had immigrated to Israel through the "family unification" process; demography experts predicted another two hundred thousand would enter over the following decade. Such an accelerated demographic shift threatened to directly undermine Israel's character and self-determination as the Jewish State.

Demographic challenges aside, the automatic immigration of Palestinians into Israel by way of marriage to an Israeli citizen posed a genuine security hazard. Israel and Palestinians had been locked in an ethno-religious-territorial conflict for nearly a century, and the 2000s kicked off with the most violent chapter yet. A situation in which Palestinians could effortlessly become full Israeli residents (halfway to citizenship) was untenable. Terror attacks were immeasurably easier to accomplish by an individual with Israeli citizenship or resident status, as they could move unhindered throughout the country. Nor was this problem theoretical: various studies at the time showed that out of terror attacks in which Israeli-Arabs (citizens or permanent residents) were involved as perpetrators, one in five included a "family unification" Palestinian immigrant. More broadly, Palestinians and Israeli-Arabs have markedly different approaches and attitudes towards the Israeli State, its institutions and its Jewish population – indeed, many have attributed modern trends of radicalization and anti-Israel sentiment among Israeli-Arabs to the influences of Palestinian immigrants. Research regarding a slew of violent riots in 2021 shows, for example, that children of Palestinian immigrants were more likely to engage in rioting and violent activities.[32]

In 2003 the Knesset passed a law which would exclude certain jurisdictions and territories from automatic conferral of spousal resident's rights. Foreign nationals belonging to countries or territories effectively at war with Israel, including Palestinians in the West Bank and Gaza, were no longer eligible for Israeli resident status on the basis of marriage to an Israeli citizen. Simply put, if you came from somewhere engaged in war with Israel, you could not simultaneously immigrate freely to Israel by marrying an Israeli. Fair or not, some might call this common sense. The rule was notably limited in numerous ways – for example, it only applied under a certain age (25 for women, 35 for men), and the Minister of Interior could approve specific exceptions on an individual basis.

The law was challenged multiple times and ended up under the judicial microscope not once, but twice. In two separate rulings, in 2006 and again in 2012, the Supreme Court upheld the law and dismissed the petitions (jointly reaching some five hundred pages).[33] The ostensibly restrained outcome was hardly reassuring – in both cases the law was saved by a single vote, coming down twice to a split bench of six Justices for dismissal against five Justices for accepting the petitions and invalidating the law. The Court had no qualms in subjecting the law to judicial review, though the issue was a non-justiciable question of core security and immigration policy; though it involved genuine risk to Israelis under the shadow of daily murderous terror attacks; and though it had the potential for far-reaching existential consequences. It seemed to many that the Court had come precariously close to subverting Israel's entire national security and the State's very viability.

The two rulings are also a prime example of the Court's simplistic and manipulative "rights" discourse – pitting a "right to family life" of the family-members demanding immigration against "security concerns" regarding potential terrorism. But this is obviously a false dichotomy and a legal fantasy. For starters, no Basic Law recognizes a "right to family life" – this was simply yet one more invention by the Court derived from the enumerated right to dignity, once again demonstrating how abstract "dignity" is the fountainhead from which any conceivable judicially-desired right or privilege may flow forth.

Further, a "right to family life" was not actually at issue, as the law did not prevent anyone from marrying whomever they chose, and the Israeli citizen could just as well move to live with their chosen Palestinian spouse or family-member. In other words, this concerned only the non-existent "right" of Palestinians to freely immigrate into Israel *en masse* – a right that is, needless to say, anathematic to the entire Zionist enterprise. Likewise, as Justice Cheshin (writing with the majority in 2006) pointedly notes, it is not "security considerations" which are on the line but rather the right to life and to physical safety of Israelis which is being compromised by unchecked Palestinian immigration via "family unification" (rights which are, refreshingly, actually specified in the Basic Law).[34]

Justice Ayala Procaccia does us a great service by providing a feverish concurring opinion (in the 2006 decision) which borders on the parodical.[35] As if trying her hardest to vindicate all critiques against subjective manipulation and exaggeration of abstract human rights (and exhibiting an acute aversion to subtlety), Procaccia contends that "the human right to family is a foundation of human existence," that "it would be hard to conceive of human rights of comparable importance and impact," and that the right "reflects the essence of human existence and the embodiment of human self-fulfillment." She describes the "constitutional protection of the human right to realize the meaning of life and the purpose of life," insisting that the "human right to family" stands at the "highest tier" among all human rights. Leaving no room for doubt, Procaccia helpfully clarifies that the right to family "takes precedence over" other rights including "the right to property, to freedom of occupation, and to privacy." Considering the latter three are enumerated rights in the Basic Law's text and the "right to family life" is a judicial fiction, this is a staggering admission. Needless to say, all this originates for Procaccia in the enumerated right to "dignity" and more broadly in the general "protection of human rights" which is the "bedrock" of Israel's "constitutional order."

Far from exceptional, Procaccia's unhinged and sweeping assertions are standard fare in Supreme Court rulings, where understated reasoning is nearly as scarce as genuine legal arguments. Need anyone go further to demonstrate just how loony an unreserved judicial reliance on "human rights" can get?

Comical as Procaccia's inflated assertions may be, it is Justice Barak who outdoes himself, though in a genre closer to horror. In the 2001 animated film *Shrek*, Lord Farquaad solemnly announces to a cheering crowd: "Some of you may die, but it's a sacrifice I am willing to make." As we shall see, Barak's opinion amounts to just about the same.

Voting to strike down the statute, Barak (true to form) presents his view as an imperative of democracy. "Democracy forfeits a certain measure of security in order to gain an incomparably greater measure of family life and equality."[36] Few arguments distill Barak's "substantive democracy" quite as well as this simple claim – for Barak, "democracy" means the judicial balancing of rights and values to produce and impose mandatory policy outcomes. If the elected and accountable legislature reaches a conclusion at odds with that of the judge, it may be dismissed as a misguided distortion of true "democracy." To Barak it simply does not occur that such "forfeit" of security is subject to the electorate's discretion.

Barak then embarks on a discussion of "risk" which is truly stupefying. He begins with the pious declaration that "there is no democracy and human rights without taking risks," and then proceeds to explain that any society must necessarily "balance" between "the need to protect the lives and safety of citizens" and the need to protect human rights. For Barak, this means that:

> "In order to protect human rights, we are required to take risks that may result in harm to innocent people. A society that wishes to uphold its democratic values and seeks to maintain a democratic regime... is not permitted to prioritize the right to life in every case where it conflicts with the protection of human rights."[37]

This passage is worth reading again. Society is "required" to take risks; it is "not permitted" to prioritize human life as it sees fit. Here we find a pure and vivid representation of Barak's supremacist jurisprudence and that of the Court. To whom is the grim task of "balancing" competing factors assigned? Who is to determine the acceptable "risk" to human life? Not the electorate, the public, the *demos*; not their representatives; not, critically, the very people who will ultimately bear the burden for any such "risk-taking." Certainly not the mutilated corpses strewn in the streets or the bereaved families of butchered victims.

No. It is a miniscule counsel of insulated ex-lawyers in gowns – and only them – who may properly determine the appropriate societal price for their own moralizing self-righteousness, a price measured and paid in grief and in blood.

Per Justice Barak, it is for unelected and unaccountable judges to dictate to society what sacrifices they must make to meet the Court's enlightened standards, and it is for the public to dutifully submit to their grim fate.

This is the grotesque face of rogue justice.

Shortly after the 2006 ruling, Justice Cheshin let his frustration with Barak slip though in a public interview: "Justice Aharon Barak is willing for scores of people to get blown up so long as we have human rights. I am not willing. He sees it one way, I see it differently. Fortunately, I was in the majority."[38] Though admirably candid, Cheshin too misses the point and is as misguided as Barak. He also considers the question to be up for judicial resolution, as though this were a disagreement of legal nuance between two jurists. Can a democratic State validly restrict immigration from a hostile foreign jurisdiction with which it is at war? How much security must the public "forfeit," the slaughter of how many innocent people must be "risked," in the name of purported human rights? Both Cheshin and Barak – and indeed, the better part of the Israeli Supreme Court in the era of supremacy – believe that it is up to them to decide.

*

For nearly four decades the Israeli Supreme Court has been striking down primary legislation, at a steadily increasing pace, based on vague abstractions from within a non-existent constitution it itself invented. The nature of these laws ranges from inconsequential minutiae to major policy and public controversies to the existential life-and-death determinations surrounding Israel's conflict with the Palestinians. The majority of these rulings had little or no legal basis and for the most part did not involve actual protection of individuals or minorities. Easily refuting Alexander Hamilton's common adage, the judicial pen is mightier than both the purse and the sword. The Supreme Court's clumsy and reckless exercise of fully-fledged constitutional power has occurred not only in the absence of any recognizable constitutional document, but without any of the mechanisms typically established to temper and counteract such formidable power and its inherent distortions and risks. As we will now observe, the consequences have been catastrophic.

II – Fallout: The Effects of a Judicial Constitution

The nuclear explosion of the constitutional revolution may be divided into several components. Most visible and perhaps most egregious is the blinding white-hot flash of hard judicial review striking down primary legislation; yet clearly the blast radius of devastation and the long-term enduring destruction in its wake are of equal significance. Far beyond the ground zero of invalidated statutes vaporized to dust, a much larger chain reaction has ripped through the Israeli legal system and governmental order. The ensuing fallout, emerging gradually, continues to ravage and poison the landscape of Israeli society.

The laws directly struck down by the Supreme Court's constitutional revolution tell only one part of the story. We may now briefly consider some of its wider systemic effects rippling and reverberating through our socio-political order. These involve both direct impact on government action, and indirect broad consequences of a less tangible nature.

Blast Radius

As an initial point of order we may note that the above list of invalidated laws is itself not exhaustive – the Court has engaged in de facto "interpretive" invalidation of laws, though such cases never make the "stricken" list of doomed legislation. These are cases in which the Court declares a provision's clear incompatibility with constitutional norms and essentially concedes that the law is irredeemably unconstitutional; yet instead of invalidating the law, the Court nonetheless "interprets" (or more accurately, "constructs" or applies) the law to conform to the Court's preference. This method effectively annuls a law and renders it a dead letter, on grounds of constitutional incompatibility, while maintaining the façade of upholding the law and of judicial restraint.

The 2003 *Herut* ruling is a case in point, in which Justice Barak killed three birds with one stone: the ruling effectively invalidated a key statute limiting the Court's jurisdiction; it dramatically expanded the scope of the judicial revolution; and it expanded the Court's substantive control of national elections.

The most important body dealing with election-related rules and disputes is the "Central Election Committee" within the Knesset. The Committee's authority encompasses almost all (non-criminal) challenges and controversies relating to election campaigns, conduct of political parties, electoral irregularities, and well beyond. The Committee is formally charged with overseeing all aspects of national elections, including issuing binding orders and addressing alleged violations of campaign laws. Critically, the Committee also approves or disqualifies particular candidates or political parties based on a defined set of statutory conditions. It is one of the most consequential organs in the Israeli electoral system, and by extension in all of Israeli democracy.

Statutory law clearly stipulates that most decisions by the Central Elections Committee are distinctly non-justiciable and are categorically not subject to judicial review of any kind. Section 137 of the 1969 Knesset Elections Act reads that "no court shall entertain a request for relief regarding such an act or omission, or in connection with a decision or directive of the Central Committee" or its associated organs (aside some exceptions explicitly defined within the same law).

The 2003 *Herut* ruling upended this clear statutory instruction. Justice Barak argued that the above provision contradicted Section 15 of "Basic Law: The Judiciary," which grants the Supreme Court (as High Court of Justice) broad authority to review any government decision. So far, so Barak. But after stating that the statutory provision contradicts the Basic Law and was therefore voidable,

Barak argued *not* to invalidate the former, but instead to "interpret" it to exclude HCJ petitions to the Supreme Court challenging Committee decisions. Needless to say, such an application of the law does not amount to "interpretation" in any sense, but rather simply ignores – and essentially annuls – the statute's literal and textual instructions ("no court shall entertain"). The Court thus pretends to leave a law intact without striking it down, while in practice "interpreting" it in direct contradiction to its clear meaning rendering the law a de facto dead letter. In doing so the Court invalidates a law for all intents and purposes, while concealing the true nature of its decision. This is not mere interpretative creativity in the "spirit" of the Basic Laws – here the Court expressly concedes that it is misapplying the law which can only be understood as contradicting a constitutional norm.

This interpretive mechanism adopted by the Court is important because it grew to become the blueprint for many other decisions. The *Herut* ruling and many others like it do not appear on any list of laws struck down by the Supreme Court.

By ignoring the statute's clear non-justiciability provision, the Court in *Herut* unilaterally subjected virtually all election-related decision-making by the Committee to the Supreme Court's supervision. But this was not the only major expansion of judicial power found in that ruling. The astute reader may have noticed that Barak claimed a violation of "Basic Law: The Judiciary." But that is not one of the two Basic Laws enacted in 1992 which were elevated to constitutional status. Indeed, the entire rationale of *Hamizrachi* was expressly limited to the 1992 laws: the ruling relied on the "substantive entrenchment" found specifically in BL:HDL, on the "formal" entrenchment in BL:FO, on the "limitation clauses" which appear only in these two Basic Laws, on the singular "constitutional moment" which existed in 1992, on the law's specific content of protecting human rights, et cetera. Barak had explicitly stated in *Hamizrachi* that other Basic Laws retained their pre-existing legal status. By the Court's own jurisprudence, "Basic Law: The Judiciary" (which is not even entrenched) enjoys no superior constitutional status.

The Court in *Herut* came up with a simple solution: just retroactively extend the "constitutional revolution" so it applied to all existing Basic Laws, such that ordinary statutes could be struck down for contradicting any Basic Law whatsoever (most of which contain no "entrenchment" or "limitation" clause). Conveniently and in typical fashion, Barak did not see fit to extend any other elements from the 1992 Basic Laws – such as the "savings clause" which precluded intervention in pre-existing statutes – in turn allowing Barak to freely subject the 1969 elections statute to the Court's judicial review. This was an extraordinary expansion of the constitutional revolution and was achieved almost as an afterthought – the Court dismissed the petitions at hand (and refused to intervene) while at the same time declaring a dramatic jurisprudential shift in *dicta*. The Court presents no explanation or rationale for this significant departure, with the ruling running only sixteen pages, and instead simply pretends it is faithfully applying the rules set out by *Hamizrachi*. With a casual flourish and a blank face, the Court just assumed that the newly acquired power of judicial review applied to all Basic Laws without even the pretense of explaining from whence this power derived or why it applied to any law outside the 1992 "constitutional" legislation.

The Court has consistently applied creative interpretation in this manner in numerous cases (some are discussed in Chapter 3), effectively invalidating laws without admitting to doing so.

The effects of the constitutional revolution have radiated throughout the legal system, in a manner which we may grant only a cursory review. Each of these paragraphs could fill a book of its own.

The Court has subjected virtually all legislation (old and new) to interpretation guided by, in accordance with, and in the spirit of, the "constitutional norms" of the Basic Laws. This has had a system-wide effect which is hard to overstate and impossible to quantify. Hundreds, perhaps thousands of cases, at all judicial tiers, regularly turn on judicial interpretation twisting and distorting statutory language, so its application conforms (in the judge's estimation) with provisions of the Basic Laws. As we have seen, the Court often violates the clear instructions of the Section 10 "savings clause" found in BL:HDL by re-interpreting pre-1992 legislation and altering associated law. Alongside the distortion of statutes and their text to conform to the Court's view on human rights, the Court has also capitalized on the "proper purpose" requirement by selectively attributing its own "objective" purpose to laws as a pretext to invalidate them. In other words, the Court can simply invent a law's purpose that has little to do with its actual purpose as intended by legislators and can then declare that the imputed purpose is "improper."*

The constitutional revolution also applies with utmost force and effect to judicial supervision of Executive action at all levels, informing the "reasonableness" standard for review and especially the "proportionality" requirement for any action affecting rights. Any executive action impacting constitutional rights (as broadly construed by the courts – think of "equality") must meet judicial standards of "proportionality" – the familiar balancing formula by which judges decide whether a policy's societal benefits outweigh any harms caused to individuals, minority groups or to just about anyone. Though this was a principle of administrative judicial review prior to the constitutional revolution, since 1995 it has grown to dramatic proportions in the scale and scope of its application. Once again, the understandable focus on legislative judicial review obscures the enormous system-wide effect of the constitutional revolution on almost all conceivable executive action.

Our discussion of the Legal Counsel to the Government in the previous chapter noted the LCG's involvement in the legislative process – just imagine how this has been impacted by the constitutional revolution. Government

---

* The Court essentially did this with some of the immigration cases discussed above. Also see the *Surrogacy* decision discussed in Chapter 3.

attorneys at the most junior level can indefinitely hold up proposed legislation (and much other government action with even greater ease) which they deem to violate constitutional norms at any level. They may allege any right (remember, "dignity" or "equality" and their vast abstract malleability), may condemn a purpose to be "improper" (including an imputed "objective" purpose existing only in the attorney's mind), or may rule out harm as "disproportionate" – all on the basis of an arbitrary whim, without so much as the semblance of judicial authority or an adjudicatory process. Put simply, all the profound flaws and outrages of the LCG's power and its application, discussed at length above, are exacerbated tenfold by the introduction of so-called constitutional evaluation.

Especially indicative of the Court's true nature is the converse stagnation of protections related to criminal procedure and law enforcement conduct. The Court has notably resisted applying most of its expansive jurisprudence to protecting individuals from abuse of State police powers by law enforcement agencies. One might think that the advent of an enumerated constitutional right to liberty, privacy, property, dignity and others, might lead to a shift in the Court's jurisprudence in criminal matters and to more robust protection of individuals from the worst excesses of arbitrary State power. Yet the latter have remained unaffected, glaringly shielded from the Court's revolutionary concern for purported human rights. To this day the state of severe abuses by Israeli law enforcement remains more abysmal than ever, not in spite of the Court and its constitutional revolution but rather very much thanks to its patronage.

Shockwaves

The most dramatic and devastating consequences of the Supreme Court's constitutional jurisprudence are found outside the sphere of the law. No comprehension of the constitutional revolution is remotely adequate without a firm grasp of its corrosive effect on Israeli societal integrity and democratic political discourse. It merits our closest attention and consideration. Though these observations apply to the Court's judicial supremacy more broadly, they are most acutely felt in the context of the Court's usurpation of ultimate legislative power by judicial review. The repercussions of Israeli judicial supremacy also contain broader lessons and insights regarding the more global phenomenon of judicial erosions of democratic culture and institutions. We therefore conclude our discussion of the constitutional revolution, and of judicial review in its name, by considering some of its most deleterious outcomes.

Destabilizing Democracy. Recalling our discussion of the "decision not to decide" and the fragmented nature of Israeli society, Israel arguably remains profoundly unprepared and ill-suited for a rigid constitution. The Court's misguided assumption (if we are to be charitable) was that imposing a constitution on the Israeli electorate would somehow resolve major political controversies, but this was fanciful wishful thinking at best. The primary outcome of the Court's unprecedented and failed experiment in coercive constitutionalism is a massive exacerbation of Israeli societal tensions throughout all fault-lines and at all levels, without any discernible or actual resolution of problems.

As sociologist Oren Soffer wrote of Israel, "it seems that the main problem is not the lack of a constitution itself, but the lack of agreement over fundamental societal values that any basic or 'thin' constitution requires in order to be formed."[39] The pre-*Hamizrachi* system of parliamentary supremacy provided Israel's fractured politics with the flexibility and agility to accommodate Israel's need for inelegant compromises, swift change and periodic reformation of its governmental infrastructure. By inventing and enforcing an imaginary "substantive" constitution the Court deprived the Israeli political order of these crucial elements and instead foisted on Israel's unwilling populace a framework of rigid, binary, uncompromising principles to be enforced by an insulated and unaccountable judiciary. To be clear, even an ideal constitution drafted by the greatest minds in statecraft history might have been a poor fit for Israel – in 1948, 1995 or 2025; but the vague, formless, lawless version artificially manufactured by the Supreme Court is drastically worse.

The inevitable result of the constitutional revolution is the subversion and destabilization of the Israeli polity in its entirety. This is caused by both the abstraction of a forced constitution and by the specific exercise of judicial review as reviewed in the previous sections. The Israeli public had essentially been informed, retroactively and irrevocably, that a binding and rigid constitution had been bestowed upon them by a benevolent judicial caste, though they had never been consulted. Such an event can only be regarded as blunt trauma to the national democratic consciousness, with a cumulative corrosive effect on the public's self-perception as sovereign citizens within a system of self-government. What is the average Israeli to conclude, when notified that their vote in the ballot box is shredded by judges on the basis of a "constitution" of which they had never heard and in which they had no part in creating or approving? How can they hold their elected representatives accountable for laws, policies and outcomes which have been defeated, distorted or diluted by incessant judicial intervention? A sensible (even if eccentric) person with agency and autonomy will quickly lose both when forcibly placed in a straitjacket. The very existence of an imposed constitution emits, by itself, a debilitating influence on the collective electoral-political psyche.

The effect of judicial review in particular cases is of course more direct. The Court's totalizing interference with the Ultra-Orthodox draft exemption has not advanced its purported cause a single inch over the course of twenty-seven years. It has succeeded only in raising the stakes, in radicalizing the public debate on all sides, in causing all parties to become more entrenched and embittered, in highlighting the most painful controversy in Israeli public life and in making the likelihood of compromise or of change far more remote. It has, in fact, effectively precluded a host of solutions and compromises which had the potential to gradually lead to lasting desirable change. This can be said in one way or another of almost any example of judicial review since the constitutional revolution – scarce gains in the face of tremendous damage.

Further still, any arrangement, rule or policy born of judicial intervention under such circumstances – that is, in the absence of any genuine recognizable constitutional authority and based on the flimsiest and shoddiest legal grounds – must irredeemably bear the mark of Cain as ill-gotten gains and as a judicially-imposed deformity. Even seemingly agreeable outcomes come permanently tainted with their dubious undemocratic pedigree, having never been subjected to meaningful public debate or assent. Lord Jonathan Sumption speaks to this point when he muses "whether it is wise to make law in this way." He points out that "the chief function of any political system is to accommodate differences of interest and opinion among citizens," yet "resolving these differences by judicial decision contributes nothing to that end." "On the contrary," Sumption continues, "characterizing something as a constitutional right removes the issue from the arena of political debate and transfers it to judges." He describes how any such judicial resolution remains controversial because it was "introduced" by "a method which relegated the wider political debate" among citizens "to irrelevance." This may or may not be true for some historical examples of controversial judicial review elsewhere, but it is undoubtedly true in the context of Israel's judicially-decreed pseudo-constitution.

The constitutional revolution and its attendant judicial review have more broadly poisoned public and political discourse on a host of issues. Instead of operating in the blurry and gray territory of negotiation and compromise, of finding common ground and mutual benefit, of each side conceding one point to gain another, the debate has shifted into the toxic, hostile and self-righteous environment of legal imperatives and moral absolutes. For one thing, meticulously crafted and hard-won public compromise cemented in legislation may well be thrown out by the Court – so what's the point? The message conveyed by such Court-induced terminations is that political actors expend their public and electoral capital for nought. Further, a judicial declaration on an issue of public controversy disincentivizes adverse parties from participating in the unattractive and unpleasant task of resolving differences – indeed, it absolves them of any duty to engage with each other at all. This is especially true for the "winning" side. If the Court has judged one's own moral and ideological position to be the only legally valid route, why bargain for it? Why settle for any less? Indeed, why bother articulating its merits and benefits, why weigh and consider counterarguments and genuine concerns and trade-offs, if one can simply assert the judicial vindication of one's own view?

This is the true "substantive entrenchment" engendered by the constitutional revolution – not legal, but dogmatic and ideological: The profound polarization of both sides as they become steadily less willing to accept the validity of the opposing view or to countenance a moderate joint accommodation. Even worse, the consistent beneficiaries of judicial supremacy develop a vested interest in upholding and maintaining the existing framework and become incapable of considering constitutional change.

Menny Mautner has chronicled and described in detail how the primary beneficiary of the Court's activism has been the Israeli political left, and how the left has heartily embraced the bear-hug of judicial coercion. He has shown how left-wing Opposition politicians consistently petitioned the Supreme Court to achieve policy aims which they failed to secure through parliamentary means, and has argued that the political left had all-but abandoned electoral persuasion and campaigning in favor of conquest by litigation, with the Court all too happy to oblige.[40] For this reason, Mautner held that the Court's pejorative nickname as the "Givat Ram *Meretz* branch" (that is, the local office of far-left political parties) is well-earned.[41] The key takeaway for Mautner is that the Court's creation of ideological winners and losers has given the political left every reason to do as it has – to forgo both the negotiation table and the ballot box in favor of lawyers and briefs, while more generally adopting an uncompromising and unforgiving posture on all key points of contention.

Alongside the polarization and toxicity of public discourse, the constitutional revolution and the Court's supremacism also altered the very nature and content of public disagreement – shifting it from reflective principle to legal pedantism. Instead of arguing over the merits and flaws of any proposed course of action the public debate itself has come to revolve around what judges might decide and around superficial quasi-legal arguments. Disputes over economic welfare policy, immigration dilemmas, proper Ministerial conduct or military strategy all devolve into inane sophistry regarding the meaning of "dignity" or "equality," instead of trying to figure out whether something is simply a good or a bad idea. As one scholar put it, "when they speak of empowering the people, they mean empowering them to petition the court."[42]

Few examples illustrate this point better than the Ultra-Orthodox draft, as the public conversation obsesses over constitutional "equality" and associated questions of justiciability, standing, enforcement, and the Court's own contested authority, instead of what might be sound or feasible short-term or long-term policy. The legal challenge to Benjamin Netanyahu's appointment as Prime Minister had a similar effect, removing the public dispute from questions of principle and propriety to the technical sphere of legal permissibility. As Jeremy Waldron has aptly noted,[43] "impotent debating about what a few black-robed celebrities might decide in the future is hardly the essence of democratic citizenship" – or of democratic debate and deliberation.

The inability to reach compromise (or to sustain compromise through the gauntlet of judicial scrutiny) leads to an ever-escalating crisis as genuine issues remain indefinitely unresolvable. Aside the individual damage cause by such unresolved enduring problems, this engenders a degree of democratic despair and nihilism as the public loses faith in its representatives, in the very system of representation, and in its own capacity for societal accommodation; in turn leading to greater reliance on judges and courts to make decisions and to resolve controversies on the public's behalf. A vicious cycle of conflict, judicial intervention, polarization and further conflict is thus born and perpetuated. The Court announces that it must "regrettably" intervene to remedy governmental inaction or incompetence without acknowledging that its own meddling has contributed to the impasse. Following the constitutional revolution the Israeli public gradually internalized that the essence of their own political activity and mobilization is reduced to petitioning the Supreme Court and to crass arguments about vacuous judicial rulings. In such a disastrous scenario – one now familiar to any Israeli – all sides of the political and ideological divide lose the most basic ability to communicate or to consider opposing views, while the notion of common accommodation as an inherent value is also eroded.

Such is the ultimate consequence of rogue justice anywhere – an enfeebled and emasculated electorate beseeching their judicial overlords for relief from the struggles and burdens of collective self-rule. Martin Loughlin alludes to this when he argues that such judicial supremacy "absolves the political branches from having to face up to intractable political questions" and "offers incentives to democratic representatives to evade their most basic civic responsibilities" by pushing "ever more political issues into an institution that is insulated from the cut and thrust of ordinary life." Unlike the clean and ordered illusion of judicial moral determinations, political struggles are "long, intense, incremental, and the product of accommodation and compromise" but their ultimate outcomes have the benefit of being "thrashed out in accountable institutions." Judicial supremacy – that is, the courts as exclusive fora "to deliver social change" – conversely "carries the danger of draining the lifeblood from democracy, not just as a system of collective decision-making but, perhaps more importantly, as a way of life."[44] This is precisely what the constitutional revolution has meant for Israel – draining the lifeblood from democracy as a way of life.

It's worth recalling the trend described by Yoav Dotan within the limited but crucial institutional context of the Knesset and the Court's incessant interventions in intra-parliamentary affairs. Discussing the *Sarid* case (Chapter 5), Dotan stresses that the Court's very engagement with certain sensitive political issues – even if it ultimately decides to "restrain" itself and does not interfere – "comes at a hefty societal cost."[45] Barak's stated goal for intervention in parliamentary affairs is to prevent harm to "the fabric of parliamentary life" – yet the Court's "medicine," says Dotan, is much worse than the "disease" it claims to cure. The judicial intervention itself causes tremendous damage to the proper functioning of the Knesset and to the Knesset's public standing. Indeed, a remedy far worse than the ailment it purports to address might just be the most accurate metaphor for the Supreme Court's overall jurisprudence since the 1980s, even when seen in the most forgiving light.

The damage to a State's democratic culture, spirit and ethos inflicted by judicial supremacy has become increasingly more apparent and acknowledged, challenging the established notion of unbounded judicial power as an indispensable feature of democracy. Discussing the judicial circumvention of political compromise and democratic decision-making, Lord Jonathan Sumption argues that "a nation cannot hope to accommodate divisions among its people unless its citizens actively participate in the process of finding political solutions to common problems." James Allan similarly warned that "judicial second-guessing of where to draw moral lines... diminishes democracy. It undermines citizens' participation in the polity. It shifts the focus from politics to the courts."[46] Such observations have become steadily more common as the West begins to emerge from the era of judicial expansionism.

Judicial supremacy doesn't only undermine the democratic accommodation of division – it also undercuts its own alleged rationale of constraining government and limiting abuse of State power. This is because supremacist courts constantly communicate the message that the way to hold government accountable or to curb its power is through cloaked lawyers reciting incantations, and not through active individual and collective participation. The public develops a misplaced faith in legal impediments to State power and in clerical law-based safeguards against governmental abuse, when in reality such idealized illusions are no substitute for popular electoral oversight over the exercise of all governmental power. Lord Jonathan Sumption stresses that defenses against abuse of government power are never guaranteed by judicial decree, but rather depend "on active citizenship, on a culture of political sensitivity and on the capacity of representative institutions to perform their traditional role of accommodating division and mediating dissent." But it is precisely all these which gradually wither under the shadow of judicial supremacy, diminishing and weakening popular constraints on government – such that the supremacist court in fact inhibits the primary goal it purports to pursue. Like with the fairies of Neverland, every time an activist judge implicitly declares they don't believe in popular government, a small light of democracy blinks out.

<u>Public Faith in the Judiciary.</u> Other effects born of the constitutional revolution are far more direct, measurable and tangible. For one thing, public faith (or trust, or confidence) in the judiciary has plummeted since the Barak-ean activist era hit its stride. Menny Mautner describes how the Court's behavior "shattered the public's trust in the Court and undermined its legitimacy even among many of its staunchest supporters."[47]

A recent comprehensive empirical study by Prof. Yehonatan Givati and Aharon Garber found that "following Israel's constitutional revolution, confidence in courts declined by two standard deviations" – that it, to an outsized and enormous degree.[48] Givati and Garber rule out alternative explanations and causes, showing a clear link between the judicialization of politics and the nosediving public estimation of the Supreme Court and its judges. This factual finding was hardly a surprise and only confirmed what many had maintained all along – the Court's critics had been warning of precisely such a decline for decades. Already in 1979 (soon after Justice Barak was appointed to the Court)

Chief Justice Moshe Landau predicted the devastating effect that lawless judicial review would have on the public's estimation of the Court and on its willingness to adhere to judicial decisions. Sensing the Court's newfound inclination towards interventionism and foreshadowing things to come, Landau issued a stark warning some might have found inexplicable at the time:

> "The courts are not capable of inventing a miracle cure for the State's severe societal and economic problems. On the contrary, if the courts attempt to do so beyond what the existing law permits and mandates... they will lose the public trust that is essential to their functioning."[49]

In that same prescient speech Landau counseled that the Court must "refrain from dealing with matters of policy, involving a choice between different worldviews on social, economic, and political issues that are subject to public controversy, whenever the Knesset has addressed one of these matters and expressed its will through the enactment of a statute." Anticipating that the Court would not heed his advice, he cautioned that annulling laws "would turn the court into a senior partner in the legislative process and would make the judges partisans in public disputes, with part of the public applauding them and another part rejecting their rulings as biased and erroneous. Thus, the court would not only come into conflict with the parliamentary majority but would also lose the broad public trust, which is an indispensable condition for its public standing."

Other scholars have made similar points on many occasions, and indeed the loss of public confidence in the judiciary has been a recurring theme amongst the Court's critics from the outset. Michal Shaked (in her 1980s critique of the novel reasonableness standard) quotes Lord Scarman, that if people get the impression judges are simply applying their "sense of what it right," "confidence in the judicial system will be replaced" by fear of judicial power becoming "uncertain and arbitrary."[50] Also writing of unreasonableness, sociologist Ronen Shamir predicted that the "inevitable result" of such judicial blending of law with moral ideology is the "increasing erosion of the Court's authoritative status" and the "growing public recognition that the Court does not possess any superior qualities whatsoever."[51] Much more recently, Yoav Dotan observed how the Court's abolishment of justiciability requirements and the "judicial engagement in sensitive political matters" have lowered the Court into the political maelstrom, "injuring its status as an apolitical judicial institute" which previously enjoyed broad public support.[52] Ruth Gavison of course made this point repeatedly throughout her years criticizing the Court, and perhaps said it best: "When the Court presumes to become the supreme moral authority it undermines its own legitimacy as the supreme legal authority."[53]

This is of course an altogether obvious and intuitive observation. Judicial power derives its legitimacy from faithful application of the law to settle disputes, and loses any such legitimacy the moment judges don't confine themselves to this particular form and function of their office. One need not be an expert in law or sociology to understand the relationship between judicial lawlessness and low public faith in courts, just as one need not be an expert in athletics or nutrition to understand that halting all exercise and starting an exclusive diet of carbohydrates and fats will result in poorer athletic performance. The cause-and-effect link here is really no great mystery.

The empirical fact of waning public confidence in Israeli courts is virtually undisputed – one of the main recurring polls supporting the data is that of the judicially-aligned Israel Democracy Institute. Yet the response of some judicial supremacists resembles the Kubler-Ross textbook stages of grief, such as denial, anger, or bargaining. In 2021, retired Chief Justice Dorit Beinisch asserted that the polls "do not reflect reality," and that anyone moving among the "un-incited" public* "will be surprised to see how much trust and great respect the Israeli street has for the Court."[54] A few scholars have expended considerable effort to argue that the Supreme Court never really underwent or initiated a legal revolution at all, and that such descriptions are inflated or a figment of our imagination (and therefore not a conceivable cause of declining public faith). Some have moved on from "denial" to the "anger" stage and project their frustration outwards – retired Justice Elyakim Rubenstein seemed to direct his anger towards the Court's critics, suggesting that declining public faith was due to "political attacks" which had "fed" and "incited" large swaths of the Israeli electorate.[55] Next comes the bargaining – in an almost embarrassing feat of intellectual acrobatics, some scholars and commentators have tried explaining why declining faith in courts isn't such a big deal, either because too much confidence in state institutions is unhealthy for a democracy (yes, really), or because the Court still enjoys higher public trust than almost all other public institutions and organs of government.[56]

This last argument is rather common and is especially obnoxious. First, it's worth noting that low public faith in Israel's elected branches – in the Knesset and in the executive Government – is almost certainly related at least partially to the relentless judicial meddling in their affairs. As many have observed, constant judicial intervention with no basis in law amounts to the infantilization of elected government and conveys a subversive message of incompetence. Small wonder that the public struggles to trust the Knesset if the Supreme Court constantly second-guesses the legal validity of its acts. Here, too, Ronen Shamir accurately described the issue already in the 1990s (as noted in our discussion of *Deri* in Chapter 6): "By speaking about the need to ensure public trust in the various branches of government, the court employs a practice whose inevitable outcome is a distrust of 'politics.'" Quashing any government decision as unreasonable and invalidating statutes as unconstitutional naturally leads to a dim public view of their elected representatives. In other words, touting the Court's higher public trust as opposed to elected branches, even though the Court itself contributed

---

* The "un-incited public" presumably means those not yet poisoned by criticism of the Court and either oblivious of it or impervious to it; this would be a delightful admission of selective sampling if Beinisch merited being taken seriously. Unfortunately, she does not.

greatly to this reduced public confidence in the same branches, requires a considerable amount of *chutzpah*.

Second, and more importantly, such an argument is deeply misguided, and grievously so. Public faith is like blood sugar: a low reading is much more dangerous for the diabetic judiciary than it is – even at nominally lower levels – for the legislative and executive branches.

Unlike courts, elected branches of government suffer low public esteem almost by design, as the cut and thrust of politics is a naturally unseemly business. Luckily, the legislature bases its legitimacy on much more concrete democratic foundations – the subjection of its members to regular elections. A parliament makes valid laws because it was chosen for a limited time by the electorate and because its members can be removed by the same electorate if they perform poorly enough – not because the public at large has any degree of trust or confidence in parliament as an institution or in its particular members. The executive enjoys a parallel but similar type of legitimacy, as they are subject to supervision which is indirect but doubled: accountable to elected politicians for their performance (whether under supervision of Government Ministers or of parliamentary committees), and accountable to courts for their adherence to the law. Crucially, both branches of government can endure – indeed even flourish – under conditions of extremely low public faith in their institutions and their members, because public faith is not the currency of their trade in the first place. Democratic mechanisms, elections chief among them, provide the periodic infusion of legitimacy and accountability which make up for any deficit in broad public faith.

The same cannot be said of the judiciary, which has no such alternate source of authority. Unresponsive to public sentiment and preference, rigidly embedded in their office, unelected and unaccountable, judges have only one thing going for them: their faithful application of the law. Without the oxygen of public faith the judiciary immediately suffocates. Any obligation of a citizen or of government to obey a court ruling is derived only from the assumption that the judge is but a conduit of the pre-existing and superior law – otherwise, on what principled basis could such judicial officers pronounce rules and issue binding orders? Certainly not by merit of democratic legitimacy or of personal accountability, of which judges and courts have neither. No, public confidence in a judge's fidelity to the law is *all the judiciary has*. Such confidence must indeed be both personal and institutional – in the absence of either, why comply with a judicial decree?

This is why the comparison with other branches of government is so perversely misleading. The Knesset and Executive can plod along with low public confidence, while the Supreme Court has no such luxury. The former two have a high tolerance level for public distrust while the latter loses its legitimacy at a much lower threshold. A judiciary losing the public's confidence poses a genuine system-wide hazard and threatens to destabilize the entire governmental order. People accept the exercise of judicial power as legitimate only to the extent they believe courts are applying the law, and not a judge's arbitrary whims or personal ideology. If courts are making and unmaking the law, or subjecting elected government to formless and contentless quasi-legal standards of review, or rendering the very notion of "law" meaningless, then the public has little reason to regard their pronouncements as valid.

James Allan describes this as "the danger that citizens will one day see the process for what it is – one where unelected judges get to impose their personal moral sentiments and beliefs on the rest of us."[57] When a court loses the people's trust that it is faithfully applying the law those same people stop obeying judicial decisions and start reaching for the pitchforks, figurative and literal. Harking back to our discussion of judicial selection in Chapter 1, this is one significant reason the issue keeps cropping up – when the public no longer trusts judges to apply the actual law, they demand that at least such judges reflect their own ideological convictions more directly. Allan lists this as precisely one such typical reaction – "the majority will insist on having judges who share its view on these moral questions." This is the natural and predictable outcome of rampant judicial activism culminating in baseless constitutional judicial review.

Abandoning the Constitution. Another related casualty of *Hamizrachi* and ensuing Supreme Court rulings is the collapse of public support for constitutionalism itself, as a viable and acceptable mechanism for democratic government. This matter of observable fact represents a spectacular self-defeating own goal of Israeli judicial supremacy. The endeavor to gradually and methodically legislate the fundamental structure of Israeli government through Basic Laws was progressing at a steady pace – the Knesset had enacted a new Basic Law every four years, on average, from 1948 until 1992. But the constitutional revolution brought Israel's constitutional project to a screeching halt. The next time a new Basic Law was enacted was over two decades later, in 2014.

In addition to eroding the public's democratic spirit and annihilating public faith in the judiciary, the constitutional revolution produced a culture of suspicion and antagonism towards constitutional legislation of almost any kind. The Court's complete distortion of the 1992 Basic Laws and the invention of an Israeli constitution out of whole cloth conveyed to the public that constitutionalism per se was an unreliable instrument of government. *Hamizrachi* made the enactment of Basic Laws an unreasonable risk: if the Court could turn two innocuous laws into a "constitutional revolution," then any legislation could be bent or broken to fit judicial whims. Constitutional legislation began to seem like a futile exercise in a system where the last word belonged to the courts regardless of what the law says.

As described by Yoav Dotan, this consequence became apparent almost immediately: as soon as 1996, three additional Basic Law bills (enshrining additional individual rights) were rejected due to "suspicion and hostility" towards the constitutional revolution.[58] The draft legislation opponents "expressly tied their objections" to their "lack of confidence" in the Court, stating they considered the Court a "political actor" which was exploiting Basic Laws as "an instrument to achieve political outcomes against the wishes of the general public." In the deliberations surrounding those same draft bills, veteran Ultra-Orthodox politician Aryeh Deri perhaps best expressed this sentiment, when he memorably quipped that even if the biblical Ten Commandments were proposed as a Basic Law, he would vote against them. After noting he finds nothing substantially wrong with the "innocent-looking" proposed bills, Deri's objections reflect the legislative mindset for a generation to come: "But who interprets these laws?... How can I rely on the Court to interpret these laws?... Through this pinhole [of Basic Laws] they have injected anything they desire."

Indeed, the only new Basic Laws since 1992 serve to strengthen the point: One Basic Law in 2014 established a mandatory referendum for any relinquishment of sovereign territory, reflecting skepticism towards opportunistic government but also towards judicial enforcement of legal constraints; the other in 2018 (which we will soon discuss) was an initial effort to counter *Hamizrachi*, by balancing the Court's clear progressive and universalistic bent with a Basic Law that sought to prioritize Israel's character as a Jewish national home.

In fact, the entire trajectory of Basic Law legislation swung in the direction of undoing what the Court had done. This was clearly on display immediately after Justice Barak had started proclaiming the "constitutional revolution" at every opportunity and even before *Hamizrachi*: a draft Coalition agreement between left-wing Labor and Orthodox Shas in 1994 already envisioned amending the new Basic Laws to explicitly exclude all "status quo" (religion and State) arrangements from the law's effects and from judicial interference.[59] Going forward, the Knesset effectively abandoned the idea of gradual constitution-making and shifted its focus to damage mitigation and inter-branch trench warfare. In true "revolutionary" fashion, *Hamizrachi* was the guillotine by which the constitutional project met its premature demise.

Absurd Outcomes

The judicial insistence that the Israeli polity conduct itself as though it possesses a constitution yields a host of oddities. These are, if you will, the deformed genetic mutations born of our constitutional fallout.

On the one hand the Court insists Israel has a "constitution" and proceeds almost nonchalantly – along with the broader legal community – as though this were an unremarkable fact. Yet as noted previously, this so-called constitution lacks many, almost all, of the most basic elements necessary for its definition as such, and for its effective and stable administration. In a 1997 essay exploring and predicting some of the systemic flaws arising out of a non-constitution, Yoav Dotan reminds the reader that "it is not superfluous to reiterate that even after the constitutional revolution, we do not have an actual constitution."[60] Or as Mautner stresses in his 2011 book, "it should be borne in mind that Israel does *not* have a written constitution."[61] (Emphasis in source.)

At the most rudimentary level, there is no agreed body of text comprising this constitution – where does it begin, and where does it end? No one can say for certain. There is no "user manual" or clearly defined amendment process – at least in principle, Basic Laws are enacted via the same method as ordinary legislation, but this is far from a recognized process of constitutional amendment. This also means that the very same "constitution" created by the Court is infinitely malleable and is subject to comprehensive and immediate change by any Knesset majority. These and other substantive flaws and omissions have been covered extensively in previous sections. Judicial supremacists routinely refer to the Israeli "Constitution" while ignoring the colossal elephant of its manifest nonexistence.

One obvious point of distortion is the Court's exercise of judicial review – freely and callously striking down legislation on the thin grounds of a "substantive" constitution. As many scholars have pointed out, the force and degree of judicial review ought to be inexorably linked to the strength of the constitutional text it relies on. Dotan explains:

> "The strength of judicial review and the degree of legitimacy it provides to the court ultimately depend on the force and status of the constitutional text itself. That is: if the constitutional text is partial, limited, and fragmented, and if its normative status – which is supposed to confer binding authority – is unstable, then the standing of judicial review based on that text may also be compromised."

Yet the Supreme Court never seemed to take the constitution's fundamental weakness into account, and preferred to proceed with judicial review as though Israel had a constitution like any other. Such a degree of blasé indifference is remarkable, considering the obvious reality that "the 'constitution' – if the term can even be applied in this context – produced by the 'constitutional revolution' is partial, unstable, and problematic."[62] Echoing a similar sentiment and for reasons of both substance and prudence, Ruth Gavison argued that the Court should have adopted a position of "cautious passivity" following the 1992 legislation. Needless to say, the Court exhibited no such judgment in *Hamizrachi* or since.

Yoav Dotan also argues a point addressed in previous sections – that the Supreme Court decreed a "substantive" constitution containing all ultimate judicial authority, yet with few accompanying justifications, tempering effects or balancing mechanisms. This is a critical flaw which is both theoretical and practical. The "unencouraging conclusions" which arise from examining the legal reality, per Dotan, is that the Court's constitutional framework "suffers most acutely from the many flaws and problems typical" of textual constitutions, "without being able to overcome the objections or mitigate their force through the arguments commonly made" in their favor.[63] Any constitution in the world must contend with a host of justified and principled objections; most constitutional jurisdictions successfully contend with these by utilizing various balancing mechanisms (such as a clear popular amendment process, or overtly political judicial selection) and by relying on competing justifications (such as grounding the constitution in clear democratic consensus, or such as an underlying federative or presidential system). Conversely, the judicially-invented Israeli constitution has done away with (or never had) any conventional constrains and counterbalances, while retaining the many inherent flaws that inevitably exist within any constitution.

It's not only that as far as the Court is concerned, "with great power comes no responsibility"; it's that a constitution devoid of its characteristic trappings is fundamentally unstable and has a profoundly disruptive effect on its surrounding environment. The recurring reference to "stability" is instructive, as that too is reminiscent of the science and literature of atomic chain reactions. To risk overusing our nuclear metaphor, the Israeli constitution since 1995 resembles the Chernobyl reactor – an overheating core, seething beneath the surface, all red lights flashing, mere steps away from a catastrophic meltdown, with the cloaked judicial engineers shrugging off any warning signs as "not great, not terrible."* Save for the white lab-coats replacing black judicial robes, the two scenarios are remarkably similar.

Another key distortion caused by the Court's constitution is the regularity and callousness – the "unbearable ease"[64] – with which the Knesset amends the purported constitutional text. Here we regard not theoretical ability, but actual prevalent practice. Basic Laws are supposed to be the core textual element of Israel's "substantive" constitution, yet they are altered or swapped at the drop of a hat. Almost every newly formed Coalition tweaks and fiddles with constitutional arrangements – sometimes dramatically so – without a second thought. Sweeping changes are introduced to reflect unattractive temporary (or permanent) compromises and to accommodate immediate, shortsighted, and mundane political circumstances of the day.

Criticism towards legislators for this seeming transgression is misplaced. MKs are engaged in the inevitable administration of statutory arrangements which are constitutional only in name, not in nature, and were never designed as such. The Knesset, in fact, simply continued to conduct itself after 1995 just as it always had done; but somehow the same practice had become "constitutional." The Court imposed the label "constitution" on a slew of laws and on a type of legislation which bear no resemblance to a constitution, and which beg frequent and heavy-handed amendments; a label which was immediately contradicted by the day-to-day reality and needs of Knesset legislative practice. The point is that accepting Basic Laws as Israel's constitution produces precisely this kind of bizarrely anomalous system – a so-called constitution that is freely and regularly amended by any majority for any reason.

To be clear, this "unbearable ease" of legislation makes perfect sense. New or old, whether as originally enacted or as later amended, the Basic Laws are no masterpiece of statecraft. No one pretends that these laws complement humankind

* A phrase immortalized by Anatoly Dyatlov in the HBO miniseries "Chernobyl."

or represent a serious degree of considered judgment. Given all the historical constraints, the convoluted legal background, the relative lack of expertise and experience of most legislators involved, and especially, the absence of a unified and consolidated system of holistic complimentary governmental arrangements, the rules set out in Israel's Basic Laws are for the most part clumsy, imprecise and ineffectual, meant to serve transient interests. In the worst case, such rules make for governing institutions and arrangements which are extremely poorly designed and are inconducive to good governance, or which are specifically geared toward benefiting one political faction over another. Even in the most charitable view they require, at the very least, constant revision and adaptation to changing circumstances, and the Israeli constitutional order was always predicated on precisely this assumption.

Two points become clear under such circumstances. The first is that one can hardly fault the Knesset for regular modification of Basic Laws. The second, more importantly, is that a desire to "constitutionalize" such arrangements as they stand is plainly bonkers. By announcing Basic Laws to be Israel's constitution, the Court freezes them mid-air and leaves in perpetual malformation. Necessary statutory changes now bear the gravity (and stigma) of "constitutional amendments," such that they are harder to enact or justify; repairing flawed arrangements becomes far more complicated. Doing so also romanticizes the statutory text of Basic Laws (to the extent the Court is capable of taking any text seriously), demanding the text be regarded as hallowed constitutional ground instead of what it really is – a muddy gutter of opportunistic political haggling.

Martin Loughlin (quoting Christopher Eisgruber) criticizes the "fetishism" surrounding constitutional texts, especially in the American context, as it "promotes a culture of uncritical devotion towards the text."[65] Regardless of whether Loughlin's criticism is justified for the United States, his description easily applies to Israel – by elevating sloppy and mediocre Basic Laws to a constitution, the Court creates an "aesthetic fallacy," ignoring the text's nature as a "compromise between practical politicians" which is in places "vague, turgid or redundant" or which contains "pedestrian provisions and unfortunate errors." This is likely truer for Israeli Basic Laws than it can be for any conventional constitution.

Another related disruptive consequence of the same origin is the way shallow political quibbling seeps into so-called constitutional legislation. The fact that the easily-amended Basic Laws have become a "constitution" simply reduced the latter to the gladiator pits of ordinary legislation. Instead of representing an elevated, aloof form of detached and enlightened deliberation, the purported constitution became sullied by the mundane trivialities and obnoxious vulgarities of ordinary politics. Yoav Dotan describes this as the "routine use of constitutional instruments and arguments" in "daily political struggles." Instead of "constitutionally-guided politics," laments Dotan, the Court created the "politicization of constitutionalism."[66]

One of Dotan's most insightful contentions in his 1997 essay was that the constitutional revolution armed both the Knesset and Supreme Court with "non-conventional" weapons – not only to legislate and interpret as had previously been the case, but also to mutually alter the fundamental "rules of the game" for any ad hoc purpose within their mutual struggle for ultimate authority.[67] This had, in Dotan's words, made the political game "immeasurably less stable and more dangerous."[68] The Court did this by creating a bizarre framework of constitutional government, under which (by the Court's own theory) the Knesset has unlimited power to effortlessly change the most fundamental constitutional arrangements; while at the same time, the Court itself became a de facto constituent authority, establishing both the constitution itself and constantly shaping its norms and application. In this way each branch possessed the power, at least in principle, to inflict devastating damage on the other. Crucially, rather than develop a "Mutually-Assured-Destruction" balance of terror in which both parties avoid use of their considerable non-conventional arsenal for fear of the consequences, the constitutional revolution created the expectation in both camps that each institution eagerly and vigorously exercise its non-conventional authority.

"At the empirical level," Dotan explains, this meant that "the results of the constitutional revolution" are the opposite of what its supporters might have hoped for – the Supreme Court suffered a public legitimacy crisis far more severe than anything prior to 1995, and further still, the Knesset came increasingly closer to reversing specific judicial outcomes and to downgrading the Court's broader institutional authority.[69] In this sense, the awkward and ill-fitting notion of a "substantive" constitution raised the political and societal stakes, and triggered a vicious cycle of escalation and counter-escalation with no end in sight.

Who Overrides Whom?

A significant part of the problem created by the constitutional revolution is the absence of crucial tie-breaking mechanisms. Any well-designed constitutional model must include a method for resolving deadlock – some avenue by which when an impasse is reached, one side of an argument may prevail under the applicable rules, the other side concedes defeat, and everyone moves on. This is especially true regarding tensions between elected branches and the embedded judiciary. Such tiebreakers can be targeted to address a particular issue – such as "notwithstanding" clauses (allowing the legislature to make exceptions to constitutional rules and rulings) or popular referendums on a particular measure; or they may be of a more systemic nature, such as constitutional amendments or judicial appointments which ultimately neutralize opposition on the court. Some easy examples are the United States, where constitutional change may be effected by a clear amendment process or by presidential appointment of the federal judiciary; or Switzerland, where the voting public can directly initiate independent ballot measures and even constitutional amendments. The benefits of tiebreakers are twofold: on a principled level they ensure that the law of the land ultimately reflects the will of a consistent democratic majority, while on a pragmatic level they are able to end prolonged and sustained inter-branch standoffs.

Israel, extraordinarily, has no real tiebreaking mechanism since the constitutional revolution, but is rather doomed to endless (and often escalating) rounds of conflict between the Supreme Court and the elected branches. The only way such clashes are resolved is when one institution or organ backs down before the other. The pre-*Hamizrachi* era of parliamentary supremacy had a clear answer – the Knesset was supreme and its explicit directives prevailed. But since 1995 Israelis no longer have a way to translate electoral success into judicially-disfavored policy. Simply put, the Israeli public has no recourse, no recognized or established route to get its way and to exercise its democratic autonomy, no viable method to prevail over judicial opposition.

Let that sink in for a moment. If a significant majority of the electorate wants to radically change Israeli immigration policy in a manner unacceptable to the Court, what is it to do? The public has almost no influence on judicial appointments and the Court's makeup; there are no mechanisms for public-initiated ballot measures or referendums. The effectiveness of amending Basic Laws is questionable – just think of the attempts to annul the Deri Doctrine, ignored by the Court – and the ability to do so is judicially-limited (we'll soon return to this point). Any reasonable observer must ask, what known recourse does the public have to enforce its will, to receive final say on policy and values?

The Ultra-Orthodox draft exemption is of course another case in point. A clear electoral and political majority desire a particular policy; such policy confers a benefit on a demographic minority and harms no tangible individual rights. Aside the hollow claim of abstract "equality," the policy violates no substantive constitutional norm (however odious or objectionable many find it to be). Nonetheless, over the course of thirty years the Supreme Court has insisted on nullifying the draft exemption again and again: ruling it justiciable in 1988, requiring primary legislation in 1998, holding that it violated "equality" in 2006, and finally striking down legislation in 2012 and again in 2017. With every single groundless ruling the Court thwarted the valid democratic will of an electoral majority while wreaking havoc on the Israeli political system. All this raises the simple question: What recourse is available to the same electoral majority? The answer, as things stand under Israeli law and jurisprudence, is "none."

This brings us to yet another anomaly caused by the non-constitution – the infamous and much-derided "override" mechanism. As the reader may recall, Yehudit Karp had argued already in 1993 that any power of judicial review would be limited by the Knesset's explicit refutation. Her (ambitious) reading of the 1992 Basic Laws was that the Court could exercise judicial review for legislation that violated rights implicitly or indirectly, while a statute that reflected a deliberate and explicit intent to contradict the Basic Laws was immune from the Court's scrutiny. And indeed, something along these lines came to pass – at least for Basic Law: Freedom of Occupation. The 1994 controversy surrounding the importation of Kosher meat produced an unusual compromise, championed by none other than Justice Aharon Barak himself. The end result was that the 1994 legislative overhaul of BL:FO included a clear "override" clause: Section 8 allows for an ordinary law to infringe upon freedom of occupation, "provided it is included in a law passed by a majority of Knesset Members and it explicitly states that it shall be valid notwithstanding the provisions of this Basic Law." Any such law needs to be renewed every four years to retain its immunity from judicial review.

Indeed, Barak glorifies and extols override clauses in *Hamizrachi*, citing these favorably as "weakening" any argument against the counter-majoritarian nature of judicial review. Specifically noting BL:FO, Barak approvingly describes such override clauses as a "constitutional opening" for "the current political majority" to circumvent constitutional rules. For Barak this is a valid "constitutional route" allowing "today's majority" to fulfill its constitutional aspirations "even while infringing upon" certain values and rights protected by the constitution.[70] Critically, for Barak this point serves to support his establishment of judicial review, as in his view an override clause neutralizes the arguments that judicial review undermines public will and popular democracy.

As the Court's pursuit of judicial supremacy became more apparent and the Court's legislative interference became more aggressive, the idea of additional "override" clauses gained more traction. An "override" mechanism of one form or another is not an Israeli invention – often called a "notwithstanding" clause, they may be found in various jurisdictions, with Canada as perhaps the most notable example. Under such a scheme, the legislature may reject a judicial determination of constitutional invalidity by explicitly stating its desire to render a statute immune from judicial review. This can be done retrospectively (re-legislating a law which was previously struck down) or prospectively (enacting an immune law in anticipation it might otherwise be struck down). The straightforward justification is that for certain issues and in certain circumstances, a handful of robed ex-lawyers are not better judges (so to speak) of abstract constitutional norms than a majority of elected representatives, nor can their ultimate "final say" authority on controversial issues be squared with republican democracy and popular sovereignty. The argument is especially valid regarding abstract notions such as "dignity" or "equality," and in cases in which the court itself is starkly divided. If nearly half the bench thinks a particular law is constitutionally valid, for instance, ought not the elected legislators have the prerogative to make their own determination on the matter?

It's worth noting that an "override" of this kind is not to be confused with general legislative correction of disputed judicial decisions. At least in principle,* any legislature may override almost any ruling which is based on interpretation or on pre-existing law, in the sense that the legislature may clarify existing statutes or make new law. If parliament disagrees with a judicial decision it can simply enact a new statute which says otherwise, or can pass more specific legislative language which leaves far less room for judicial discretion and directs judges to

* As we know, the Court is fully capable of simply ignoring such legislative clarifications or even new laws it dislikes.

the preferred outcome in future cases. A court is bound by new legislation and must adjust its rulings accordingly, *especially* if such legislation is a direct response to previous rulings. This is a basic element of parliamentary democracy and of separation of powers and does not require further elaboration. Israeli discourse on the matter often conflates such routine legislative rerouting of judicial decisions, and the more intense "override" mechanism regarding judicial invalidation of a statute on constitutional grounds.

The "override" mechanism crops up every few years and has been floated, fairly consistently, in almost every elections since 1995. Some proposals would add such a clause to BL:HDL, while others would legislate a broader "override" ability for all judicial review. The concept gradually became a controversial flashpoint in Israeli legal and political circles. Polls indicate that the idea enjoys substantial public support, while on the other hand, politicians on both sides of the aisle seem reluctant to pursue such proposals with vigor. One reason is that an "override" clause makes constitutionalists and legal conservatives genuinely uneasy on principled grounds – there are obvious objections to providing the majoritarian legislature a veto over judicial protection of rights and liberties. Other concerns are more tactical, as some argue that the practical hurdles to exercising any "override" authority would be so considerable that it would hardly ever be used (as is indeed the case in Canada); while at the same time its existence would embolden the Court even further, as the Court could claim that the "override" adds greater popular oversight and therefore increases the legitimacy of its decisions. In other words, even critics of the Court's expansionism are skeptical of adopting an "override" mechanism.

Such dilemmas aside, the mainstream debate surrounding the "override" clause obscures its core justification and the warped reality it reflects. The need for an "override" is itself another distortion caused by the absurd scenario of judicial review with no constitution, no constitutional text, no public mandate and consensus for supreme law and its enforcement, no clear amendment process, and no electoral input into judicial selection. Far from a deviation which is "notwithstanding" a firm constitutional rule, an Israeli "override" clause represents legislative rejection of far-fetched and half-baked judicial application of faux-constitutional law. While ordinary constitutional democracies might deliberate whether an "override" clause is appropriate for their circumstances, the average Israeli may rightly ask – how can we possibly *not* have an override clause? How can a democratic society tolerate final say authority seized by an unelected self-perpetuating oligarchy, without any known or legal ability to deviate from its diktats? A Supreme Court which vetoes legislation based on a fabricated non-constitution and an electorate wholly powerless to do anything about it is a reality unjustifiable in principle and untenable in practice. Something's got to give.

Whatever one thinks of an Israeli "override" clause, we must recognize that it is just one more byproduct of the constitutional revolution, just one more lopsided solution to a much more severe problem. This may be said of many of the legislative attempts at restricting the Court's exceptional powers. What seems most peculiar is the habit of judicial supremacists to complain of such efforts. Not only are these a direct outcome of the Court's constitutional revolution; they are also predicated on the same theoretical and practical basis which the Supreme Court itself developed and championed. If a small minority of oblivious legislators could inadvertently spawn a constitution with hard judicial review, surely the same legislature can then – deliberately and with broader support – fashion additional, alternative and contrary constitutional arrangements. In other words, the very foundation offered by the Court to legitimate its constitutional revolution, both in substance and in form, must necessarily also legitimate subsequent exercises of "constituent powers" by the Knesset. In this sense supremacist opponents of the "override" clause can't possibly reject its legal premise – they just dislike the taste of their own medicine. Yoav Dotan put it presciently and succinctly in 1997:

> "Those who 'enact' a 'constitution' through deceptive parliamentary maneuvers should neither be surprised nor offended when it becomes clear that they must stand guard to defend such 'constitution' from opposing political maneuvers. Nor should they be surprised if political groups who… feel that they were the targets of such deception refuse to stand silent or to join the 'festivities,' but instead attempt to 'reverse the decree' by all political means at their disposal."[71]

*

The events of the constitutional revolution happened three decades ago. Much water has flowed under the bridge since that time. The fact of the matter is that the Supreme Court regularly exercises an authority of judicial review and strikes down Knesset legislation, while the legal and political order have largely come to begrudgingly accept this as an existing feature of the Israeli system of government. One might reasonably ask – if the constitutional revolution is "settled" and an established legal reality, what's the point of all this, and why does it matter? Why relitigate so much legal history and rehash these scholarly debates? Shouldn't bygones be bygones? Can we not put the matter to rest and move on?

The answer is that the critiques and flaws apply today with as much force and relevance as they did in November of 1995, and every day since. As this chapter has shown, the Supreme Court's constitutional revolution and its interference with primary legislation is not an isolated blow which a victim may shrug off, not an injury from which one naturally recovers with the passage of time. Its profoundly debilitating effects permeate every corner of Israeli law, culture and politics – and the cumulative harm it creates is rapidly increasing, not diminishing. The Court's power and practice of lawless and limitless judicial review is an untended festering wound at the heart of Israel's national existence. As time passes the legal infection spreads, and the polity's condition worsens. The rot gradually begins to compromise critical systems, with ever-deteriorating cycles of convulsion and resuscitation. The notion that such an ailment will "heal with time" is a dangerous delusion: either the contagion is properly diagnosed and urgently treated with the utmost vigor and resolve, or the patient will ultimately succumb to the strain of judicial supremacy.

Chapter 11

Lawless

Judicial Supremacy and Ultimate Final Say

"*This ruling represents a peak moment of judicial activism on a global scale... Israel experienced a regime change at the start of 2024 and can no longer be considered a democracy but rather a juristocracy.*"
— Prof. Moshe Cohen-Eliyah[1]

The Constitutional Revolution 2.0

The 2024 *Reasonableness* ruling has made for an unlikely recurring character in our exploration of Israeli judicial supremacy. When this book had first been contemplated and initiated the ruling had not yet been born, still existing prenatally only in contested litigation briefings and in the pregnant minds of Supreme Court Justices. Yet it has reliably made its appearances at various points throughout the previous chapters, each time illuminating or demonstrating a particular aspect of the Court's behavior or jurisprudence. While its fleeting entries have been instructive and useful, we have mostly skirted around (or have entirely avoided) the decision's primary substance and its most important ramifications. As we now arrive at our final discussion, the *Reasonableness* ruling may properly take center stage, and reveal itself as both the harbinger of ultimate judicial power and as the death knell of Israeli constitutional law in its entirety.

To fully explicate the essence and significance of the *Reasonableness* ruling we must commence with an exceedingly simple and straightforward question. Can the Supreme Court strike down a Basic Law as unconstitutional or invalid?

This question has no doubt been nagging the astute reader for some time now, as despite its near-obvious consequence it has so far gone unacknowledged and unaddressed. After all, one might ask, what's the big deal? If the Knesset can legislate and amend any Basic Law by any majority; and if the Basic Laws are the State's de facto "constitution" since *Hamizrachi* by the Court's jurisprudence; and if the Court's power of judicial review is derived of the Basic Law's supreme status and text; then does this not simply mean that the Knesset still retains final-say authority? Does it not mean that the Knesset is at liberty to freely undo what the Court has done? This resembles Professor Nimmer's critique of *Bergman* in the 1970s – if Basic Laws are a constitution but the Knesset may enact or amend them as it pleases, is this not indistinguishable from parliamentary supremacy? And if this is the case, then what's all the hullabaloo?

The question is well taken. Our discussion so far would reasonably lead us to conclude that the answer is "no" – the Court may not strike down a Basic Law. If the Knesset exercises original "constituent power" by enacting Basic Laws, and if the Court can strike down ordinary statutes due to their unconstitutional violation of Basic Laws, then surely the Court has no conceivable authority to review the legality of Basic Laws themselves. Indeed, according to everything we've described so far in the previous chapters, the Knesset may annul "Basic Law: Human Dignity and Liberty" without even an absolute majority; it may disband the Supreme Court and establish a different institution in its stead, not to mention simply altering the judicial selection process; it may render certain Government decisions to be categorically nonjusticiable and beyond the reach of the Court – and so on. No "override" clause would ever be necessary, as in principle the Knesset could simply re-enact the invalidated statute as a new Basic Law, or could immunize a statute to begin with the same way. In short, if the Court is bound by Basic Laws and is powerless to invalidate them, then the Knesset remains supreme – at least when push comes to shove – taking much of the sting out of the constitutional revolution.

To all this we may ruefully answer as did the Coen brothers – "would that it were so simple."*

In a process that began in 2017 and culminated in the 2024 *Reasonableness* ruling, the Supreme Court developed a series of doctrines to justify and enable their interference with – and ultimate domination of – Basic Laws. In doing so, the Court arrogated to itself the most significant norm-making power within the Israeli constitutional order and pulled the rug out from under the constitutional revolution with all its premises and rationales. It is to this most recent dramatic development that we now turn our attention.

Unlimited Original Constituent Power

Even with all its faults and failings, with all its distortion and implausibility, the constitutional revolution had a single and central premise of some discernible coherence and internal logic. *Hamizrachi* was based on an intuitive and straightforward proposition: That Basic Laws are Israel's constitution created by the exercise of the Knesset's original constituent authority, and that the Supreme Court was merely enforcing said constitution by judicial review of incompatible inferior legislation. If we suspend all our objections to the legal validity and justifications of the premise itself, we may recognize its elegant, hierarchical and uncomplicated nature. Indeed, the Court and many of its supporters often present the argument in such simple terms. This foundational thesis stands at the core of

---

* From the 2016 film "Hail, Caesar!"

the constitutional revolution and of (almost) all of the Court's constitutional jurisprudence since 1995. It has been repeated to exhaustion in judicial rulings, speeches, scholarly writings, media interviews, and anywhere else conceivable, hundreds if not thousands of times. It flows directly and immediately from all the convoluted and elaborate theories of the constitutional revolution.

From the People to the Knesset to the Basic Laws. In this sense the Court had always sought to frame its power of judicial review as the uncomplicated, inevitable and natural outcome of applying a democratic constitution. Grounding the constitutional revolution on this foundation represents the Court's efforts at maintaining the democratic pedigree of its constitutional jurisprudence, even if loose and implausible. This simple (or even simplistic) formula conforms, at least superficially, to the most fundamental constitutional principle of supreme law derived from popular sovereignty – the conventional framework of established constitutional thought throughout the democratic world.

The second key element or premise of the constitutional revolution is the Knesset's unlimited and supreme authority to enact constitutional legislation. Chief Justice Shamgar posited such authority explicitly – he called his theory "the Knesset's unlimited authority" – and argued that this included the ability of self-restriction and of creating distinct tiers of superior and inferior legislation, in turn enabling judicial review. Chief Justice Barak's theory, which swiftly became the dominant and official view, was that the Knesset acting as constituent authority could impose limits and restraints on the Knesset acting as legislature. Critically, on Barak's view, the Knesset exercises *original* constituent powers, that is, it is equivalent to a constitutional assembly drafting an original constitution, and does not exercise mere post-establishment "amendment" power (we will return to this momentarily). In both versions, and in essence, under any theory capable of supporting the constitutional revolution, the Knesset possesses limitless power to shape and reshape Israel's constitutional norms.

These two elements – Basic Laws as a constitution and the Knesset's unlimited constitutional powers – are not mere technicalities or accidents, but are necessary for the Court's entire construct of the constitutional revolution enabling judicial review. It is only based on these two fundamental components that the Court could claim that the 1992 Basic Laws, legislated casually and almost accidentally without fanfare or public sanction, could serve as a de facto constitution. Without both combined, the Court can rely on nothing but thin air.

The first element has already been discussed at length, and a handful of quotes will suffice to illustrate the point. In Section 1 of his *Hamizrachi* opinion, Barak establishes the "core" of the constitutional revolution in no uncertain terms, as "the recognition that, under our constitutional structure, the Knesset holds the constitutional authority to grant Israel a constitution."[2] A few pages later he writes: "The theory of the Knesset's constituent authority has, at its base, the conception that its constituent power derives from the sovereign – that is, from the people. By virtue of this constituent authority, the Knesset grants Israel its constitution (in the form of Basic Laws)."[3] This in turn serves as Barak's basis for judicial review: "By exercising judicial review the court fulfills the constitution and the Basic Laws."[4] Barak and others reiterated the claim time and again – a decade later, Barak stressed: "We presently have a constitution. Our extant constitution is the Basic Laws."[5] When the Court strikes down laws, it does nothing but humbly enforce the constitutional rules set out by Basic Laws enacted by the democratic Knesset wielding its constituent power. These are the core propositions – distinguished by their relative simplicity, consistency and clarity – which summarize the overarching legal theory of the constitutional revolution adopted by the Court and by the legal establishment.

Yet a key aspect of this argument is often overlooked or misunderstood. The idea of unlimited Knesset constitutional power is not only legal, doctrinal or theoretical – it was and remains a critical component of the Court's practical effort at recruiting public and political legitimacy for the constitutional revolution. This was a defensive, prospective, *forward-looking* justification. Perhaps the legal *authority* of the Basic Laws rested on the Knesset's past exercise of its constituent powers; but the democratic *legitimacy* of the constitutional revolution depended on the future ability of the Knesset to freely change or enact further constitutional norms.

The point of prospective unlimited constitutional powers does of course have normative implications. As a doctrinal or philosophical argument, democratic representatives retain continued legitimacy not because they were previously elected, but primarily because they are subject to repeated future reevaluation by the electorate. A core insight of ongoing representative democracy is that a legislator's legitimacy is derived from the next elections at least as much as from the previous ones. Similarly, the authority of any democratic constitution might rest on some past historical moment, but its legitimacy is predicated on the ultimate ability of the People to amend or replace it, one way or another. The distinction here is arguably semantic, in the sense that both authority and legitimacy are one and the same – the democratic rationale for the validity of a supreme law is the same rationale for the people retaining power to change or replace such law. The point remains the same, and was reiterated by the Court to justify the constitutional revolution.

A related but crucial factor is the idiosyncratic nature of the "ongoing" Israeli constitutional revolution. No one in the mainstream of Israeli judicial supremacy – certainly not Barak or the Court – has claimed that the Israeli constitution is complete. The 1992 Basic Laws, and those that came before or after, were recognized by the Court as individual enforceable "chapters" of a constitution still deep in the process of its own formulation. This view has been reiterated by the Court time and again, including in recent cases such as the *Reasonableness* ruling. Flaws of such a construct (discussed at length above) notwithstanding, it is universally agreed that under the Court's theory, when the Knesset amends or enacts Basic Laws it is exercising *original* constituent power (as though it were the 1949 constitutional assembly itself) and not some derivative or delegated amendment power. For this reason, any future Knesset continues to possess the same constitutional powers it did in 1992 or at any other time. In other words, analytically, the underlying rationale of the constitutional revolution – that of piece-meal, fractional, gradual constitution-making – necessarily entails that the Knesset retains unlimited future constitutional power, at least until a full and comprehensive constitution is adopted and recognized (an event that virtually all agree has not yet transpired). Without the Knesset's unlimited constitutional authority there could be no constitutional revolution in the first place – remove that premise and the entire construct comes tumbling down.

But most importantly, touting the Knesset's unlimited power to enact and change Basic Laws was a pragmatic persuasion tactic for the Court to defend the constitutional revolution, to preserve public legitimacy, to assuage its critics and to allay the fears of the political establishment. The core of the Court's argument was that it was not usurping constitutional or legislative power, nor was it establishing a system of judicial supremacy based on arbitrary will, because ultimate authority still remained solely in the hands of the elected, accountable, responsive Knesset. Even after the constitutional revolution (and in keeping with its theoretical basis) the Knesset may continue to shape the Israeli constitution as it sees fit, such that the link to popular sovereignty remains intact and the overall democratic framework is maintained. Indeed, the Court contended that it was empowering and defending the Knesset, not usurping its power. The Court essentially reassured the Knesset that as a practical matter it could always respond to the Court's judicial decisions and that it would have the clear upper hand. Furthermore, this meant that in a worst-case scenario the Knesset could in fact reverse the constitutional revolution itself in its entirety – it could annul the 1992 laws, enact specific legislation ruling out judicial review, reconstitute the Supreme Court or establish a separate constitutional court for judicial review, and so on.

Critically, the Court also clarified and reiterated that the definition of a constitutional norm – that is, of a Basic Law – is binary, and the designation of legislation as "Basic Laws" is subject to the absolute discretion of the Knesset, as had always been the case. In other words, the Knesset remained the sole body authorized to enact "constitutional" legislation without any substantive or procedural limitations (save the exception of procedural-numerical entrenchment for specific provisions).*

Adopting this position had two strong practical implications. First, it lent additional legitimacy to individual instances of judicial review and gave the Court more leeway. If the Knesset disliked a particular case in which a law was struck down, the Knesset could always simply reverse the Court's decision by re-legislating the same law anew as a Basic Law. As such the Court could maintain that there was an additional democratic check on its own exercise of judicial review, which could be employed with less restraint. Second, the argument generally takes much of the sting out of critiques against the constitutional

* We will return to this point in our later discussion of the *Shafir* case.

revolution. If the Knesset retains final-say power all along, is the constitutional revolution really that bad, really so usurpative and undemocratic? If the Knesset could, in principle, disband the Court or fundamentally remake the constitutional order, is the constitutional revolution really so terrible? Stating that the Knesset remained the ultimate constitutional authority conveyed the message that the democratic balance of power had not been upended.

A more subtle implication relates to the Court's incentives against radical rulings. The Knesset's ability to negate the Court's rulings and even to unilaterally upend the constitutional order has an undeniable tempering effect on the Court's most activist and supremacist tendencies. At least in theory, the Court would exercise a modicum of care in the knowledge that if it pushed the envelope too hard it could elicit a genuinely devastating legislative backlash. The Knesset's ultimate constitutional authority was thus a critical check on judicial power, not only in the event of a showdown but rather especially as it could moderate judicial decision-making to avoid such showdowns altogether.

This overall key component of the Court's constitutional theory is critical to understanding the Knesset's response to *Hamizrachi* and to subsequent cases, or lack thereof. The Knesset and its elected politicians were consistently reassured that Basic Laws were immune from judicial review, and that as such their ultimate authority was not undercut. They were willing to tolerate certain judicial antics confident in the knowledge that, at least in theory, they could hit the "abort" button at any time.

This view was most effectively and explicitly expressed by none other than Justice Aharon Barak. One especially illustrative example deserves our closest attention. In 2003 the public and Knesset were slowly coming to terms with the constitutional revolution, as its implications and consequences had only just begun to emerge. Only three relatively inconsequential laws had been struck down so far, but the legal and public debate was increasing in its extent and intensity. New governing Coalitions had begun consistently appointing Justice Ministers overtly critical of the Court's expansionist activism. On this backdrop, Barak took the opportunity to articulate the prevailing view on unlimited Knesset authority.

In a speech to the annual convention of the Israel Bar Association, which was later published as a law review article, Chief Justice Barak took great pains to emphasize the Knesset's unlimited constitutional power. Echoing the first "premise" discussed above, Barak explained that when the Court had adopted the power of judicial review in 1995, it had "expressed the supremacy of the Knesset as constituent authority." Any restriction enforced by the Court was "a restriction the Knesset itself created, and is an expression of the Knesset's supreme constituent power." Per Barak, the Court's role is to "interpret the Knesset's most supreme norm – the Basic Laws," to "interpret ordinary legislation," and to "determine whether there is a contradiction" between the two. As such, "when recognizing such a contradiction the Court is enforcing the Knesset's supreme norm – the Basic Laws." Barak maintains that "this does not trespass on the Knesset's authority, but rather protects the Basic Law constituted by the Knesset against infringement." Barak then summarizes and reiterates his core contention of *Hamizrachi*: "When the Court annuls a law passed by the Knesset because it contradicts a Basic Law, it does not deny the sovereign its democratic authority; the sovereign is the people. The Court gives expression to the will of the sovereign (the people) through their representatives in the Knesset, as reflected in the Basic Law."[6]

Barak then spells out, in the clearest terms possible, what this means for the Knesset's ability to enact Basic Laws, reflecting our second "premise" above:

> "If the Knesset does not agree with the court's ruling interpreting a Basic Law, it has the authority to amend the Basic Law and establish a different constitutional arrangement… Thus, at the pinnacle of the normative pyramid stands the Knesset as a constituent authority. It acts above the Knesset as a legislative authority. The judge's role is to interpret the provisions enacted by the Knesset as both a constituent and legislative authority, and to determine whether they are compatible; in doing so, the judge protects the Knesset itself."

The quote is well worth reading a second time and filing away for future reference. "*At the pinnacle of the normative pyramid stands the Knesset as a constituent authority.*" It encapsulates in a nutshell the entire conception of Knesset supremacy and the idea that the Knesset retains unlimited constitutional power, acknowledged even (and especially) after the constitutional revolution.

Later that year, Chief Justice Barak made similar statements to a group of senior jurists that had assembled for a conversation, at the Knesset, regarding inter-branch tensions. Again, expressing the ultimate authority retained by the Knesset, Barak did not mince words:

> "The Knesset may pass a Basic Law annulling constitutional judicial review, and the Court could not overturn such a rule… If the Court strikes down a law as unconstitutional, the Knesset could override such a ruling by re-enacting the law anew as a Basic Law."[7]

Barak's point here reflects the two parallel aspects of Knesset supremacy – both the ability to reverse judicial review by enacting Basic Laws which are immune from judicial scrutiny, and the ultimate power of constitutional legislation, including "annulling" judicial review altogether.

Critically, Barak's statements in both examples from 2003 were plainly uncontroversial and drew little attention. Barak in his capacity as Chief Justice was stating the obvious reality, known and acknowledged by all relevant actors, including the Court. The undisputed fact that the Knesset could freely enact Basic Laws as it saw fit, and that no court could review the legality or validity of Basic Laws, flowed naturally and inevitably from the core logic of the constitutional revolution and from the clear and unequivocal reassurances of the Court, its members and its leader.

The fundamental premise of an omnipotent Knesset (when acting as constituent authority) was thus not only a product of the constitutional revolution – it was and remains one of its only conceivable defenses. Though the Court's power of judicial review is devoid of legal merit and has been routinely abused, it could perhaps be somehow endured, through gritted teeth, as long as this premise held true. The immunity of Basic Laws from judicial scrutiny was not only an essential component of the constitutional revolution – it is the thread by which the entire edifice hangs, the Court's sole remaining lifeline of legitimacy.

Only once we have grasped the essence and centrality of this point, can we turn to consider the audacity, the absurdity – indeed, the treachery – of its inversion and annihilation by the Supreme Court, by subjecting the Knesset's constituent power to judicial review and declaring Basic Laws unlawful.

Just how radical and paradoxical would such an attempt by the Court be? Yoav Dotan had identified the potential for such a development already in 1997, explaining that any such approach by the Court would necessitate deviating from the "textual" foundation it had adopted in *Hamizrachi* (i.e., the Basic Laws are the constitution), and relying on a profoundly problematic "meta-textual" jurisprudence (i.e., the Court does as it pleases based on abstract moral ideals). In Dotan's words (emphasis added):

> "Any attempt by the Court to limit the Knesset's future constituent authority would presumably have to be based on meta-textual foundations. If the Court were to go down that route… its approach would likely encounter significant difficulties. On the theoretical level, *adopting any such judicial position would contradict the textualist theory on which the Court itself relied.* On the practical level, a judicial stance of this kind would likely face a sharp backlash from both the public and the political system alike. This is not only because *the Court would have to explain how it is reversing its course*, and censoring the very same "constitution" whose status the Court itself had previously elevated to great heights within our legal system; but especially because it is probable that such an explanation would have to be offered against a tense and problematic political backdrop, formed by the same circumstances causing the collision between Court and Knesset."[8]

Some twenty-seven years later, when the Court voted to strike down the Basic Law *Reasonableness* amendment, Justice David Mintz pointed out this very same categorical contradiction:

> "Doctrines applying judicial review to the content of the constitutional text [i.e., to Basic Laws] undermine the very foundation recognizing the constituent authority. This is not a technical or procedural difficulty; it is a substantive difficulty that challenges fundamental, deep-rooted conceptions. The annulment of Basic Laws based on their content, in light of certain supreme foundational principles, stands in direct and

> severe contradiction to the theoretical basis upon which the authority to conduct judicial review was established in *Hamizrachi*, according to which the Knesset, in its capacity as constituent authority, is the body that determines constitutional norms."

Despite all this, the Court methodically developed two routes to achieve judicial review of Basic Laws, as we shall presently see.

Judicial Review of Basic Laws I: Abuse of Constituent Power

Starting in 2017, the Supreme Court began seriously entertaining the idea of striking down Basic Laws. Within seven short years, by 2024, the previously unimaginable had morphed into the Court's formal jurisprudence. We may describe these developments and their key doctrinal and factual elements in broad strokes, before finally settling on the 2024 *Reasonableness* ruling.

The Court utilized and developed two parallel doctrines for its evaluation of Basic Laws: "Abuse (or Misuse) of Constituent Power" (which we may call *Abuse*) and "Unconstitutional Constitutional Amendments" (which we may call *UCA*). One common theme for both is that in certain circumstances a constitutional amendment may be deemed unlawful and rendered invalid by a court, even if all procedural amendment requirements are met. Another common theme is that the "amendment power" was exercised in a way which somehow violates the constitution itself or its overarching framework.

UCA essentially contends that an "amendment power" – that is, the power granted within a constitution to amend it – is not a "replacement" power and is distinct from the original power wielded by a constituent assembly that formed the constitution. Any "amendment power" is itself a creature of the constitution and must be exercised within the constraints the constitution defines. As such, there are judicially-enforceable limits to the substance of constitutional amendments – certain elements of the constitution which cannot be violated or changed. A court might identify such limits by three main indicators: 1) An "eternity clause" might explicitly prohibit particular changes or might cement certain provisions from any amendment whatsoever. A classic example is found in Article 79(3) of the German constitution, which establishes that certain fundamental principles may never be violated, even by constitutional amendment. 2) Some constitutions might enumerate particular overarching core principles, such that even without an "eternity clause," the violation of such principles might be deemed an impermissible amendment. 3) A court can deduce implicit or inherent principles of a constitution, even if these are not explicitly stated or listed, and can consider their violation to be impermissible. This is often referred to as the "Basic Structure" doctrine. Under *UCA*, a court looks at the substantive content of a constitutional amendment and evaluates whether the amendment violates some superior constitutional rule and is therefore invalid.

The *Abuse* doctrine holds that the "amendment power" is reserved for changes of a genuine constitutional nature, and does not extend to certain changes which don't fit that description. The doctrine has a number of variations, but its Israeli brand focuses on the exercise of the amendment power for improper or ill-fitting purposes. Typical characteristics of "proper" constitutional provisions might include permanency, principled determinations, arrangements serving long-term goals, first-order rules that go to the heart of the regime, broad rules of a general nature, and more. Consequently, under this doctrine, a constitutional amendment might be an "abuse" of power and invalid if its application is temporary, if it serves short-term or immediate political needs, if it regards high-resolution details of government mechanisms, and so on.

It might be tempting to consider the *Abuse* doctrine as softer or less aggressive than *UCA*, but the two are virtually indistinguishable, with the former arguably representing an even higher degree of judicial interference. The *Abuse* doctrine essentially assumes certain "fundamental principles" such as the permanent or principled nature of constitutional provisions – and in this sense is simply a variation of the second or third type of amendment limitation under *UCA*. Further, the two doctrines amount to performing an identical function – a court striking down a constitutional amendment. Perhaps the only discernible difference between these doctrines is that *UCA* must somehow, at least in theory, make a rational argument appealing to the unamendable substantive provisions or principles of a constitution; that is, it assumes some form of legal reasoning. A claim of *Abuse*, on the other hand, has no such restriction – a court has immeasurably greater leeway in selecting the "proper" features of a constitutional provision and in rejecting non-conforming amendments as invalid. In this sense, though often presented as more subtle and formalistic, the *Abuse* doctrine is arguably more extreme in the discretion claimed and exercised by judges in evaluating constitutional amendments.[9]

Judicial review of constitutional amendments raises a host of obvious philosophical, legal and practical issues which may be set aside for now. One can scarcely imagine a version of judicial activism more extreme than annulling a duly-adopted constitutional amendment.* Suffice to say that such doctrines would be considered unacceptable and unthinkable in the vast majority of Western democracies, and in most jurisdictions have generally been either ignored or rejected out of hand. The handful of cases in which a court has directly applied such doctrines belong mostly to the undeveloped third-world, or to emerging and nominal democracies with a dubious and precarious commitment to popular sovereignty or the rule of law.

It will likely come as no surprise to the reader that much of the academic and scholarly literature on this topic in recent years has been pioneered by Israeli jurists, with a marked uptick from 2017 onwards. One such Israeli was Aharon Barak. Another was Professor Yaniv Roznai, a Barak protégé who in 2017

---

* With the exception of a judicially-invented constitution, of course.

published the definitive book on the subject and who is regarded as one of its preeminent global experts.

Whether applying such doctrines to Israel and its Basic Laws can be justified will be considered more carefully later on. For now we turn to review the gradual process by which the Supreme Court debated and developed its method of annulling Basic Laws. The key rapid-fire rulings were issued in 2017, 2021, and 2024.

The year 2017 indeed marked the entrance of super-constitutional judicial review onto the Israeli legal stage, and the timing was far from accidental. Over two decades had passed since *Hamizrachi* and opposition to the constitutional revolution seemed to be mounting steadily. Following the 2015 elections, Ayelet Shaked served as the first in a string of Ministers of Justice overtly opposing the constitutional revolution, and had brought criticism of the Supreme Court to the forefront of the public debate. Towards the end of 2016 Shaked published a comprehensive intellectual essay outlining her ideological support for judicial restraint and her practical agenda to curb the Court's rampant activism. Daniel Friedmann's groundbreaking book *The Purse and the Sword* had been published in 2013, with its effects rippling across the legal and political arenas and influencing a new generation of fresh law students and lawyers. The Court had invalidated a second draft-exemption law in 2017, sowing political chaos and all but guaranteeing an inevitable legislative response.

Sensing the brewing storm which threatened to challenge judicial hegemony, and keeping faith with the Supreme Court *modus operandi* of creeping jurisprudential change, the Court and legal establishment embarked on a campaign advocating – and gradually adopting – judicial review of Basic Laws. In a blitz of academic articles, in tangential *obiter dictum* discussions and non-binding minority opinions, in moot rulings with no practical effect, and in minor cases receiving little public attention, the Court and its allies eroded the hard legal immunity of Basic Laws until it existed only in name, to be finally brushed aside in the 2024 *Reasonableness* decision.

The 2017 *Biennial Budget* case revolved around "Basic Law: The State Economy" (BL:SE), a 1975 Basic Law which defines the process by which the Knesset passes the State Budget alongside other core elements of the Israeli economy. Section 3 of the Basic Law mandates that the Knesset pass an "annual" State Budget – that is, the Knesset must approve the budget separately for each fiscal year. In 2009 the Knesset enacted "temporary" legislation, amending the Basic Law to allow for a biennial budget; the amendment had a sunset clause, such that it would expire automatically after a limited timeframe and allowed for a joint biennial budget only for the fiscal years of 2009-2010. The Knesset then consistently extended the same temporary arrangement several times, to allow a biennial budget again for 2011-2012, 2013-2014, 2015-2016, and finally for 2017-2018.

These amendments were challenged by a flurry of petitions on various grounds. One line of argument was that this was a bona fide "unconstitutional" constitutional amendment because it violated fundamental democratic principles relating to the Knesset's ability to supervise the executive Government. The annual budget is considered by some to be a key oversight mechanism, because failure to pass a budget typically disbands the current Knesset and triggers new elections. A biennial budget was therefore said to undermine the Knesset's control of Government action (though this was a weak claim: the Knesset can always dismiss the Government and call for new elections with a majority vote).

Another line of argument contended that "temporary" legislation is unfitting for Basic Laws, which as a "constitution" ought to contain permanent or more stable and long-term rules. Such legislation is therefore either invalid on these grounds alone, or has a lower normative status than other Basic Laws and ought to be regarded as ordinary legislation (which is susceptible to judicial review and invalidation).

In the 2011 *Bar-On* decision (a precursor to the main 2017 ruling), the Supreme Court dismissed petitions against the biennial budget but took the opportunity, in laborious *dicta*, to deliberate whether such amendments could be struck down and according to which doctrine. Justice Beinisch expressed misgivings about the use of "temporary" amendments to Basic Laws and issued a "warning" that they could not withstand judicial scrutiny for long. In typical fashion, the immaterial musings of *Bar-On* were to be regarded later as binding doctrine and served as the basis for future rulings.

Following numerous extensions of the biennial budget mechanism and matching renewed petitions, the Court finally pulled the trigger with the 2017 *Biennial Budget* ruling – essentially initiating the first stage of a new constitutional revolution. In a unanimous seven-member decision penned by Justice Rubenstein, the Court issued an official "invalidation warning" – not quite striking down the amendment, but holding it to be unlawful such that future extensions or similar amendments would not be tolerated and would be deemed automatically invalid. Relying on *dicta* of the prior *Bar-On* decision, the Court wholeheartedly adopted and embraced the "Abuse of Constituent Power" doctrine while pretending it was applying established precedent and was doing nothing out of the ordinary. The Court held that the use of "temporary" measures was inappropriate for constitutional legislation and that such legislation could therefore not properly be regarded as a "Basic Law," but rather as an ordinary statute – subject to ordinary judicial review. In other words, according to the Court, just because the Knesset calls something a "Basic Law," that doesn't make it so – and the Court can retroactively downgrade a Basic Law enacted by the Knesset to the inferior status of ordinary legislation.

The implications of the 2017 ruling were staggering. The Court had put a significant dent in the fundamental premise of Basic Law supremacy and of the Knesset's ability to enact constitutional norms. In doing so the Court accomplished a double feat – first, by opening the floodgates to judicial review of Basic Laws; and second, by rejecting the entire existing paradigm that "Basic

Laws" were designated as such exclusively by the Knesset, and were identified according to their title in binary fashion. If under *Hamizrachi* the Knesset could choose to act either as legislature or as constituent authority, this new ruling essentially revoked the Knesset's prerogative to decide which type of power it was exercising. According to the Court, it was its Justices that would now decide whether a Basic Law enacted by the Knesset was in fact as advertised, or whether it was really an imposter, an ordinary statute masquerading as a Basic Law which needed to be stripped of its undeserved constitutional status.

Another key element was the Court's reversion to abstract subjective principles. If judicial review of legislation purported at least to rely on (albeit preposterous) interpretation and application of Basic Laws, the Court was now conjuring super-constitutional principles out of pure ether. The Court pretends to circumvent this problem by demoting a Basic Law to an ordinary statute (and then striking it down as routine judicial review), but of course this very demotion is only enabled by judicially-invented standards devoid of any legal or constitutional anchor. In other words, the Court's determination (or assumption) of what does or does not qualify as sufficiently "constitutional" is itself a super-constitutional question, the answer to which the Court makes no effort in deriving from existing constitutional text or doctrine.

The decision had only limited immediate consequences, in two ways. It regarded an issue at the fringes of public attention – whether the State Budget could be enacted biennially or had to be enacted annually; and it had a deferred effect, such that the current legislation remained intact, and only potential future legislation of a similar nature was preemptively invalidated (this was of course touted by judicial supremacists as "restraint"). By this point critics of the Court had become well acquainted with the latter's habit of creeping constitutional change, and recognized precisely where the Court's jurisprudence was heading. Nonetheless, their vocal objections notwithstanding, the decision failed to provoke any substantial public or political reaction.

The ruling was also the fruit of another strategic case previously discussed – the 2003 *Herut* decision which elevated all existing Basic Laws to constitutional status, and not only the 1992 laws concerning human rights. This allowed the Court to effectively prevent the Knesset from enacting critical changes to institutional and infrastructural legislation, despite these having nothing to do with human rights or with minority protections, and despite those Basic Laws having no "entrenched" or "limitation" clauses (which served as the core legal justification for "constitutionalizing" the 1992 Basic Laws). The 2017 *Biennial Budget* ruling casually treated "Basic Law: The State Budget" as an ostensibly superior constitutional norm – so superior that temporary amendments were deemed impermissible.

A side point worth briefly noting is that the Court's substantive argument seems completely nonsensical on principled grounds. There is nothing inherently "anti-constitutional" in temporary (or "expiring") amendments. As has been discussed at length above, a measure of flexibility and malleability is an essential component of many constitutions, and it has been perhaps the most dominant and prominent feature of Israeli constitutionalism since the State's founding. More specifically, as the Government had argued in its defense, a "temporary" amendment is in many senses more stable and prudent than "permanent" constitutional change. The Knesset desired to alter a specific mechanism to meet a particular need and wanted to do so experimentally – with a set expiration, such that the Knesset would need to consciously enact further legislation to retain the new mechanism. A "permanent" amendment would arguably simply remain in place without any immediate impetus to revert to the previous budgetary rules.

Another point of interest is, as we have become accustomed, the poor and ineffectual representation afforded to the Government. In both 2011 and 2017 cases the Legal Counsel to the Government offered a half-hearted defense, conceding that temporary amendments were "deeply problematic." Critically, the government lawyers did not seem to allege at any point that *any* review of Basic Laws was *categorically* beyond the scope of judicial authority and directly contradicts the entire framework and foundation of the constitutional revolution.

One final point is the Court's refusal to consider or recognize that the very problem at the case's heart was the inevitable outcome of *Hamizrachi*'s inherent flaws. Justice Rubenstein laments the Knesset's irreverent disregard for Basic Laws as constitutional norms, but does not stop to reflect for a moment on the Court's contribution to this reality. Here Rubenstein's tone is almost whining: "Behold – a Basic Law, in name and in claim, a constitutional document – and yet, here it lies, like a trampled threshold, emptied of meaning by every prevailing economic or political wind, cast towards experiments and wandering, in practice yielding more aimless wanderings than experiments. If such is a Basic Law, then its base is fundamentally unstable." But such "trampling" of Basic Laws is nothing more than another bizarre and avoidable consequence, of the Court's unrelenting and patently irrational insistence on designating a "constitution" that which is manifestly not so. The Basic Laws were not designed as a constitution, do not conform to any notion of a constitution, and are utterly inapt and incapable of serving as a constitution. Instead of calling a spade a spade, the Court calls it "Excalibur" and is appalled when farmers continue using it for shoveling fertilizer. Needless to say, neither Rubenstein nor anyone on the Court is willing to concede that this was the only conceivable outcome of its redesignation of important but ordinary laws, and their artificial and unnatural elevation to constitutional status.

What Makes a Constitution – The *Shafir* Ruling

The next dramatic development of the *Abuse* doctrine came with the 2021 *Shafir* case. At the height of COVID-19 and following three fruitless election cycles, 2020 saw the formation of a novel unity Government led by Netanyahu's Likud party and Benny Gantz's "Blue and White" party. The newly formed Government envisioned a form of power-sharing in which almost any significant legislative or executive initiative required bi-partisan consensus, and in which the Prime Minister's role would be "rotated" between both party leaders, including the creation of a new "Alternate Prime Minister" role. This unprecedented model of dual-party joint government required massive amendments to core institutional and governmental mechanisms, especially within "Basic Law: The Government" and other key Basic Laws. The legislation had the distinction of being sweeping and penetrating on the one hand, while also idiosyncratic and narrowly tailored to the specific unusual circumstances at hand.

The unity-government soon enough began to unravel. One significant stumbling block was the Coalition's inability to agree upon and enact a State Budget. According to "Basic Law: The Knesset," the unity Government had until August of 2020 to pass a budget, or otherwise the Knesset would automatically disband. As the date approached, trying to avoid the Government's collapse and new elections, the Coalition reached a unique compromise – the Knesset would extend the budget deadline to December of 2020, to allow the Coalition parties a final chance to formulate a bi-partisan budget. To facilitate this compromise the Knesset legislated additional temporary amendments to "Basic Law: The Knesset" and to "Basic Law: The State Economy." To allow the executive Government to continue to function without an approved State Budget, additional amendments were introduced to allow for rolling state expenditures based on the pre-existing approved budget. The legislation was passed by an overwhelming majority and was effectively also supported by the Opposition, who conceded that a fourth round of elections (within two years) at the height of the COVID-19 pandemic crisis was not in the country's best interests.

In the end the deadline extension turned out to be insufficient – the Coalition did not pass a budget, the Government collapsed in December of 2020, and new elections were called.

The *Shafir* case revolved around this last temporary amendment which had extended the budget deadline and which allowed for continued governmental spending without an approved State Budget. We may already observe some hallmark features common to many instances of the Court's new expansionism. The named plaintiff was Stav Shafir – a former Member of Knesset that of course had not the remotest claim of standing or of individual grievance. The legislation in question had nothing to do with human rights or protection of minorities, and could not be said to somehow undermine fundamental democratic principles. The amendment to the Basic Law was trying to address unprecedented circumstances, within the dual crises of political turmoil and a global pandemic, and had received bi-partisan support recognizing this much. The standards for judicial review were now firmly embedded in judicial fantasy, without even the pretense of some solid legal foundation for the Court's deliberation and decisions.

Perhaps most conspicuous was the utter mootness of the case. The legislation in question applied to a specific timeframe that had come and gone; it also failed to have any sustained tangible effect, as the Knesset disbanded anyway. The budgetary provisions were now irrelevant, as the Knesset's disbandment and new elections triggered a preexisting statutory framework of government spending, which was of uncontested validity. The amendment was produced by circumstances which were unlikely to ever repeat themselves. The Court was obviously in no rush to issue its decision – the primary hearing was held in February 2021, long after it was clear that any ruling would have no operative consequences whatsoever. Nonetheless, the Court was clearly determined not to waste such a valuable opportunity.

The Supreme Court ruled in May of 2021, by a majority of six Justices versus three dissenting, to strike down (by a preemptive "invalidation warning") the Basic Law amendments. The Court relied on the *Abuse* doctrine, holding that the amendments failed to meet the standards befitting constitutional legislation; the new legislation could therefore not be considered "Basic Laws" and was rendered invalid.

The *Shafir* ruling is extraordinary in many respects. Though it builds on the (vacuous) foundation of the previous two *Abuse* rulings, the majority opinion penned by Chief Justice Hayut admirably attempts to explicate, concretize and specify the *Abuse* doctrine and its applicability to Basic Laws in much greater detail. In this sense the Court offers a more thorough account of its newfound constitutional jurisprudence than it had presented thus far. Unfortunately for the Court, its argument and analysis not only fail, but backfire spectacularly.

First, Hayut describes the core features which characterize a constitutional norm and make it classifiable as such. These "tests," according to Hayut, enable the Court to identify constitutional rules and potentially to reject a rule's claim of constitutional status if these standards are not met. The tests are: 1) Stability – whether the rule is a permanent, long-term, future-facing arrangement, or is temporary with expiring applicability; 2) Generality – whether the rule is of a broad-systemic nature, or serves a specific purpose of meeting limited or immediate circumstances; 3) Compatibility – is the rule consistent with the overall constitutional "fabric" of other existing constitutional norms, or is it an outlier, foreign to such "fabric." Justice Daphne Barak-Erez offers a slightly modified variation in her concurring opinion, but the essence remains the same.

Hayut, and the majority with her, ultimately concludes that the Basic Law amendments in question ran afoul of all three tests – they were temporary; they served the localized, short-term purposes of the specific Government that had enacted them; and they were in disharmony with the overall constitutional fabric consisting of other Basic Laws. The amendments therefore could not be regarded or treated as "Basic Laws."

The constitutional "recognition" test articulated by the Court in *Shafir* is striking, both in its contradiction of *Hamizrachi* and in its glaring omission of the most fundamental feature of any constitutional norm – the norm's originator and procedure of enactment. As noted above, *Hamizrachi* set out the definition of Israeli constitutional norms in unambiguous and binary terms: a Basic Law is a chapter in the Israel constitution, period. Its designation as such is identified by it bearing the title of "Basic Law" – that is, by the Knesset's deliberate decision to classify legislation as constitutional. A "Basic Law" label was the sufficient, exclusive, defining criteria to endow legislation with constitutional standing. Barak called this the "form" test and embraced it unreservedly. The "form" test is not only "formal" as the name suggests but rather stems from the Court's overall theory of the Knesset as constituent authority. More to the point, Barak's "form" test is the bedrock on which the entire constitutional revolution rests because the 1992 Basic Laws were otherwise devoid of any distinguishing factors, as discussed above – hardly recognized as constitutional by anyone in real time, under the radar of public debate, enacted by a small majority of legislators, and BL:HDL not even possessing an entrenchment clause. In other words, even (and especially) under the Court's elaborate theory, the title "Basic Law" was the only real argument in favor of recognizing the 1992 laws as "constitutional."

Here is how Barak put it in *Hamizrachi*:

> "The Knesset holds constituent authority. By virtue of this authority, it granted Israel a constitution. It did so chapter by chapter, in accordance with the "Harari Resolution." Each Basic Law constitutes a chapter in the constitution of the State of Israel. Each chapter stands at the top of the normative pyramid... Indeed, Israel has a constitution – the Basic Laws.
>
> ... The status of a norm within the normative pyramid *is determined by the nature of the authority that created it*."[10] (emphasis added)
>
> Barak then continues:
>
> "The Knesset is authorized to grant the state a constitution. How does it do so? When is a norm created by it considered to have constitutional status, and when is it said to be an "ordinary" law? ... The answer is that the Knesset exercises its constituent authority when it gives external expression to this intent in the title of the norm *and designates it as a Basic Law.*" (emphasis added)

In other words, per the Court in *Hamizrachi* and ever since, a law is "constitutional" because the Knesset (as constituent authority) said so; and the Knesset says so, by appending the title "Basic Law" to any legislation. Sweet and simple.

The Court in *Shafir* throws this entire framework out the window without a backward glance. All of a sudden, whether a norm is "constitutional" no longer derives from the Knesset's constituent power and its decision to designate it as such but is rather subject to the arbitrary judgment of nine Supreme Court Justices. Hayut and the Court present this radical shift casually, as though they had not just shattered the bedrock of their original constitutional revolution.

At a deeper level, Hayut's (and the Court's) method for recognizing constitutional rules reflect an even greater perversion – it is profoundly, manifestly antithetical to constitutionalism itself. As discussed at length above, the theoretical, legal and political foundation of any constitution is its democratic sanction, and by extension the constitutional authority of the body or institution which creates, enacts and approves constitutional rules. A rule is to be recognized as "constitutional" because the democratically-engaged organ vested with constitution-making powers determined it to be so. The first thing that endows a rule with constitutional status is its *origin* – the identity of the rule maker (or as Barak put it, "the nature of the authority that created it"). This tenet of constitutional democracy is obvious to any first-year student of law or politics. Barak himself reiterates the same in *Hamizrachi*: "The constitution is a creation the People, whether directly (such as through a referendum) or indirectly by delegating constituent authority to a governing institution."

This flaw of course had existed in *Hamizrachi* as well, with the Court glossing over the clear factual fallacies and democratic deficit in its designation of the 1992 Basic Laws as a "constitutional revolution." As noted earlier, Justice Shamgar also neglected to include constitutional authority or popular sanction when he listed the typical "elements" by which to identify a constitutional rule. Yet *Hamizrachi* and its constitutional revolution still sought to operate – at least nominally and for the sake of appearance – within the bounds of accepted constitutional theory and practice. Though reflecting a distortion of Israeli law and jurisprudence, though twisting the existing facts of Israeli Basic Laws and the 1992 legislation, the theoretical framework of *Hamizrachi* still adhered to the fundamental conception of constitutional power deriving exclusively from the people and their designated agents.

This is what makes the *Shafir* requirements so jarring – unlike Justice Shamgar's tangential and hypothetical ruminations on the elements of constitutional rules (in *Hamizrachi*), the *Shafir* "tests" of constitutional validity make up the heart of its judicial determination and form the basis for invalidating a Basic Law. By omitting any mention (and thus denying the centrality) of the law's "originator," the Court in *Shafir* effectively abandons the most basic foundation of all constitutional thought. Its "tests of recognition" are a categorical repudiation of constitutionalism itself.

Thus, more than anything else, the theoretical argument declared in *Shafir* exposes the Court's ignorance of (or disregard for) elementary democratic principles, and its contempt for its own jurisprudence established in *Hamizrachi*.

<u>Second</u>, the *Shafir* ruling also disproves the misrepresentation of the *Abuse* doctrine as a benign, formalistic or technical instrument of judicial power. Hayut quotes a concurring opinion from the 2017 *Biennial Budget* ruling, alleging that the Court "[does] not examine the substance of the Basic Law legislation" and is not "concerned with [its] desirability or meaning."[11] But *Shafir* reveals this to be

patently false – the entire "test" presented by Hayut reflects a particular opinion on the "desirability" of different kinds of norms within a constitution (e.g., general rules are desirable and specific or conditional rules are undesirable). And the Court does indeed "examine the substance" of legislation to decide whether it conforms to any one of the test's standards. More broadly, the Court imposes a contrived requirement for generality on no discernible legal grounds, and then evaluates whether the Basic Law's content is sufficiently "general" – determinations of the highest order which are patently "substantive." As noted above, judges seizing the power to designate norms as constitutional or "ordinary" based on arbitrary abstract principles is arguably more extreme and egregious than striking down constitutional provisions due to contradiction with other parts of the constitution.

It's worth also observing that the Court's theory is simply (again) unfounded on its merits. The "tests" stipulated by Hayut do not reflect some universal imperative or conventional truth; they do not derive as a logical inevitability from the nature of constitutions. Constitutional provisions can certainly be temporary, or tailored to specific purposes (even of pedestrian political convenience), or anomalous. Sometimes constitutional arrangements require ad hoc alterations to meet specific demands and challenges. Indeed, it is often in the face of extreme or extraordinary circumstances that flaws or shortcomings of governing institutions, rules and mechanisms are fully exposed, requiring urgent and targeted modification – such that "tailored" or "ad hoc" constitutional amendments are not only a natural feature in the course of political life, but actually make a great deal of sense. This is all the more applicable to imperfect, short-sighted, partial and poorly-designed constitutional arrangements which none consider to be of high quality or value from the outset. Such arrangements would inevitably require regular "topical" remedies and changes to match new scenarios as they crop up. Thus the claim that constitutional amendments which address a particular issue at a particular time are categorically invalid is simply preposterous.

While we might agree some of features described by the Court are desirable (such as a "generality" requirement under leading conceptions of the rule of law), this does not make them binding principles to be enforced by judges against the electorate. The entire argument by Hayut and the majority that these are somehow obligatory legal rules is pure fiction.

Third, *Shafir* really disintegrates when it comes to grappling with the simple issue of judicial authority. Philosophical musings and claims about "recognition" of constitutional norms are all well and good, but the Court in *Shafir* had to contend with a more concrete and preliminary legal question – what grants the Court authority to review Basic Laws? In other words, before the Court can apply any elaborate theory of "Abuse of Constituent Power," it must show it has legal authority to consider the validity of Basic Laws.

Since *Hamizrachi*, the Court had a straightforward answer regarding the source of authority to review ordinary legislation – that answer was "the Basic Laws." As described above, this conformed to an intuitive and clear hierarchy of distinct legal norms. Any exercise of judicial power must necessarily point to some superior legal norm which it is applying, and which, by definition, takes precedence over the action or decision annulled by the Court. Any determination of invalidity must indicate a higher legal norm, the contradiction of which renders the challenged act or law invalid. And so the simple question remains: within the Israeli constitutional order, what is the source of authority for the Court to review Basic Laws?

Here the Court offers a stunning answer: The Court's authority to review Basic Laws is part of "the core of the judicial role" anchored in "the rule of law." In just two curt and cryptic sentences the Court swats away the most essential legal issue, like the nuisance the Court perceives it to be. Chief Justice Hayut proclaims:

> "The task of identifying a norm as a legal norm within a specific normative hierarchy – including the constitutional hierarchy – lies at the core of the Court's function… This judicial authority is embedded at its root in the principle of the rule of law."[12]

That's it. Never mind the fact that scholars, statesmen and jurists had been debating this question for decades, almost universally conceded to be an insurmountable obstacle to judicial review of Basic Laws. Never mind that no court in the world has yet claimed authority to strike down (sorry, "demote") constitutional amendments as an inherent feature of "the rule of law." Never mind that, if anything, the rule of law requires that State power (including judicial power) be grounded in recognized and clear legal norms – not arbitrary whims – and that a court claiming the power to annul constitutional provisions because of its "core function" is the diametric opposite of any notion of the rule of law.* As Prof. Richard Ekins has explained in the context of British judicial activism, this kind of reasoning is "flatly contrary to the rule of law's concern that positive law should frame and limit the exercise of public power, including judicial power."[13] For Hayut and the Court, such inexplicable, meaningless and paradoxical drivel passes as sufficient justification to wield the ultimate power of final judicial supremacy over the State's only recognized mechanism of constitutional change. Few passages demonstrate the Court's legal sloppiness and intellectual laziness (at best) or the Court's desperate and dishonest attempts to seize supreme constitutional power (at worst) more effectively than this one. To again echo Ekins' criticism on similar grounds, Hayut's claim is "so antithetical to the rule of law" and "so unrooted" in the Israeli constitutional tradition "as to be a lawless grab for power."

As if to prove this last point, Hayut added final insult to injury by not even

---

* The Court has an illustrious history of abusing the term "rule of law," including its jurisprudence regarding the LCG, discussed briefly in Chapter 8.

bothering to contend with the substantial dissenting opinions aligned against her own – not even going through the motions as a perfunctory gesture. Justices Solberg, Mintz and Elron all penned devastating critiques of the majority opinion, its novel doctrines, its lack of legal grounding, its deviation from existing precedent, and its sheer imprudence. Hayut takes the time to address the concurring opinion of her colleague and ally Daphne Barak-Erez (debating intricacies of their shared "recognition" tests) but refuses to even acknowledge any of the dissenting opinions. This is despite the fact that there was no rush or time constraints (the case was moot to begin with), and that such cross-Justice inter-opinion engagement is a staple feature of the Court's rulings and can be found in virtually any judicial decision of consequence. Such a snub, in such an important and groundbreaking case based on rickety and controversial legal arguments, is unprecedented in the Supreme Court's history.

The *Abuse* doctrine was employed by the Supreme Court again in 2024, this time to much more practical and immediate effect. In the *Incapacity* case, the Court "deferred" the application of a Basic Law amendment so that it would not apply to the current Knesset and Government. As briefly discussed in the context of the Legal Counsel to the Government in Chapter 8, the Knesset had amended "Basic Law: The Government" in order to clarify that "incapacity" meant physical or medical inability to function as a matter of fact, and not any other form of "substantive" legal incapacity which the LCG was implicitly pursuing and which the Court seemed to indicate it could support. The context was the ongoing criminal trial of Benjamin Netanyahu and the claim of his opponents that the Prime Minister could be unilaterally declared "incapacitated" by the LCG, due to the trial's disruptive effects (both actual and "legal") on Netanyahu's ability to perform his duties. Though this interpretation of "incapacity" was always ludicrous – distorting the meaning of the word "incapacity" and empowering an unelected bureaucrat to effectively fire the Prime Minister based on arbitrary and subjective judgment – such was the lack of faith in both the LCG and the Court that the Knesset was compelled to amend the Basic Law so as to make the (obvious and pre-existing) legal situation unequivocally clear.

Once again relying on the *Abuse* doctrine, the Court ruled that the amendment's "particular-personal" element – that is, that it sought to influence the law's application to a specific person at a specific time – rendered it an "abuse of constituent power" and therefore invalid, to the extent that it could only take effect at a later time. By prohibiting the law's immediate effect on current circumstances, the Court had essentially struck down the Basic Law amendment, thwarting both the unambiguous textual content and the unequivocal legislative intent behind it. The 212-page decision divided the Court with six Justices in the majority and five dissenting.

In the 2024 *Incapacity* ruling we find the culmination of the Court's *Abuse* doctrine in all its deformities, and the final abandonment of the Court's constitutional jurisprudence and of any semblance of legal argumentation. Relying on the three previous cases – all of them moot, immaterial, or *dicta*, and all of them relating to obscure budget-related amendments – the Court now casually applied the *Abuse* doctrine as though it were settled and established precedent. It did so to meddle with a constitutional rule of the highest order – who gets to dismiss the Prime Minister, how, and on what grounds – on the staggeringly dubious basis that addressing immediate and practical concerns was an impermissible exercise of constituent authority. By using the language of "deferral," the Court also deceptively tried to evade public backlash and to obscure the fact that it had effectively annulled the amendment, which had specifically sought to remove the current threat of the LCG declaring the Prime Minister as "incapacitated."

On the merits, the Court's reasoning fails the most casual assessment. Laws are regularly "personal" in the sense that they often seek to address a particular problem in time and space. Such problems often emerge or are acutely felt due to "personal" circumstances of specific individuals or scenarios. Such laws have been enacted numerous times, without incident, both in Israel and throughout the democratic world. Further, even where a valid limitation on "personal" legislation exists, it regards a law's actual effect and application, not its motives or incentives. A law is only "personal" if it applies to some specific beneficiary and not to others – in the *Incapacity* case, the clarified rule obviously applies to all future Prime Ministers in a host of conceivable situations. Finally, and ironically, it is the Court's decision that is inherently "personal." The Court in effect ruled that a constitutional provision will apply generally, universally and indefinitely *except* to Benjamin Netanyahu until mid-2026, such that the *Incapacity* ruling is far more "personal" than the law it deferred.

It's also worth recalling that the Court itself had a vested institutional interest in the case's outcome. The outrageous claim of "substantive incapacity" was directly linked to the legal reform proposals of the previous year. The threat of "incapacity" was constantly held by the LCG over Netanyahu's and the Government's head, and some argued that the reforms themselves were sufficient to trigger a declaration of "incapacity." Thus the prospect of "incapacity" plainly served the scheme of judicial supremacy and the Court's interest in preserving power. Tolerating the absurd idea of "substantive incapacity" – now formally validated by the Court – was, if anything, an obvious abuse of judicial power in order to retain yet another non-conventional warhead in its legal arsenal.

The legal and practical implications of the Court's decision are mind-boggling. As discussed above, the claim that a constituent authority may not address particular or immediate needs is simply bogus and bonkers – devoid of any rational, theoretical, comparative or legal basis. In the Court's view the Knesset, ostensibly the "constituent power" which authorized judicial review and which vested the 1992 (and all other) Basic Laws with constitutional status, is legally prohibited from enacting a simple and straightforward amendment dealing with the State's most fundamental allocation of executive governing power. Any notion of the Knesset functioning as a constituent authority had now officially and formally become subject to selective and deeply partisan judicial discretion. This was a microcosm of the Court's paradoxical jurisprudence in all its absurdity – the Knesset wields limitless constituent authority to empower the judiciary and its proxies, yet in almost any other respect wields a handicapped constituent power subject to permanent judicial approval and veto.

Needless to say, the fact that the LCG and the Court itself were developing ad hoc, loony legal doctrines such as "substantive incapacity" for profoundly personal-particular purposes – that is, within the clear partisan and political context of Benjamin Netanyahu and efforts at unilaterally reversing his sustained electoral success – is never deemed a relevant or problematic factor by the Court. Radically novel first-order constitutional rules which are tailored to serve specific political circumstances are fine, so long as these are conjured by the Legal Counsel to the Government or by Justices of the Supreme Court, and not by the elected and accountable constitution-making Knesset.

The *Incapacity* ruling once again demonstrates how the *Abuse* doctrine may be leveraged by the Court to interfere with constitutional legislation which is otherwise manifestly valid by even the most activist and supremacist perspective. Here was an amendment with no effect on individual rights and liberties, no harm to electoral minorities, and which clearly advances fundamental democratic norms. A constitutional amendment which clarifies that a Prime Minister may be dismissed only by legislature or electorate is disqualified by the Court under an amorphous, malleable, subjective and utterly fabricated doctrine, all while the Court maintains it is applying some technical form-based limitation on the Knesset's power to enact constitutional rules.

Judicial Review of Basic Laws II: Unconstitutional Constitutional Amendments

Parallel to its development of the *Abuse* doctrine the Supreme Court – backed by its supremacist allies – advanced a fully-fledged doctrine of "Unconstitutional Constitutional Amendments." In a concerted effort led by Aharon Barak, a key group of legal academics started publishing regular pieces on the inherent "limits" of the Knesset's constituent powers. Around the same time, the Court began routinely entertaining petitions against the validity of Basic Laws with Justices musing about the potential applicability of *UCA* to Israeli circumstances.

The *Abuse* cases discussed above address *UCA* only in passing, typically distinguishing the latter from the former and rejecting its relevance. This made tactical sense: The Court presented *Abuse* as more technical, benign and restrained while rejecting *UCA* as a more forceful doctrine reserved for extreme circumstances, allowing the Court to gradually introduce the idea of invalidating Basic Laws even while it "dismissed" claims of *UCA*.

Additional cases discussed *UCA* more directly yet reiterated its problematic nature and its prima facie irrelevance for the Israeli legal system. One significant example was the 2018 *Removal* case. The Knesset had passed a Basic Law amendment which would authorize the Knesset to remove a Member of Knesset (that is, an elected legislator) from office under certain conditions and only by an overwhelming (ninety-member) majority. Petitions challenging the amendment claimed that it was unconstitutional due to its infringement of democratic representation rights, along with other violations of fundamental democratic principles. The Court could not rely on the previous *Abuse* rulings because the amendment on its face was almost certainly not an "abuse" of constituent power: it was not temporary, regarded a central constitutional mechanism, and clearly did not serve the immediate interests of a particular Government or political faction.

As had become already routine practice, the case was entirely hypothetical – there was no aggrieved or injured party as the new provision had not even been employed against any MK. The named plaintiff himself was just another useful activist attorney and serial petitioner. This of course did not deter the Court from exercising pure abstract ex ante review of constitutional legislation. Neither justiciability nor standing were raised or considered.

Though the Court ultimately dismissed the petitions and upheld the amendment, it conducted the most significant discussion to date (at the time) regarding the *UCA* doctrine in its own right. Writing for the majority, Chief Justice Hayut expressed doubts as to the applicability of *UCA* within the framework of Israeli constitutional law (a point we will soon revisit), but also indirectly outlined some basic conditions for judicial review of Basic Laws. These might involve a Basic Law which violates "fundamental supreme principles," which "negates the State's core democratic identity" or which "shakes the foundations" of Israel's "constitutional structure." Hayut then leaves the question "to be resolved at a later time" in light of her conclusion upholding the amendment.[14]

The *Removal* case was thus another step in the Court's incremental (but relatively rapid) erosion of the supremacy of Basic Laws, another step closer towards the day on which the Court might strike down a Basic Law due to its incompatibility with super-constitutional norms.

The next stage came quickly enough. Only two months after the *Removal* ruling, the Knesset enacted the 2018 "Basic Law: Israel as the Nation-State of the Jewish People," otherwise known as the "Nation State Law" and which we may call "BL:NS." This law was a major legislative initiative that had been brewing for at least seven years under three separate Knessets. It was easily the most significant "constitutional" legislation since the 1992 Basic Laws and the constitutional revolution. The law articulated a variety of Israel's fundamental values and priorities as a Jewish State, investing them with explicit constitutional status. Though the law's underlying ideology almost unquestionably enjoyed broad electoral support and reflected overwhelming public consensus, the law itself became deeply controversial. Objections to the law centered on its alleged privileging of the Jewish majority at the expense of other ethnic and religious minorities, and on its omission of additional fundamental values such as democracy or equality. Following a lengthy and heated public and political debate, the law was enacted by an absolute majority of sixty-two Members of Knesset.

Multiple petitions against BL:NS provided the Court with the perfect opportunity to fully consider the doctrine of "Unconstitutional Constitutional Amendments" and to develop a robust theory for judicial review of Basic Laws. Unlike the *Removal* case, the Court now clearly considered BL:NS to be the appropriate "later time" to "resolve" the complex associated questions.

The public controversy surrounding the Nation-State Law was perhaps understandable, given the ongoing polarization of Israeli politics, but the judicial wrangling over its legality was peculiar – or at least would be in any other jurisdiction. The law's content was wholly declarative and had virtually no operative provisions with immediate or overtly practical implications. As described by one leading Israeli legal scholar, the law "consists of symbolic and declarative statements that are not legally enforceable and have long been in the Israeli consensus."[15] Not only was there very little legal substance to latch on to, but the challenge and debate was itself "legal" only in name, as no tangible harm was (or could be) alleged by any of the petitioners. Neither the law's content nor its application to date had any adverse effect on any of the parties or on anyone else – the entire case revolved around *speculation* of *potential* harms and grievances in the future. Much like the *Removal* case, the *Nation State* ruling was profoundly inappropriate and ill-suited as a basis for developing constitutional jurisprudence.

Menny Mautner and Or Bassok (an Israeli constitutional scholar and protégé of Ruth Gavison) pointed this out after a hearing in the case, stating that "one thing was missing from the oral arguments: the law."[16] Indeed, as Mautner and Bassok observed, even the Justices eventually had to express their exasperation. Justice Hayut berated one attorney, saying "sir, you are in a court of law; you must offer a legal proposition"; and later exclaimed "what does this argument have to do with legal matters? God!" Needless to say, the Court's rebuke rings hollow considering its own contribution to such a bizarre reality, by entertaining petitions based solely on abstract philosophizing and speculative future harm – or as Mautner and Bassok put it, "the Justices should point their finger at themselves."

Mautner and Bassok further note the deeply inappropriate remarks emanating from the bench, as some Justices felt free to simply opine on their degree of affection or disapproval for the new Basic Law. The two scholars "find it hard to think of another national high court in the world in which Justices make similar remarks from the bench." Such unrestrained and undisciplined judicial behavior is inevitable in such circumstances, stemming from the highly theoretical nature of the case, where the court functions as "a Platonic philosopher-king seeking to determine the proper regime for a state, rather than a court of law examining a particular infringement of a right or the violation of a protected interest." In this sense the case was remarkably devoid of legal substance, even by the wild standards of Israeli judicial supremacy. Anyone watching the live-streamed hearing might have mistaken it for a Knesset sub-committee debating the merits of legislation, or might have confused the judges with grandstanding politicians – with every passing case the line between jurisprudence and political ideology was getting vanishingly thin.

The *Nation-State* ruling was issued by the Supreme Court in July of 2021, some three years after BL:NS was enacted. In a 200-page majority decision, ten Justices voted to uphold the Basic Law with one Justice dissenting. Yet within the ten-member majority there were profound differences. Chief Justice Hayut and most of the panel concluded that they had the legal authority to invalidate Basic Laws, in principle. Justice Mintz expressed skepticism as to such a conclusion while referencing his detailed dissent in *Shafir*, but did not elaborate on the matter due to the near-unanimous view that the law in question did not approach any threshold for invalidation. Justice Solberg, on the other hand, laid out a comprehensive critique of the majority opinion and against the Court's claim of authority over Basic Laws, in what amounted to a thorough and principled dissent (concurring with the case's practical outcome but passionately disputing the Court's reasoning).

Writing again for the majority, Chief Justice Hayut reiterated her reservations regarding the relevance and applicability of the *UCA* doctrine to Israeli constitutionalism, yet this time she did not stop there. Hayut reasoned that even if *UCA* could not apply, the Knesset's authority as "constituent power" was not unlimited. In the absence of a comprehensive *UCA* doctrine, the Knesset as constituent authority was bound by a "single, narrow" limitation – it is "unable to negate, by a Basic Law, Israel's character as a Jewish and Democratic State."[17] Per Hayut, this limitation was derived from the "overall constitutional framework" of which Israel's "Jewish and Democratic" identity is the "beating heart."[18] Hayut offers a variety of potential arguments supporting her claim, though does not select any specific one as determinative. This limit on the Knesset's power proscribes any constitutional rule that would deal a "fatal blow" to Israel's Jewish or democratic character.

Though the terms "Jewish" and "democratic" are inescapably abstract and vague, as discussed earlier in this chapter, Hayut was kind enough to enumerate several inviolable democratic principles. These include, inter alia: "free and fair elections; a recognition of core human rights; separation of powers; the rule of law; and an independent judiciary." Per Hayut and the Court, if a Basic Law were to "deny" or "directly contradict" these "core features," which embody the "minimum definition" of Israel as Jewish and democratic, then "we may say that the Knesset has exceeded its constituent authority."[19]

Hayut then considers whether such inherent substantive limits necessarily imply a power of judicial oversight – that is, whether such limits grant the Supreme Court authority to strike down Basic Laws. Much like in *Shafir*, Hayut dedicates only the briefest discussion to this foundational question, noting two primary justifications in favor of such an authority: First, because "one of the main roles of the court is to protect the Basic Laws, which stand at the core of our legal order." Hayut does not bother grounding this assertion in any statute or in any recognizable legal rule or norm, presenting a near-perfect example of question-begging. What is the source of the Court's authority to strike down Basic Laws? The Court's role of protecting Basic Laws. Second, Hayut notes that the "need" for judicial review of constitutional provisions "perhaps arises" especially in jurisdictions where constitutional legislation is relatively flexible[20]. We will return to these points, and to a broader critique of the Court's approach, in the next section.*

Further following her own example in *Shafir*, Hayut entirely ignored Justice Solberg's dissenting opinion, elevating her intellectual evasion to something of a tradition. This was despite the case being perhaps the most significant and consequential since *Hamizrachi* in 1995, and despite the various points of contention going to the core of Israel's constitutional character. The fact that the two agreed on the case's outcome is immaterial – take for example the *Hamizrachi* ruling, the bulk of which was extensive debate between the various concurring opinions of Justices Barak, Shamgar and Cheshin. As we shall see again in the *Reasonableness* ruling, Hayut's legacy as Chief Justice may well be the demise of principled, reasoned, sincere inter-judicial debate, more than any rickety constitutional jurisprudence.

The Court ultimately dismissed the petitions, ruling that the new Basic Law in question did not amount to a "fatal blow" justifying judicial intervention.

As an aside, it's worth noting that though the law was not struck down, the *Nation State* ruling certainly yielded concrete and immediate legal outcomes. The Court explained that any of the law's supposed inconsistencies with existing constitutional norms – such as "equality" – could be resolved by creative purposive interpretation. This was a central element in its reasoning upholding the law. In doing so the Court essentially declared it would ignore the main provisions of BL:NS so that they "conform" to the Court's existing jurisprudence, ideology and priorities. Though the Nation State Law was an explicit effort to realign the Court's substantive jurisprudence and to curb the Court's imbalanced interference with heavily contested societal dilemmas, the Court conveniently chose to render the law a dead letter.

In the 2021 *Nation State* ruling the Court once again upheld a law and assumed a posture of "restraint," while effectively erecting the most radical supremacist mechanism of political power wielded by judges. The Court presented its expansionism in innocuous terms – after all, who could object to the claim that Israel's core character was "Jewish and democratic"?

Yet the Court's decision was anything but benign. To anyone paying attention

* Hayut's explanation also contains a characteristic analytical error. She describes these justifications as "deriving" from the inherent limits on the Knesset's authority, but then makes no arguments as to why this is so. Her claims are, on the contrary, rational or principled claims in favor of her proposition, not "derived" in any sense from her earlier conclusion.

the Court's ploy was decidedly transparent. By establishing "Jewish and democratic" as the standard for substantive judicial review of Basic Laws the Court had now armed itself with an open-ended and essentially unrestricted power to annul constitutional legislation, on almost any conceivable grounds. Hayut gives up the game when she includes "human rights," "judicial independence," "separation of powers" and "the rule of law" within her catalogue of Israel's unalterable democratic features – terms which in the Court's capable hands become vessels for any principle or policy the Court fancies. The insertion of "the rule of law" was of particular significance, as it implied that any legislative (and constitutional) limits on judicial power or on the Supreme Court's institutional autonomy could indeed be an impermissible violation. The Court had now fortified its defenses against any legislative regulation of its exceptional and unparalleled power. Indeed, many commentators (across the political spectrum) publicly speculated that the purpose of the *Nation State* ruling was to enable future judicial review of any change to the judicial appointments process – an initiative that had been consistently raised by politicians for decades and which seemed increasingly inevitable.

Whether one supports the 2018 "Nation-State Law" or finds it deeply objectionable is completely immaterial. The Knesset was adhering to the framework established by the Court in *Hamizrachi* by exercising its constituent power to "write another chapter" in the State's emerging constitution. It did so in a patently non-confrontational way – promulgating positive substantive values by which it expected the Court and other State organs to abide. Though the Nation State Law was to some extent a repudiation of the Court's expansionism and an effort to counter it, it was also a tacit acknowledgment of the constitutional revolution, with the Knesset now willing to play by the rules set out by the Court. The Knesset implicitly respected the Court's sincerity and good-faith in applying Basic Laws and contributed fresh statutory constitutional provisions to be observed and advanced by the Court. More so, it avoided the kind of structural or overt changes to judicial authority seen in the 2023 proposals for legal reform. The problem with the *Nation-State* case was thus not whether the new Basic Law was good or bad, but rather the Court's radical assumption that it was capable and authorized to provide the answer to such a question.

In the lead-up to the ruling, numerous critics of the Nation-State Law nonetheless objected to the Court's contemplation of striking down Basic Laws and argued that any petitions ought to be dismissed outright. On this view, those finding fault with the Nation-State Law could voice their concerns and attempt to modify or scrap it through the customary democratic channels of the political-electoral process; judicial intervention under such circumstances was not only legally and morally unsound, but socially ruinous. Simply put, no genuine democrat can plausibly argue that such determinations are supposed to be settled by a miniscule cohort of judges. In other jurisdictions a court striking down a similar law would be unthinkable.

In 2019 Ruth Gavison and Or Bassok warned that "fixing the Nation-State Law" was "not the Supreme Court's job" even though they opposed the law itself, and that "the questions it raises should be debated in Israel's political and civil society and should not be decided by the Supreme Court." The Court's very willingness to entertain the petitions was a "grave mistake," and the threshold doctrine of non-justiciability existed precisely in order to avoid instances of such judicial involvement in fraught public controversies. Gavison and Bassok list the reasons the Court must pull back from considering the petitions. These include the absence of any legal basis for judicial review of Basic Laws, the law's ideological and non-legal subject-matter declaring the State's vision and identity, and the resulting further erosion of the Court's public standing.

Menny Mautner and Or Bassok also wrote a joint op-ed in 2020 (prior to the one mentioned above) in which they make similar points.[21] They argue that "the court should avoid ruling on this question," as the petitions "present a grave danger to the future of Israeli democracy," despite BL:NS being (in their view) "a bad law." In addition to the case creating a lose-lose scenario in which no outcome is beneficial, Bassok and Mauter warned that "a ruling that the court indeed has the authority to review the legality of Basic Laws – even while denying petitions aimed at striking down this particular one – would mean that the Justices have the last word when it comes to the contents of the constitution." If the Court took such a "radical step," it would not only be an admission that the "constitutional revolution" truly was a judicial invention all along but would also mean that the Court "is now the institution demarcating the limits of that revolution."

These exhortations and many others were of course not heeded by the Court, which proceeded with single-minded focus, strategic dedication and admirable precision. The trajectory of the Court's rulings and their overall purpose served one paramount objective – setting the stage for the ultimate moment in which the Court would strike down a Basic Law. Any level of internal consistency and integrity, any commitment to the concrete principles and rationales of *Hamizrachi*, would have led to the immediate and automatic dismissal of all petitions against Basic Laws, the most definitively "non-justiciable" norms in the Israeli legal order. But the Court knew precisely where it was going and how to get there. By entertaining petitions, holding hearings, dangling the threat of invalidation and writing laborious opinions, all while professing contrived restraint, the Court methodically normalized the notion of striking down Basic Laws.

The Court rightly calculated that as long as its new radical jurisprudence involved moot cases or theoretical *dicta* it would elicit no backlash from the public and its elected representatives. These cases were small beans, pawns to be sacrificed in pursuit of the real prize – a Basic Law which would materially affect the Court's domination of the Israeli governmental order. The checkmate move could then be presented as following established precedent, as a natural evolution of previous rulings, as but a small and inevitable step on the same path. As one Israeli jurist put it succinctly in 2018: "The oxymoron of a 'Basic Law approved by the Supreme Court' will begin to roll off the tongue and become a familiar refrain. The rhetoric, according to which the court is authorized to approve or strike down Basic Law legislation, will gain more and more supporters and will come to be perceived as a model of the rule of law."[22] This was precisely the intended effect.

*

Thus 2021 saw the final preparatory phase in anticipation of the Court's second constitutional revolution and the attainment of genuine judicial supremacy. *Shafir* was issued in May, the *Nation State* ruling just six weeks later. Both rulings could have been published at any time, before or long after – *Shafir* was moot and regarded circumstances the recurrence of which were not on any horizon; the *Nation State* case had been ongoing for three years and regarded speculative, potential harms. Yet the Court's timing was impeccable. *Shafir* was handed down soon after it became clear, on May 5th, that Israel's right-wing parties were not able to form a Coalition in the Knesset following elections, such that the threat of legislative retaliation was dramatically diminished. The *Nation State* ruling was released days after the new Bennett-Lapid Government – intensely sympathetic to the Court's supremacy – had been officially formed. As a popular Israeli saying playfully goes, "timing is a matter of timing."*

Having sufficiently developed and established the doctrines of *Abuse* and *UCA*, having primed its newfound instrument of devastating constitutional enforcement, the Court was now poised to strike when the need arises. That moment finally arrived with the 2023 amendment to Basic Law: The Judiciary which sought to restrict the Court's use of "extreme unreasonableness."

Applying *UCA* to Israeli Basic Laws

As we approach the 2024 *Reasonableness* ruling and the final phase of judicial supremacy in Israel, we must pause to lay out the obvious and devastating objections to the Supreme Court striking down Basic Laws.

The notion of any court striking down a constitutional provision or amendment raises clear democratic concerns. The problems with an unelected court invalidating duly-enacted constitutional provisions don't need much elaboration. As discussed above, in the vast majority of jurisdictions it is considered unthinkable or has been explicitly rejected by the courts and by the legal community alike – considered something of a disreputable theory entertaining primarily by excitable academics seeking to stand out. Proponents of this practice typically rely on examples of doubtful relevance – either from third-world countries, or from jurisdictions with limited democratic experience, deficient democratic culture and a highly questionable commitment to democratic principles of popular sovereignty.

---

* The Hebrew original is more amusing, with the first part of the sentence in Hebrew and the final word in English, though the first and last word bear the same meaning.

As a matter of comparative and universal practice these doctrines have some clear common features. In the rare cases in which the doctrine of "Unconstitutional Constitutional Amendments" was adopted or applied, it has relied entirely on explicit constitutional text – such as express "eternity" clauses or clear procedural requirements for amendments. The cases in which a court recognized implicit limitations on constitutional amendments are even more rare, and rely either on "principles" stipulated by the constitution or on the constitution's alleged overall "fundamental character" or "basic structure" (which is by definition the product of judicial reasoning). The doctrine of "Abuse of Constituent Authority" essentially exists only in theory – virtually no court has ever applied it directly, in isolation from additional doctrines and as independent grounds for invalidation. It is considered, at best, supplemental grounds which are tacked on to more concrete and tangible justifications (such as an explicit "eternity" clause), and may be better described as a supporting rationale for *UCA* than as a distinct doctrine.

Yet one critical element of both *UCA* and *Abuse* doctrines stands out in the context of their potential applicability to Israel. Both in theory and practice, any such doctrine relies exclusively, as its core assumption and precondition, on the existence of a conventional constitution. This is because all versions and instances of these doctrines, on their own terms, claim to enforce *the constitution itself* and not some higher philosophical norm. This is easily evident with explicit constitutional clauses limiting its own amendments. But it is equally the case for judicial enforcement of alleged "principles," whether delineated in the constitutional text or whether "emerging" from the totality of the constitution's provisions; the court claims to defend such inviolable "principles" – found in the constitution itself – from violation. It is also equally the case for preventing "abuse" of constituent power, as the authority to amend the constitution is itself derived from (and therefore potentially limited by) the constitution. In any variation of *UCA* and *Abuse*, on their own terms, the underlying fundamental justification is that the court is merely requiring compliance with the constitution itself. No court has ever presumed (at least overtly) to subject constitutional amendments to the superior claims of abstract morality or universal values.

In his classic textbook on the subject, Yaniv Roznai makes this point in unequivocal terms. Implied limitations "derive from within the constitutional order rather than from a source external to the constitutional order."[23] That is, such limitations are grounded in the constitutional text itself, even if implicitly so. Roznai indeed rejects the notion of limitations to constitutional amendments based solely on abstract moral theories not based on the constitution itself – even if "binding, objective moral principles exist in every society… there is no basis to regard them as a yardstick for determining the *legal validity* of an amendment." Somewhat understating the obvious objection, Roznai continues: "Subjecting the legal validity of constitutional norms to moral thresholds would undermine certainty in law and detract from its authoritative nature" as it would "necessitate the *a priori* resolution of contentious moral questions."[24]

Adjacent to this core feature are two parallel and complementary assumptions. First, that "constituent power" is distinct from "amendment power," in the sense that an original constitution is created by the former wielding supreme constitutional authority, while subsequent amendments to that same constitution are enacted by the latter which stands on a slightly lower footing.* Because the existing constitution defines the amendment process, and essentially establishes and delegates the very power to amend, exercise of such delegated amendment authority is itself subject to the constraints of the existing constitution. On this view, the proponents of *UCA* like to explain that the authority to *amend* the constitution is not the same as (and is inferior to) the power to *replace* the constitution. As such there are inherent (and enforceable) limits to what constitutional amendments can do, because the amending power is *not* authorized to alter some fundamental features (or to violate certain principles) of the constitution. Put differently, under *UCA*, the constitution has both an "author" and an "editor"; the latter is bound by the constitution itself and fills a role which is more limited in both scope and substance. The same theory applies equally to *Abuse*, because the "amending power" delegated by the constitution must be used in a particular manner and for specific appropriate purposes.

The second parallel assumption is that the constitution being enforced is an integral, documentary, comprehensive, unified constitution – i.e., a conventional written constitution – without which no overarching "principles" or "core" may be asserted. The idea of a constitution having an inherent and unalterable "character" at its hearts only makes sense if there is an entire "constitution" to begin with. Different constitutional provisions might easily be in tension or even contradict one another; different governmental arrangements balance each other out; it is only the complete apparatus, viewed as a whole, from which one might derive "principles" and which give any such principles credence and force. Put differently, the fundamental "principles" of any constitution (whether explicitly stated or not) are a product and mirror of the sum of its substantive and concrete provisions. The proposition is otherwise illogical – how can one deduce the character of a constitution, if only a half of it is known and the other half is either unknown or does not exist? Could one deduce the core "principles" of the U.S. Constitution by reading only articles one, three, five and seven, while ignoring articles two, four, and six?

The second assumption is directly relevant to the first – if there is no complete constitution in the typical sense, there is no distinction between a constitution's creator and its amender. There is no "delegated" amendment power which is inferior to an "original" creation power, because there is simply no "original" constitution (yet). A subsequent change cannot be said to impermissibly "replace" an existing constitution, because no such constitution exists. In other words, the distinction between (unlimited) creation power and (limited) amendment power can only be supported within the framework of a conventional, written,

* Scholars tend to call this "primary" and "secondary" constituent power.

comprehensive constitution.

These assumptions might seem obvious but are in no way trivial. Regardless of whether they are true or compelling, they serve as the basic justification and the prerequisites for *UCA* or *Abuse*. Applying either doctrine in the absence of an actual constitution would be risibly outrageous. It would be a contradiction in terms. In Israel it becomes downright grotesque.

For convenience, going forward we will refer to both doctrines jointly as *UCA*.

Subjecting Basic Laws to *UCA* within the Israeli constitutional order fails any rational evaluation and directly contradicts the core assumptions described above. As we have observed countless times and as the Supreme Court itself concedes, Israel doesn't really have a constitution per se. Even by the most generous and sympathetic interpretation, the Israeli pseudo-constitution is decidedly partial and incomplete in an elementary sense – there might be a chunk of a constitution, but the rest is still in the drawn-out process of being formed. By all accounts, what Israel has is three slices of an unbaked constitution-pizza pie.

Further, as has been explored in great deal, under *Hamizrachi* and the Court's constitutional revolution the Knesset exercises *original* constituent power. This cannot be stressed enough – according to the Court's own jurisprudence, when the Knesset enacts Basic Laws it is acting as though it were the first constituent assembly, as if it were creating the constitution anew. The Knesset is clearly not an "amending" power exercising some "secondary amendment authority" delegated by, and under the regime of, a fully-fledged constitution. It is wielding an ultimate and supreme power which predates any specific Basic Law (be it in 1958 or 1992 or 2023) and which continues to exist thereafter. This is true regardless of whether the legislation in question technically alters a Basic Law or enacts a new one. The Knesset's original constituent authority is directly related to the "incomplete" nature of the Israeli constitution – the Knesset is steadily enacting new constitutional chapters or reshaping existing ones, and it can only do so from the outset as an originator, not as an amender, of constitutional norms. In other words, the Knesset remains the "author," not the "editor," of the Israeli constitution, creating new chapters and rewriting existing ones as the Knesset sees fit.

Recall once again that these are not disposable or tangential elements of *Hamizrachi* but rather serve as its foundation. The Supreme Court could only recognize the 1992 Basic Laws (and later, all preexisting Basic Laws) as Israel's "constitution" under the premise that this was a partial constitution, still in the making; and the Court could only endow such Basic Laws with constitutional status by positing that the Knesset possessed the authority to create constitutional norms out of thin air. This is the Court's own argument justifying its power of judicial review.

For these reasons alone, individually and jointly, any form of *UCA* is simply inapplicable to Israel and its Basic Laws on the most basic theoretical and doctrinal level. The doctrine of *UCA* does not claim, under any formulation, to bear relevance to an incomplete constitution or to the original constituent assembly creating it. What are the inherent unalterable "principles" of an unfinished constitution consisting of a handful of Basic Laws? Indeed, how can there be any such principles when all agree that many critical Basic Laws have yet to be enacted? A partial constitution-in-the-making cannot possibly have binding "principles" limiting the future content of its prospective provisions, because such "principles" only emerge out of the final totality of a whole constitution. Similarly, the base rationale behind all *UCA*, that it restricts the amendment power, is categorically inapplicable to the Knesset's exercise (under *Hamizrachi*) of original constituent power. As the Knesset is not amending the constitution, but is rather writing it from scratch, Basic Laws simply fall outside the scope of *UCA*. In the absence of a complete constitution to enforce against its offending amender *UCA* collapses into irrelevancy. This is the only conceivable outcome of faithfully and consistently applying any *UCA* doctrine to the Supreme Court's straightforward jurisprudence since 1995.

The Court's insistence on striking down Basic Laws due to their supposed violation of overriding principles is preposterous even by the radical standards of *UCA*. Imagine a court telling the U.S. Constitutional Convention in Philadelphia – or any other constitutional assembly – during their deliberations that certain draft provisions were "unlawful" because they were inconsistent with other previously discussed draft provisions, or with the "overarching principles" of the yet-unwritten constitution. The idea is simply absurd.

The Supreme Court is acutely aware of this categorical, definitional, outright contradiction, and concedes the problem at various stages throughout the cases discussed above. The Justices time and again repeat the inherent "challenges" in applying *UCA* in the absence of an actual constitution. In the 2011 *Bar-On* ruling, Justice Beinisch emphasizes that the "constitutional project" is "still incomplete," and that "to a considerable extent" the constitution "is still in the process of formation."[25] Justice Hayut writes in the 2018 *Removal* decision that: "Given the current state of Israel's constitutional project as an unfinished endeavor… there is considerable difficulty in adopting a comprehensive doctrine concerning unconstitutional constitutional amendments."[26] In the 2021 *Nation-State* ruling, Hayut observed the obvious point that *UCA*, "as its name implies," had exclusively been used in other jurisdictions where a "complete constitution exists," such that the doctrine applies "in relation to the authority to amend such a constitution"; as opposed to Israel, where "the process of constitution-making has yet to be completed." Hayut continues to note that until "the completion of the Basic Laws project into a full constitution," such doctrines "are not applicable… to our system."[27] Indeed, already back in a 2011 article Aharon Barak explained that *UCA* "has no place in Israel" as a "comprehensive" doctrine, because "the very concept of a constitutional amendment" is "problematic in the Israeli context"; the constitution "remains a work in progress," with "the task not yet completed."[28]

The Court's solution in the *Nation-State* case onwards is nothing short of astonishing. To circumvent this colossal inconvenience the Court simply proceeds to apply the doctrine by a different name. In the same breath as disavowing *UCA* the Court announces matter-of-factly that the Knesset's authority as constituent power is nonetheless "not unlimited," due to the "narrow" prohibition on denying Israel's Jewish and democratic character. This is an impressive feat of sophistry and logical acrobatics even by the Court's standards – after essentially admitting that *UCA* cannot apply to Israel both in theory and in practice, the Court just restates the doctrine and pretends it is doing something else. In this way the Court legitimates and normalizes the *idea* of striking down constitutional provisions, and then neatly sidesteps the fact that none of those legitimating factors can possibly apply to the matter at hand.

To be clear, the doctrine of "unconstitutional constitutional amendments" is an umbrella concept used to describe judicial review of constitutional provisions. To the extent the doctrine has any validity whatsoever, it is within the narrow confines set out by a handful of theorists and by the practice of a bare few courts which have engaged in this type of extreme judicial review. A judicial decision to strike down constitutional amendments doesn't magically become any less an application of *UCA* just because a judge claims to be doing something else.

When the Israeli Supreme Court subjects Basic Laws to judicial review it irrefutably employs *UCA*, lock, stock and barrel; but without even the pretense of relying on any existing recognized justification and without the remotest resemblance to other comparable jurisdictions. Throwing around euphemisms such as "inherent limits" and insisting these are more "narrow" than conceivable alternatives doesn't change a thing. The Court applies *UCA* to its fullest extent immediately after declaring the doctrine inapplicable, hoping no one notices this bizarre "bait and switch" tactic. Cutting through the fog, the main upshot from the Court's analysis is that it is, by its own account, the only court in the world willing to invalidate constitutional provisions enacted by the *original* constituent power *during* the process of constitution-making and in the absence of a conventional constitution, in complete deviation from even the most radical related doctrines. To the Court's credit it at least has the decency to be somewhat embarrassed and to pretend this is not the case.

Calvinball and Bad Faith Constitutionalism

So much for principle and theory. Yet it is on the practical plane that the Court's transgressions emerge as truly egregious, far worse than any doctrinal flaw.

As demonstrated at length in the current and previous chapters, the constitutional revolution was justified in large part by the Court and its supporters precisely *because* of the Knesset's ability to change Basic Laws and to remake the constitution as it saw fit. When accused of anti-democratic usurpation of legislative authority, the Court's most effective and compelling defense was that the Knesset still retained ultimate lawmaking power. The Knesset could, for example, annul the Court's ability to conduct judicial review of any kind. As Barak stressed repeatedly, the Knesset remained the "pinnacle of the normative pyramid."

The Knesset, the legal system, the electorate and indeed the entire political order in turn relied on the Court's declarations of subservience to Basic Laws enacted by the Knesset in its role as constituent authority. They took the Court's assurances at face-value and responded accordingly. If there is any single, isolated reason that the constitutional revolution survived in the first few years after 1995, it is this explicit and unequivocal pledge by the Court to respect the Knesset's supreme authority to enact constitutional norms. The Knesset and political system grudgingly tolerated the constitutional revolution, playing by the new rules unilaterally and unlawfully dictated by the Court, all under the assumption that the Court would honor its own jurisprudence.

Yoav Dotan describes the constitutional revolution as including a "promissory note" – that is, a check for future redemption. On the one hand of the deal was the Court's groundless creation of a constitution (and judicial review), and on the other hand was the assurance that the Knesset "could alter and shape the content" of that same constitution, as it saw fit and without limitation. When the Knesset turned to do precisely that – to enact significant constitutional change via new or amended Basic Laws – it was cashing the check tendered in 1995 and reaffirmed by the Court for decades. Referring specifically to the proposed reforms in 2023, Dotan notes that "no special intellectual effort was required" of the Knesset to establish its authority to embark on constitutional reform, as all it needed was "to rely on the Knesset's constituent power as recognized by the Supreme Court in countless rulings" and indeed as "developed and championed by the Court itself" over the course of decades.[29]

The Court's subsequent decisions that it can strike down Basic Laws thus constitute a shocking, jaw-dropping reversal of its original position, a remarkable display of bad-faith, hypocrisy and disingenuity. In doing so, the Court defaulted on the check which stood at the heart of its dubious deal with the Israeli people, backtracking on the most fundamental element enabling and legitimizing the constitutional revolution. Either the original Court never meant a word of its earlier commitments, exposing them to be nothing more than deceptive lip service meant to sedate opposition; or the modern Court blatantly and consciously flouted its prior explicit guarantees to the Knesset in the service of whatever immediate legal outcome the Court desired.

Some commentators at the time characterized the Court's methodology as "Jewish Poker."[30] In a well-known 1955 sketch by legendary Israeli comedian Ephraim Kishon, the hapless narrator plays "Jewish Poker" against his friend and quickly discovers to his dismay that his friend makes up new rules as they go along, each time to the friend's benefit and to the narrator's detriment. Perhaps just as accurate a description would be the game of "Calvinball" – in the classic comic strip "Calvin and Hobbes" by Bill Waterson, the titular characters play a game in which the only rule is that there are no rules. The players make up the absurd and ridiculous game as they go along, the only guiding principle being that "you can never play it the same way twice." The Supreme Court's reversal seems to take a page out of both, dastardly as the former and farcical as the latter. When judges subject Basic Laws to judicial review they throw their own rulebook out the window and invent new rules as they go along. All other players are effectively prevented from ever winning, though they scamper around naively trying to conform to the Court's fluctuating and self-serving jurisprudence.

A separate but related point focuses on the ease with which the Knesset can amend the "constitution." Supporters of judicial supremacy on and off the bench often stress the "unbearable ease" of Basic Law legislation as a justification for constitutional judicial review. The fact that the Knesset could effortlessly change constitutional norms, so the argument goes, means that there is greater risk of abuse or of ill-considered amendments, therefore requiring judicial oversight of constitutional legislation. While possessing some initial intuitive appeal, this finer point is equally hypocritical in its inversion of the Court's original framework since 1995. The constitutional revolution was defended not merely on the grounds that the Knesset was *able* to change the constitutional order, but specifically that it could do so *easily*. Aharon Barak himself explicitly spells this out in *Hamizrachi*: "To the extent that these methods of [constitutional] amendment are not particularly difficult, they allow the majority of the day to express its views, thereby softening the force of the argument that relies on a formalistic conception of democracy."[31] Justice Barak essentially argued that the easier it is to enact constitutional change, the less valid democracy-based (or majoritarian) objections become, because popular sovereignty is still exercised and translated into constitutional content relatively easily. In other words, the ease of changing a constitution is portrayed as a positive and democratic counterbalance to judicial power.

Extraordinarily, the Court and its supporters upended this argument and claimed the exact opposite without batting an eyelid. In 2011 Justice Beinisch dwelt at length on the "damage" caused to the constitutional status of Basic Laws due to the ease of their amendment, though she did not expressly argue that this supported their subjection to judicial supervision. Justice Rubenstein repeated the point in 2017. Then in a 2018 article, two prominent scholars carefully suggested that "the more the process of enacting constitutional norms... is no more demanding than that of ordinary legislation, the greater the willingness ought to be to allow judicial review of constitutional amendments."[32] The Court latched on to this passage and repeated it ad nauseum across its subsequent *UCA* rulings.

In *Shafir* the Court used the constitution's supposed malleability to vaguely support its claim as enforcer of "the rule of law"; in the *Nation-State* decision the "flexibility" argument took center stage, touted as one of only two justifications for judicial review of Basic Laws (and really the only justification, as the other one was a circular claim based on the Court's "role" as "protector" of Basic Laws). Justice Hayut patiently explains how "the need for judicial review of the content of constitutional norms" arises especially "where the process of enacting and amending constitutional norms is not subject to a rigid and distinct procedure, thereby enabling a transient majority to fundamentally alter the existing constitutional order with relative ease."[33]

One must marvel at the Court's audacity in completing such a total reversal of its analytical position. In *Hamizrachi* and later, the flexibility of Basic Laws was a democracy-based *defense* of judicial review in the name of electoral final say, a valid and worthy check on arbitrary judicial power; but as the Court hurtled towards supremacy, the ease of legislating Basic Laws was rebranded as a danger which needed to be contained. First the Court argued: "Don't worry about judges seizing power, the elected Knesset can always change things easily." Then, when this was no longer expedient, the Court's tone shifted to: "Oh dear! The elected Knesset can change things too easily; judges must seize power to mitigate this."

Needless to say, the "unbearable ease" with which the Court itself can nullify a constitutional provision (immeasurably greater than the Knesset's) is never considered by supremacists as objectionable or problematic. Extreme constitutional flexibility is only a menace when exercised by an elected parliament, not when exploited by unaccountable former lawyers in gowns.

The Court's analytical farce is especially ironic, in light of its consistent historical disregard for the method and procedure of constitution-making. As noted above, the Court has time and again disregarded the process of enactment as a feature of constitutional norms; the question of "how" a constitution is made has always been of minimal concern. The idea that this is a fundamental element conferring constitutional status on a legislative provision is conspicuously absent from Shamgar's 1995 list in *Hamizrachi* and from Hayut's 2021 list in *Shafir.* Indeed, if the "ease" of legislating Basic Laws is so "unbearable" to the Court, why did it elevate the 1992 Basic Laws – enacted effortlessly and clumsily – to constitutional status? How convenient, then, that the Court suddenly discovered the problematic nature of "flexible" Basic Laws in the *UCA* cases. It would seem that the method or process of constitutional legislation only matters to the Court when serving the goal of extending judicial power.

Analytical contradictions aside, the Supreme Court's bewildering about-face regarding the ease of amending Basic Laws is disingenuous on a broader and more fundamental level. The flexibility of enacting Basic Laws was a primary argument employed by the Court's critics *objecting* to the 1995 constitutional revolution. Constitutionalizing the Basic Laws was a grievous error for a variety of reasons, but chief among these was the fact that their enactment and amendment was no different from ordinary legislation, such that Basic Laws enjoyed neither democratic legitimacy to serve as supreme law nor the stability appropriate for constitutional norms. In other words, the flaws which the Court now finds so troubling were precisely the reason the Basic Laws should never have been artificially elevated to constitutional status to begin with.

The Court's reversal is in this sense all the more mind-boggling. After declaring the Basic Laws a "constitution" despite their utter unsuitability to assume that role, the Court then weaponizes that very same unsuitability to block future provisions it dislikes. One has to read it to believe it. Justice Beinisch in *Bar-On* (2011) decries the "significant gap in Israel's constitutional system" due to "the process of enacting Basic Laws." Knesset legislative procedures "do not contain any special provision distinguishing between" ordinary and constitutional legislation. Beinisch laments that "Basic Laws can be enacted by any majority in the Knesset" and "amended by any majority."[34] Fast forward to Justice Mazuz in the 2021 *Nation-State* ruling, who argues that "it is precisely the absence of a complete constitution, and the existence of an exceptional situation in which constitutional norms in Israel are, in practice, enacted through an ordinary legislative process… that underscores the need for, and the importance of, imposing limitations on the exercise of constituent authority…" Mazuz further bemoans the "utterly unprecedented" ease of constitutional legislation in Israel.[35]

Such observations are superficially compelling until one remembers that this was the argument *against* constitutionalizing Basic Laws in the first place. It was the Court that absurdly insisted on creating the "exceptional situation" of a faux constitution which may be amended with "utterly unprecedented" ease. After charging forward with the truly indefensible invention of a half-baked constitution unfit for purpose, ignoring the frantic warnings and myriad obvious flaws, the Court turns around and exclaims – "hey, this constitution is really not great. We need to save it from itself!" A popular Hebrew biblical phrase asks, "have you murdered and also inherited?" Here the Court commits the crime and then has the gall to claim the reward.

As a separate practical and analytical point, the relative "ease" of enacting constitutional provisions in fact undermines the case for their judicial review, precisely because of their potential for future reversal. A rigid and inflexible constitutional amendment, perhaps entrenched by some exacting procedural requirement, might raise greater concerns regarding its potential damage to liberal-democratic principles. A clear majority (and perhaps even a supermajority) "stuck" with an objectionable and damaging constitutional arrangement is at least partially undesirable. There is, at least in theory, a risk that might justify judicial prevention mechanisms. Yet in Israel no such risk exists. The ease of constitutional legislation means that any subsequent Coalition and Government – as soon as the next elections – can effortlessly reverse such objectionable measures. The more harmful a Basic Law, the more likely it is that the following elections will render a legislative coalition interested in altering it for the better. Indeed, this is what the Opposition has consistently maintained since the advent of the 2023 legal reforms – that they will cancel and annul any related Government legislation after they win the next elections and take control of the Knesset. In such a system there is no need for judicial risk-mitigation in the form of preemptive judicial review over Basic Laws. The political process itself rectifies the worst excesses of problematic constitutional provisions, and the "ease" of doing so is an argument *against* judicial review of Basic Laws, not for it.

Finally, subjecting Basic Laws to judicial review removes one of the sole moderating influences on the Court's jurisprudence after the constitutional revolution. If previously the Court had to exercise some caution lest its activism invoke the wrath of legislators and voters, the Court can now live out its most extreme supremacist fantasies, safe in the knowledge that it can swat away even constitutional legislation by the Knesset. To use Dotan's metaphor, if after *Hamizrachi* both Court and Knesset possessed "non-conventional" weapons which enabled a certain co-deterrence, now the Court had disarmed the Knesset's only available retaliatory measure, leaving the Court alone possessing a doomsday machine. While the Knesset's deterrent and tempering effect was not an explicit justification articulated by the Court, it was certainly an implicit assumption in the background of the constitutional revolution and essentially in all the Court's ensuing rulings. In this sense too, the Court's jurisprudential reversal is all the more dramatic and jarring.

A last point to consider revolves around the substantive grounds for evaluating the validity of constitutional legislation. Even after resolving that the Knesset's constituent powers are limited and that the Supreme Court may strike down Basic Laws, the question remains – what is the standard against which the Court can measure Basic Laws in order to determine their legality, and where is such a standard found? In other words, what is the legal norm which, if violated, renders a constitutional provision impermissible?

Any answer divides between two broad categories. One approach finds such norms outside the existing legislative framework, in eternal and metaphysical rules of democracy and morality inherent to the Israeli governmental and societal order. Another approach finds the answer within the existing Basic Laws themselves – either within their text or within their broader legal spirit. On brief examination both approaches emerge as equally absurd.

The first approach is in some senses more analytically coherent but also easier to reject. No court in the civilized world has claimed the authority to strike down primary legislation – much less so, constitutional provisions – based solely on the force of "democracy" or any other pure moral principle. No jurisdiction has yet recognized or enforced a substantive "super-constitution" that exists above and beyond all recognizable legal norms. Courts have always attempted to anchor such decisions on some foundation within the legal and constitutional text, however implausible such claims may be. Courts and judges ultimately do one thing – they apply the law. In the absence of even a prima facie claim to some applicable and enforceable legal norm, a court making any order or decision on the basis of distilled "democracy," "truth," "wisdom," "justice," "decency," "equality," "enlightenment" or any other laudable concept engages in nothing less than arbitrary tyranny. Such conduct is also of course indistinguishable from a court ruling on the basis of Aryanism, Salafist Islam, the Inquisition, Communism, or Bolshevism (to name a few). Even if all were to agree that such principles exist and supersede all legal (or constitutional) norms, a handful of judges still clearly have no superior claim to apply or enforce these, compared to the electorate or to a constitutional assembly. Without elaborating further, suffice to say that the impossibility of this approach is obvious to anyone familiar with the Western tradition of liberal democracy.

The Israeli context presents an even more extreme difficulty. The Supreme Court in 1995 elected to establish its judicial review on the "textual" basis of Basic Laws created by a supreme constituent power wielded by the Knesset. It explicitly rejected the model of abstract morality for obvious reasons (although the model was briefly contemplated by Barak in his 1989 *Laor* ruling). If it were to now adopt the notion of enforcing abstract principles of "democracy" to strike down Basic Laws, the Court would need not only to overcome the considerable principled objections to any such tyrannical power, but would also need to explain (as noted by Dotan above) why it is diverging from nearly three decades of hard jurisprudence.

Unfortunately for the Supreme Court, the second approach – of measuring new Basic Laws against existing ones – is neither more plausible nor more valid than the first. It would entail privileging earlier Basic Laws over newer ones, either by enforcing specific existing provisions against future ones (including against amendments to the very same provision), or by extracting some overarching principles collectively derived from the overall framework of all prior Basic Laws combined. This is indeed the broad direction the Court has adopted in its *UCA* cases, when it identifies the State's core character as "Jewish and democratic" based on the same vague phrase which appears in several Basic Laws, and on the broader spirit allegedly characterizing all Israeli constitutional legislation. In this way the Court could, on some level, at least pretend that its decisions rely on some distinguishable tangible legal norm.

The theoretical flaws and contradictions of judicial "editing" of constitutional provisions, in the context of an incomplete constitution still in the process of being enacted, have been discussed above. But grand constitutional theory aside, any such endeavor by the Court also raises immediate practical objections and challenges. First, there seems no plausible reason to privilege older Basic Laws over newer ones following the simple universal interpretive rules of *lex posterior* and *lex specialis* – for rules or laws on the same tier, new trumps old and specific trumps general. If Basic Laws are "the constitution," then limiting new provisions so that they conform to old ones is inconsistent with the most fundamental canons of Western legal thought as we know them.

Far more importantly, if the constitutional revolution is to be afforded any significance and if *Hamizrachi* is to be applied with a shred of consistency, then surely any Basic Law enacted from 1995 onwards ought to be afforded *greater* constitutional weight than preexisting laws. After all, even by the most optimistic and sympathetic standard, any Basic Law from before 1995 was enacted within the highly ambiguous constitutional conditions of the Harari Resolution and under the assumption that these were not a rigid, binding, enforceable constitution. However, following 1995 and *Hamizrachi*, one can plausibly argue that the Knesset and political order grudgingly accepted the new constitutional framework created by the Court. As a result, the Knesset began to engage in constitutional legislation in a manner far more conscious and deliberate than ever before. It is only after *Hamizrachi* that we may say with confidence that the Knesset was put "on notice" by the Court regarding its role as constituent power, and that only after (or at least, especially after) *Hamizrachi* the Knesset legislated Basic Laws fully aware of their constitutional nature and of the legal implications of such legislation.

In this critical sense, any Basic Law (enacted or amended) after 1995 reflects a much higher, more forceful and more explicit degree of constitutional authority. This is true both in principle and in practice. Unlike prior legislation and unlike even the 1992 Basic Laws, all such new laws were regarded as bearing constitutional status, and were drafted, debated, and enacted (or rejected) precisely as such. This is undeniably evinced by the historical and parliamentary record for virtually any Basic Law legislation since 1995, but the two most controversial Basic Laws are a case in point. The 2018 Nation-State Law and the 2023 Reasonableness Amendment were drafted, championed and enacted as fully-fledged new constitutional provisions. They were the products of prolonged legal consideration, intense legislative debate and unprecedented public controversy. They were both supported by a significant and absolute majority of Knesset Members. None of this can be said of the 1992 laws or of any previous Basic Laws.

Further still and similarly, most prior Basic Laws related to judicial authority in ways which were implicit or ambiguous at best.* Their text and underlying intent typically did not directly contemplate their impact on the scope and limits of judicial power. Yet the post-1995 Basic Laws could not be more explicit – with both BL:NS and the Reasonableness Amendment overtly aimed, in letter and in spirit, at directing or limiting judicial authority. That is, the newer Basic Laws contain much clearer and more detailed instructions for the Court in its enforcement of constitutional norms, reflecting unequivocal legislative objectives.

All this amounts to an almost-obvious argument, that if there is to be any disparity between the status of conflicting Basic Laws then the newer ones must undoubtedly prevail. The Court's elevation of pre-1995 Basic Laws to super-constitutional status at the expense of any future adverse Basic Law is wildly inconsistent with any rational and faithful application of its own constitutional jurisprudence. There is simply no legally sound way to evaluate the validity of new or amended Basic Laws, because there are no discernible substantive norms which are plausibly superior to new Basic Law legislation.

*

The Court's embrace of *UCA* (or whatever euphemism it chooses for the same) is utterly devoid of theoretical basis or justification; contradicts global practice; and

* An obvious exception being Basic Law: The Judiciary.

most importantly, violates and negates the Court's own fundamental jurisdiction and doctrine established in *Hamizrachi* and the constitutional revolution. At least in *Hamizrachi* the Court was able to pretend that its revolution was precipitated by the two new Basic Laws enacted in 1992; here it could have no such excuse. Astoundingly, from 2017 onwards the Court dismantled the entire constitutional order it had itself erected over the two previous decades, this time without the slightest legislative provision, societal development or textual hook to rely on as even a contrived impetus.*

One last point of critical importance is that the Court's subjection of Basic Laws to judicial review is not just another layer of rabid judicial activism, not just another escalation in the power contest between juridical and elected government. By declaring that it may invalidate Basic Laws (and ultimately by exercising such authority) the Court razes the edifice of *Hamizrachi* to the ground. The two constitutional frameworks – Knesset wielding unlimited original constituent power or Court as enforcing supreme unalterable values – are profoundly contradictory. They are paradoxical. As an analytical, rational, philosophical and practical matter, they cannot simultaneously coexist. One necessarily and categorically cancels the other. Either the Knesset functions as constituent authority which ostensibly created the constitutional revolution and judicial review in the first place, and the Knesset can therefore freely use such authority as it desires; or the Knesset is bound by abstract judicially-concocted "principles" enforced by unelected and insulated judges, is not a constituent authority in any sense and by any standard and does not possess genuine constitution-making power – meaning that the 1995 constitutional revolution could never have relied on this (flimsy) foundation to begin with.

The dilemma for the Court here is obvious – to invalidate Basic Laws, it must abandon the *Hamizrachi* framework entirely; yet in doing so, it undermines and essentially destroys the only coherent argument which ever could have supported its most ambitious expansion of judicial power to date, while also sacrificing what little integrity and prestige it still retains. Subjecting Basic Laws to judicial review would spell the end of Israeli constitutional law as a distinct discipline and the advent of a new era of sheer judicial lawlessness, in which judges wield ultimate final say regarding any issue of governmental, public or societal consequence, without even the pretense of legal authority or legitimacy. As we shall presently see, this is precisely what the Court elected to do.

The *Reasonableness* Ruling

In July of 2023 the Knesset enacted an amendment to "Basic Law: The Judiciary" which expressly limited the scope and application of the judicially-created standard of "extreme unreasonableness." The law essentially prohibited the use of reasonableness to evaluate the legality of decisions made by the Prime Minister,

---

* I am grateful to Matanel Bareli for this observation.

by Government Ministers individually, and by the collective Government (i.e., Cabinet) itself. The newly enacted provision reads, in full:

> 15(D1). Notwithstanding anything stated in this Basic Law, anyone vested with judicial authority under the law – including the Supreme Court acting as High Court of Justice – shall not hear a case concerning the reasonableness of a decision made by the Government, the Prime Minister, or any other Minister, and shall not issue an order in such a matter; for the purposes of this section, "decision" includes any decision, including those regarding appointments or a decision to refrain from exercising any authority.

The controversial law was immediately challenged – on the very same day – by a host of petitions to the Supreme Court. Needless to say, no petitioner could allege any tangible harm or personal grievance, as the law had only existed for a few hours. Despite the abstract and hypothetical nature of the arguments against the amendment, the Court set an unprecedented and rushed litigation schedule – demanding the Government respond almost immediately, skipping a first preliminary hearing, issuing a provisional order *nisi* on the strength of written briefs alone just two weeks after the law was passed, and setting the primary hearing for one month later.* Chief Justice Hayut determined that the case would be heard by all fifteen Justices, en banc, for the first time in the Court's history.

A single hearing for oral argument was held on September 12th, 2023. Just a few months later, on January 1st, 2024, the Supreme Court published the *Reasonableness* ruling, and by a majority of eight versus seven Justices struck down the Basic Law amendment as an impermissible violation of Israel's core democratic character. The decision is, at least as of now, the most important and consequential single ruling in Israel's legal and political history. Thus the Court completed its second constitutional revolution and indisputably established itself at "the pinnacle of the constitutional pyramid."

Some initial observations merit our brief attention before we consider the ruling's substance. Many months before the Reasonableness Amendment was passed and in response to the first announcement of the proposals for legal reform, Chief Justice Hayut expressed her clear disapproval of the contemplated legislation in a fiery public speech. The impropriety of any Justice declaring their views on pending legislation – which at the time had not yet even been drafted or presented to the Knesset for deliberation – was of course lost on her and on much of the Israeli legal establishment.

In the January 2023 speech at a legal conference, Hayut lambasted the

---

* For comparison, a recent challenge to another Amendment to the same Basic Law (regarding the Judicial Selection Committee) is plodding along at a leisurely pace. The law was passed in March of 2025; in July the Government had not yet even responded, and no hearing date has yet been set.

proposed reforms (which had so far only been outlined in vague terms) as an "unrestrained assault on the judiciary, as if it were an enemy to be attacked and subdued" and as "a plan to dismantle the judiciary." Hayut continued that the proposals were "intended to deliver a fatal blow to the independence and impartiality of the judicial branch." If adopted, the reforms would render 2023 as "the year in which Israel's democratic identity suffered a grievous blow." She concluded her speech by warning that "the meaning" of the proposals was "a transformation of State's democratic character beyond recognition."[36]

Whether Hayut's evaluation was justified is beside the point.* Here, the Chief Justice used the strongest terms to publicly criticize the Knesset's primary legislative initiative, even though she would almost certainly be later required to preside over a petition challenging the very same legislation. Hayut's wild violation of any known *sub judice* principle yields two useful insights. First, Hayut's position – indeed reflecting the Court's institutional position – had been determined long before any concrete details were known, before any law had been drafted and let alone enacted. Specifically, the argument of a "grievous blow" to Israel's "democracy" was clearly tailored to the prior *Nation-State* ruling which held that even a Basic Law could not violate Israel's core democratic character. The harm to Israel's "democracy" was a forgone judicial conclusion, despite the fact that no law had yet been drafted and that the details of the reform's several components were yet undefined and unknown (even to its proponents). Such statements cast the Court's ultimate ruling in a profoundly prejudicial light.

Second, Hayut's imprudence also likely affected her decision to assign the entire Supreme Court roster to the case panel. The Chief Justice's fiercely and vocally adverse position against potential legislation (which had not yet even been born) did not quite inspire confidence in the Court's impartiality, neutrality or objectivity. Numerous scholars argued that Hayut's unprecedented en banc assignment was a form of PR damage control – assigning the full bench to the case panel and allowing for a fully "diverse" decision was supposed to balance out Hayut's own proclaimed prejudice. Far from a recognition of the gravity and importance of the case, it was a way to compensate for her manifest bias by signaling that she was not using panel-composition to manipulate the case outcome.

Alas, the temptation of procedural engineering of a predetermined outcome was still too much to withstand – not (only) by panel assignment, but (also) by

---

* In all fairness, Hayut is not known for intellectual depth or nuance. In 2019 Hayut dismissed the entirety of conservative legal thought with the following observation: "Conservatism, according to the commonly accepted definition, is a worldview that opposes social change, sanctifying stability and continuity, alongside entrenchment of the existing order. Such a worldview does not align with the very essence of the law, which never remains static, is dynamic by nature and requires constant development and change, as it is intended to reflect the social order necessary in an ever-evolving reality." Such a confused view contrasting law with stability as incompatible opposites would be laughable (and embarrassing) in any other jurisdiction.

scheduling maneuvers. The *Reasonableness* case was indeed administered in record time, but for all the wrong reasons. Most judicial review cases in Israel have taken years to run their course, often for desirable reasons that make sense. Parties and judges ought to have sufficient time to develop their positions, argue their cases, and consider their decisions – especially in a system with immediate access to Supreme Court litigation with no "percolation" process. Such cases typically involve some factual assertion of harm – infringement of rights, for instance – which often justifies a measured and patient approach to observe a statute's actual real-world effects. At times changing political fortunes supply their own solution by amending the offending law, whether due to political compromise or to the law's opponents gaining parliamentary power. All these factors and others contribute to courts taking their time – in Israel and elsewhere – when considering the constitutionality of laws. They apply all the more forcefully to judicial review of constitutional legislation. The *Nation-State* ruling was issued some three years after the law was enacted. Even *Hamizrachi* took some two years to make its way (via civil appeal) to the Supreme Court.

More than the proceedings being condensed into a short and rushed timeframe, the timing of the *Reasonableness* decision itself was incredibly contentious. War had broken out on October 7th following the vicious and cowardly attack by Hamas, one month after the oral hearings. The government proposals for legal reform had been set aside and the public controversy surrounding them had mostly subsided. A National Unity Government had been formed which included the Court's supporters. Israel was fighting for its survival in a war that was already clearly the most significant in its history and which would define Israel's future for generations. Many argued that there was no sense and no justification in publishing the ruling under such circumstances, and that it would do much more societal and political harm than any ostensible legal good.

Why, then, was Chief Justice Hayut desperate to dispose of the *Reasonableness* case so quickly? Why the hasty proceedings and abysmally timed decision? The appalling answer is, unfortunately, no mystery. Hayut was scheduled to retire on October 13th, 2023, upon reaching the mandatory retirement age of 70. Another supremacist Justice, Anat Baron, was retiring one day earlier. The oral hearing had to take place beforehand for the two to participate. As statutory law requires that a judge complete their "involvement" in a case within three months of retirement, the ruling had to be published by January 12th. Thus, the most important case in Israeli legal history had to be rushed, and the ruling had to be issued at a profoundly inappropriate moment, ostensibly so that the two eminent jurists Esther Hayut and Anat Baron could participate in the case.

This argument, hinging on an insignificant legal technicality, is just as unconvincing now as it was for the 1995 *Hamizrachi* ruling, issued mere days after the assassination of Prime Minister Yitzhak Rabin under similar pretenses. The resemblance between the timing of the two cases is in fact remarkable. The sheer falsity and absurdity of this argument has been covered already in our discussion of *Hamizrachi* such that here we may revisit the point only in passing.

The rule in question (limiting judicial involvement to three months after retirement) can be interpreted such that the Court could issue a ruling long after a judge has retired; indeed, the statute could also simply be ignored, utilizing any of the Court's many mechanisms used to circumvent the legal text when it so pleases, and few would find fault with the Court postponing its decision under such extraordinary circumstances. Further, the Court's sudden commitment to procedural rigor is less credible while in the very same breath it yet again upends the entire Israeli constitutional order. If the Court is comfortable with annulling constitutional provisions without the remotest legal basis, it can darn well extend a statutory deadline for issuing rulings by retired judges.

A far simpler and achingly obvious solution was in fact available: Hayut could have excluded herself and Baron from the case in the interest of justice, propriety, honesty, rigor and much besides. Chief Justice Hayut had total discretion in appointing the case panel. None would have balked at a thirteen-member panel instead of fifteen, to serve the national public interest. This was true the moment the petitions were filed in July of 2023, when it was clear that including Hayut and Baron would yield unnecessarily and improperly rushed proceedings; and it was all the more true when the war broke out in October and the draft opinions were likely not yet written – Hayut and Baron could have announced their withdrawal from the case at that time to enable the ruling's deferral. It would seem, though, that such noble thoughts never crossed their minds.

Hayut's reckless and senseless insistence on her and Baron's participation in the *Reasonableness* case was not about ego alone – there were, evident to any observer and openly discussed, darker considerations at play. The majority and minority Justices in the ruling divided along predictable and relatively predetermined ideological lines, and all agreed the ruling would likely turn on the opinion of one or two "swing" Justices. Consequently, it was clear already at the outset that the votes from Hayut and Baron would be decisive. The ruling eventually played out precisely so – of the eight-Justice majority, Hayut and Baron provided the critical two votes to invalidate the Reasonableness Amendment, though they had already retired.

In this important sense the *Reasonableness* ruling dramatically differs from *Hamizrachi* in 1995, which had no operative effect (and upheld the statute being challenged) and which had the support of an overwhelming majority on the bench. Though benefitting the Court in terms of public perception and attentiveness, *Hamizrachi's* strategic timing and composition did not materially affect the case outcome, which would have remained the same even if it were published later or if the retired Shamgar were excluded from the panel.

The *Reasonableness* case could not be more different – if Hayut and Baron were not on the panel, the ruling would have swung the other way and the Basic Law amendment would have been upheld. Indeed, extraordinarily, at the time the ruling was published Hayut and Baron were *no longer serving* on the Court, and the decision no longer commanded the majority supporting its outcome. The majority of *active* (non-retired) Justices on the panel actually voted to uphold the

Reasonableness Amendment when the ruling was issued. Wrap your head around that for a moment.

The sinister timing of the Court's final ruling does, however, mirror that of *Hamizrachi* in terms of the grieving national mood and the state of political disarray. Ascribing this to procedural rigidity or even to callous indifference is, unfortunately, too naively generous an estimation of the Court and its machinations. There is no question, as a matter of objective fact, that the Court benefitted from the ruling's publication in January of 2024, at the peak of Israel's bloodiest and most horrific war. Public attention was focused on the ongoing day-to-day battles in Gaza and Lebanon; most people recoiled at the idea of rekindling the societal conflict of yesteryear. The political forces, chief among them the Knesset and Government, were bruised and battered from their failure to protect the country on October 7th, and clearly lacked the electoral capital to muster any kind of immediate legislative response – not to mention being preoccupied by managing a multi-front all-encompassing military campaign. A National Unity Government made any meaningful political backlash even less likely. This proved too valuable an opportunity for the Court to pass up.

It is difficult to describe the impression of judicial underhandedness and bad faith, and the sensation of acute betrayal, felt by many when the ruling was finally published. Such vague descriptions of the Israeli public mood cannot do justice to the raw, searing, mind-numbing pain and disorientation felt by most Israelis in the leadup to January of 2024. Some anecdotal details may serve to provide more tangible context: In December of 2023 Israel was still literally burying bodies from the October 7th massacre, with many victims yet unidentified and with new information on barbarous atrocities emerging every day. Hundreds of hostages continued to languish in Hamas terror tunnels, and on December 15th three hostages were misidentified and accidentally killed by Israeli troops. On December 29th South Africa brought a case against Israel before the International Court of Justice, alleging that Israel was committing genocide. December saw some of the most intense fighting to date as part of the ground incursion into Gaza – with one hundred and ten Israeli soldiers killed in that month alone. These included Elisha Levinshtern, age 38, son of my elementary school vice principal, killed in action on December 3rd; Yakir Schenkolewski, age 21, the cousin of my wife's cousins, killed in action on December 4th; Gil Daniels, age 34, brother of an old friend, killed in action on December 4th; and Lior Sivan, age 32, my former student at our local youth movement, killed in action on December 19th. May their memory be a blessing.

These were the things on most Israelis' minds on the eve of 2024. The Court could have chosen to rise to the moment. It could have easily postponed the ruling. It could have prioritized integrity, transparency, societal unity and the public interest, not to mention professional and intellectual diligence. Instead, infuriatingly and shamefully, the Court chose to capitalize on Israel's distracted and vulnerable state in the pursuit of its own power and petty public relations. In a feat of transparent procedural manipulation, the Court – and especially the Chief Justice – engineered its desired outcome.

Democracy = Judicial Supremacy

The *Reasonableness* ruling needed to answer two simple questions: First, can the Court strike down Basic Law amendments, and on what basis? Second, is the constitutional amendment in question invalid? With fifteen learned judicial opinions spanning a whopping 738 pages,* the Supreme Court answered "yes" to both with an eight-over-seven majority. A full analysis of the Court's justifications, doctrines and jurisprudence is beyond the scope of our current discussion. Suffice to say that any such analysis likely dignifies the ruling far more than its opinions merit. We will therefore contend ourselves with some cursory observations.

On the first question, a larger majority of Justices reasoned that the Knesset's constitution-making power was limited, and that the Court could enforce such limits by invalidating Basic Laws. The Court's prior efforts with the *UCA* rulings were now paying off, as Justices trotted out the tired tropes parroted in previous cases. True to form, the Court regarded *dicta*, minority opinions and academic writing as binding law, and could proclaim that the question had already been resolved in the *Nation-State* case and that it was merely applying settled precedent. Here the Supreme Court could finally utilize all its painstakingly developed theories, and for the first time followed through with the direct invalidation of a Basic Law. The ludicrousness and ramifications of such a holding by the Court have been discussed at length in the preceding sections and do not need repeating. Having decreed its own power to veto any part of the Israeli constitution, the Court was now truly Supreme, not only by doctrine, but in practice.

Though the Court majority agreed that the Knesset was prohibited from altering the "Jewish and democratic" character of the State, any semblance of uniformity or of coherence ends there, as does the meaning of a "majority opinion." Remarkably, *no two Justices* could agree on the underlying legal theory yielding limits on the Knesset's constituent powers and granting the Court authority to subject Basic Laws to judicial review. Every single concurring Justice presented their own idiosyncratic version of how and why the Court could strike down constitutional legislation – from the "fundamental values of the system," to the text of disparate prior Basic Laws, to abstractions of "the rule of law," to the Court's (statutory) authority to administer "justice," to the Declaration of Independence, to Hans Kelsen's "Basic Norm," to archaic splinters of legislation from the British Mandate and beyond. Fantastically, Justice Amit simply announces that he sees "no practical significance" to identifying a source of super-constitutional authority insofar as "all paths lead" to the same outcome of judicial

* Consider that the ruling is significantly longer than this book.

limits to constitution-making power. The overall impression is of a group of fresh law students eagerly inventing creative solutions to a tricky assignment.

This is one sense in which the ruling simply defies rational legal analysis. Why bother dissecting each opinion if the Justices themselves can't seem to agree on a single theory? Justice Solberg stresses the point, noting that the majority opinions "do not agree, in the slightest" about the source of the authority they claim to exercise. If one were to inquire about the State's "most supreme constitutional norm," Solberg muses, on the basis of which the Court strikes down a Basic Law enacted by the constituent power, they would find "no clear answer" in the majority opinions.[37]

The significance of this matter alone cannot be overstated. The fragmented nature of the Court's reasoning speaks volumes as to the strength of its arguments. One need not be a seasoned scholar to recognize that the most momentous ruling in a Court's history ought to have some degree of consistency, some common underlying understanding shared by the deciding majority. Yet the *Reasonableness* ruling contains nothing of the sort. Each of the Justices didn't seem particularly convinced by their colleague's philosophical creativity. The variety and diversity of outlandish opinions within the disjointed majority leave the impression of mismatching cheap tableware at a seedy second-hand antique shop, where both the unkempt proprietor and his bogus merchandise seem equally unreliable. The fact that no two Justices could agree on the most fundamental question at issue – the source of their super-constitutional authority – tells the reader all they need to know about the plausibility and legitimacy of the Court's core argument.

In answering the second question, the Court invalidated the Reasonableness Amendment and essentially elevated the "unreasonableness" standard to super-constitutional status. The Court held that the Knesset's restriction of unreasonableness review amounted to an impermissible violation of Israel's core democratic character.

To describe such an astonishing conclusion as bizarre would be a wild understatement. One can argue many things about both the reasonableness standard and about the legislative attempt to limit its applicability, but to claim that it is an inviolable pillar of "democracy" – in Israel or elsewhere – is plain bonkers. It is a juvenile and facile insult to the intelligence of any sentient being. Though the Court's crude reasoning can hardly justify a close analysis, we may take a step back to evaluate some key aspects of the Court's overall judgment.

As noted above, the 2023 Reasonableness Amendment limits the scope of the "extreme unreasonableness" standard so that it does not apply to the apex of elected, accountable executive government. Aside its implications for substantive government policy, this would also have an obvious dramatic effect on judicial review of executive appointments (and dismissals), would essentially nullify the Deri Doctrine of judicial impeachment, and would significantly curtail the power of the Legal Counsel to the Government over high-level executive action.

Whether these are desirable measures and outcomes, whether they are beneficial or detrimental to the Israeli constitutional order, can be a matter of legitimate debate. But an impermissible violation of core features of democracy? The suggestion is risible, but was gravely contemplated and earnestly embraced by the Court.

As has been exhaustively demonstrated in Chapter 5, the unreasonableness standard places all conceivable executive government power – policymaking, appointments, the very act of governing itself – in the hands of unelected and unaccountable judges and their equally insulated proxies. Judges evaluate whether any policy or decision "properly" and "correctly" balanced the competing considerations and factors, as though this were a technical legal question and not the core function of government itself. Clawing back some degree of such power and restoring it to the stewardship of elected politicians who alone bear electoral responsibility may be many things, but only a fool or a charlatan could call it "undemocratic." By the Court's twisted logic, "democracy" demands that the core functions of executive government be exercised or supervised by a supreme legal priesthood, while by the same token "democracy" prohibits the assignment of governing authority to actual elected officials and the formal institutions representing popular will. Again, one need not be an expert on the Western democratic tradition to understand just how ludicrous a claim this is.

Justice Elron conveys a similar point in his dissenting opinion – if the Reasonableness Amendment is a grievous violation of Israel's democratic character by the Court's vague standard, then so is just about any potential legislation that a petitioner might choose to challenge.[38] So implausible is the "democratic" claim against the amendment, that striking it down on such grounds simply proves the Court's standard to be devoid of any substance.

Zooming further out, it's worth recalling that contemporary Israeli unreasonableness is a judicially-created standard, entirely and exclusively developed by the Supreme Court. Not only is it absent from any constitutional provision (e.g., Basic Laws), it has no basis even in statutory law. Unlike potential changes to other contentious arrangements (such as the judicial selection process), the Reasonableness Amendment doesn't actually amend any existing statutory provision – it adds a new one to counter pure judicial doctrine. The Court couldn't even pretend that the Knesset was altering some longstanding sacred foundational legal text, because no such text exists. The contest in this case was not between conflicting iterations of the democratic process and popular sovereignty channeled by the Knesset, between old and new expressions of legislative or constitutional power; it was rather a contest between sheer judicial rulemaking and the State's sole recognized lawmaking authority. In any other democratic jurisdiction this would be no contest at all – legislative will defeats judicial invention by knockout.

In the same vein, the unreasonableness standard is ultimately a doctrine of *administrative* law governing executive officials and agencies, and is consistently described as such by the Court itself. As noted at the end of Chapter 6, such rules are universally considered to be under the prerogative and discretion of the legislature (especially in a parliamentary system in which the executive is appointed by parliament and not directly elected). That is, it is the elected legislature which makes the laws governing the conduct and confines of executive action – this is typically uncontroversial. Yoav Dotan states this unequivocally:

> "The accepted view in comparative legal systems is that as a general rule, the legislature has the authority (in principle) to deny or to restrict administrative judicial review, or to define the scope of judicial review and its grounds and standards."[39]

Judges have no business telling parliament how to direct and supervise the executive.

These two points combined underscore just how wacky the Court gets in its *Reasonableness* ruling. In any normal jurisdiction a constitutional provision to limit the use of "unreasonableness" would be superfluous overkill – an ordinary statute would be entirely sufficient, and any court would be compelled to retreat before a plain rule of administrative law duly stipulated by express legislation, all the more so if it were emphatically repudiating a judicial rule. Yet per the Supreme Court, a standard of administrative law wholly invented and developed by judges prevails over an explicit contrary instruction by the Knesset. More amazingly still, the former prevails even over a constitutional amendment. This is the Court's vision of "democracy" – judges formulating paramount legal rules of executive conduct, which can be overcome neither by statute nor by constitution.

Judge Richard Posner captured this point nearly two decades earlier, when describing Barak's "usurpative" approach to judicial legislation. For Barak, "common-law judging" meant judges freely making law while unbeholden to any other source of legal authority:

> "Barak's method, lacking as it does any but incidental references to enacted provisions, may seem the method of the common law… except that common-law rules are subject to legislative override, and his rules are not. The significance of this point seems to elude him. He takes for granted that judges have inherent authority to override statutes. Such an approach can accurately be described as usurpative."

Little did Posner know how much the Barak-ean Supreme Court would prove him right.

How, then, could the Court possibly argue that the reasonableness standard was at the "core" of Israeli democracy? Easily enough. This was the third-act smoking gun foreshadowed by Hayut including "separation of powers" and "the rule of law" as features of Israeli substantive democracy in first-act earlier rulings. The Court arbitrarily infused the term "democracy" with whatever subjective values it seems to favor, though they bear no necessary terminological, analytical or theoretical link. Then, in a feat of typical and familiar Orwellian newspeak, the

Court interprets these to convey the opposite of their plain meaning: "Separation of powers" is not the allocation of exclusive government power to each respective appropriate branch, but rather the exercise of judicial power unconstrained by any other rule or institution, effectively superior to any other branch, insulated from and impervious to the products of democracy. Thus judges effectively exercising supreme executive and legislative power is the epitome of "separation of power." Similarly, "the rule of law" is not the subjection of all State (including judicial) action to known articulated rules, but rather primacy of judicial arbitrary discretion over any government authority and institution. Using such terms and others, the Court incorporates untouchable judicial supremacy into the fabric of so-called democracy, and *viola* – any curb on judicial power is *ipso facto* a violation of democracy itself. Simply put, the Court effectively defines democracy as the *de facto* and *de jure* rule of judges – no more, no less.

From here onwards the Court's conclusion is inevitable. A restriction on the outrageous and lawless reasonableness standard indeed undermines "democracy" so conceived.

A final noteworthy point is that the Reasonableness Amendment doesn't even fall afoul of familiar expansive notions of democracy – such as *Hamizrachi's* flimsy definition of "substantive" democracy founded on protection of minorities and human rights. This is because the amendment simply does not impact the adjudication of rights' violations or of minority protections. Any harm to human rights (which include, one might stress, the measureless right to "dignity" and "equality" as reviewed above) automatically falls under the purview of "proportionality" review, not "unreasonableness," and as such would be unaffected by the amendment. The same goes for any primary legislation which might adversely impact minorities, as statutory law is not (and never has been) subject to the administrative reasonableness standard. In other words, the Court could not even pretend that the Reasonableness Amendment undermined its original definition of democracy which had served to justify the constitutional revolution.

Similarly, the amendment left all other existing grounds of judicial review intact – including those of arbitrariness, discrimination, bad faith, procedural flaws, natural justice, immaterial considerations, and of course *ultra vires* (illegality or excess of authority) above them all. Any executive action would still have been subject, without exception, to the full confines of the law and to all the conventional instruments of administrative judicial supervision. Even if the amendment had been upheld and followed faithfully, executive government could still only operate within the firm framework defined by statutory law and enforced by courts. As such, the common argument (routinely repeated by majority Justices) that the amendment renders executive government "lawless" or somehow absolves them of adherence to genuine legal rules is baseless and nonsensical.

This simple point is clearest on an intuitive level and does not require much elaboration. An amendment which has no bearing on individual rights, which ensures de facto governing power is retained by elected officials and which leaves in place all traditional legal limits on government power, simply cannot be branded "anti-democratic." The Court's central finding that the amendment violates Israel's core democratic character is manifestly, excruciatingly absurd.

Perhaps more than anything else, the split decision itself strongly indicates just how weak of an argument the majority espoused. If the Reasonableness Amendment truly was a "grievous" blow destroying Israel's core democratic essence, then this would have been obvious also to the seven dissenting Supreme Court Justices. The majority's claim inherently requires a degree of unequivocalness – the colossal, devastating harm to Israeli democracy as described by the majority opinions would need to be unmistakable in order to be true. It's not that a close call and split court automatically negate a judicial majority's views; it's that in the *Reasonableness* case, if the majority was right then the minority Justices could not possibly disagree and no close call could exist. The fact that nearly half of all presiding Justices were unconvinced utterly eviscerates the majority's central contention of undeniable democratic destruction.

Though we will not conduct a thorough review of the various individual opinions in the *Reasonableness* ruling, a few anecdotal remarks are justified. Unfortunately, at the time of this writing, thc only portion translated into English is Hayut's majority opinion.

Justice David Mintz offers what is by far the most comprehensive, eloquent and compelling refutation of the Court's majority position. He denies the Court's authority to review Basic Laws, rejects the Court's invalidation of the amendment, and even dares to question the Court's power of judicial review and the entire constitutional paradigm since *Hamizrachi*. His opinion is presented with methodical clarity, analytical rigor and jurisprudential integrity. Any reader seeking an irresistibly persuasive counter to the Court's majority ruling need look no further than Mintz's opinion.

Enlisting support from Israel's greatest jurists of yore, Justice Noam Solberg concedes that he may be in the minority (in the *Reasonableness* ruling) but that he stands firmly with the majority of all previous Supreme Court Justices. Solberg recites a litany of quotes from the Court's most renowned Justices over the generations, all of whom expressly rejected the notion of judicial review over Basic Laws and who unequivocally recognized the Knesset's ultimate and final authority as the bedrock of the Israeli governmental order. In doing so Solberg highlights just how sharply the Court was deviating from its own conventional jurisprudence. He advocates, almost pleadingly, that the Court "come ashore" to the "safe harbor" of the flimsy but coherent framework established by *Hamizrachi*, recognizing and warning against the irreversible devastation the Court was about to visit upon all of Israeli constitutionalism.

Justice Alex Stein, widely regarded as one of the Court's most principled and stalwart conservative Justices, disintegrates with a profoundly disappointing (and to many, disillusioning) opinion, showing that even a working clock sometimes runs out of batteries. Though a "dissent" in the sense that Stein votes to uphold the amendment, he joins the majority in finding that the Knesset's power as constituent authority is limited and that the Court may rightfully strike down Basic Laws. Dismissing the abstract theories proposed by other Justices, Stein pedantically traces the sources and limits of all legislative-constitutional power in Israel and thus arrives at his own technical, mechanical yet entirely novel argument. Stein of course cannot escape the obvious problem plaguing Israeli constitutionalism since the State's inception – that its governing order rests precariously on a hodgepodge jumble of trivial components – and thus he eventually reaches back to several obscure British-Mandate ordinances and early-State legislation, inexplicably upgrading them to be Israel's legal foundation. Stein, the avowed critic of Barak's purposive interpretation, the fearless censor of unfounded LCG authority, argued that from the first moment of its creation in 1949 there were things that the Knesset – and any other conceivable Israeli constitutional organ – was not legally permitted to do, by any majority and even unanimously. The result of Stein's ostensibly formalist inquiry, by which a handful of insignificant and provisional governmental decrees are vested with eternal super-constitutional status, is underwhelming as it is unconvincing. Of this far-fetched theory (never before seriously advanced by other jurists and not adopted even by the most supremacist Justices), we may note the observation made by Judge Richard Posner that "activists frequently adopt the formalist style to conceal the degree to which they are asserting judicial power."[40]

A final dishonorable mention must be reserved for Justice Anat Baron (who, as noted above, had already retired by the time the ruling was issued). Baron begins her opinion by comparing the Reasonableness Amendment to, no less, the October 7th terror assault by Hamas. One needs to steel themselves before reading:

> "Existential threats currently loom over the State of Israel, both external and internal…
>
> The State of Israel is engaged in a bloody war against a barbaric enemy that has risen against us to destroy us. These threats shall be overcome…
>
> Today Israeli democracy faces an internal threat, embodied in the amendment to Basic Law: The Judiciary – a measure intended to bring about fundamental regime change in the State of Israel."[41]

An external existential threat which murdered, raped and pillaged its way through Israeli towns leaving over a thousand corpses in its wake is juxtaposed, by Baron, with the internal "existential threat" of democratic Knesset legislation limiting the reasonableness standard. The State of Israel had been brought to its knees. Children had been slaughtered before their parents; entire families burned alive; women and children taken captive. Shiri Bibas and her red-headed toddlers Ariel and Kfir had already been killed. For Anat Baron, these were equivalent to an absolute majority of elected legislators voting to reduce the application of a contrived and unparalleled judicial doctrine.

It's enough to make the blood boil. One can scarcely imagine a more abhorrent comment made by a sitting Supreme Court Justice in an official judicial ruling – which was surely considered, reviewed and revised numerous times before final submission. Baron's comparison is a useful indication and reminder of the poor quality of judicial character and the low degree of intellectual sophistication too-often found on the Supreme Court. Substance aside, the fact that a Justice would permit themselves such depraved vulgarity reflects some persistent failings of the contemporary Court's judicial culture – a penchant for gross alarmism and loss of perspective, an absence of refinement and stylistic judgment, and at times even questionable mental faculties.

Baron will likely be forever remembered in collective Israeli history for this single deliberate remark (not that her judicial career leaves much else of distinction). It was also clearly no momentary imprudence or lapse of judgment – only a few weeks after the ruling was published, Baron repeated the claim of an "existential threat" posed by the effort to curb judicial power in an interview for the *Haaretz* newspaper.[42] In that interview the retired Baron expressed policy prescriptions and ideological positions unmistakably aligning her with the extreme left of Israeli politics: Describing the so-called occupation in the West Bank as the most "urgent and critical" problem facing the country, calling for an immediate end to the war in Gaza in exchange for a return of hostages, proclaiming a judicially-controlled Commission of Inquiry as the (exclusively) correct mechanism for investigating the leadup to the war, and placing some of the blame for October 7th on the preceding proposals for legal reform. She also made numerous verifiably false claims, such as that opponents of the 2023 legal reforms had never called for avoiding military reserve-duty as an act of protest. As one journalist pointed out, even Aharon Barak never expressed such blatantly partisan sentiments in the two decades since his retirement, knowing that this type of indiscreet statement shatters the illusion of judicial subject-matter neutrality and erodes what little remains of public trust in the courts.

Baron's bizarre claim is instructive in another way. She was, after all, merely channeling a core Barak-ean element of judicial supremacy: *L'État, c'est moi*. The Supreme Court is the State, or at least its most sublime manifestation; criticizing the Court or limiting its power is an attack on the State itself. Through such a warped paradigm, the physical annihilation of Israel and the legal restriction of Israeli judicial power really do amount to the same thing. Few examples better demonstrate the degree to which some Justices conflate the Court with the sovereign State.

*

The Demise of Constitutional Law

And so on January 1st, 2024, the Court finally attained true judicial supremacy.

By directly striking down a Basic Law it had not only removed the last impediment to unfettered ultimate judicial power, but had also effectively annulled the very existence of Israeli constitutional law. From that moment onwards, the metaphysical and mystical abstractions of arbitrary judicial decree became the law of the land, permeating the Israeli legal system and political order at every conceivable level. The oath sworn by every new Israeli judge – to keep faith with the laws of Israel – has been rendered meaningless. As can only be expected, the petitions against new Basic Law legislation are already rolling in.

The Court's decision to subject constitutional provisions to judicial review demolished the pre-existing legal structure erected by the Court itself in *Hamizrachi*. Though the Court might like to pretend otherwise, this development is irreversible – a canon that can only be fired once. In its wake none can plausibly claim that Israel continues to have a constitution comprised of Basic Laws, enacted by the Knesset, and interpreted or enforced by the judiciary. That particular argument was incinerated when the eighth Justice put pen to paper and signed their opinion in the *Reasonableness* ruling. The Israeli pseudo-constitution and its accompanying law and jurisprudence no longer exist in any meaningful sense. To paraphrase John Cleese in Monty Python's "Dead Parrot" sketch: "This constitution is no more. It has ceased to be. It has expired and gone to meet its maker. It's a stiff. Bereft of life, it rests in peace. It has kicked the bucket, it has shuffled off its mortal coil, run down the curtain and joined the bleedin' choir invisible. This is an ex-constitution."

There is some irony in the inelegant and unceremonious execution of the "substantive constitution" by the Court's own hand. Like Robespierre meeting his own fate by guillotine, so the Israeli constitution was temporarily useful as a vehicle for the initial revolutionary act of establishing lawless judicial review in a system of parliamentary supremacy; yet the moment it became an impediment and a liability to the objective of unlimited judicial power, the same constitution was devoured by the very revolution it had borne.

The simplest way to understand the Court's renewed constitutional revolution is through the prism of *recourse*. The concept of judges striking down parliamentary legislation in a democracy rests on the assumption that the public can do something about it – that it can respond and potentially reverse the decision. Indeed, the public's ultimate ability to bring about its desired policy or rules is one of the classic justifications for judicial review and its primary defense against claims of supremacy and counter-majoritarianism. Any other jurisdiction in the world invariably offers some solution to this tension: constitutional power can be asserted by the electorate by enacting direct constitutional amendments through a defined process; or in other cases, by appointing apex-court judges that are willing to effect the required constitutional change. There is often a balance between the two options. Constitutional change is notoriously difficult in the United States, but voters have the option of gradual modification (or correction) through presidential elections and ensuing judicial appointments to the Supreme Court, which ultimately and cumulatively reflects public sentiment over time. At the other end of the spectrum, voters in Switzerland can unilaterally trigger a referendum on a proposed constitutional amendment, and only an ordinary voting majority is required for its approval. Both such systems are geared not only towards producing outcomes which ultimately conform to popular will, but also specifically towards empowering the public to counter unwanted judicial action. It is not uncommon to find judicial appointments or constitutional amendments which are explicitly targeted at undoing some prior judicial mischief.

One especially instructive example is found in Slovakia. Following interbranch tensions, the Slovakian parliament enacted a constitutional amendment in 2014 which pertained to the process of judicial selection. In 2019 the Slovakian Constitutional Court ruled the amendment to be unlawful and invalid, expressly adopting the "unconstitutional constitutional amendment" doctrine. But things didn't end there: in 2020, the Slovakian parliament responded and passed a new constitutional amendment, stating that the Constitutional Court had no authority to review or strike down constitutional provisions. In other words, the Slovakian electorate was able to respond to the Court by lawful means, explicitly rejecting *UCA* in the constitutional text and asserting its final-say authority. The public had recourse, which it exercised by rescinding the Court's self-granted short-lived power to review constitutional provisions.

The Israeli *Reasonableness* ruling thus begs a natural, inevitable question – what course of action or reaction, what recourse, is now available to the Knesset, the electorate, the *demos*? Under the Court's new jurisprudence, the answer is – none. At least formally, there is no conceivable lawful way for the Israeli democratic process to produce an outcome intended by the Reasonableness Amendment, or any other outcome to which the Court sufficiently objects. The option simply does not exist. In the new framework created by the Court, the Justices possess final-say authority in the most pure and technical sense.

Take, for example, a Basic Law that explicitly prohibits judicial review of Basic Laws, much like the one enacted by Slovakians. One would be naïve or a fool to think that the Court would not strike it down as a "violation" of Israel's "core democratic character." The same is likely true, at least to some extent, of many other conceivable constitutional efforts, such as changing the judicial appointments process, limiting petitioners' standing or even establishing a separate constitutional court. If the Supreme Court decides a Basic Law does not satisfy its requirements of judicial supremacy (or any other standard it fancifully ties under the label of "democracy"), the public is categorically powerless to challenge such decision by any recognized lawful method.

Before 2024, Israelis could still delude themselves that the Supreme Court's radically supremacist jurisprudence was grounded, at least partially, in its sincere effort to apply and enforce Basic Laws serving as Israel's pseudo-constitution and as its supreme legal norm. Israelis could still tell themselves that their so-called constitution was a product of their will and was subject to alteration if they so desired, and that the Court's decisions conformed to some level of logical coherence and consistency. After the *Reasonableness* ruling such illusions are no longer tenable. There is no higher "law" which guides or restricts the Justices; and there is no institutional body or power above the Court.

The Supreme Court's decision to invalidate a Basic Law must inevitably be regarded as a spectacular act of self-immolation.

Perhaps some on the bench genuinely believed that they possessed the rightful authority to strike down constitutional legislation, or that the "unreasonableness" standard truly is an indispensable and universal requirement of democracy. But we may afford some Justices the courtesy of assuming they are not so dim as to believe their own hokum. Many in the *Reasonableness* majority may well have proceeded with their opinion as a calculated risk, in the hope that it would put an end to constant escalating tensions between judicial and elected branches. On this view, even though the substantive arguments were themselves implausible (to put it mildly), the Court was expressing its determination to make a stand, drew its battle lines, and presented a zero-tolerance, scorched-earth approach. A blinding "Hiroshima" to end the war.

Even at this level, and adopting the Court's supremacist institutional perspective, the decision was an obvious tactical blunder. A wiser course of action for the Court would have been to uphold the amendment, to once again "recognize" its authority over Basic Laws, but to reserve its exercise for a more clear-cut case with more substantial (even if debatable) "democratic" objections. The Court, led by Chief Justice Esther Hayut, could have thus demonstrated restraint and shown deference to the ostensible "constituent authority" of the Knesset, gaining significant public and legal credibility. At the same time, the Court could have subsequently applied the amendment in a manner greatly minimizing its effects, while still utilizing a host of other grounds for administrative judicial review in ways sufficiently creative to substantially impose judicial whim over executive discretion. The result would have been the Court taking the high road with only limited damage to show for it, and being much better positioned for its next tussle with the Knesset. When another disliked Basic Law comes along – such as an amendment to the judicial appointments process – the Court would have possessed the high ground, having proven its capacity for restraint and deference, and having shown that its test of "democratic character" had some genuine substance. The Court would likely have also found a more stable and sizeable majority on the bench to support an eventual decision to strike down a Basic Law, instead of the hairline provisional majority it commanded for the *Reasonableness* ruling.

Alas, it was not to be. The temptation for the supremacist Justices proved irresistible, and the rest is history. Some argue that this was the goal of the 2023 legal reform all along. On this theory, the legislators behind the reform proposals knew that such legislation would throw the Court off-balance – causing it to miscalculate, to overstep, to issue a profoundly damaging ruling undermining its own power-base and achievements. If this is true (though I have my doubts), they certainly succeeded.

By striking down the Reasonableness Amendment and subjecting Basic Laws to judicial review, the Court severed the only real branch holding its considerable weight in the withering tree of Israeli constitutionalism. Like the Wile E. Coyote cartoon character after running off a cliff, the Court now hangs suspended mid-air, moments away from gravity catching up.

Yoav Dotan has aptly described the post-*Reasonableness* reality as "a total constitutional dystopia." The Supreme Court of Israel is the only court in world history to unilaterally declare and thus invent a constitution; to strike down primary legislation contradicting said non-existent constitution; and then to renounce its own creation by invalidating provisions of the same constitution. As things stand the only de facto constituent authority in Israel, with the power to create and mold constitutional norms in its image, is found in the flesh-and-blood Justices of the Supreme Court. They are, in a very literal sense, Israel's "living constitution."

Conclusion

During the 2023 upheaval surrounding the Government's proposals for legal reform, some described the state of affairs as approaching a "constitutional crisis." The label was fair but overdue. The truth is that Israel has been caught up in an ongoing full-blown constitutional crisis for several decades, as this book has hopefully illuminated in detail. Israel's crisis extends at least as far as 1995, when the Supreme Court unilaterally willed a constitution into being and proceeded to impose it on the electorate. This crisis more accurately started further back in the 1980s, when Aharon Barak's Court dramatically shifted from neutral arbitrator of legal disputes to supremacist arbiter of all social and political conflict. Long before 2023 Israel had already undergone major "legal reform," but one initiated and defined by judges, a "reform" persistently and methodically effected by brute judicial power.

In this sense Israel's current constitutional woes were eminently predictable, a crisis forty years in the making. They are the inevitable result of a judiciary gone rogue, of judges and courts abandoning law in the most profound, systematic and comprehensive way. They were also undoubtedly assisted by the complacency – and at times incompetence – of the public's democratic representatives and of those electing them. The tale of Israel's legal system and constitutional order as refashioned by its courts is thus a cautionary one. The Supreme Court's experiment with unbridled judicial supremacy has yielded results which can only be considered catastrophic, and which show little sign of abating. Let our folly be a warning.

The 2023 Legal Reforms

After winning national elections in November of 2022, the Likud-led parliamentary Coalition announced its intent to embark on a broad effort at reforming Israel's legal system and judiciary. The initial plan put forward by Justice Minister Yariv Levin involved four proposals, with some key elements that remained consistent throughout their various permutations, though the specifics of the reform proposals varied over time. They were, in a nutshell, as follows.

1) Judicial appointments: Eliminating the judicial veto or reducing judicial influence over the selection process, and enhancing the role of elected officials and their representatives within the selection committee.

2) Reasonableness: Annulling or curbing the use of "extreme unreasonableness" with regard to decisions made by senior Executive officials.

3) Legal Counsel to the Government: Clarifying the LCG's role as purely "advisory," such that their opinion does not bind or obligate the Government.

4) Judicial Review: Reducing and limiting the Court's power of judicial review while equipping the Knesset with greater ability to assert its superior claim to democratic authority. The proposal regarding judicial review in turn included four components: The Court could strike down only ordinary legislation and not Basic Laws; judicial review of legislation would require an expanded panel and an enlarged majority on the bench (such as two thirds or three quarters); the Court could only invalidate a law based on its violation of an expressly enumerated (i.e., textual) right and not based on a contradiction with an unenumerated (i.e., judicially-deduced) right; and finally, the Knesset could "override" the Court's judicial review by deliberate decision of some enlarged majority.

The book you are reading did not set out to defend or justify the proposals for legal reforms, nor does it intend to. Nonetheless, in light of all that has been discussed in the preceding chapters, several observations are in order.

Thoughtful, informed, intelligent people may reasonably disagree as to the desirability and utility of such reforms. Some might find them warranted, others might consider them detrimental and objectionable, while others still might find them inadequate. Yet one misguided and disingenuous argument which must be rejected outright is that the reform proposals undermine Israeli democracy. This claim, which stood (and remains) at the center of the anti-reform and pro-judiciary protest movement, was aptly described by Prof. Adam Tomkins as "obviously preposterous."[1]

Without the need for a comprehensive exposition of the matter, consider these simple irrefutable facts. First, Israel was a perfectly valid democracy in 1990 (before the Court's supremacy) and indeed in 1980 (before the Court's ascendancy). A partial reversion to this preexisting legal state of affairs can hardly be considered the demise of Israeli democracy, if Israel was democratic well before (and without) the "reasonableness" standard and judicial review of legislation. To suggest that Israel would cease to be a democracy without the features of judicial supremacy is to assert that it was not a democracy in 1980 or 1990 – a claim which is demonstrably false.

Second, the various proposals would bring Israel closer in line with other Western democracies. By any objective measure and parameter, each and every reform would lessen some of Israel's diversion from conventional global democratic practice and would make Israel resemble other democracies more strongly. This is why Prof. Alan Dershowitz, who opposed the reform proposals and argued against them as "ill-advised," still maintained that even if they were enacted they "would make Israel more like Great Britain, Canada and even the United States, and not at all like Hungary, Poland, and Turkey."[2]

Third, and perhaps most importantly, the reform proposals – each one in its way and as a matter of objective fact – would undeniably divert some degree of governing power away from unaccountable bureaucrats and towards elected officials and legislators. Such a shift may be called many things, but "anti-democratic" is not one of them. The reform proposals can be disliked for numerous reasons without resorting to the canard that reserving ultimate governing power for the people is "undemocratic." Many rabid judicial supremacists similarly dubbed the legal reforms a "coup," a libelous term widely adopted by many of the plan's opponents including most media outlets and much of legal academia. Yet "coups" typically involve some insulated and unaccountable elite or group illegally seizing governmental power at the expense of the public and their ability of self-government. Indeed, Israel's 2023 reforms would be the first anti-democratic coup in history to have transferred *more* power to the electorate and their accountable representatives.

There is of course considerable irony in the weaponization of "democracy" by the camp of judicial supremacy. As this book has painstakingly demonstrated, few have eroded and corrupted Israeli democracy more than the Supreme Court, its proxies and its allies. A miniscule group of unelected senior judges lawlessly seizing control of ultimate de facto governing power might even be called, by some, a "coup."

Whatever the valid arguments against the legal reforms proposed in 2023,* their purported destruction of Israeli democracy has always been a malicious perversion of truth and inversion of reality. Israel is one of only twenty countries in the world that have been consistent democracies since the 1950s – it deserves some benefit of the doubt. More than anything else, leveling the "democracy" allegation primarily served to stifle any serious (and desperately needed) public debate about the Court's transgressions, the many harms these have caused, and the steps required to rectify them. Saving Israeli democracy became a smokescreen so that judicial supremacists could once again avoid contending with the profound flaws inherent in Israel's legal system consistently exacerbated by the Court's raging lawlessness.

Aside its manifest falsity, we must also recognize what this confusion says about the way Israelis – and especially Israel's legal elites – understand the core ideas of democratic government. Yoav Dotan observed that "for large swaths of the Israeli public, the legal system and the Supreme Court at its head have become the institute most symbolizing the essence of democracy."[3] I was once asked whether Israelis really prefer rule-by-judges over democracy; I answered that many genuinely don't know there's a difference. Constitutional scholars and judges deliberately abusing their status and propagating a narrative they know to be false is one thing. But the fact that so many well-meaning and patriotic citizens have been duped – sincerely believing that democracy means irrevocably

* Yoav Dotan, who opposed the reforms, called some of the academic arguments against them "patently absurd and indeed confounding."

consigning the State's most contentious and consequential points of public disagreement to the exclusive final determination of a handful of unelected ex-lawyers in robes – does not bode well for actual Israeli democracy, and for our ability to resolve ever-intensifying societal conflicts and disputes.

The Supreme Court's undermining of Israeli democracy and the rule of law, and its concrete decisions and policymaking, have had a direct and tangible detrimental effect in a host of distinct areas and fields extending far beyond strictly legal matters. These include Israeli military, defense and national security; the economy, financial industry, business and commerce; the fragile balancing of religion-and-State issues; illegal immigration; Jewish-Arab relations; and much more. With no basis in law, the Court's rulings and jurisprudence have undermined Israeli security, destabilized its economic system, violated delicate arrangements between religious and secular groups, and exposed Israel to crippling demographic threats. Each of these topics requires separate detailed treatment which ranges well beyond the scope of this book, though they are an important component of Israeli judicial supremacy and its impact.

Where do we go from here?

If there is ever to be hope of any mitigation – and even resolution – of the profound flaws discussed in this book, it surely must begin with a clear-eyed and sober recognition of their severity and their origins. My aim has been to provide some modest contribution to this crucial first step.

Prescriptions and predictions for the future are a fool's errand in the volatile and combustible reality of Israeli law, politics, and culture. Nonetheless some initial observations naturally arise from the previous chapters.

For all its faults and foibles, Israeli society and its political order would have been far, far better off without the lawless, corrosive and enfeebling judicial intervention of the past four decades. The trajectory and state of judicial supremacy in Israel has always been unjustifiable in principle and unsustainable in practice. As such, part of any mission to heal our ailing legal system is to undo much that has been done. This is no trivial conclusion. One common suggestion is to set all differences aside, to let bygone be bygones, to "work it out," to focus on the future and not on the past. Such trite advice is all well and good, and nothing in my view justifies a vendetta against the Court, its Justices or the legal establishment. But the sheer scope and degree of the harm caused by the Supreme Court and its supremacist jurisprudence necessarily yield two critical points, separate from the principled arguments against unlimited judicial power.

First, to return to any measure of acceptable normality by Western democratic standards, a substantial amount of genuine "dismantling" is absolutely necessary, involving meticulous legislative action, uncompromising executive fortitude, and thorough public outreach. The Court has established and entrenched its power in a variety of methods and institutions, all which require careful treatment – curing the disease without sacrificing the patient. On the one hand, there is no silver bullet, no single law or measure which can erase forty years of the methodical, systematic, strategic construction of Israel's sprawling web of judicial supremacy; on the other, a handful of marginal, superficial or symbolic tweaks will not move the needle. Restoring the Israeli judiciary and democracy requires neither bulldozer nor chisel, but must inescapably involve the diligent application of numerous sledgehammers.

This puts the 2023 reform proposals in important perspective. Whether such solutions are "extreme" (as some have described them) depends a great deal on the magnitude of the problem they are trying to address. The most extreme and radical reform has already been initiated and implemented by the Supreme Court itself; any effort to effectively reverse even a fraction of the Court's actions must, by definition, mirror them in scale and substance to at least some degree. In this sense the 2023 proposed legal reforms may or may not have been "extreme"; but they were undeniably far less extreme than anything the Court had already done. Some might even argue that they were relatively benign. The Coalition in 2023 could just as well have advanced a far more robust agenda which more closely resembled the Court's own advances since the 1980s: Rescinding the 1992 Basic Laws entirely, or expressly prohibiting judicial review of any and all legislation; shifting Supreme Court (and other) judicial appointments to a direct Knesset vote; making all Government appointments categorically non-justiciable with an exception for highly-technical grounds; annulling the role of LCG and establishing a new, separate institution for governmental legal counsel; and so on. Such reforms are far more "extreme" than the ones actually proposed, though they amount to little more than dismantling the Court's own array of prior unilateral lawless reforms.

All this is to say, that any realistic solution will unavoidably require far-reaching and fundamental changes spanning the length and breadth of Israeli law and government.

Second, on a pragmatic level, the vast system of judicial supremacy erected by the Court has created clear winners and losers. Just like any imbalance of power, none are too keen to surrender their ill-gotten gains. The beneficiaries of the current apparatus – many of whom belong to Israel's cultural, economic and military elite or are firmly embedded at the center of bureaucratic government – have a clear vested interest in maintaining the situation as it is (or at least they believe so, which amounts to the same thing). As such, governing power will not be wrested from judicial hands without a fight, much as has been proven throughout the 2023 protest movement against the legal reforms. Both the Court and its supporters have demonstrated (and indeed at times have explicitly declared) that they will go to extreme lengths in their fight to defend judicial supremacy. Indeed, none should be surprised that Israeli legal academia – the vanguard and cheerleaders of judicial supremacy – were unyielding in their rejection of even the most watered-down versions of legal reform advanced by the Israeli President (Isaac Herzog) in negotiations he sponsored. Despite some claims that the reforms would have elicited less resistance if only they were presented differently, or adopted through a more inclusive process and dialogue, the obvious truth is that any significant attempt to challenge the Court's power was always going to be met with ugly resistance. Reformers must accept that in the effort to fix Israel's broken judiciary, things are likely to get worse before they get better.

This bears directly on the necessity of undoing much of the Court's prior mischief, simply because it is the only route to an eventual consensus-based commonly agreed resolution. The current beneficiaries of judicial supremacy have little incentive to negotiate, let alone compromise. As such the notion of a "clean slate," of restarting societal bargaining regarding Israel's desired constitutional framework *de novo*, is utterly fanciful. The current state of affairs created by the Court is such that compromise is impossible so long as the Court reigns, well, supreme. The point cannot be overstated: To achieve societal consensus and an agreed framework of government, the Court's power must first be curbed. This will likely entail further determined unilateral action by the Knesset with a slim majority. Paradoxically, enabling compromise and consensus will first require government initiative which is one-sided, decisive and uncompromising. In order to de-escalate inter-branch conflict, the electorate and their representatives must first escalate dramatically to level the playing field.

The prospect of compromise between judicial supremacists and genuine democrats brings us to a related point. Many well-meaning solutions, old and new, propose the adoption of a constitution. "Just get a constitution!" has become a familiar refrain – and the reader may have understandably entertained similar thoughts.

As already discussed at length, the desirability and feasibility of Israel enacting *any* constitution remains very much in question. The arguments against an Israeli constitution (and the absence of critical preconditions) arguably apply now just as much as they did in 1948. But setting such doubts aside, the generic appeal to enacting a constitution does little to resolve its many underlying challenges.

Connecting to our earlier point, genuine constitutional negotiation and compromise are not possible under the duress of judicial supremacy (or of cultural elites threatening to sacrifice the State itself at the altar of judicial power). Even assuming that the different segments of Israeli society are theoretically capable of reaching a mutual accord, no progress can be made towards a constitution as long as major societal elements have nothing to gain and much to lose by cooperating. The Israeli political order is not in a vacuum or behind a veil of ignorance. Perhaps a constitution would have been a good idea in 1948; but in present circumstances, at least some of the primary stakeholders have no incentive to come to the table and every reason to avoid constitutional compromise. In other words, no constitution is on the books as long as the deck is stacked in the Court's favor. Not for the first time, judicial supremacy essentially prevents what slim chances there may have been for adopting a constitution.

Further, and perhaps somewhat obviously, a call for "a constitution" too-often rings superficial and simplistic, because the question then becomes: *which* constitution? Different proponents of a written conventional constitution mean very different things. As the wide variety of draft Israeli constitutions proposed by various parties over the years shows, "a constitution" becomes code for whatever a particular group or individual happens to think is a beneficial arrangement. One might propose a constitution that, for instance, precludes judicial review of legislation altogether, as is the case in Switzerland and the Netherlands – an arrangement others would find intolerable and a non-starter. In short, nothing in the abstract support for "a constitution" can actually resolve the genuine first-order and second-order dilemmas at the heart of Israeli societal conflict.

I will nonetheless hazard to suggest some potential avenues for reconciliation and progress.

The vast majority of solutions proposed for Israel's legal woes have been particular, substantive ideas – a specific piece of legislation, a new institution, a change to the electoral system, or a comprehensive expertly-drafted written constitution. These have typically been misguided though well-intended. The story of Israeli politics and jurisprudence has been one of shortcuts – prudent shortcuts taken in the formation of the State's governing framework, sloppy shortcuts taken by the Knesset and legislators over the years, and especially, reckless shortcuts incessantly imposed by the Supreme Court. Any genuine solution cannot simply add yet another layer of rickety ad hoc scaffolding to the precarious structure of Israeli law.

Menny Mautner says it well in the context of the Court's artificial and contrived invention of the constitutional revolution in 1995:

> "If Israel wishes to have a constitution, no 'shortcuts' are available: Israelis will have to tackle all the fundamental questions that currently divide them, and in a long and painstaking process hammer out a document that embodies the compromises necessary for them to unite behind one shared credo. Until that happens, if ever, the advent of the constitutional revolution discourse cannot but be interpreted as just one more measure initiated by an activist Court… in the ongoing struggle over the shaping of Israel's culture."[4]

Rivka Weill makes a similar point: "There are no shortcuts. One does not simply stand in the buffet line to be served a constitution on a tray; there are significant in-depth processes that every society must navigate, each in its own way."[5]

I propose two such processes which I believe might be conducive towards ultimate societal stability and mutual compromise.

Democratic Literacy

The first proposal regards the improvement of democratic, constitutional and legal literacy among Israel's citizenry and especially its legal and political class. No democratic system can survive, let alone flourish, if large parts of the body politic believe that "law" means subjective judicial whim; that "democracy" means arbitrary limits on popular will by unelected judges; that "separation of powers" means judicial coercion of all other branches and judicial immunity from the rule of law itself; or that the role of courts is to "bridge the gap between law and society." The same is true of a belief in unaccountable Platonic "gatekeepers" with unlimited governing power, or in a "substantive" super-constitution existing only in the hearts and minds of a priestly caste of judges (to borrow the term from Lord Sumption). These utter distortions of Western, liberal, democratic thought, among many others, have firmly taken hold among much of Israeli society and especially within its ruling elites. The doctrines and ideology of judicial supremacy, meticulously designed and cultivated by the Supreme Court, must be challenged, countered and eventually relegated to the fringes of legal and political discourse – the same place it occupies in any functioning, healthy democracy.

To that end, organizations like the Israel Law & Liberty Forum play a crucial role in public education, in fostering informed debate, in exposing Israeli jurists to alternative viewpoints, and in creating a diverse community for genuine proponents of democracy and the rule of law. I am proud to have been deeply involved in its founding in 2019 and its initial growth, and am pleased to observe its continued success and pivotal impact on the Israeli legal debate. For the ILLF and for others, there is still much more work to be done. Repairing the entrenched culture and DNA of any professional or intellectual community is a gargantuan, generational task – those pursuing it need all the help they can get. It is perhaps high time for the formation of a dedicated philanthropic fund that supports those challenging judicial supremacy and pursuing genuine democratic ideals in the legal realm.

Beyond supporting the work of the ILLF and similar organizations, non-Israelis can assist this effort in several ways. One is in the delicate education of Israelis regarding fundamental democratic norms as understood elsewhere in the world. Basic insights taken for granted elsewhere – such as that arbitrary subjective judicial lawmaking is incompatible with "the rule of law," or that popular sovereignty exercised through majority rule is the only true bedrock of democratic government – are not obvious to many Israelis. Some might be open to hearing an adverse view from those outside the tumult of our own polarized political discourse. Another way to help is in recognizing the profound complexity of the controversial issues and debates surrounding Israeli law and constitutionalism. Such recognition ought to yield, at the very least, a sense of humility and caution when approaching such matters from the outside. The option can sometimes be to sit it out – "hands off" – and to let Israeli societal convulsions run their course without the (presumably) well-intended but disruptive intervention of external parties.

A Constitutional Assembly

My second proposition might seem more ambitious but is in many senses more straightforward. It seeks to avoid the failed approach of shortcuts and isolated substantive solutions, and to focus on a genuine *process* – one which could potentially yield acceptable, lasting, and commonly-agreed constitutional arrangements. I submit that the time is nigh for the revival of that elusive institute which Israel possessed for only a fleeting moment in its infancy: A constitutional assembly.

In The Federalist 22, Hamilton argues that the nation's constitutional fabric "ought to rest on the solid basis of the consent of the people" and that "the streams of national power ought to flow immediately from that pure, original fountain of all legitimate authority." The original sin of Israeli jurisprudence and constitutionalism is easily found in the 1949 decision by the first Constitutional Assembly, by which the Assembly essentially dismissed itself and became the familiar First Knesset. In that fateful moment the sole institution established and elected for the purpose of enacting a constitution abrogated its chief designated task, sowing the seeds of chaos for generations to come. In doing so, the 1949 Assembly severed the only connection between the prospective Israeli constitution and the "pure, original fountain" of popular consent. The action required to remedy this blunder has been staring at Israel in the face ever since – not a new constitution, but a new constitutional *assembly* to set things right. Sometimes the simplest solution – the most obvious, banal and conventional – is the correct one.

Every few years some new putative constitution is drafted and touted by scholars and politicians; or yet another novel ad hoc mechanism is advanced to address some particular failing. But what such proposals get wrong is their attempt to deliver a solution, while ignoring that the process of formulating any such solution is the most central component of the final product itself. What Israel needs is not a ready-made prefab constitution, but rather a workshop with the ability to produce one. Israel may or may not be ready for a constitution; its socio-political composition and circumstances may or may not preclude one; and certain constitutional arrangements may or may not be wise or beneficial for the Jewish State. But the fact of the matter is that Israel has never attempted to find out using the standard and ordinary way for doing so.

It is somewhat remarkable that the notion of a new constitutional assembly has been raised so rarely in the Israeli legal-political debate. A constitutional assembly (or "convention" as it is sometimes called) is after all hardly inventing the wheel; it is the tried-and-tested, familiar, default, go-to method for enacting any constitution. Yet Israelis keep trying to come up with strangely elaborate schemes instead of using the single most obvious route. As they say in the military and in tech: "keep it simple, stupid."

A constitution itself and the governing mechanisms contained within are often extremely complex, but the formal *process* of arriving at a constitution can be relatively straightforward. And though there is no one right way to go about administering a constitutional assembly, there is certainly a broadly-accepted general framework: A distinct institution is established solely for the task of drafting and enacting a constitution; its members are elected by the public with a specific mandate to do so; and the proposed constitution must be approved or rejected by public referendum. Already back in 1970, Melville Nimmer observed that though questions regarding the content of a future Israeli constitution are "unanswerable," the basic "procedure" for its adoption is clear enough and "must contain two prime elements." These are "profound deliberation by the constitution makers" and "popular approval or rejection" by the electorate.[6]

Without getting too specific or technical, here is one potential model outlined in broad strokes. The Knesset enacts "Basic Law: The Constitutional Assembly" which establishes the new institution and lays out its mission and governing parameters. The Assembly possesses the sole authority of enacting a constitution – nothing more, nothing less. The Assembly is granted a precise and detailed timeline, disconnected from any other political and electoral schedule, to fulfill its duties – say, two years for establishment and elections, four years for deliberation and drafting, and two years for approval by referendum. Two-hundred and forty (double the current number of Knesset Members) Assembly members are appointed by the public in national elections which are separate from the routine Knesset elections.

The Assembly deliberates, debates, and eventually drafts a comprehensive written constitution, to be approved by a supermajority of three-fifths of the Assembly. If approved, the constitution must then be ratified by three-fifths of the voting public in a national referendum, with at least fifty percent of eligible voters casting a vote. If the Assembly fails to complete its task within the allotted timeline, it disbands, and the process starts over with new Assembly elections – though no outgoing Assembly member can serve two consecutive terms. Renewed elections perhaps serve as an "exit" point in which the Knesset has the opportunity to tweak particular arrangements (or to scrap the endeavor altogether). If the public rejects the constitution submitted by the Assembly, the existing Assembly has the chance to alter the proposed constitution and resubmit it for another referendum; if rejected again, the Assembly disbands as though it failed to propose a constitution. The Knesset sets out the Assembly's default procedural rules, though once established the Assembly can alter its own rules as it sees fit by three-fifths majority vote, with such changes requiring Knesset approval. Finally, the Knesset has no authority (aside explicit exceptions) to interfere with the Assembly's work and procedures; and all aspects of the Assembly's work are categorically non-justiciable and not subject to judicial review of any kind, by any court.

One critical caveat is that the Assembly will be entitled to enact a "thin" constitution if it deems that to be preferable or if it concludes that a comprehensive constitution is not feasible. Without formulating a full constitution, the Assembly could stipulate some core constitutional rules regarding key governmental mechanisms (such as judicial review). Indeed, the Assembly need not approach the Israeli constitutional order as a *tabula rasa*, but can rather deliberately and consciously address critical controversial issues at the heart of the public debate, such as judicial appointments, the Legal Counsel to the Government, reasonableness review of executive action, and so on. These rules or such a "thin" constitution would be enacted by the same majority and process as a full constitution. Whatever the content of such rules ends up being, they will have the benefit of an undeniable democratic sanction from elected representatives not involved in the direct administration of government and from the public itself via referendum. In other words, such rules would enjoy an immeasurably higher degree of stability, longevity and legitimacy (both in principle and in practice) than those presently governing our legal and political system.

This is of course an oversimplification and there are many other details to consider; but again, one need not be particularly original, with ample global experience and expertise surrounding constitutional assemblies.

Such a process will likely yield a system of government for Israel which is significantly superior to the current one (a low bar to exceed) and which enjoys broad public support due to voters being afforded an equal opportunity for meaningful participation and input. A constitution produced by an original Constitutional Assembly would certainly *not* resolve all the flaws and shortcomings of the Israeli legal system and political order; but it will answer some important fundamental questions, and can provide an agreed framework for accommodating disagreement and for peaceful resolution of existing and future disputes – precisely the purpose of any democratic constitution. Putting some foundational (or at least structural) matters to rest, the political process and electorate will be better equipped to resolve other outstanding issues.

Israel must do that which it neglected to do in 1948 and has refused to do ever since. It must undergo the ordered and disciplined process of vesting a dedicated institution with constitutional power, and of finally formulating constitutional rules in the universally-recognized by-the-book manner of doing so.

Rivkah Weill raises an adjacent point in a paper titled *Shall We Ask the People*, where she critiques the lack of direct electoral participation in the creation of constitutional norms in Israel (in the context of a legislative bill which had caused a stir at the time). Yet she herself does not go so far as to explicitly propose a new constitutional assembly. Another jurist, Rivki Dabash, has advocated for increased use of ad hoc "people's councils" for similar purposes. But the fact remains that the idea of a contemporary constitutional assembly is broadly absent from Israeli legal literature and from the constitutional public debate, both historically and contemporarily. This is of course relatively unsurprising – the legal establishment had long since abandoned "the people," and a mechanism of popular debate and authority would be overtly counter-productive to judicial supremacy and counter-intuitive to its adherents.

Even the unprecedented upheaval surrounding the 2023 reform proposals and the anti-reform protest movement failed to generate much interest in a constitutional assembly or momentum in its favor. Though the circumstances might have been the most conducive to recognizing the need for major constitutional overhaul (and that the current system was irredeemably faulty), the idea of a new constitutional assembly simply did not make any significant appearance throughout the stormy and vigorous public debate. The one notable exception is an initiative introduced by several academics and community leaders who explicitly called for a new constitutional assembly – the first such major suggestion since 1949. The endeavor was spearheaded by the eminently reasonable and sensible Prof. Netta Barak-Corren, a rising (or risen) academic star and one of the only remaining non-supremacist Israeli constitutional scholars not branded as a "conservative." Still, this admirable initiative is very much the exception that proves the rule – a new constitutional assembly remains far outside mainstream legal and political discourse.

In any case, the push for a new constitutional assembly can only come from a concerted effort of elected politicians. The fact that such ideas have never been advanced by the legal establishment poses no great mystery – the judicial-supremacist camp has nothing to gain and everything to lose from a constitutional assembly, as virtually any conceivable outcome would result in a net reduction of judicial power (suffice to say that no existing constitution in the world comes close to Israel in its conferral of judicial power). This is why Barak-Corren's 2023 initiative and others like it will never gain the mainstream support of Israeli legal experts, constitutional scholars and senior judges. Yet if the Knesset were to propose legislation like the one outlined above, purported constitutionalists and democrats would be compelled to either grudgingly get on board or expose themselves as genuine judicial-supremacist theocrats (those that have not already done so).

Some might argue that elected politicians themselves would not countenance surrendering ultimate power to a parallel competing institution, but I beg to differ. An overwhelming majority of the Israeli electorate recognizes the need for dramatic change to our legal system and political order. Despite any misleading impression created by the 2023 protests, numerous elements of constitutional reform have been consistently endorsed by the Israeli political center and center-left – with easy examples such as Daniel Friedmann, Haim Ramon, Tommy Lapid and even his son Yair Lapid. At least on paper, some form or other of constitutional reform enjoys a two-thirds majority among legislators and voters. Furthermore, similar to the legal establishment, a serious proposal for a new constitutional assembly would put obstinate political opposition in a bind. Unlike some other countries with high levels of electoral polarization, most Israelis still view "national unity" as a fundamental virtue and as a worthy cause. Refusing an opportunity for genuine and neutral political reconciliation is not a good look for any party or candidate. Simply put, judicial supremacists in law and in politics will have a difficult time objecting to a bona fide proposal for a new constitutional assembly. Finally, all but the blindest supporters of judicial supremacy – even those on the Supreme Court – realize that the tide is turning. Prudent advocates of maximal judicial power will recognize that a constitutional assembly might be their last best chance to capitalize on their successes so far and to participate in the formation of a constitution on relatively higher ground. They otherwise risk further escalations in the struggle between judiciary and electorate, the favorable outcome of which is far from guaranteed.

In sum, a constitutional assembly can provide Israel the reset it needs by focusing on the process of enacting a constitution based on consensus and popular legitimacy – so conspicuously missing from all the Court's unilateral and usurpative reforms over the past forty years – and not on the *deus ex machina* of proposals for substantive top-down constitutional rules.

What's At Stake

The State of Israel faces genuine existential threats. Its long-term viability and survival are not to be taken for granted. As a tiny embattled country surrounded by enemies, plagued by internal strife and beset with other immense challenges, Israel does not have the luxury to drift aimlessly with a leaky hull in the hope that things will work themselves out before the ship starts to sink. Israel must recognize, address and resolve the menace of judicial supremacy, before it threatens to compromise the Zionist enterprise in its entirety.

The type of social unrest and political polarization engendered by the Court's interference poses a genuine risk to the security of all Israelis and to the viability of the Jewish State. Israel's uniquely precarious geostrategic reality requires constant military readiness (and indeed, sacrifice) which in turn relies on a high degree of civic commitment. For Israel to prevail, its citizens must be by-and-large earnestly devoted to the country despite all differences and divisions. Such commitment or devotion cannot possibly persist if the people do not retain actual ultimate authority over their own government and in the absence of effective and legitimate mechanisms for collective decision-making and compromise. Israelis can rise to the challenges facing them only as masters of their own collective fate, "a free people in our land," not subject to the benevolent tyranny of a select few. Judicial supremacy doesn't only undermine democracy and the rule of law; in Israel, it erodes the State's existential foundation and gambles with our prospects of survival.

Ultimately, the precondition of any solution to Israel's ongoing legal and judicial crisis is a basic understanding of its core elements and of its primary causes. The relative cultural and linguistic isolation of Israeli society and its governmental order means that outside observers must overcome considerable barriers if they are to even begin to comprehend the history, the nature, and the extent of judicial supremacy in Israel. In this book I had set out to provide the reader with a clear yet detailed account which may assist them in assessing and evaluating current affairs and future developments surrounding the Israeli judiciary and legal system. I hope I have managed to do so.

Acknowledgements

This book would not have been possible without, and was made considerably easier with, the assistance and support of numerous individuals. What follows is only a partial list.

Randy Barnett and the Center for the Constitution at Georgetown University for inviting me to join the Center, for suggesting this ambitious project and for much else besides. The Center leadership and staff including Stephanie Barclay, Elana Shapiro and Arielle Vertsman. Leonard Leo for his generous and stalwart support, along with Roger Hertog. The Tikvah Fund – namely Roger Hertog, Elliot Abrams, Eric Cohen, Amiad Cohen and especially Aylana Meisel-Diamant – for their vision and courage in founding and sustaining the Israel Law & Liberty Forum in which I had the honor to take part. Dean Reuter and Ilya Shapiro for much recurring sound advice. Daniel Friedmann for his inspiration and mentorship. Jeremy Rabkin for illuminating insights during the writing process and for penetrating comments on the first draft. Many others have shared counsel and insights throughout the research and writing process, including (in no particular order): Peter Berkowitz, Ed Whelan, Yuval Levin, Richard Epstein, Larry Solum, Adam White, Greg Dolin, David Sloss, Roger Zakheim, Tevi Troy, Josh Hammer, Uriel Charlap, Andrew DeLoach, Simcha Rothman, Oren Tamir, Gil Bringer, Katie Green (thanks mom!), Aryeh Green (thanks dad!), and Matanel Bareli. This book owes much to the uncompromising scholarly writings on which it has relied – especially those of Daniel Friedmann, Yoav Dotan, Menny Mautner, Shimon Nataf, Rivkah Weill, Joshua Segev, Yehonatan Givati, Gil Bringer and Eitan Levontin. Keren Burlan Dahari for the arresting cover design.

Paul du Quenoy at Academica Press. A small cohort of dedicated law students and attorneys who assisted with case law compilation and summaries: Ilya Kesselman, Naor Peretz, Shira Pinchas, Ido Kerem, Ariel Klein, Malachi Arama, Shimon Bamberger, Tzur Prag. Special thanks to my dedicated research assistant Uriel Charlap.

Shira and the kids who shared the considerable burden of this book and who make it all worth it.

Any errors are mine alone.

Appendix

The 1992 Basic Laws, As Amended

The following is an unofficial and non-binding translation of the full text of the amended 1992 Basic Laws, offered by the Israeli Knesset. This is roughly the version of the two laws after they had been amended (or re-enacted), primarily in 1994, and in their current form today. The translation is imperfect (I believe that partial translations which appear throughout the book are superior) but sufficient, and I preferred to include the complete Knesset translation with its original wording.

Basic-Law: Human Dignity and Liberty

Basic principles (Amendment No. 1)	1.	The basic human rights in Israel are based on the recognition of the value of the human being, the sanctity of his life, and his being a free person, and they shall be upheld in the spirit of the principles included in the Declaration of the Establishment of the State of Israel.
Purpose	1a.	The purpose of this Basic Law is to protect human dignity and liberty, in order to embed the values of the State of Israel as a Jewish and democratic state, in a basic law.
Preservation of life, body and dignity	2.	One should not violate the life, body, or dignity of a human being as such.
Protection of property	3.	The property of a human being shall not be violated.

Protection of life, body and dignity	4.	Every human being is entitled to protection of his life, body and dignity.
Personal liberty	5.	The liberty of a human being shall not be taken or restricted, by means of imprisonment, detention, extradition, or in any other manner.
Departure from the State of Israel, and entry to it	6.	(a) Every person is free to exit Israel. (b) Every Israeli citizen who is abroad is entitled to enter Israel.
Privacy and intimacy	7.	(a) Every person has a right to privacy and to intimacy in his life. (b) There shall be no entry into the private premises of a person, without his permission. (c) No search shall be held on the private premises of a person, upon his body, in his body, or among his private effects. (d) The confidentiality of conversation of a person, his writings or his records shall not be violated.
Violation of rights (Amendment No. 1)	8.	One is not to violate the rights accorded by this Basic Law save by means of a law that corresponds to the values of the State of Israel, which serves an appropriate purpose, and to an extent that does not exceed what is required, or on the basis of a law, as aforementioned, by force of an explicit authorization therein.

Reservation regarding the security forces	9.	The rights of persons serving in the Israel Defense Forces, the Israel Police, the Prisons Service, and other security organizations of the State, shall not be limited under this Basic Law, nor shall these rights be subject to conditions, save by virtue of a law, or by regulation enacted by virtue of a law, and to an extent that does not exceed what is required by the essence and nature of the service.
Retention of laws	10.	This Basic Law shall not affect the validity of any law that existed prior to the inception of the Basic Law.
Applicability	11.	Each and every government authority is obliged to respect the rights in accordance with this Basic Law.
Stability of the law	12.	Emergency regulations do not have the power to change this Basic Law, to temporarily suspend it, or to lay down conditions to it. However, when a state of emergency exists in the State, by virtue of a declaration under article 9 of the Law and Administration Ordinance 5708-1948, emergency regulations may be enacted on the basis of the said article, that will involve denial or limitation of rights under this Basic Law, provided that the denial or limitation shall be for a worthy purpose, and for a period and an extent that do not exceed the required.

Basic-Law: Freedom of Occupation

Basic principles	1.	The basic human rights in Israel are based on the recognition of the value of the human being, the sanctity of his life, and his being a free person, and they shall be upheld in the spirit of the principles in the Declaration of the Establishment of the State of Israel.
Purpose	2.	The purpose of this Basic Law is to protect the freedom of occupation, in order to establish the values of the State of Israel as a Jewish and Democratic state, in a basic law.
Freedom of occupation	3.	Every citizen or inhabitant of the State is entitled to engage in any occupation, profession or trade.
Violation of the freedom of occupation	4.	The freedom of occupation is not to be violated, save by a law that corresponds to the values of the State of Israel, which is designed to serve an appropriate purpose, and to an extent no greater than required, or on the basis of a law, as aforementioned, by force of an explicit authorization therein.
Application	5.	Each one of the government authorities is obliged to uphold the freedom of occupation of every citizen or resident.
Stability	6.	Emergency regulations do not have the power to change this Basic Law, to temporarily suspend its validity, or to subject it to conditions.

Rigidity	7.	This Basic Law is not to be changed save by a basic-law that was adopted by a majority of the Knesset Members.	
The validity of a divergent law (Amendment No. 2)	8	(a)	A provision of the law that violates the freedom of occupation, shall be valid even though it does not correspond with article 4, if it was included in a law that was adopted by a majority of the Knesset Members, and explicitly states that it is valid despite what is stated in this Basic Law. The validity of a law, as stated, shall expire at the end of four years from its inception, unless an earlier date was prescribed in it.
		(b)	The provision regarding the expiration of validity, as stated in clause (a), shall not apply to a law adopted before the end of a year from the inception date of this Basic Law.
Repeal	9.	Basic-Law: Freedom of Occupation [5752 - 1992] is repealed.	
Temporary provision (Amendments Nos. 1 & 2)	10.	Legislative provisions, which in the absence of this Basic- Law, or the Basic Law that was repealed as stated in article 9, were valid on the eve of the inception of this Basic Law, shall remain in force until the 1st of Nisan 5762 (March 14, 2002), unless they were repealed beforehand, but the interpretation of the said provisions shall be construed in the spirit of this Basic-Law.	

Amendment of Basic- Law: Human Dignity and Liberty	11.	[Was integrated into Basic law: Human Dignity and Liberty]

Sources

I have endeavored to rely on English-language sources as much as possible, and so the reader will find numerous references to English books and articles, both historical and contemporary. This is in the hope that curious readers will be able to further enrich themselves by direct access to such sources. Nonetheless, a great many of the references cited herein are unavoidably in Hebrew. With modern translation tools, a determined reader should be able to obtain a reasonable translation of Hebrew texts with relative ease. Israeli case law and Supreme Court decisions are occasionally available in English. Some are official translations by the Court's own initiative and appear on the Court's English website; others are available via the Israeli Supreme Court Project (known as "Versa") by the Yeshiva University Cardozo School of Law. Some citations refer to English translations of case law for the reader's convenience, though I have mostly relied on the original Hebrew or have somewhat improved on the cited translation, and have typically provided my own accurate translation (which can conceivably deviate from the cited English translation to a small degree).

Notes to Preface and Introduction

[1] Menachem Mautner, *Law and the Culture of Israel* (Oxford University Press, 2011), 167 (emphasis in original).

[2] Phillips, N. Taylor. "Rev. Gershom Mendez Seixas: 'The Patriot Jewish Minister of the American Revolution.'" *The American Jewish Year Book* 6 (1904): 40–51. http://www.jstor.org/stable/23600099.

[1] HCJ 5658/23 Movement for Quality Government in Israel v. Knesset, Versa (January 1, 2024), https://versa.cardozo.yu.edu/opinions/movement-quality-government-israel-v-knesset, Hayut CJ. pp. 179, 183.

[2] Jonathan Sumption, *Trials of the State: Law and the Decline of Politics* (Profile Books, 2019), Martin Loughlin, *Against Constitutionalism* (Harvard University Press, 2022); Robert H. Bork, *Coercing Virtue: The Worldwide Rule of Judges* (AEI Press, 2003); Ran Hirschl, *Towards Juristocracy: The Origins and Consequences of the New Constitutionalism* (Harvard University Press, 2007).

[3] Loughlin, *Against Constitutionalism*, 199.

[4] Amnon Rubinstein, "Farewell to Barak," *Maariv*, September 15, 2006, https://amnonrubinstein.com/%D7%A4%D7%A8%D7%99%D7%93%D7%94%D7%9E%D7%91%D7%A8%D7%A7.html.

[5] Rivka Weill, "The Strategic Common Law Court of Aharon Barak and its Aftermath: On Judicially-led Constitutional Revolutions and Democratic Backsliding," *Law & Ethics of Human Rights* 14, no. 2 (2018): 232.

[6] Nomi Levitzky, *The Supremes: Inside the Supreme Court* [in Hebrew] (HaKibbutz HaMeuhad, 2017), 383.

[7] Jeremy Waldron, "The Crisis of Judicial Review," May 25, 2023, https://www.univ.ox.ac.uk/wp-content/uploads/2023/06/HLA-Hart-Memorial-Lecture-2023.pdf.

[8] Richard A. Posner, "The Meaning of Judicial Self-Restraint," *Indiana Law Journal* 59, no. 1, (1983), https://www.repository.law.indiana.edu/ilj/vol59/iss1/1.

Notes to Chapter 1

[1] Steven Calabresi, "Comparative Aspects of the Reform of the Judicial System in Israel," [title in Hebrew] virtual lecture, March 30, 2023, by Israeli Law and Liberty Forum, YouTube, https://youtu.be/nxMhP7JZa9E.

[2] Ruth Gavison, "The Constitutional Revolution: Reflecting Reality or a Self-Fulfilling Prophecy?" [in Hebrew] *Mishpatim* 28 (1997): 21-141.

[3] Yoav Dotan, "Constitutional Judicial Review: The Question of Accountability - A Comparative Perspective," [in Hebrew] *Mishpat UMimshal* 10 (2006): 508.

[4] Dotan, "Constitutional Judicial Review," 503.

[5] Oren Soffer, "Judicial review of legislation in Israel," *Israel Affairs* 12, no. 2 (2006): 310-311.

[6] Dotan, "Constitutional Judicial Review," 510.

[7] Shai-Nitzan Cohen, Shimon Nataf, and Aviad Bakshi, *Selecting Judges to Constitutional Courts – A Comparative Study* (Kohelet Policy Forum, 2021), https://en.kohelet.org.il/publication/selecting-judges-to-constitutional-courts-a-comparative-study.

[8] Einat Berkowitz, "Towards the Supreme Court Appointments Round: Internal Disagreements on the Question of Future Judicial Bench Composition," [in Hebrew] *Globes*, December 25, 2002, https://www.globes.co.il/news/article.aspx?did=646720.

[9] Yair Lapid (@yairlapid), "Yariv Levin offered nothing but destruction and devastation," [in Hebrew] Twitter (now X), December 14, 2024, https://x.com/yairlapid/status/1868031069464981708.

[10] Shlomo Piotrkowski, "Supreme Court Justices Changed the Decision: Levin Will be Able to Submit a Reply Affidavit," [in Hebrew] *Makor Rishon*, September 15, 2023, https://www.makorrishon.co.il/news/668507/.

[11] Alexander Hamilton, *The Federalist No. 81*, in *The Federalist Papers*, ed. Jim Miller (Dover Thrift, 2018), 396.

[12] Yonatan Green, *Regulation of Lawyers in Israel – Analysis and Proposal for Reform* [in Hebrew] (Kohelet Policy Forum, 2020), https://www.kohelet.org.il/wp-content/uploads/2024/03/KPF_00108_Attorneys-Analysis-

Reform_60_Electronic.pdf.

13 § 4(c), Basic Law: The Judiciary, https://m.knesset.gov.il/EN/activity/documents/BasicLawsPDF/BasicLawTheJudiciary.pdf.

14 See generally: Stephen J. Choi, G. Mitu Gulati, and Eric A. Posner, "Professionals or Politicians: The Uncertain Empirical Case for an Elected Rather than Appointed Judiciary," *Journal of Law, Economics, and Organization* 26, no. 2 (2008): 290–336; Charles G. Geyh, "Methods of Judicial Selection and Their Impact on Judicial Independence," *Dædalus* (Fall 2008): 86–101.

15 James Allan, "Is Talk of the Quality of Judging Sometimes Strained, Feigned or Not Sustained?" in *Judicial Independence: Contemporary Challenges, Future Directions*, ed. Rebecca Ananian-Welsh and Jonathan Crowe (Federation Press, 2016), 66.

16 Menachem Mautner, *Law and the Culture of Israel* (Oxford University Press, 2011), 166.

17 Yossi Dar, "Beinish – Chief Justice on a Broken Road," [in Hebrew] News 1, August 28, 2005, https://www.news1.co.il/Archive/003-D-11765-00.html; Moshe Gorali, "A Mediocre Student or a Real Justice Warrior," [in Hebrew] *NRG*, April 18, 2004, https://www.makorrishon.co.il/nrg/online/1/ART1/074/837.html.

18 Moshe Gorali, "If a flame has fallen among the cedars," [in Hebrew] *NRG*, May 18, 2005, https://www.makorrishon.co.il/nrg/online/19/ART/1/823/935/279.html.

19 Gorali, "A Mediocre Student or a Real Justice Warrior."

20 Nomi Levitzky, *The Supremes: Inside the Supreme Court* [in Hebrew] (HaKibbutz HaMeuhad, 2017), 396.

21 Aviram Zino, "Beinisch: 'Friedmann will bring politicization to judicial appointments,'" [in Hebrew] *Ynet*, January 2, 2008, https://www.ynet.co.il/articles/0,7340,L-3489600,00.html.

22 Itamar Levin, "Barak Calls on Supreme Court Justices to Resign if Veto on Appointments is Lifted," [in Hebrew] News 1, December 2, 2016, https://www.news1.co.il/Archive/001-D-385619-00.html.

23 Jeffrey Heller, "Israeli Justice Minister Rebuked by Supreme Court Chief Justice," *Reuters*, November 3, 2016, https://www.reuters.com/article/idUSKBN12Y1PI/; Tova Tzimuki, "Supreme Court Chief Justice to Justice Minister: 'You Have Placed a Gun on the Table,'" [in Hebrew] *Ynet*, November 3, 2016, https://www.ynet.co.il/articles/0,7340,L-4873966,00.html.

24 Netael Bandel, "'An Unbridled Attack on the Judicial System': The Supreme Court Chief Justice's Full and Extraordinary Speech," [in Hebrew] *Israel HaYom*, January 12, 2023, https://www.israelhayom.co.il/news/law/article/13576332.

25 Moshe Gorali "The First Shot Through the Heart of Democracy: The Government Will Appoint Judges," [in Hebrew] *Calcalist*, February 9, 2023,

https://www.calcalist.co.il/local_news/article/hynkirbps.

[26] Gidi Weitz, "'Make No Mistake, Israel's Coup Is Alive and Kicking': A Stunning Warning by Supreme Court Justice Anat Baron," *Haaretz*, June 28, 2024, https://www.haaretz.com/israel-news/2024-06-28/ty-article-magazine/.highlight/israels-coup-is-alive-and-kicking-a-stunning-warning-by-justice-anat-baron/00000190-5b0a-dc65-abff-7b2b72f50000.

[27] Brian T. Fitzpatrick, "The Politics of Merit Selection," *Missouri Law Review* 74, no. 3 (2009): 675-710.

[28] HCJ 5973/92 Association for Civil Rights in Israel v. Minister of Defense, Versa, (January 28, 1993), https://versa.cardozo.yu.edu/opinions/association-civil-rights-israel-v-minister-defense.

[29] Philip Hamburger, Letter to the editor, *Wall Street Journal*, February 26, 2023, https://www.wsj.com/articles/israeli-judicial-independence-supreme-court-reform-bcfa3589.

[30] Allan, "Strained, Feigned or Not Sustained," 71.

[31] *Ibid.*

[32] Jonathan Sumption, "The Reith Lectures 2019: Law's Expanding Empire," BBC Radio 4, May 25, 2019, https://www.bbc.co.uk/programmes/m00057m8.

[33] Revital Hovel, "Secret Committee Disqualifies Judicial Promotions Without Legal Authority," [in Hebrew] *Haaretz*, August 18, 2025, https://www.haaretz.co.il/news/law/2015-08-18/ty-article/.premium/0000017f-e745-df5f-a17f-ffdf6c650000.

[34] *Advisory Committee to Examine Possibilities for the Promotion of Magistrate Judges*, [in Hebrew] 1-19 Procedural Order of the President of the Supreme Court, (July 23, 2019), https://supreme.court.gov.il/Documents/%D7%A0%D7%95%D7%94%D7%9C%20%D7%A0%D7%A9%D7%99%D7%90%D7%94%201-19.pdf.

[35] Moshe Landau, "Granting Israel a Constitution by Way of Judicial Decree," [in Hebrew] *Mishpat UMimshal* 3 (1995): 697-712. Available in English at *Publius,* https://publius.co.il/wp-content/uploads/2025/03/Landau_Hamizrachi_English.pdf.

Notes to Chapter 2

[1] Yoram Shachar, "On the Structure of the Supreme Court of Israel," [in Hebrew] *Bar-Ilan Law Studies* 19, no. 2 (2003): 397–411, http://www.jstor.org/stable/24273695.

[2] Author's rough translation from contemporary news reports. Moshe Gorali, "This is a Bug we Must Squash While Still Small," [in Hebrew] *Globes*, March 22, 2001, https://www.globes.co.il/news/article.aspx?did=478539; Moshe Gorali, "In the End, Everyone Discussed 'How Barak Stuck It to the Professors,'" [in Hebrew] *Haaretz*, April 11, 2002, https://www.haaretz.co.il/misc/2002-04-11/ty-article/0000017f-dbf9-db5a-a57f-dbfbe75f0000.

[3] Aviram Zino, "Former justice: 'I shall cut off the hand of one who limits power

of the court,'" *Ynet*, July 2, 2007, https://www.ynetnews.com/articles/0,7340,L-3362271,00.html.

[4] H. W. Perry, Jr., *Deciding to Decide: Agenda Setting In the United States Supreme Court* (Harvard University Press, 1991), 230.

[5] Gal Forer, "How the High Court Came to Run the Country," [in Hebrew] *Mida*, January 16, 2023, https://mida.org.il/2023/01/26/%D7%9B%D7%9A-%D7%94%D7%A4%D7%9A-%D7%91%D7%92%D7%A5-%D7%9C%D7%9E%D7%A0%D7%94%D7%9C-%D7%94%D7%9E%D7%93%D7%99%D7%A0%D7%94/.

[6] Friedrich A. Hayek, *The Constitution of Liberty: The Definitive Edition* (University of Chicago Press, 2011), 320.

[7] Avraham Bloch, "The Surprising Numbers in the Judicial System: How Many Cases Were Opened and How Many Were Closed?" [in Hebrew] *Maariv*, July 4, 2023, https://www.maariv.co.il/news/law/Article-1020106.

[8] Ehud Guttel, Liat Dasht, and Yuval Procaccia, "Coordinated or Complementary? Tort Law and High Court Case Law," [in Hebrew] *Mishpatim* 50 (2021): 713-757, https://lawjournal.huji.ac.il/article/12/1835.

[9] Daniel Friedmann, "Formalism and Values – Legal Certainty and Judicial Activism," [in Hebrew] *HaMishpat* 11 (2007): 9-25, https://hamishpat.colman.ac.il/wp-content/uploads/2018/11/A_DFridman_1.pdf.

[10] A sporadic example: Stephen B. Burbank, "Procedure and Power," *Journal of Legal Education* 46, no. 4 (1996): 513–17, http://www.jstor.org/stable/42898242.

[11] Joshua Segev, "Reforming the Israeli High Court of Justice: Proposed versus Desirable," *Israel Law Review* 56, no. 3 (2023): 440–55, https://doi.org/10.1017/S0021223723000237.

[12] Keren Weinshall-Margel, "Attitudinal and Neo-Institutional Models of Supreme Court Decision Making: An Empirical and Comparative Perspective from Israel," *Journal of Empirical Legal Studies* 8, no. 3 (2011): 556-586.

[13] Miriam Naor, "Speech by the Chief Justice of the Supreme Court at the Opening Ceremony of the Bar Association Conference at the Dan Hotel in Eilat," [in Hebrew] *News1*, May 22, 2017, https://www.news1.co.il/Archive/004-D-120224-00.html.

[14] Miron Gross and Yoram Shachar, "To the Question of the Methods of Assigning Supreme Court Justices – Quantitative Analyses," [in Hebrew] *Mishpatim* 29 (2000): 567

[15] Yehonatan Givati and Israel Rosenberg, "How Would Judges Compose Judicial Panels? Theory and Evidence from the Supreme Court of Israel," *Journal of Empirical Legal Studies* 17, no. 2 (2020): 317-341.

[16] Joshua Segev "Reforming the Israeli High Court of Justice."

[17] HCJ Rehearing 60/23 Belen v. The Executor of the Will of the Late Raymond Litwinski, [in Hebrew] Nevo Legal Database, 75 (December 12, 1961).

[18] Gross and Shachar, "To the Question of the Methods of Assigning Supreme

Court Justices – Quantitative Analyses."

[19] HCJ 5693/18 Siam v. Prime Minister, [in Hebrew] Nevo Legal Database (August 26, 2018).

[20] Joshua Segev "Reforming the Israeli High Court of Justice," 5; Omer Dekel Cross Examination in the High Court of Justice and the Administrative Court," [in Hebrew] Tel-Aviv University Law Review 35, (2022): 160, https://papers.ssrn.com/sol3/papers.cfm?abstract_id=3001932.

[21] § 30, Courts Act, 5744–1984, [in Hebrew] SH 1123 195, 202, https://www.nevo.co.il/law_html/law00/74849.htm.

[22] Yehonatan Givati and Israel Rosenberg, "Why do Judges Grant Rehearing Requests? Evidence from the Supreme Court of Israel." *Journal of Institutional and Theoretical Economics* 179, no. 1
(2023): 6-22.

[23] CivM 1481/96 Nahmani v. Nahmani, [in Hebrew] 49(5) PD, 598, 611 (1996).

[24] Yoel Sussman, *Civil Procedure,* [in Hebrew] 7th ed, (Aminon 1995), 871.

[25] Respectively: HCJ Rehearing 5026/16, Gini v. Chief Rabbinate of Israel, [in Hebrew] Nevo Legal Database (September 12, 2017); CivA Rehearing 4960/18, Zeligman v. Phoenix Insurance, [in Hebrew] Nevo legal Database, July 4, 2021; HCJ Rehearing 8537/18, Jane Doe v. The Great Rabbinical Court in Jerusalem, [in Hebrew] Nevo Legal Database, June 24, 2021; CrimA Rehearing 5387/20, Rotem v. The State of Israel, [in Hebrew] Nevo Legal Database, (December 15, 2021); CrimA Rehearing 1062/21, Urich v. The State of Israel, [in Hebrew] Nevo Legal Database (January 11, 2022).

[26] Aviad Glickman (@aviadlickman), "Elron's announcement causes a storm in the Supreme Court." [in Hebrew] Twitter (now X), August 30, 2023, https://x.com/aviadglickman/status/1696934433851379749?s=20; Dina Zilber, "Why Would a Supreme Court Justice Want to Neuter the Judicial System?" [in Hebrew] *Haaretz*, September 1, 2023, https://www.haaretz.co.il/ news/law/2023-09-01/ty-article/.premium/00000 18a-4d2c-d775-a79a-5dbd bcfe0000; Tova Tzimuki, "The Judge Who Is Aiming to be Supreme Court Chief Justice," [in Hebrew] *Ynet*, August 30, 2023, https://www.ynet.co.il/news/article/bjlgutha2; Ido Baum, "Elron Violated Constitutional Custom and Ought to be Suspended" [in Hebrew] *The Marker*, August 30, 2023, https://www.themarker.com/law/2023-08-30/ty-article/.premium/0000018a-470c-d6ae-a5da-df3ee03a0000; Yuval Yoaz, "With His Own Hands, Judge Elron Introduced Politicization to the Supreme Court," [in Hebrew] *Zman*, August 31, 2023, https://www.zman.co.il/ 419108/popup/; Guy Peleg, "Elron is not worthy of being a Supreme Court Justice," [in Hebrew] *N12*, August 31, 2023, https://www.mako.co.il/news-columns/2023_q3/Article-e7e1955016a4a81026.htm; Susie Navot, "What's Wrong with Seniority?" [in Hebrew] *Israel Democracy Institute*, September 1, 2023, https://www.idi.org.il/articles/50676; Mordechai Kremnitzer, "The Association of Supreme Court Justice Elron with the Coup Plotters is a Step Forward on the Path to Eliminating the Rule of Law in Israel," [in Hebrew]

Haaretz, August 30, 2023, https://www.haaretz.co.il/news/law/2023-08-30/ty-article/.premium/0000018a-46c4-d252-abdf-57ecde700000.

[27] HCJ 4703/14, Sharon v. The Chief Justice of the Supreme Court, [in Hebrew] Nevo Legal Database, (November 30, 2014), Rubinstein J., 10.

[28] Observed March 24, 2024.

[29] Yitzhak Zamir, "Without the Seniority System, the Government Would Have Almost Unlimited Power," [in Hebrew] *Haaretz*, January 9, 2024, https://www.haaretz.co.il/opinions/2024-01-09/ty-article-opinion/.premium/0000018c-edc6-df1e-a5ff-eddf3f010000.

[30] Shuki Segev, "Reporting Live from the Supreme Court: USA and Israel," [in Hebrew] *Reshut HaRabim*, April 23, 2020, https://journal.lawforum.org.il/segev-live/.

[31] Yinon Magal (@YinonMagal), "Judge Melzer Reveals: This is How the High Court Promotes an Agenda," [in Hebrew] Twitter (now X), May 19, 2024, https://x.com/YinonMagal/status/1792213941730308489.

[32] Ronen Shamir, "The Politics of Reasonableness: Discretion as Judicial Power," [in Hebrew] *Theory and Criticism* 5 (1994): 10.

Notes to Chapter 3

[1] Kashrut (Prohibition of Deceit) Law, 5743-1983, LSI 37 147.

[2] HCJ Rehearing 5026/16, Gini v. Chief Rabbinate of Israel, [in Hebrew] Nevo Legal Database (September 12, 2017), Naor C.J. 17.

[3] HCJ 7803/06, Abu Arfa v. Minister of Interior, [in Hebrew] Nevo Legal Database (September 13, 2017).

[4] Edward H. Levi, *An Introduction to Legal Reasoning*, rev. ed. (University of Chicago Press, 1962).

[5] Alex Stein, "Probabilism in Legal Interpretation," *Iowa Law Review* 107 (4) (2022): 1389-1437. https://www.proquest.com/scholarly-journals/probabilism-legal-interpretation/docview/2672062119/se-2.

[6] See for example, Lawrence B. Solum, "Legal Theory Lexicon 063: Interpretation and Construction," *Legal Theory Lexicon*, April 27, 2008, https://lsolum.typepad.com/legal_theory_lexicon/2008/04/legal-theory-le.html.

[7] CrimA 53/54 ASD v. Legal Counsel to the Government, [in Hebrew] 8 PD 785, 819 (1954).

[8] CivA 61/48 Zevulon v. Melech, [in Hebrew] 2 PD 464 (1949).

[9] CivA 406/46 Perel v. Zaltzman, [in Hebrew] 2(1) PD 114, 119 (1949).

[10] Uri Yadin, "On the Interpretation of Knesset Laws," in *The Attorney – The Jubilee Book: 50 Years of 'The Attorney' 1943–1993*, [in Hebrew] ed. Arnan Gabrieli and Miguel Deutsch (Israel Bar Association Publishing House, 1993), 483.

[11] HCJ Sefer v. Minister of Interior, [in Hebrew] 10 PD 1213, 1221 (1956).

[12] HCJ Rehearing 3/62 Minister of Interior v. Musa, [in Hebrew] 16 PD, 246, 2479 (1962).

[13] *Ibid.*
[14] Yoel Sussman, "Some Interpretive Rationales," in *Pinchas Rosen Jubilee Book*, [in Hebrew] ed. Haim Cohen (The Copying Factory, 1962), 156.
[15] Eliahu Likhovski, "The Courts and the Legislative Supremacy of the Knesset," *Israel Law Review* 3 (1968): 353.
[16] Rivka Weill, "The Strategic Common Law Court of Aharon Barak and Its Aftermath: On Judicially-Led Constitutional Revolutions and Democratic Backsliding," *Law & Ethics of Human Rights* 14, no. 2 (November 2020): 236.
[17] *Ibid.*
[18] Aharon Barak, "General Principles of Law in Legal Interpretation," in *The Weissman Book: Legal Studies in Honor of Yehoshua Weissman*, [in Hebrew] ed. Shalom Lerner and Daphne Levinson-Zamir (The Harry and Michael Sacher Institute for Legislative Studies and Comparative Law, 2002), 2.
[19] Aharon Barak, "A Judge on Judging: The Role of a Supreme Court in a Democracy," *Harvard Law Review* 116, no. 1 (2002): 74.
[20] Barak, "General Principles of Law in Legal Interpretation," 3.
[21] Barak, "A Judge on Judging," 68.
[22] *Ibid.*, 71.
[23] *Ibid.*
[24] *Ibid.*
[25] *Ibid.*, 73.
[26] *Ibid.*, 74.
[27] *Ibid.*, 76.
[28] *Ibid.*, 75.
[29] *Ibid.*
[30] *Ibid.*, 77.
[31] *Ibid.*, 75.
[32] *Ibid.*, 69.
[33] *Ibid.*, 74.
[34] *Ibid.*, 77.
[35] *Ibid.*, 78.
[36] *Ibid.*, 70.
[37] Barak, "General Principles of Law in Legal Interpretation," 3.
[38] CrimA 787/79 Mizrahi v. State of Israel, [in Hebrew] 35(4) PD 421 (1980).
[39] Weill, "The Strategic Common Law Court," 235 (emphasis in origin).
[40] See generally Rafi Reznik, "The Rise of American Conservatism in Israel," *Penn State Journal of Law and International Affairs* 8, no. 2 (2020): 383-472.
[41] Stein, "Probabilism in Legal Interpretation."
[42] Barak, "A Judge on Judging," 72.
[43] Richard A. Posner, "Enlightened Despot," *The New Republic*, April 23, 2007, https://newrepublic.com/article/60919/enlightened-despot.
[44] Barak, "General Principles of Law in Legal Interpretation," 9.
[45] Barak, "A Judge on Judging," 75.

[46] Thomas A. Balmer, "What's a Judge to Do?" *Yale Journal of Law & the Humanities* 18 (2006): 139, 141.
[47] Stanley Fish, "Intention Is All There Is: A Critical Analysis of Aharon Barak's Purposive Interpretation in Law," *Cardozo Law Review* 29 (2007): 1109.
[48] *Ibid.*, 1138.
[49] *Ibid.*, 1114.
[50] *Ibid.*, 1136.
[51] *Ibid.*, 1129.
[52] *Ibid.*, 1145.
[53] Barak, "A Judge on Judging," 73.
[54] Antonin Scalia, *A Matter of Interpretation: Federal Courts and the Law* (Princeton University Press, 1997), 17.
[55] Scalia, *A Matter of Interpretation*, 31.
[56] Scalia, *A Matter of Interpretation*, 34.
[57] Barak, "General Principles of Law in Legal Interpretation," 9.
[58] CivM 1481/96 Nahmani v. Nahmani, [in Hebrew] 49(5) PD, 598 (1996).
[59] Lawrence B. Solum, "Legal Theory Lexicon 026: Rules, Standards, Principles, Catalogs, and Discretion," *Legal Theory Lexicon*, March 07, 2004.
[60] CivA 2112/95 Tariffs and VAT Department v. Elka Holdings, [in Hebrew] 53(5) PD 769 (1999).
[61] *Ibid.*, Strasbourg-Cohen J. 5-8.
[62] HCJ 4562/92 Zandberg v. Broadcasting Authority, [in Hebrew] 50(2) PD 793 (1992), Barak J. 19.
[63] HCJ 9098/01 Ganis v. Ministry of Building and Housing, Versa (November 22, 2004), https://versa.cardozo.yu.edu/opinions/ganis-v-ministry-building-and-housing, Beinisch J. 2.
[64] Yaniv Roznai "Retroactivity – Not Only a Matter of Time! Thoughts on Analyzing Retroactive Legislation Following Ganis," [in Hebrew] Mishpat VeAsakim 9 (2008): 433, https://runilawreview.org/2008/02/01/volume09_roznai/, cited by Shimon Nataf, *Interpretation of Legislation in Israel* [in Hebrew] (Bursi, 2023), 121, n. 348.
[65] HCJ 1892/14 The Association for Civil Rights in Israel v. Minister of Public Security, Versa, (June 13, 2017), https://versa.cardozo.yu.edu/opinions/association-civil-rights-israel-v-minister-public-security, Rubenstein J. 112.
[66] HCJ 294/89, The National Insurance Institute v. The Appeals Committee under Section 11 of the Victims of Hostile Action (Pensions) Law, 5730-1970, [in Hebrew] 45(5) PD 445 (1991).
[67] Shimon Nataf, *Interpretation of Legislation in Israel*, 94.
[68] HCJ 781/15 Arad Pinkas v. Committee for Approval of Embryo Carrying Agreements under the Embryo Carrying Agreements (Agreement Approval & Status of the Newborn Child) Law, 5756-1996, [in Hebrew] Nevo Legal Database (February 27, 2020).
[69] HCJ 5119/23 Movement for Purity of Virtue v. The Knesset [In Hebrew] Nevo Legal Database (October 26, 2023), Vogelman J. 62.

[70] Daniel Friedmann, "The Deri-Pinhasi Doctrine and Basic Principles in Legal Interpretation: Following HCJ 2592/20 The Movement for Quality Government in Israel v. Legal Counsel to the Government," [in Hebrew] *Tel Aviv University Law Review Online* 44, (2020): 6, https://www.taulawreview.sites.tau.ac.il/44fridman2.

[71] *Ibid.*, 16.

[72] CivA 4628/93 State of Israel v. Aprofim Housing and Promotions (1991) Ltd, Versa, (April 6, 1995), https://versa.cardozo.yu.edu/opinions/state-israel-v-apropim.

[73] Daniel Friedmann, "The Deri-Pinhasi Doctrine," 21.

[74] CivAC 3961/10 National Insurance Institute v. Sahar Claims Company Ltd., [in Hebrew] Nevo Legal Database (February 26, 2012).

[75] Joshua Segev, "Detaining Unlawful Enemy Combatants in Israel: A Matter of Misinterpretation?" in *Constitutionalism Under Extreme Conditions: Law, Emergency, Exception*, ed. Austin Sarat, 121–137 (Springer, 2020), https://www.researchgate.net/publication/345483869_Detaining_Unlawful_Enemy_Combatants_In_Israel_A_Matter_of_Misinterpretation.

[76] *Ibid.*, 131.

[77] Benjamin N. Cardozo, *The Nature of the Judicial Process* (Yale University Press, 1921), 141.

[78] *Terminiello v. City of Chicago*, 337 U.S. 1 (1949) (Frankfurter, J., dissenting).

[79] Barak, "A Judge on Judging," 82.

Notes to Chapter 4

[1] Aharon Barak, "A Judge on Judging: The Role of a Supreme Court in a Democracy," *Harvard Law Review* 116, no. 1 (2002): 98.

[2] HCJ 45/49 Unterricht v. Chairman of Haifa Municipality Election Committee, [in Hebrew] Nevo Legal Database (September 12, 1949).

[3] HCJ 107/50 Ariav v. Shazar, [in Hebrew] 5 PD 523 (1951).

[4] HCJ 295/65 Oppenheimer v. The Interior Minister, [in Hebrew] 20(1) PD 309 (1966).

[5] HCJ 287/69 Miron v. The Labor Minister, [in Hebrew] 24 PD 337 (1970).

[6] HCJ 26/76 Bar Shalom v Zorea, [in Hebrew] 31(1) PD 796 (1977).

[7] HCJ 65/51 Jabotinsky v. Weizmann, Versa (July 20, 1951), https://versa.cardozo.yu.edu/opinions/jabotinsky-v-weizmann.

[8] 186/65 Reiner v. Prime Minister of Israel, [in Hebrew] 19(2) PD 485 (1965).

[9] 561/75 Ashkenazi v. Minister of Defense, [in Hebrew] 30(2) PD 309 (1977).

[10] HCJ 2592/20 Movement for Quality Government v. Legal Counsel to the Government, [in Hebrew] Nevo Legal Database (May 6, 2020) Hayut C.J. 19.

[11] Yoav Dotan, *Judicial Review of Administrative Discretion*, [in Hebrew] vol. 1 (Nevo, 2023), 120.

[12] *Ibid.*, 121.

[13] *Ibid.*, 122.

[14] HCJ 40/70 Becker v. The Minister of Defense, [in Hebrew] 24(1) PD 238 (1970). Most quotes from pages 246-247.
[15] HCJ 448/81 Ressler v. Minister of Defense, [in Hebrew] 35 PD 81, 89 (1981).
[16] HCJ 2/82 Rehearing Ressler v. Minister of Defense, [in Hebrew] 36(1) PD 708 (1982).
[17] HCJ 179/82 Ressler v. Minister of Defense, [in Hebrew] 36(4) PD 421 (1982).
[18] HCJ 910/86 Ressler v. Minister of Defense, 42(2) PD 441 (1988), https://versa.cardozo.yu.edu/opinions/ressler-v-minister-defence.
[19] Dotan, *Judicial Review,* 121.
[20] Ressler, 42(2) PD, 441.
[21] *Ibid.*, 477.
[22] Aharon Barak, "The Essence of Judicial Activism," [in Hebrew] *Tel Aviv University Law Review* 17(1993): 477 (on Hebrew); See Menachem Mautner, *Law and the Culture of Israel* (Oxford University Press, 2011), 60.
[23] Barak, "A Judge on Judging," 98.
[24] Dotan, *Judicial Review,* 122.
[25] *Ibid.*, 123-124.
[26] Joshua Segev, "The Standing Doctrine: What Went Wrong?" in *Oxford Handbook of the Israeli Constitution*, ed. Aharon Barak, Barak Medina, and Yaniv Roznai (Oxford Academic, forthcoming), https://papers.ssrn.com/sol3/papers.cfm?abstract_id=4010860.
[27] Dotan, *Judicial Review,* 259.
[28] Richard A. Posner, "Enlightened Despot," *The New Republic*, April 23, 2007, https://newrepublic.com/article/60919/enlightened-despot.
[29] Dotan, *Judicial Review,* 266.
[30] Menachem Mautner, "On the Limits of the Court – Part I," The Hearing Podcast, May 25, 2021, Spotify, https://open.spotify.com/episode/4L8Bc7RIpHLoznFhjGc44r.
[31] Mautner, *Law and the Culture*, 60.
[32] Ressler, 42(2) PD, 477.
[33] Dotan, *Judicial Review,* 255-258.
[34] Jonathan Sumption, *Trials of the State: Law and the Decline of Politics* (Profile Books, 2019), 3.
[35] Ressler, 42(2) PD, 479.
[36] Rivka Weill, "The Strategic Common Law Court of Aharon Barak and its Aftermath: On Judicially-led Constitutional Revolutions and Democratic Backsliding," *Law & Ethics of Human Rights* 14, no. 2 (2018): 244, 248.
[37] Dotan, *Judicial Review,* 254.
[38] *Ibid.*, 125.
[39] *Ibid.*, 125; Mautner, *Law and the Culture*, 61-68.
[40] Dotan, *Judicial Review,* 241.
[41] *Ibid.*, 298.
[42] *Ibid.*, 134.
[43] Segev, "The Standing Doctrine."

[44] HCJ 3123/99 Hilman v. Minister for Internal Security, [in Hebrew] Nevo Legal Database (May 11, 1999).
[45] Ressler, 42(2) PD, 523.

Notes to Chapter 5

[1] Menachem Mautner, "The Reasonableness of Politics," [in Hebrew] *Theory and Criticism* 5 (1995): 39.
[2] HCJ 8397/06 Wasser v. Minister of Defense, Versa (June 28, 2007), https://versa.cardozo.yu.edu/opinions/wasser-v-minister-defense, Beinisch C.J., 11.
[3] *Ibid.*, 14.
[4] Menachem Mautner, *Law and the Culture of Israel* (Oxford University Press, 2011), 71.
[5] Yoav Dotan, "The (Supra-)constitutional Status of Administrative Law in Israel," [in Hebrew] *Mishpatim*, (forthcoming).
[6] Henry William Rawson Wade, *Administrative Law,* 4th ed. (Clarendon Press, 1980), 38; quoted in Michal Shaked, "Comments on the Reasonableness Review in Administrative Law," [in Hebrew] *Mishpatim* 12 (1982): 117.
[7] Yoav Dotan, *Judicial Review of Administrative Discretion*, [in Hebrew] vol. 1 (Nevo, 2023), 117.
[8] Shaked, "Comments on the Reasonableness," 104.
[9] See *Ibid.*, and the cases mentioned in footnotes 6 to 9.
[10] HCJ 16/48 Baron v Prime Minister, [in Hebrew] 1 PD 109, 112-13 (1948). Translation from Mautner, *Law and the Culture*, 68 n. 76.
[11] HCJ 311/60 Miller v. Minister of Transportation, [in Hebrew] 15 PD, 1989, 1996 (1961).
[12] Associated Provincial Picture Houses Ltd v. Wednesbury Corp [1948] 1 KB 223.
[13] Council of Civil Service Unions v. Minister for the Civil Service [1984] UKHL 9, at 45, [1985] 1 AC 374, at 410.
[14] Wade, *Administrative Law*, 347; quoted in Shaked, "Comments on the Reasonableness," 113.
[15] HCJ 910/86 Ressler v. Minister of Defense, 42(2) PD 441, 481 (1988), https://versa.cardozo.yu.edu/opinions/ressler-v-minister-defence.
[16] Dotan, *Judicial Review*, 876.
[17] HCJ 389/80 Dapei Zahav v. The Broadcasting Authority, [in Hebrew] 35(1) PD 421, 437 (1980).
[18] HCJ 840/79 Israel Contractors and Builders Centre v. Government of Israel, [in Hebrew] 34(3) PD 729 (1980).
[19] Mautner, *Law and the Culture,* 69.
[20] Dapei Zahav, 35(1) PD, 431-32.
[21] Israel Contractors, 34(3) PD, 751.
[22] Shaked, "Comments on the Reasonableness," 113.
[23] *Ibid.*, 116.

[24] Dotan, *Judicial Review*, 126-127.
[25] Mautner, *Law and the Culture,* 68.
[26] Rivka Weill, "The Strategic Common Law Court of Aharon Barak and its Aftermath: On Judicially-led Constitutional Revolutions and Democratic Backsliding," *Law & Ethics of Human Rights* 14, no. 2 (2018): 238.
[27] Yoav Dotan, "Two Concepts of Restraint – and Reasonableness," [in Hebrew] *Mishpatim* 51, (2022): 673-712.
[28] Dapei Zahav, 35(1) PD, 441.
[29] Shaked, "Comments on the Reasonableness," 114.
[30] Mautner, "The Reasonableness of Politics," 43.
[31] Shaked, "Comments on the Reasonableness," 118-121.
[32] HCJ 5853/07 Emunah – National Religious Women's Organization v. Prime Minister, Versa, https://versa.cardozo.yu.edu/opinions/emunah-v-prime-minister (6 December 2007) Grunis J. 9-10. See also Dotan, *Judicial Review*, 866-867.
[33] Dapei Zahav, 35(1) PD, 438.
[34] Weill, "The Strategic Common Law Court," 238.
[35] Dapei Zahav, 35(1) PD, 441.
[36] HCJ 935/89 Ganor v. The Legal Counsel to the Government, [in Hebrew] 44(2) PD 485, 503 (1990).
[37] HCJ 5853/07 Emunah – National Religious Women's Organization v. Prime Minister, Versa, https://versa.cardozo.yu.edu/opinions/emunah-v-prime-minister (6 December 2007) Grunis J. 10.
[38] Mautner, *Law and the Culture,* 175.
[39] Shaked, "Comments on the Reasonableness," 105.
[40] Dotan, *Judicial Review*, 874.
[41] Yoav Dotan, "The Wonders of Reasonableness," [in Hebrew] *Haaretz*, June 19, 2019, https://www.haaretz.co.il/opinions/2019-06-19/ty-article-opinion/.premium/0000017f-e191-d568-ad7f-f3fb8f8a0000.
[42] Netael Bandel, "Senior Law Professor Goes on The Attack: 'The High Court is Turning Itself into a Second Government,'" [in Hebrew] *Israel Today*, January 1, 2023, https://www.israelhayom.co.il/magazine/hashavua/ article/13627780.
[43] Jonathan Sumption, "The Reith Lectures 2019: Law's Expanding Empire," BBC RADIO 4, May 25, 2019, https://www.bbc.co.uk/programmes/m00057m8.
[44] HCJ 1635/90 Zarzevsky v. Prime Minister, [in Hebrew] 45(1) PD 749, 854(1991).
[45] Ressler, 42(2) PD, 492.
[46] Mautner, "The Reasonableness of Politics," 38.
[47] Shaked, "Comments on the Reasonableness," 116, 118.
[48] *Ibid.*, 121.
[49] *Ibid.*, 126.
[50] Oliver Wendell Holmes Jr., "The Path of the Law," *Harvard Law Review* 10,

no. 8 (1897): 457–478.

[51] Dotan, *Judicial Review*, 866, 868, 870.

[52] Shaked, "Comments on the Reasonableness," 126 nn. 106–07; Benjamin N. Cardozo, *The Nature of the Judicial Process* (Yale University Press, 1921), 67.

[53] Shaked, "Comments on the Reasonableness," 122, quoting Alfred Tennyson, *Aylmer's Field*, in The Literature Network, accessed August 11, 2025, https://www.online-literature.com/tennyson/4085 (Line 441).

[54] Shaked, "Comments on the Reasonableness," 122.

[55] HCJ 5853/07 Emunah – National Religious Women's Organization v. Prime Minister, Versa, https://versa.cardozo.yu.edu/opinions/emunah-v-prime-minister (6 December 2007) Grunis J. 9.

[56] See generally Mautner, *Law and the Culture,* chap. 4, though his writing in Hebrew on the subject is far more comprehensive.

[57] Antonin Scalia, *A Matter of Interpretation: Federal Courts and the Law* (Princeton University Press, 1997), 25.

[58] Ronen Shamir, "The Politics of Reasonableness: Discretion as Judicial Power," [in Hebrew] Theory and Criticism 5 (1994): 20.

[59] Weill, "The Strategic Common Law Court," 237.

[60] Mautner, *Law and the Culture*, 60-61.

[61] Yoav Dotan, "The (Supra)constitutional Status of Administrative Law in Israel," [in Hebrew] *Mishpatim*, (forthcoming).

[62] Ressler, 42(2) PD, 479.

[63] Dotan, *Judicial Review*, 257.

[64] *Ibid.,* 259.

[65] Ressler, 42(2) PD, 481.

[66] Ressler, 42(2) PD, 482.

[67] Moshe Landau, "On Justiciability and Reasonableness in Administrative Law," [in Hebrew] *Tel Aviv University Law Review* 18, no. 1(1989): 12-13.

[68] HCJ 1635/90 Zarzevsky v. Prime Minister, [in Hebrew] 45(1) PD 749, 764 (1991).

[69] *Ibid.,* 766.

[70] *Ibid.,* 770.

[71] *Ibid.,* 771.

[72] *Ibid.,* 773.

[73] LAA 7216/18 Alqasem v. Ministry of the Interior and The Hebrew University, Versa (October 18, 2018), https://versa.cardozo.yu.edu/opinions/alqasem-v-ministry-interior-and-hebrew-university. Hendel J. 18.

[74] HCJ 2964/18 The Parents Circle – Families Forum (PCFF) v. Minister of Defense, Nevo Legal Database (Apr. 16, 2018).

[75] HCJ 3052/19 Fighting for Peace Ltd. And The Parents Circle - Families Forum (PCFF) v. Minister of Defense, Nevo Legal Database (May 6, 2019).

[76] HCJ 3030/23 Fighting for Peace Ltd. v. Minister of Defense, [in Hebrew] Nevo Legal Database (April 23, 2023).

[77] HCJ 2199/21 Committee for the Israel Prize v. Minister of Education, [in Hebrew] Nevo Legal Database (August 12, 2021).

[78] HCJ 8076/21 Committee of the Israel Prize v. Minister of Education, [in Hebrew] Nevo Legal Database (March 29, 2022).

[79] HCJ 2205/97 Massala v. Minister of Education and Culture, [in Hebrew] 51(1) PD 233 (1997).

[80] HCJ 5124/18 Tnuva Cooperative Center for the Marketing of Farm Produce in Israel Ltd. V The Minister of Finance, [in Hebrew] Nevo Legal Database (March 4, 2019).

[81] HCJ 4862/18 The National Initiative to Eradicate Smoking – Smoke Free Israel v. Minister of Finance, [in Hebrew] Nevo Legal Database (December 24, 2018).

[82] See generally, Rivka Weill, "Twilight Period: On the Powers of a Transitional Government," [in Hebrew] *Mishpat UMimshal* 13 (2011): 211-212: https://law.haifa.ac.il/wp-content/uploads/2021/11/05-weill.pdf.

[83] See for example Gil Bringer, "The Supreme Court's Double Standard Regarding the Appointment of Judges During an Election Period," [in Hebrew] *Globes,* January 22, 2021, https://www.globes.co.il/news/article.aspx?did=1001358017.

[84] HCJ 306/81 Flatto Sharon v. The House Committee, [in Hebrew] 35 PD 118, 132 (1981).

[85] *Ibid.*, 135. Quoting HCJ 96/81, Abu Atiya v. Commander of the Judea and Samaria Region, [in Hebrew] 37(2) PD 19 (1981).

[86] HCJ 652/81 Sarid v. Chairman of the Knesset, 36 PD 197 (1982), https://versa.cardozo.yu.edu/opinions/mk-sarid-v-chairman-knesset.

[87] Quoted in Mautner, *Law and the Culture,* 61.

[88] Dotan, *Judicial Review*, 273-75.

[89] HCJ 2144/20 Movement for Quality Government in Israel v. Knesset Speaker, Versa (March 23, 2020), https://versa.cardozo.yu.edu/opinions/movement-quality-government-israel-v-speaker-knesset.

[90] See generally Yonatan Green "HCJ Edelstein: Case Note," [in Hebrew] *Mishpatim Online* 17 (2022): 90-134; Rivka Weill, "The Yuli Edelstein Decision and the History of the Balance of Power Between the Knesset and the Government in Israel," [in Hebrew] *Tel Aviv University Law Review* 44 (2021): 322-62.

[91] AAA 662/11 Sela v. Yehieli, Versa (September 9, 2014), https://versa.cardozo.yu.edu/opinions/sela-v-yehieli, Vogelman J. 21.

[92] Yoav Dotan, "Judicial Conservatism and Intellectual Courage: A Homage to Chief Justice (ret.) Asher Grunis," *Versa,* March 24, 2015, https://versa.cardozo.yu.edu/viewpoints/judicial-conservatism-and-intellectual-courage-homage-president-ret-asher-grunis. Other quotes in this section are from the same source.

[93] HCJ 5658/23 Movement for Quality Government in Israel v. Knesset, [in Hebrew] Nevo Legal Database (January 1, 2024), Amit J. 123.

[94] Dotan, *Judicial Review*, 880.

Notes to Chapter 6

[1] Yoav Dotan, "Judicial Impeachment of Elected Officials under Constitutional Scrutiny," [in Hebrew] *ICON-S-IL Blog*, May 4, 2020, https://israeliconstitutionalism.wordpress.com/2020/05/04/%D7%94%D7%93%D7%97%D7% 94-%D7%A9%D7%99%D7%A4%D7%95%D7%98%D7%99%D7%AA-%D7%A9%D7%9C-%D7%A0%D7%91%D7%97%D7%A8%D7%99-%D7%A6%D7%99%D7%91%D7%95%D7%A8-%D7%91%D7%9E %D7%91%D7%97%D7%9F-%D7%97%D7%95%D7%A7%D7%AA/.

[2] Yoav Dotan, "The (Supra)constitutional Status of Administrative Law in Israel," [in Hebrew] *Mishpatim* (forthcoming): 15.

[3] HCJ 6163/92 Eisenberg v. Minister of Building and Housing, Versa (March 23, 1993), https://versa.cardozo.yu.edu/opinions/eisenberg-v-minister-building-and-housing, Barak J. 39.

[4] *Ibid.,* 52.

[5] *Ibid.,* 64.

[6] Yoav Dotan, "Impeachment by Judicial Review: Israel's Odd System of Checks and Balances," *Theoretical Inquiries in Law* 19, no. 2 (2018): 723.

[7] *Ibid.,* 725.

[8] *Ibid.,* 724.

[9] *Ibid.*

[10] *Ibid.*

[11] Dotan, "Judicial Removal of Elected Officials."

[12] Ruth Gavison, "Emphatic but Unconvincing," [in Hebrew] *Hadashot*, September 9, 1993.

[13] Kalman Liebskind, "Following Mandelblit's Tapes: Where's Netanyahu's Responsibility for the Malfunctions in the Law Enforcement System?" [in Hebrew] *Maariv*, October 17, 2020, https://www.maariv.co.il/journalists/Article-795994.

[14] Dotan, "Impeachment by Judicial Review," 739.

[15] *Ibid.,* 741. Dotan likely meant "contours" and not "counters."

[16] *Ibid.,* 742.

[17] Yoav Dotan, "'Deri Doctrine' Has Become a Tool for Political Elimination," [in Hebrew] *Haaretz*, May 3, 2020.

[18] Dotan, "Impeachment by Judicial Review," 730.

[19] HCJ 2592/20 Movement for Quality Government v. Legal Counsel to the Government, [in Hebrew] Nevo Legal Database (May 6, 2020) Amit J. 22.

[20] Ronen Shamir, "The Politics of Reasonableness: Discretion as Judicial Power," [in Hebrew] *Theory and Criticism* 5 (1994): 18.

[21] For example, the term "including" is usually regarded as preceding a non-exhaustive list of examples, and application of the statute is not limited to the expressly enumerated examples. See Antonin Scalia and Bryan A. Garner, *Reading Law: The Interpretation of Legal Texts* (Thomson/West, 2012), 132.

[22] *Ibid.,* 93.

[23] HCJ 1993/03 The Movement for Quality Government in Israel v. The Prime Minister, Versa, https://versa.cardozo.yu.edu/opinions/movement-quality-government-israel-v-prime-minister-mr-ariel-sharon (October 9, 2003), Rivlin J. 23 (emphasis in source).

[24] *Ibid.*, Cheshin J. 23.

[25] HCJ 2592/20 Movement for Quality Government v. Legal Counsel to the Government, [in Hebrew] Nevo Legal Database (May 6, 2020) Hayut C.J. 9.

[26] Daniel Friedmann, "The Deri-Pinhasi Doctrine and Basic Principles in Legal Interpretation: Following HCJ 2592/20 The Movement for Quality Government in Israel v. The Legal Counsel to the Government," [in Hebrew] *Tel Aviv University Law Review Online* 44, (2020): 16, https://www.taulawreview.sites.tau.ac.il/44fridman2.

[27] *Ibid.*, 6.

[28] Scalia and Garner, *Reading Law*, 107.

[29] *Ibid.,* 174.

[30] Friedmann, "The Deri-Pinhasi Doctrine," 16.

[31] HCJ 3997/14 Movement for Quality Government in Israel v. Minister of Foreign Affairs, [in Hebrew] Nevo Legal Database (April 12, 2015), Grunis C.J. 24.

[32] Dotan, "Impeachment by Judicial Review," 728.

[33] HCJ 2592/20 Movement for Quality Government v. Legal Counsel to the Government, [in Hebrew] Nevo Legal Database (May 6, 2020) Mintz J. 3.

[34] HCJ 4921/13 OMETZ – Citizens for Good Governance and Social Justice v. The Mayor of Ramat Hasharon, Versa, https://versa.cardozo.yu.edu/opinions/ometz-%E2%80%93-citizens-proper-administration-and-social-justice-israel-v-rochberger (October 14, 2013) Arbel J. 5.

[35] Rinat Kitai-Sangero, "The Israeli Case for the Applicability of the Presumption of Innocence to Indicted Public Officeholders," *Cal. W. Int'l L.J.* 52, no. 1 (2021): 197.

[36] *Ibid.,* 191.

[37] *Ibid.,* 206.

[38] *Ibid.,* 201.

[39] *Ibid.,* 204.

[40] *Ibid.,* 195.

[41] Dotan, "Impeachment by Judicial Review," 734.

[42] *Ibid.,* 734.

[43] Daniel Friedmann, *The Purse and the Sword: The Trials of Israel's Legal Revolution* (Oxford University Press, 2016), 288.

[44] HCJ 5853/07 Emunah – National Religious Women's Organization v. Prime Minister, Versa, https://versa.cardozo.yu.edu/opinions/emunah-v-prime-minister (6 December 2007) Grunis J. 7.

[45] Dotan, "Impeachment by Judicial Review," 711.

[46] *Ibid.,* 727.

[47] *Ibid.*, 725.

[48] *Ibid.*, 727.

[49] *Ibid.*, 737.

[50] HCJ 1993/03 The Movement for Quality Government in Israel v. The Prime Minister, Versa, https://versa.cardozo.yu.edu/opinions/movement-quality-government-israel-v-prime-minister-mr-ariel-sharon (October 9, 2003).

[51] HCJ 5853/07 Emunah – National Religious Women's Organization v. Prime Minister, Versa, https://versa.cardozo.yu.edu/opinions/emunah-v-prime-minister (6 December 2007), Procaccia J. 28.

[52] HCJ 4921/13 Ometz – Citizens for Proper Administration and Social Justice in Israel v. Rochberger, [in Hebrew] Nevo Legal Database (October 14, 2013), Naor J. 57-58.

[53] HCJ 2592/20 Movement for Quality Government v. Legal Counsel to the Government, [in Hebrew] Nevo Legal Database (May 6, 2020) Meltzer J. 22.

[54] William P. Barr, "Remarks by Attorney General William P. Barr at Hillsdale College Constitution Day Event" (Washington, DC, September 16, 2020), https://www.justice.gov/archives/opa/speech/remarks-attorney-general-william-p-barr-hillsdale-college-constitution-day-event.

[55] Friedmann, *Purse and the Sword*, 34.

[56] See for example *Procedure for Handling the Prevention of Conflicts of Interest of Ministers and Deputy Ministers*, Legal Counsel to the Government, https://www.gov.il/BlobFolder/generalpage/float-page-files/he/supports-tests_files_ministers-conflict-of-interests.pdf.

[57] HCJ 3056/20 Movement for Quality Government in Israel v. Legal Counsel to the Government, [in Hebrew] Nevo Legal Database (March 25, 2021), 30.

[58] Friedmann, *Purse and the Sword*, 292.

[59] Ido Nordan, "This Is Not What Democracy Looks Like," [in Hebrew] interview by Hadas Tzuri, *INN*, April 18, 2024, https://www.inn .co.il/news/635065.

[60] Ehud Olmert, *In Person* (Miscal, 2018).

[61] HCJ 2592/20 Movement for Quality Government v. Legal Counsel to the Government, [in Hebrew] Nevo Legal Database (May 6, 2020) Amit J. 4.

[62] See *Update of the Procedure for Examining the Suitability of a Candidate for a Position in the Civil Service (Candidates with a Criminal or Disciplinary Record, and Candidates Against Whom Criminal or Disciplinary Proceedings Are Pending)*, [in Hebrew] Civil Service Commission Directive (January 13, 2015), https://www.gov.il/BlobFolder/policy/2010506/he/2010 506.pdf.

[63] Yair Lapid, "Against the Legalization of Marijuana," [in Hebrew] interview on Political Status, Channel 10, YouTube, https://www.youtube.com/watch?v= 62-ZFeovFy0.

[64] HCJ 2592/20 Movement for Quality Government v. Legal Counsel to the Government, [in Hebrew] Nevo Legal Database (May 6, 2020) Mazuz J. 1.

[65] HCJ 3095/15 The Movement for Quality of Government v. The Prime Minister of Israel, [in Hebrew] Nevo Legal Database (13 August, 2015), Hayut J. 23.

[66] HCJ 232/16 Movement for Quality Government in Israel v. Prime Minister, Versa, https://versa.cardozo.yu.edu/opinions/movement-quality-government-israel-v-prime-minister (May 8, 2016), Joubran J. 45.

[67] HCJ 8948/22 Sheinfeld v. Knesset, [in Hebrew] Nevo Legal Database (January 18, 2023).

[68] Daniel Friedmann, "The Judiciary Opened a New Chapter of Unjustified Abuses Against Deri," [in Hebrew] *Maariv*, January 16, 2021, https://www.maariv.co.il/journalists/opinions/Article-815236.

[69] Nir Yasslovitz, "The Tiny Mouse That Gave Birth to a Mountain: Politicization Contaminated the Deri Case," [in Hebrew] *Globes*, December 30, 2021, https://www.globes.co.il/news/article.aspx?did=1001396785.

[70] Guy Peleg, "Mandelblit on the Deri Case: 'The Result Is Not Good; Not Even a Mouse Was Born from This Case,'" [in Hebrew] *N12*, December 8, 2021, https://www.mako.co.il/news-law/2021_q4/Article-292178978ba9d71026.htm.

[71] Moshe Mizrahi and Amit Kriegel, "Contrary to Claims, Aryeh Deri Was Neither Accused Nor Convicted of Tax Evasion," [in Hebrew] *Globes*, November 29, 2022, https://www.globes.co.il/news/article.aspx?did= 1001431113.

[72] HCJ 37830-08-24 Louis Brandeis Institute v. the Government of Israel, [in Hebrew] Nevo Legal Database (May 12, 2025).

[73] HCJ 54321-03-25 Zulat v. the Government of Israel Nevo Legal Database (May 21, 2025).

[74] Yoav Dotan, *Judicial Review of Administrative Discretion*, [in Hebrew] vol. 1 (Nevo, 2023), 127.

[75] Dotan, *Judicial Review,* 236.

Notes to Chapter 7

[1] Reuven Rivlin, "I Am Torn," Interview by Ari Shavit, [in Hebrew] *Haaretz*, June 3, 2003, https://www.haaretz.co.il/misc/2003-06-03/ty-article/0000017f-e10a-d75c-a7ff-fd8f35480000

[2] CrimA Rehearing 5387/20 Rotem v. The State of Israel, [in Hebrew] Nevo Legal Database (December 15, 2021).

[3] Russell A. Shalev, "Israel Needs to Talk About the Arab Riots of May 2021," [in Hebrew] *Fathom*, March 2022, https://fathomjournal.org/israel-needs-to-talk-about-the-arab-riots-of-may-2021/.

[4] Netael Bandel, "Two Years After the Guardian of the Walls Riots: Most Defendants Escaped Heavy Punishments," [in Hebrew] *Israel Hayom*, July 13, 2023, https://www.israelhayom.co.il/magazine/hashavua/article/14381809.

[5] Avi Cohen, "Court Rules: The Incident in Which Yigal Yehoshua Was Killed in Lod Was Nationally Motivated," [in Hebrew] *Israel Hayom*, April 28, 2025, https://www.israelhayom.co.il/news/law/article/17843499.

[6] Amit Segal, "Amsalem Against Al-Sheik: 'An Attempted Coup,'" [in Hebrew] *N12*, February 8, 2018, https://www.mako.co.il/news-law/crime-q1_2018/

Article-784d134ef347161004.htm.

[7] "Supreme Court chief calls for probe of 'worrying' leaks from Netanyahu case," *The Times of Israel,* September 14, 2020, https://www.timesofisrael.com/supreme-court-chief-calls-for-probe-of-worrying-leaks-from-netanyahu-case/; Jacob Magid, "Ombudsman Calls on AG to Probe Cops Leaking Contents of Interrogations to Press," *The Times of Israel,* November 5, 2019, https://www.timesofisrael.com/ombudsmancalls-on-ag-to-probe-cops-leaking-contents-of-interrogation-to-press/; "Attorney General resists opening probe into leaks from Netanyahu case," *The Times of Israel,* October 2, 2020, https://www.timesofisrael.com/ag-resists-opening-probe-into-leaksfrom-netanyahu-case/.

[8] Reported in Amit Segal, Telegram, May 28, 2024.

[9] *See* Thomas Weigend and Khalid Ghanayim, "Human Dignity in Criminal Procedure: A Comparative Overview of Israeli and German Law," *Israel Law Review* 44 (2011): 209–11.

[10] Joshua Segev and Israel Zvi Gilat, "The Decline of Habeas Corpus in Israel," *Pace Law Review* 42, no. 2 (2022): 273-321.

[11] Itamar B.Z., "The Extreme Boundary of the Sphere of Legitimacy," [in Hebrew] *The Seventh Eye*, February 1, 2023, https://www.the7eye.org.il/4 77477.

[12] Netael Bandel and Lior El-Hai, "Nir Hefetz Sues for 10 Million Shekels: 'Harsh Detention Conditions and Harmful Investigative Actions,'" [in Hebrew] *Ynet*, February 12, 2025, https://www.ynet.co.il/news/ article/rkecjxctjl.

[13] Matan Wasserman, "The Cases Against Efi Nave and Judge Kraif Were Closed Due to Concern That the Evidence Would Not Hold Up in Court," [in Hebrew] *Maariv*, March 21, 2021, https://www.maariv.co.il/news/law/Article-829201.

[14] CrimA Rehearing 1062/21 Urich v. The State of Israel, [in Hebrew] Nevo Legal Database (November 1, 2021).

[15] CrimA 4039/19 Nachmani v. The State of Israel, [in Hebrew] Nevo Legal Database (March 17, 2021), Amit J. 102.

[16] Jerome Hall, *General Principles of Criminal Law*, 2nd ed. (The Lawbook Exchange, 1960), 59, as quoted by Justice Antonin Scalia in Rogers v. Tennessee, 532 U.S. 451, 468 (2001).

[17] CrimA 205/73 Steven Ivan Ross v. The State of Israel, [in Hebrew] 27(2) PD 365, 372 (1973).

[18] Boaz Sangero, "Expansive Interpretation in Criminal Law?! On the Supreme Court Chief Justice as a Super-Legislator and Eulogizing the 'Strict Construction Rule,'" [in Hebrew] 3 *Alei Mishpat* 165 (2003): 173.

[19] CrimA 787/79 Mizrahi v. State of Israel, [in Hebrew] 35(4) PD, 421 (1980).

[20] *Ibid.*

[21] Boaz Sangero, "Expansive Interpretation in Criminal Law?!" 165–190.

[22] CrimA 3583/20 A. v. State of Israel, Nevo Legal Database (September 11, 2020).

[23] Office of the State Attorney, *2021 Yearly Report Summary* (2022), 38-42,

https://www.gov.il/BlobFolder/news/report2021/he/2021-year-report.pdf.

[24] Ido Abger, "Data on the Demographic and Occupational Background of Judges," [in Hebrew] Knesset Center for Research and Information (2020), 3, https://fs.knesset.gov.il/globaldocs/MMM/e95db6db-1d12-eb11-8108-00155d0aee38/2_e95db6db-1d12-eb11-8108-00155d0aee38_11_16514.pdf.

[25] Yoav Dotan, *Judicial Review of Administrative Discretion*, [in Hebrew] vol. 1 (Nevo, 2023), 307.

[26] HCJ 943/89 Ganor v. Legal Counsel to the Government, [in Hebrew] 44(2) PD 485 (1990).

[27] HCJ 4845/17 Hamdan v. Legal Counsel to the Government, [in Hebrew] Nevo Legal Database (October 28, 2019).

[28] HCJ Rehearing 7491/19 Hamdan v. Legal Counsel to the Government, [in Hebrew] Nevo Legal Database (November 12, 2019).

[29] HCJ 3090/22 Hamdan v. Legal Counsel to the Government, [in Hebrew] Nevo Legal Database (May 29, 2023).

[30] Gil Bringer, "Who Needs the Legal Counsel to the Government, and What Is Netanyahu's Curse?" [in Hebrew] *Globes*, November 15, 2019, https://www.globes.co.il/news/article.aspx?did=1001307330.

[31] CrimAC 6477/20 Shaham v. State of Israel, [in Hebrew] Nevo Legal Database (Nov. 15, 2021), Hendel J. 15.

[32] *Ibid.*, Hendel J. 15.

[33] § 284, Penal Code, 5737-1977.

[34] Law Commission, *Misconduct in Public Office*, Law Com. 397 (Law Commission, December 4, 2020), https://www.lawcom.gov.uk/project/misconduct-in-public-office/.

[35] Miriam Gur-Aryeh, "Moral Panic and Political Corruption: The Expansion of the Criminal Offense of Breach of Public Trust over Disciplinary and Ethical Areas," [in Hebrew] *Mishpat VeAsakim* 17 (2014): 447-67, https://www.runi.ac.il/media/qwph2xe4/gur-arye.pdf.

[36] Daniel Friedmann, *The Purse and the Sword: The Trials of Israel's Legal Revolution* (Oxford University Press, 2016), 233-36; Moshe Gorali, "How the Crime of Breach of Trust Was Abolished," [in Hebrew] *Haaretz*, February 6, 2003, https://www.haaretz.com/2003-02-06/ty-article/how-the-crime-of-breach-of-trust-was-abolished/0000017f-e344-df7c-a5ff-e37ebf990000; Yuval Karniel, "Breach of Trust of a Public Servant – A Proposal for Interpretation Based on the Value Protected by the Offense," [in Hebrew] *Mishpat UMimshal* 7 (2004): 415.

[37] Miriam Gur-Aryeh, "Breach of Trust by Public and Elected Officers – Is it a Crime?" [in Hebrew] *Plilim* 8, (1999): 271.

[38] CrimA Rehearing 1397/03 State of Israel v. Shimon Sheves, [in Hebrew] PD 59(4) 385 (2004).

[39] *Ibid.*, Barak C.J. 44.

[40] *Ibid.*, Barak C.J. 32.

[41] *Ibid.*, Barak C.J. 39.

[42] *Ibid.*, Barak C.J. 30.

[43] *Ibid.*, Beinisch J. 2.

[44] Kalman Liebskind, "First Report: What Appears in the 'Yitzhaki Dossier' Held by the Police Concerning MKs," [in Hebrew] *Maariv*, July 21, 2018. https://www.maariv.co.il/journalists/Article-652251.

[45] Gadi Taub, "The Yitzhaki Method Is More Alive and Dangerous Than Ever," [in Hebrew] *Mida*, September 9, 2022, https://mida.org.il/2022/09/09/%D7%A9%D7%99%D7%98%D7%AA-%D7%99%D7%A6 %D7%97%D7%A7%D7%99-%D7%97%D7%99%D7%94-%D7%95%D7%9E%D7%A1%D7%95%D7%9B%D7%A0%D7%AA-%D7%9E%D7%AA%D7%9E%D7%99%D7%93/.

[46] Yishai Porat, "Brigadier General Guy Nir on the Gal Hirsch Affair: Dormant Investigations Are Used for Political Elimination," [in Hebrew] *Ynet*, November 12, 2018, https://www.ynet.co.il/articles/0,7340,L-5398443,00.html; Amir Levi, "Gal Hirsch Is a Victim of a Targeted Assassination, and This Is Not the Only Case," [in Hebrew] *Mida*, November 12, 2018, https://mida.org.il/2018/11/12/%d7%92%d7%9c-%d7%94%d7%99%d7%a8%d7%a9-%d7 %94%d7%95%d7%90-%d7%a7%d7%95%d7%a8%d7%91%d7%9f-%d7%9c%d7%a1%d7%99%d7%9b%d7%95%d7%9c-%d7%9e%d7%9e%d7%95%d7%a7%d7%93-%d7%95%d7%96%d7%94-%d7%9c%d7%90-%d7%94 /; Amir Levi, "The Only Righteous Man in Sodom: Guy Nir Is the True Gatekeeper," [in Hebrew] *Mida*, December 26, 2018, https://mida.org.il/2018/12/26/%D7%94%D7%A6%D7%93%D7%99%D7%A7-%D7%94%D7%99% D7%97%D7%99%D7%93-%D7%91%D7%A1%D7%93%D7%95%D7%9 D-%D7%92%D7%99%D7%90-%D7%A0%D7%99%D7%A8-%D7%94%D7%95%D7%90-%D7%A9%D7%95%D7%9E%D7%A8-%D7%94%D7% A1%D7%A3/.

[47] § 59, Criminal Procedure Code, 5742-1982.

[48] Friedmann, *Purse and the Sword*, 219.

[49] Amir Levi and Guy Peleg, "Exclusive: Mandelblit Tapes – 'This Jerk Won't Decide My Case,'" [in Hebrew] *N12*, October 13, 2020, https://www.mako.co.il/news-israel/2020_q4/Article-4f96b1a25722571026.htm.

[50] Ombudsman for Public Complaints Against State Representatives in Courts, *2015 Annual report*, (2015), [in Hebrew] 15, https://www.gov.il/BlobFolder/reports/annual_report_2014/he/finel_report2015.pdf.

[51] Moshe Lichtman, "How Did Ruth David Manage to Close the Case in Just a Few Days?" [in Hebrew] *Globes*, November 20, 2017, https://www.globes.co.il/news/article.aspx?did=1001212454; Tova Tzimuki, "Former District Attorney Ruth David Closed the Case Within Three Days: 'Serious Concern About a Cover-Up,'" [in Hebrew] *Ynet*, November 20, 2017, https://www.ynet.co.il/articles/0,7340,L-5045481,00.html.

[52] 388/15 Summary of Decision, [in Hebrew] Ombudsman for Public Complaints on State Representatives in Courts (November 10, 2017), https://www.gov.il/BlobFolder/dynamiccollectorresultitem/essence-108/he/natam_20112017.

pdf.

[53] Moshe Lichtman, "The Tax Authority Corruption File Was Destroyed for an Unknown Reason," [in Hebrew] *Globes*, May 21, 2018, https://www.globes.co.il/news/article.aspx?did=1001237132.

[54] *Ibid.*

[55] Sharon Pulwer, "The Legal Counsel to the Government Ordered the Closure of the Case Against Former Tel Aviv District Attorney Ruth David," [in Hebrew] *Haaretz*, March 1, 2016, https://www.haaretz.co.il/news/law/2016-03-01/ty-article/0000017f-e260-d7b2-a77f-e36721a00000.

[56] A useful summary of the affair may be found here: Yasmin Guetta-Lekov, "The Case That Dragged On, the Intervention of David Rosen – and the File That Was Destroyed Under Mysterious Circumstances," [in Hebrew] *The Marker*, November 28, 2017, https://www.themarker.com/law/2017-11-28/ty-article/0000017f-dc91-d856-a37f-fdd1179c0000.

[57] Itamar Levin, "The Recurring Lies of Shai Nitzan," [in Hebrew] *News 1*, May 29, 2019, https://www.news1.co.il/ShowArticles.aspx?DocID= 134399 &SubjectID=24&ShowAll=true.

[58] Amit Segal, "Shai Nitzan Prevented an Investigation Against Al-Sheikh and Ruled: His Behavior Was Scandalous – But No Action Will Be Taken Because It Would Help Netanyahu," [in Hebrew] *N12*, September 7, 2020, https://www.mako.co.il/news-law/2020_q3/Article-31677483d1a6471027.htm.

[59] "Former Deputy Head of the Police Investigations Department Claims: Nitzan and Mandelblit Protected Al-Sheikh 'Because of Netanyahu's Cases,'" [in Hebrew] *Haaretz*, July 25, 2022, https://www.haaretz.co.il/news/law/2022-07-25/ty-article/.premium/00000182-3684-ddb5-ad8e-f7a72deb0000; Amit Segal, "'Al-Sheikh Obstructed, Nitzan Covered Up, Mandelblit Looked On': Senior Police Investigations Official in Exclusive Interview," [in Hebrew] *N12*, July 25, 2022, https://www.mako.co.il/news-law/2022_q3/Article-00f21bcb8763281027.htm.

[60] Revital Hovel and Roni Linder, "The Prosecution Tries to Sabotage the Appointment of a Doctor Who Testified in Favor of Zadorov," [in Hebrew] *Haaretz*, May 16, 2014, https://www.haaretz.co.il/news/law/2014-05-16/ty-article/.premium/0000017f-efb8-d487-abff-fffe8d0e0000.

[61] Revital Hovel and Roni Linder, "The Struggle is Over: The Prosecution Will Compensate the Pathologist from the Zadorov Case," [in Hebrew] *Haaretz*, March 1, 2015, https://www.haaretz.co.il/news/law/2015-03-01/ty-article/.premium/0000017f-e4b1-dc7e-adff-f4bd35470000.

[62] Mor Shimoni, "The State Comptroller on the Prosecution: Flaws in Shai Nitzan's Conduct in the Zadorov Trial," [in Hebrew] *Maariv*, December 21, 2015, https://www.maariv.co.il/news/israel/Article-518698.

[63] Maya Forman, "This Is How the Prosecution Almost Destroyed My Career," [in Hebrew] interview by Revital Hovel, *Haaretz*, December 14, 2017, https://www.haaretz.co.il/magazine/2017-12-14/ty-article-

magazine/.premium/0000017f-db50-d3ff-a7ff-fbf04a8e0000.

[64] Some useful overviews of the saga: Omri Maniv, "The Forman Case: Closure for the Expert in the Zadorov Trial Who Was Persecuted by the Prosecution," [in Hebrew] *N12*, April 2, 2023, https://www.mako.co.il/news-law/2023_q2/Article-5aca802a17f3781027.htm; Ayelet Kahana and Atara German, "'The System Protects Itself': The Connection Between Zadorov's Acquittal and Judicial Reform," [in Hebrew] *Makor Rishon*, March 30, 2023, https://www.makorrishon.co.il/news/599135/; Ronen Bergman, "Zadorov's Acquittal, the Victory of the Forensic Medicine Institute," [in Hebrew] *Ynet*, April 2, 2023, https://www.ynet.co.il/news/article/ryvpuguwh.

[65] § 255, Penal Code, 5737–1977.

[66] Evelyn Gordon, "Is It Legitimate to Criticize the Supreme Court?" [in Hebrew] *Azure Online*, Winter 1998, no. 3, http://www.azure.org.il/article.php?id=397&page=all.

[67] Friedmann, *Purse and the Sword,* 225.

[68] Yehoshua (Josh) Breiner, "The New Head of the Police Investigations Department: Our Role Is to Serve the Police; Arrests of Officers Should Be Avoided as Much as Possible," [in Hebrew] *Haaretz*, June 29, 2018, https://www.haaretz.co.il/news/law/2018-06-29/ty-article/.premium/0000017f-db95-d3ff-a7ff-fbb582990000.

[69] Itzik Saban, "Deputy Head of the Police Investigations Department in Sharp Attack Against Department Head: 'Prevented the Arrest of Officers,'" [in Hebrew] *Israel Hayom*, January 4, 2021, https://www.israelhayom.co.il/news/local/article/7214586.

[70] Editorial, "Bar-Menahem is Unfit" [in Hebrew] *Haaretz*, January 11, 2021, https://www.haaretz.co.il/opinions/editorial-articles/2021-01-11/ty-article-opinion/.premium/0000017f-db12-df9c-a17f-ff1a1dce0000.

[71] Globes Service, "Judge Gerstel: 'The Prosecution Is Sick; Innocent People Are in Prison,'" [in Hebrew] *Globes*, January 25, 2017, https://www.globes.co.il/news/article.aspx?did=1001173689.

[72] Chen Ma'anit and Netael Bandel, "Prosecution Ombudsman to *Haaretz*: 'If the Law Is Not Amended, It Is Better to Close the Ombudsman's Office,'" [in Hebrew] *Haaretz*, August 16, 2021, https://www.haaretz.co.il/news/law/2021-08-16/ty-article/.premium/0000017f-e241-d38f-a57f-e65393580000.

Notes to Chapter 8

[1] HCJ 1843/93 Pinhasi v. The Knesset, [in Hebrew] 49(1) PD 661, Barak C.J. 42 (1995).

[2] Shlomo Avineri, "Decentralize Now," *Haaretz*, October 25, 2009, https://www.haaretz.com/2009-10-25/ty-article/decentralize-now/0000017f-e2ac-df7c-a5ff-e2fe36640000.

[3] "The 2015 Naveh–Mandelblit Tapes: How the LCG Appointment Was Tailored for Him," [in Hebrew] *Ynet*, September 4, 2024, https://www.ynet.co.il/news/article/skphfqi2c.

[4] Yoav Dotan, *Judicial Review of Administrative Discretion*, [in Hebrew] vol. 2 (Nevo, 2023), 863.

[5] Gil Bringer, "The Silent Power-Grab: From Legal Advisors to Gatekeepers," [in Hebrew] *Hashiloach,* September 2018, https://hashiloach.org.il/% D7%94 %D7%9E%D7%97%D7%98%D7%A3-%D7%94%D7%A9%D7% A7%D7 %98-%D7%9E%D7%99%D7%95%D7%A2%D7%A6%D7%99%D7%9 D -%D7%9E%D7%A9%D7%A4%D7%98%D7%99%D7%99%D7%9D-%D 7%9C%D7%A9%D7%95%D7%9E%D7%A8%D7%99-%D7%A1%D7%A 3/.

[6] Ruth Gavison, "The Legal Counsel to the Government: A Critical Assessment of New Trends," [in Hebrew] *Plilim* 5, no. 2 (1996): 95.

[7] Eitan Levontin, "A Critical Introduction to the Representation of the State in Courts," [in Hebrew] *Mishpatim* 52 (2024): 45.

[8] Daniel Friedmann, "An Advisor Who is Legislator, Judge, and Prosecutor," [in Hebrew] in *Essays on Law In Honor Of Avigdor V. Levontin*, ed. Yehoshua Weissman, Barak Medina and Celia Wasserstein Fassberg (Nevo, 2013), 185.

[9] Yuval Yoaz and Daniel Ben Uliel, "Legal Counsel to the Government – Chronicles of the Controversy: A Conversation with Aharon Barak," [in Hebrew] *Mishpat UMimshal* 18 (2017): 495-517.

[10] HCJ 4247/97 Meretz Faction in the Jerusalem Municipal Council v. Minister of Religious Affairs, [in Hebrew] 52 (5) PD 241, 278 (1998).

[11] CivA 3350/04 Director General of the Ministry of the Interior v. Shanen, [in Hebrew] Nevo Legal Database (June 13, 2007), 14.

[12] HCJ 4646/08 Lavi v. the Prime Minister, [in Hebrew] Nevo Legal Database (October 12, 2008), Beinisch C.J. 37.

[13] Friedmann, "An Advisor Who is a Legislator," 202.

[14] HCJ 5403/22 Lavi – Civil Rights, Proper Administration and Encouragement of Settlements v. Prime Minister, [in Hebrew] Nevo Legal database (September 22, 2022).

[15] Moshe Cohen-Eliya, "Israel's Juristocracy," *Law and Liberty*, March 4, 2024, https://lawliberty.org/israels-juristocracy/.

[16] *The Legal Counsel to the Government's Response to the Draft Memorandum of Basic Law: The Judiciary*, Legal Counsel to the Government Letter (February 2, 2023).

[17] "Constitution, Law, and Justice Committee Held Another Discussion on Basic Law: The Judiciary – The Reasonableness Standard," [in Hebrew] *Knesset*, June 6, 2023, https://main.knesset.gov.il/news/pressreleases/pages/press 26.06.23j.aspx.

[18] Gili Cohen and Tamar Almog, "Legal Counsel to the Government to Netanyahu: 'A Commission of Inquiry into the War Must Be Established Immediately,'" [in Hebrew] *KAN*, June 6, 2024, https://www.kan.org.il /content/kan-news/ politic/758472/.

[19] Yonatan Lis, Noa Shpigel, and Bar Peleg, "Following a Discussion Convened Under the Guidance of the Supreme Court, the Government Decided Not to

Establish a State Inquiry Commission at This Stage," [in Hebrew] *Haaretz*, May 5, 2025, https://www.haaretz.co.il/news/politics/2025-05-05/ty-article/00000196-9fbd-d9bf-a1b6-ffbd2d7b0000.

[20] Anna Reiba-Breski, "Sharp Clash Between Mandelblit and Ohana: The Coronavirus Cabinet Meeting Was Almost Canceled," [in Hebrew] *Maariv*, September 22, 2020, https://www.maariv.co.il/news/politics/Article-791444.

[21] Yoav Dotan, *Lawyering for the Rule of Law: Government Lawyers and the Rise of Judicial Power in Israel* (Cambridge University Press, 2014), 87.

[22] Submission of Evidence by Affidavit in Civil Proceedings on Behalf of the State, 6.1007, [in Hebrew] Legal Counsel to the Government Guideline (April 9, 2018).

[23] HCJ 4646/08 Lavi v. the Prime Minister, [in Hebrew] Nevo Legal Database (October 12, 2008), Beinisch C.J. 37.

[24] Movement for the Quality of Government in Israel v. Israel Lands Council, [in Hebrew] Nevo Legal Database (November 14, 2016).

[25] Gil Bringer, "The Silent Power-Grab: From Legal Advisors to Gatekeepers."

[26] Gavison, "The Legal Counsel to the Government."

[27] Dotan, *Lawyering for the Rule of Law,* 87.

[28] Yoav Dotan, "'Pre-HCJ' and Constitutional Dilemmas Regarding the Role of the State Attorney's Office in the Framework of Litigation in the HCJ," [in Hebrew] *Mishpat UMimshal 7* (2004): 171-72.

[29] Levontin, "A Critical Introduction," 39.

[30] Shimon Nataf, "The Binding Opinion of the Legal Counsel to the Government," [in Hebrew] *Bikurei Mishpat* 1 (2020): 1-37.

[31] AdminA 6329/20 Zomer v. The Commissioner for Freedom of Information at the Ministry of Justice, [in Hebrew] Nevo Legal Database (July 6, 2022).

[32] David Peter, "The Legal Advice: Binding but Confidential – Following the Zomer Supreme Court Ruling," [in Hebrew] *Reshut HaRabim*, August 3, 2022, https://journal.lawforum.org.il/zomer/.

[33] Quoted in Levontin, "A Critical Introduction," 4, n. 8.

[34] Quoted in Aharon Garber, "The 'Legal Prevention' of the Legal Counsel to the Government – Critique and Assessment," [in Hebrew] *Reshut HaRabim*, February 7, 2021, https://journal.lawforum.org.il/garber-ag/.

[35] *Ibid.*

[36] Lior Gutman, "Zilber to CEO of the Companies Authority: Do Not Cancel the Board Team; Amsalem Responds: 'Arrogant and Insolent,'" [in Hebrew] *Calcalist*, December 17, 2020, https://www.calcalist.co.il/local/articles/0,7340, L-3882511,00.html.

[37] Idan Yosef, "Amsalem Refuses to Sign a Power of Attorney for the Companies Authority," [in Hebrew] *News1*, December 26, 2020, https://www.news1.co.il/Archive/001-D-435157-00.html.

[38] HCJ 1182/20 Israeli Democracy Guard v. Minister of Justice, [in Hebrew] Nevo Legal Database, February 24, 2020; "*High Court order freezes panel probing internal police investigations*," *The Times of Israel* February 24, 2020,

https://www.timesofisrael.com/high-court-orders-freezes-panel-probing-internal-police-investigations/.

[39] § 23, Government Service Law (Appointments), [in Hebrew] 5719-1959, SH 279, 86, https://www.nevo.co.il/law_html/law01/p221k1_001.htm#_ftn1.

[40] *Appointment of Adv. Orly Ben-Ari as Acting State Attorney*, [in Hebrew] Legal Counsel to the Government Letter (17 Dec 2019), https://pic-upload.ynet.co.il/news/171219.pdf.

[41] HCJ 34680-08-24 Movement for the Quality of Government in Israel v. Minister of Communications, [in Hebrew] Nevo Legal Database (October 14, 2024) Kabub J. 6, 12.

[42] Guide for Legislation, [in Hebrew] Office of Legal Counsel and Legislative Affairs, https://www.gov.il/BlobFolder/generalpage/legislation_guide/he/guide.pdf.

[43] HCJ 8987/22 Movement for Quality Government in Israel v. Knesset, [in Hebrew] Nevo Legal Database (January 2, 2025) Vogelman J. 71.

[44] Yuval Erel, "The Horror Script: When the Head of Mossad, the Chief of Staff, and the Police Commissioner Will Have to Decide Whom to Obey," [in Hebrew] *N12*, March 9, 2023, https://www.mako.co.il/news-n12_magazine/2023_q1/Article-f20fdb544a0c681027.htm.

[45] Shlomo Piotrkowski, "The Nightmare Scenario: What Will Happen on the Day of a Direct Clash Between the Court and the Government," [in Hebrew] *Makor Rishon*, March 8, 2023, https://www.makorrishon.co.il/news/588759/.

[46] See Barak Medina and Ilan Saban, "Conflict of Interest of a Prime Minister, Defensive Democracy and the Authority to Declare Incapacity," [in Hebrew] *ICON-S-IL Blog*, October 11, 2020, https://israeliconstitutionalism.wordpress.com/2020/10/11/%d7%a0%d7%99%d7%92%d7%95%d7%93-%d7%a2%d7%a0%d7%99%d7%99%d7%a0%d7%99%d7%9d-%d7%a9%d7 %9c-%d7%a8%d7%90%d7%a9-%d7%9e%d7%9e%d7%a9%d7%9c%d7%94-%d7%93%d7%9e%d7%95%d7%a7%d7%a8%d7%98%d7%99%d7%94-%d7%9e%d7%aa/.

[47] HCJ 3056/20 Movement for Quality Government in Israel v. Legal Counsel to the Government, [in Hebrew] Nevo Legal Database (March 25, 2021), Meltzer J. 3.

[48] HCJ 2412/23 Movement for the Quality of Government in Israel v. Knesset, [in Hebrew] Nevo Legal Database (January 3, 2024).

[49] High Court 43471-11-24 Shela Oren v. Prime Minister, [in Hebrew] Nevo Legal Database (December 4, 2024), Ronen J. 9.

[50] See Barak in HCJ 1843/93 Pinhasi v. The Knesset, [in Hebrew] 49(1) PD 661 (1995); for another articulation (among hundreds), see HCJ 5124/18 Tnuva Cooperative Center for the Marketing of Farm Produce in Israel Ltd. V The Minister of. Finance, [in Hebrew] Nevo Legal Database (March 4, 2019), Mazuz J. 2.

[51] Aharon Garber, "'Did it happen or not:' Is there a conceivable 'Precedent' to Give the Legal Counsel to the Government a Monopoly on Representation?"

[in Hebrew] *Tel Aviv Law Review Online* 44 (2021): 10.

[52] Levontin, "A Critical Introduction," 28.

[53] Eitan Levontin and Ruth Gavison, "The 'Binding' Opinions of the Legal Counsel to the Government," in *The Shamgar Book,* [in Hebrew] ed. Tova Alshtein, vol. 5 (Israel Bar Association Publishing House, 2003), 221–286.

[54] Aharon Garber, "Did it Happen or Not,'" 23.

[55] Levontin, "A Critical Introduction," 67.

[56] Yoav Dotan, "Judge Stein Against the Wall of Suppression," [in Hebrew] *Haaretz*, March 9, 2019.
https://www.haaretz.co.il/opinions/2019-03-09/ty-article-opinion/.premium/0000017f-e1f3-d804-ad7f-f1fb846f0000.

[57] Levontin, "A Critical Introduction," 46.

[58] Levontin and Gavison, "The 'Binding' Opinion of the Legal Counsel to the Government," 30.

[59] HCJ Rehearing 3660/17 General Association of Merchants and Self-Employed Persons v. Minister of Interior, Versa, https://versa.cardozo.yu.edu/opinions/general-association-merchants-and-self-employed-persons-v-minister-interior (October 26, 2017), Naor C.J. 45.

[60] HCJ 8076/21 Judges Committee of the Israel Prize v. Minister of Education, [in Hebrew] Nevo Legal Database (March 29, 2022), Willner J. 16.

[61] HCJ 8451/18 Woman to Woman Haifa Feminist Center v. Minister of Public Security, [in Hebrew] Nevo Legal Database (October 18, 2020).

[62] HCJ 8451/18 Woman to Woman Haifa Feminist Center v. Minister of Public Security, [in Hebrew] Nevo Legal Database (April 27, 2022).

[63] HCJ 158/21 Physicians for Human Rights v. Minister of Public Security, [in Hebrew] Nevo Legal Database (January 31, 2021).

[64] HCJ 433/24 Movement for the Quality of Government in Israel v. Minister of National Security, [in Hebrew] Nevo Legal Database.

[65] HCJ 31238-09-24 Minister of National Security v. Legal Counsel to the Government, [in Hebrew] Nevo Legal Database (March 9, 2025).

[66] Avraham Bloch, "In an Extremely Rare Move: The Legal Counsel to the Government Filed a Petition to the Supreme Court," [in Hebrew] *Maariv*, November 22, 2024, https://www.maariv.co.il/news/law/article-1150332.

[67] Manchin v. Browning, 170 W. Va. 779 (1982).

[68] Pub. Util. Comm'n of Texas v. Cofer, 754 S.W.2d 121, 125 (Tex. 1988).

[69] Warren E. Burger, "Tribute to Wade McCree," *Loyola of Los Angeles Law Review* 21 (1988): 1051-2.

[70] Rivka Weill, "The Strategic Common Law Court of Aharon Barak and its Aftermath: On Judicially-led Constitutional Revolutions and Democratic Backsliding," *Law & Ethics of Human Rights* 14, no. 2 (2018): 230

[71] Friedmann, *Purse and the Sword*, 290.

[72] Mordechai Kremnitzer, "To Split or Not to Split the Role of the Legal Counsel to the Government?" [in Hebrew] *Israel Democracy Institute*, August 26, 2021, https://www.idi.org.il/articles/36227.

[73] Itzhak Zamir, "Splitting the Legal Counsel to the Government Role Will Harm Democracy," [in Hebrew] *Haaretz*, July 15, 2021, https://www.haaretz.co.il/opinions/2021-07-15/ty-article-opinion/.premium/0000017f-db1a-df0f-a17f-df5b37020000.

[74] Netael Bandel, "Mazuz: The Initiatives to Split the Role of the LCG Are Intended to Weaken the Judicial System," [in Hebrew] *Haaretz*, June 1, 2021, https://www.haaretz.co.il/news/law/2021-06-01/ty-article/.premium/0000017f-db6f-df62-a9ff-dfffe1850000.

[75] Avraham Bloch, "Miriam Naor: Netanyahu's Trial – Mandelblit's Trial," [in Hebrew] *Srugim*, September 3, 2020, https://www.srugim.co.il/486342-%D7%9E%D7%A8%D7%99%D7%9D-%D7%A0%D7%90%D7%95% D7%A8-%D7%94%D7%9E%D7%A9%D7%A4%D7%98-%D7%A9%D7%9C-%D7%A0%D7%AA%D7%A0%D7%99%D7%94%D7%95-%D7%9E%D7%A9%D7%A4%D7%98%D7%95-%D7%A9%D7%9C-%D7%9E%D7%A0%D7%93.

[76] Shlomo Avineri, "Split the Office of the Legal Counsel," [in Hebrew] *Haaretz*, July 1, 2021, https://www.haaretz.co.il/opinions/2021-07-01/ty-article-opinion/.premium/0000017f-eb34-dc91-a17f-ffbd2a3d0000.

[77] Levontin, "A Critical Introduction," 41.

[78] Yoav Dotan, "Hired Guns and Ministers of Justice: The Role of Government Attorneys in the United States and Israel," *Israel Law Review* 49, no. 1 (2016): 16.

[79] Dotan, *Lawyering for the Rule of Law*, 189.

[80] Yoav Dotan, "Hired Guns," 16.

[81] *Ibid.*

[82] Dotan, *Lawyering for the Rule of Law*, 189.

[83] Friedmann, "An Advisor Who is a Legislator," 188.

[84] Dotan, *Lawyering for the Rule of Law*, 189.

[85] Levontin, "A Critical Introduction," 22.

[86] Friedmann, "An Advisor Who is a Legislator," 202.

[87] HCJ 5658/23 Movement for Quality Government in Israel v. Knesset, [in Hebrew] Nevo Legal Database (January 1, 2024), Ronen J. 39-40.

[88] *Ibid.*, Barak-Erez J. 40-42.

[89] Martin Edelman, "Israel," in *The Global Expansion of Judicial Power*, ed. C. Neal Tate and Torbjörn Vallinder (New York University Press, 1997), 413-17.

[90] Robert D. Cooter and Thomas Ginsburg, "Comparative Judicial Discretion: An Empirical Test of Economic Models," *Int'l Rev. L. & Econ.* 16, no. 3 (1996): 300.

Notes to Chapter 9

[1] Richard A. Posner, "Enlightened Despot," *The New Republic*, April 23, 2007, https://newrepublic.com/article/60919/enlightened-despot.

[2] Martin Loughlin, *Against Constitutionalism* (Harvard University Press, 2022),

1.

[3] *Ibid.*, 3.

[4] *Ibid.*, 33.

[5] For various examples, see: Amos Shapira, "Why Israel Has No Constitution, but Should, and Likely Will, Have One," *Saint Louis University Law Journal* 37, no. 2 (Winter 1993): 283-290, Joshua Segev, "Who Needs a Constitution? In Defense of the Non-Decision Constitution-Making Tactic in Israel," *Albany Law Review* 70, no. 2 (March 3, 2007): 55–116.

[6] David Ben-Gurion, "Against Court and Constitution: A Never-Before-Translated Speech by David Ben-Gurion, *Mosaic,* March 10, 2021, https://mosaicmagazine.com/observation/israel-zionism/2021/03/against-court-and-constitution-a-never-before-translated-speech-by-david-ben-gurion/.

[7] Shani Schnitzer, "Ben-Gurion, the High Court and the Constitution that Never Was," [in Hebrew] *Mishpatim* 53 (forthcoming).

[8] Robert A. Dahl, *On Democracy* (Yale University Press, 1998), 149-55.

[9] Loughlin, *Against Constitutionalism*, 113.

[10] Jonathan Sumption, "The Reith Lectures 2019: Rights and the Ideal Constitution," BBC RADIO 4, June 15, 2019, https://www.bbc.co.uk/programmes/m0005t85.

[11] Loughlin, *Against Constitutionalism*, 143.

[12] Jonathan Sumption, "The Reith Lectures 2019: In Praise of Politics," BBC Radio 4, June 1, 2019, https://www.bbc.co.uk/programmes/m0005f05.

[13] Joshua Segev, "Who Needs a Constitution?"

[14] Eliahu Likhovski, "Can the Knesset Adopt a Constitution Which Will Be the 'Supreme Law of the Land'?" *Israel Law Review* 4, no. 1 (1969): 67, https://doi.org/10.1017/S0021223700001722 (emphasis in source).

[15] Segev, "Who Needs a Constitution?" 430 (quoting Daphne Barak Erez).

[16] For a detailed exploration of these issues, *see*: series of essays by Martin Kramer in Mosaic magazine and responses there: Martin Kramer, "The Most Significant Document Composed by Jews since Antiquity," *Mosaic*, April 14, 2021, https://ideas.tikvah.org/mosaic/observations/the-most-significant-document-composed-by-jews-since-antiquity; Eugene Kontorovich and Yonatan Green, "Why the Declaration of Independence is Not, and Should Not Be, Israel's Constitution: Two Views," *Mosaic*, November 22, 2021, https://ideas.tikvah.org/mosaic/essays/responses/why-the-declaration-of-independence-is-not-and-should-not-be-israels-constitution-two-views.

[17] Rivka Weill, "Dicey Was Not Diceyan," *The Cambridge Law Journal* 62, no. 2 (2003): 474–93. http://www.jstor.org/stable/4509005.

[18] A. V. Dicey, *Introduction to the Study of the Law of the Constitution*, 10th ed. (Macmillan, 1959), 3–5.

[19] Jonathan Sumption, "The Reith Lectures 2019: Shifting the Foundations," BBC Radio 4, June 22, 2019, https://www.bbc.co.uk/programmes/ m00060vc.

[20] Eliahu Likhovski, "The Courts and the Legislative Supremacy of the Knesset," *Israel Law Review* 3, no. 3 (1968): 345–67. https://doi.org/10.1017/S002122

3700001564.

[21] David M. Sassoon, "The Israel Legal System," *The American Journal of Comparative Law* 16, no. 3 (1968): 405–15. https://doi.org/10.2307/838665.

[22] Martin Chancey, "The Legal System of Israel," *The American Journal of Comparative Law* 18, no. 4 (1970): 870–873.

[23] Amos Shapira, "Why Israel Has No Constitution," *St. Louis University Law Journal* 37, no. 2 (1993): 283–290.

[24] Bernard Susser, "Toward a Constitution for Israel," *St. Louis University Law Journal* 37, no. 4 (Summer 1993): 939–971.

[25] HCJ 188/63 Bassul v. Minister of Interior, [in Hebrew] 19(1) PD 337 (1965).

[26] HCJ 108/70 Manor v. Minister of Finance, [in Hebrew] 24(2) PD 442 (1970).

[27] CivA 228/63 Azuz v. Azar, [in Hebrew] 17 PD 2541 (1963).

[28] HCJ 306/81 Flatto Sharon v. The House Committee, [in Hebrew] 35 PD 118, 132 (1981).

[29] HCJ 163/57 Lubin v. Tel-Aviv-Jaffa Municipality, [in Hebrew] 12 PD 1041 (1957).

[30] HCJ 120/73 Tobis v. Government of Israel, [in Hebrew] 27(1) PD 757 (1973).

[31] HCJ 10/48 Zeev v. Commissioner of the Tel Aviv Urban District, [in Hebrew] 1 PD 85 (1948).

[32] HCJ 7/48 Al-Kharboutly v. Minister of Defense, [in Hebrew] 2 PD 5 (1948).

[33] Chancey, "The Legal System of Israel," 870.

[34] See Ruth Gavison, "The Constitutional Revolution: Reflecting Reality or a Self-Fulfilling Prophecy?" [in Hebrew] *Mishpatim* 28 (1997): 109.

[35] The two scholars most associated with this view were Benjamin Akzin and later Claude Klein.

[36] Loughlin, *Against Constitutionalism*, 3.

[37] See for example, Peter Elman, Claude Klein, and Benjamin Akzin, "Judicial Review of Statute," *Israel Law Review* 4, no. 4 (1969): 559–78. https://doi.org/10.1017/S0021223700002193.

[38] Melville B. Nimmer, "The Uses of Judicial Review in Israel's Quest for a Constitution," *Columbia Law Review* 70, no. 7 (1970): 1217-60.

[39] Mark Tushnet, "The Universal and the Particular in Constitutional Law," *Columbia Law Review* 100, no. 5 (2000): 1327-46.

[40] Nimmer, "The Uses of Judicial Review," 1228.

[41] See generally: Alison L. Young, *Constitutional Entrenchment and Parliamentary Sovereignty*, (Institute for Government, 2022), https://www.bennettinstitute.cam.ac.uk/wp-content/uploads/2023/03/constitutional-entrenchment.pdf.

[42] HCJ 98/69 Bergman v. The Minister of Finance, [in Hebrew] 23(1) PD 963 (1969).

[43] Claude Klein, "How it all Started: Bergman Decision – First Responses," [in Hebrew] *Alei Mishpat* 3 (2004): 391-404.

[44] Moshe Landau, "A Constitution as Supreme Law for the State of Israel," [in Hebrew] *HaPraklit* 27 (1972): 30-41.

[45] Klein, "How it all Started."

[46] HCJ 148/73 Kaniel v. Minister of Justice, [in Hebrew] 27(1) PD 794 (1973).

[47] HCJ 246/81 Derech Eretz Association v. Broadcasting Authority, [in Hebrew] 35(4) PD 1 (1981), https://versa.cardozo.yu.edu/opinions/agudat-derekh-eretz-v-broadcasting-authority; HCJ 141/82 MK Rubinstein v. Chairman of the Knesset, Versa, https://versa.cardozo.yu.edu/opinions/mk-rubinstein-v-chairman-knesset; HCJ 142/89 La'Or Movement - One Heart and One Spirit v. Central. Elections Committee for the Sixteenth Knesset, [in Hebrew] 44(3) PD 529 (1990).

[48] See Segev, "Who Needs a Constitution?" 433 and accompanying references.

[49] Aharon Barak, "A Constitutional Revolution: Israel's Basic Laws," *Forum Constitutionnel* 4 (1992-1993): 83.

[50] Aharon Barak, "A Constitutional Revolution: Protected Fundamental Rights," [in Hebrew] *Mishpat UMimshal* 1 (1992):9-35.

[51] Rivka Weill, "Twenty Years Since Bank Hamizrachi: On the Piquant Story of the Hybrid Israeli Constitution," [in Hebrew] *Tel Aviv University Law Review* 38 (2016): 546.

[52] Aharon Garber, "From Revolution to Crisis – Between Theory and Practice," [in Hebrew] *Reshut HaRabim,* November 17, 2021, https://journal.lawforum.org.il/garber-hamizrahi/.

[53] Weill, "Twenty Years Since Bank Hamizrachi," 503.

[54] Rivka Weill, "The Strategic Common Law Court of Aharon Barak and its Aftermath: On Judicially-led Constitutional Revolutions and Democratic Backsliding," *Law & Ethics of Human Rights* 14, no. 2 (2018): 250.

[55] "Constitution and Basic Laws," [in Hebrew] *The Knesset*, https://main.knesset.gov.il/about/lexicon/pages/heb_mimshal_hoka.aspx.

[56] "Being powerful is like being a lady. If you have to tell people you are, you aren't." Cited at Jena McGregor, *Margaret Thatcher, in Her Own Words*, *The Washington Post*, April 8, 2013, https://www.washingtonpost.com /national /on-leadership/margaret-thatchers-best-quotes/2013/04/08/97abce78-a07d-11e2-82bc-511538ae90a4_story.html.

[57] Segev, "Who Needs a Constitution?" 488.

[58] Daniel Friedmann, *The Purse and the Sword: The Legal Revolution and Its Collapse* [in Hebrew] (Miskal Publishing, 2013), 587 (Hebrew edition).

[59] Weill, "Twenty Years Since Bank Hamizrachi," 545.

[60] *Ibid.*, 546.

[61] Weill, "The Strategic Common Law Court," 250.

[62] Gary J. Jacobsohn, *Apple of Gold* (Oxford University Press, 1993), 249.

[63] Weill, "Twenty Years Since Bank Hamizrachi," 519.

[64] Haim Ramon, *Against the Wind,* [in Hebrew] (Yediot Books, 2020), Chapter "Is this the Rule of law?"

[65] Haim Ramon, "'The Fools Didn't Understand': How Aharon Barak Carried Out the Constitutional Revolution – and Changed the Country," [in Hebrew] interview with Akiva Bigman, YouTube, 1:01 https://www.youtube.com/

watch?v=yWli5GPTlIc.

[66] Yehudit Karp, "Basic Law: Human Dignity and Liberty – A Biography of Power Struggles," [in Hebrew] *Mishpat UMimshal* 1, (1993): 375-77.

[67] *Ibid.*, 326.

[68] *Ibid.*, 357.

[69] *Ibid.*, 340.

[70] *Ibid.*, 343-44.

[71] *Ibid.*, 365-66.

[72] *Ibid.*, 327-28.

[73] *Ibid.*, 325.

[74] *Ibid.*, 324.

[75] *Ibid.*, 331-32.

[76] *Ibid.*, 371.

[77] *Ibid.*, 339.

[78] Ran Baratz, "The Coup and the Failure: The Conspiracy That Gave Birth to the Constitutional Revolution," [in Hebrew] *Mida*, July 21, 2017.

[79] Karp, "Basic Law: Human Dignity and Liberty," 361.

[80] Ariel Bendor, "Defects in the Enactment of the Basic Laws," [in Hebrew] *Mishpat UMimshal* 2 (1995): 445-447.

[81] Weill, "Twenty Years Since Bank Hamizrachi," 547.

[82] *Ibid.*

[83] See for example, Michel Troper, "Marshall, Kelsen, Barak and the Constitutionalist Fallacy," *International Journal of Constitutional Law* 3, no. 1 (2005): 24-38.

[84] Fred Foldvary, "Democracy, Constitutional," in *Encyclopedia of Global Justice*, ed. D. K. Chatterjee (Dordrecht: Springer, 2011), 232, https://doi.org/10.1007/978-1-4020-9160-5_42.

[85] CivA 6821/93 United Mizrahi Bank Ltd. v. Migdal Cooperative Village, [in Hebrew] 49(4) PD 221, 398 (1995).

[86] *Ibid.*, 423.

[87] Aharon Barak, "Constitutional Judicial Review of Statutes and the Status of the Knesset," [in Hebrew] *HaPraklit* 47 (2003): 5-8.

[88] *Ibid.*

[89] Jonathan Sumption, "The Reith Lectures 2019: Rights and the Ideal Constitution," BBC RADIO 4, June 15, 2019, https://www.bbc.co.uk/programmes/m0005t85.

[90] Richard A. Posner, "Enlightened Despot," *The New Republic*, April 23, 2007, https://newrepublic.com/article/60919/enlightened-despot.

[91] Dan Avnon, "The Israeli Basic Laws' (Potentially) Fatal Flaw," *Israel Law Review* 32, no. 4 (1998): 540–42.

[92] C. S. Lewis, "Screwtape Proposes a Toast," *Saturday Evening Post*, December 19, 1959.

[93] Barak Medina, "Does Israel have a Constitution? On Formal and Liberal Democracy," [in Hebrew] *Tel Aviv University Law Review* 44 (2021): 5-48.

[94] Ido Porat, "The Institutional Problem in the Essentialist Approach," [in Hebrew] *Tel Aviv University Law Review Online* 44 (2021): 1-5; Raif Zarik, "Dworkin in Jerusalem," [in Hebrew] *Tel Aviv University Law Review Online* 44 (2021): 1-6.

[95] Eretz Nehederet, "First Lesson in Democracy," [in Hebrew] Facebook, https://www.facebook.com/watch/?v=945417242325032.

[96] Avigdor Klagsbald, "Democracy Under Fire," [in Hebrew] Reichman University, interview by Amit Segal, YouTube, 30:30. https://youtu.be/SmiqQeRYHvM?si=8xidc9AWcyLKuRac.

[97] Avraham Landsberg, "Justice Amit: 'Majority Rule? A Fourth-Grade Democracy,'" [in Hebrew] *Channel 14*, May 11, 2025, https://www.c14.co.il/article/1210191; Gilad Morag and Gilad Cohen, "Justice Amit: If the Majority Can Do Everything, It's a Fourth-Grade Decoration Committee-Level Democracy," [in Hebrew] *Ynet*, September 12, 2023, https://www.ynet.co.il/ blogs/bagatzruleofreason/article/rkmsdpt0h.

[98] Karp, "Basic Law: Human Dignity and Liberty," 376.

[99] Oren Soffer, "Judicial Review of Legislation in Israel," *Israel Affairs* 12, no. 2 (2006): 314.

[100] Troper, "Marshall, Kelsen, Barak," 32.

[101] CivA 6821/93 United Mizrahi Bank Ltd. v. Migdal Cooperative Village, 49 (4) PD 221, 416 (1995) (in Hebrew).

[102] Troper, "Marshall, Kelsen, Barak," 35.

[103] Karp, "Basic Law: Human Dignity and Liberty," 377-79.

[104] Aharon Barak, "A Constitutional Revolution," 22.

[105] Karp, "Basic Law: Human Dignity and Liberty," 380-81.

[106] CivA 6821/93 United Mizrahi Bank Ltd. v. Migdal Cooperative Village, 49(4) PD 221, 417 (1995) (in Hebrew).

[107] Aharon Barak, *A Judge in a Democracy* (Princeton University Press, 2006), 131-35.

[108] Weill, "The Strategic Common Law Court," 266.

[109] Moshe Landau, "Granting Israel a Constitution By Way of Judicial Decree," [in Hebrew] *Mishpat UMimshal* 3 (1995): 697-712. Available in English at *Publius*, https://publius.co.il/wp-content/uploads/2025/03/Landau_Hamizrachi_English.pdf.

Notes to Chapter 10

[1] G.K. Chesterton, *Heretics* (John Lane, 1905), 61.

[2] Hillel Sommer, "In Praise of Judicial Restraint in the Constitutional Sphere," [in Hebrew] *Mishpat VeAdam – Mishpat VeAsakim* 19 (2012): 155–182.

[3] Yoav Dotan, *Judicial Review of Administrative Discretion*, [in Hebrew] vol. 2 (Nevo, 2023), 927.

[4] *Ibid.*, 928-929.

[5] James Allan, "Portia, Bassanio or Dick the Butcher? Constraining Judges in the Twenty-First Century," *King's College Law Journal* 17, no. 1 (2006): 15.

[6] Cruzan v. Dir., Mo. Dep't of Health, 497 U.S. 261, 301 (1990) (Scalia, J., concurring).

[7] Sommer, "In Praise of Judicial Restraint," 178.

[8] Yoav Dotan, "The (Supra-)constitutional Status of Administrative Law in Israel," [in Hebrew] *Mishpatim*, (forthcoming).

[9] HCJ 10662/04 Salah Hassan v. National Insurance Institute, Versa, https://versa.cardozo.yu.edu/opinions/hassan-v-national-insurance-institute (February 28, 2012) Beinisch C.J. 71.

[10] HCJ 366/03 Commitment to Peace and Social Justice Society v. Minister of Finance, Versa, https://versa.cardozo.yu.edu/opinions/commitment-peace-and-social-justice-society-v-minister-finance (December 12, 2005).

[11] Karp, "Basic Law: Human Dignity and Liberty," 336-37.

[12] Moshe Landau, "Granting Israel a Constitution By Way of Judicial Decree," [in Hebrew] *Mishpat UMimshal* 3 (1995): 697-712. Available in English at *Publius*, https://publius.co.il/wp-content/uploads/2025/03/Landau_Hamizrachi_English.pdf.

[13] Sommer, "In Praise of Judicial Restraint."

[14] HCJ 3267/97 Rubinstein v. The Minister of Defense, Versa, https://versa.cardozo.yu.edu/opinions/rubinstein-v-minister-defense (December 9, 1998), Barak C.J. 31.

[15] Sommer, "In Praise of Judicial Restraint."

[16] HCJ 6427/02 Movement for Quality Government in Israel v. Knesset, [in Hebrew] 61(1) PD 619, Grunis C.J. 15 (2006).

[17] HCJ 4124/00 Ornan Yekutieli v. the Minister for Religious Affairs, Versa, https://versa.cardozo.yu.edu/opinions/yekutieli-v-minister-religious-affairs (June 14, 2010).

[18] HCJ 616/11 The National Union of Israeli Students v. The Government of Israel 66(3) PD 819 (2014).

[19] HCJ 8300/02 Nasser v. The Government of Israel, Nevo Legal database (May 22, 2012).

[20] HCJ 7146/12 Adam v. the Knesset, Nevo Legal database (September 16, 2013).

[21] HCJ 8665/14 Desta v. Knesset, Versa, https://versa.cardozo.yu.edu/opinions/desta-v-knesset (August 11, 2015).

[22] HCJ 6942/19 Chevano v. Minister of Interior, [in Hebrew] Nevo Legal Database (July 12, 2023).

[23] Robert A. Dahl, On Democracy (Yale University Press, 1998), 147-48.

[24] HCJ 2996/17 Union of Journalists in Israel v. The Prime Minister, [in Hebrew] Nevo Legal Database (January 23, 2019), Meltzer J. 39.

[25] HCJ 1661/05 Gaza Beach Regional Council v. Knesset of Israel, [in Hebrew] 59(2) PD 481 (2005).

[26] Sosa v. Alvarez-Machain, 542 U.S. 692 (2004).

[27] HCJ 8276/05 Adalah Legal Center for Arab Minority Rights in Israel v. Minister of Defense, Versa, https://versa.cardozo.yu.edu/opinions/adalah-legal-center-arab-minority-rights-israel-v-minister-defense (December 12, 2006).

[28] CrimAM 8823/07 A v. State of Israel, Versa, https://versa.cardozo.yu.edu/opinions/ v-state-israel-0 (11 February 2010).

[29] HCJ 5239/11 Avneri v. Knesset, Versa, https://versa.cardozo.yu.edu/opinions/avneri-v-knesset (April 15, 2015).

[30] HCJ 1308/17 Silwad Municipality v. Knesset, [in Hebrew] Nevo Legal Database (June 9, 2020).

[31] HCJ 3390/16 Adalah v. The Knesset, Nevo Legal Database (July 8, 2021).

[32] Russell A. Shalev, "Israel Needs to Talk About the Arab Riots of May 2021," [in Hebrew] *Fathom*, March 2022, https://fathomjournal.org/israel-needs-to-talk-about-the-arab-riots-of-may-2021/.

[33] HCJ 466/07 Gal-On v. Legal Counsel to the Government, [in Hebrew] Nevo Legal Database (January 11, 2012); HCJ 7052/03 Adalah v. Minister of Interior, Versa, https://versa.cardozo.yu.edu/opinions/adalah-legal-center-arab-minority-rights-israel-v-minister-interior (May 14, 2006).

[34] *Ibid.*, Cheshin J. 120.

[35] *Ibid.*, Procaccia J. 2, 6.

[36] *Ibid.*, Barak C.J. 93.

[37] *Ibid.*, Barak C.J. 111.

[38] Yuval Yoaz, "Cheshin on Barak: 'He Is Willing for 30–50 People to Explode, But There Should Be Human Rights,'" [in Hebrew] *Haaretz*, May 24, 2006, https://www.haaretz.co.il/misc/2006-05-24/ty-article/0000017f-ef2e-dc28-a17f-ff3f68310000.

[39] Sommer, "In Praise of Judicial Restraint," 315.

[40] Menachem Mautner, *Law and the Culture of Israel* (Oxford University Press, 2011), 172.

[41] Menachem Mautner, "Why Israel's High Court Is Considered Left-wing," *Haaretz*, October 26, 2010, https://www.haaretz.com/2010-10-26/ty-article/why-israels-high-court-is-considered-left-wing/0000017f-e04a-df7c-a5f f-e27aaa4c0001; see also: Joshua Segev, "The Standing Doctrine: What Went Wrong?" in *Oxford Handbook of the Israeli Constitution*, ed. Aharon Barak, Barak Medina, and Yaniv Roznai (Oxford Academic, forthcoming), 11, https://papers.ssrn.com/sol3/papers.cfm?abstract_id=4010860.

[42] Ronen Shamir, "The Politics of Reasonableness: Discretion as Judicial Power," [in Hebrew] *Theory and Criticism* 5 (1994): 19, quoting Michael Mandel.

[43] Jeremy Waldron, *Law and Disagreement* (Clarendon Press Publication, 1999), 291.

[44] Loughlin, *Against Constitutionalism*, 168.

[45] Dotan, *Judicial Review*, 274.

[46] Allan, "Portia, Bassanio or Dick the Butcher?" 25.

[47] Mautner, *Law and the Culture of Israel*, 163.

[48] Yehonatan Givati and Aharon Garber, "Juristocracy in the Court of Public Opinion," *American Law and Economics Review* (Forthcoming), https://papers.ssrn.com/sol3/papers.cfm?abstract_id=5127967.

[49] Moshe Landau, "Constitutional Law: The Power of the Court and Its Limits,"

[in Hebrew] *Mishpatim* 10, (1980), 196–201.

[50] Michal Shaked, "Comments on the Reasonableness Review in Administrative Law," [in Hebrew] *Mishpatim* 12 (1982): 127.

[51] Shamir, "The Politics of Reasonableness," 22.

[52] Dotan, *Judicial Review*, 266.

[53] Ruth Gavison, "The Paradox is that When the Court Claims to be a Supreme Moral Authority, it Undermines its Legitimacy as a Supreme Legal Authority," [in Hebrew] interview by Ari Shavit, *Haaretz*, November 12, 1999.

[54] Dorit Beinisch, "Public Trust in the Judicial System – Lecture at the Annual Conference in Memory of Amnon Lipkin-Shahak," [in Hebrew] *ICON-S-IL Blog*, June 27, 2021, https://israeliconstitutionalism.wordpress.com/2021/06/27/%D7%90%D7%9E%D7%95%D7%9F-%D7%94%D7%A6%D7%99%D7%91%D7%95%D7%A8-%D7%91%D7%9E%D7%A2%D7%A8%D7%9B%D7%AA-%D7%94%D7%9E%D7%A9%D7%A4%D7%98-%D7%94%D7%A8%D7%A6%D7%90%D7%94-%D7%91%D7%9B%D7%A0%D7%A1/.

[55] Elyakim Rubinstein, "Trust in the Institutions of the Rule of Law," [in Hebrew] *Globes*, February 14, 2022.

[56] Adam Shinar, "The decline of trust in the courts: Sounding the alarm or much ado about nothing?" in *Menachem (Meni) Mazuz Book*, ed. Yoram Rabin, Yaniv Vaki, Alon Rhodes and Guy Rubinstein (forthcoming), https://papers.ssrn.com/sol3/papers.cfm?abstract_id=4943833.

[57] Allan, "Portia, Bassanio or Dick the Butcher?" 25.

[58] Yoav Dotan, "A Constitution for the State of Israel? – The Constitutional Dialogue After the 'Constitutional Revolution,'" [in Hebrew] *Mishpatim* 28 (1997): 196.

[59] *Ibid.*, 194.

[60] *Ibid.*, 179.

[61] Mautner, *Law and the Culture of Israel*, 178.

[62] Dotan, "A Constitution for the State of Israel," 182.

[63] *Ibid.*, 182.

[64] Ariel Bendor, "Defects in the Enactment of the Basic Laws," [in Hebrew] *Mishpat UMimshal* 2 (1995): 445-447.

[65] Loughlin, *Against Constitutionalism,* 141.

[66] Dotan, "A Constitution for the State of Israel," 199.

[67] *Ibid.*, 189.

[68] *Ibid.*, 209.

[69] *Ibid.*, 193.

[70] CivA 6821/93 United Mizrahi Bank Ltd. v. Migdal Cooperative Village, [in Hebrew] 49(4) PD 221, 423 (1995).

[71] Dotan, "A Constitution for the State of Israel," 200.

Notes to Chapter 11

[1] Moshe Cohen-Eliya, "Israel's Juristocracy," *Law and Liberty*, March 4, 2024.

[2] CivA 6821/93 United Mizrahi Bank Ltd. v. Migdal Cooperative Village, [in Hebrew] 49(4) PD 221, 354 (1995).

[3] *Ibid.,* 355.

[4] *Ibid.*, 423.

[5] Quoted in Menachem Mautner, *Law and the Culture of Israel* (Oxford University Press, 2011), 178.

[6] Aharon Barak, "Constitutional Judicial Review of Statutes and the Status of the Knesset," [in Hebrew] *HaPraklit* 47 (2003): 5-6.

[7] Barak, "Only the Knesset Can Remove Judicial Review by Way of Basic Law," [in Hebrew] *Globes*, November 20, 2003.

[8] Yoav Dotan, "A Constitution for the State of Israel? – The Constitutional Dialogue After the 'Constitutional Revolution,'" [in Hebrew] *Mishpatim* 28 (1997): 186.

[9] See Rivkah Weill, "On Abuse of Constituent Authority and an Unconstitutional Constitutional Amendment," [in Hebrew] *ICON-S-IL Blog*, October 6, 2019, https://israeliconstitutionalism.wordpress.com/2019/10/06/%d7%a2%d7%9c-%d7%a9%d7%99%d7%9e%d7%95%d7%a9-%d7%9c%d7%a8%d7%a2%d7%94-%d7%91%d7%a1%d7%9e%d7%9b%d7%95%d7%aa-%d7%9e%d7%9b%d7%95%d7%a0%d7%a0%d7%aa-%d7%95%d7%aa%d7%99%d7%a7%d7%95%d7%9f-%d7%97%d7%95%d7%a7/.

[10] CivA 6821/93 United Mizrahi Bank Ltd. v. Migdal Cooperative Village, [in Hebrew] 49(4) PD 221, 404 (1995).

[11] HCJ 5969/20, Shafir v. Knesset, [in Hebrew] Nevo Legal Database (May 23, 2021), Hayut C.J. 31 (in Hebrew).

[12] *Ibid.*

[13] Richard Ekins and Graham Gee, "Putting Judicial Power in its Place," *University of Queensland Law Journal* 36, no. 2 (2018): 387.

[14] HCJ 5744/16 Shachar Ben Meir v. Knesset, [in Hebrew] Nevo Legal Database (May 27, 2018).

[15] Abraham Bell "The Counter-Revolutionary Nation-State Law" *Israel Studies* 25, no. 3 (2020): 240–55, https://doi.org/10.2979/israelstudies.25.3.21.

[16] Or Bassok and Menachem Mautner, "Israeli High Court's Pursuit of a Constitutional 'Gospel,'" *Haaretz*, January 14, 2021, https://www.haaretz.com/opinion/2021-01-14/ty-article-opinion/.premium/israels-high-courts-pursuit-of-a-constitutional-gospel/0000017f-e5d6-dea7-adff-f5ff3ba50000.

[17] HCJ 5555/18 MK Akram Hasson v. The Knesset of Israel, [in Hebrew] Nevo Legal Database (July 8, 2021), Hayut C.J. 16.

[18] *Ibid.*, Hayut C.J. 18.

[19] *Ibid.*, Hayut C.J. 29.

[20] *Ibid.*, Hayut C.J. 34.

[21] Menachem Mautner and Or Bassok, "On Thorny Nation-State Issue, Israel's High Court Faces a Tragic Dilemma," *Haaretz*, December 20, 2020, https://www.haaretz.com/opinion/2020-12-20/ty-article-

opinion/.premium/on-thorny-nation-state-issue-israels-high-court-faces-a-tragic-dilemma/0000017f-def2-df9c-a17f-fefac4f20000.

[22] Aharon Garber, "The Supreme Court Has No Authority to Rule on a Basic Law," [in Hebrew] *Israel Hayom*, August 20, 2018, https://www.israelhayom.co.il/opinion/581609.

[23] Yaniv Roznai, *Unconstitutional Constitutional Amendments: The Limits of Amendment Powers* (Oxford University Press, 2017), 70.

[24] *Ibid.*, 80.

[25] HCJ 4908/10 MK Ronnie Bar-On v. Israel Knesset, Versa, https://versa.cardozo.yu.edu/opinions/bar-v-knesset (April 7, 2011), Beinisch C.J. 19.

[26] HCJ 5744/16 Shachar Ben Meir v. Knesset, [in Hebrew] Nevo Legal Database (May 27, 2018), Hayut C.J. 25.

[27] HCJ 5555/18 Hayut C.J. 14-15.

[28] Aharon Barak, "A Constitutional Amendment That Is Unconstitutional," in *Gabriel Bach Book*, [in Hebrew] ed. David Haan, Dana Cohen Lekah, and Michael Bach (Nevo, 2011), 361-82.

[29] Yoav Dotan, "The (Supra-)constitutional Status of Administrative Law in Israel," [in Hebrew] *Mishpatim*, (forthcoming): 38.

[30] Garber, "The Supreme Court Has No Authority."

[31] CivA 6821/93 United Mizrahi Bank Ltd. v. Migdal Cooperative Village, [in Hebrew] 49(4) PD 221, 423 (1995).

[32] Suzi Navot and Yaniv Roznai, "On the Authority for Judicial Review of Basic Laws," [in Hebrew] *ICON-S-IL Blog*, November 4, 2018, https://israeliconstitutionalism.wordpress.com/2018/11/04/__trashed-4/.

[33] HCJ 5555/18 MK Akram Hasson v. The Knesset of Israel, [in Hebrew] Nevo Legal Database (July 8, 2021), Hayut C.J. 34.

[34] HCJ 4908/10 MK Ronnie Bar-On v. Israel Knesset, Versa, https://versa.cardozo.yu.edu/opinions/bar-v-knesset (April 7, 2011), Beinisch C.J. 20.

[35] HCJ 5555/18 MK Akram Hasson, Mazuz J. 5.

[36] Tova Tzimuki and Eitan Glickman, "The Supreme Court Chief Justice's Unprecedented Attack: The Full Speech of Justice Hayut," [in Hebrew] *Ynet*, January 12, 2023.

[37] HCJ 5658/23 Movement for Quality Government in Israel v. Knesset, [in Hebrew] Nevo Legal Database (January 1, 2024), Solberg J. 130-131.

[38] *Ibid.*, Elron J. 6.

[39] Dotan, "The (Supra-)constitutional Status of Administrative Law.

[40] Richard A. Posner, "The Meaning of Judicial Self-Restraint," *Indiana Law Journal* 59, no. 1 (1983): 1-24.

[41] HCJ 5658/23 Movement for Quality Government in Israel, Baron J. 1.

[42] Gidi Weitz, "'Make No Mistake, Israel's Coup Is Alive and Kicking': A Stunning Warning by Supreme Court Justice Anat Baron," *Haaretz*, June 28, 2024, https://www.haaretz.com/israel-news/2024-06-28/ty-article-magazine/.highlight/israels-coup-is-alive-and-kicking-a-stunning-warning-by-justice-

anat-baron/00000190-5b0a-dc65-abff-7b2b72f50000.

Notes to Conclusion

[1] Adam Tomkins, "It Is Preposterous to Assert That Israeli Democracy Is at Stake," *The Jewish Chronicle*, March 28, 2023.

[2] Alan Dershowitz, *War Against the Jews: How to End Hamas Barbarism* (Skyhorse Publishing, 2023).

[3] Yoav Dotan, "The (Supra-)constitutional Status of Administrative Law in Israel," [in Hebrew] *Mishpatim* (forthcoming): 44.

[4] Menachem Mautner, *Law and the Culture of Israel* (Oxford University Press, 2011), 180.

[5] Rivka Weill, "Twenty Years Since Bank Hamizrachi: On the Piquant Story of the Hybrid Israeli Constitution," [in Hebrew] *Tel Aviv University Law Review* 38 (2016): 508.

[6] Melville B. Nimmer, "The Uses of Judicial Review in Israel's Quest for a Constitution," *Columbia Law Review* 70, no. 7 (1970): 1256.

Index

A

B

C

I

J

K

T

U

www.ingramcontent.com/pod-product-compliance
Lightning Source LLC
Chambersburg PA
CBHW070156310326
41914CB00104B/2060/J

9781680533132